Encyclopedia of

Islam

and the

Muslim World

Editorial Board

Encyclopedia of

Islam
and the
Muslim World

Editor in Chief
Richard C. Martin

Volume 2
M-Z, Index

**MACMILLAN
REFERENCE
USA**™

THOMSON
★™
GALE

New York • Detroit • San Diego • San Francisco • Cleveland • New Haven, Conn. • Waterville, Maine • London • Munich

THOMSON ™
GALE

Encyclopedia of Islam

Richard C. Martin, Editor in Chief

Library of Congress Cataloging-in-Publication Data

Encyclopedia of Islam and the Muslim world / edited by Richard C. Martin.
     p. cm.
Includes bibliographical references and index.
   ISBN 0-02-865603-2 (set) — ISBN 0-02-865604-0 (v. 1) — ISBN 0-02-865605-9 (v. 2)
   1. Islam—Encyclopedias. I. Martin, Richard C.
BP40.E525 2003
909'.097671—dc21

2003009964

This title is also available as an e-book.
ISBN 0-02-865912-0
Contact your Gale sales representative for ordering information.

Printed in the United States of America
10 9 8 7 6 5 4 3 2

M

MADANI, 'ABBASI (1931–)

Algerian Islamic activist and opposition leader, 'Abbasi Madani was born in 1931 in Sidi 'Uqbah, in southeastern Algeria. An early member of the National Liberation Front (Front de Libération Nationale, or FLN), Madani was imprisoned throughout the eight-year war against the French. After the independence in 1962, Madani joined the Qiyam (Islamic values) association and took a critical stance against the socialist and secular orientation of the FLN. He received a religious education, then studied philosophy and psychology, and in 1978 received a Ph.D. in education in Britain. Madani upheld the ideas of Algeria's reformist movement and criticized the state's secular policies, calling for Islamic revival and the Arabization of the predominantly francophone educational system.

Madani ascended the political ladder during anti-FLN riots in October 1988. The following year he founded the religiously inspired Islamic Salvation Front (Front Islamique du Salut, or FIS), which quickly became the opposition party, representing the vast majority of the urban poor. Madani's first electoral victory came in June 1990, during Algeria's first multiparty municipal elections, and subsequently he emerged as the potential successor to the then-president Chadli Benjedid. In May 1991, Madani called for an indefinite general strike to protest against a new electoral legislation, but was arrested soon thereafter. During his incarceration, military intervention against FIS's success in the first round of the December 1991 national elections resulted in the party's ban and years of civil violence. He was freed in July 1997. Madani endorsed the beliefs of many Islamic modernists who call for an Islamic solution to the crisis of modernity and, through the FIS, brought Islam to the forefront of Algerian national identity.

See also **Islamic Salvation Front; Political Organization; Reform: Arab Middle East and North Africa.**

BIBLIOGRAPHY

Burgat, Francois, and Dowell, William. *The Islamic Movement in North Africa.* Austin: Center for Middle Eastern Studies, University of Texas at Austin, 1993.

Ciment, James. *Algeria. The Fundamentalist Challenge.* New York: Facts on File, 1997.

Claudia Gazzini

MADHHAB

Lexically, the term *madhhab* denotes a "way of going," and by extension a "manner followed," an "ideology" or "movement." Most commonly, the term and its plural (*madhahib*) refer to the different "schools" of Islamic law.

The classical Sunni schools of law emerged in the late ninth and early tenth centuries C.E.; they were built on the legal opinions of certain local authorities from the late eighth and early ninth centuries. By the late tenth and early eleventh centuries, the legal opinions of scholars identified as "followers" (*ashab*) of people like Malik b. Anas, Abu Hanifa, and al-Shafi'i were condensed into compendia that represented the perspectives of the five main schools: Maliki, Hanafi, Shafi'i, Hanbali (following Ahmad b. Hanbal), and the Zahiri (following Da'ud b. Khalaf). The followers of local authorities such as al-Awza'i, Sufyan al-Thawri, and others, did not materialize into institutionalized schools of law beyond the tenth century though their opinions continued to play a role in the legal theory of the other schools.

Following the eleventh century, each school continued to develop distinct legal theory while maintaining constant interaction and dialogue with the other schools. Divisions among the schools were often characterized not only in terms of general approaches to the authoritative sources (*usul*) and methods of interpretation, but also in terms of legal rulings on specific issues or practices.

The Hanafi *madhhab* is sometimes called the "followers of opinion" (*ashab al-ra'y*), denoting a perception of their greater reliance on logic and reasoning, as opposed to the label "followers of the hadith" (*ashab al-hadith*) applied to the Shafi'i and Hanbali *madhahib*s. Other schools, such as the Zahiri *madhhab*, were known for their eschewing of reason and logic, relying instead on the "literal" interpretation of authoritative sources. The Maliki *madhhab* asserted its authority as a continuation of the practices that originated with the prophet Muhammad at Medina. It was not uncommon, however, for individual jurists to belong to different *madhhab*s, such as Muhammad b. Khalaf (d. 1135), who was called "Hanfash" because he was first a Hanbali, then a Hanafi, and finally a Shafi'i.

It has been remarked that the later developments of the schools lacked innovation and fluidity, being too reliant on imitation of earlier legal opinions. Much of the postclassical scholarship did take the form of commentaries (*shuruh*) upon earlier texts, and in both premodern and modern times there were attempts to codify the "law" of a particular *madhhab*. The epistemological and methodological structure of Islamic jurisprudence (*fiqh*) in conjunction with changing social circumstances seemed to require a continual rethinking and examination of the authoritative sources. Each *madhhab* has its own distinct means for authorizing such change and for linking new legal opinions with past precedents.

In addition to the Sunni *madhahib*, there are Shi'ite *madhahib* that emerged at various times due to changes in the authority of certain Shi'ite imams. The best known of these Shi'ite *madhahib* is the "Twelver" or "Imami" Shi'i *madhhab* that was established after the greater occultation of the twelfth imam in 941. The Twelver Shi'ite *madhhab* is characterized by greater juristic authority and formal hierarchy but conforms in many ways to the principles governing the shape of the Sunni *madhahib*.

See also **Abu Hanifa; Ibn Hanbal; Kalam; Law; Malik Ibn Anas; Shafi'i, al-; Shi'a: Imami (Twelver).**

BIBLIOGRAPHY

Chamberlain, Michael. *Knowledge and Social Practice in Medieval Damascus, 1190–1350.* Cambridge, U.K.: Cambridge University Press, 1994.

Melchert, Christopher. *The Formation of the Sunni School of Law, 9th–10th Centuries C.E.* Leiden: E. J. Brill, 1997.

Stewart, Devin J. *Islamic Legal Orthodoxy: Twelver Shiite Responses to the Sunni Legal System.* Salt Lake City: University of Utah Press, 1998.

Weiss, Bernard G. *The Spirit of Islamic Law.* Athens, Ga., and London: University of Georgia Press, 1998.

Brannon M. Wheeler

MADRASA

Madrasa, is an Islamic college, literally a "place of instruction," especially instruction in religious law. In medieval usage the term referred to an institution providing intermediate and advanced instruction in Islamic law and related subjects. This contrasted with elementary schools, which provided basic Qur'an instruction, and nonreligious institutions, which provided instruction in such subjects as medicine. In modern usage the term usually applies to schools offering Islamic religious instruction at any level. The madrasa can be considered as a building, as a legal entity, and as an educational institution. As a rule, the medieval madrasa served male students who were past the elementary level and who intended to acquire credentials as ulema, religious scholars. Elementary schools and schools offering vernacular or practical education were usually known by other names.

Description and Architecture

A typical Islamic madrasa contained rooms for students, a prayer hall, and classrooms and would likely also contain a residence for one or more professors, a library, and sanitary facilities. It was usually attached to a mosque, and large mosque complexes, such as those in Istanbul, might contain several madrasas. The typical Middle Eastern madrasa was a square building of one or two stories surrounding a courtyard. The student rooms opened onto the courtyard, and if the madrasa had two stories, the student rooms might be on the upper floor with classrooms and service rooms on the ground floor. Sometimes the central courtyard was replaced by a domed central hall. In their architecture madrasas are closely linked with other kinds of Islamic public buildings, notably mosques and caravansaries. There is, however, a great deal of variation in the design of madrasas. Some of the earliest surviving madrasas have few student rooms or none, perhaps because they served little more than a neighborhood, in contrast to great royal foundations that drew students from far away. Many madrasas, especially in Egypt, contain the mausoleums of their founders, with the madrasa proper being almost an afterthought. In crowded cities a cramped or irregular site often resulted in modification of the traditional plan. The fact that a madrasa's prayer hall might serve as a neighborhood mosque sometimes resulted in the addition of a minaret and the separation of the student rooms from the rest of the madrasa. When, as in the great Ottoman mosque complexes, the madrasa was closely associated with a mosque, the prayer hall shrank to make room for other facilities. When a madrasa was intended for more than a single legal school, separate teaching facilities were provided for each professor, so that there are cruciform madrasas providing symmetrical facilities for professors of each of the four Sunni schools of law. Finally, a house or some other existing building might simply be used as a madrasa without any special modifications.

The Medieval Madrasa

The madrasa appears as an institution in about the eleventh century and evolved from the informal schools that operated in mosques or teachers' homes. Islamic education was usually a distinctly personal and informal matter, and prior to the rise of the madrasa, as is still often the case, religious scholars would teach in a convenient mosque, perhaps teaching more advanced students, or controversial subjects, in their homes. It was customary for medieval Muslim students of the religious sciences to travel extensively to study with well-known teachers, and teachers also often traveled long distances seeking opportunities to teach, receive patronage, and further their own studies. A well-known hadith attributed to Muhammad says, "seek knowledge, even in China." A mosque, however, was not a suitable place for professors or significant numbers of students to live for long stretches, so by the tenth-century *khans*, inns, were being built adjacent to mosques. The first great burst of madrasa construction occurred in the eleventh century in the Seljuk empire and is associated with the name of the great wazir Nizam al-Mulk, who founded a number of madrasas known as Nizamiya, the most important of which, the Nizamiya in Baghdad, became one of the greatest educational institutions in the Islamic world. Whatever Nizam al-Mulk's philanthropic goals may have been, he probably also intended his madrasas to combat the threat posed to Sunni Islam by various forms of more or less revolutionary Shi'ism. The institution of the madrasa soon spread across the Islamic world and became the dominant form of institution of higher learning. It was not the only form of educational institution; there were also Qur'anic schools for younger pupils; Sufi monasteries; hospitals; observatories; vernacular schools for the children of merchants, shopkeepers, and artisans; and various forms of private tuition for the children of government officials.

Legal Status

A madrasa was legally a *waqf*, a charitable endowment. The founder would donate property, from whose proceeds the madrasa was built and maintained. The income from the endowment supported one or more professors, various servants and functionaries, and the students, who received room, board, and perhaps a small stipend. The founder's instructions governed such matters as the legal school to which the professor would belong. The extensive legal literature relating to madrasas deals with predictable problems of defining an adequate stipend, absentee professors, stipends for students who did not live at the madrasa, financial shortfalls, and responsibility for maintenance of the facilities. Madrasas as institutions did not issue degrees or diplomas. The closest counterpart to the Western degree was the *ijaza*, the license to teach a particular book or subject issued by an individual teacher. Madrasas had several advantages for donors. First, whereas the founder of a mosque had very little control after its establishment, the founder of a madrasa had a good deal of discretion in the terms of the endowment, so that in practice one could use the endowment of a madrasa to support one's

descendants. Second, a madrasa was less expensive to build and endow than a mosque, putting it within reach of those of more modest wealth or allowing a ruler to build a larger number of institutions. Finally, a madrasa could be an ideological tool, a way to help Islamize newly conquered territories or to combat the influence of a rival sect.

Curriculum and Instruction

The madrasa education was intended to teach the student how to deduce religious law from the authoritative Islamic texts. The students who went through the whole course were qualified to be judges and religious scholars, but most students doubtless dropped out earlier, becoming mosque imams or pursuing secular careers with the added prestige of a religious education. The method of instruction was scholastic and dialectical: intense debate about the interpretation and difficulties of a set of standard textbooks. Students came to the madrasa knowing the Qur'an by rote and a fair amount of Arabic. Students studied Arabic, logic, and the core subjects of the Islamic religious sciences: *fiqh* (Islamic law), Qur'an interpretation, and the hadith, sayings of the Prophet. Better students went on to study *usul al-fiqh* (jurisprudence), along with some theology, philosophy, mathematics, astronomy, and sometimes medicine.

Modern Developments

The arrival of modern educational institutions was a major challenge to the madrasas. Colonial administrators, nationalists, and Islamic reformers alike dismissed the scholastic madrasa education as out-of-date. Traditional sources of income dried up. Talented students sought new opportunities in modern universities and professions. Islamic revivalists complained of the rationalist character of the traditional madrasa curriculum and its neglect of core religious subjects. Postcolonial governments sometimes attempted to close or co-opt madrasas, fearing that they might become centers of opposition. This was the case in Turkey, where Ataturk closed the madrasas, and Indonesia, where the government tried to reduce the influence of the madrasas, known there as *pesantran*s, by controlling the curriculum, giving teachers government salaries, and establishing rival institutions. In many cases, standards of instruction and numbers of students declined precipitously, though in most places the major institutions survived. The attempts of the Pahlavi regime in Iran to control the madrasas failed, creating bitter opposition to the government among the ulema.

The Islamic revival of the late twentieth century has resulted in the revival of madrasas in a number of countries. The Iranian revolution of 1978–1979 was organized by ulema, so after the establishment of the Islamic Republic of Iran the Iranian madrasas, especially in Qom, received a huge influx of new students and financial support. Saudi Arabia, through both its government and wealthy individuals, has subsidized madrasas in many countries, thus increasing the influence of Saudi-style Wahhabi literalist Islam at the expense of both

In Jammu, India, Muslim children read the Qur'an at a madrasa, a religious Islamic school. Hindu groups have criticized Indian madrasas for preaching Islamic fundamentalism. In Pakistan, poor families often send their sons to one of the the tens of thousands of madrasas established by Islamic groups, in part because room and board are free. AP/WIDE WORLD PHOTOS

rationalist and mystical approaches to Islam. In the subcontinent the major Islamic revivalist movements have competed through their educational institutions since the nineteenth century. The most important of these was the Deoband movement. Its founders established a large educational complex in Deoband, near Delhi, devoted to propagating a revived, hadith-oriented Islam. The Deobandis thus opposed not only the new European-style education system of British India and the modernist Islamic Aligarh Muslim University but also the traditional Islamic religious education of India associated with the Firingi-Mahall educational complex in Lucknow, which was strongly rationalist and also closely associated with Sufism. Religious competition through madrasas has been particularly pronounced in Pakistan, where various Islamic groups have established tens of thousands of madrasas on the elementary, secondary, and university level. The Taliban (lit. "students") movement in Afghanistan in the late twentieth century was an outgrowth of madrasa training in Pakistan. These institutions are appealing to poor families, both because of the prestige of Islamic education and because, unlike the usually inadequate government schools, the madrasas provide room and board and charge no fees. Their quality varies tremendously and is, in general, quite poor. Finally, immigrant Islamic communities in Europe and North America have begun establishing their own religious schools, usually on the model of Sunday schools but sometimes as independent parochial schools. There are no schools training ulema outside of the Islamic world.

The madrasas have not kept their monopoly on training ulema. Increasingly, advanced Islamic education is taking place in modern universities. In the late nineteenth century the University of the Punjab in Lahore began granting Islamic clerical degrees. There are now faculties of theology in many universities in Islamic countries producing Islamic legal scholars and religious leaders. Finally, it is not uncommon for more talented madrasa students to go on for graduate degrees in secular universities in fields such as Arabic, Islamic studies, and philosophy.

See also **Aligarh; Azhar, al-; Deoband; Education.**

BIBLIOGRAPHY

Eccel, A. Chris. *Egypt, Islam, and Social Change: Al-Azhar in Conflict and Accommodation.* Berlin: K. Schwarz, 1984.

Makdisi, George. *The Rise of Colleges: Institutions of Learning in Islam and the West.* Edinburgh: Edinburgh University Press, 1981.

Metcalf, Barbara D. *Islamic Revival in British India: Deoband, 1860–1900.* Princeton, N.J.: Princeton University Press, 1982.

Mottahedeh, Roy P. *The Mantle of the Prophet: Religion and Politics in Iran.* New York: Simon and Schuster, 1983.

Sufi, G. M. D. *Al-Minhaj, Being the Evolution of Curriculum in the Muslim Educational Institutions of India.* Lahore: Shaikh Muhammad Ashraf, 1941.

Tibawi, A. L. *Islamic Education: Its Traditions and Modernization into the Arab National Systems.* London: Luzac, 1972.

John Walbridge

MAGHAZI *See* Military Raid

MAHDI

The Mahdi, meaning "the guided one," is the honorary title of the expected deliverer or messianic figure in Islam. Although the term and concept is not found in the Qurʾan, both Sunni and Shiʿa hadith collections mention it among the prophetic traditions concerning crises (*fitan*). These traditions often contain eschatological material, and frequently speak of a figure who will come at the end of time to combat the forces of evil led by the one-eyed Dajjal. This righteous individual is said to be one who "will fill the earth with justice after it has been filled with injustice and tyranny." The Mahdi's coming will lead the forces of good in a final apocalyptic battle, where the good will triumph. Jesus will also return to earth at this time, according to some reports, and fight alongside the Mahdi or rule after him. All of these events are predicted to take place shortly before Judgment Day.

In Twelver Shiʿite Islam, due to the community's minority status and continuing sense of persecution and injustice, the Mahdi symbol developed into a powerful and central religious idea and became combined with the figure of the last of the twelve Imams, Muhammad al-Mahdi, who is believed to have disappeared around 874. He was born in Samarra, son of Hasan al-Askari and the lady Nargis. He is also known as the ruler of the time (*sahib al-zaman*), the one who will restore justice (*qaʾim*), and the awaited one (*al-muntazar*).

Lists of the qualities of the expected one were drawn up, including his name being Muhammad, his descent from the Prophet, his appearance (*zuhur*) or rising, his rule (for either seven, nine, or nineteen years), and his mission to restore justice on earth. After the last imam disappeared as a child, Shiʿite sources identified a lesser occultation (disappearance)

of some seventy years, during which a series of four deputies was said to have consulted with him. After that time, the Mahdi, or Hidden Imam, entered the greater occultation that is still in force, remaining alive but not meeting with representatives. The fact that Shiʿite religious scholars are believed to continue to receive his blessings and guidance gives them a greater charisma and authority than their Sunni counterparts. Shiʿite political theory traditionally declared all temporal power illegitimate in the absence of the imam, only recently allowing the concept of a caretaker government of religious authorities (*wilayat al-faqih*) that underlies today's Islamic republic in Iran.

Claimants to the role of the Mahdi have not been absent from Islamic history. The first was Muhammad al-Hanifiyya (d. 700), son of ʿAli from a wife other than Fatima, whose role as the Mahdi was promoted by al-Mukhtar (d. 687). Although al-Mukhtar was killed and his movement crushed, ideas that Muhammad al-Hanafiyya did not die and would one day return continued to circulate and later attached themselves to subsequent imams. More recent claimants have arisen in both Shiʿa and Sunni contexts, including Muhammad Mahdi of Jaunpur in India (d. 1504), whose followers continue as a separate Muslim sect, the Mahdavis, and the Sudanese Mahdi, Muhammad Ahmad (d. 1885), who rose against the British occupiers and was killed at the battle of Omdurman. Contemporary Islamist or Sufi movements may occasionally evoke the anticipated return of the Mahdi as a means of encouraging millenarian expectations among their followers. In Shiʿa Islam, expectation and eager anticipation of the Mahdi's return is a central theme of piety and discourse.

See also **Fitna; Hadith; Imam; Mahdist State, Mahdiyya; Religious Beliefs; Shiʿa: Early; Shiʿa: Imami (Twelver).**

BIBLIOGRAPHY

Blichfeldt, Jan-Olaf. *Early Mahdism: Politics and Religion in the Formative Period of Islam.* Leiden: E. J. Brill, 1985.

Sachedina Abdulaziz, *Islamic Messianism.* Albany: State University of New York, 1981.

Marcia Hermansen

MAHDI, SADIQ AL- (1936–)

Sadiq al-Mahdi is a Sudanese political leader and intellectual, and a descendant of the nineteenth-century Islamic revolutionary known as "the Mahdi," Muhammad Ahmad. Sadiq received a traditional Muslim education as well as a modern one, graduating from Oxford University in 1957. When his father, Siddiq al-Mahdi, died in 1961, Sadiq became the head of the Mahdist-supported Umma Party. He was prime minister of Sudan from 1966 to 1967, and following the military coup by Jaʿfar Numayri in 1969, Sadiq went into exile. He returned to Sudan during a national reconciliation in 1977, but was jailed for his opposition to Numayri's 1983 decrees imposing a form of Islamic law on the country. Following the overthrow of Numayri, Sadiq al-Mahdi was again prime minister (1986–1989), and his government was overthrown by Islamist military officers in 1989. He was a leader in the movements of opposition to the Islamist regime but, at the beginning of the twenty-first century, Sadiq al-Mahdi engaged in efforts to reconcile government and opposition. He has written numerous books advocating effective *ijtihad* (independent reasoning) in understanding Islam's message in the contemporary world. He is an advocate of democracy in an Islamic context and has provided a contemporary understanding of what messianic leadership (the mission of the Mahdi) means in the modern world.

BIBLIOGRAPHY

Sidahmed, Abdel Salam. *Politics and Islam in Contemporary Sudan*. New York: St. Martin's Press, 1996.

John O. Voll

MAHDIST STATE, MAHDIYYA

The Sudanese Mahdi became known in the eastern Sudan (*bilad al-Sudan*) in June 1881 when he began to dispatch letters to local leaders proclaiming himself the Expected Mahdi. He was Muhammad Ahmad ibn 'Abdallah and about forty years old. He had been a member of the Sammaniyya sufi *tariqa* in the north of the country, but due to dissatisfaction with one of his teachers he moved to the Nile River island of Aba, south of Khartoum. There he established himself with a small band of followers, among whom was his future successor, 'Abdullahi ibn Muhammad.

The Sudan was then an Ottoman-Egyptian colony, and the regime was known locally as the *Turkiyya*. By the 1870s, however, the colonial state was thoroughly neglected by the rulers based in Egypt, creating opportunities for revolt. The administration and significant sectors of the colonial economy had substantial European participation right up to the level of governor. A few Sudanese were part of the government but most of the indigenous peoples resented their foreign rulers. The exclusion of Muslim Sudanese from leading roles in the colony, but the inclusion of non-Muslim Europeans, also disturbed pious Muslims such as the Mahdi. Slavery was under attack by the British, and abolition threatened the livelihoods of many northern Sudanese slave traders. These slave-traders threw their weight behind the mahdist movement.

The Mahdi came to address what he and his followers thought was an oppressive authority, and one that was contravening Islamic precepts. They challenged this situation and believed that a movement would emerge throughout the land to overthrow the regime. The Mahdi's calculation, however, that a countrywide revolt would follow his calls was never realized. This political failure was offset by success in the sphere of religious influence. Much support for the Mahdi was based on the belief that he was a divinely inspired figure. The religious dimension of his mission was perhaps more significant than its political impact.

The Mahdiyya was an indigenous northern Sudanese phenomenon, but the Mahdi modeled himself and his movement on the early Islamic community of the Prophet of Islam in the Arabian Peninsula. His followers were called *ansar* (helpers), just as the Prophet's supporters in Medina were named. The Mahdi preached jihad against the infidels, collected *zakat* (tax on wealth) instead of the range of colonial taxes, and strove to impose *shari'a* prohibitions and punishments. His successor, who was appointed when the Mahdi was on his deathbed, was given the title *khalifa* (caliph), as was the Prophet's successor. Indeed, Khalifa 'Abdullahi was named *khalifa al-Siddiq*, the latter term usually associated with the first caliph of Islam, Abu Bakr.

For the first two years of his mission, the Mahdi was confined to the province of Kordofan, but soon his forces began to spread slowly to the north along the Nile River. Thereafter his supporters increased and brought large parts of the west and east of the country under their control. Important towns such as El-Obeid, the main city of Kordofan, fell in January 1883, and the defeat of the expedition of Colonel William Hicks at Shaykan in September of the same year bolstered the movement tremendously.

The already weak government in Cairo was unable to do much to stem the tide of the Mahdi's success, and the British, who had recently occupied Egypt (in 1882), were hesitant to act. When General Charles Gordon was dispatched to the Sudan, he was sent with contradictory instructions: to restore "good government" and to evacuate the colony. When he reached Khartoum he wrote to the Mahdi, offering him the sultanship of Kordofan. The Mahdi rejected the offer, for he had much bigger ambitions that transcended mere political authority, especially when that authority was confined to an isolated province.

In October 1884 the Mahdi arrived on the banks of the Nile River opposite Khartoum and laid siege to the capital. In January of the following year Khartoum fell to the Mahdists. Instead of installing himself there, the Mahdi established a new capital, called Omdurman, opposite the old one. There he died in June 1885. His body was buried and a tomb was built over his gravesite. But the Mahdi's tomb was destroyed, and his body disinterred in the reconquest of the Sudan by Sir Herbert Kitchener in 1898.

The reign of the Mahdi's successor, Khalifa 'Abdullahi, opened with the new state's armies engaged on multiple fronts: in the west to pacify the state of Dar Fur, on the Ethiopian marches against the Christian state, and on the

The tomb of the Mahdi at Omdurman, Sudan. The original tomb, along with much of the city, was destroyed in 1898 when the Anglo-Egyptian forces of Lord Kitchener defeated the Khalifa and thus ended the Mahdist state in Sudan. GETTY IMAGES

Egyptian border. Against the Ethiopian fighters the Mahdists were successful, but elsewhere they met defeat. The Khalifa also had to deal with a number of pretenders, "false mahdis" who sought to claim his position. Furthermore, internal schisms surfaced between various layers of supporters who were dissatisfied with the Khalifa's policies. The *ashraf*, from the Mahdi's own kinsmen, were dissatisfied with the hegemony of the Ta'aisha, the Khalifa's clan. There were also a series of ecological challenges, including bad harvests and epidemics that led to famine between 1889 and 1990. As a result, by the early 1890s the Khalifa's armies were easily beaten in numerous engagements. Their final defeat came at the hands of Lord Kitchener, beginning in August 1897 and continuing until the last battle at Karari, outside Omdurman, in September 1898. Thousands of Sudanese fighters were

killed or wounded, whereas the Anglo-Egyptian losses numbered fewer than fifty dead and four hundred wounded.

This was the end of the Mahdiyya, but its influence did not end there nor in the Sudan. Rather, it spread throughout the *Bilad al-Sudan*. Right into the late 1920s the new colonial state had to deal with smaller mahdist revivals undertaken by local spiritual leaders (called *feki*s in the Sudan), often done in the name of 'Isa (Jesus). The religious idea in these uprisings was that *nabi 'Isa* (prophet Jesus) would appear after the death of the Mahdi, to herald the end of time.

In its short history the Mahdist state was able to put in place the foundations of a coherent and workable administration. There was a judiciary, and judgments were based on the classical Islamic methods of juristic thought, although the Mahdi also sometimes relied on his own intuition as the Mahdi, a man with divinely inspired authority. There was a *bayt al-mal* (roughly, a Department of Finance or Treasury) which kept detailed records, taxed the subjects, and distributed wealth. The state minted its own coins for the local economy. In addition there was the military.

Under the Khalifa, the administration that had been put in place by the Mahdi lost its reputation and drifted into corruption. The Khalifa, for instance, acquired a private army for himself and a separate share of the *bayt al-mal*. However, the state under the Khalifa was not as wholly corrupt as it has sometimes been judged, although it did divert from the strictly puritanical path of the its founder. The Mahdist state relied on local personnel and expertise and generated a huge body of correspondence, declarations, and other written material that has made it possible for historians to study this rare example of an African Muslim millernarian movement and state.

See also **Africa, Islam in; Islam and Other Religions; Mahdi; Muhammad Ahmad ibn 'Abdullah; Zar.**

BIBLIOGRAPHY

Holt, P. M. *The Mahdist State in the Sudan 1881–1898: A Study of Its Origins, Development and Overthrow.* Oxford, U.K.: Clarendon Press, 1958.

Holt, P. M.; and Daly, M. W. *A History of the Sudan: From the Coming of Islam to the Present Day,* 5th ed. Essex, U.K.: Longman, 2000.

Trimingham, J. Spencer. *Islam in the Sudan.* London: Oxford University Press, 1949.

Shamil Jeppie

MAHR

Mahr is a gift that the Muslim bridegroom offers the bride upon marriage. It is also called *sadaq*, an Arabic term that implies "friendship." In English, *mahr* has commonly been translated as "dower." *Mahr* is an integral part of every Islamic marriage contract: there can be no marriage without it. It becomes the exclusive property of the bride after marriage, and she can dispose of it in whatever way she wishes. The exact amount of *mahr* is often agreed upon prior to marriage and is specified in the contract—*mahr al-musamma* (definite *mahr*). If the amount is not specified, the bride is entitled to *mahr al-mithl* (average *mahr*), which is determined on the basis of her personal qualities, her family position, and the prevailing *mahr* among her people. *Mahr* can also be divided into two portions, the "prompt" portion, which is paid at the time of marriage, and the "deferred" portion, which is payable only if the husband divorces his wife, or dies. If a man dies without paying his wife's *mahr*, it is considered as a debt to be paid from his estate.

There is a general and implicit agreement among the different schools of Islamic law that *mahr* is a corollary of the exchange element of the marriage contract. Classical jurists often speak of it as a price/compensation (*'awad*, sometimes *'iwad*) that the man pays for the exclusive right to the sexual and productive faculties of a woman, analogous to the price paid in the contract of sale. Modern writers, however, regard *mahr* as an expression of honor for a woman's worth and as a means of providing her with economic security during and after marriage. The rules regulating *mahr* negate this view: It is linked merely to the act of consummation, not to any other aspect of the marriage contract. For example, a woman becomes entitled to *mahr* only after the consummation of the marriage; at the same time, she can refrain from sexual submission unless she receives her *mahr* in full.

Despite the uniformity among all schools of Islamic law on the definition of *mahr* and the rules governing it, Muslim societies vary greatly as to its practice. In some countries, like Morocco, the bulk of the *mahr* is paid to the father of the bride, who uses it to provide her with a trousseau for her wedding, and the deferred portion is nominal. In other countries, like Iran, no transfer of wealth takes place at the time of marriage and *mahr* becomes payable only if and when divorce occurs: It is seen as a safeguard, and a woman can effectively use her *mahr* as a negotiating card to obtain either a divorce or custody of her children in the event of the breakdown of the marriage. The value and practice of *mahr* also varies with social class, and with the wealth of the families. As marriages are usually arranged by the parents of the spouses, they often agree on the amount of *mahr*. In many cases, a woman has no control over her *mahr*, as the entire amount is received by her father who might use it to secure brides for his sons. Throughout the Muslim world, moreover, there are a number of customary payments and exchanges made on the occasion of marriage, which bear little or no relation to the formal legal requirement of *mahr*.

See also **Divorce; Law; Marriage.**

BIBLIOGRAPHY

Maghniyyah, Muhammad Jawad. *Marriage According to Five Schools of Islamic Law.* Tehran: Department of Translation and Publication, Islamic Culture and Relations Organization, 1997.

Mir-Hosseini, Ziba. *Marriage on Trial: A Study of Islamic Family Law; Iran and Morocco Compared.* London: I. B. Tauris, 1993.

Ziba Mir-Hosseini

MAITATSINE *See* **Marwa, Muhammad**

MAJLIS

The term *majlis* (assembly) has been used for elected parliaments in the Near and Middle East since the 1860s. The first modern constitution in the Muslim world, proclaimed by the bey of Tunis in 1861, provided for a grand assembly, but it was to be selected by the king and was intended for the supervision of administration and adjudication. The first elected *majlis*, which was inaugurated in Egypt in 1866, was purely consultative, but the Ottoman parliament was given some legislative power a decade later. The Ottoman parliament was created by the Ottoman constitution of 1876 and included representatives from the Balkan and Arab provinces, as well as the Turkish of the Ottoman Empire. It was dissolved, however, in less than two years. The ruler of Egypt was forced by constitutionalist parliamentarians to proclaim a more liberal constitution than the Ottoman one in 1882, but the effort came to naught with the British occupation of Egypt later that year.

The next wave of constitutionalism in the Middle East began with the revolution of 1906 in Iran, which forced the shah to proclaim a constitution that included a parliament with full legislative power. The Iranian National Consultative Assembly (Majles-e Shura-ye Melli) was elected in the same year. After the Islamic revolution, Iran was declared an Islamic Republic, but its new constitution of 1979 retained the *majlis*, and it was only after it met in 1980 that the *majlis* changed its name to the Islamic Consultative Assembly.

In 1908, the Young Turks revolution forced the sultan to restore the Ottoman constitution. A year later, the constitution was amended to make ministers fully responsible to the parliament. After the Kemalist revolution, the last Ottoman parliament was dissolved by the sultan in 1920, and was replaced by the Grand National Assembly (Buyuk Millet Mejlisi) of Turkey, which passed the republican constitution of 1924.

In the period between the two world wars, constitutional monarchies with elected parliaments were established in independent Egypt (1923) and in Iraq (1925) and Jordan (1928) under the British mandate. In 1938, the emir of Kuwait proclaimed a five-article constitution. It included an assembly whose president was to have executive authority, but the assembly was soon dissolved and the experiment abandoned. A new Kuwaiti constitution was promulgated in 1962.

Republican constitutions came to force in Syria and Lebanon in 1943, Egypt in 1956, Tunisia in 1959, and Algeria and Yemen in 1962, whereas the Moroccan constitution of 1962 declared the nation to be a monarchy. Ministerial responsibility to parliament had been the main bone of contention between the executive branch of government and parliaments under constitutional monarchy, and parliaments had usually lost the contest. Securing meaningful accountability of the executive became even more difficult under the republican constitutions of the postcolonial era, which weakened the rights provisions by their commitment to the ideologies of socialism and nationalism and gave the presidents emergency powers and the right to rule by decree.

The Gulf states other than Kuwait gained their independence from Britain in the 1970s with constitutional documents, but usually without elected parliaments, except for Bahrain and, more recently, Qatar. Oman promulgated a constitution in 1991, and Saudi Arabia in 1992—sixty years after it had first been promised. A Palestinian parliament was set up in accordance with the 1993 Oslo Accords. With rare exceptions, Near and Middle Eastern parliaments have remained weak institutions, and have not succeeded in taking the initiative in legislation or in establishing enduring accountability of the executive branch of their respective governments.

See also **Modernization, Political: Constitutionalism; Political Organization.**

BIBLIOGRAPHY

Brown, Nathan J. *Constitutions in a Nonconstitutionalist World.* Albany: State University of New York Press, 2002.

Saïd Amir Arjomand

MAJLISI, MUHAMMAD BAQIR (1627–1698)

Muhammad Baqir b. Muhammad Taqi Majlisi, known as the second Majlisi or the author of the *Bihar*, was a renowned Iranian Twelver Shi'ite jurist of the late seventeenth century. Acting as the prayer leader and *shaykh al-Islam* of Isfahan under the Safavid monarchs, Shah Suleiman (r. 1666–1694) and Shah Sultan Husayn (r. 1694–1722), he suppressed philosophy and Sufism and reestablished clerical authority under his leadership. He devoted great efforts to the collection and translation of Shi'ite hadith from Arabic into Persian to benefit the laity. He opposed the conventional reliance on Arabic as the main medium of instruction and publication for religious scholars and emphasized the need for doctrinal and legal works in Persian, which could be accessible to the public. He fervently upheld the concepts of "enjoining the good" and "prohibiting evil" and renewed the impetus for conversion from Sunnism to Shi'ism. His legal method drew upon both the *akhbari* (traditionist) and *usuli* (rationalist) schools, as such accepting both the authority of Shi'ite traditions and the role of reason in arriving at a legal opinion. He is mostly known for his monumental work, a Shi'ite encyclopedia of hadith, *Bihar al-Anwar*, completed in 1692.

Rula Jurdi Abisaab

MAKASSAR, SHAYKH YUSUF (C. 1626–1699)

Traditional Makassarese sources report that 'Ali (Shaykh) Yusuf was born in 1626 to a princess of South Sulawesi and raised in the palace of the king of Tallo. He studied under some of the most prominent Arab Muslim scholars in Sulawesi before traveling to continue his education in Banten, Gujarat, the Yemen, Mecca, and Syria. In Damascus he was inducted into the Khalwatiyya order of Sufism, which he worked to spread in Southeast Asia after returning from the Middle East.

In 1664 he settled in Banten where he taught various branches of the Islamic sciences. In 1682 the sultan's son rose against his father's authority with the backing of the Dutch East India Company. Shaykh Yusuf took up an opposition campaign that he pursued for over a year until his capture by the Dutch. He was imprisoned in Batavia and later exiled to Sri Lanka, where he continued his role in advocating resistance against the Dutch via correspondence with the Muslim communities of Indonesia. In 1693 some of these communications were intercepted, and he was thus re-exiled to the Cape of Good Hope. He arrived there on 2 April 1694 and became a founding figure of the Muslim community in South Africa, where he remained until his death. In 1705 the ruler of Makassar petitioned for the repatriation of Shaykh Yusuf's remains, and today his tombs in both Sulawesi and South Africa remain active centers of pilgrimage. Since the 1980s Shaykh Yusuf has become an increasingly popular figure in both Indonesia and South Africa, where Nelson Mandela hailed him as a hero in the history of struggles against oppression.

See also **Africa, Islam in; Southeast Asia, Islam in; Tariqa.**

BIBLIOGRAPHY

Feener, R. Michael. "Shaykh Yusuf and the Appreciation of Muslim 'Saints' in Modern Indonesia." *Journal for Islamic Studies* 18–19 (1999): 112–131.

R. Michael Feener

MALCOLM X (1925–1965)

An extraordinary orator, a self-taught intellectual, and a deeply spiritual man, Malcolm X was one of the most prominent African American political and religious leaders of the civil rights era. After being released from prison in 1952, where he had become a follower of Nation of Islam leader Elijah Muhammad, Malcolm worked as a minister for the organization, most successfully in Harlem, New York. By the late 1950s, Malcolm had become Elijah Muhammad's chief representative, helping to build the movement into black America's most visible Muslim group. Famous for his fiery rhetoric, he was dubbed "America's angriest Negro" as he sought to convert blacks to Elijah Muhammad's separatist Islam. Malcolm also gained national attention as a critic of pro-integration civil rights leaders. In 1964, however, Malcolm left Elijah Muhammad's movement and made the hajj, the annual pilgrimage to Mecca, an occasion during which he publicly embraced Sunni Islam and distanced himself from Elijah Muhammad's teachings. He also visited West Africa and became an advocate of pan-Africanism, the movement that called for the cultural and political unification of black persons around the world.

Until his brutal assassination in 1965, Malcolm worked as both a Sunni Muslim missionary in the United States and as founder of the Organization for Afro-American Unity, which espoused black solidarity. *The Autobiography of Malcolm X* (1965), which was coauthored by Alex Haley, was published shortly after his death. Today, Muslims continue to debate the meaning of Malcolm's life, often disagreeing about whether Malcolm overemphasized the importance of racial identity in his quest for black liberation.

See also **American Culture and Islam; Conversion; Farrakhan, Louis; Muhammad, Elijah; Nation of Islam.**

BIBLIOGRAPHY

DeCaro, Louis A., Jr. *On the Side of My People: A Religious Life of Malcolm X.* New York: New York University Press, 1996.

Haley, Alex, and Malcolm X. *The Autobiography of Malcolm X.* Reprint. New York: Ballantine, 1987.

Edward E. Curtis IV

MALIK, IBN ANAS (C. 708–795)

Malik Ibn Anas, who was born between 708 and 716 C.E., was the most famous jurist from Medina by the time of his death in 795. Malik composed one of the first books of Islamic law, the *Muwatta'*.

Malik studied with several experts on Islamic tradition (hadith), some of whose parents knew the Prophet. He was renowned for his knowledge of hadith, but his teachings were unique for his championing of the practice (sunna) of the inhabitants of Medina. Malik attracted students from all over the Islamic world, and the *Muwatta*' was taught in all medieval centers of learning, especially Egypt, Baghdad, North Africa, and Spain.

Under the caliph al-Mansur in 762 and 763 Malik was punished for his support of Muhammad b. 'Abdallah, an 'Alid pretender to the throne. But later in life the Abbasid caliph Harun al-Rashid tried to make the *Muwatta*' the basis for a unified code of law. The sources agree, however, that these political intrigues were aberrations, and that Malik lived a simple life devoted to teaching, surrounded by a close group of devotees who collected his opinions on every conceivable subject.

The *Muwatta*' has survived in several versions and includes hadith from the Prophet and his Companions as well as legal opinions of Malik and other famous scholars from Medina. It is organized in chapters and covers all aspects of ritual and social life. It is still part of the required curriculum of many Islamic universities today, especially in North and West Africa where the Maliki school (one of the four *madhhab*s of Sunni law) predominates. Several other books, some recently uncovered, contain extensive collections of Malik's opinions not found in the *Muwatta*'.

See also **Africa, Islam in; Law; Madhhab.**

BIBLIOGRAPHY

Goldziher, Ignaz. *Muslim Studies.* Edited by S. M. Stern and translated by S. M. Stern and C. R. Barber. Albany: State University of New York Press, 1972.

Schacht, Joseph. "Malik b. Anas." In *Encyclopaedia of Islam.* New ed. Edited by H. A. R. Gibb, et al. Leiden: E. J. Brill, 1962.

Jonathan E. Brockopp

MA'MUN, AL- (786–833)

Abu 'l-'Abbas 'Abdallah al-Ma'mun (r. 813–833) was the seventh caliph of the Abbasid Dynasty (750–1258). He came to power in the wake of Islam's fourth civil war and is best known for his theological interests and for instituting an inquisition, the *Mihna*, on the doctrine of the createdness of the Qur'an.

During the reign of his father, Harun al-Rashid (r. 786–809), al-Ma'mun served as the governor of Khurasan, in northeastern Iran. He was appointed by al-Rashid as his second successor, after al-Ma'mun's half-brother, Muhammad al-Amin (r. 809–813). But the relations between the two brothers deteriorated rapidly after the death of al-Rashid, which led to a protracted and destructive civil war and eventually to the defeat and death of al-Amin. Al-Ma'mun stayed in Khurasan for several more years after the civil war, before moving back to the Abbasid capital, Baghdad, in 818. The civil war was an episode of major proportions: The long siege of Baghdad and the unrest that followed its fall to al-Ma'mun's troops left large parts of the city in ruins; and the killing of al-Amin, the first time in Abbasid history that a caliph had been murdered, cast a long shadow over the victorious caliph's legitimist claims.

Al-Ma'mun's reign is also noted for the distinctly pro-'Alid policies he pursued. The 'Alids, the descendants of the Prophet's cousin and son-in-law, 'Ali ibn Abi Talib (d. 661), considered themselves to be the rightful claimants to the caliphate, and saw not just the Umayyads (661–750) but also the Abbasids as usurpers—claims viewed unfavorably by caliphs from both houses. While still in Khurasan, al-Ma'mun, in an unprecedented move that startled and dismayed many in his Abbasid clan, had in 817 nominated 'Ali b. Musa al-Rida (d. 818) as his successor. This was justified by the caliph on grounds that al-Rida—"the acceptable one," whom the later Twelver Shi'a reckon to be their eighth imam—was the person most qualified for the political leadership of the community. The caliph also adopted the 'Alid green to replace black as the official color of the Abbasids. And later in his career, he had 'Ali ibn Abi Talib publicly declared "the best" person after the prophet Muhammad, thus denying the superiority of Muhammad's first two successors, Abu Bakr and 'Umar, a point that was then evolving as a matter of dogma among the early Sunnis. 'Ali al-Rida mysteriously died before al-Ma'mun's return to Baghdad, though the caliph continued his pro-'Alid stance until the end of his reign.

The episode, however, which left the most lasting impression on subsequent generations was neither the civil war nor the caliph's pro-'Alid sympathies. Nor was it even al-Ma'mun's patronage of ancient Greek learning, which later came to be associated specifically with his name. Rather, what came to be remembered as the most famous, and controversial, facet of the caliph's reign and of his legacy was the Mihna, an inquisition seeking to enforce the doctrine of the createdness of the Qur'an. This was a doctrine attributed in particular to two early theologians, Ja'd b. Dirham (d. 743) and Jahm b. Safwan (d. 745), and to the latter's putative followers, the Jahmiyya. The Mu'tazila—the most famous of Islam's rationalist theologians, who enjoyed unprecedented political influence under al-Ma'mun and his two successors—espoused it as well; they were also closely associated, during the years of the Mihna (833– c. 851), with the abortive caliphal effort to implement this doctrine as a matter of state policy.

In 827, al-Ma'mun had publicly announced his support for the createdness of the Qur'an. Five years later, and shortly before his death, he decreed that the judges and the scholars of hadith be made to publicly assent to it. A number of explanations have been offered to explain this ultimately abortive venture into state sponsorship of a theological doctrine, but it appears that the caliph's interest in asserting his position as the arbiter of right belief, and in thereby checking the increasing influence in society of the populist scholars of hadith, had much to do with the institution of the Mihna.

The caliph lived for only about four months after he had begun the Inquisition. He died in Tarsus in 833, while on a campaign against the Byzantines, and was succeeded by his brother al-Muʿtasim (r. 833–842). The Inquisition continued under him as well as under the latter's successor, al-Wathiq (r. 842–847), and was finally brought to an end—along with the political influence of the Muʿtazila—during the reign of al-Mutawakkil (r. 847–861). The debate on the theological controversies the Mihna had brought to the fore, as well as on the controversial caliph who had instituted it, continued for many centuries.

See also **Caliphate; Fitna; Mihna; Muʿtazilites, Muʿtazila; Succession.**

BIBLIOGRAPHY

Cooperson, Michael. *Classical Arabic Biography: The Heirs of the Prophets in the Age of al-Maʾmun.* Cambridge, U.K.: Cambridge University Press, 2000.

Ess, Josef Van. *Theologie und Gesellschaft im 2. Und 3. Jahrhundert Hidschra.* Berlin: Walter de Gruyter, 1991–1997.

Gutas, Dimitri. *Greek Thought, Arabic Culture: The Graeco-Arabic Translation Movement in Baghdad and Early ʿAbbasid Society (2nd-4th/8th-10th Centuries).* London: Routledge, 1998.

Hibri, Tayeb, el-. *Reinterpreting Islamic Historiography: Harun al-Rashid and the Narrative of the ʿAbbasid Caliphate.* Cambridge, U.K.: Cambridge University Press, 1999.

Tabari, al-. *The History of al-Tabari.* Vols. 31–32. Albany: State University of New York Press, 1987–1992.

Muhammad Qasim Zaman

MANAR, MANARA

At its simplest, a minaret (Ar. *manar(a), miʾdhana, sawmaʿa*) is a raised structure attached to a mosque from which a muezzin gives the call to prayer, known in Arabic as the *adhan.* Minarets give a distinctive "Islamic" look to the skylines of cities in the Muslim world and indicate from afar the presence of a mosque below. Minarets are commonly tall and slender towers—sometimes polygonal or square but most often cylindrical—supporting one or more balconies for the muezzin. In some parts of the Muslim world, notably Upper Egypt, East Africa, and Kashmir, minarets were either unknown or took a more modest form.

In most times and places minarets were built only with mosques, but occasionally they were attached to other structures, such as the Taj Mahal, a magnificent seventeenth-century tomb at Agra in India, which is surrounded by four towers. Muslim architects have built minarets out of brick or stone or even wood; they have left them plain or covered them with tiles and carving bearing geometric, arabesque, and epigraphic motifs. They have placed them either singly, or in pairs, to flank a doorway or a facade, or in groups of four or more to surround an important building, such as the sanctuary around the Kaʿba in Mecca. The origins of the minaret have been sought in the monumental columns and lighthouses of the late antique Mediterranean lands, the ziggurats of ancient Mesopotamia, and the stupas and commemorative columns of India, but it seems most likely that the minaret was wholly an Islamic invention of the ninth century, meant to draw attention to the mosque as a center of religious life.

See also **Adhan; Architecture; Masjid.**

BIBLIOGRAPHY

Bloom, Jonathan. *Minaret: Symbol of Islam.* Oxford, U.K.: Oxford University Press, 1989.

Sheila S. Blair
Jonathan M. Bloom

MANICHEANISM

Manicheanism was a gnostic religious movement founded by Mani (c. 216–274 or 276), an Iranian religious figure who believed that he had received divine instruction from a spiritual "Twin." The Twin revealed to him "the mystery of light and of darkness" and "the battle which darkness stirred up" when its demons attempted to invade the kingdom of light and entrapped light particles in material bodies. In 240, the Twin commanded him to become the apostle of a new religion and church. The Manichean community was composed of the Elect, whose rituals and strictly regulated behavior helped liberate light particles, and the Auditors, who led less austere lives and provided the Elect with nourishment. To this essentially dualistic religion, and in an attempt to create a truly universal faith, Mani and his followers deliberately added elements drawn from other religions they encountered, including Mithraism, Christianity, and Buddhism. Mani won the support of the Sassanian ruler Shahpur I (239–270) for his far-ranging missionary activities but aroused the enmity of the Zoroastrian clergy, led by the high-priest Kartir, who eventually persuaded Bahram I (271–274) to imprison Mani. Mani either died in prison or was executed. Manicheanism was thereafter ruthlessly suppressed both in the Sasanian East and the Christian West.

The Muslim conquests temporarily ended persecution of Manicheanism in the land of its birth. The Umayyad governor of Iraq, al-Hajjaj b. Yusuf (d. 714), apparently sought to accord Manicheans protected (*dhimmi*) status and to regulate the affairs of their community through an *archegos* based in Ctesiphon (Mada'in). Efforts were also made to heal the sectarian schism that had developed between the Mesopotamian Manicheans and those in the east (known as the Dinawariyya). The Abbasid caliphs, however, were increasingly intolerant of religious diversity, and al-Mahdi (775–785) and al-Hadi (785–786) carried out a systematic purge of individuals suspected of *zandaqa*. This term was virtually a synonym for Manicheanism, and it is claimed that those accused of *zandaqa* had to prove their innocence by spitting on a portrait of Mani. Yet only one of the victims of this campaign has been shown to have actually been a Manichean proper; the Abbasid repression was rather directed against Manichean tendencies in Islam and more generally against nominal Muslims suspected of holding Persianizing, dualistic, syncretistic, subversive, free-thinking, or atheistic ideas. It did make the practice of Manicheanism more difficult and led to a new migration of Manicheans from Iraq to Central Asia. According to al-Nadim, the last leader of the Manichean community in Iraq fled to Khurasan in the time of al-Muqtadir (908–932). He further indicates that he had personally known some three hundred "Zindiqs" in Baghdad during the time of the Buyid emir Mu'izz-al-Dawla (946–967), but this number had dwindled to less than five a quarter-century later.

Manicheanism was strongest in eastern Iran and Central Asia, where Sogdian merchants served as able missionaries for the faith. Its position was strengthened when, in about 762, it became the official religion of the Uighur khaghanate. According to al-Nadim, the "ruler of Khurasan" (presumably one of the Samanids) wanted to follow the Abbasid lead and exterminate the Manicheans in his kingdom but was restrained by the threats of the Uighur khaghan ("lord of the Tughuzghuz") to retaliate against the Muslims in his lands. A Manichean text in Parthian from this period shows that Manicheans were attempting to assimilate the terminology and concepts of Islam, just as they had in the case of other religions. From the tenth century onward, Sufi missionaries, including al-Hallaj, actively proselytized among the Manichean and Turkish communities. By Mongol times, Manicheanism had been supplanted in Central Asia by either Islam or Buddhism.

An unresolved question is the extent to which Manicheans and Manichean tendencies (mixed with neo-Mazdakism) may have been involved in anti-Abbasid revolts in Central Asia. It is suggestive, for example, that the famous revolt of al-Muqanna' (c. 777–783) took place in Sogdia and was supported by the Turks; he and his followers were known as "wearers of white" (reminiscent of the traditional garb of the Manichean Elect), believed in the transmigration of souls, and made much use of the imagery of light. There is, however, no direct evidence linking the revolt to Manicheans, and the dietary and sexual practices attributed to the rebels were certainly non-Manichean.

Mani and Manicheanism are mentioned in numerous Islamic historical and literary texts. They sometimes depict Mani as a prototypical arch-heretic, but he is also often treated as a genuine religious leader and, especially in Persian works, remembered as an acclaimed artist (as he was in fact the founder of the rich Manichean tradition of illustrated manuscripts and fresco paintings).

See also **Islam and Other Religions.**

BIBLIOGRAPHY

Decret, François. *Mani et la tradition manichéenne.* Paris: Seuil, 1974.

Flügel, Gustav. *Mani, seine Lehre und seine Schriften.* Leipzig: Brockhaus, 1862.

Henning, Walter B. "Persian Poetical Manuscripts from the time of Rudaki." In *A Locust's Leg: Studies in Honour of S. H. Taqizadeh.* Edited by W. B. Henning and E. Yarshater. London: Percy Lund, Humphries, and Co., 1962

Klimkeit, Hans-Joachim. *Gnosis on the Silk Road: Gnostic Texts from Central Asia.* San Francisco: HarperCollins, 1993.

Lieu, Samuel N. C. *Manichaeism in the Later Roman Empire and Medieval China: A Historical Survey.* Manchester, U.K.: Manchester University Press, 1985.

Nadim, al-. *The Fihrist of al-Nadim: A Tenth-Century Survey of Muslim Culture.* Edited and translated by Bayard Dodge. New York: Columbia University Press, 1970.

Vajda, Georges. "Les Zindiqs en pays d'Islam au début de la période abbaside." *Rivista degli Studi Orientali* 17 (1937–1938):173–229.

Widengren, Geo. *Mani and Manichaeism.* Translated by Charles Kessler. New York: Holt, Rinehart and Winston, 1965.

Elton L. Daniel

MANSA MUSA (? –1337)

One of the most famous emperors of the medieval Western Sudanic kingdom of Mali, Mansa Musa reigned from about 1312 to 1337. He extended the kingdom of Mali by bringing under its suzerainty many non-Mandingo people of the Sahel. Many sources, including the Arabic author al-'Umari (1301–1394), described Mansa Musa as a pious Muslim, and as one of the medieval rulers whose contribution to the spread of Islam in the Western Sudan was the most significant.

One of the most noted events of Mansa Musa's reign was his pilgrimage to Mecca in 1312. On his way, he visited Egypt during the reign of the Mamluk sultan, Nasir b. Qala'un.

Mansa Musa, it has been reported, was accompanied by thousands of peoples and camels laden with gold. He gave huge quantities of gold to the sultan of Egypt. His stay in Egypt was one of the main events of the year 1312. He distributed so much gold that the price of this precious metal dropped. Perhaps because of the notoriety he gained by this pilgrimage, Mali started to appear in maps drawn by European cartographers.

Mansa Musa's reign supported a flowering in Malian scholarship and architecture. He commissioned al-Sahili, the Andalusian poet and man of letters, to design mosques and other buildings in Mali. Mansa Musa attracted scholars and brought back books of Islamic jurisprudence to the libraries Mali. He also began sending students to Islamic universities in North Africa. He built Qur'anic schools, and established the Friday congregational prayer in Mali.

See also **Africa, Islam in.**

BIBLIOGRAPHY

Clark, P. *West Africa and Islam: A Study of Religious Development from the 8th to the 20th Century.* London: Edwards Arnold, 1982.

Hiskett, M. *The Development of Islam in West Africa.* London and New York: Longman, 1984.

Ousmane Kane

MAQASSARI, TAANTA SALMANKA AL- *See* **Makassar, Shaykh Yusuf**

MARJA' AL-TAQLID

Marja' al-taqlid (Persian *Marja'-e taqlid*) literally means "the source of imitation." *Marja' al-taqlid* is a title given to the highest-ranking cleric within Twelver Shi'ism. The conception of a single leading scholar who both directs and leads the ulema was not absent in Shi'ism, but the *marja'* institution did not emerge until the nineteenth century. The first universally recognized *marja'* was the influential *mujtahid* Murtada al-Ansari (d. 1864). He was followed by a series of scholars whose level of support as *marja'* varied, and a number of scholars at the same time could be put forward as "sources" (*maraji'*) simultaneously. There is no formal means whereby a *marja'* is selected: it seems he emerges as the "most learned" (*a'lamiyya*). There is also much dispute of the level of his authority (as a spokesperson, or as an authority to be obeyed by other scholars and the community). In 1979, Ayatollah Khomeini led a revolution in Iran arguing that a single "supreme jurist" should control both the religious and the political affairs of the Shi'a. His success changed the institution of *marja' al-taqlid*, politicizing it and making disobeying the orders of the supreme jurist similar to treason. After Khomeini died in 1989, there were political and religious disputes among the Shi'a over the role of the *marja' al-taqlid*. This dispute contributed to the declaration by the Iranian government, in 1994, that Ayatollah Sayyed 'Ali Khamane'i (a former close associate of Khomeini) was the single *marja' al-taqlid* when the then undisputed *marja'* Ayatollah Khu'i died. This move was undoubtedly linked to the need to establish the position of "leader of the revolution" (*rahbar*) in Iran. Ayatollah Khamene'i's position as the *Marja' al-taqlid* has, however, remained a matter of dispute.

See also **Shi'a: Imami (Twelver); Taqlid; Ulema.**

BIBLIOGRAPHY

Amanat, A. "In Between the Madrasa and the Marketplace: The Designations of Clerical Leadership in Modern Shi'ism." In *Authority and Political Culture in Shi'ism.* Edited by S. A. Arjomand. Albany: State University of NewYork Press, 1988.

Lambton, A. K. S. "A Reconsideration of the Position of the *Marja' Taqlid* and the Religious Institution." *Studia Islamica* 20 (1964): 115–135.

Robert Gleave

MARRIAGE

In Muslim societies marriage is a contract regulated by a code of law rooted in religious precepts—the *shari'a.* The relations between the precepts and the law are complex, the interpretations of the law vary considerably, and the social practices of marriage constitute a major part of the rich cultural diversity of the Muslim world. Moreover, marriage rules and customs have been central to ongoing debates over issues of modernity and women's status in Islam, starting with the anticolonial and nationalist movements of the early twentieth century. The codification and reform of *shari'a* rules governing marriage in the first part of the century, and the more recent emergence of Islamist movements and their demand for a return to *shari'a*, have highlighted the ideological dimension of the legal regulation of marriage.

Marriage in Islamic law is based on a strong patriarchal ethos, imbued with religious ideals and values. It is one of the few contracts that straddles the boundary between the two main categories: *'ibadat* (spiritual/ritual acts) and *mu'amalat* (social/private acts). In spirit, marriage belongs to *'ibadat*, in that Muslim jurists define it as a religious duty. In form, it comes under the category of *mu'amalat*, is defined as a civil contract, and is patterned after the contract of sale, which has served as a model for other contracts. In this respect, there is no difference among the various schools: all share the same conception of marriage. If they differ, it is to the extent to which they translate this conception into legal rules.

In its legal structure, marriage (*nikah*) is a contract of exchange, with fixed terms and uniform legal effects. Its essential components are the offer (*ijab*), which is made by the woman or her guardian (*wali*), the acceptance (*qabul*) by the man, and the payment of dower (*mahr* or *sadaq*), a sum of money or any valuable that the husband pays or undertakes to pay to the bride before or after consummation. With the contract, a wife comes under her husband's *'isma* (dominion and protection), entailing a set of defined rights and obligations for each party—some supported by legal force, others by moral sanction. Those with legal force revolve around the twin themes of sexual access and compensation, embodied in the concepts of *tamkin* (submission) and *nafaqa* (maintenance). *Tamkin*—defined as unhampered sexual access—is the husband's right and thus the wife's duty; whereas *nafaqa*—defined as shelter, food, and clothing—is the wife's right and the husband's duty. A wife is entitled to *nafaqa* only after consummation of the marriage, and she loses her claim if she is in a state of *nushuz* (disobedience).

The contract establishes neither a shared matrimonial regime nor identical rights and obligations between the spouses: The husband is sole provider and owner of matrimonial resources and the wife is possessor of *mahr* and her own wealth. The only shared space is that involving the procreation of children, and even here the wife is not legally compelled to suckle her child unless it is impossible to feed it otherwise. Likewise, only a man can enter more than one marriage at a time (four permanent contracts in Sunni schools of law; and, in Shi'a law, as many temporary ones as he desires or can afford). Only the husband can terminate each contract at will: He needs no grounds and neither the wife's presence nor her consent. Wives can, however, through the insertion of stipulations in the contract, modify some of its terms and acquire, for example, the right to choose the place of residence or to work, or the delegated right to divorce if the husband contracts another marriage.

Muslim jurists claim that this construction of marriage, based on their readings of the sacred texts, is divinely ordained. But marriage as lived and experienced by Muslims involves a host of customary obligations and social relationships that have always gone far beyond juristic constructions. Some of these are rooted in the ideals of the *shari'a* and enjoy its moral support, though they are not reflected in legal rulings. In Muslim societies, marriage in practice not only creates a matrimonial regime but takes a wide range of forms, varying according to customary practices, individual inclinations and characters, the social origins (rural/urban, class) of the partners, and their economic resources. Men's unconditional legal rights to divorce and polygamy are often checked in practice by social mores, the pressures of the extended family, and the stigma usually attached to both polygamy and divorce.

With the emergence of modern nation-states and the creation of modern legal systems in the early part of the twentieth century, the juristic rules of marriage were selectively reformed, codified, and grafted onto a unified legal system (as in most Middle Eastern and Asian Muslim countries) or were left intact to be applied by Islamic judges (as in most African and Persian Gulf countries). Turkey was the only state in the Muslim world to introduce a Western code to replace juristic rules, though these continued to govern marriages in rural areas and among religious groups. In most Muslim countries during the twentieth century, as women's access to education and work, and consequently their aspirations for equality, increased, so did the gap between juristic and social notions of marriage widen. On the whole, until the rise of political Islam in the 1970s, marriage was acquiring a more egalitarian legal structure in the Muslim world. More recently, the patriarchal juristic model has been widely reasserted. Despite wide-ranging variations and changes in practice, the jurists' notions continue to dominate both the reality of marriage in contemporary Muslim societies and debates about the issue. Not only do most Muslims believe the juristic conception to be divinely ordained, but it informs the legal rules in most Muslim countries.

An image of a young Muslim couple in traditional wedding attire appears in the volume two color insert.

See also **Divorce; Gender; Law; Mahr.**

BIBLIOGRAPHY

'Abd Al 'Ati, Hammudah. *The Family Structure in Islam.* Indianapolis: American Trust Publication, 1977.

El Alami, Dawoud. *The Marriage Contract in Islamic Law.* London, Dordrecht, and Boston: Graham & Trotman, 1992.

Anderson, J. N. D. "The Eclipse of the Patriarchal Family in Contemporary Islamic Law." In his *Family Law in Asia and Africa.* London: George Allen & Unwin, 1968.

Mir-Hosseini, Ziba. *Marriage on Trial: A Study of Islamic Family Law: Iran and Morocco Compared.* London: I. B. Tauris, 1993.

Nasir, Jamal J. *Islamic Law of Personal Status.* 2d edition. London: Graham & Trotman, 1990.

Ziba Mir-Hosseini

MARTYRDOM

The idea of martyrdom in Islam is rooted in the fact that from the beginning of the religion, Muslims died in the struggle to establish and expand the Islamic state, and their deaths in the course of this struggle were remembered and celebrated. The

Qur'an encourages martyrdom by assuring believers that death is illusory: "And say not of those slain in God's way, 'They are dead'; rather they are living, but you are not aware" (2:154).

God also promises ample rewards to those who die *fi sabil Allah*, "in the way of God":

Count not those who were slain in God's way as dead, but rather living with their Lord, by Him provided, rejoicing in the bounty God has given them, because no fear shall be on them, neither shall they sorrow, joyful in blessing and bounty from God, and that God leaves not to waste the wage of the believers. (3:169–171)

Other passages elevate death in the course of struggle for Islam (e.g. 3:157–158, 4:74; 9:20–22; 47:4–6; and 61:11).

Martyrdom in Early Islam

While the idea of martyrdom is clearly rooted in the Qur'an, the technical terms for martyr, *shahid*, and for martyrdom, *shahada*, arise from a different context. When the term *shahid* appears in the Qur'an, as it does frequently, it never means martyr, but only "witness," in the legal sense or in the ordinary sense of "eyewitness." The extension of the meaning of *shahid* to martyrdom was likely a borrowing from Syrian Christians for whom the connection of martyrdom with an act of witnessing was deep rooted and reflected in linguistic usage. The terms *martys* in Greek and *sahda* in Syriac both carried the dual meaning of witness and martyr, and A. J. Wensinck and Ignaz Goldziher plausibly argued that the Arabic *shahid* is borrowed from the Syriac.

This connection between martyrdom and witness made sense to Christians, for the Christian martyrs were those who witnessed by their manner of death to the reality of heaven and the inevitable victory of God. But for Muslims the connection was a stretch for the simple reason that the Qur'anic idea of death in the way of God required no act of witnessing. Muslims were thus left with the uncomfortable problem of discovering a link between the two ideas, and they came up with a variety of creative suggestions: Martyrs are called "witnesses" because their souls witness Paradise, their deaths are witnessed by angels, they will serve as witnesses against those who rejected God's prophets, Muhammad will be a witness on their behalf at the Day of Judgment, or their wounds will testify to their exalted status in the afterlife. The awkwardness of these suggestions, as Keith Lewinstein points out, suggests that later Muslims had no idea why the two ideas came together and that the connection had to be invented to explain linguistic usage.

Early Islamic martyrdom, then, was an inevitable corollary not of witnessing to the truth but of struggling on its behalf. Thus jihad, or struggle, provides the chief context for the earliest ideas of martyrdom in Islam. Accounts of the earliest Muslim martyrs reflect this context. The martyrs most celebrated in biographies of the Prophet are those who threw themselves into battle with courage and abandon. Ibn Ishaq's account of the Muslim victory at Badr (623/624 C.E.), for example, is peppered with accounts of martyrdom. In one account, 'Umayr was eating some dates when he heard the Prophet promise Paradise to any who died in battle. At this he immediately flung the dates aside and threw himself into the battle exclaiming, "Is there nothing between me and entering Paradise save to be killed by these men?" Another Muslim, 'Asim, asked Muhammad, "What makes the Lord laugh with joy at His servant?" Muhammad answered, "When he plunges into the midst of the enemy without mail." At this 'Asim threw off his mail coat, plunged into the battle and was killed.

Incentives for this kind of battlefield martyrdom are colorfully elaborated in the tradition literature. Martyrs are first of all spared from the normal pain of death. They then proceed directly to the highest station in Paradise, without waiting for the Day of Judgment, and without enduring interrogation in the grave by the angels Munkar and Nakir. Once in Paradise they share the place closest to the throne of God with the prophets, wear jeweled crowns, and are each given seventy *houris* (virgins of paradise). Martyrs are purified of sin and do not require the Prophet's intercession—indeed, according to some traditions, martyrs are themselves second only to the prophets as intercessors.

While fighting unbelievers on the battlefield has remained a basic and consistent emphasis in Muslim understandings of martyrdom, conflicts within the Muslim community took the idea in new directions. Martyrdom was an especially potent ideal among some Kharijite Muslims who called themselves *shurat*, or vendors, in reference to Qur'anic praise for those who sell their earthly lives in exchange for Paradise (4:74; 9:112). The idea of deliberately seeking martyrdom (*talab al-shahadat*) by "selling" one's life came to be especially associated with Kharijites. One Kharijite ideologue, for instance, exhorts his followers to strive against "the unjust leaders of error, and to go out (*khuruj*) from the Abode of Transience to the Abode of Eternity and join our believing, convinced brothers who have sold (*ba'u*) this world for the next, and spent their wealth in quest of God's good pleasure in the final reckoning" (Lewinstein, 2002, p. 85). As this exhortation makes clear, the conflicts that provided the Kharijites with opportunities for martyrdom were not struggles against unbelievers, but struggles for justice and purity in the Muslim community. More importantly, martyrdom was not merely an inconvenient by-product of struggle for which the martyr needs to be compensated, but a goal worth pursuing in its own right.

The Shi'a and Martyrdom

Internal struggles within the *umma* also shaped the construction of martyrdom among Shi'ite Muslims, for whom the death of the Prophet's grandson Husayn became the defining event of their history as a community. Husayn was martyred in 680 at Karbala in Iraq when his small band, accompanied by women and children, was attacked and massacred by the army of the Umayyad ruler, Yazid. Shi'ite interpretations of Karbala took Muslim ideas of martyrdom in completely new directions. Husayn's suffering and death came to be seen not just as an individual contribution to the struggle against injustice, meriting individual reward, but as a deliberate redemptive act of cosmic significance. By choosing martyrdom Husayn ensured the ultimate victory of his community and earned the place of mediator for his people. Martyrdom became such a central value for the Shi'a that all the Shi'ite imams were held to have been martyrs, and the major ritual and devotional expressions of Shi'ism are celebrations of martyrdom.

Types of Martyrdom

To celebrate martyrdom is not the same as to seek it, however. Shi'ite scholars were happy to revere Husayn but they resisted the impulse to emulate him. In this they were part of a broader scholarly tendency to dilute the value of martyrdom. In the hands of mainstream scholars, both Sunni and Shi'ite, the category of martyr was enlarged to include many kinds of death, including drowning, pleurisy, plague, or diarrhea. According to other traditions martyrs also include those who die in childbirth, those who die defending their property, those who are eaten by lions, and those who die of seasickness. A special category of martyr is made up of those who suffer the pangs of unexpressed and unrequited love, patiently keeping their passions concealed to death. The trend culminated in the transference of the value of martyrdom to other pious acts, so that death was no longer the most important prerequisite. The band of martyrs came to include anyone who conscientiously fulfills his or her religious obligations, those who engage in the "greater jihad" against their own evil tendencies, and, significantly, scholars who engage in the "jihad of the pen." According to one well-known hadith, the ink of the scholars will outweigh the blood of the martyrs.

The incongruity of equating battlefield martyrs with victims of unrequited love or those who died quietly in bed did not go unnoticed by legal scholars. Thus battlefield martyrs are put in a special category as "martyrs in this world and the next" and are honored with special burial rites. The martyr's body, in most circumstances, is not washed; he is to be buried in the clothes in which he was killed. Some hold that no prayers over the martyr are necessary since he is automatically purified from sin. The lesser categories of martyrs are "martyrs of the next world" meaning, chiefly, that they are not eligible for special burial rites but must be satisfied with divine approbation and the rewards of Paradise.

Even if battlefield martyrs retained a special status, however, the trend in medieval Muslim treatments of the subject was to render the major benefits of martyrdom common currency, readily available to any pious believer. Several characteristics of medieval Islam contributed to the trend: the pervasive influence of Sufism with its characteristic focus on the spiritual value of an act rather than its externals, scholarly quietism in reaction to the militancy of the Kharijites and other Islamic rebels, and the simple fact that opportunities for martyrdom in the struggle against unbelievers were severely diminished after the initial century of conquest.

Outside the definitions of martyrdom discussed in the legal literature, an independent tradition of martyrdom was kept alive among Sufis. The paradigmatic Sufi martyr was Ibn Mansur al-Hallaj (d. 922), who was crucified by Muslim authorities in Baghdad on the charge of blasphemy. Al-Hallaj, along with other Sufi martyr heroes like Suhrawardi (d. 1168), 'Ayn al-Qudat (d. 1131), and Ibn Sab'in (d. 1269), died the victim of his own inordinate love for the Divine, thus exemplifying the Sufi ideal of extinction in the Divine and acting out the tragedy of the mystic lover, caught between the conflicting demands of love and law. This style of martyrdom belonged to the spiritual virtuosi, however. For the ordinary Muslim, the benefits of martyrdom are only experienced secondhand, by visiting a martyr's shrine, or *mashhad*, or for Shi'a, by reenacting the passion of Husayn in *ta'ziya* celebrations during the month of Muharram.

Militancy and Martyrdom

The sublimation of the martyr ideal in pious devotion has continued in Muslim societies, but the modern experience has also given some Muslims abundant reason to revive more militant ideas of martyrdom. Modern Muslim treatments of martyrdom have been intertwined with changing attitudes toward jihad, and are shaped by reaction against the quietism of the medieval tradition. Whereas for medieval jurists both jihad and martyrdom were spiritualized and internalized, the colonial experience suddenly gave the idea of militant struggle new relevance. Thus a common early response to colonialism was the emergence of anticolonial jihad movements like that of Sayyid Ahmad in India. Nineteenth-century Muslim apologists and modernists like Sayyid Ahmad Khan (1817–1898), Chiragh 'Ali (1844–1895), and Muhammad 'Abduh (1849–1905) departed from the medieval tradition in a different way by reinterpreting jihad to accord with Western preconceptions. Jihad, the modernists argued, amounts to no more than the right of a state to defend itself against attack. The effect was to encourage a secularization of martyrdom whereby any soldier who died for his country could be counted a martyr.

Against both the quietism of medieval scholars and the apologetics of modernists, revivalists have called for a return to militant jihad and a revival of the ideals of physical martyrdom. Hasan al-Banna (1906–1949), founder of the Muslim Brotherhood and a celebrated martyr in his own right, offers a stirring invitation to martyrdom:

Brothers! God gives the *umma* that is skilled in the practice of death and that knows how to die a noble death an exalted life in this world and eternal felicity in the next. What is the fantasy that has reduced us to loving this world and hating death? If you gird yourselves for a lofty deed and yearn for death, life shall be given to you . . . . Know, then, that death is inevitable, and that it can only happen once. If you suffer in the way of God, it will profit you in this world and bring you reward in the next. (Hasan al-Banna, 1978, p.156).

For al-Banna and other revivalists, waging jihad is held to be an individual duty (*fard 'ayn*) of all Muslims. It is thus incumbent on every Muslim to prepare him- or herself for martyrdom, and it is on the basis of this duty that al-Banna calls on Muslims to become skilled at dying and to master "the art of death" (*fann al-mawt*). Since all must die, the wise will learn how to get the most benefit out of the exchange (Q. 4:74). Such advocacy of martyrdom echoes the ideology of the Kharijites and comes close to encouraging the seeking out of martyrdom, *talab al-shahada*, a practice condemned in classical scholarship. The recent pattern of suicide bombings sponsored by militant Islamic movements, many of them offshoots of the Muslim Brotherhood, fits comfortably into the framework of the call of Hasan al-Banna to be "skilled in the practice of death."

Modern Shi'ite treatments of martyrdom have tended to run along parallel lines, emphasizing the ideological value of martyrdom. When an individual gives his or her life for a cause, according to 'Ali Shari'ati (1933–1977), this life becomes valuable in proportion to the value of the cause for which it is spent. A martyr expends his or her whole existence for an ideal, and that ideal is given life through martyrdom. Martyrs thus exchange their lives for something greater and more lasting, leaving behind a permanent and valuable legacy. Similarly, Ayatollah Taliqani (1910–1979) invokes the Sufi poet Jalaluddin Rumi (1207–1273) to argue that martyrdom is part of a chain of sacrifice whereby the imperfect is perfected. Just as vegetation is eaten by a lamb and becomes flesh and blood, so a martyr loses his existence to partake in a higher cause.

These justifications for martyrdom are clearly modern in their emphasis on the ideological value of martyrdom. Such ideas have more than theoretical relevance. Modern conflicts in Palestine, Afghanistan, Kashmir, Chechnya, Iraq, and Iran have produced a large crop of martyrs, along with a huge volume of popular literature celebrating their deeds. Consequently, activist and militant forms of martyrdom tend to be the most visible and dramatic expressions of the idea in the modern Islamic world. The prominence of such militant forms should not, however, be allowed to obscure the continued importance of other enduring expressions of martyrdom in popular devotion and especially in Shi'ite ritual.

See also **Banna, Hasan al-; Expansion; Husayn; 'Ibadat; Imamate; Jihad; Kharijites, Khawarij; Ta'ziya.**

BIBLIOGRAPHY

Ayoub, Mahmoud. *Redemptive Suffering in Islam: A Study of the Devotional Aspects of 'Ashura' in Twelver Shi'ism.* The Hague: Mouton, 1978.

Banna', Hasan al-. *Five Tracts of Hasan al-Banna' (1906–1949): A Selection from the Majmu'at Rasa'il al-Imam al-Shahid Hasan al-Banna'.* Translated by Charles Wendell. Berkeley: University of California Press, 1978.

Goldziher, Ignaz. *Muslim Studies.* Edited and translated by C. R. Barber and S. M. Stern. London: Allen & Unwin, 1971.

Husted, W. R. "Karbala' Made Immediate: The Martyr as Model in Imami Shi'ism." *Muslim World* 83 (1993): 263–278.

Kohlberg, E. *Medieval Muslim Views on Martyrdom.* Amsterdam: Noord-Hollansche, 1997.

Lewinstein, Keith. "The Revaluation of Martyrdom in Early Islam." In *Sacrificing the Self: Perspectives on Martyrdom and Religion.* Edited by Margaret Cormack. Oxford, U.K.: Oxford University Press, 2002.

Massignon, Louis. *The Passion of al-Hallaj: Mystic and Martyr of Islam.* Princeton, N.J.: Princeton University Press, 1982.

Rosenthal, Franz. "On Suicide in Islam." *Journal of the American Oriental Society* 66 (1946): 239–259.

Shariati, Ali. *Martyrdom: Arise and Bear Witness.* Translated by Ali Asghar Ghassemy. Tehran: Ministry of Islamic Guidance, 1981.

Smith, Jane I., and Haddad, Yvonne Yazbeck. *The Islamic Understanding of Death and Resurrection.* Albany: State University of New York Press, 1981.

Taleqani, Mahmud; Muttahhari, Murtaza; and Shari'ati, 'Ali. *Jihad and Shahadat: Struggle and Martyrdom in Islam.* Edited by Mehdi Abedi and Gary Legenhausen. Houston: Institute for Research and Islamic Studies, 1986.

Wensinck, A. J. "The Oriental Doctrine of the Martyrs." In *Semietische Studien uit de Nalatenschap.* Leiden: A. W. Sijthoff, 1941.

Daniel W. Brown

MARWA, MUHAMMAD (D. 1980)

Muhammad Marwa (Maitatsine) was a Qur'anic teacher from Cameroon in West Africa who followed *shari'a* (Islamic law). After he moved to Nigeria, his teachings inspired a religious, millennial revolt against the government in the northern province of Kano in 1980. A mystic, he resembled the Mahdi of Sudan in that he claimed revelatory knowledge, which supplemented, and even superseded, the teachings of the prophet Muhammad. In 1979, he apparently declared himself a prophet greater than Muhammad. The movement, also known as Yan Tatsine (the followers of Maitatsine), was nominally Muslim but unorthodox, rejecting established authorities, both religious and secular. It had a strong element of political protest in it, attracting mostly the urban poor, young men who had moved to the city and could not fit in with established groups.

Marwa recruited from Qur'anic schools, rejecting the authority of all books aside from the Qur'an, including the hadiths. Followers kept their own mosques and schools. The movement was hostile to women, many of whom were kidnapped and kept in Marwa's compound for months. Tensions with the government exploded in a series of riots, apparently instigated by attacks that Marwa's followers made on members of the local Muslim community in December 1980 in Kano (resulting in 4,177 deaths) and again in 1982 in Kaduna and Maiduguri, after which the movement was suppressed. It was blamed for further uprisings in the early 1980s, which the government used as an excuse to increase state control. Marwa was among those killed in the 1980 riots.

See also **Africa, Islam in; Kano; Mahdi.**

BIBLIOGRAPHY

Callaway, Barbara, and Creevey, Lucy. *The Heritage of Islam: Women, Religion and Politics in West Africa.* Boulder, Colo.: Lynne Rienner Publishers, 1994.

Kastfelt, Niels. "Rumours of Maitatsine: A Note on Political Culture in Northern Nigeria." *African Affairs* 88, no. 350 (1989): 83–90.

Paula Stiles

MARWAN (623–685 C.E.)

Marwan b. al-Hakam b. Abi al-'As, Abu 'Abd al-Malik, the eponym of the Marwanid branch of the Umayyads, reigned for several months in 684 and 685 C.E. He was one of the Companions of Muhammad and the cousin of 'Uthman b. 'Affan (r. 644–656), the third caliph of Islam. Marwan was appointed secretary to 'Uthman during his caliphate because of his knowledge of the Qur'an and became the caliph's closest advisor. He probably encouraged the caliph to compile the Qur'an. Much of Marwan's wealth came from the rich plunder he obtained during an expedition to North Africa, which he invested in properties in Medina. Despite objection from many Medinans, Marwan influenced 'Uthman to appoint his brother, Harith b. Hakam, to oversee the market of Medina.

Marwan was viewed as an ambitious man and his influence on the caliph was generally regarded as negative. When Egyptian malcontents negotiated a political settlement with

'Uthman, Marwan is believed to have written a letter ordering the execution of the Egyptians concerned. It was the discovery of this letter by the Egyptians that led to 'Uthman's being besieged and murdered in his home in 656. This event is remembered as "the battle of the house," or *yawm al-dar*. Marwan was wounded while trying to protect 'Uthman. He later fought in the Battle of the Camel with 'A'isha against 'Ali, for 'Ali would neither investigate nor punish the murderers of 'Uthman. Later, Marwan swore allegiance to 'Ali, but joined the ranks of Mu'awiya when 'Ali was murdered. He was appointed governor of Medina by the caliph Mu'awiyya b. Abi Sufyan (r. 661–680), and served in this capacity from 661 to 668 and again from 674 to 677.

Mu'awiyya was succeeded by his son, Yazid, who died in 683, followed by Yazid's son, Mu'awiya II, who died a few months later. Meanwhile, the hostility provoked by Yazid during his brief caliphate, which saw the death of Husayn b. 'Ali, the battle of the Harra (a stronghold in Medina), and the onslaught against Mecca, had brought 'Abdullah b. al-Zubayr great popularity. Al-Zubayr was acclaimed caliph of the region extending from the Hijaz (a region in western Saudi Arabia) to Iraq. The Umayyads were thus forced to look beyond the Sufyanid family for a leader.

At this point, frustrated by inadequate leadership, tribal loyalties that had been submerged by the uniting forces of Islam emerged once again. The faction led by Ibn Bahdal, chief of the Kalbi clan, proclaimed Marwan caliph, while the faction led by al-Dahhaq b. Ways al-Fihri supported Ibn al-Zubayr. When the two factions met at the battle of Marj Rahat it was Marwan who won the day

Marwan immediately consolidated his position: He married Fakhita bt. Abi Hashim, the widow of Yazid, vowing that the latter's son, Khalid b. Yazid, would be his successor. Once appointed caliph, however, he first replaced Egypt's Zubayrid governor with his son, 'Abd al-'Aziz. Then, reneging on his promise to Fakhita, he named his eldest son, 'Abd al-Malik, heir to the caliphate. Finally, having defeated Mus'ab b. al-Zubayr, the brother of his rival caliph in Mecca, he sent his general, 'Ubayd Allah b. Ziyad, to capture Iraq.

Marwan died in 685, murdered by his wife, Fakhita, before Iraq was taken. His son, 'Abd al-Malik (r. 685–705), successfully consolidated the Umayyad caliphate under the Marwanid banner.

See also **Caliphate; Succession.**

BIBLIOGRAPHY

Dixon, A. A. *The Umayyad Caliphate 65–86/684–705.* London: Luzac, 1971.

Hawting, Gerald. *The First Dynasty of Islam.* Carbondale: Southern Illinois University Press, 1987.

Madelund, Wilferd. *The Succession to Muhammad.* Cambridge, U.K.: Cambridge University Press, 1997.

Kennedy, Hugh. *The Prophet and the Age of the Caliphates.* London: Longman, 1986.

Rizwi Faizer

MASCULINITIES

The academic study of masculinity has recently emerged as a parallel to feminist strategies of deconstructing historical, cultural, class, religious, and other factors shaping notions of maleness. In the case of Islam and Muslim societies, elements contributing to masculinities are normative pronouncements of the religion, the models of the Prophet and his companions, as well as philosophical, ethical, and social discourses and practices.

The Qur'an seems to privilege the male as being "a degree higher" and gives him responsibility over females. Nonetheless, feminist scholars such as Asma Barlas have been trying to recover an underlying antipatriarchal ethos behind the stories of the sacred text, for example, in Abraham's breaking with traditional models of patriarchy through rejecting his father's gods. The Prophet himself embodied traits of strength and gentleness, and served both as a warrior and tender husband and father. 'Ali, the fourth caliph, as a heroic male figure embodies both military prowess and spiritual wisdom, whereas 'Umar, the second caliph, projects the harsh and uncompromising enforcement of social control while dispensing impartial justice.

Both pre- and post-Islamic Arabic cultures contain well-developed concepts of *muruwwa*, or manliness, combining moral notions of integrity, fidelity, valor, chastity, and honor. In medieval Muslim societies and Sufi spheres, the ethical code of *futuwwa* (Arabic) or *jawanmardi* (Persian) was enacted by societies or guild-like alliances of young men bonded around ethics of honor and companionship. A sort of Persian cult of male strength and chivalry is still performed in the *zurkhana*, or "house of strength," where gymnastic exercises are carried out to the background of the chanted national epic, the *Shahnameh.*

Contemporary studies of film and literature from the Muslim world explore their themes of male competition, violence, and coming of age in a highly gendered social world. Certain tropes, such as the wily woman who deprives males of virility and the constant need to preserve and control female honor, play on male anxieties. Some anthropological and literary studies have highlighted the role of the wedding night in Arab societies, where in traditional contexts male sexual performance and female virginity were expected and verified, giving further clues into the psychological background of asserting male potency as a quasi-sacrificial blood ritual.

Further research analyzes how maleness is inculcated through rituals such as circumcision which, in certain Muslim societies such as Turkey, may be a prepuberty ritual accompanied by public display and celebration, including dressing the boy in a military-type uniform. The cultural significance of male attributes such as beards and mustaches, which may also have a religious or political valence, is another dimension of the Muslim embodiment of maleness. Variations in conceptions of the ideal masculine have also merited attention in terms of homosexual identities, black Muslim male embodiment, the effect of colonialism and the colonial gaze on Muslim constructions of the masculine, and so on.

See also **Body, Significance of; Feminism; Gender; Homosexuality.**

BIBLIOGRAPHY

Cornwall, Andrea, and Lindisfarne, Nancy, eds. *Dislocating Masculinity: Comparative Ethnographies.* London and New York: Routledge, 1994.

Ghoussoub, Mai, and Sinclair-Webb, Emma. *Imagined Masculinities: Male Identity and Culture in the Modern Middle East.* London: Saqi Books, 2000.

Marcia Hermansen

MASHHAD

Mashhad is a major city of Iran, and the capital of Khorasan, the country's largest province with six million inhabitants. In 1996, 2.25 million of the province's population lived in Mashhad. It is the country's most important pilgrimage site, visited annually by over thirteen million pilgrims from Iran and abroad. The shrine of 'Ali b. Musa al-Rida (Reza) (764–818 c.e.), the eighth and the only imam buried in Iran, is in Mashhad. The imam was buried in an orchard by the grave of the Abbasid caliph Harun al-Rashid at Sinabad, a hamlet near Nawghan, one of the districts of the city of Tus. The Mongol assault in the early thirteenth century, followed by the attack of the Timurid Miran Shah in 1385, were major blows that led to the gradual extinction of Tus, so much so that we find no mention of it in the sources since the middle of the fifteenth century. While Tus gradually disappeared, the hamlet of Sinabad grew into a town, first called Mashhad-e Razavi and then Mashhad-e Tus, as large numbers of Shi'a settled there because of the imam's shrine, known for centuries as "Mashhad al-Razavi."

The shrine and its upkeep received the attention of Samanid, Ghaznawid, and Seljuk rulers who held the Alawid in reverence despite their Sunni creed. Mashhad received special royal attention during the reign of the Timurid ruler Shahrukh. He visited the imam's shrine for *ziyara* in 1406 and it was during his reign that the famous Gawharshad Mosque, completed for his wife in 1418, and other buildings in the shrine complex were constructed. After establishing Safavid control of Khorasan, Shah 'Abbas showed a special reverence for Mashhad and in 1601 made a pilgrimage on foot, having set out from Isfahan, to fulfill a vow. The shrine received greater patronage during the reign of the Safavids and the Qajars, and most of the inscriptions pertaining to the repairs and new construction are extant. A new plan for the extension of the shrine complex was put into effect in the years before the Islamic Revolution in the course of which bazaars and houses in a large surrounding area were demolished. New construction is still occurring in the open space around the shrine.

In the past the shrine's upkeep and administration of the enormous endowments pertaining to it lay with an administrator (*mutawalli*), traditionally a sayyid from the descendants of Imam Reza appointed by royal decree. Since the Islamic Revolution, the appointment of the administrator lies within the jurisdiction of the supreme jurist (*valiye faqih*). The shrine as an architectural complex consists of the central building and its gilded dome, which houses the mausoleum and a one-thousand-year-old mosque (Masjid Balasar), twenty-three halls, several courtyards of different sizes, eight minarets, and two towers, each with its own particular history. It also maintains a major library, one of the oldest in Iran and dating from tenth century, with 26,400 manuscripts, 2,820 Qur'an manuscripts, and over 300,000 printed books now kept in a newly built structure (inaugurated in 1995), as well as a museum and several subsidiary buildings housing various facilities. The *Astan-e Quds* (Holy Threshold), the establishment which manages the shrine complex and the related endowments, is a huge conglomerate that administers, in addition to a university, scores of academic, cultural, and economic institutions that play an important role in the life of the province.

Mashhad has a center of learning (*hawzah 'ilmiyya*) next only to that of the Qom in size and importance. Leading scholars of this *hawzah* have enjoyed a regional following as "sources of emulation" (*marja' al-taqlid*).

See also **Pilgrimage: Hajj; Pilgrimage: Ziyara; Shi'a: Imami (Twelver).**

Rasool Ja'fariyan

MASJID

The term *masjid* refers to the customary place for performing the obligatory ritual prayer (*salat*) in the Muslim tradition. The Arabic verbal root *s-j-d* from which the noun derives, denotes the action of bowing down or prostration. Its close cognates in other Semitic languages, meaning a place of worship, predate Islam and allude to sacred venues belonging to other religions.

The Qur'an contains over twenty references to *masjid*, in singular and plural, offering ample evidence for the importance of this space in the life of Muslims from the time of the Prophet, although its form and its significance have undergone extensive elaboration as the Islamic civilization took shape and expanded. Thus a variety of related institutions have emerged that are embraced by this same term, normally rendered as mosque in English.

In the Qur'an, the word most frequently refers to the sanctuary at Mecca, *al-masjid al-haram*, indicating its uniqueness and centrality while several passages refer to the practices prescribed for it as a site of cult and pilgrimage (e.g., 2:196, 9:28, 48:27).

The first *masjid* built by Muhammad consisted of the enclosed empty courtyard of his house at Medina. Not only did his followers gather there for collective prayer and preaching, but for many other activities. As the effective seat of government, it served as the center of civil and military administration while also providing space for instruction, social gatherings, and hospitality to strangers. During the Prophet's lifetime the establishment of other *masjid*s for local use appears to have been infrequent as believers were encouraged to regard everyplace as available for the conduct of prayer, although later, *masjid*s began to arise quickly, starting with those locales where it was remembered the Prophet had prayed.

With the spread of Islam beyond the Arabian Peninsula, new *masjid*s arose, especially in the principal cities such as Kufa, Basra, Damascus, and Cairo, which sought to reproduce the model of Medina. Thus the seat of government and the space for collective prayer were closely conjoined. This architectural fusion of religious and secular functions, in conformity with Islamic teachings, was also represented in the nature of leadership. In time, however, the caliphs and their governors in the provinces ceased to preside at public prayer and to preach themselves, relegating these tasks to pious scholars instead, although these two realms of authority remained linked in Islamic theories of rule.

Hence, the preaching of the sermon (*khutba*) at the Friday noon prayer—which was initially restricted to one large central *masjid* in the major cities (a *masjid* of the type that came to be known as a *jami'*, or Friday Mosque)—always entailed the installation of a *minbar*, a raised platform or pulpit, which symbolically associated the preacher as the spokesman of the legitimate ruler. Later historical transformations, with profound effects on political organization and social structure, redefined this relationship such that today a gathering for the weekly congregational prayer and sermon may occur in almost any *masjid*. Nevertheless, the classical ideal envisaging a unity of sacred and civil order not only continues to inspire many Muslims, but it is formalized as law in most lands with a majority Muslim population.

A street near the Iman Reza shrine in Mashhad, Iran. Over thirteen million people per year make the pilgrimage to this shrine. © Brian Vikander/Corbis

In addition to the paradigm of Medina, a second key influence affecting the development of *masjid*s derives from the example of the sanctuary at Mecca. This affiliation appears symbolically in the directional orientation of a *masjid*, namely the *qibla*, and in the placement of the empty niche or *mihrab*, which believers face when praying. But it also resonates in numerous ornamental motifs, such as Qur'anic calligraphy and in certain expressive patterns of devotion, including localized pilgrimage practices, that emphasize rituals of reverent recollection or *dhikr*, colorful festivals honoring saints, and a variety of spiritual exercises associated with Sufi teachings.

The construction styles and, to some degree, the uses of *masjid*s have been adapted creatively over the centuries to conditions prevailing in the many settings where Islam was implanted and flourished. In the earlier period, many churches, synagogues, and temples that were converted into *masjid*s contributed significant influences to aspects of subsequent *masjid* design, helping give rise to highly distinct indigenous idioms exhibited in the size, the shapes, and the lines of minarets, domes, facades, arcades, floor plans, portals, and the internal furnishings characteristic of such particular styles identified, for instance, as Arab, Andalusian, Persian, Mongol, Mamluk, or Ottoman. More recently, a variety of notable contemporary *masjid*s have been erected, not only in the old

Islamic heartlands and its periphery, but in Europe and America, often achieving a distinctive synthesis of modern and authentic form.

The rich history of Islamic intellectual life is also deeply rooted in *masjid*s, which often served as schools in addition to their social, political, and religious functions. Frequently under the tutelage of a teacher also fulfilling the role of the local imam or designated prayer leader, *masjid*s not only provided training for children, with a curriculum concentrated on the memorization of the Qur'an and the acquisition of basic literacy skills, but less formally these same institutions provided advanced instruction, legal counsel, and spiritual guidance to members of the community at large.

A related development inseparable from *masjid*s involves their pivotal place in the establishment and the flourishing of the great medieval centers of learning throughout the Islamic world. This capacity to provide and to maintain fruitful settings for scholarship and inquiry owed much to the privileges traditionally accorded to *masjid*s, which included various juridical protections of resources derived from donations, patronage, or endowments. Although modern schools in the Muslim world, including most universities, follow Western curricular models, *masjid*s retain their distinctive impact in

In New Delhi, thousands of Muslims pray at the Jami' Masjid, also known as the Mosque of the Mogul emperor Shah Jahan, during 'Id al-Fitr (Festival of Breaking the Fast) at the end of Ramadan in 1999. The Mosque was built in 1650. AP/WIDE WORLD PHOTOS

the formation of religious professionals and others seeking to deepen their knowledge of the tradition.

In today's world, most *masjid*s have substantially reduced or shed the wide range of practical involvements that once integrated them on multiple levels into the whole fabric of society. Centralized bureaucracies under state authority have generally taken over the tasks of education, social welfare, the administration of justice, or the maintenance of order, designating specialized institutions and personnel as responsible for providing these services. In most cases, *masjid*s have likewise tended to restrict their work to a more explicitly defined set of religious activities. This trend has been especially evident in traditional Islamic lands, where their construction and supervision is typically funded and managed by a government ministry that appoints those who hold positions in *masjid*s and oversees their operations.

However, this widespread movement toward the incorporation of *masjid*s into national regulatory systems has been accompanied by an array of elite and popular responses featuring the establishment of privately funded *masjid*s, some locally sponsored, others affiliated with larger regional groupings or transnational organizations that may share resources and provide important forms of assistance not readily otherwise available. Many such independent *masjid*s, evincing various ideological orientations and seeking to recover the active autonomy of *masjid*s belonging to a prior era, have come to play a dynamic part in efforts to forge new bases of public participation, promote social improvement, religious renewal, and political reform.

See also **'Ibadat; Khutba; Manar, Manara; Mihrab; Minbar (Mimbar); Religious Institutions.**

BIBLIOGRAPHY

Affes, Habib, et al. *La Mosquée dans la Cité*. Paris: Éditions La Medina, 2001.

Frishman, Martin, and Khan, Hasan-Uddin, eds. *The Mosque: History, Architectural Development and Regional Diversity*. London: Thames and Hudson, 1994.

Joseph, Roger. "The Semiotics of the Islamic Mosque" *Arab Studies Quarterly* 3, no. 3 (1981): 285–295.

Pedersen, Johannes. "Masdjid" In *Encyclopaedia of Islam*. 2d ed. Leiden: Brill, 1960.

Patrick D. Gaffney

MASLAHA

Maslaha is an Arabic term that, in law and social ethics, means "the common social good or welfare." Medieval jurists and theologians defined *maslaha* in contrast to its antonym, *mafsada*, which means "that which causes or constitutes a harm." According to historical and legal texts, it was the second caliph, 'Umar ibn al-Khattab (r. 634–644), who applied the principle of pursuing public policies that contribute to the common good over those that do not, although he did not use the term *maslaha*, as such. The issue arose over the booty taken by Muslim militias during the conquest of Iraq and beyond during his reign: how should captured land be divided? In many cases, material goods and property taken in battle were distributed among the warriors as payment for their actions on behalf of Islam. The caliph 'Umar ruled that, in the case of the rich alluvial land in southern Iraq between the two rivers Tigris and Euphrates, the land should remain under the control of the state, to serve as a source of tax income. This would allow a land tax (*kharaj*) to be levied against owners, to be used for the general good (*'umum al-naf'*) of Muslim believers.

The medieval theologian and jurist, Abu Hamid al-Ghazali (d. 1111), argued that *maslaha* is the main intent of *shari'a*, the sacred law of Islam. It is the purpose of the law to offer guidance and governance in establishing a state in which the religious and material welfare of Muslim believers is maintained and preserved. Ghazali and other medieval theorists held that, while the general welfare of Muslims with respect to needs and improvements should be linked to the *shari'a* through legal reasoning, that which was deemed in context to be necessary to the welfare of the community required no other justification for implementation.

The nineteenth-century Egyptian reformer and modernist theologian, Muhammad 'Abduh (d. 1905), also found great value in the legal conceit of *maslaha*. Like Ghazali eight centuries earlier, 'Abduh was a seminal thinker who gave clear articulation to the intellectual currents of his age. In nineteenth-century Egypt and elsewhere, Western legal thought and colonial rule was having an enormous influence on Islamic laws and courts, in effect challenging their authority and relevance. 'Abduh argued that the demands on Muslims to find religious guidance in the ever-changing social circumstances of modern society necessitated giving preference to those meanings which contributed to the common social good of the Muslim *umma* (community), thus following Ghazali and medieval jurists but for modernist purposes.

For 'Abduh, *maslaha* took precedence over the sources of the law in cases of necessary social reform. He and other modernists took the concept of *maslaha* a step further by using it as an argument against prophetic traditions (hadith) and religious practices that were difficult to justify in modern times. Islamist critics of the modernists rejected the notion of permitting any principle other than those contained in the *shari'a* to take precedence over the sources of the law. Nonetheless, the principle of *maslaha* remains of vital interest and discussion among Muslim jurists, theologians, and social theorists in contemporary Islamic thought.

See also **'Abduh, Muhammad; Ethics and Social Issues; Ghazali, al-; Law; Shari'a.**

BIBLIOGRAPHY

Kerr, Malcolm H. *Islamic Reform: The Political and Legal Theories of Muhammad 'Abduh and Rashid Rida*. Berkeley: University of California Press, 1966.

Richard C. Martin

MATERIAL CULTURE

This article describes and discusses some aspects of the material culture of Islam to underscore and appreciate the diversities of Islamic societies and emphasize the ability of Islamic communities to use objects, artifacts, and forms of expression as media on and with which to express faith, identity, and status. The importance of sacred spaces, such as the mosque; aesthetic expressive forms like art and music; and identity types including dresses, garbs, and regalia, are discussed with a clear vision that their importance in Islamic societies emanates from their conformity with teachings on Islamic law, morality, theology, and mysticism.

The material culture of Islam includes objects, artifacts, and facets of Islamic arts created in diverse Islamic communities in the continents of Asia, Africa, Europe, and the Americas. Comprising cultural products of spiritual reflections, they are embedded in the Muslim ethos and worldview but also function to facilitate learning and mediation of social interactions and relations. Broadly, the utility derived from such products and their performance is expected to conform to acceptable Islamic symbolism and communicative functions.

Architecture

The mosque or *masjid* is a center for community prayer throughout Muslim society that communicates sacred space or history as exemplified in the Ka'ba in Mecca. Mosques also reveal a complexity of issues including the expressions of the diversity of faith and its practicality as manifest in the multiple identities in Muslim societies. Exemplifying Muslim aesthetics grounded in the religions, epistemology, the mosque is situated and created not as an obsolete innovation but as the product of the thoughts, experiences, and environments of its interlocutors. As works of art, mosques are not created ex nihilo but their sophistication in form and image represents the very essence and symbolism of Islamic cultures of sacred space.

Clothing

The religious symbolism expressed in sacred buildings also manifests in the material cultures exemplified and traced through clothing and adorned regalia. Muslim conventions of dress and garb form potent symbols of identification and lifestyles. Some historical apparel probably worn for special occasions was preserved in respectful memories of its genteel or famous owners, usually rulers and their progenitors. Other garbs are worn for their ascribed powers, especially their ability to protect the wearer and ward off evil. Famous in this category of protective regalia are the talismanic shirts worn by various sultans of the Ottoman Empire. Embroidered in expensive silks and calligraphic verses of the Qur'an and other paraphernalia, talismanic shirts were gowns and garbs attributed with sacred qualities, but they also embodied the very essence of mysticism and the magico-religious aspects of Islam. Sacred garbs also include the *khirqa*, literally meaning "a robe worn," which are actually garments or specialized cloaks worn and revered by the ascetic class, the Sufi. In Sufism aspirants in stages of spiritual pedagogy were bestowed with *baraka* (blessing) once they were given the *khirqa* symbolizing that the wearer possesses special qualities from the master. The felt is a woolen fabric of great social significance that appeared in regions dominated by the Ottoman Empire; it played an important part in the lives of Turkomens, who traditionally lived in tents made of white and black felt symbolizing wealth and poverty. The Kazakhs lived in felt tents known as *kiyiz uy*. Felt-making was widespread among the Seljuk and Ottoman Turks and their craftsmen played an important role in the mystic trade organization known as *ahi*. One of the most pronounced felt products is the stiff felt cloak, the *kepenek*, a distinctive garment worn by shepherds to protect themselves from heat in summer and from cold and wet in winter. The most famous felt garment of all is the tall conical cap, *sikke*, made in the city of Konya in Turkey and worn by the Mevlevi dervishes.

The long-sleeved white gown (*thob*) and headcoverings (*taqiyya* and *khafiya*) of the Arabian peninsula accompanied Islam as it spread and became almost hallmarks of Islamic identity. African Muslim communities have internalized and indigenized some of these gowns, including the East African loose caftan top for men, the *kanzu*, and the cap, or *kofia*. The cap is the most visible communicator of identity and religious authority among male Muslims. A West African Muslim male would hardly venture outside without his *hula*, and the Swahili man is incomplete if he does not have his *kofia* during social occasions. Any Muslim may wear a cap but the position attributed to the individual is also gathered from the expressive importance of the quality of fabrics and the ornate designs of the *kofia* or *hula*. Those with intricate patterns like *jani la mbaazi* (the green pea leaf), or *chapa msikiti* (the mosque design), are the most adorned in East African Islam. Among Hijaz Arabs the *ghutra* (white scarf) is a modern innovation of official dress when topped with the *'igal*, or black rope crown, while men in Iraq, Jordan, and Palestine usually wear a white or red- or black-checked *kufiyya* with the *'iqal*. Historically, among urban men the most common form of headcovering was the *taqiyya*, a small cap, covered by an *'imama*, an embroidered silk scarf that was larger than the *ghutra*, and was wrapped tightly around the head. This practice largely died out as men started wearing fezzes in the twentieth century, and now most male city dwellers in Arab cities leave their heads bare.

Decorative Arts, Writing, and Music

Islamic material culture also embraces varied facets of visual and decorative arts. These items have no ascribed tangible value but are useful in expressing and transmitting remembered emotions and have a role in evoking intense social reactions. For example, Turkish *kilim* (rugs) hanging on the walls of living rooms have no tangible meanings, except for the memory of a glorious past visit to Istanbul. The expression of wealth and power could be exhibited through panoplies of objects and repertoires of gestures showing privileged knowledge. The handheld staff, *bakora*, carried by members of Swahili communities, is usually made of wood. It may be engraved in gold or laced with ivory, and functions to negotiate and symbolize masculine power just as the sword displays authority in the process of negotiating for privileges and personal identity among Arab groups. In the spiritual realm, the handheld *tasbihi* (prayer beads) are a symbol of piety.

The material culture of Islam may include the written arts represented by a variety of script forms. Writing developed in Islamic societies because of the need to record every syllable of the revelation of the Qur'an. Thus, the written script was revered and its mastery became an accomplishment for any Muslim. In its nascent development as a liturgical script form, writing depended on Sufi expressions of piety as its calligraphic form became the manifestation of spirituality, that is, of inward perfection. Calligraphy attains levels of religious consecration because its production entails notions that purity of writing is purity of soul, thus making stern ascetic demands on the master calligrapher. Works of Islamic calligraphy are revered objects of material cultures, exhibited in museums, homes, and other places of historical preservation.

Various musical genres have developed in Islamic communities and one type, the *taarab*, is popular among Muslims

In Islamabad, Pakistan, traditional caps are displayed at a market. AP/WIDE WORLD PHOTOS

in East Africa. *Taarob*, which means "to be moved, or agitated by the sound of music," includes both vocal and instrumental forms like the *bashraf*, which is played with a variety of instruments, such as the *nai*, *udi*, and *zeze*.

The material culture of Islam ranges widely and represents a cross-fertilization of common ideas and religious expressions in global Islamic communities, nevertheless displaying unity in diversity.

See also **African Culture and Islam; American Culture and Islam; Architecture; Art; Calligraphy; Central Asian Culture and Islam; Clothing; European Culture and Islam; Music; South Asian Culture and Islam; Southeast Asian Culture and Islam.**

BIBLIOGRAPHY

Dilley, R. "Tukolor Weaving Origin Myths: Islam and Reinterpretation." *The Diversity of the Muslim Community: Anthropological Essays in Memory of Peter Lienhardt.* Edited by Ahmed Al-Shahi. London: Ithaca Press, 1987.

Hodder, Ian. *The Meaning of Things: Material Culture and Symbolic Expressions.* London and Boston: Unwin Hyman, 1989.

Miller, Daniel. *Material Culture and Mass Consumption.* Oxford, U.K., and New York: Blackwell, 1989.

Stillman, Yedida Kalfon. *Arab Dress: A Short History from the Dawn of Islam to Modern Times.* Edited by Norman A. Stillman. Leiden Boston: Brill, 2000.

Hassan Mwakimako

MATURIDI, AL- (?–944)

Al-Maturidi, a major figure among Hanafite scholars of the Transoxiana (Mawara al-nahr) region of Central Asia, and the founder of the Maturidite school of *kalam*, was known as Abu Mansur Muhammad b. Muhammad. He was born in Maturid (or Maturit), a neighborhood close to Samarqand, in present-day Uzbekistan, in the second half of ninth century and died there in 944. Sources name Abu Bakr Ahmad al-Juzjani and Abu Nasr Ahmad b. al-ʿAbbas al-Iyadi among his teachers.

Al-Maturidi had an extensive knowledge of other beliefs and responded to views of Christians and Jews regarding the doctrines of trinity and prophecy, as well as to Dualists, Manichaeans, Zoroastrians, and other ancient Persian or Indian religions. Moreover, al-Maturidi is a primary source for modern researchers on some controversial thinkers in Islamic intellectual history such as Ibn al-Rawandi, Abu Isa al-Warraq, and Muhammad b. Shabib.

He wrote many works, among which *Kitab al-tawhid* (On divine unity) is the main source of his theology. His Qur'anic commentary *Ta'wilat al-Qur'an* includes rational interpretations on theological and juridical verses. Among his lost books, *Kitab al-maqalat* was about early Muslim theological groups, and *Ma'Khadh al-Shar'i'* and *Kitab al-Jadal* were on Islamic legal methodology. Three of his other books in the list given by al-Nasafi are refutations of Abu'l-Qasim al-Balkhi's works, who is known as al-Ka'bi; two are against the principles (*usul*) and derivations (*furu*) of al-Qaramita; one is against al-Bahili's *Usul al-khamsa*; and another is against Mu'tazilism.

Al-Maturidi had a high standing among the Hanafite jurists of his age in Central Asia and their followers. He took a middle position between the Mu'tazila and the Ash'ariyya in some controversial subjects, such as free will, the attributes of God, and so on. His doctrine was in some cases more rationalist than Ash'ari's and closer to Mu'tazilism. On the issue of predestination and human will, as the best examples of his thought, Maturidi tried to preserve both human freedom and divine omniscience without resorting to fatalism or a deistic approach. According to al-Maturidi, since the Qur'an gives moral responsibility to each person, human beings possess free will. There is no imposition by God on human actions, but human beings cannot create their actions or realize their potential without God's will and permission, which is the difference between al-Maturidi and the Mu'tazilites on this issue. Maturidi's formula about human actions was formed of free intention (*kasb*) of an action by a human and creation (*khalq*) of this action by God if He wills. Human acts are thus acts of God in one respect, yet in another aspect (in reality not metaphorically) humans' acts are by their free choice (*ikhtiyar*). A person's power to act is valid for opposite acts of right and wrong. God's creation of human acts according to their own choice does not prevent human freedom, because human capacity (*istita'a*) is already limited.

Al-Maturidi's school begins with his immediate follower, associate and student Abu 'l-Hasan al-Rustughfeni (d. 956). Abu Nasr al-Iyazi's two sons, Abu Ahmad Nasr and Abu Bakr Muhammad, were both students of al-Maturidi's and al-Rustughfeni. However, the outstanding followers of his school were from a later generation. Abu 'l-Yusr al-Pazdavi (d. 1099), a chief qadi of Samarkand at the end of the eleventh century and the author of *Usul al-din*, was the first among them. Another follower, Abu 'l-Muin al-Nasafi (d. 1115), was considered the second founder of Maturidism, and his role in that school is compared to that of al-Baqillani among Ash'arites. Maturidite scholars differ from Ash'arites, the other Sunni *kalam* school, on a few theological questions such as whether bringing into existence (*takwin*) is a divine attribute, whether the actions of God are created, or whether good and bad are rationally known, and so on. But these differences are not major and are usually regarded as methodological.

See also **Ash'arites, Ash'aira; Central Asia, Islam in; Kalam; Mu'tazilites, Mu'tazila.**

BIBLIOGRAPHY

Ceric, Mustafa. *Roots of Synthetic Theology in Islam: A Study of the Theology of Abu Mansur al-Maturidi.* Kuala Lumpur: ISTAC, 1995.

Frank, Richard M. "Notes and Remarks on the Taba'i' in the Teaching of al-Maturidi." In *Mélanges d'Islamologie.* Edited by Pierre Salmon. Leiden: E. J. Brill, 1974.

Özervarli, M. Sait. "The Authenticity of the Manuscript of Maturidi's Kitab al-Tawhid: A Re-examination." *Turkish Journal of Islamic Studies* 1 (1997): 19–29.

Pessagno, J. Meric. "Intellect and Religious Assent." *The Muslim World* 69, no. 1 (1979): 18–27.

Watt, W. Montgomery. "The Problem of al-Maturidi." In *Mélanges d'Islamologie.* Edited by Pierre Salmon. Leiden: E. J. Brill, 1974.

M. Sait Özervarli

MAUDUDI, ABU L-A'LA' (1903–1979)

It was in the 1930s that Abu l-A'la' Maududi from Aurangabad, India formulated his political ideas about state and government, which had a great impact on the Muslim world. Maududi was, like many Islamists of his time, an autodidact and an intellectual. He started his career as a journalist working for the Deobandi-based political party Jam'iyat-e 'Ulama-e Hind (JUH), but soon distanced from the party and in 1932 founded his own Urdu-language journal *Tarjuman al-Qur'an* in Hyderabad, India. In contrast to the JUH, which postulated composite nationalism (*muttahida qaumiyyat*), and also in contrast to Muhammad Iqbal's idea of a Muslim state (territorial nationalism), Maududi postulated a third alternative when he began to Islamize the political discourse of the nationalists and freedom fighters: An Islamic state must correspond to the Islamic ideology through which the divine order can be realized on earth. A Muslim should believe in the sovereignty of God rather than in the idea of a government of the people, through the people, and for the people. Hence, Muslims did not represent a nation, but the party of God, which acts as God's agent on earth (*khalifa*). For this aim, he considered self-purification a prerequisite. Toward the end of the 1930s he was convinced that the creation of a Muslim state would not be the right method of reform, because the un-Islamic politicians were not able to create an Islamic state.

To put his ideas into practice, in 1941 the Islamic classicist Maududi founded the Jamaʿat-e Islami (Islamic Community)—which he led until 1972 as its president—and postulated the sovereignty of God on Earth (hakimiyat-e ilahi) in a universal, ideologically Islamic nation. After 1947, he tried to materialize this idea of an imagined community in the constitution of Pakistan, where he, along with the majority of his community, eventually emigrated. Hence he accepted the idea of a nation-state, which he had rejected formerly. His Jamaʿat won much influence, especially among young intellectuals and the middle class in the years to come.

Maududi was the first to work toward an Islamic constitution, and his endeavors were partly incorporated in the Objectives Resolution of 1949, which was incorporated in turn into the constitution of the Islamic Republic of Pakistan, according to which Pakistan was to be an Islamic state. His rather state-apologetic interpretation of Islam, on which he had elaborated in his *Islamic Law and Constitution* (1955), made him and his party collaborate with the government at several instances—for example, during the reign of Zia ul-Haq—though Maududi himself was imprisoned several times on the charge of being disloyal to Pakistan.

His argument was that the wrong interpretation of the Qurʾan's basic principles had led the people astray, which had resulted in the loss of religious and cultural identity, due to misguided mystics (Sufis) among others. It was important to leave the *jahiliyya* (the pre-Islamic state of ignorance) behind and return to the righteous society here and now. The reconstruction of an idealized pure Islamic society would guarantee the iteration of the original Muslim community (*umma*). This required Muslims to live according to the sunna of the Prophet, based on a transnational view of the golden age of the Prophet and the first generations. It implied a reinvention of tradition. With this argument Maududi created a new normative and formative past, and an absence of historical records allowed him to regard himself an exponent of the projected imagined Islamic society, or *jamaʿat*, as the avant-gardist, who considered himself authorized to establish renewal (*tajdid*). *Ijtihad*, for example, the maximum effort to ascertain, in a given problem or issue, the injunction of Islam and its real intent, was the proper channel for that process. The concept of history informed by the notion of constant decay, already developed in his *Muslims and the Present Political Crisis* (1937–1939), was the basic motivation for his activism, which he wanted to implement through education.

Maududi gained great fame throughout the Islamic world and became a member of several societies and a founding member of the Rabitat al-ʿAlam al-Islami in 1961.

See also **Jamaʿat-e Islami; Political Islam.**

BIBLIOGRAPHY

Ahmad, Khurshid, and Ansari, Zafar Ishaq, eds. *Islamic Perspectives; studies in honour of Mawlana Sayyid Abul Aʿla Mawdadi.* London: The Islamic Foundation, 1979.

Nasr, Seyyed. *Vali Reza: Mawdudi and the Making of Islamic Revivalism.* New York: Oxford University Press, 1996.

Jamal Malik

MAZALIM

The word "*mazalim*" is the plural of *mazlima*, which means iniquity, act of injustice, or wrong doing. In terms of Islamic judicial system, *mazalim* denotes a special type of court, where sessions for hearing cases of injustices are held or supervised by the supreme political authority, or by one of his close deputies or other high-ranking authority.

In the view of al-Mawardi (d. 1058), the institution of *mazalim* existed in the pre-Islamic Arab community and also under the Sassanid regime. Mawardi mentions Caliph ʿUmar Ibn ʿAbd al-ʿAziz of the Umayyads, as well as caliphs al-Mahdi, al-Hadi, al-Rahsid, al-Maʾmun, and al-Muhtadi of the Abbasids as important leaders who employed hearings in the *mazalim* to distribute justice.

A session of *mazalim* requires the presence of five types of assistants. These are the guards, the *qadi*s, the *faqih*s, the secretaries (to keep records), and the notaries (to witness). The jurisdiction of this court extends to the adjudication of abuse of power related cases involving both officials and non-officials. It also deals with the issues of restitution of properties taken by force, the supervision of *waqf* (pious endowments), the enforcement of public order that exceeds ordinary internal security measures, the enforcement of judgments that exceed the authority of the ordinary judges, the enforcement of public duty issues such as Friday prayers, feasts, pilgrimage, jihad, and other extraordinary events. The *mazalim* is also called to provide arbitration between conflicting parties.

The main difference between the *mazalim* and the ordinary judicial courts is that the supervisor of *mazalim* (*sahib al-mazalim* or *nazir al-mazalim*) has extra discretionary power. The ordinary judge is bound by the limitations of conventional judicial system, whereas the supervisor of *mazalim* enjoys greater procedural latitude. For instance, he may obtain evidence in ways might be unacceptable to an ordinary court's judge. The supervisor of the *mazalim* also is free to impose arbitrational settlements that are binding on the contesting parties. This option is unavailable to the judge in an ordinary court. In other words, the uniqueness of the *mazalim* lies in the breadth of its supervisors' discretionary power and political authority.

See also **Caliphate; Law; Religious Institutions.**

BIBLIOGRAPHY

Liebesny, Herbert, J. *The Law of the Near and Middle East: Readings, Cases, and Materials.* Albany: State University of New York Press, 1975.

Nielsen, J. S. "Mazalim." In Vol. VI, *The Enyclopaedia of Islam.* Edited by C. E. Bosworth, et al. Leiden: E. J. Brill, 1990.

Osman Tastan

MAZRUI, MAZRUʿI

Although historically associated with the city of Mombasa, Kenya, originally the Mazrui (Ar. Mazruʿi) were native to the Rustaq region of Oman. By the early eighteenth century, they began settling the coast of Kenya and Pemba Island until, altogether, fourteen Mazrui clans came to be represented in East Africa. Mazrui accounts claim that the imam of Oman sent Nasir bin ʿAbdallah Mazrui as his representative (*liwali*) in Mombasa soon after capturing Fort Jesus from the Portuguese in 1698. However, other sources suggest Nasir arrived around 1727.

Beginning with Nasir, the Mazrui administered Mombasa as its principal ruling family until the Busaidi sultan of Zanzibar, Sayyid Saʿid bin Sultan, replaced them with his own representative in 1837. Altogether, the Mazrui provided Mombasa with a succession of eleven *liwalis*, which was terminated when Saʿid kidnapped and murdered Rashid bin Salim and twenty-four tribal elders. In 1741, Liwali Muhammad bin ʿUthman Mazrui had refused to acknowledge the Busaidi tribe as the new imams of Oman. Further acts of Mazrui defiance damaged their already poor relations with the Busaidi, making a violent outcome inevitable.

Much remains controversial about Mazrui rule in Mombasa. A Mazrui history claims they exercised a true mastery over Mombasa's affairs, and that their dominion extended over "most of the Swahili country." However, a careful reading of all available sources indicates that their rule was totally contingent on support and alliances with Mombasa's Swahili citizens and their Mijikenda neighbors. Loss of this support in 1835 quickly led to the Mazrui downfall. Imperialist ambitions to widen their influence through interference in the affairs of neighboring coastal states like Tanga, Wasin, and Pate were resented and frequently resisted. Also, the Mazrui not only allowed a considerable trade in slaves at Mombasa, but most probably participated in it. In later years, like many coastal Muslims, they exploited slave labor in the areas they settled around Mombasa and Takaungu.

Although they lost Mombasa, after 1837 the Mazrui continued to resist Omani and European imperialism and to play a significant part in the history of Kenya. To avoid Busaidi predominance in Mombasa, many resettled in Pemba, Gazi, and Takaungu after 1837. One, Mbaruk bin Rashid of Takaungu, never rendered tribute to the Busaidi, nor recognized their sovereignty over East Africa, and Busaidi attempts in the 1850s and the 1870s to force his submission were both failures. Active resistance ended when a final, pointless Mazrui uprising was defeated by British forces in 1896, forcing Mbaruk to end his days exiled in another colonial possession, German East Africa.

Even before Mbaruk's defeat, some Mazrui had discovered intellectual resistance to be effective. Originally Ibadi Muslims, like the Busaidi and their Omani allies, in the 1800s many Mazrui converted to the Shafiʿi sect prevalent in East Africa. One in particular, ʿAbdallah b. ʿAli, made the hajj and converted soon after 1837. His descendants, including ʿAli b. ʿAbdallah and al-Amin bin Ali Mazrui, became some of the most influential Shafiʿi *qadis* in Kenya. More recently, scions of this particular family have enjoyed considerable popularity in Africa and the United States as educators and modernizers of African institutions.

See also **Africa, Islam in; Zanzibar, Saʿidi Sultanate of.**

BIBLIOGRAPHY

Mazrui, Al-Amin bin Ali. *A History of the Mazruʿi Dynasty of Mombasa.* London: Oxford University Press, 1995.

Nicholls, Christine. *The Swahili Coast.* New York: Africana, 1971.

Pouwels, Randall L. *Horn and Crescent: Cultural Change and Traditional Islam on the East African Coast: 800–1900.* Cambridge, U.K.: Cambridge University Press, 1987.

Salim, Ahmad Idha. *The Swahili-Speaking Peoples of Kenya's Coast, 1895–1965.* Nairobi: East African Publishing House, 1973.

Randall L. Pouwels

MECCA *See* Holy Cities

MEDICINE

Medicine has been an integral part of Islamic intellectual life and social institutions from the time of the Prophet. This brief description will touch on the diverse origins of medical knowledge in Islam; the development of hospitals, medical practice, and medical knowledge during the Islamic "Golden Age" (the latter half of the seventh century through the thirteenth century C.E.); the role of the Islamic world in protecting, elaborating, and reintroducing Hellenic medicine to Europe after the Dark Ages; and contemporary issues including the development of Islamic medical organizations dedicated to the assertion and protection of the religious context of the practice of medicine.

Medicine in the Time of the Prophet

The tribes that inhabited what is now Saudi Arabia at the time of the prophet Muhammad had a great deal of traditional medicine. As medical thinking and knowledge became explanatory and inductive with the parallel development of scientific thought in general, much of this traditional knowledge was preserved and some of it expressed in religious thinking. At the same time, distinct medical traditions were well developed in India, Persia, China, and Greece. Early Islamic medicine drew upon all of these traditions. The Qur'an itself contains limited specific medical text, although there is important guidance in prescribing breastfeeding as the right of every child, in proscribing intoxicants and the meat of certain animals, and in commentary on the beneficial health effects of some natural foods. However, the hadith (authenticated sayings and deeds of the Prophet) and its interpretations contain rich and detailed material on preventive and curative medicine, dietetics, and spiritual health. Early in the Islamic tradition these sources were collected and eventually became known as al-Tibb al-Nabawi (Medicine of the Prophet, or Prophetic Medicine). These collections remained distinct from the Persian, Indian, and Greek sources that early Islamic physicians drew upon, although they interacted with these traditions through their work. The best-known version is that of Ibn Qayyim al-Jawziyya, writing in Damascus in the late eleventh century c.e. Translated into many languages and widely accessible to Muslims the world over, the Medicine of the Prophet forms the rationale for many aspects of everyday Muslim life in terms of health protection and promotion—for example, injunctions against overeating; prescriptions for the spiritual and psychological care of the bereaved and traumatized; encouragement of moderation in all things; and much specific instruction on everyday food, drink, rest, and sexual behavior.

The Development of Islamic Medicine

The schisms within European Christianity in the fourth and fifth centuries c.e. paved the way for a shift of focus outside Europe for development of the profession. When Nestorius, the Patriarch of Byzantium, and his followers were forced out of Europe a large pool of intellectuals moved to the Middle East, many to Jund-e Shapur, a city in what is now southwestern Iran that was already home to a thriving intellectual community including Syrians, Persians, and Jews and where a medical school was well established. When Justinian I (527–565 c.e.) expelled "heathen philosophers" from Athens, the Hellenic medical tradition based on Galen and others was transplanted to the fertile soil of Jund-e Shapur where it thrived amid a community of scholars who translated the Greek medical works into Arabic either directly or through translations into Syriac. Manuscripts from other regions including India and China were also translated and when Islam expanded into Egypt, Greek manuscripts from Alexandria also became available. A short time before, the Persians had been conquered by Muslim armies under the first caliph, giving the Muslims access to Jund-e Shapur.

In 765 c.e., an eminent Christian physician who headed the medical school at Jund-e Shapur, Jurjis Bukhtishu, was invited to Baghdad by the caliph al-Mansur to treat him. He did this successfully, and was appointed to the court. Although he returned to Jund-e Shapur, his son migrated to Baghdad and set up a successful medical practice. Other prominent medical men and their offspring soon joined an emigration to Baghdad, which became a medical focal point with many hospitals and medical centers and a great deal of scientific and intellectual activity of all sorts, most of which drew on Greek intellectual tradition. That the medical experts of Jund-e Shapur and later of Baghdad were accomplished linguists who opened the Islamic empire to knowledge from the rest of the world and made Arabic the primary language of the time for documentation in medicine, science, philosophy, and many other fields.

During the several centuries that followed, hospitals and medical schools were established and thrived throughout the Islamic world, with the largest and most notable in Damascus, Cairo, and Cordoba. These facilities established traditions of treatment free of charge to the patient and acceptance of all in need of treatment without regard to means, religion, age, or gender. The development, enrichment, and encyclopedic documentation of medicine in the Islamic world of the time was led by a series of individuals, some of whom were true "Renaissance men" of their times. The guidance of several of these (al-Razi, al-Zaharwi, Ibn Sina) will be briefly mentioned, but they are among many other eminent contributors to medicine from this period.

Abu Bakr Mohammed ibn Zakariyya al-Razi (known as Rhazes in the West) was born near what is now Tehran in middle of the seventh century c.e. Al-Razi was accomplished in many spheres, and came to the study of medicine relatively late in life after a visit to Baghdad and a hospital there, which he later directed. There are many stories about al-Razi's skill as a practitioner. One famous account addresses his knack for environmental health. The story goes that he was asked at some time during his career to choose the location for a new hospital in Baghdad. He did this by observing fresh meat hanging in various parts of the city and choosing the area based on where the meat took the longest to spoil. He was a diligent teacher, a skilled diagnostician, and a prolific writer. His written works number in the hundreds. The largest, which is a huge compilation of case studies and notes edited and published by al-Razi's students after his death, has been called al-Hawa (the Continent); a thirteenth-century Latin translation was entitled Continens. This work summarized essentially all of the medical writings preceding al-Razi's time as well as his own observations. His most famous piece was a much shorter monograph in which he distinguished smallpox, chicken pox, and measles; this work translated to Latin was called de Pestilentia and formed the basis for much future work on these highly contagious diseases.

Several centuries later, the dual influence of al-Zahrawi in the West and Ibn Sina in the East were pivotal. Abu 'l-Qasim al-Zahrawi lived from about 930 to 1013 c.e. and was known as the "greatest surgeon of Islam." Zahrawi lived in the western caliphate, near Cordoba, and attended the University of Cordoba. He is most famous for his command of analgesia and anesthesia, utilizing opium and other natural narcotics and depressants, and the theory and practice of surgery. He invented many surgical instruments and wrote what is no doubt the first textbook of surgery. Although ignored throughout most of the eastern part of the Islamic world at the time, his influence on Europe was very significant.

Ibn Sina (known as Avicenna in the West) lived just a bit later (980–1037 c.e.). He was born in Persia in what is now Isfahan, Iran. Like many medical men of his time, he was an intellectual in a complete sense, writing on philosophy, music, military strategy, mathematics, and other subjects as well as medicine. His greatest medical work was the *Qanun fi al-tibb*, a five-volume treatise based on Greek knowledge and including Ayurvedic writings from India, some Chinese medicine, and other available sources. The *Qanun* included discussions of almost all ailments imaginable, as well as health promotion focusing on diet, the environment, and climate; it also included a huge *materia medica* including many medicinal plants and the drugs that could be derived from them. His theory of infection by "traces," together with the Prophet's earlier injunction to avoid travel to or from places in which plague was present, led to the introduction of quarantine as a means of limiting the spread of infectious diseases. Although he also wrote in his native Persian, Ibn Sina's medical works were penned in Arabic, which faciliated the reintroduction of scientific medicine in Europe as the Dark Ages gave way to the European Renaissance. This process paralleled a period of decline in Islamic influence and hegemony.

The Re-Introduction of Medical Science to Europe

The Arabic text of Ibn Sina's *Qanun* was published in Rome in 1593, and was one of the first Arabic books to be printed. The entire text had been translated into Latin two centuries earlier. This encyclopedic work soon became the preeminent medical text in Europe and was depended upon for four hundred years by the major medical schools on the continent. It was published in no less than sixteen editions, in Milan, Padua, and Venice throughout the 1400s and 1500s; the last edition for textbook use was published in 1658. Ibn Sina's writings, and the antecedent Islamic works on which he drew, thus formed the route by which the Arabic repository of Hellenic medicine, greatly expanded and enriched, was reintroduced to Europe. The subsequent major scientific advancements that came with Claude Bernard's (quite compatible) theory of the internal milieu, van Leewenhoek's discovery of the microscope, and other advances quickly pushed medicine to a secular, empirical basis and the importance of the contributions of the Arabic texts was largely forgotten.

Medicine in Contemporary Islam

Today, the infrastructure and content of medicine as it is practiced in the Islamic world is compatible with and even formed in the image of European and other Western models. Ironically, the only part of the world in which the corpus of (largely Greek) theory that constituted the medical knowledge of early Islamic history is still taught is in South Asia, where there are schools and licensure for practitioners of "Tibb Unani" ("Greek Medicine"). In most of the Muslim world, however, medical education and practice is largely consistent with that in the West, with a structure of specialties, supervisory responsibility and liability, curricula, and requirements for continuing medical education for practitioners. However, the last several decades have seen a movement toward development of consciously Muslim perspectives in medicine.

A notable recent change has been the reentry of women into medicine throughout the Muslim world. There has never been a prohibition on female physicians, nor on the treatment of patients of either gender by a male or female doctor. Aside from the doctrine that "necessity overrides prohibition," the hadith states clearly that treatment should depend solely on the needs of the patient and the capability of the doctor. Indeed, the precedent for female doctors was set by the Prophet's own entirely female medical corps that accompanied his armies into battle. As medicine became an intellectual pursuit requiring literacy and education, skills that were the province of men in most Muslim societies, the profession became almost entirely male. As education has more recently included women, they have moved back into medicine without formal barriers and with enthusiasm.

Recently there has been particularly active dialogue and introspection around issues of bioethics and the conduct of the Muslim medical practitioner in the religious context. Noteable in this context is the Islamic Organization for Medical Sciences (IOMS) (<http://www.islamset.com>), established in 1984 in Kuwait with an objective of serving the entire Muslim world. In its brief history IOMS has held multiple conferences on the heritage of Islam in medicine, established a World Health Organization Collaborating Research Center focused on traditional medicinal plants, and published a number of works focusing on ethical issues including Muslim definitions of the beginning and end of life, the use of newer reproductive technologies, care of the aged, and, recently, the impact of globalization on health and health care in the Islamic world. An Islamic Oath of the Doctor was developed by an IOMS conference, and is now widely published and used.

An early anatomical drawing appears in the volume two color insert.

See also **Body, Significance of; Ethics and Social Issues; Falsafa; Science, Islam and.**

BIBLIOGRAPHY

Bakar, Osman. *The History and Philosophy of Islamic Science.* Cambridge, U.K.: Islamic Texts Society, 1999.

Hathout, Hassan. *Islamic Perspectives in Obstetrics and Gynecology.* Kuwait: Islamic Organization for Medical Sciences, 1986.

Islamic Organization for Medical Sciences. *Overview of the Islamic Organization for Medical Sciences.* Kuwait: IOMS, 1987.

Jawziyya, Ibn Quyyim al-. *Medicine of the Prophet.* Translated by Penelope Johnstone. Cambridge, U.K: Islamic Texts Society, 1998.

Rosenthal, Franz. *Science and Medicine in Islam.* Brookfield, Vt.: Gower Publishing Company, 1990.

Wright, David Lionel. *The Legacy of Arabic Medicine during the Golden Age of Islam.* Kuwait: Islamic Organization for Medical Sciences, 1996.

Gail G. Harrison
Osman M. Galal

MEDINA *See* Holy Cities

MIHNA

"Mihna" is the Arabic term for a test or a trial. In its most common historical usage, Mihna refers to the inquisition launched by the seventh Abbasid caliph, al-Ma'mun (r. 813–833) toward the end of his reign to enforce the doctrine of the createdness of the Qur'an. The Mihna has loomed large in the way medieval historians represented the reign and the legacy of al-Ma'mun, and modern scholars have often seen the Mihna and its eventual failure as a major episode in the religious and political history of the first centuries of Islam.

History

In 833, while at Raqqa in northern Mesopotamia, al-Ma'mun wrote to his governor of Baghdad, ordering him to examine the views held by his judges and the scholars of hadith regarding the Qur'an. The caliph believed that, contrary to what "ignorant" people thought, the Qur'an was not eternally existent—for this was an attribute that belonged only to God—but created by Him, and that this was how God Himself had spoken of it. Therefore, al-Ma'mun believed, supposing the Qur'an to be uncreated and eternal threatened to compromise the unity (*tawhid*) of God, and thus to undermine the very foundations of religion. As he lamented in his letters to his governor, most people were too ignorant of the reality of religion to hold sound beliefs about it, and yet they—and the demagogues who aspired to their leadership— claimed to be the most assiduous followers of Muhammad's normative example, the hadith. As one entrusted with knowledge, and with the obligation to uphold "God's right[s]," al-Ma'mun wanted therefore to see to it that false beliefs about the Qur'an were rectified.

Most of those who were examined on the question of the Qur'an's createdness—by al-Ma'mun's governor of Baghdad, by the caliph himself, or by his officials in the provinces— ended up declaring their adherence to the caliphal position. The most famous dissenter, however, was the noted hadith scholar of Baghdad, Ahmad ibn Hanbal (d. 855). He, alongside another recalcitrant scholar, was sent to al-Ma'mun's military camp in Tarsus to be interrogated, but the caliph died before he could attend to the matter and Ibn Hanbal was returned to Baghdad. This, however, was only the beginning of the Mihna, and of Ibn Hanbal's long and much-celebrated ordeal.

In the history of Islamic theology, the doctrine of the uncreatedness of the Qur'an (*khalq al-Qur'an*) is associated primarily with the rationalist Mu'tazila school. However, several other theologians also held this position. These theologians have often been characterized in Islamic heresiography as the "Jahmiyya," for their putative association with doctrines held by an early and much-maligned figure named Jahm b. Safwan (d. 745). Al-Ma'mun himself was not a Mu'tazili, for he did not share the Mu'tazila's characteristic doctrine of free will, but he agreed with them on the createdness of the Qur'an. Already in 827, the caliph had publicly declared his support for this doctrine, though it was only in 833 that he went on to institute the Mihna.

On his deathbed, al-Ma'mun left instructions that his successor, Abu Ishaq al-Mu'tasim (r. 833–842), continue to uphold his position on the Qur'an. During the latter's reign, Ibn Hanbal was interrogated and flogged for refusing to accept the Qur'an's createdness. A central figure during the Mihna years was the Mu'tazili chief judge, Ahmad Ibn Abi Du'ad (d. 854), who is represented in Sunni historiography as being far more anxious to continue the Inquisition than the caliphal successors of al-Ma'mun themselves might have been. Later historians also lay much of the responsibility for the flogging of Ibn Hanbal on Ibn Abi Du'ad. For his part, Ibn Hanbal is reported to have remained steadfast despite the flogging, after which he was released and left alone by the prosecutors of the Mihna. His release is usually explained in Sunni historiography as being due to fears of popular commotion against his persecution, though some (largely unfavorable) sources claim the real reason for it to have been that he too had eventually capitulated to the authorities. This, however, seems unlikely, in view of the severity with which Ibn Hanbal himself later treated many of those who had acknowledged the doctrine of the Qur'an's createdness during the Mihna.

The Inquisition continued under al-Mu'tasim's successor, al-Wathiq (r. 842–847), who appears to have pursued it rather more vigorously than had al-Mu'tasim. Indeed, he went so far as to interrogate Muslim prisoners in Byzantine captivity about their view of the Qur'an before deciding whether or not they were to be ransomed. The harshness of the state's inquisitorial policies led some people of Baghdad to attempt a revolt, but the plot failed and its leader, Ahmad ibn Nasr al-Khuza'i, who was closely associated with the scholars of hadith, was executed (c. 845–846). Soon, however, with the accession of a new caliph—al-Mutawakkil (r. 847–861)—the Mihna itself began to unravel. In 849, this caliph forbade disputations about the Qur'an, and in the same year he ordered several leading scholars to narrate hadith to the people, refuting the doctrines of the Mu'tazila and the Jahmiyya. A more decisive demonstration of the shift in caliphal policy came when, in 851, the Mu'tazili chief judge, Ibn Abi Du'ad, and his son (also a judge in the then-Abbasid capital of Samarra) were removed from office and their property was confiscated. This, for practical purposes, signaled the end of the Mihna, though the doctrine of the createdness of the Qur'an would continue to be debated in theological circles for centuries.

Interpretations of the Mihna

Modern scholars have much debated the meaning and significance of the Mihna, and there is no consensus on why al-Ma'mun so insisted on the doctrine of the Qur'an's createdness. Al-Ma'mun's own explanation was that it was his calling, as caliph and imam, to provide guidance to his subjects and, in particular, to rectify their dangerously wayward beliefs about the Qur'an. Yet modern scholars have often discerned motives behind the Mihna which go beyond a specific theological controversy. In *God's Caliph*, Patricia Crone and Martin Hinds have argued that al-Ma'mun was really trying, through the Mihna, to make a last-ditch effort to reclaim a religious authority that had belonged to earlier caliphs but which had been eroded by the growing influence of the scholars of hadith and of the ulema in general. To these scholars, religious authority was enshrined, not in the will or verdicts of the caliphs, but rather in the hadith of the Prophet, and of this the ulema claimed to be the sole interpreters. This position was unacceptable to al-Ma'mun, and the Mihna represented a vigorous if ultimately abortive effort to make the scholars subservient to the caliphs.

It is not clear, however, if the Abbasid caliphs prior to al-Ma'mun did claim the sort of overarching religious authority that Crone and Hinds impute to them. The Mihna is perhaps better interpreted not as the decisive culmination of a struggle over the form or locus of authoritative religious guidance but, instead, as a break with the evolving patterns of caliphal patronage under the early Abbasids. Rather than co-opt or draw close to the emerging scholars of hadith, al-Ma'mun sought to rein in their influence and assert his own authority as the arbiter of right belief. These scholars, best represented by Ibn Hanbal, were the principal target of the caliph's ire and of his effort to assert his authority.

As the names of those questioned indicate, however, scholars of hadith were not alone in their tribulation. Some of those examined also had a record of political opposition to the caliph, and this suggests that the Mihna's uses extended beyond theological speculation and even beyond the caliph's assertion of religious authority. For instance, several recent authors have observed that Ibrahim b. al-Mahdi was among those interrogated during the Mihna. Ibrahim was not a religious scholar but, rather, a prominent member of the Abbasid family and he had been declared caliph in Baghdad following the civil war between al-Amin and al-Ma'mun. Even some of the scholars who were questioned during the Mihna were suspect on political grounds. For instance, the widely respected scholar Abu Mushir al-Ghassani (d. 833) of Damascus had sided with an anti-Abbasid revolt in Syria. Ahmad b. Nasr al-Khuza'i's execution during the reign of al-Wathiq owed more to his abortive revolt than to his views on the Qur'an, even though it was ostensibly for the latter that he was killed. In general, it seems fair to say that a variety of factors were involved in the institution and continuation of the Mihna, as well as in the choice of those who were interrogated during its course.

Modern scholarly interpretations of the larger significance of the Mihna are necessarily shaped by how it is seen in relation to Abbasid history, and to early Islamic history in general. If early Abbasid history is viewed as a continuing contest over religious authority between "God's caliph" and the emerging ulema, then the Mihna assumes the character of a watershed event, the failure of which permanently divested the caliphs of any significant role in religious life and established a lasting "separation" between the political and the religious authorities. However, there is little evidence for such a contest between the caliphs and the ulema prior to al-Ma'mun, just as there are many indications of caliphal participation in the community's religious life after the Mihna. Caliphs could still undertake the Qur'anic obligation of "commanding right and forbidding wrong." The caliphs al-Qadir (r. 991–1031) and al-Qa'im (r. 1031–1075) led efforts to devise a theological creed against the Mu'talzila and other unwelcome groups; and caliphs could still participate in the deliberations of the jurists. It is also worth noting that, in his influential treatise on constitutional theory, al-Mawardi (d. 1058) should have listed juridical expertise among the necessary qualifications for the caliphate, for even if such a stipulation was more wishful thinking than a realistic expectation, it still reveals something about how jurists viewed the caliphate two centuries after the Mihna. It is true, of course, that as the ulema's scholarly specializations evolved—a process already unmistakably underway before al-Ma'mun—there was progressively less space for caliphs to authoritatively shape religious discourses in the community over which they presided. Yet the constraining of that space is better analyzed not with reference to any decisive impact the Mihna itself may have had on it, but rather in light of the long and complex history of the ulema and, of course, that of the caliphate.

If the failure of the Mihna did not remove the caliphs from religious life, the entire protracted episode and its aftermath did nevertheless contribute to the vigor and identity of the emerging ulema. The end of the Mihna brought to a close the political ascendancy of the Mu'tazili theologians, who were replaced in caliphal favor by the scholars of hadith. Ibn Hanbal was much sought after by Caliph al-Mutawakkil and his officials; and though he is reported to have been much perturbed by what he saw as this unwanted attention, there can be little doubt that royal patronage was one of the factors contributing, in the succeeding generations, to the growing prominence of Ibn Hanbal's followers in the religious life of Baghdad. The scholars of hadith had already, during the Mihna, shown themselves to have considerable popular support. Indeed, such increasing prominence may, arguably, have provoked at least some of al-Ma'mun's suspicions of them in the first place. The end of the Mihna further deepened and extended the populist roots of early Sunnism and, in particular, of those adhering to the school of law that came to be identified with the name of Ahmad b. Hanbal.

In theological terms, a major facet of the Mihna's significance lies in its contribution to the articulation of the "orthodox" Sunni view on the nature of the Qur'an. Al-Ma'mun had accused his opponents of believing the Qur'an to be co-eternal with God but, as Madelung—following the medieval Hanbali jurist and theologian Ibn Taymiyya (d. 1328)—has observed, early hadith scholars had usually been content to characterize the Qur'an as God's speech and to leave the matter there. In response to the doctrine al-Ma'mun wanted to enforce, however, the traditionists came to hold that the Qur'an was indeed uncreated. This dogma then became a defining feature of Sunni theology, though there continued to be much disagreement, long after the Mihna, on its precise meaning and implications.

See also **Caliphate; Disputation; Ibn Hanbal; Imamate; Ma'mum, al-; Mu'tazilites, Mu'tazila; Qur'an.**

BIBLIOGRAPHY

Abou El Fadl, Khaled. *Rebellion and Violence in Islamic Law.* Cambridge, U.K.: Cambridge University Press, 2001.

Cooperson, Michael. *Classical Arabic Biography: The Heirs of the Prophets in the Age of al-Ma'mun.* Cambridge, U.K.: Cambridge University Press, 2000.

Crone, Patricia, and Hinds, Martin. *God's Caliph: Religious Authority in the First Centuries of Islam.* Cambridge, U.K.: Cambridge University Press, 1986.

Ess, Josef van. *Theologie und Gesellschaft im 2. und 3. Jahrhundert Hidschra.* Berlin: Walter de Gruyter, 1991–1997.

Hinds, Martin. "Mihna." In *The Encyclopaedia of Islam.* 2d ed. Leiden: E. J. Brill, 1960.

Lapidus, Ira M. "The Separation of State and Religion in the Development of Early Islamic Society." *International Journal of Middle East Studies* 6 (1975): 363–385.

Madelung, Wilferd. "The Controversy on the Creation of the Koran." In *Orientalia Hispanica sive studia F. M. Pareja octogenario dedicata.* Edited by M. M. Barral. Leiden: E. J. Brill, 1974.

Nawas, John A. "A Reexamination of Three Current Explanations for al-Ma'mun's Introduction of the Mihna." *International Journal of Middle East Studies* 26 (1994): 615–629.

Patton, Walter M. *Ahmad ibn Hanbal and the Mihna.* Leiden: E. J. Brill, 1997.

Tabari, al-. *The History of al-Tabari.* Vol. 32: *The Reunification of the 'Abbasid Caliphate.* Translated by C. E. Bosworth. Albany: State University of New York Press, 1987.

Zaman, Muhammad Qasim. *Religion and Politics under the Early 'Abbasids.* Leiden: E. J. Brill, 1997.

Muhammad Qasim Zaman

MIHRAB

The semicircular niche in the wall of a mosque that faces Mecca is known as the *mihrab.* Introduced in the Prophet's mosque in Medina when it was rebuilt by the Umayyad caliph al-Walid I (r. 705–715), the *mihrab* may have been originally intended to commemorate the place of the Prophet, but it soon became ubiquitous and is generally understood to indicate the direction of prayer (*qibla*). The earliest complete example to survive is believed to be a monolithic marble *mihrab* dated to the mid-eighth century and reused in the Khassaki Mosque in Baghdad. Later examples were often made of other precious materials, including stone or glass mosaic, carved or joined wood, and glazed tile.

See also **Architecture; Art; Devotional Life; Masjid.**

BIBLIOGRAPHY

Fehervar, G. "Mihrab." In *Encyclopaedia of Islam,* 2d ed. Edited by H. A. R. Gibbs, et al. Leiden: E. J. Brill, 2002.

Sheila S. Blair
Jonathan M. Bloom

MILITARY RAID

The raid, which is essentially a form of brigandage, was viewed in the Bedouin pastoral milieu as one of the few manly occupations. Termed *ghazwa,* (pl. *maghazi*), in Arabic, its purpose was plunder, not bloodshed, and it was not permitted during the sacred months: Dhu-l-Qa'da, Dhu-l-Hijja, and Muharram (the last two and first months of the year), which were set aside for religious observances, and Rajab (the fourth month), which was set aside for trade.

Islamic literature, however, when referring to the *ghazwa* of the prophet Muhammad, makes no distinction between battle and raid. Before attacking a community, the Muslims would first proclaim a *da'wa* or invitation, calling their opponents to accept Islam. Only those male polytheists who refused to convert were fought to the death; women and children were taken captive. "People of the book," such as Jews and Christians, were permitted to practice their faith, if they agreed to pay a poll tax, or *jizya*.

The title *Maghazi* is given to compilations which tell of the numerous raids and battles that Muhammad undertook to establish Islam in Arabia. The term has thus come to represent the achievements of Muhammad, and become synonymous with his life's work. *Maghazi* and *ghazwa* therefore are also used to signify events in the life of Muhammad. For example, "*Ghazwat al-Hudaybiyya*" concerns the conclusion of a peace agreement between Muhammad and the Meccans.

Muslim b. al-Hajjaj (d. 875), the famous compiler of hadith (traditions concerning the Prophet), listed the battles and raids of the Prophet under the title jihad, which literally means to struggle or strive in the path of God. Incorrectly translated as holy war, the term "jihad," in fact, is best understood in a spiritual context and includes such activities as fasting, charity, and meditation. The term *Fath* (pl. *Futuh*) is more appropriately used for wars of expansion such as the Arab conquests of Egypt, Syria, and Persia.

See also **Conflict and Violence; Da'wa; Expansion; Jihad.**

BIBLIOGRAPHY

Baladhuri, Ahmad b. Yahya. *Futuh al-Buldan.* Edited by M. J. De Goeje. Leiden: E. J. Brill, 1866.

Faizer, Rizwi. "Expeditions and Battles." In Vol. 2, *Encyclopaedia of the Qur'an.* Edited by Jane McAuliffe. Leiden: E. J. Brill, 2002.

Hitti, Philip K. *History of the Arabs*, 9th ed. London: Macmillan, 1966.

Jones, J. M. B. "The *Maghazi* Literature." In *Arabic Literature to the End of the Umayyad Period.* Edited by A. F. L. Beeston. Cambridge, U.K.: Cambridge University Press, 1983.

Rizwi Faizer

MINARET *See* **Manar, Manara**

MINBAR (MIMBAR)

The *minbar* is the elevated seat of honor in the mosque and it represents religio-political authority. It is similar, but not identical to, the place and function of the pulpit in Christian churches. Not only is the Muslim Friday sermon (*khutba*) delivered from its base by the local preacher, but important public pronouncements are also made from it. For instance, in the past the Qur'anic prohibition on wine was delivered from the *minbar*. Muslim rulers (caliphs), as well as provincial governors or their representatives sat on it and delivered the Friday sermon. In the twentieth and twenty-first centuries, preaching from the *minbar* has been used to oppose political authority as well as to support it. In Egypt and Saudi Arabia, *minbar* sermons in local mosques critiquing the government have been taped and widely distributed. In 1979, *minbar* sermons were instrumental in mobilizing revolutionary activity against the shah of Iran. However, the main function of the *minbar* has always been ethical rather than political, with sermons providing guidance on worship, family life, education, and cordial human relations.

Sermons and announcements delivered from the *minbar* assume greater consequence in part because the *minbar* is located next to the prayer niche (*mihrab*) in the most sacred part of the mosque. *Minbar*s are composed of a platform with steps with a seat at the top and a balustrade, all usually made of wood and sometimes, in urban mosques, they may be elaborately carved and decorated.

See also **Masjid; Mihrab.**

BIBLIOGRAPHY

Borthwick, Bruce. "The Islamic Sermon as a Channel of Political Communication." *The Middle East Journal* 21, no. 3 (1967): 299–313.

Gaffney, Patrick. *The Prophet's Pulpit: Islamic Preaching in Contemporary Egypt.* Berkeley: University of California Press, 1994.

Richard T. Antoun

MINORITIES

DHIMMIS
Patrick Franke

OFFSHOOTS OF ISLAM
Robert Gleave

DHIMMIS

From the beginning of Islam up to present day, many Islamic societies have been characterized by the presence of more or less numerous non-Muslim minorities. Whereas in practice the status and treatment of these minorities have varied greatly over time and space, Islamic law provides a certain theoretical framework that has remained quite constant throughout the time: According to this all non-Muslim people are considered infidels (*kuffar*, sing. *kafir*). However there is a basic distinction between the polytheists (*mushrikun*, sing. *mushrik*) on the one hand, with whom social intercourse is forbidden, and who were to be fought until they either converted or were killed or enslaved and the "people of the book" (*ahl al-kitab*) on the other, whose faith was founded on revelation, who were to be granted protection, and with whom social intercourse was allowed. Originally only Jews and Christians were conceived as *ahl al-kitab*; later, however, this term was extended to a sect known as the Sabeans, the Zoroastrians, and, in India, even to Hindus. Concerning the legal status of these "people of the book," Islamic law makes another distinction between the *dhimmi* living as a protected person in Islamic territory, the *harbi* who lives in non-Muslim lands (*dar al-harb*), and the *musta'min* who as a foreigner is granted the temporary right of residence in an Islamic territory. The status of the *dhimmi*s was secured by a legal institution called *dhimma* ("protection"), which guaranteed safety for their life, body, and property, as well as freedom of movement and religious practice on condition of their acknowledging the domination of Islam. This included the payment of various taxes, the most important being the so-called *jizya*, a poll-tax levied on all able-bodied free adult *dhimmi* males of sufficient means.

It is the attitude of the prophet Muhammad who, after the expansion of his authority across Arabia, concluded agreements of submission and protection with Jews and Christians of other localities which serves as precedent for the *dhimma* institution. In the course of the Arab conquests under the "rightly guided" caliphs similar agreements were reached with the non-Muslims of Mesopotamia, Syria, Persia, and North Africa who surrendered their cities to the Arab armies. Muslim jurists later compiled these individual treaties into a coherent, sophisticated legal system conceding to the *dhimmi* communities almost complete autonomy under their respective religious leaders. It has to be pointed out, however, that the doctors of Islamic law tended to draw rather distinct boundaries between Muslims and non-Muslims, and to interpret the subjection of *dhimmi*s to Islamic authority as a justification for discriminating and humiliating measures imposed upon them. Thus, according to Islamic law, a Muslim could marry a *dhimmi* woman, but a *dhimmi* could not marry a Muslim woman; a Muslim could own a *dhimmi* slave, although the reverse was not allowed; at the frontier the *dhimmi* merchant would pay double the tariff rate paid by the Muslim (10% and 5%, respectively) and in criminal law it was commonly considered that the blood-wit (*diya*) for a *dhimmi* was less (one-half or two-thirds) than that for a Muslim; finally, the *dhimmi* had to wear distinguishing clothing, in particular the *zunnar* belt, and there were various limitations on the outward expressions of worship such as processions, the use of bells, and the construction and repair of religious buildings. A famous document authorizing many of these restrictions is the so-called "Covenant of 'Umar," a list of pledges allegedly given to the second "rightly-guided caliph," 'Umar ibn al-Khattab (634–644), by the Christians of the cities conquered by him.

In the classical centuries of Islam persecution of *dhimmi*s was very rare: One single case has been recorded, that of the Fatimid caliph al-Hakim (r. 996–1021) who in 1009 ordered the destruction of the Holy Sepulcher in Jerusalem. In the late Middle Ages, however, there was a general hardening of attitudes against *dhimmi*s in Muslim countries. In the West, the Almohads adopted an intolerant policy, while in the East the government of the Mamluk state could not resist the pressure of jurists, such as Ibn Taymiyya, who insisted on an increasingly vexatious interpretation of the law regarding *dhimmi*s. It was the legal system of the expanding Ottoman Empire that in the sixteenth century restored the classical Islamo-*dhimmi* symbiosis. This lasted until the middle of the nineteenth century, when under strong European pressure the provisions of Islamic law were increasingly replaced by new legislations that were intended to free the non-Muslims from their inferior status of "protected people" and to make them full citizens. Today most written constitutions of Muslim states confirm the principle of equality of all citizens irrespective of religion, sex, and race. Certain militant Islamic groups, however, advocate the reimposition of the *jizya* and the *dhimma* regulations.

See also **Minorities: Offshoots of Islam.**

BIBLIOGRAPHY

Braude, Benjamin, and Lewis, Bernard. *Christians and Jews in the Ottoman Empire: The Functioning of a Plural Society.* New York: Holmes & Meier, 1982.

Krämer, Gudrun. "Dhimmi or Citizen? Muslim-Christian Relations in Egypt." In *The Christian-Muslim Frontier. Chaos Clash or Dialogue?* Edited by Jorgen S. Nielsen. London and New York: Tauris, 1998.

Tritton, A. S. *The Caliphs and their Non-Muslim Subjects: A Critical Study of the Covenant of 'Umar.* London: Oxford University Press, 1930.

Patrick Franke

OFFSHOOTS OF ISLAM

Defining where the boundaries of Islam can be drawn, and which groups can be placed outside of that boundary, is, of course, a normative procedure. In the history of Islam, a number of scholars and groups have been subjected to *takfir*—the declaration of unbelief—and hence might be classed as offshoots of Islam. If one takes a strict definition of right belief, such as that proposed by Ibn 'Abd al-Wahhab, or in the more recent past, by Sayyid Qutb, many of those who call themselves Muslims do not deserve the term. Nonetheless, these groups, religious at base and tracing their origins to Islam, consider themselves Muslim despite the majority community refusing to accept them as such.

The emergence of radical alternatives to the dominant Sunni expression of Islam is normally located (by Sunni scholars at least) in the first civil war (*fitna*), during the caliphate of ʿAli (r. 656–661). Two alternative views of the nature of the Muslim community emerged at this time. First were the Shiʿites, who themselves later divided into a variety of competing groups. The Shiʿites not only considered ʿAli as the rightful caliph, but also defended the doctrine that only the descendants of ʿAli could be legitimate leaders of the Muslim community. Second were the Kharijites, who withdrew their support for ʿAli following his willingness to negotiate with his opponent Muʿawiya. The Kharijites (literally, "those who withdrew") developed an exclusive view of Islamic identity, declaring all sinners to be non-Muslims. The mainstream of Sunni Islam took a more forgiving attitude toward those who failed to obey the law of Islam in every detail. The strict Kharijite view undoubtedly contributed to the relatively small number of Kharijites in Muslim history. Elements of Kharijite doctrine, however, survive today within the Ibadi community, which is restricted to Oman and small communities in North Africa. Both the Ibadis and the Shiʿites have lived as minorities in Sunni-dominated milieux.

Many offshoots of Islam are centered upon the charismatic authority of a particular individual teacher. This charisma is at times successfully transferred to the leader's successor. Perhaps the most enduring of these offshoots is the Druze religion, which has its roots in the doctrines of Muhammad al-Darazi (d. 1020) concerning the Fatimid (Shiʿite) caliph of the time, al-Hakim bi-Amr Allah (d. 996). Darazi, with other Ismaili Shiʿite scholars, made claims of divinity for al-Hakim. This entailed an inevitable break with Islam, which has been maintained ever since. The modern-day Druze form a separate, non-Muslim religious community in Syria, Lebanon, Jordan, and Israel.

In the modern period, the Ahmadiyya, a community based around the teachings of the Indian leader Hazrat Mirza Ghulam Ahmad (d. 1908), provide an instructive example of individual charisma within Islam. Ahmad made a number of different claims regarding his theological status, including the assertion that he was the Promised Messiah of the Muslims. Though the community did maintain its unity after his death, it eventually divided in 1914 along theological lines. The different groups, which still exist today, claimed different levels of authority for Ahmad. Some viewed him as a prophet (*nabi*) while others tried to ameliorate the tension with mainstream Islam by calling Ahmad a *mujaddid* (renewer). The Ahmadiyya's minority status as non-Muslims was confirmed in Pakistan by a 1984 decree that prevented them from using Islamic forms of worship and legalized their prosecution.

A similar pattern can be seen in Shiʿite offshoots such as Babism and Bahaʾism. The former, led by ʿAli Muhammad Shirazi ("the Bab," executed in 1850), began in 1844, when Shirazi proclaimed himself the Gate to the Hidden Imam. He proceeded to establish a network of missionaries across Iran, who hoped to persuade the mainly Twelver Shiʿite population to recognize the Bab. The Bab's self-understanding developed further, and in 1848 he declared the advent of a new religion, with a new code of practice (which he controversially termed a *shariʿa*) to replace that of the prophet Muhammad. It is clear he adopted the role of a prophetic figure, though he was careful not classify himself as a *nabi*.

The Babis instigated a number of uprisings in the late 1840s, culminating in the Bab's execution in 1850. The Bahaʾi faith emerged out of the collapse of Babism. Bahaʾallah Husayn ʿAli Nuri, one of Shirazi's closest companions, promoted himself as a messianic figure who had been foretold by the Bab. His message consisted of a bundle of doctrines, including the unity of all religions, the institution of a new covenant which abrogated Islam, pacifism and the desire for world peace, and the role of himself and his descendants as conduits for revelation, blessed with spiritual insights which were passed to the people through new revelatory texts. Elements of early Bahaʾi doctrine are clearly influenced by Shiʿite Muslim theology and law. However, the Bahaʾis have incorporated Western notions of democracy and human rights into their belief system.

Bahaʾis consider themselves to be quite distinct from their Muslim parent religion. The feeling is mutual, as Bahaʾis are generally regarded as schismatic heretics by Shiʿite Muslims. The success of Bahaʾism as an independent religion has, in the main, rested upon its ability to gain converts in Western Europe and North America. Undoubtedly, Bahaʾis and perhaps even some Babis (called Azalis) continue to exist as minorities in Iran, although their numbers are difficult to estimate because open adherence brings inevitable discrimination and persecution.

Smaller groups, such as the Ahl-e haqq and the Yazidis (sometimes called "Devil-worshippers"), both based in Kurdistan, might also be classified as offshoots of Islam. Their theologies show a certain syncretism of the various mystical elements of the Middle Eastern milieu. The various Afro-American Muslim movements, such as the Nation of Islam, might also be considered as offshoots of Islam. These various offshoots display a variety of attitudes toward Islam, some wishing to be considered Muslims, while others prefer to be regarded as a separate from, and superior to, Islam.

See also **Ahmadiyya; Ahmad, Babiyya; Bab, Sayyed ʿAli Muhammad; Bahaʾallah; Bahaʾi Faith; Kharijites, Khawarij; Minorities: Dhimmis; Mirza Ghulam.**

BIBLIOGRAPHY

Amanat, Abbas. *Resurrection and Renewal: The Making of the Babi Movement in Iran, 1844–1850.* Ithaca, N.Y.: Cornell University Press, 1989.

Betts, Michael. *The Druze.* New Haven, Conn.: Yale University Press, 1988.

Calder, Norman. "The Limits of Islamic Orthodoxy." In *Intellectual Traditions in Islam*. Edited by Farhad Daftary. London: I. B. Tauris, 2000.

Cole, Juan R. I. *Modernity and the Millennium: The Genesis of the Baha'i Faith in the Nineteenth-Century Middle East*. New York: Columbia University Press, 1998.

McCloud, Amina Beverly. *African-American Islam*. London: Routledge, 1995.

Robert Gleave

MIRACLES

Miracles in the Islamic tradition play less of an evidentiary role than in some other religions since the prophet Muhammad's humanity is stressed. The miracles of prophets mentioned in the Qur'an are known there as signs (*ayat*) and include Abraham's not being harmed by the fire he was thrown into (21:69), as well as Jesus' speaking as a baby (19:30–33), bringing birds made of clay to life (3:49, 5:110), and healing powers (3:49). The Qur'an itself is often said to be the main miracle of Muhammad since an untutored or illiterate (*ummi*) person could not have been the source of this most compelling and eloquent message.

The sayings of the Prophet and his biography (*sira*), as they developed provide examples of various miraculous occurrences during the life of the Prophet including the childhood opening of his breast and cleansing of his internal organs by an angel, his night journey from Jerusalem through the seven heavens, his splitting of the moon, multiplication of food, and bestowal of blessings generally.

In later Muslim sources prophetic miracles were termed *mu'jizat*, or "things which render the detractors or opponents incapable or overwhelmed." In other words, acts incapable of being imitated as in the doctrine of the *i'jaz al-Qur'an*—its incomparable eloquence and content. In theological or philosophical discussions the term *kharq al-'ada*—a break in God's customary order of things—is used to indicate the miraculous. In the case of Sufi saints miracles are usually termed *karamat* (gifts or graces). They have the ambiguous role of both confirming spiritual attainments and potentially distracting from the ultimate goal of service of God. Classical authors struggled to differentiate prophetic and saintly miracles, and those who were inclined toward Sufism saw the saintly miracles as emerging and continuing the prophetic legacy. Al-Hakim al-Tirmidhi (d. 930) argued that the signs of the prophets emanated from the divine power while the *karamat* of the saints emanated from the divine generosity. Other Sufi commentators differentiated the public nature of prophetic miracles from the secretive aspects of saintly powers. Later Sufis, however, did not hesitate to openly enumerate the graces they received as in the *Lata'if al-minan* of al-Shar'ani or the many accounts of saints performing miracles

that led to mass conversions on the frontiers of Islamic expansion. South Asian saints' lives often consecrate chapters to *waqi'at* or "events" of a paranormal nature including mind reading and predicting future events.

More recent reformists and some classical theologians, such as the Mu'tazila, were more skeptical of miracle stories, given their rationalist proclivities, in some cases denying saintly miracles altogether. Debates over the physical reality of prophetic miracles such as the night journey or moon splitting still engage Muslim commentators.

A color plate of the Seven Sleepers of Ephesus *appears in the volume two color insert.*

See also **Mi'raj; Muhammad; Prophets.**

BIBLIOGRAPHY

Gramlich, Richard. *Die Wunder der Freunde Gottes*. Stuttgart: Steiner Verlag, 1987.

Gril, Denis. "Le Miracle en islam, critère de la sainteté." In *Saints Orientaux*. Edited by Denise Aigle. Paris: de Boccard, 1995.

Marcia Hermansen

MI'RAJ

Early Islamic sources preserve references to Muhammad's extraordinary journey from Mecca to Jerusalem and/or from the earth to the heavens. The narrative of the night journey (*isra'*) and ascension (*mi'raj*) developed its own unique form in the hadith reports of the eighth and ninth centuries.

The Qur'anic proof-text for the Mi'raj is the elliptic opening verse of Sura 17: "Glorified be the one who caused his servant to journey by night from the sacred prayer-site to the furthest prayer-site whose precincts we have blessed in order to show him some of our signs. . . ." Muslim consensus reads the verse as a reference to Muhammad's miraculous journey from the Ka'ba ("the sacred prayer-site") to either the Temple in Jerusalem or a heavenly temple ("the furthest prayer-site"). The sound hadiths of Bukhari and Muslim show that both the terrestrial and the celestial night journeys were considered potentially authentic by early traditionists.

Early exegetes such as Muqatil b. Sulayman al-Balkhi (d. c. 767) and Muhammad b. Jarir al-Tabari (d. 923) collated the "night journey verse" (17:1) with the visionary passage from the beginning of the Sura of the Star (53:1–18). The latter passage describes a pair of visions, one at "a distance of two bows or nearer," the other at "the lote tree of the boundary." Exegetes disagree about whether these verses describe Muhammad's vision of God or of Gabriel, but they generally agree in placing the "lote tree of the boundary" in the heavens and thus in relating the passage to the Mi'raj.

At least some early Muslims considered the night journey and ascension to refer to two separate events. The biography of the Prophet by Ibn Ishaq (d. c. 767) in the recension of Ibn Hisham (d. 833) treats the two separately but in succession. The biographer Ibn Sa'd (d. 845) goes even further by attaching two different dates to the events. While the date of the journey(s) remained a source of controversy, the idea that the journey from Mecca to Jerusalem was immediately followed by the ascension from Jerusalem through the seven heavens became the majority opinion in the centuries that followed.

The night journey and ascension narrative begins typically with the Prophet asleep in Mecca and awakened by one or more angels. In some versions, these angels open the Prophet's chest and cleanse his heart (94). Then the magical beast Buraq bears Muhammad to Jerusalem where he performs the prayer at the Temple in the company of Abraham, Moses, and Jesus. Muhammad is offered a choice of two or three cups of different drinks. He proves his right guidance by avoiding the wine and selecting the milk.

The angel Gabriel then takes Muhammad up through the heavens. At each level an angelic gatekeeper interrogates Gabriel before allowing entrance. In each Muhammad encounters one or more Abrahamic prophets, offers his greeting, and then departs for the next level. The typical order of encounter, already present in Ibn Hisham's account, consists of Adam in the first heaven, Jesus and John the Baptist in the second, Joseph in the third, Enoch (Idris) in the fourth, Aaron in the fifth, Moses in the sixth, and Abraham in the seventh. After meeting Abraham in the seventh heaven near the celestial temple known as the frequented house (al-bayt al-ma'mur), Muhammad arrives at the lote tree, experiences a revelation, and receives the ritual duty to pray fifty times a day. He descends to Moses, who sends him back to request that the burden be reduced. God removes a portion of the duty, but Moses sends Muhammad back again and again until the number of daily ritual prayers is reduced to five. Some accounts include Muhammad's return and his efforts to prove his experience to a skeptical Meccan community.

By the ninth century this spare narrative was amplified by storytellers. Evidence for this popular tradition can be found in the extended narratives preserved in the Qur'an commentaries on the "night journey verse" by al-Tabari and the early Shi'ite exegete 'Ali b. Ibrahim al-Qummi (d. c. 919). The account of Muhammad's young companion Ibn 'Abbas (d. c. 687) circulated widely and remains highly popular.

The Mi'raj tradition served to bring various modes of Islamic literature into conversation. The pivotal Sufi traditionists Abu 'Abd al-Rahman al-Sulami (d. 1021) and 'Abd al-Karim al-Qushayri (d. 1072) each composed important works on the early mystical interpretations of Muhammad's night journey and ascension. Mystics such as Abu Yazid al-Bistami (d. c. 850), Muhyi al-Din Ibn 'Arabi (d. 1240), and Farid al-Din 'Attar (d. c. 1220) made the Prophet's journey into a paradigm for their own journey toward mystical union. For philosopher Ibn Sina (d. 1037), the Mi'raj serves as a neoplatonic allegory. For the litterateur Abu 'Ala' al-Ma'arri (d. c. 1058) it stimulated an imaginative parody of contemporary attitudes toward literature, linguistics, and morality.

The Mi'raj also became a site of literary and cultural contestation and intercourse among different religious and geographical worlds. The thirteenth-century Latin and old French translations of the Liber Scale indicate the story's influence among European intellectuals, including Dante. In the East, it was translated into Persian and Turkish and inspired numerous poetic works. A fifteenth-century eastern Turkish manuscript accompanied by stunning Persian miniatures illustrates the story's influence on painting. At some point Muslims began to commemorate the night of the ascension during the month of Rajab, which has become an important popular holiday. Some Islamic Mi'raj material shows clear signs of engagement with other traditions. One Mi'raj narrative attributed to al-Bistami draws upon material from Jewish Merkava and Hekhalot ascent narratives of the Jewish mystics describing journeys through celestial palaces to the divine throne. Christian apocalyptic writings such as the Apocalypse of Paul also contain important parallels, as do inter-testamental and apocryphal texts such as the Ethiopic Book of Enoch. The initiatic features of the Mi'raj (e.g., ritual dismemberment, meeting past elders, receiving a divine commission) has led some to note similarities to patterns from shamanic tradition.

In general, the Mi'raj interpretation of the visions of Qur'an 53 offers a paradigm of "ascent" by the Prophet toward revelation in contrast to the dominant Qur'anic motif of "descent" (tanazzul) of the revelation toward the Prophet, two contrasting paradigms that were in similar play throughout late antiquity and the Middle Ages. One could read many Mi'raj traditions as expressions of a symbolic cosmology that served as a common cultural language for religious, philosophical, literary, and cultural contact and as a symbolic field that differing cultural worlds attempted to appropriate as their own.

An interpretation of Muhammad's vision of ascension appears in the volume two color plates.

See also **Buraq; Holy Cities; 'Ibadat; Miracles.**

BIBLIOGRAPHY

Amir-Moezzi, Mohammad, ed. *Le Voyage initiatique en Terre d'Islam.* Louvain-Paris: Peeters, 1996.

Asin Palacios, Miguel. *La escatalogia musulmana en la Divina Comedia.* Madrid and Granada: Consejo Superior de Investigaciones Cientificas, 1919.

Bencheikh, Jamel Eddine. *Le Voyage nocturne de Mahomet.* Paris: Imprimerie Nationale, 1988.

Ghayti, Najm al-Din al-. "The Story of the Night Journey and the Ascension." In *A Reader on Islam*. Edited and translated by Arthur Jeffrey. The Hague, Netherlands: Mouton and Co., 1962.

Heath, Peter. *Allegory and Philosophy in Avicenna (Ibn Sina)*. Philadelphia: The University of Pennsylvania Press, 1992.

Hyatte, Richard. *The Prophet of Islam in Old French: The Romance of Muhammad (1258) and The Book of Muhammad's Ladder (1264)*. Leiden: E. J. Brill, 1997.

Ibn Hisham, ʿAbd al-Malik. "The Night Journey and Ascent to Heaven." In *The Life of Muhammad*. Edited and translated by Alfred Guillame. Oxford, U.K.: Oxford University Press, 1955.

Piemontese, Angelo. "Le Voyage de Mahomet au Paradis et Enfer: une version persane du Miʿraj." In *Apocalypses et en Voyages dans l'Au-delà*. Edited by Claude Kappler. Paris: Les Editions du CERF, 1987.

Samarrai, Qassim. *The Theme of Ascension in Mystical Writings*. Baghdad: National Printing Company, 1968.

Schimmel, Annemarie. "The Prophet's Night Journey and Ascension." In *And Muhammad is His Messenger*. Chapel Hill: University of North Carolina Press, 1985.

Seguy, Marie-Rose. *The Miraculous Journey of Mahomet*. Translated by Richard Pevear. New York: George Braziller, 1977.

Sells, Michael. *Early Islamic Mysticism: Sufi, Qurʾan, Miʿraj, Poetic and Theological Writings*. New York: Paulist Press, 1996.

Tabari, Muhammad b. Jarir al-. "Muhammad's Night Journey and Ascension." Translated by Rueven Firestone. In *Windows on the House of Islam*. Edited by John Renard. Berkeley: University of California Press, 1998.

Widengren, Geo. *Muhammad, the Apostle of God, and his Ascension (King and Savior V)*. Uppsala: A. B. Lundequistska, 1955.

Frederick Colby
Michael Sells

MIRZA HUSAYN ʿALI NURI

See Bahaʾallah

MODERNISM

Modernism is a movement to reconcile Islamic faith with modern values such as nationalism, democracy, rights, rationality, science, equality, and progress. Islamic modernism is distinguished from secularism by its insistence on the continuing importance of faith in public life; it is distinguished from other Islamic movements by its enthusiasm for contemporary European institutions. The movement emerged in the middle of the nineteenth century as a response to European imperialism, which pitched the Islamic world into crisis, but also—in the view of the modernists—offered solutions to the crisis. Influential early figures included Sayyid Jamal al-Din al-Afghani (1838–1897), Muhammad ʿAbduh (1849–1905), and Sayyid Ahmad Khan (1817–1898). Islamic modernism generated a series of novel institutions, including schools that combined Islamic education with modern subjects and pedagogies; newspapers that carried modernist Islamic ideas across continents; theaters, museums, novels, and other cultural forms that were adapted from European models; constitutions that sought to limit state power; and social welfare agencies that brought state power into ever more sectors of social life.

Islamic modernism justified each of these institutions as being more consistent with the original spirit of Islam than were the existing institutions of the Islamic world. In some regions Islamic modernism declined in the mid-twentieth century, losing popularity to revivalist and secularist movements. Yet it appeared to have revived in the late twentieth century, spurred in part by a dramatic global increase in modern education.

See also ʿAbduh, Muhammad; Afghani, Jamal al-Din; Ahmad Khan, (Sir) Sayyid; Iqbal, Muhammad; Liberalism, Islamic; Modern Thought; Rahman, Fazlur.

BIBLIOGRAPHY

Kurzman, Charles, ed. *Modernist Islam: A Sourcebook, 1840–1940*. New York: Oxford University Press, 2002.

Charles Kurzman

MODERNITY

The European penetration of the Near East and India and the decline of Muslim ascendancy in these regions in the nineteenth century precipitated the crisis that defined the responses of Muslim intellectuals to European modernity. The key thinkers in the nineteenth century, who continue to influence contemporary attitudes in the Islamic world to modernity, were the so-called Islamic modernists, such as Jamal al-Din Afghani (1839–1897), Muhammad ʿAbduh (1849–1905), and Sir Sayyid Ahmad Khan (1817–1898). Although there were some differences between these thinkers, their work was governed by the same project, which was to show that Islam was consistent with the rationality of the European enlightenment and the development of modern science. As such, they argued that there was no fundamental incompatibility between modernity and its narrative of progress, and Islam as a religion. They tended toward a rationalist interpretation of the Qurʾan, in which whatever appeared to be in contradiction to rationality could be interpreted symbolically and allegorically. As a consequence of this they argued that the meaning of the Qurʾan was accessible to everyone. In other words, there was no need to rely on the technical and elaborate procedures of *tafsir*, in which the ulema trained in the traditional Islamic sciences were conversant.

These two tendencies in Islamic modernism also reflected in part the major impact of print on the Islamic world in the modern period. From the nineteenth century onward, the availability of the Qur'an in print, and its concurrent translation into local languages, struck at the very heart of the traditional system of the oral transmission of knowledge, in which the charisma of the teacher as a living embodiment of knowledge was crucial. The multiplication of texts through printing made unsupervised reading possible. This in turn meant that it was possible to engage with religious texts without the mediation of the formally trained ulema.

These tendencies in Islamic modernism, and the impact of print, lie behind the works of a number of important Muslim thinkers in the twentieth century, in which the engagement with European modernity was a key theme. It is particularly evident in the commentaries on the Qur'an by Sayyid Abu l-A'la' Maududi, the founder of the fundamentalist Jama'at-e Islami. Maududi himself was not a formally trained *'alim*, but it is precisely because of this that his ideas and thought played a crucial role in the development of what is called Islamic fundamentalism. These tendencies are similarly evident in Muhammad Iqbal's (1893–1938) *The Reconstruction of Religious Thought in Islam* (1934). This work exemplifies Islamic modernism's response to European modernity both in its style and its content. It purports to show how the Qur'an is entirely consonant with the major discoveries of European science, and it is wide-ranging in its eclectic use of European thinkers. Iqbal's engagment with the Qur'an is singular and unmediated by any sense of *tafsir* in the traditional sense of the word.

Islam's relationship with modernity has been the defining theme of the work of major Muslim thinkers of the nineteenth and twentieth centuries. The strategies of interpreting the Qur'an, and its relocation as a sacred text in the act of individual and unmediated reading, are in fact among the major consequences of the impact of modernity on Islam. However, the role of modernist thinkers as spokesmen for Islam vis-à-vis European modernity also points to some other features of the impact of modernity on the Islamic world.

First, it is clear that there are a multiplicity of Islamic voices engaging with European modernity. This in part is also a consequence of the abolition of the caliphate in 1924 by Ataturk, so that even symbolically there is no single figurehead in the Islamic world. This, together with the undermining of the authority of the formally trained ulema, has meant that there are competing voices for Islam with no clear procedures or authorities to adjudicate between them.

Secondly, Islamic engagements with modernity can be read in two overlapping ways. In part, the relationship of

This Cairo bus ferries passengers past a billboard for director Magdi Ahmed 'Ali's 2001 *Girls' Secrets,* a film in which a middle-class family faces its teenage daughter's pregnancy. The film has been acclaimed for its portrayal of contemporary Egypt's struggle to balance tradition and religion with modernity and science. AP/ WIDE WORLD PHOTOS

Islamic thought to European thought is mimetic; that is to say, in the work of Afghani, 'Abduh, Iqbal, and others, such as the poet Altaf Husayn Hali (1837–1914), Islam is refashioned into a mirror of European modernity. At the same time, though, Islamic modernism also teases out, generally unself-consciously, the contradictions in European modernity itself. Islamic engagements with modernity are at times ambivalent, rather than mimetic alone. As such, these engagements can be read alongside the works of European philosophers, such as those of the Frankfurt School and Michel Foucault, who have explored the tensions in modernity, arguing that it is less a narrative of progress than one of repression.

Thirdly, nowhere is this ambivalence to modernity more evident than in the attitude to the nation-state demonstrated by the thinkers mentioned above. There is an obvious tension between the modernist attempts to define a pan-Islamic, worldwide community, theoretically made possible through innovations in technologies of communication, and the fundamental reality of the nation-state, some with Muslim populations that are hostile to each other. The very attempts by Afghani, 'Abduh, Iqbal, and others to reinterpret Islamic law as a legal system in keeping with a modern state is indicative of the powerful reality of the nation-state as the organizing principle of the world in the twentieth century. Furthermore, given the fact that the nation-state tends toward monopolizing all sources of authority, as long as it remains in existence, it is unlikely that the ulema will recover the authority they enjoyed in the pre-modern Islamic world.

The engagement of Islam with modernity remains open-ended and multivocal. Having said that, it is important to note that no Muslim thinker has argued for rejecting European modernity in toto in the way that the famous Indian nationalist leader, Mohandas Gandhi (1869–1948), tried to do in his life's work. Although there may be problems regarding the feasibility of Gandhi's position, the fact that the possibility of any alternatives to European modernity has not been explored in any depth in Muslim thought is powerful testimony to the sway that European modernity has held over the Islamic world since the early nineteenth century.

See also 'Abduh, Muhammad; Afghani, Jamal al-Din; Ahmad Khan, (Sir) Sayyid; Iqbal, Muhammad; Liberalism, Islamic; Maududi, Abu l-A'la'; Modern Thought.

BIBLIOGRAPHY

Ahmad, Aziz. *Islamic Modernism in India and Pakistan 1857–1964.* London: Oxford University Press, 1967.

Azmeh, Aziz, al-. *Islams and Modernities.* London and New York: Verso, 1993.

Cooper, John; Nettler, Ronald; and Mahmoud, Mohamed, eds. *Islam and Modernity. Muslim Intellectuals Respond.* London: I. B. Tauris, 1998.

Hourani, Albert. *Arabic Thought in the Liberal Age, 1798–1939.* Cambridge, U.K.: Cambridge University Press, 1983.

Robinson, Francis. "Technology and Religious Change: Islam and the Impact of Print." *Modern Asian Studies* 27, no. 1 (1993): 229–251.

Shackle, Christopher, and Majeed, Javed. *Hali's Musaddas. The Flow and Ebb of Islam.* Delhi: Oxford University Press, 1997.

Javed Majeed

MODERNIZATION, POLITICAL

ADMINISTRATIVE, MILITARY, AND JUDICIAL REFORM
Aslam Farouk-Alli

AUTHORITARIANISM AND DEMOCRATIZATION
Claudia Stodte
Anne-Sophie Froehlich

CONSTITUTIONALISM
Sohail H. Hashmi

PARTICIPATION, POLITICAL MOVEMENTS, AND PARTIES
Quintan Wiktorowicz

ADMINISTRATIVE, MILITARY, AND JUDICIAL REFORM

The modern states of the Middle East are remnants of the Ottoman (Turkish) and Safavid (Persian) dominions, the last of the great Muslim empires. These countries not only share common religious and historical legacies but have also experienced very similar colonial and postcolonial influences. The term "Middle East" in fact alludes to the colonial encounter and was coined by the Allied forces (the British, Free French, and Americans) during the Second World War to indicate a single military theater for operational and supply purposes. The area in question thus encompasses the Arab world as well as the non-Arab countries of Turkey and Iran. To fully appreciate developments in the post-independence period—after 1945—events that led to the modern state system must be briefly charted.

World War I resulted in the collapse of the Ottoman Empire and the creation of mandate territories run as colonies. This gave rise to strong anti-colonial, nationalist movements, especially in Turkey and Iran, which emerged as independent states in 1923 and 1921, respectively. Egypt gained independence in 1922, when the British withdrew from direct control, and Saudi Arabia attained sovereignty in 1926. The period after World War II was characterized by rapid independence, and between 1945 and 1946 Syria, Lebanon, and Jordan all witnessed the disappearance of the European presence. However, the authority of the West still weighed burdensomely upon the region and determined the manner in which these countries reconstituted themselves in light of modern developments. This influence continues to the present day.

Three of the most significant factors challenging reform and growth in the region have been the discovery of oil, the strengthening of the United States' position after World War II, and the creation of the state of Israel. These factors had, and continue to have, a direct impact upon reform initiatives, manifesting themselves differently depending upon the social and cultural conditions of the individual countries of the region,

Iran

Reza Shah Pahlevi (1925–1941) was able to create a strongly centralized state by using the army, thereby leaving an enduring legacy of military intervention in Iranian politics right up to the Islamic revolution in 1979. Muhammad Reza, who succeeded his father in 1941, initially indulged party politics, but soon followed his father's example and used his control over the army to re-establish royal authority. Prior to this however, Iranian politics (between 1945 and 1953) was extremely turbulent, due to both internal and external factors.

Throughout the 1940s, the political scene was driven by British, Soviet, and American interests competing for influence. The United States was able to forge close ties with the Iranian army, while Britain sought a privileged position for its oil interests. The placing of Iran's economic and military development in the hands of foreigners created growing consternation among Iranian nationalists, and in 1950 a group of politicians led by Mohammed Mosaddeq were able to obtain sufficient support in the *Majlis* (parliament) to act against the Anglo-Iranian oil company, nationalizing its Iranian assets. In 1951 the *Majlis* nationalized the oil industry altogether, and also elected Mosaddeq as prime minister. However, his reform efforts were short-lived and he was overthrown in a U.S.–assisted coup in 1953, largely due to American fears of Soviet influence over Iran. Mosaddeq's overthrow enabled the shah to create his royal dictatorship, and with the assistance of U.S. and Israeli advisors he formed SAVAK, his notorious secret police service.

From 1953 to 1979 there was absolutely no political freedom in Iran. In 1963 the shah was severely criticized by a then still-obscure member of the religious establishment, Ayatollah Ruhollah Khomeini. Khomeini was arrested by SAVAK in June 1963 and deported to Turkey in 1964. In the following year he was deported to Iraq, where he stayed, preaching and writing. In 1978 he was forced to go to France. However, Khomeini returned to Iran in triumph in 1979, as leader of one of the most spectacular and unexpected revolutions in modern history.

The shah's dictatorial policies robbed Khomeini of all political legitimacy and were ultimately responsible for his downfall. Most of his 1961 to 1963 White Revolution reforms centered on huge military spending and benefits offered to appease the officer corps. By 1976 Iran had the fifth largest military force in the world. Khomeini's efforts at economic and social development were miserable failures, with the exception of the literacy drive, which enjoyed measurable success. In 1975 he scrapped the two-party system and introduced the single National Resurgence Party. It was ultimately the shah's brutal response to unarmed protests in 1978 that ignited the revolution. The clergy were able to effect large-scale uprisings, and emerged as the representatives of the masses.

The new government, under the leadership of Ruhollah Khomeini, initially made efforts to include secular elements. Mehdi Bazargan, the secular reformist, was made the first prime minister of the Islamic Republic of Iran. Ultimately, however, the idea that social, political, and economic change could only be achieved by the renewal of an Islamic order prevailed, ushering in the Khomeini era, in which Iran was transformed into a theocracy ruled by the clergy.

Khomeini died in 1989, and the post-Khomeini period has once again surprised analysts with the emergence of liberal-minded reformists. At the turn of the twenty-first century, Iran's president, Mohammad Khatami, has even called for increased powers of the elected assembly over the ulema's Council of Guardians, and he appears to be trying to reconcile a deeply religious political ethos with the principles of representative government.

Turkey

After independence in 1923, Turkish politics was dominated by the single-party rule of Mustafa Kemal Ataturk's authoritarian Republican People's Party (RPP). His successor, who assumed office in 1938, departed from Ataturk's economic policies and lessened government sponsorship of industrial development. This was largely in response to pressure from the Turkish business sector, which sought more freedom for private entrepreneurial activity, and pressure from the peasantry, which was displeased with the government's bias in favor of industrialization over agricultural development. Government also responded to pressure from intellectuals and politicians critical of the single-party dispensation by allowing greater political freedom. As a result, four members of the national assembly defected from the RPP in 1946 and formed a new party, called the Democratic Party (DP).

Although the democrats were only able to win sixty-five seats in the 1946 elections, they were able to extend their influence tremendously over the next four years and won 396 of the 465 seats in the national assembly in 1950. The DP showed greater sensitivity to religious sentiments and restored the public call to prayer in Arabic (which had previously been banned), maintained and developed mosques, and offered religious instruction to all Muslim students in primary schools on a voluntary basis. It still, however, strongly upheld the principal of secularism.

Economic policies instituted by the democrats were geared towards agricultural reform in order to appease their support-base among the peasantry, but when the economy began to suffer they came under severe public criticism. The government responded harshly by introducing extremely repressive restrictions against the press, and even brought in the army to quell violent protests. They further exploited ruling-party privilege by using the army to disrupt RPP campaign rallies. Such irresponsibility met with a severe backlash, and on 27 May 1960 the military stepped in to institute the first coup d'état.

Military intervention became commonplace in Turkish politics, but remains unique in that power was always handed back to civilian politicians. The military establishment was primarily concerned with upholding the principle of Kemalism, but equally committed to the system of multi-party politics. The 1960 intervention lasted for only eighteen months, in which time the constitution was revised to protect the rights of individuals and assert the principle of secularism.

The period between 1961 and 1983 witnessed the proliferation of political parties, with attendant political upheaval and instability. The military instituted two more coups, in 1971 and 1980, and further constitutional amendments were introduced. In addition to the rise and fall of various coalition governments, civil order was also threatened by Kurdish separatist aspirations and by the rise of Islamic revivalism, led by the National Salvation Party. Islamist parties have had to constantly re-invent themselves under different guises due to the military's censure of "anti-secular" politics. This trend has set contemporary Turkish politics to sway between two poles: that of a re-emergent Islamist ideal versus a secular-liberal ideal seemingly on the wane. Just below the surface, however, lies the powerful military, which keeps the powers-that-be decisively in check.

In 1997 the Islamist Refah (Welfare) Party's leader was forced to step down due to pressure from the National Security Council, and the party itself was closed down the following year on charges of anti-secular activities. Refah re-constituted as the Fazilat Party, which was also banned in 2001. In spite of this, the 2002 elections were won by the Justice and Development Party, which emerged from the modernizing wing of the Fazilat Party. Although enjoying overwhelming support from the masses, the Justice and Development Party will have to constrain its constituency's aspirations or face the fate of all its Islamist predecessors.

The Arab States
In contrast to the relatively effective constitutional regimes of Iran and Turkey, the Arab States of the Middle East are ruled by either monarchies or military dictators. It is important to note that the regions' dictatorships are a result of the social and political processes of the twentieth century. The Arab defeat at the hands of Israel in the 1967 war and the changing structure of global politics due to Cold War competition were the main factors responsible for the polarization of the Arab states and the tempering of Arab Nationalist sentiments that were so strongly evoked by the Egyptian leader Jamal 'Abd al-Nasser, especially between 1953 and 1967.

By 1945 the massive influx of wealth into the Arab states, primarily due to oil revenues, served as the single impetus for development, especially in terms of infrastructure and nation-building. However, progress was undermined by defeat in the first Arab-Israeli war from 1948 to 1949, as well the failure to cope with internal political, economic and social pressures. The resultant backlash brought about a series of military coups: in Syria in 1949, Egypt in 1952, Sudan and Iraq in 1958, North Yemen in 1962, and Libya in 1969. The remaining countries, including Morocco, Jordan, Saudi Arabia, and the Gulf States, were all monarchies and effectively one-party states. The only exception was Lebanon, where the existence of parliamentary or party politics has been essential in order to balance the interests of both Christians and Muslims.

The sharp rise in oil prices in the early 1970s led to ambitious programs of social and economic development, and even had a positive impact upon the non-oil producing states like Egypt, Syria, and Jordan, which were able to benefit from the new wealth through workers' remittances and financial aid. In the 1950s and 1960s, the military was seen as an instrument of modernization and change, but by the 1970s this image was severely damaged largely due to defeats on the battlefield and failed agrarian and industrialization reform policies.

The two major home-grown ideologies up to this point were Nasserism and Ba'thism, impacting most significantly upon Egypt, Syria, and Iraq. Egypt under Nasser embodied the aspirations of the Arab world, facing a future freed of the imperial past, newly independent and equally assertive. From the time of the Free Officers' coup in 1952 up until the Arab-Israeli War in June of 1967, Nasser was seen as a dynamic president who had set in motion a positive process of national transformation. As a result Egypt exercised profound regional influence in this period.

However, Nasserism as a doctrine tried to satisfy too many conflicting aspirations. As such, it was able to position itself neither as religious nor secular, democratic nor authoritarian, socialist nor capitalist. It contained aspects of all but faltered in privileging any one of these as the most important. The defeat in 1967 marked the true end of Nasserism. Hereafter, Nasser allowed the Soviet Union to acquire dominant influence in the military. He dropped the quest for Arab unity and the hopes he had raised were finally shattered with his death in 1970. His successor, Anwar Sadat (1918–1981), was left to fill the void.

Although lacking the charisma of Nasser, Sadat was able to reorient Egyptian domestic and foreign policy in ways that were every bit as profound as Nasser's. He realigned Egypt with the superpowers in favor of the United States by expelling Soviet military advisors and by courting peace with Israel, not before redeeming Egyptian honor by defeating the Israelis in the October 1973 war. Sadat's U.S.–brokered treaty with Israel earned him the discontent of militant Islamic groups in Egypt. His clampdown on these groups ultimately led to his assassination on 6 October 1981.

Ba'thism, in contrast to Nasserism, was characterized by a more sharply defined set of principles. Michel 'Aflaq (1910–1989), the cofounder of the Ba'th Party, defined its role in stirring and romantic language. The party was conceived of as an instrument of social justice and was supposed to be at the vanguard of Arab unity. It attracted young Arabs of the post-independence era eager to restore Arab dignity, especially in Syria and Iraq.

Aflaq was, however, in no way comparable to Nasser in terms of leadership qualities. Lacking a politician of ability to implement its vision, the party's plans were thwarted as it divided into regional groupings and quarreling factions. Ambitious men like Syria's Hafiz al-Asad (1930–2000) and Iraq's Saddam Husayn (1937–) used the party's apparatus and ideology to serve their own ends. In the hands of al-Asad and Husayn the Ba'th became a means of survival their respective regimes and they utilized it as an effective instrument of control and indoctrination.

As such, the party lost its pan-Arab mission and developed rival Syrian and Iraqi branches. Common to both, however, was severe political repression, although social reforms were in some instances significant. Syria still remains an authoritarian dictatorship under Bashar al-Asad (b. 1965), Hafiz al-Asad's son and heir, whereas the political future of Iraq after the U.S.-led overthrow of Saddam Husayn in April of 2003 is uncertain.

In the 1980s, the biggest challenge that faced the Arab regimes was the re-emergence of Islamic reformism, which was greatly influenced by the Islamic revolution in Iran. The Islamic reform movements were largely unsuccessful due to the foreign support offered to the various regimes in order to protect their own interests. A striking example is the overthrow of the Islamic Salvation Front (FIS) in Algeria by the military after a landslide victory in the first round of parliamentary elections held in December 1991. Voters had rejected the National Liberation Front that had ruled the country as a single party for thirty years. The Islamic Salvation Front was poised to gain a decisive parliamentary majority, but the military intervened, declaring the elections null and void. A notable exception, however, was the successful establishment of an Islamic regime in Sudan in 1989.

The United States in the early twenty-first century exercises undisputed influence over the Middle East, and it is difficult to envisage the flourishing of any popular movement representative of the political aspirations and ambitions of the civilian populations in these countries. This is borne out by the United States' heavy-handed policies towards countries with well-established systems of representative government, like Sudan and Iran, and its tolerance and open allegiance to repressive regimes like Egypt, Saudi Arabia, and Tunisia, which are notorious for their gross violations of human rights. American support for Israel in terms of massive financial assistance and the turning of a blind eye to the occupation of Palestine also leaves little hope for resolving conflict and diffusing tensions in the region as a whole. The U.S.–led invasion of Iraq in April of 2003 only signals the perpetuation of the old colonial paradigm of political, military, and economic domination and exposes the divide between the vested interests of a powerful center and ultimate regional self determination on the periphery. These are but some of the major factors that hinder positive reform and progress in the Middle East.

Judicial Reform

The process of judicial reform in the Middle East had already begun in the nineteenth and early twentieth centuries, when the Ottoman Empire and Egypt began appropriating Western legal codes that were mostly derived from French and British models. The immediate effect of these measures was the reduction of the scope of Islamic law or *shari'a*, jurisdiction.

With the dismantling of the Ottoman Empire and the rise of the modern republic of Turkey, a fairly complete secularization of the law code was effected in that country, even in matters of personal status. The *shari'a* was effectively purged from the new statute books. However, developments in the neighboring regions were far more gradual.

Iran, under Reza Shah Pahlevi, adopted a version the Swiss family law code that remained in effect until after the revolution. The shah's obsession with Western models of development drove his reform initiatives, and some of the family protection laws instituted between 1967 and 1975 granted women greater legal equality within marriage. Unlike the case of Turkey and Tunisia, however, the shah did not abolish polygamy. However, the husband was required to take the consent of his current wife in order to marry another.

The most significant reform initiative in the Arab states was the introduction of the new Egyptian civil code, framed by 'Abd al-Razzaq al-Sanhuri in 1949. Al-Sanhuri drew upon existing legislation, contemporary Western codes, and the *shari'a* in formulating the code, although its final shape was more French than Islamic. Other Arab states also amended their codes and continued to increase the centralization of their courts. The Egyptian model inspired many of these efforts. Al-Sanhuri was also called upon to formulate the Iraqi and Kuwaiti codes later on.

A notable exception to the reform trend is seen in Saudi Arabia and Yemen. Neither of these countries came under British protection and the early Ottoman reforms were not that far-reaching. As such, the pre-existing *shari'a* system was never restricted. In more recent times Yemen has made efforts to centralize and codify its legal system, whereas in Saudi Arabia the *shari'a* courts still retain general jurisdiction.

The period of malaise in the Middle East after 1967 prompted militants and ordinary citizens alike to express desire for the re-establishment of the *shari'a*. Muslim intellectuals have generally favored the idea that rulers are subject to and must therefore enforce laws that are not entirely of their own making. This is but one strong inclination that ensures the continuing appeal for calls to re-introduce the *shari'a* and its role in future legal reforms cannot be easily dismissed or discounted.

See also **'Abd al-Nasser, Jamal; 'Abd al-Razzaq al-Sanhuri; Ataturk, Mustafa Kemal; Iran, Islamic Republic of; Islamic Salvation Front; Khomeini, Ruhollah; Modernization, Political: Participation, Political Movements, and Parties; Mosaddeq, Mohammad; Muhammad Reza Shah Pahlevi; Revolution: Islamic Revolution in Iran.**

BIBLIOGRAPHY

Brown, Leon Carl, ed. *Imperial Legacy – The Ottoman Imprint on the Balkans and Middle East.* New York: Columbia University Press, 1996.

Brown, Nathan J. *The Rule of Law in the Arab World – Courts in Egypt and the Gulf.* Cambridge, U.K.: Cambridge University Press, 1997.

Brumberg, Daniel. *Reinventing Khomeini: The Struggle for Reform in Iran.* Chicago: University of Chicago Press, 2001.

Cleveland, William L. *A History of the Modern Middle East.* Boulder, Colo.: Westview Press, 1994.

Edge, Ian, ed. *Islamic Law and Legal Theory.* New York: New York University Press, 1996.

Hourani, Albert; Khoury, Philip S.; and Wilson, Mary C., eds. *The Modern Middle East.* London: I. B. Tauris, 1993.

Humphreys, R. Stephen. *Between Memory and Desire: The Middle East in Troubled Age.* Cairo: The American University in Cairo Press, 2000.

Owen, Roger. *State, Power, and Politics in the Making of the Modern Middle East.* London: Routledge, 1992.

Aslam Farouk-Alli

AUTHORITARIANISM AND DEMOCRATIZATION

In the Middle East, liberal democracy is a rarity. There is no democracy in the Western sense, that is, characterized by the right to form political parties; the possibility of changing government by election; the freedoms of the press, belief, and association; the protection of individual rights; the separation of powers; and secularism.

One reason for the lack of democratic structures lies in the experience of colonialism and neocolonialism. Most Arab countries achieved independence only after World War II, and the borders were in many cases fixed by the colonial powers; therefore, the people in the new political entities did not necessarily share a national identity. For some decades there was a strong movement toward "Arab unity" or pan-Arabism. However, actual attempts to form a greater nation, like that of Egypt, Syria, and Yemen (1958–1961), came to nothing.

Even in countries that never were colonies, like Iran and Afghanistan, Western and Soviet interference, respectively, prevented democratic development. The success of the Iranian revolution of 1978 and 1979 is partly due to the repeated defeat of attempts at democratization. The ongoing Israeli-Arab conflict stymies liberalization, and plays into the hands of extremist groups.

Another reason for the lack of democratic structures lies within the extremely patriarchal Middle Eastern societies themselves and their tradition of authoritarianism. The latter has its roots in the patronage system of the tribal Arab societies as well as in the Islamic theory of power with its ideal of the just sovereign.

The political landscape since the 1970s has been dominated by two forms of governance: conservative monarchies and military or single-party republics. Even countries that established an ideologically founded republic (e.g., Algeria, Tunisia, and the People's Democratic Republic of Yemen, or South Yemen) or abolished monarchy through military coups d'état (e.g., Egypt, Iraq, and Libya), later developed a highly authoritarian, personalized leadership. If presidential elections are held, people do not really have a choice between different candidates; the "presidential monarch" is usually reelected with close to 100 percent of the votes (e.g., in 1999: Yemen 96%, Egypt 94%, Tunisia 99%). Nowhere else do governors stay in power so long: The average reigning time for rulers in the Arab world was twenty-one years in 1998.

With many Arab societies still divided into tribes (most notably in Yemen) or sects (Lebanon), it is hard to establish political parties at all. Moreover, members of minority factions often prefer authoritarian regimes that protect their existing freedoms.

A possible exception to the failure of democracy is Turkey, defined as a secular republic in 1923—by the patriarchal rule of Mustafa Kemal (Ataturk). Since the end of the single-party system in 1945, there has been a wide range of political parties, and governments have been changed by elections. The democratic character of the republic is limited, however, by the strong position of the military, which took over power three times between 1960 and 1980. Its influence as well as the continuing violation of human rights are obstacles to Turkey's bid for membership in the European Union.

Other countries in the region are, at least to some extent, free and democratic. Since 1989 Jordan has developed a relatively unfettered press and has installed an elected parliament with real opposition parties, while remaining a hereditary monarchy. Morocco also established a parliament, although the real political power still lies with the king. In states like Egypt, Tunisia, and the reunited Yemen, there are parliaments and elections, but the presidents—relying on a strong secret service or military—determine most developments and still refuse to grant rights to political movements, parties, or groups.

Syria and Iraq, where branches of the socialist Ba'ath (Rebirth) party came to power in the 1960s, soon became extremely autocratic states with quasi-hereditary presidencies. The same thing happened to the political system created by Mu'ammar al-Qadhafi in Libya in 1969, combining elements of grassroots democracy and socialist ideas with a totally autocratic style of governance.

The oil-rich Arab kingdoms and emirates of the Persian Gulf combined economic modernization with strict autocratic governance. As if in compliance with the principle "no taxation without representation," these wealthier states could afford to keep their population calm without granting democratic rights. The United Arab Emirates have no parliamentary structures at all; Saudi Arabia suppresses all opposition by force.

Throughout the Middle East, the 1980s were characterized by the rise of political Islam. It evolved primarily according to domestic factors, often as a reaction against authoritarianism and corruption. Some states are trying to include the Islamists in their democratization efforts: In Jordan and Yemen the major opposition parties in parliament are Islamist. But most states consider them a fundamental threat to the political system. In Algeria the democratization process ended with the annulment of the relatively free elections in December 1991, when it became evident that the Islamist Front Islamique du Salut (FIS) was going to win most parliamentary seats. The army took over with international approval and a decade of savage civil strife ensued.

Other states made concessions to political Islam. They revived, for example, the principle of consultation (*shura*), which in reference to Qur'an passages 3:159 and 42:38 provides some kind of participation. Even Saudi Arabia has had a *shura* council since 1993; every four years its 120 members are appointed by the king. If broadly applied (as in Jordan), this principle of consultation can be helpful in achieving political participation and pluralization.

The Islamic Republic of Iran (1979) is an interesting case. Although an Islamic state, governed by the principle of *velayat-e faqih* (i.e., the absolute authority of the religious jurist), it has republican structures—a constitution, a parliament, and elections. Since 1997 the results of the elections, though still controlled, show a great demand for democracy, especially among women and young voters.

With the deaths of three veteran rulers in 1999 (the kings of Jordan and Morocco, and the emir of Bahrain) and of Syria's Hafiz al-Asad in 2000, a new generation of Arab leaders gained power, and more such changes will follow. These new rulers were partly educated in the West, and the aspirations for more democracy under their governance are high. They will probably not change the political systems completely, but they are taking steps to open their countries, economically and otherwise. Shaykh Hamad bin Khalifa al-Thani, who came to power in 1995, not only decreed that Qatar was to become a democracy, but also abolished censorship and launched al-Jazeera, the freest television channel in the Arab world. As one of its moderators put it, "the main obstacle to progress in the Middle East is the lack of free media. In our society, the rubbish has been swept under the carpet far too long."

See also **Ataturk, Mustafa Kemal; Modernization, Political: Administrative, Military, and Judicial Reform; Modernization, Political: Constitutionalism; Political Islam; Qadhafi, Mu'ammar al-; Reform: Arab Middle East and North Africa; Reform: Iran; Revolution, Modern.**

BIBLIOGRAPHY

Brynen, Rex; Korany, Bahgat; and Noble, Paul, eds. *Political Liberalization and Democratization in the Arab World.* Vol. 1, *Theoretical Perspectives.* Vol. 2, Comparative Experiences. Boulder, Colo.: Rienner, 1995, 1998.

Gerner, Deborah J., and Schrodt, Philip A. "Middle East Politics." In *Understanding the Contemporary Middle East.* Edited by Deborah J. Gerner. Boulder, Colo.: Rienner, 2000.

Claudia Stodte
Anne-Sophie Froehlich

CONSTITUTIONALISM

Virtually all the Arab countries, as well as Turkey and Iran, have promulgated formal, written constitutions. As they and other Muslim nations have learned, however, a constitutional document does not always reflect or ensure constitutionalism, just as constitutionalism does not always require a written constitution. Constitutionalism is the idea that political order ought to be subject to a higher authority beyond the arbitrary human will expressed through an autocrat, a minority faction, or a democratic mob. Although constitutionalism is commonly identified with liberal democracy, any regime that provides for limited and accountable government, adherence to the rule of law, and the protection of fundamental rights to all its citizens may be said to be constitutionalist. Defined in this way, constitutionalism has had a troubled history in the countries of the Middle East, and no country has to date fully implemented constitutionalist principles.

The earliest constitutionalist experiments in Arab states occurred in Tunisia and Egypt. In 1857, under pressure from European governments, Muhammad Bey issued the 'Ahd al-Aman, or Fundamental Pact, under which all residents of Tunisia were granted equal rights of security, legal redress, and employment. In 1861, Tunisia promulgated the first constitution in the Muslim world, under which the legislative and judicial powers of the bey and his ministers were limited by the establishment of a Grand Assembly. The assembly consisted of sixty members, appointed by the bey for five-year terms, and all drawn from the country's elite. The constitutional experiment lasted but three years, collapsing in 1864 in the wake of popular demonstrations in the provinces.

Constitutional reforms would not resume until 1955, as the French protectorate over Tunisia was nearing an end. The constitution promulgated in June 1959 declared Tunisia a republic, with executive power vested in a president and legislative power in a National Assembly, both elected by universal suffrage. The judiciary was declared to be independent. The constitution was significantly amended in 1988 to strengthen executive control over the legislature, and to specify that the prime minister succeeds the president in case of death or disability.

Egyptian constitutionalism gained ground during the reign of the Khedive Isma'il, fueled mainly by the notables' growing concern with Egyptian indebtedness to European powers. In 1866, Isma'il agreed to create the Consultative Assembly of Deputies, comprised of Egyptian notables, and in 1878 he formed the Council of Ministers, to which he transferred a great deal of executive authority. In 1882, when Isma'il's successor, Tawfiq, attempted to reverse his predecessor's concessions, the Assembly of Deputies pressured the khedive to approve their draft constitution. Under this document, the Assembly was to be an elective body whose members served five-year terms. Both it and the Council of Ministers could initiate legislation, subject to the final approval of the khedive. Most importantly, the prime minister could be summoned and questioned by the Assembly, and if a conflict arose between the two, the Assembly's will was to prevail.

The 1882 constitution was never fully implemented, and when the British occupied Egypt the same year, it was suspended. Shortly after independence, Egypt promulgated a new constitution in April 1923, which established the supremacy of the king over the cabinet and the parliament. Following the Free Officers' overthrow of the monarchy in 1952, a new constitutional charter was enacted in January 1956 that declared Egypt a republic, with most powers vested in the president. A new constitution was drafted in 1971, soon after Anwar Sadat's assumption of the presidency. This document retains a strong presidency but adds provisions for an expanded role for the judiciary, including the creation of a Supreme Constitutional Court. The courts' powers have effectively been curtailed, however, by the invocation of Emergency Laws by Hosni Mubarak, ostensibly to combat terrorism within the country.

Iraq's constitution was drafted and promulgated in 1925, while the country was still under a British mandate. It created a constitutional monarchy, with a strong king and a bicameral legislature. Once the British mandate ended, the king's authority over the cabinet was enhanced through constitutional amendments in 1943. The July 1958 revolution that ended monarchical rule effectively ended constitutionalism as well. From 1958 to 2003, the country was run by the Revolutionary Command Council (RCC). The RCC's authoritarian rule was formalized in the 1970 "interim" constitution adopted by the Ba'thists, which continued in place until it officially became Iraq's constitution in 1990. Amendments in 1995 made the election of the president subject to national plebiscite, but in effect bolstered the authoritarian rule of Saddam Husayn by eliminating the RCC's ability to dismiss the president.

The Lebanese constitution is among the most intriguing of all the Arab republics. Given the deep sectarian cleavages in the Greater Lebanon that was created under the French

'Abd al-Hamid II (1842–1918) was the Ottoman sultan from 1876 to 1909. He was responsible for building schools, roads, railroad lines, and other public works during a time of Ottoman decline. Though he accepted the first constitution in 1876, he suspended it from 1878 until 1908 and enforced his autocratic rule through secret police. The Armenian massacres of 1894–1896 were perpetrated during his reign. THE ART ARCHIVE/TOPKAPI MUSEUM ISTANBUL/DAGLI ORTI

mandate, the 1943 National Covenant established a consociational democracy. Seats in the Chamber of Deputies were divided according to a 6:5 formula, giving the Christian population a permanent majority in the legislature over the Muslims. The president had to be a Maronite Christian, the prime minister a Sunni Muslim, and the speaker of the parliament a Shi'ite Muslim. This "elite cartel" continued to function until the outbreak of the civil war in 1975. Under the Ta'if Agreement of 1989 that ended the civil war, the sectarian apportionment of high offices was retained, but the Christian-Muslim allocation of seats in the legislature was brought to parity and the powers of the prime minister relative to those of the president were substantially increased.

All of the extant Arab monarchies, including Morocco, Jordan, Kuwait, and the other emirates of the Persian Gulf, have adopted constitutional instruments that make token attempts at creating popularly elected legislatures, but which retain effective powers in the hands of the monarch. Kuwait is a notable, but qualified, exception; the emir has battled parliaments demanding a greater role since the 1960s. The parliament's authority was enhanced following the liberation of Kuwait from Iraqi control in 1991. As for Saudi Arabia, no real constitutional document was enacted until 1992, when the Basic Laws codified the complete dominance of the Saudi ruling house in the country's administration. The king appoints the Consultative Council and heads the Council of Ministers.

Turkey's experience with constitutionalism began with the Ottoman constitution of 1876, which formalized the central place of the sultan in the government of the empire, but created a bicameral parliament to share the sultan's legislative functions. Sultan 'Abd al-Hamid II suspended this constitution within months of its enactment. It was revived, with modifications that enhanced executive powers, following the Young Turks revolt in 1908. Turkey's transformation to a secular republic began with constitutional enactments passed by the Grand National Assembly following the empire's defeat in the First World War. In January 1921, the Law of Fundamental Organizations vested legislative authority in the Grand National Assembly. Another decree in November 1922 abolished the sultanate. Finally, on 20 April 1924, following the abolition of the Ottoman caliphate, the constitution of the Turkish republic was announced.

By the 1950s, Turkey had evolved firm republican and what seemed to be strengthening democratic institutions, going so far as to see the triumph of an opposition party in the 1950 general elections. Increasing paralysis in the parliament caused by party differences led to the first military intervention in 1960. The military seized power again in 1971 and 1980, leading to the proclamation of a constitution that legitimated the military's political role in 1982. In 1995, with Turkey attempting to join the European Union, constitutional amendments attempted to lessen the political profile of the military.

Iran's constitutional revolution of 1906 launched that country's attempt at constitutional monarchy. In 1925, the constitution was amended to effectuate the transfer of monarchical authority from the Qajar dynasty to the new Pahlevi dynasty that was founded by the erstwhile minister of war, Reza Khan. The only period during the Pahlevi era when constitutional practices were even partially implemented was from 1941 to 1953, when the young Muhammad Reza Shah was not strong enough to exert his will against the *Majlis*, the national parliament. Through the late 1960s and early 1970s, the shah's rule became increasingly despotic.

In January 1979, the monarchy was overthrown in the Islamic revolution led by Ayatollah Khomeini. The constitution of the Islamic Republic of Iran was enacted in December 1979. Its most notable feature was the implementation of direct rule by the Shi'ite religious scholars, chiefly in the institution of the *vali-ye faqih*, or the supreme religious guide of the nation. Significant amendments were made in 1989 to allow for a transfer of supreme authority after Khomeini's impending death. The changes did nothing, however, to alleviate the fundamental tension built into the 1979 constitution, namely, the rivalry between two executive authorities, the president and the supreme religious guide.

See also **Majlis; Modernization, Political: Administrative, Military, and Judicial Reform.**

BIBLIOGRAPHY

Arjomand, Saïd Amir. "Constitutions and the Struggle for Political Order: A Study in the Modernization of Political Traditions." *Archives Européennes de Sociologie* 33 (1992): 39–82.

Brown, Nathan J. *Constitutions in a Nonconstitutional World: Arab Basic Laws and the Prospects for Accountable Government*. Albany: State University of New York Press, 2002.

Brown, Nathan J. *Dustur: A Survey of the Constitutions of the Arab and Muslim States*. Leiden: Brill, 1966.

Sohail H. Hashmi

PARTICIPATION, POLITICAL MOVEMENTS, AND PARTIES

A profound tension has plagued attempts at political modernization and reform in the Middle East. On the one hand, leaders face enormous pressures to democratize. During the 1970s and 1980s, economic crises eroded regime legitimacy, creating grassroots demands for political rights and civil liberties. These local pressures coincided with growing international norms of democracy and human rights, supported by the United Nations and nongovernmental organizations. Accustomed to political control, however, leaders in the region feared that democracy would unleash hostile political movements and sweep the ruling elite from power. Pressures for democratization were thus pitted against a desire to remain in power.

In the first few decades after World War II, most regimes in the region were concerned with building new governments, asserting independence from Western countries, and securing hegemony over fractious societies. In an effort to establish control, a number of leaders asserted populist ideologies tied to socialist principles and Arab nationalism, which emphasizes the unity of Arabs irrespective of their country of residence. Perhaps the most central figure in the Arab nationalist camp was Jamal 'Abd al-Nasser (d. 1970) of Egypt, who created the Arab Socialist Union in 1962 as a vehicle to mobilize the masses. Nasser's charisma and powerful leadership inspired movements that threatened regime power in other countries. The fusion of Arab nationalism and socialism manifested itself in Syria and Iraq as well. Both countries spawned movements rooted in Ba'th ideology, which combines socialism and its emphasis on income redistribution and nationalization with visions about the glory of historical Arab unity. Ba'th parties in Syria and Iraq had to contend with strong communist movements but managed to consolidate power and gain control of government.

The influence of Arab nationalism waned during the 1970s and was replaced by the rapid ascendance of Islamic movements, which became a central force of opposition in the Middle East. The most spectacular Islamic challenge emerged in Iran in the late 1970s. Muhammad Reza Shah Pahlevi's repression and failed modernization program prompted opposition from a wide consortium of social groups, which mobilized demonstrations under the leadership of the Islamic clergy in the late 1970s. The protest movement overthrew the shah, and an Islamic state was established in 1979.

The Iranian Revolution sent shock waves throughout the Middle East, and regimes became increasingly concerned about the rising power of Islamic movements. Because the growth of Islamic activism coincided with external and internal pressures for democratization, incumbent elites faced a conundrum—how to release some of the building societal pressure for political reform while preventing Islamic movements from taking power.

Two responses to this dilemma predominated. First, a number of regimes implemented an inclusionary model of controlled political liberalization. In this strategy, opposition movements, including Islamic groups, were allowed to participate in national elections, but the regime retained ultimate power and executive authority. In 1989, for example, King Hussein (d. 1999) of Jordan held elections to the Chamber of Deputies (the lower house of parliament) for the first time since 1966. Although several political movements participated, the Islamic movement dominated the campaign and won thirty-four of the eighty seats, creating the single largest bloc in parliament. The movement later joined the government cabinet during the Persian Gulf War in 1991, formed a political party (the Islamic Action Front) in 1993, and supported democratic principles (even while boycotting elections in 1997). The monarch, however, remained the ultimate authority. A similar response occurred in Kuwait after the Gulf War in 1991. Because of considerable pressure from the international community and former Kuwaiti exiles, Shaykh Jaber al-Ahmed al-Sabah held parliamentary elections in October 1992, the first since parliament was dissolved in 1986. Opposition movements openly contested the elections, and various Islamic factions won nineteen of the fifty seats in 1992, seventeen seats in 1996, and twenty in 1999. Despite this participation, the emir retained executive power.

But not all regimes gambled their political survival on the incorporation of Islamic groups through parties, elections, and political participation. Instead, they opted for an alternative exclusionary model. In this response, regimes enacted limited political liberalization measures and elections, but Islamic groups and other powerful political movements were excluded and repressed. This was the strategy in Egypt. Although the mainstream Muslim Brotherhood movement had long been prevented from forming a political party, it forged alliances with other parties and successfully won seats in parliament (eight seats in the 360-member parliament in 1984 and thirty-six in 1987). Under Hosni Mubarak in the mid-1990s, however, the regime initiated a crackdown against the movement and imprisoned fifty-four of its leading members, including many candidates who ran in the 1995 elections. Activists from more radical Islamic groups, such as the Gamaʿa Islamiyya (Islamic Group) and Islamic Jihad, attempted to form political parties in the late 1990s, but were denied permits.

Other regimes fluctuated between inclusionary and exclusionary responses to democratizing pressures and political movements. For example, following austerity riots in 1988, the Algerian regime initiated political reforms, including a number of policies that seemed to support the Islamic movement. A variety of Islamic factions reacted by forming the Islamic Salvation Front (Front Islamique du Salut, or FIS), which was legally recognized in 1989. In 1990, the FIS won stunning victories in municipal and regional races; and although the regime subsequently repressed the movement, the FIS still dominated the 1991 parliamentary elections and was poised to control parliament with a comfortable majority. The regime quickly shifted to draconian exclusionary policies and canceled election results in early 1992, banned the FIS, and imprisoned Islamic leaders. The repression incited an Islamic rebellion that led to more than 150,000 deaths during the 1990s. A similar shift from inclusionary to exclusionary strategies can be seen in Turkey, where the Islamic-oriented Welfare Party installed its leader, Necmeddin Erbakan, as the prime minister in a coalition government in 1996. While this initially indicated an inclusionary strategy, the military eventually intervened and the coalition collapsed. The Welfare Party was subsequently closed and Erbakan was banned from politics for life. The Welfare Party and its successor, the Virtue Party, were banned. Yet a third reconstructed Islamic party, Justice and Development, won the largest number of seats in the Turkish parliament and formed a government in 2002. Such examples point to variation in strategies as leaders calculate the risks of political movement participation.

See also **Communism; Erbakan, Necmeddin; Ikhwan al-Muslimin; Modernization, Political: Authoritarianism and Democratization; Nationalism: Arab; Nationalism: Iranian; Nationalism: Turkish; Pan-Islam; Political Islam; Socialism.**

BIBLIOGRAPHY

Batatu, Hanna. *The Old Social Classes and the Revolutionary Movements of Iraq.* Princeton, N.J.: Princeton University Press, 1978.

Langhor, Vickie. "Of Islamists and Ballot Boxes: Rethinking the Relationship between Islamisms and Electoral Politics." *International Journal of Middle East Studies* 33, no. 4 (2001): 591–610.

Norton, Augustus Richard. "The Challenge of Inclusion in the Middle East." *Current History* 94 (1995): 1–6.

Quintan Wiktorowicz

MODERN THOUGHT

A complex of ideologies that emerged unevenly in the nineteenth and twentieth centuries—including revivalism, rationalism, empiricism, pluralism, constitutionalism, and egalitarianism—drawing heavily on European inspirations and seeking to anchor itself in Islamic precedent.

Origins

Modern Islamic thought emerged during the period of European colonial expansion. Beginning in the eighteenth century, and accelerating in the nineteenth century, the Islamic world began to bear the brunt of this expansion. The Ottoman Empire and the Qajar dynasty in Iran lost territory and were forced to sign humiliating treaties of "capitulation" that granted extraterritorial and monopoly rights to Europeans. Other Islamic lands, from West Africa to Southeast Asia, were colonized outright. By the early twentieth century, virtually the entire Islamic world was in the grip of Europe.

Europe's self-understanding at this time, notwithstanding variations and contradictions, involved the ideology of modernity. Indeed, this ideology had developed in part as an attempt to distance Christians from Muslims: Early modern political theorists contrasted the emerging constitutionalism in Europe with the "Oriental despotism" of the Islamic world; Enlightenment thinkers contrasted European religiosity with Muslim "fanaticism"; Orientalist scholars contrasted European science with Muslim "irrationality."

In response to the threat posed by Europe, many Muslims sought to adopt aspects of modernity, to make modernity serve their interests rather than the interests of the colonizers. This process was not specific to the Islamic world—in Europe and elsewhere, interstate competition also spurred the development of modern institutions. The first institutions to be modernized were the militaries, whose reorganization, reoutfitting, and retraining—along European lines, often with European instructors—were ordered by rulers such as Muhammad 'Ali of Egypt (r.1805–1849), Mahmud II of the Ottoman Empire (r.1808–1839), and Ahmad Bey of Tunisia (r.1837–1855). A second wave of modernization involved the bureaucratization of other state institutions under reformist ministers such as Amir Kabir in Iran (1848–1851), Midhat Pasha in the Ottoman Empire (1860s–1870s), Khayr al-Din in Tunisia (1873–1877), and Abu Bakar of Johore in Malaya (1862–1895). Some of these reformers did not last long in office, but their project of state-building continued after their departure. A further wave of modernization involved economic institutions, which were transformed by their entry into the global economy. While some guilds were able to survive in their traditional forms, many peasants were forced from their lands and deposited in the modern capitalist workforce. Fortunes accumulated in the hands of Muslim industrialists, such as the Azerbaijani businessmen who collaborated and competed with European investors in the Islamic world's first oil boom, in the 1870s in Baku.

These modern institutions sponsored, sometimes unintentionally, the creation of the new class of intellectuals associated with modern Islamic thought. Muhammad 'Ali of Egypt, for example, sent students to study in France; the religious guide appointed for the group, Rifa'a Rafi' al-Tahtawi (Egypt, 1801–1873), returned after five years to write an influential book extolling the virtues of French technology, society, and politics. State-run secular schools in the Ottoman Empire and elsewhere generated modern-oriented graduates such as Ali Suavi (Turkey, 1839–1878), who incorporated Western concepts such as "democracy" and "constitutionalism" into the Islamic lexicon. Industrialists in Baku and throughout the Islamic world funded modern schools, newspapers, and cultural institutions that provided cadres, jobs, and audiences for the new breed of intellectuals.

Yet modernist thinkers, for all their novelty, also considered themselves to be authentic representatives of Islamic heritage. Modern Islamic thought appealed to aspects of this heritage that it viewed retroactively as precursors to modernity. In particular, modern movements framed their ideals as the recovery of the lost piety and glory of the early years of Islam.

Revivalism

The theme of revival—also termed renewal, rebirth, and reform—permeates much of modern Islamic thought. "There is no doubt that in the present age distress, misfortunate, and weakness besiege all classes of Muslims from every side," wrote Sayyid Jamal al-Din al-Afghani (Iran, 1838–1897), perhaps the most influential activist of the modernist Islamic movement. The Islamic world awaits a "sage and renewer" to "reform the minds and souls of the Muslims, repel the unforeseen corruption, and again educate them with a virtuous education. Perhaps through that good education they may return to their former joyful condition" (pp. 123–129). This joyful condition existed in the early years of Islam, before "complete intellectual confusion beset the Muslims," according to Muhammad 'Abduh (Egypt, 1849–1905), the most prominent student and collaborator of al-Afghani's. Confusion can only be cured by returning to "the essential nature" of Islam, as "interpreted according to the understanding of those among whom it was sent down [from heaven] and to the way they put it into practice" (pp. 39, 153–154) "Truly, we are in a dire need for renewal and renewers," wrote Rashid Rida (Syria-Egypt, 1865–1935), 'Abduh's most prominent student and collaborator, citing the saying of the Prophet, "God sends to this nation at the beginning of every century someone who renews its religion" (Kurzman et al., p. 78).

The most important precedent for the earliest modern renewers was Ibn Taymiyya (Syria, 1263–1328), who along with his student Ibn al-Qayyim al-Jawziyya (Syria, 1292–1350) railed against the corrupt practices of Muslims of their era. While these figures remain important for modern revivalism, they have been eclipsed somewhat by the example of Muhammad Ibn 'Abd al-Wahhab (Arabia, 1703–1787), the religious leader of a movement to purify Muslim practices—demolishing shrines, for example, which they took to represent false idols. Other Islamic movements of purification and renewal emerged about the same time in West Africa, South Asia, Southeast Asia, and China. Hostile observers often label revivalists "Wahhabis" to emphasize their premodern roots, while contemporary followers of such movements generally identify themselves as Muwahiddun (Unitarians, or believers in divine unity) or Salafiyyun (imitators of the ancestors, that is, the early generations of Muslims).

Yet modern revivalism differs significantly from its premodern predecessors. It emerged most often in regions that are highly modernized, including the Muslim diaspora in western Europe and North America. Its leaders frequently have modern educations—for example, Hasan al-Banna (Egypt, 1906–1949), the most prominent follower of Rida and founder of the Muslim Brotherhood in Egypt, was trained as an educator, as was Sayyid Qutb (Egypt, 1902–1966), the Muslim Brotherhood's most influential theoretician of radical revival. Usama bin Ladin (Saudi Arabia, born 1957), the most notorious revivalist of the present time, was trained in civil engineering. Al-Afghani and Abu l-A'la' Maududi (India-Pakistan, 1903–1979), the leading South Asian revivalist of the twentieth century, had seminary training but hid their traditional backgrounds, not wishing to be identified with such institutions (in al-Afghani's case, because he attended Shi'a seminaries and later passed as a Sunni). In addition, modern revivalism presented itself as an ideology, comparable to other ideologies in the modern world (though preferable to them, according to its supporters). Revivalist slogans like "Neither East (that is, communism) nor West" and "Islam is the solution" placed Islamic revival within the field of global ideological debates, in a way that premodern revivalism did not. Finally, many revivalists also adopted other strands of modern thought, such as the ones discussed in the following sections.

In the first generations of modern Islamic thought, revivalism and these other strands were seamlessly woven together. By the 1930s, however, the seams had begun to show. Revivalism remains central in modern Islamic thought, but some revivalists downplay modern ideals, while some modernists downplay revivalist ideals. Today a distinction can be drawn between Islamic ideologies that approach modernity as a means toward revivalism, and those that approach revivalism as a means toward modernity.

Rationalism

Debates within modern Islamic thought take place on the ground of rationalism. Even thinkers who disagree with one another share the underlying premise that educated, informed Muslims should devise reasoned justifications for their positions, and may the best argument win. This premise differs from premodern limits on rationality (as opposed to faith), suspicion of novelty (vulnerable to accusations of heresy), and reliance on authority (particularly the genealogy of one's spiritual teacher). The distinction is not absolute: Certainly novel arguments were developed in premodern times, and some modern thought denies that it does anything more than revive the insights of its predecessors. But in general, the distinction holds, demarcated symbolically by the concept of *ijtihad*.

The concept of *ijtihad*, derived from an Arabic root meaning "effort" or "struggle," was for centuries limited to a fairly technical meaning, referring to the intellectual effort of trained Islamic scholars to arrive at legal rulings on matters not covered in the sacred sources. The modernist Islamic movement of the nineteenth century adopted the term as a rallying cry, transforming its meaning into the more general task of "rational interpretation" that they held to be incumbent upon all educated Muslims. The opposite of *ijtihad*, in this view, was *taqlid*, literally "following," which modernists took to mean "blind obedience to authority." Al-Afghani, for example, urged Muslims to "shun submission to conjectures and not be content with mere *taqlid* of their ancestors. For if man believes in things without proof or reason, makes a practice of following unproven opinions, and is satisfied to imitate and follow his ancestors, his mind inevitably desists from intellectual movement, and little by little stupidity and imbecility overcome him—until his mind becomes completely idle and he becomes unable to perceive his own good and evil; and adversity and misfortune overtake him from all sides" (p. 171). 'Abduh sought "to liberate thought from the shackles of *taqlid* to return, in the acquisition of religious knowledge, to its first sources, and to weigh them in the scales of human reason, which God has created in order to prevent excess or adulteration in religion" (Hourani, 140–141). Sayyid Ahmad Khan (India, 1817–1898), the chief organizer of the modernist Islamic movement in South Asia in the nineteenth century, argued that Islam is "in full correspondence with reason" (Troll, 257).

Modernists cited premodern precedents for this view. Ahmad Khan, for example, praised the broadened use of *ijtihad* by Shah Wali Allah (India, 1703–1762). Muhammad Iqbal (India, 1877–1938), the great poet and philosopher, relied on Shah Wali Allah, Muhammad b. 'Ali al-Shawkani (Yemen, circa 1760–1839), and other, older theorists of *ijtihad.* Fazlur Rahman (Pakistan–United States, 1919–1988), the most prominent Islamic modernist of late twentieth century South Asia, cited a long-standing legacy running through Wali Allah and Iqbal. Many modernists trace rationalism back to a saying of the prophet Muhammad: When Muhammad appointed Muʿadh b. Jabal as ruler of Yemen, he asked Muʿadh how he planned to make decisions. "I will judge matters according to the Book of God," said Muʿadh. "But if the Book of God contains nothing to guide you?" Muhammad asked. "Then I will act on the precedents of the Prophet of God." "But if the precedents fail?" "Then I will exercise my own *ijtihad.*" Muhammad praised Muʿadh for his response.

Modern Islamic rationalism universalized such precedents. Whereas premodern thought had generally limited the use of *ijtihad* to qualified scholars, modernists consider all Muslims—or, in some theories, all educated Muslims—to be capable of rational interpretation. Modern thinkers nonetheless differ as to the matters to which rationalism may legitimately be applied, with some exempting matters whose treatment in the Qurʾan and the precedent of the prophet Muhammad they consider to be unambiguous. Other thinkers, such as ʿAbd al-Karim Sorush (Iran, b. 1945), hold that even seemingly unambiguous revelation is subject to human—and thus variable and fallible—interpretation, and therefore that rational analysis is required on all matters.

Empiricism

In modern Islamic thought, rationalism is not limited to textual exegesis, but operates also on the empirical world. Scientific observation is required of Muslims, in this view, both for its own sake and for the benefits it can bestow upon the welfare of the Islamic world. Ismaʿil Bey Gasprinskii (Crimea, 1851–1914), one of the founders of modern Islamic thought in the Russian Empire, considered science to be crucial to the survival of Islam, which had fallen hundreds of years behind Europe, he argued, because of its failure to keep up with Western scientific advances. Rizaeddin bin Fakhreddin (Ar. Rida al-din bin Fakr al-din) (Tatarstan, 1858–1936), one of the chief seminary-trained collaborators of the Russian-educated Gasprinskii, likened the sciences in the Islamic world to "a factory standing idle," and argued that "it is futile to resist machines and struggle against nature" (Kurzman, 239). Abdalrauf Fitrat (Ar. ʿAbad al-Raʿuf Fitrat) (Bukhara–Soviet Union, 1886–1938), who helped to bring Ottoman and Tatar modernism to Central Asia, urged Muslim schools to abandon "the nonsense of studying obscure points of Arabic grammar" in favor of "the new sciences, which produce rapid results and great benefits, [and which] the Christians possessed to make them victorious over you" (Kurzman, 245).

These figures and their colleagues were instrumental in reforming and founding Islamic schools—known as "New Method" (Usul-e Jadid) schools—throughout the Russian Empire to encourage the teaching of empirical subjects: natural sciences, particularly physics and chemistry; human sciences, particularly history and geography; and language arts, particularly literacy in Arabic and local languages. By the time the Russian Empire collapsed in 1917, there were hundreds of such schools, only to be destroyed through the economic disasters, political purges, and civil conflicts of the early Soviet era. In other regions, however, similar school reform movements survived. Ahmad Khan's Anglo-Muhammadan College in Aligarh, India, was one of several new institutions that trained generations of modernist Muslims in South Asia. The Muhammadiyya movement in Southeast Asia established a network of new schools that exist to this day. Postcolonial states throughout the Islamic world have frequently required traditional schools to introduce scientific subjects, while also incorporating religious education as a subject in the new state-run educational systems. Empiricism has become widely entrenched both as a worldview and as a pedagogy.

The Islamic justification for empiricism cites both scriptural and historical grounds, as well as the pragmatic grounds of progress and survival. Modernists describe in glowing terms the scientific advances of the early centuries of Islam, including such figures as Abu Jaʿfar al-Khwarazmi (Baghdad, c. 800–847), who invented algebra; Ulugh Beg (Central Asia, 1394–1449), whose astronomical observations were used throughout the world for centuries; and Ibn Khaldun (Tunisia, 1332–1406), widely considered a precursor to modern historiography and social science. The relative lack of comparable paragons in later years poses the central problem for modern Islamic empiricism. Modernists have also collected numerous verses of the Qurʾan and sayings of Muhammad in support of empirical study, including the saying, "Seek knowledge, even though it be in China." Indeed, one strand of Islamic empiricism argues that all significant scientific discoveries were prefigured in the Qurʾan—not only is scientific knowledge fully consistent with Islam, in this view, but Islam had it first.

Egalitarianism

Empirical claims, according to modern Islamic thought, are to be judged by their content, not by the social position of the speaker. In the words of ʿAbd al-Qadir al-Jazaʾiri (Algeria–Syria, c. 1807–1883), an anticolonial military leader who turned to a modernist form of Sufism during his decades of retirement: "People should be measured according to the truth, not the truth according to [the reputation of] people" (Kurzman, 135).

Other modernists extended this egalitarian sentiment to many arenas of social life, for example, ethnicity. ʿAbd al-Rahman al-Kawakibi (Syria, 1854–1902) and others criticized Ottoman Turkish discrimination against Arabs in governmental and social affairs; Syeikh Ahmad Surkati (Sudan–Java, 1872–1943) and others objected to Arab discrimination against Southeast Asians; Chandra Muzaffar (Malaysia, b. 1947) and others protested against Southeast Asians' discrimination against non-Muslim communities in the region, such as the Chinese. In these and similar cases, egalitarianism sought to replace traditional forms of hierarchy with a new form of community, sometimes defined in religious terms (the *umma*, or Islamic community as a whole), but more frequently in national terms. Arab, Southeast Asian, and other nationalisms cast individuals as citizens with equal rights and responsibilities.

One of the most contentious aspects of egalitarianism involved the extension of this ideology to gender. At the turn of the twentieth century, feminists—both male and female—began to argue that patriarchal practices offended Islamic faith. Qasim Amin (Egypt, 1863–1908), the Islamic world's most famous male feminist, argued that Islamic law originally treated men and women equally, with the exception of polygamy, granting women rights still not achieved by many Western women. Halide Edib Adivar (Turkey, 1882–1964), arguably the Islamic world's most famous female feminist, argued the reverse, suggesting that Islamic family law was inherently anti-egalitarian on gender matters and had to be replaced with Western laws. The debate between these positions continues, with men and women on both sides of the fence. However, feminists have won near unanimity on several crucial points: that women have historically been oppressed by men; that this oppression has often been defended with misguided interpretations of Islam; that such justifications must be countered, either by the reform or removal of traditional laws and practices; and that women deserve, at the very least, equal access to education.

Another controversial extension of egalitarianism involves economic rights, especially those associated with the socialist movements that emerged in the Islamic world in the early twentieth century. In the Dutch East Indies—later Indonesia—the Islamic Union Party combined nationalist goals with redistributive ones, using an Islamic discourse of *zakat*, or tithing. To the left of this movement was an Islamic Communist Party, which criticized the Islamic Union Party and others on Islamic grounds, as in the comments of Hadji Mohammad Misbach (Java, circa 1876–1940): "To be sure, they perform the precepts of the religion of Islam, but they pick and choose those precepts that suit their desire. Those that do not suit them they throw away. Put bluntly, they oppose or defy the commands of God—and rather fear and love the will of Satan—that Satan whose evil influence is apparent in this present age in [the system of] Capitalism" (Shiraishi, 285). Socialist thought, drawing on Islamic and non-Islamic discourses, was embedded in the independence movement in Indonesia, as in Pakistan and several others around the Islamic world. In parts of the Middle East, Islamic socialism became particularly popular in the 1960s, expressing itself in both pro-Soviet and nonaligned manifestations. Soon thereafter—in the Islamic world as in the West—a counter-movement set in, with leftist sentiments ceding to dreams of individual and national capital accumulation.

Constitutionalism

A special case of egalitarianism involves political rights, civil liberties, and the rule of law, all of which were bundled in the movement for constitutional government—*mashrutiyat*, a nineteenth-century neologism derived from the Arabic root *shart* (conditionality) and the French term *charte* (constitution). Namik Kemal (Ottoman Turkey, 1840–1888), one of the leading activists in the constitutionalist movement of the 1860s and 1870s, quoted Qur'anic injunction such as, "And seek their council in the matter" (3:159), and concluded that "the salvation of the state today is dependent upon the adoption of the method of consultation" (Kurzman, 140). ʿAli ʿAbd al-Raziq (Egypt, 1888–1966), a scholar at al-Azhar University in Cairo, took another tack, arguing that the sacred sources do not require democratic government, but rather permit it. The Qur'an and the precedent of the Prophet leave the form of government to human devising, "for the trusteeship of Muhammad, peace be upon him, over the believers is the trusteeship of the Message, untainted by anything that has to do with government" (Kurzman, 36). These novel arguments for constitutionalism were controversial in their day. Namik Kemal served on the Council of State that prepared the short-lived Ottoman constitution of 1876, but suffered banishments before and after that time. ʿAbd al-Raziq was fired from al-Azhar for his controversial views.

Yet constitutionalism gradually became the norm in Islamic lands. Egypt promulgated a constitutionalist document in 1860, and a fuller constitution in 1882; Tunisia briefly in 1861 and then, after the colonial interlude, in 1959; Iran briefly in 1906, then again in 1909; and so on. Upon decolonization, almost all countries in the Islamic world drew up constitutions, the last one to do so being Saudi Arabia, whose monarch announced a Basic Law modeled on Western constitutions in 1992. Some of these documents, including Saudi Arabia's, provide far fewer rights and limits on state power than is common in Western constitutions of the same period. But it is indicative of the spread of modern thought that even traditional monarchs have felt the need to draw up a codified statement of rights and obligations. At the same time, states in the Islamic world often disregard the constitutions that are nominally in force. Many such regimes are secular in orientation, not Islamic, but a correlation persists between Muslim population and low levels of democracy.

In the face of ongoing repression, even some radical Islamic movements have adopted the discourse of constitutionalism. In Turkey, the Welfare Party—banned and reconstituted under several different names—portrayed itself as an "Islamic-Democrat" movement analogous to the Christian-Democrat parties in several western European countries. In Egypt, the Muslim Brotherhood began to mobilize on behalf of civil liberties in the 1980s, as did the Islamic Salvation Front in Algeria, the Renaissance movement in Tunisia, and the Justice and Charity movement in Morocco. Uncharitable observers have expressed skepticism about the sincerity of this discourse, but these movements have generated a substantial written record elaborating their constitutionalist ideologies in Islamic terms. These writings brought the radicals closer in some ways to Islamic liberalism.

Pluralism

Alongside political pluralism stands religious pluralism, the notion that multiple interpretations of the sacred are possible and legitimate. In the last quarter of the twentieth century, proponents of this approach emerged around the Islamic world. Among the most influential is the philosopher ʿAbd al-Karim Sorush (Iran, born 1945): "Religion is divine, but its interpretation is thoroughly human and this-worldly," Soroush wrote. "The text does not stand alone, it does not carry its own meaning on its shoulders, it needs to be situated in a context, it is theory-laden, its interpretation is in flux, and presuppositions are as actively at work here as elsewhere in the field of understanding. Religious texts are no exception" (Kurzman, 245). Similarly, the philosopher Hassan Hanafi (Egypt, b. 1935) argued, "There is no one interpretation of a text, but there are many interpretations given the difference in understanding between different interpreters. An interpretation of a text is essentially pluralistic. The text is only a vehicle for human interests and even passions" (Kurzman, 26). Fazlur Rahman, cited above, suggested that "To insist on absolute uniformity of interpretation is neither possible nor desirable" (144). Amina Wadud-Muhsin (United States, b. 1952) wrote that "when one individual reader with a particular world-view and specific prior text [the language and cultural context in which the text is read] asserts that his or her reading is the only possible or permissible one, it prevents readers in different contexts from coming to terms with their own relationship to the text" (Kurzman, 130). ʿAbdullahi An-Naʿim (Sudan, b. 1946) wrote that "there is no such thing as the only possible or valid understanding of the Qurʾan, or conception of Islam, since each is informed by the individual and collective orientation of Muslims." (An-Naʿim, 233). Few if any of these authors had read one another's work; pluralism sprouted independently in multiple locations.

Some writers consider the millennium of coexistence of multiple schools of thought in Islamic jurisprudence to be precedent for contemporary pluralism. Others go back further, to the earliest years of Islam. Mohamed Talbi (Tunisia, born 1921) quoted Sura 5, Verse 51 of the Qurʾan: "To each among you, have We prescribed a Law and an Open Way. And if God had enforced His Will, He would have made of you all one people." Muhammad Asad (Austria-Pakistan, 1900–1992) quoted the saying of the prophet Muhammad, "The differences of opinion among the learned within my community are [a sign of] God's grace." Farid Esack (South Africa, b. 1959) cited the words of ʿAli b. Abi Talib, Muhammad's son-in-law and fourth successor: "this is the Qurʾan, written in straight lines, between two boards [of its binding]; it does not speak with a tongue; it needs interpreters and interpreters are people." Esack translates this into contemporary terms: "Every interpreter enters the process of interpretation with some preunderstanding of the questions addressed by the text—even of its silences—and brings with him or her certain conceptions as presuppositions of his or her exegesis" (p. 50). Leading pluralists have suffered threats and worse, as their arguments pose a challenge to other modern trends in Islamic thought that believe a single correct interpretation of Islam is achievable and ought to be enforced.

Conclusion

The contrast between pluralists and revivalists reminds one that modern thought is frequently self-contradictory. Constitutionalism is consistent with both authoritarianism and democracy. Empiricism breeds competing analyses. Socialism and capitalism are both modern phenomena, as are "third way" ideologies. Indeed, the label *modern* is sometimes used so elastically that virtually all ideas expressed in the past two centuries fall under this rubric. Other definitions, such as the one presented here, are more restrictive. Others leave the definition open, considering an idea as modern only if its authors consider it so.

Similar definitional dilemmas are associated with the term *Islamic*. Some of the writings quoted in this piece are not considered Islamic by other Muslims, even if their authors consider them so. A further body of thought is self-consciously non-Islamic, though its authors are Muslims.

At stake in these definitional disputes is the frame of reference for any given analysis. Calling something "modern" associates it with the entire package of modern institutions, an association that some Muslims desire and others abhor. Calling something "Islamic" associates it with the divine revelation and generations of followers of Islam, an association that some Muslims would like to monopolize. Bringing the two terms together, as in "modern Islamic thought," suggests that the two frames overlap, and that Muslims have contributed to the construction of modernity.

See also **ʿAbd al-Karim Sorush; Afghani, Jamal al-Din; Ahmad Khan, (Sir) Sayyid; Capitalism; Communism; Feminism; Gender; Iqbal, Muhammad; Liberalism, Islamic; Modernism; Pluralism: Legal and Ethno-Religious; Pluralism: Political; Qutb, Sayyid; Rahman, Fazlur; Science, Islam and; Secularization; Shariʿati, ʿAli; Wali Allah, Shah.**

BIBLIOGRAPHY

ʿAbduh, Muhammad. *The Theology of Unity (Risalat al-tawhid).* Translated by Ishaq Masaʾad and Kenneth Cragg. London: Allen & Unwin, 1966.

Afghani, Sayyid Jamal ad-Din al-. *An Islamic Response to Imperialism: Political and Religious Writings of Sayyid Jamal ad-Din al-Afghani.* Translated by Nikki R. Keddie. Berkeley: University of California Press, 1968.

Ahmad, Aziz. *Islamic Modernism in India and Pakistan, 1857–1964.* London: Oxford University Press, 1967.

Ahmed, Leila. *Women and Gender in Islam: Historical Roots of a Modern Debate.* New Haven, Conn.: Yale University Press, 1992.

An-Na'im, Abdullahi. "Toward an Islamic Hermeneutics for Human Rights." In *Human Rights and Religious Values: An Uneasy Relationship?* Edited by Abdullahi A. An-Na'im, Jerald D. Gort, Henry Jansen, and Hendrik M. Vroom. Grand Rapids, Mich.: William B. Eerdmans Publishing Company, 1995.

Azmeh, Aziz al-. *Islams and Modernities.* 2d ed. London: Verso, 1996.

Berkes, Niyazi. *The Development of Secularism in Turkey.* 2d ed. London: Hurst & Co., 1998.

Brown, Daniel W. *Rethinking Tradition in Modern Islamic Thought.* Cambridge, U.K.: Cambridge University Press, 1996.

Esack, Farid. *Qur'an, Liberation, and Pluralism.* Oxford, U.K.: Oneworld, 1997.

Esposito, John L., and Voll, John O. *Makers of Contemporary Islam.* New York: Oxford University Press, 2001.

Göle, Nilüfer. *The Forbidden Modern: Civilization and Veiling.* Ann Arbor: University of Michigan Press, 1996.

Hourani, Albert. *Arabic Thought in the Liberal Age, 1798–1939.* London: Oxford University Press, 1962.

Keddie, Nikki R. *Sayyid Jamal ad-Din "al-Afghani": A Political Biography.* Berkeley: University of California Press, 1972.

Khalid, Adeeb. *The Politics of Muslim Cultural Reform: Jadidism in Central Asia.* Berkeley: University of California Press, 1998.

Kurzman, Charles, ed. *Liberal Islam: A Source-Book.* New York: Oxford University Press, 1998.

Kurzman, Charles, et al., eds. *Modernist Islam, circa 1840–1940: A Source-Book.* New York: Oxford University Press, 2002.

Martin, Richard C., and Woodward, Mark R., with Atmaja, Dwi S. *Defenders of Reason in Islam: Mu'tazilism from Medieval School to Modern Symbol.* Oxford, U.K.: Oneworld, 1997.

Rahman, Fazlur. *Islam and Modernity: Transformation of an Intellectual Tradition.* Chicago: University of Chicago Press, 1982.

Shiraishi, Takashi. *An Age in Motion: Popular Radicalism in Java, 1912–1926.* Ithaca, N.Y.: Cornell University Press, 1990.

Troll, Christian W. *Sayyid Ahmad Khan: A Reinterpretation of Muslim Theology.* New Delhi: Vikas Publishing House, 1978.

Charles Kurzman

MOJAHEDIN-E KHALQ

Mojahedin-e Khalq (Ar. Mujahidin; The People's Warriors) is a popular name for the Sazman-e Mojahedin-e Khalq-e Iran (Organization of the Iranian People's Religious Warriors), a group of Shi'ite Islamic-Marxist revolutionaries that formed in Iran during the 1960s in opposition to the regime of Muhammad Reza Shah (r. 1953–1979).

The Mojahedin constituted one of several opposition movements, ranging from the Marxist left to the liberal center to the religious right, that led popular support against the transparent authoritarianism of the shah's regime and its dependency on the United States, particularly after the shah's violent repression of demonstrations against his program of economic and social modernization, known as the White Revolution, in June 1963. The Mojahedin drew its membership from the urban intelligentsia, mostly middle-class, college-educated young men with degrees in engineering. During the 1970s, it conducted a guerrilla war against the monarchy, but gradually declined in the face of internal divisions and external force. They experienced a resurgence, however, under the leadership of Mas'ud Rajavi (b. 1947) after the 1978 and 1979 revolution, when they attacked Ayatollah Khomeini and his cadre of Shi'ite mullahs who were consolidating their control of the country. Nearly ten thousand Mojahedin members were exterminated by the Khomeini regime between 1981 and 1985. Saddam Husayn allowed surviving members to organize an armed Iranian opposition movement in Iraq, which subsequently fell under the control of American occupation forces there in April 2003.

Their ideology is based on a radical reinterpretation of traditional Shi'ite concepts in light of Marxist sociology and anticolonial rhetoric. Ervand Abrahamian notes that they transformed terms like *jihad, mujahid, shahid* (martyr), *tawhid* (monotheism), and *umma* (community of believers) to mean "liberation struggle," "freedom fighter," "revolutionary hero," "egalitarianism," and "dynamic classless society," respectively (1989, p. 96). They echoed many of the ideas of 'Ali Shari'ati, widely considered the chief ideologue of the Iranian revolution after Khomeini.

See also **Iran, Islamic Republic of; Khomeini, Ruhollah; Political Islam; Shari'ati, 'Ali.**

BIBLIOGRAPHY

Abrahamian, Ervand. *The Iranian Mojahedin.* New Haven, Conn.: Yale University Press, 1989.

Keddie, Nikki R., and Monian, Farah. "Militancy and Religion in Contemporary Iran." In *Fundamentalisms and the State: Remaking Polities, Economies, and Militance.* Edited by Martin E. Marty and R. Scott Appleby. Chicago: University of Chicago Press, 1993.

Juan Eduardo Campo

MOJAHIDIN *See* **Mujahidin**

MOJTAHED-SHABESTARI, MOHAMMAD (1937–)

Born in 1937, Mohammad Mojtahed-Shabestari attended Qom Seminary at the age of fourteen. During his eighteen years of study in Qom, he was influenced by the new philosophical and theological currents that were gaining popularity among the younger generation of theologians. Subsequently, he expanded his learning to the conventional secular curriculum and independently studied contemporary Western philosophies and languages. In 1970, he moved to Germany where he later succeeded Ayatollah Beheshti as the director of the Hamburg Islamic Center, a post he held until the 1979 Iranian Revolution. After the revolution, he was elected to the first Islamic Consultative Assembly and is a faculty member of the School of Theology and Islamic Studies at the University of Tehran.

Mojtahed-Shabestari is one of the leading Iranian advocates of the hermeneutic approach to Islamic theology. In his book, *Hermenutik, Ketab Va Sunnat* (*Hermeneutics, the Book and Tradition*), he advances a theology largely extricated from earlier apologetic Islamic modernism. Influenced by the German theologian Paul Tillich and German phenomenology of religion, he argues that theological innovations emerge from the religious experiences of each generation of believers rather than from doctrinal debates. The interpretation of the divine text is mediated by history, society, body, and language. While a hermeneutic approach acknowledges these contingencies, it also endeavors to transcend them. However, this transcendence can never be total and, accordingly, truth-claims may never be absolute. Truth belongs to God and remains inaccessible to human faculties.

See also **Reform: Iran.**

BIBLIOGRAPHY

Farzin Vahdat, "Postrevolutionary Discourses of Mohammad Mojtahed Shabestari and Mohsen Kadivar: Reconciling the Terms of Mediated Subjectivity," *Critique*, no. 16 (Spring 2000): 31–54.

Behrooz Ghamari-Tabrizi

MOLLA

Molla comes from the Arabic term *mawla*, which is most often used to mean religious leader. The term *molla* is used primarily in Iran and parts of Asia to refer to Muslim religious scholars, or ulema, who serve various clerical functions. It is used as a generic term for a Muslim cleric. The term *akhund* is a synonym for it in Persian and related languages. *Molla*s receive a religious education as a child in a *maktab* (Ar. *kuttab*). They study the Qurʾan, hadith (sayings of the prophet Muhammad), and basic aspects of belief and practice. At the highest level of training *molla*s receive the equivalent of a doctorate in theology from a theological seminary, called a madrasa or *howzah ʿilmiyya*. *Molla*s serve a series of social and religious functions: prayer leader in a mosque, reciter of the Qurʾan, religious teacher for children or a professor, jurist or judge, administrator of religious endowments and sites, community leader, politician, scholar of religion, and sometimes as scribes or even bookkeepers. They also preside over various rituals including marriage contracts, and other religious rituals. Not all *molla*s are employed full-time in this profession. Many of them have other occupations along with their religious duties. It is not uncommon, especially in the past and in rural areas, for the term *molla* to be applied to a cleric with far more limited education, perhaps limited to some basic knowledge of the Qurʾan and hadith.

See also **Ulema.**

BIBLIOGRAPHY

Meir, Litvak. *Shiʿi Scholars of Nineteenth-Century Iraq: The "Ulama" of Najaf and Karbala*. New York: Cambridge University Press, 1998.

Momen, Moojan. *An Introduction to Shiʿi Islam*. New Haven, Conn.: Yale University Press, 1985.

Waldbridge, Linda S., ed. *The Most Learned of the Shiʿa: The Institution of the Marjaʿ Taqlid*. New York: Oxford University Press, 2001.

Kamran Aghaie

MOLLABASHI

The Mollabashi was the head of the religious institution in Iran under the late Safavid rule. It is a synthetic title from the Arabic word, *mawla*, meaning "lord," and the Turkish, *bashi*, or "head." The title of Molla refers to any Muslim scholar who has acquired a certain degree of religious education. During the last years of the Safavid rule, the Mollabashi was the head of the religious institution and a leading member of the Safavid administration system. In the earlier period of the Safavid kings, this title belonged to the most learned scholar of the time, who was considered as the Mollabashi.

The office of Mollabashi was created by the Safavid shah Sultan Hosayn, who ascended the throne as king of Persia in 1694. He instituted the office during the last years of his rule. The Mollabashi was nominated by the king himself and held held the post at the king's will.

As the chief of the Mollas, during the royal assembly the Mollabashi had a definite place near the king, closer than that of any other religious scholar. The Mollabashi did not interfere in any state affairs except for soliciting pensions for religious students and scholars. The Mollabashi also pleaded to the king directly on behalf of the aggrieved and oppressed, and for individuals convicted of crimes.

After the collapse of the Safavid state and during the reign of the Afsharid dynasty, the prerogatives of the Mollabashi office increased because the Mollabashi was the most powerful figure in the court. But by the fall of the Afsharid state and during the reign of the Qajar dynasty, the role of the Mollabashi was limited to that of tutor of the royal princes.

See also **Empires: Safavid and Qajar; Molla; Nader Shah Afshar; Ulema.**

BIBLIOGRAPHY

Arjomand, S. A. "The Office of Mullabashi in Shi'ite Iran." *Studia Islamica* 57 (1989): 135–146.

Mansur Sefatgol

MONARCHY

Neither the Qur'an nor Muhammad made any specific provisions for the organization of government for the Islamic community. Muhammad's successors, who ruled Arabia and a vast empire conquered by the Muslims during the quarter of century after the Prophet's death, were called caliph (*khalifa*) and assumed the title of "Commander of the Faithful": (*amir al-mu' minin*). After a civil war that ended the period of the four "rightly-guided" caliphs in 661, the caliphate became hereditary in the Umayyad Dynasty until 750, and in the Abbasid Dynasty from 750 until 1258. The administrative and fiscal systems of the Byzantine (Roman) and Sassanian (Persian) empires were taken over by the caliphate. The bureaucratic class that carried out the fiscal and administrative tasks for the caliphs were eventually ordered to use Arabic instead of Persian and Greek in the closing decade of the seventh century, and some decades thereafter also began to translate Persian works on statecraft into Arabic. Through these translations, the idea of monarchy was absorbed into the public law and Arabic literature on statecraft, as can be seen in the Book of Sovereignty (*Kitab al-sultan*) by the famous ninth-century author, Ibn Qutayba.

This term first occurs as a substantive, meaning "authority" in the Qur'an, and came into usage with reference to the palaces housing the caliph's central administration. In the latter part of the ninth century, independent royal dynasties were established in Iran and in Egypt and chose to remain under the suzerainty of the caliphs. In this period, we find the term *sultan* first used to refer to a specific person: the caliph's brother, who was the commander of a special army. This haphazard use of the term to refer to a person became systematic when the Buyids (Buwayhids), Shi'ite mercenaries from the Caspian region, captured Baghdad in the mid-tenth century, without, however, overthrowing the Abbasid caliphate. The Buyids became the first of a series of secular independent rulers to assume the title of sultan. The bifurcation of sovereignty into caliphate and sultanate became permanent, however, and underscored the new autonomy of monarchy from the caliphate.

In Iran, where the Buyids ruled independently of the caliph, they assumed the pre-Islamic Persian titles of *shah* (king), and even the imperial *shahanshah* (king of kings). The Turkish Seljuks, who replaced the Buyids in Baghdad in 1055 and proceeded to defeat the Byzantine emperor and create a vast empire from the Oxus to the Mediterranean, assumed the titles of both sultan and shahanshah. The subsequent Turkish dynasties, including the Ottomans, attached the title of sultan to their names, also using additional Persian terms such *shah* and its variant, *padshah*. Local rulers in Iran used the title of *shah*, and those in the Arab countries, the equivalent term *malik* (king). Turkish dynasties established a Muslim monarchy in northern Indian in the thirteenth century, with Delhi as its capital. The Dehli Sultanate lasted for some three centuries, until the Mogul conquest in 1526, which established a larger Muslim empire in India. The sultanate spread eastward into Asia, and survives to this day in the federal states of Malaysia and in Brunei. With the spread of Islam into sub-Saharan Africa, some of the Muslim local rulers assumed the title of sultan, and in 1841, the sultan of Oman transferred his court to Zanzibar across the Indian Ocean.

Monarchy (*saltana[t]*, *padshahi*, *mulk*) was legitimated independently of the caliphate, and primarily on the basis of justice. The function of monarchy was the maintenance of order and ruling with justice. As such, monarchy was compared to prophecy, the function of which was the salvation of humankind. Kings were thus required by the divine constitution of cosmic order, just as were the prophets. As stated in a tradition (hadith) attributed to Muhammad, "the ruler (*sultan*) is the shadow of God on earth." A distinct literary genre on political ethic and statecraft grew, grounding the legitimacy of monarchy in its justice. This literature absorbed a philosophical strand that idealized monarchy on the Platonic model of the philosopher-king. A major synthesis of the Persian and the philosophical traditions, written in the thirteenth century by Nasir al-Din Tusi, *Akhlaq-e Naseri*, had many imitators and became the standard work on political ethic and statecraft in the great modern empires of the early modern period: the Ottoman, the Safavid, and the Mogul.

King Hussein of Jordan (1935–1999) represented the Hashimite monarchy in Jordan, which was established in 1921. Upon Hussein's death he was succeeded by his son 'Abdallah II. The Hashimites claim legitimacy as *sharifs*—descendants of the prophet Muhammad. AP/WIDE WORLD PHOTOS

After the overthrow of the Abbasid caliphate by the Mongols in 1258, the rulers of Muslim lands typically added caliph to sultan as their titles, except in Mamluk Egypt (1260–1517), when a shadow Abbasid caliph was maintained by the Mamluk sultans. The Ottomans claimed the last Abbasid (shadow) caliph gave them the mantle of the Prophet and transferred the caliphate to them when they conquered Cairo in 1517.

The idea of constitutional monarchy was introduced into the Islamic world in the process of political modernization, with the Ottoman constitution of 1876 and the Iranian constitution of 1906. With the creation of the modern state of Turkey, the Ottoman sultanate was abolished in 1922, and the caliphate in 1924. In Iran, the monarchy was overthrown with the Islamic revolution of 1979. A number of Muslim monarchies have survived to the present, notably in Morocco, Saudi Arabia, and Jordan.

See also **Caliphate; Political Organization.**

BIBLIOGRAPHY

Arjomand, Saïd Amir. "Medieval Persianate Political Ethic." *Studies on Persianate Societies.* 1 (2003): 7–33.

Barthold, W. "Caliph and Sultan." *Islamic Quarterly* 7 (1963): 117–135.

Lambton, A. K. S. "Justice in the Medieval Persian Theory of Kingship." *Studia Islamica* 17 (1962): 91–119.

Saïd Amir Arjomand

MORAVIDS

This movement, which was to make Muslims in the Sahara and Spain more conscious of the distinctiveness of their religion, and which began a tradition of the Muslim scholar as militant reformer. The Moravid movement had its origins in the western Sahara in the 1030s when several tribes of camel breeding Sanhaja nomads broke their return journey from the pilgrimage (hajj) to Mecca to study in Cairouan—then the intellectual center of North Africa outside of Egypt. Greatly inspired by the teachings of the Sufi (mystic) and Maliki jurist, Abdullah b. Yasin, and by those of a former pupil of his, 'Abdallah Ibn Yasin al-Jazuli (henceforth: Ibn Yasin), they decided, once back in the western Sahara, to establish a house of retreat (Ar. *al-Murabitun*) where they studied and trained to become scholars and efficient warriors in the name of Islam.

By the mid-1050s a militant Almoravid movement swearing allegiance to the caliphs of Baghdad, and under the leadership of Abu Bakr ibn 'Umar, who took the title of emir (supreme leader, c. 1055–1108), rapidly extended its control outward from its new capital Marrakesh, over much of Morocco and modern Algeria. Sections of the movement pushed further southward across the Sahara and waged jihad, possibly unsuccessfully, against the Soninke of the kingdom of Ancient Ghana. Some historians believe that these incursions laid the foundations of a tradition of jihad that was to become a marked feature of Senagambian Islam in centuries to come and particularly from the late seventeenth century to the present. The Almoravid movement is also thought to have made its way eastward across the Sahel to Aier.

Invited to Spain in 1086 by the Muslim rulers of al-Andalus, the Almoravids, led by Yusuf ibn Tashufin, defeated the army of Alphonso VI at Zalaqa. Yusuf returned to Spain in 1090 and took control of al-Andalus before extending Muslim rule further north over the important Christian strongholds of Badajoz (1094), Valencia (1102), and Saragossa (1112).

Almoravid success in Spain was short-lived. By 1118 Saragossa had been retaken by Alfonso I of Aragon and this was followed by successful excursions further south. Popular rebellions in 1144 and 1145 ended Almoravid rule in Spain.

See also **Andalus, al-.**

Peter B. Clarke

MOSADDEQ, MOHAMMAD (1882–1967)

Mohammad Mosaddeq was an Iranian liberal-nationalist prime minister (1951–1953) overthrown by an Anglo-American-sponsored coup d'état. Born into a prominent family of notables and educated in Tehran, France, and Switzerland, where he gained a doctorate in law, Mosaddeq returned to Iran in 1914 where he taught, occupied various ministerial and other high-ranking posts, and achieved national prominence as a nationalist and constitutionalist parliamentarian. His opposition to the autocracy of Reza Khan (later shah) resulted in his exclusion from political life and virtual house arrest from 1936 onward.

Following Reza Shah's abdication in 1941, Mosaddeq returned to the political scene to represent Tehran twice in the parliament, receiving the highest number of votes cast in the capitol. The failure of negotiations to revise the British oil concession eventually resulted in the nationalization of the Anglo-Iranian Oil Company. The leadership of Mosaddeq and the National Front, formed by him in this process, led to his premiership in late April 1951.

Vehemently opposed to Mosaddeq and his oil policy, the British concentrated on destabilizing his government, while the shah refused to accept the role of constitutional monarch as defined by the premier. The relentless opposition of pro-British and royalist elements and the shah's refusal to transfer the War Ministry to the prime minister resulted in Mosaddeq's resignation in July 1952, but a popular uprising returned him to power a few days later. The intractable oil question continued, however, to aggravate the government's problems. Some of its supporters joined the opposition, while the activities of the pro-Soviet Tudeh Party enabled the government's opponents, including the religious forces, to claim that a communist takeover was imminent. The British and American secret services, aided by Mosaddeq's domestic opponents, eventually engineered his downfall in August 1953.

Following three years of imprisonment, Mosaddeq was confined for the rest of his life to his country home away from the capital. While cognizant of the place of Islam in the inherited culture of Iran, Mosaddeq was primarily a secular democrat and a civic nationalist, dedicated to promoting Iranian national sovereignty.

See also **Nationalism: Iranian.**

BIBLIOGRAPHY

Azimi, Fakhreddin. *Iran: The Crisis of Democracy, 1941–53.* New York: St. Martin's Press, 1989.

Katouzian, Homa. *Musaddiq and the Struggle for Power in Iran.* London: I. B. Tauris & Co., Ltd., 1990.

Fakhreddin Azimi

MOSQUE *See* **Adhan; Architecture; Jami';
Manar, Manara; Masjid; Minbar (Mimbar);
Religious Institutions**

MOTAHHARI, MORTAZA (1920–1979)

Born in Iran in 1920, Mortaza Motahhari was assassinated on 1 May 1979 by members of Forqan, a radical Muslim anticlerical group. He attended the prestigious Mashhad seminary and in 1936 moved to Qom to pursue his interest in Islamic philosophy. However, philosophical issues were seldom discussed in Shi'ite seminaries. Both philosophy and mysticism were subjects marginalized in favor of jurisprudence. In 1944, he studied jurisprudence with Ayatollah Borujerdi; one year later he embarked on studying seminal philosophical texts with Ayatollah Khomeini; and finally he attended 'Allama Tabataba'i's seminars on the philosophies of Mulla Sadra and Ibn Sina.

Motahhari is considered to be one of the most influential modernist clerics in contemporary Iran. Although Motahhari was a disciple of Ayatollah Ruhollah Khomeini and one of his closest aides during the first months of the Islamic revolution, he remained critical of Khomeini's juridical conception of *velayat-e faqih*. He emphasized the role of reason in the comprehension and practice of religion, and admonished traditional jurists for their promotion of a blind imitative faith. Motahhari believed that the orthodoxy that dominated Shi'ite seminaries alienated pensive youth from religion and created a fertile soil for the growth of Marxism. Accordingly, he intended to advance a Shi'ite philosophical rationalism, which engaged contemporary issues and was accessible to modern intellectuals.

See also **Khomeini, Ruholla; Reform: Iran; Revolution: Islamic Revolution in Iran; Velayat-e Faqih.**

BIBLIOGRAPHY

Dabashi, Hamid. *Theology of Discontent: The Ideological Foundations of the Iranian Revolution.* New York: New York University Press, 1993.

Motahhari, Mortaza. *Fundamentals of Islamic Thought: God, Man, and the Universe.* Translated by R. Campbell. Berkeley, Calif.: Mizan Press, 1985.

Behrooz Ghamari-Tabrizi

MSA *See* **Muslim Student Association of North America**

MUʿAWIYA (?–680)

Muʿawiya ibn Abi Sufyan was the first Umayyad caliph (661–680 C.E.). Muʿawiya's father, Sakhr ibn Harb ibn Umayyah—popularly known as Abu Sufyan—led the Quraysh army against the Prophet in the battles of Uhud and Khandaq. He later embraced Islam. His mother, Hind, the daughter of a prominent Quraysh chief, ʿUtbah ibn Rabiʿa, was also hostile to Muhammad before her conversion to Islam.

Some sources suggest that Muʿawiya accepted Islam before the conquest of Mecca in 630 but concealed it until later; the general view is that he accepted Islam after the conquest. This explains why he is included among the *tulaqaʾ* (those who were pardoned by the Prophet after the conquest).

Muʿawiya and his father, Abu Sufyan, were also included among what Qurʾan refers to as the *muʾallafat al-qulub* (those to whom the Prophet gave alms as a way of reconciling their hearts to Islam). The fact that Muʿawiya was literate ensured his appointment by the Prophet as his scribe.

In 634 the first caliph of Islam, Abu Bakr, sent Muʿawiya to Syria, where he was appointed as a commander of one division of the army led by his brother, Yazid, against the Byzantines. On Yazid's death in 639, the second caliph, ʿUmar, appointed him as commander of the army, collector of taxes, and governor of Damascus.

The third caliph, ʿUthman, confirmed Muʿawiya's appointment as governor of Syria, which became an important front for the defense of the caliphate against the Byzantines. Muʿawiya established garrisons all along the coast and for the first time Muslims engaged in naval warfare.

When ʿUthman was besieged in Medina by dissidents who demanded the instatement of ʿAli as caliph, he requested assistance from Muʿawiya. As soon as he assumed the caliphate after the assassination of ʿUthman, ʿAli sought to dismiss Muʿawiya, who refused to pay allegiance to him until ʿUthman's murderers had been punished.

The deadlock between ʿAli and Muʿawiya led to the Battle of Siffin in 657 C.E. The battle was brought to an end when Muʿawiya, whose army was on the verge of defeat, proposed that the conflict be resolved through negotiation. The two parties agreed to arbitration (*tahkim*).

The decision of the arbiters that both ʿAli and Muʿawiya be relieved of their posts did not resolve the conflict. ʿAli's supporters, in particular, rejected the outcome of the arbitration.

In the meanwhile, Muʿawiya had succeeded in gaining the support of the Syrians. In 658 he dispatched ʿAmr ibn al-ʿAs to conquer Egypt on his behalf. While Muʿawiya's position was strengthened by the conquest of Egypt, ʿAli's position in Iraq (where his capital was based) was considerably weakened.

After ʿAli was assassinated by a Kharijite dissident in 661, he was briefly succeeded by his son Hasan. Soon Muʿawiya convinced him to accept compensation for abdicating in his favor; thereby inaugurating Umayyad rule in 661. The seat of the caliphate was transferred to Damascus.

Muʿawiya's rule, according to most historians, was characterized by peace and justice. Governors were granted full civil and military authority. However, toward the end of his life, he nominated his son Yazid to succeed him. This move met with a great deal of opposition, especially from ʿAbdallah ibn Zubayr and ʿAli's son, Husayn ibn ʿAli.

Muʿawiya was accused of turning the caliphate into a kingship. The legitimacy of Yazid's succession was debated and contested by many, including Husayn ibn ʿAli. Husayn's march with his followers to challenge Yazid met a tragic end at Karbala, an event that is commemorated to this day by the Shiʿa as well as many Sunni Muslims.

Muʿawiya has been held responsible for the emergence of the first schisms in Islam. His refusal to acknowledge ʿAli's caliphate and his appointment of Yazid as heir not only resulted in the introduction of hereditary succession in Muslim polity, but also in the emergence of the Khawarij and consolidation of the Shiʿa.

While Muʿawiya has been vilified by Shiʿa throughout Muslim history, Sunni Muslims respect his political sagacity, justice, impartiality, forbearance, and resolution of character. It is said that he granted his subjects free access to him as well as freedom of expression. He was reputed for his oratory and his ability to turn adversaries into allies.

See also **Caliphate; Karbala; Kharijites, Khawarij; Succession.**

BIBLIOGRAPHY

Hawting, G. R. *The First Dynasty of Islam: The Umayyad Caliphate AD 661–750.* London and New York: Routledge, 2000.

Ibn Hisham, Abd al-Malik. *The Life of Muhammad: A Translation of Ishaq's Sirat Rasul Allah.* Introduction and notes by A. Guillaume. Karachi, Pakistan, and New York: Oxford University Press, 1997.

Tabari, al-. *Between Civil Wars: The Caliphate of Muʿawiyah.* Translated and annotated by Michael G. Morony. Albany: State University of New York Press, 1987.

Suleman Dangor

MUFTI

The mufti, or jurisconsult, stands between man and God, and issues opinions (*fatwa*, pl. *fatawa* or *fatwas*) to a petitioner (*mustafti*) either with regard to the laws of God or the deeds of man. In early Islam the mufti operated as a privately funded, free agent who was independent of state control. As successor to Muhammad in his role as jurist, the mufti was to exemplify sound juridical wisdom and moral rectitude. His knowledge of the Arabic language, the Qur'anic sciences, and hadith traditions had to be thorough, as did his grasp of legal reasoning. Such idealized standards eventually yielded to societal needs, until, by the turn of the tenth century, the office of the mufti required that he be thoroughly grounded in no more than juridical precedent within a given school of law.

A mufti is distinct from a judge (*qadi*) in several ways. The judge's authority is generally delegated by the state, whereas the mufti's is delegated by his peers; the judge's ruling is final, or subject to limited appeal, whereas that of a mufti is but one of many competing juridical opinions; and the mufti rules most often on questions of law, whereas the *qadi* rules on fact.

A mufti must always appear dignified and neatly dressed, for he serves as a model of good behavior in public. He must avoid delivering opinions when angry, ill, or weary, and also when there appears to be a conflict of interests.

See also **Fatwa; Qadi (Kadi, Kazi).**

BIBLIOGRAPHY

Masud, Muhammad Khalid; Messick, Brinkley; and Powers, David S., eds. *Islamic Legal Interpretation: Muftis and their Fatwas*, Cambridge, U.K.: Cambridge University Press, 1996.

Muneer Goolam Fareed

MUHAMMAD (570–632 C.E.)

Abu al-Qasim Muhammad ibn (henceforth b. meaning the son of) 'Abdullah b. 'Abd al-Muttalib, of the clan of Hashim, of the tribe of Quraysh, is acknowledged by more than one billion Muslims as the last messenger of God. It was through him that the Qur'anic passages, which his followers believe present the word of God, had been revealed to guide the nascent community through its predicaments. The religion that Muhammad preached is called Islam, meaning submission to God; its creed asserts that there is but one God and that Muhammad is the Messenger of God.

The Life of Muhammad

Recognized before his prophethood as *al-Amin* (the trustworthy), the Prophet of Islam is largely known to us through the lore of the early Muslim community from oral traditions

Muhammad's migration to Yathrib. XNR PRODUCTIONS/GALE

(hadiths) that were later written down. Though not always in agreement, these traditions come together to tell us about an Arab who was born around the end of the sixth century in the oasis of Mecca, a sanctuary town built around a cubical "house of God," the Ka'ba. He was nursed in his infancy by Halima, a Bedouin woman of the Banu Sa'd, as was customary among the Quraysh. Muhammad lost his mother, Amina bint (henceforth bt. meaning daughter of) Wahb, a few years after he was reunited with her at the age of six. He was then cared for by his grandfather 'Abd al-Muttalib and, then by his uncle Abu Talib, who granted him protection and stood by him in troubled times. Interestingly, Abu Talib never converted to Islam.

It was Abu Talib who introduced Muhammad to the camel-caravan trade, which became his occupation. This, in turn, led him to employment by a wealthy widow Khadija bt. Khuwaylid, who, though older than him, was impressed by his personality and subsequently married him. She bore him two sons who died in infancy, and four daughters: Zaynab, Ruqayya, Fatima (who alone survived her father), and Umm Kulthum.

Around age forty (610 C.E.), increasingly troubled by the social conditions of his fellow Meccans, Muhammad began to make regular trips to Mount Hira' for prayer and meditation. On one such occasion, he claimed the angel Gabriel came to him with words written upon a banner of brocade. "Recite!" commanded the angel, and Muhammad, feeling an enormous pressure upon his chest, finally pronounced the words:

Recite in the name of the Lord who created

Man from blood coagulated.

Recite! Thy Lord is wondrous kind

Who by the pen has taught mankind

Things they knew not. (96)

When Muhammad awoke from this vision, the words seemed to be etched in his heart and he feared he was possessed. For a brief moment he contemplated suicide, but then a voice came to him from the skies, hailing him as the apostle of God. Returning home, Muhammad informed Khadija of what had happened. With the help of her Christian cousin, Waraqa b. Nawfal, who interpreted Muhammad's vision as a spiritual experience, Khadija persuaded Muhammad to have faith in himself.

At first Muhammad communicated his message only to those very close to him: Khadija; his young cousin, 'Ali b. Abi Talib; his adopted son, Zayd; and Abu Bakr b. Abi Quhafa, a merchant and friend. They are believed to have been the first Muslims. A few years later, Muhammad took his message to the people of Mecca informing them of a life after death and of a just and fair God who would reward humans according to their deeds in this world. 'Umar b. al-Khattab and 'Uthman b. 'Affan were two important Meccans who accepted his teachings at this time, though generally it was the less well-to-do youth who were attracted to his call. Most Meccans, however, resented the deprecation of their gods, the gods of their forefathers, and the rejection of their beliefs by the youth that Muhammad's teachings encouraged. Moreover, the Meccans depended on the income derived from worship at the Ka'ba and feared that Muhammad would destroy the numerous idols that brought the pilgrims there. They opposed Muhammad, and made plans to kill him. Muhammad knew he had to leave Mecca when, in approximately 619 C.E., Abu Talib and Khadija passed away within a year of each other and there was no one left who was willing to grant him the protection and moral support he required.

Meanwhile, the people of Yathrib, unable to reconcile their differences and learning of Muhammad's fair and honest ways, decided to invite him to live among them as their judge and arbitrator. Muhammad immediately seized the opportunity to leave Mecca, and after sending his followers ahead, secretly followed them with Abu Bakr as his companion. This event, known as the *hijra*, is believed to have taken place in 622 C.E., a date that was later adopted as the beginning of the Muslim calendar. For Muslims, it marks the dawn of the "Age of Islam," as distinct from pre-Islamic times, which were termed the "Age of Ignorance," or *jahiliyya*. Muhammad now asserted leadership over a community based, not on tribal ties, but on its shared faith in One God. Jews, too, were included in this community. Soon, Yathrib came to be known as Medinat al-nabi (the city of the Prophet) or Medina. The Meccans who emigrated with Muhammad became known as Muhajirun, and the Medinans who welcomed and helped them as the Ansar.

Muhammad was encouraged in his immigration to Medina by the presence of Jews, who, he hoped, as monotheists would approve of his teachings. Even before arriving in Medina, Muhammad explained that he too worshipped the God of Moses and Jesus, and turned to face Jerusalem in prayer. Such was his reverence for Jerusalem that he had a mystical experience that had led him there. When the Jews of Medina rejected his teachings, however, Muhammad decided to distinguish his community from theirs, and changed the direction of prayer towards the Meccan Ka'ba. Then he fought a series of battles against the Meccans and as well as the Medinan Jews, until finally Islam was secure in Medina.

At the same time, Muhammad established Medina as his home. He married as many as fourteen wives, and Muhammad's situation was more complex than the number suggests. Among his wives were 'A'isha, daughter of Abu Bakr, the only virgin he ever married; Hafsa, the widowed daughter of 'Umar (an early Meccan companion); and Zaynab, bt. Jahsh, a divorcee, previously married to his adopted son, Zayd. Tradition also mentions a concubine, Maria the copt, who bore him a son who died in infancy. It is worth noting that while the Qur'an permits four wives to every man—provided he treats them all equally—it also informs us that the Prophet was permitted more wives because of his special circumstances. Yet, we are told that Muhammad asked 'Ali, husband to his daughter, Fatima, to refrain from taking a second wife. Polygamy had complex meaning and was not established as a pattern based on the Prophet's example.

Muhammad decided to venture back to Mecca on pilgrimage to the Ka'ba, which he believed had originally been consecrated by Abraham. At first, Meccan resistance led Muhammad to secure a peace treaty at al-Hudaybiyya (628 C.E.) for a period of ten years. By the terms of this treaty Muhammad agreed to let the Meccans trade freely, while the Meccans consented to let him make the lesser pilgrimage to Mecca (*'umrah*) in the following year. The peace enabled Muhammad to conquer the Jewish fortresses of Khaybar and to conclude a treaty whereby the surrendering Jews handed over all their property in exchange for their lives. They were permitted to continue farming the land in return for half of their produce. The Qur'anic verse 9:29 corroborates Muhammad's decision; it commands that monotheist *ahl al-kitab* (people of the book) be permitted to practice their faith in Islamic lands, on payment of a poll tax.

The following year, Muhammad, learning that Bedouin allies of the Meccans had attacked some of his followers, determined to lead an army against Mecca. Because the Jews were no longer available as allies, the Meccans decided to surrender, and Abu Sufyan, the Qurayshi leader of the Meccans, and his wife Hind, finally acknowledged that Muhammad was

God's prophet. A few weeks later, when several tribes led by the Hawazin decided to challenge Muhammad at Hunayn, the newly converted Meccans joined with Muhammad to defeat them.

Around 632 c.e., Muhammad, having established his authority over the Arabian Peninsula, made the hajj pilgrimage to Mecca, circumambulating the Ka'ba, and established the ritual according to which Muslims to this day perform the hajj. It is recognized as the Farewell Pilgrimage. Muhammad died a few days later in Medina, in the house of 'A'isha, where he was buried. Muslims suffered a great loss when Muhammad died. Their deep love and gratitude are reflected in the blessings (*tasliya*) they ask God to shower upon him whenever they mention his name.

Religious and Political Influence of Muhammad

The religion that Muhammad taught was called Islam, meaning submission to God. Asserting that "there is no God but Allah, and Muhammad is His prophet," it commanded that every believer pray five times daily; fast during the month of Ramadan; contribute an annual tithe, or *zakat*, for the benefit of the poor; and, if possible, make the hajj pilgrimage at least once in a lifetime. Mindful of the ethical purpose of monotheism, it also denied believers the addictive pleasures of alcohol and gambling that had such disastrous effects on family life. Traditions also convey Muhammad's respect for the ease of the larger community. For example, he wore perfume when he went to the mosque and refrained from taking garlic before attending a gathering.

Muhammad preached that Islam was the original religion brought by Moses and Jesus, but that it had become corrupted by the people. He taught that Jews should recognize Jesus as a prophet, and that Christians should understand that Jesus was neither God, nor His son but, rather, a prophet. Nevertheless, Muhammad held that all monotheists must be permitted to practice their faith, as long as they paid a tax in acknowledgment of Islam's political dominance. The activism of Islam that was demonstrated by Muhammad in both words and deeds requires a careful investigation as to when aggression might be justified. Importantly, the justification for holy war (often identified with jihad, which means to strive), is usually understood to be defensive. The Qur'anic declaration, "There is no compulsion in religion" (2:256) suggests an attitude of tolerance.

By acknowledging God's unique otherness, Muhammad claimed that all humankind, of whatever race, ethnicity, tribe, or color was equal before the Lord, and that each would be judged justly according to his or her deeds at the end of time. While slavery and concubinage were recognized, it was recommended that such persons be set free. Nevertheless, women were not considered equal to men. This is exemplified through the Qur'anic requirement that the testimony of two women is required to challenge that of one man (2:282).

Just as troubling is the permission given to men to reprimand their wives, affirming their dominance.

Islam's paternalistic attitude towards women is an issue of contention, particularly in the context of today's feminism. Nevertheless, the consideration granted by Islam to women, in the context of seventh century Arabia, was significant: Islam permitted women to keep control of their property even after marriage and inheritance rights were granted to wives, daughters, mothers, and aunts. Women were not only given a say in their marriages, but their sexual needs and desires were acknowledged. It is perhaps surprising to find listed among the inadequacies of men, for instance, the act of having intercourse with one's wife "before talking to her and gaining her intimacy, and satisfying his need from her before she satisfied her need from him" (Daylami, *Musnad al-firdaws*).

Muhammad's influence on subsequent religious and political life was significant. He had brought monotheism to the Arab world. Both Judaism and Christianity had already visited the Arabian Peninsula, but neither had ever quite captured it. Neither the Old nor the New Testament was in Arabic, nor had they yet been translated into Arabic. Moreover, Orthodox, Byzantine Christianity rejected the Arab Monophysites and Nestorians as heretics, and as for Judaism, there is no evidence of any communication between the rabbinical schools and the Jews of Arabia.

In contrast, the Qur'an brought by Muhammad was in Arabic; it delivered a message that the people of the region could understand, through a prophet who was one of them. It united the fractious tribes of Arabia, providing them with the political will to go far beyond their boundaries, to travel into North Africa and Spain in the west, and through Syria, Iraq, Persia, and into India, in the east. In a sense, Muhammad had provided the Arabs with inspiration for the making of an Arab empire, within which, for several centuries, Jews, Christians, and Muslims would make Arab culture their own.

Muhammad's Succession

There was, however, a problem. The Prophet had never overtly proclaimed his heir. There were two choices. One possibility was Muhammad's young cousin, 'Ali, roughly thirty years of age, who had lived with the Prophet ever since 'Ali's father, Abu Talib, had fallen into financial difficulties. 'Ali had fought bravely at the Prophet's side and, as husband to Fatima, was also father to Muhammad's beloved grandsons, Hasan and Husayn. Significantly, Muhammad chose 'Ali to pronounce the Qur'an verses of Bara'a, at the conclusion of the pilgrimage in 631 c.e., which put an end to polytheist pilgrimages to the Ka'ba. Unfortunately, 'Ali, who had spent most of his adult years in Medina, had little recognition from the Meccan Quraysh.

The alternative was Muhammad's dear friend and father-in-law, Abu Bakr, roughly two years his junior, whom Muhammad had sought to lead the prayers during his last illness. The tradition of Ghadir Khumm, cited in the Musnad of Sunni scholar Ibn Hanbal, has the Prophet declare, "Of whomsoever I am lord, then 'Ali is also his lord." The Shi'ites claim that this indicates Muhammad's appointment of 'Ali as his successor. The Sunnis insist, however, that it was merely the Prophet's way of reconciling 'Ali, who was extremely unpopular at the time, with the community.

At Muhammad's death (632 C.E.), Abu Bakr, with the support of 'Umar, went forward to be selected as successor to the Prophet (khalifat rasul Allah). The appointment had political ramifications and family ties were rejected as a basis for succession. The precedent that the caliph should be a companion of the Prophet, of the tribe of the Quraysh, and approved by them, was established at that time. Thus, Abu Bakr appointed 'Umar as his successor, and 'Umar designated a group of twelve to select one among themselves as his successor.

More serious, however, was Abu Bakr's insistence that Muhammad had stated that he left no heirs and his rejection of Fatima's claims to her father's property. The act effectively isolated Fatima and led her husband, 'Ali, to refuse his consent to Abu Bakr's authority until after Fatima' death six months later. This is probably what led to the formation of the *Shi'at 'Ali*, the partisans of 'Ali, a significant minority who asserted that Abu Bakr's leadership was illegitimate. It was the cause of a rent so deep in the Muslim community that even today mediation between the two communities is difficult.

The Denominations of Islam and Their Images of Muhammad

On the basis of Muhammad's teachings, three broad denominations emerged after his death. The largest group call themselves the *ahl al-sunnah wa al-jama'a* (also called "Sunni"). They accept the legitimacy of the succession from the Prophet as it developed historically and thus believe in the legitimacy of the prophetic legacy, as preserved by those who succeeded him, as a source for knowing God. The common Sunni position that has evolved regarding Muhammad is that prophets are free from the sins that provoke repugnance and error in the transmission of divine revelation. (Prophets are considered to be susceptible to error in matters unrelated to revelation, however.) Most Sunnis believe that Muhammad did not appoint a successor before his death and they do not give recognition to a priesthood. An imam, for the Sunni, may be a political leader, but he is generally someone who merely leads the community in prayer. The position of Abu Bakr as successor to Muhammad was, importantly, not vested with religious authority.

For the Shi'ites, Muhammad's position came to be closely linked to that of 'Ali. According to the Imami Shi'ites of Iran, for instance, "Two thousand years before creation, Muhammad and 'Ali were one light before God." 'Ali is significant not only as successor to the Prophet, but also as the one from whom the Shi'ite imams, who provide religious guidance to the community, descend. The imams alone can interpret the Qur'an with any degree of certitude. Moreover, special powers of infallibility, sinlessness, and wisdom are believed to have been inherited from, or granted by, God to 'Ali and the imams who succeeded him. Importantly, the Shi'ite traditions usually rely only on the words or actions of one of their imams (Momen, 1985, p. 173).

Finally, the Sufis, or mystics, claim that God is an intimate presence in all of His creation. While Sufism is not incompatible with being either Sunni or Shi'ite, the mindset of the Sufi is quite different—more tolerant, and less legalistic. Sufis believe that humans have an innate knowledge of God within and that the Divine may be experienced through jihad (spiritual striving), such as meditation or by the ritual repetition of God's names and attributes (*dhikr*). One who has achieved this goal is known as *wali-Allah* (friend of God), and through him or her the ordinary believer might hope to negotiate with God. This has led to prayers of intercession at the graves of significant Sufis, including the Prophet, an activity that is condemned by non-Sufis as polytheistic. Like the Sunnis, the Sufis acknowledge the caliphates of the Rashidun (the Rightly Guided), i.e., Abu Bakr, 'Umar, 'Uthman, and 'Ali. The first three of these were rejected and even cursed by the Imami Shi'ites. But like the Shi'ites, the Sufis believe that the Qur'an has both an exoteric and an esoteric message.

Biographical Literature and the Changing Image of Muhammad

During his lifetime, Muhammad probably did not exaggerate the significance of his person. Certainly, he claimed to be a prophet, indeed, he claimed to be the last of the prophets of God: *Khatam al-anbiya'*. But there was a fear that his followers might deify him. Thus, theologians emphasized that Muhammad was but a man and that his only miracle was the Qur'an. To establish the miraculous nature of this achievement the Qur'anic description of Muhammad as "*ummi*" (7:157; 7:158; 62:2) was explained by exegetes as meaning that he was illiterate. Moreover, the fallibility of the Prophet is suggested by the Qur'anic verses that insinuate that he had faltered, as when he turned away from the blind man (80). Another example cited to show his fallibility is more controversial and comes from the tradition narrated by al-Tabari. According to this tradition, Muhammad agreed, for just a brief moment, to acknowledge the goddesses of the Meccans, al-Manat, al-Lat, and al-'Uzza, as subordinate deities.

There is also the tradition that recalls 'Umar's words denying that Muhammad had died, although he was immediately corrected by Abu Bakr. Many early traditions convey the miraculous happenings that punctuated the Prophet's life. Although the Qur'an points to Muhammad's fallibility, it also includes signs that God interfered on his behalf quite readily. Incidents supporting this view include the splitting of the moon (54:1), the journey to the farthest place of prayer

(17:1), and Muhammad's victory at Badr (3:123–24). The very act of being selected prophet can be viewed as a miracle.

As time passed, veneration for the Prophet gradually increased. This is reflected in the several steps taken by those in authority to preserve his memory. During the reign of 'Uthman (r. 644–656 C.E.), the Qur'an was compiled; during the reign of 'Umar II (r. 717–720 C.E.) traditions (hadiths) concerning the Prophet and the early Muslim community, which had thus far been communicated orally, were also written down and compiled. By the time of al-Shafi'i (d. 820 C.E.), the practices of the Prophet (conveyed by traditions) were being considered as significant a source as the Qur'an for the making of Islamic law.

While private collections of traditions from and about the Prophet were probably made during his lifetime, many appear to have been put together according to subject rather than chronology. With the rise of the Abbasids (750 C.E.), who encouraged polemical exchanges with Jews, Christians, and Zoroastrians, the Muslims had become acutely aware of the lacuna that existed in the recorded life of their prophet. Al-Mansur (r. 755–775 C.E.) therefore commanded Ibn Ishaq (d. c. 773 C.E.) to establish a biography of the Prophet, which in the recension of Ibn Hisham (d. 833 C.E.), under the title *Sirat rasul Allah*, is the only version that is extant in its entirety today. Ibn Ishaq compiled a narrative that informs us of the life of Muhammad as it unfolded, from his birth until his death. He soon became the most recognized biographer of the Prophet throughout the empire. Selecting traditions that would endorse a prophetic career, Ibn Ishaq shaped a narrative that presented Muhammad as the last and best of Qur'anic prophets. Placing Muhammad's birth in the Year of the Elephant (570 C.E.) the compiler affirmed his early life in sixth century Arabia. Intertwining moments of revelation throughout the Prophet's career, Ibn Ishaq endorses the community's view that it was through Muhammad alone that the Qur'an was revealed. According to Ibn Ishaq, an important aspect of his prophetic personality was his performance of miracles.

Ibn Ishaq had to take political factors into consideration as well. Al-Mansur, who was of the Sunni denomination, had come to power through a revolution. He therefore desired legitimation of his authority among Muslims, for whom association with the family of the Prophet was required, but also among the numerous Jews and Christians whose One God, the Muslims claimed, had chosen Muhammad as His last prophet. Ibn Ishaq tackled the problem by presenting al-'Abbas, the eponym of the Abbasids and an uncle of Muhammad, as one for whom the Prophet had a deep affection and by including hagiographic traditions on Muhammad that paralleled the representation of prophets and patriarchs in the Bible.

Although Muhammad had his first revelation when he was around forty years of age (610 C.E.), we are told that even at his birth there were signs of his prophetic mission. Muhammad is said to have had the "seal" of prophethood on his back, and to have been followed by clouds that sheltered him from the burning sun. Indicating Muhammad's place in the larger scheme of monotheism, Ibn Ishaq establishes Muhammad's connection to the family of Abraham through Abraham's son, Isma'il, and demonstrates similarities between the families of Abraham and Muhammad. Thus, 'Abd al-Muttalib (Muhammad's grandfather), like Abraham before him, was released from his vow (made when he faced opposition from the Quraysh to his reclaiming of the well named Zamzam) to sacrifice his son. Instead he sacrificed several camels. Muhammad, like Jacob, "dreamed" he ascended a ladder (*mi'raj*) to the heavens where he met with God. Like the biblical prophets, Muhammad also performed miracles such turning a handful of dates into a quantity sufficient to feed several companions and healing the foot of one and the eye of another.

One of Ibn Ishaq's significant contributions is the information concerning a "Constitution of Medina," according to which the Muslims of Mecca and Medina, along with their Jewish allies in Medina, agreed to support Muhammad and help him against the Meccan polytheists who opposed him. When the Jews broke their agreement, Muhammad not only fought the Meccans, but also considerably reduced the Jewish presence in Medina. The tale regarding the Jews of the Banu Qurayza, whose adult men were executed after their surrender (while their wives and children were sold into slavery), is notorious in this regard. For Ibn Ishaq, the narrative follows the biblical pattern establishing God's destruction of those who oppose His prophets.

Ibn Ishaq is careful, however. Much of the information on miraculous occurrences is qualified by phrases such as "it is alleged," or "God only knows." In the case of Muhammad's miraculous journey from Mecca to Jerusalem, Ibn Ishaq directs the reader to a tradition from 'A'isha in which it was said that only Muhammad's spirit had journeyed to "the distant place of prayer." With the passage of time, however, these miracles were revisited without such caution, as in the compilations of al-Tabari (d. 923 C.E.) and Ibn Kathir (d. 1387 C.E.), which indicated an increasing veneration of the Prophet.

A growing devotion could also be seen in the activity of the Muslims. Around 780 C.E. for instance, Kahyzuran, the Queen of al-Mahdi (775–785 C.E.), consecrated the birthplace of Muhammad as a mosque. A few years later Qur'anic scholar al-Naqqas (d. 962 C.E.) mentioned it as a place where a personal prayer of request would be satisfactorily answered by noon each Monday. (Monday was the day of the week on which the Prophet is supposed to have been born, received the first revelation, and emigrated to Medina.) The tomb of the Prophet was visited with similar intent. It compared with the Sufi practice of prayer at tombs of saints or "friends of God," who were solicited for such benefits as a recovery from illness or the birth of a son. Muhammad's role as intercessor was clearly seen to be an active one.

The timely protest of Ibn Taymiyya, who recognized in such negotiations a contamination of monotheism, was followed several centuries later by the more radical approach of Muhammad b. 'Abd al-Wahhab (d. 1791), who feared a "regression into unbelief." His cause was taken up by Sa'ud b. 'Abd al-'Aziz. Such activity did not affect the rest of the Muslim world (Egypt, India, Turkey, and the like). In those places, Sufi practices and the celebration of the *maulid* continue to take place to this day. The oil revenues that accrued in Saudi Arabia in the twentieth century have, however, enabled the export of Wahhabism to the developing world, gradually eroding the latter's more Sufi-istic heritage.

Biographical literature on Muhammad in the twentieth century has been more concerned with issues of science and modernization. The representations of Muhammad by three biographers who belong to different nations and generations—Haykal (1888–1956) an Egyptian journalist; Dashti (1896–1982) an Iranian engineer; and Mernissi (b. 1940) a Moroccan sociologist—exemplify a variety of appreciations of the Prophet's life.

In *The Life of Muhammad*, Haykal's concern is to combat nineteenth-century western critics of Islam who portray the Prophet sometimes as an epileptic and at others as a fraud. Haykal insists that the Qur'an is God's word, not Muhammad's, and justifies his belief by claiming that Muhammad was illiterate. Asserting that the Prophet performed no miracles, he explains Muhammad's journey to Jerusalem, and from there to the heavens, as an experience of the mind rather than the body. As for the story concerning the "satanic verses," Haykal rejects it, explaining that Muhammad was, as a prophet of God, "infallible," and therefore not prone to such error.

Regarding the Prophet's marriages, Haykal is apologetic and unrealistic. He insists that these were not inspired by love but, rather, required by political and social circumstances. Muhammad's marriage to Zaynab, who was previously married to Zayd, his adopted son, is justified on the grounds that the marriage was conducted to make the point that an "adopted" son is not a blood relative, and to establish an inclusive approach to divorcees. More interesting is Haykal's rejection of polygamy on the basis of Qur'an (4:123), which requires that a man treat all his wives with equality. For Haykal this was impossible and clearly meant that monogamy is what the Qur'an advocates.

For Dashti, Muhammad is inexorably human. To him, the Qur'an is Muhammad's creation. His interpretation of the satanic verses and his weakness for women are simply the marks of human frailty. According to Dashti, Muhammad's relations with his wives are a private concern, and should not

be included in an evaluation of his leadership. Moreover, the battles of Medina against the polytheists and Jews were necessary, for Islam would not have emerged as it did from Medina if Muhammad had remained the visionary that he was in Mecca. The portrait Dashti paints of Muhammad in *Twenty Three Years* is one of an extraordinary man concerned for his fellow men.

According to Fatima Mernissi, "being a prophet means pushing people to the utmost, toward an ideal society." In *The Veil and the Male Elite* she recognizes that the Prophet, despite his endeavors, held back from granting women equality with men by recommending that women hide their sexuality when going out into the streets and by giving husbands authority over them. These decrees are explained, however, as the consequence of the warring milieu and the chauvinistic attitude of the Prophet's companions.

Displaying a keen understanding of hadith criticism, Mernissi examines the misogynistic opinions reflected in the *Sahih* of al-Bukhari, and explains that these were not the opinions of the Prophet, but of al-Bukhari. According to Mernissi, the Prophet, despite his "weakness," respected women and consulted them in moments of crisis.

Finally, it is important to recognize that Muhammad is not merely the quest of believers, but of historians as well. In this regard a word of caution must be offered concerning the nature of the sources. The *hijra* (Muslim calendar) was established only during the caliphate of 'Umar b. al-Khattab (r. 634–644 C.E.). Before the *hijra*, events in Arab life were remembered in relation to more significant happenings of the recent past, such as raids and battles or through the mnemonic of numbers. Traditions in biographical literature that provide a chronology and sequence to the events that constitute the life of Muhammad are therefore suspect. Moreover the Qur'an, which is not compiled in the sequence in which it was revealed, mentions Muhammad only four times. It gives no information regarding his place of birth or death or the names of his parents, wives, and children. As for archeological remains, the Ka'ba and the Mosque of Medina were completely rebuilt within a hundred years of the Prophet's death; and, tragically, all buildings consecrated to the memory of the Prophet in Mecca were destroyed by Sa'ud b. 'Abd al-'Aziz (r. 1803–1814).

Scholarship has moved on, nevertheless. Where once the challenge had been to query the divine authorship of the Qur'an, today it has shifted to a recognition of its various threads that apparently indicate a composite structure. Where once the Qur'an seemed to be the inspiration *of* Muhammad, it is now believed by some to have been the inspiration *for* Muhammad. Many centuries ago, the bewildered believer came to terms with Muhammad's death by emphasizing his faith in God. This could well be his response even today. Perhaps more documentation will come to light in the future.

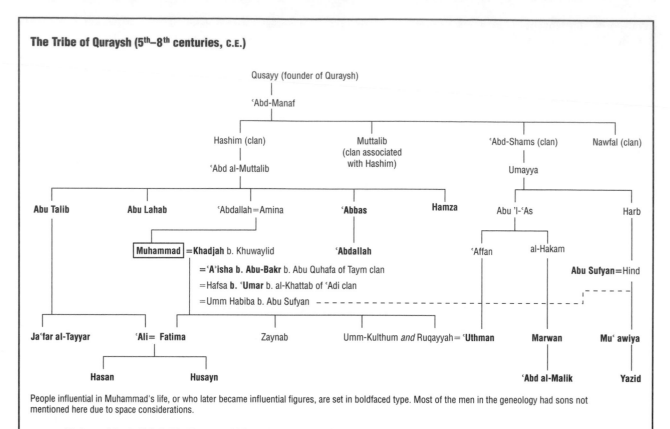

The Tribe of Quraysh (5th–8th centuries, C.E.)

People influential in Muhammad's life, or who later became influential figures, are set in boldfaced type. Most of the men in the geneology had sons not mentioned here due to space considerations.

SOURCE: Hodgson, Marshall G. S. *The Venture of Islam: Conscience and History in a World Civilization.* Vol. 1. Chicago: University of Chicago Press, 1974.

Muhammad's lineage.

See also **Arabia, Pre-Islamic; Biography and Hagiography; Caliphate; Hadith; Holy Cities; Mi'raj; Qur'an; Shi'a: Early; Succession; Sunna; Tasawwuf.**

BIBLIOGRAPHY

Cook, Michael. *Muhammad.* Oxford, U.K.: Oxford University Press, 1983.

Dashti, 'Ali. *Twenty Three Years.* Translated by F. R. C. Bagley. Costa Mesa, Calif.: Mazda Publishers, 1994.

Guillaume, Alfred. *Islam.* Baltimore: Penguin Books, 1954.

Guillaume, Alfred. *The Life of Muhammad: A Translation of Ishaq's Sirat Rasul Allah.* Karachi: Oxford University Press, 1955.

Hallaq, Wael b. *A History of Islamic Legal Theories: An Introduction to Sunni Usul al-Fiqh.* Cambridge, U.K.: Cambridge University Press, 1997.

Haykal, Muhammad Husayn. *The Life of Muhammad.* Qum, Iran: Center of Islamic Studies, 1976.

Jarrar, Maher. "*Sirat ahl al-Kisa.*" In *The Biography of Muhammad.* Edited by Harald Motzki. Leiden: E. J. Brill, 2000.

Kaptein, Nico. "Materials for the History of the Prophet Muhammad's Birthday Celebration in Mecca." *Der Islam* 69, no. 2 (1992): 193–203.

Kathir, Ibn. *The Life of the Prophet Muhammad.* Translated by Trevor Le Gassick. Reading, U. K.: Garnet Publishing, 1998.

Mernissi, Fatima. *The Veil and the Male Elite.* Translated by Mary-Jo Lakeland. New York: Addison Wesley, 1987.

Momen, Moojan. *An Introduction to Shi'i Islam.* New Haven, Conn.: Yale University Press, 1985.

Newby, Gordon. *The Making of the Last Prophet.* Columbia: University of South Carolina Press, 1989.

Rippin, Andrew. *Muslims: Their Religious Beliefs and Practices.* 2d ed. London: Routledge, 2001.

Schimmel, Annemarie. *And Muhammad Is His Messenger.* Chapel Hill: University of North Carolina Press, 1985.

Sellheim, Rudolf. "Prophet, Chalif und Geschichte. Die Muhammed-Biographie des Ibn Ishaq." *Oriens* 18–19 (1967): 3–91.

Stowasser, Barbara. *Women in the Qur'an, Traditions, and Interpretation.* Oxford, U.K.: Oxford University Press, 1994.

Tabari, Muhammad b. Jarir, al-. *The History of al-Tabari,* vols. 6–9. Edited by S. A. Arjomand. Albany: State University of New York Press, 1988.

Watt, W. M. *Muhammad: Prophet and Statesman.* Oxford, U.K.: Oxford University Press, 1961.

Watt, W. Montgomery. *Muhammad's Mecca*. Edinburgh: Edinburgh University Press, 1988.

Welch, A. T. "Muhammad's Understanding of Himself: The Koranic Data." In *Islam's Understanding of Itself.* Edited by R. G. Hovannisian, and S. Vryonis, Jr. Malibu, Calif.: Undena Publications, 1983.

Rizwi Faizer

MUHAMMAD AHMAD IBN 'ABDULLAH (1844–1885)

Muhammad Ahmad b. 'Abdullah, known as al-Mahdi, was born in 1844 in northern Sudan and died on 22 June 1885 in Omdurman. He did not follow his family's profession of boat building, embarking instead on a religious and political career. He studied Qur'anic and other religious sciences and joined the Sammaniyya mystical brotherhood. Besides his religious and ascetic fervor, he was imbued with a strong sense of social justice and reform-mindedness that filled him with a firm commitment to eradicate the colonial Turco-Egyptian regime and establish an Islamic state (1820–1885).

The regime's oppression and injustices, the loss of the class of religious *shaykhs* (masters) of the privileged status they had hitherto enjoyed, and the discontent of the influential northern merchant class, all contributed to the creation of a revolutionary situation. Furthermore, there was an eschatological expectation among many people of the imminent coming of a *mahdi* (the guided one).

Muhammad Ahmad's declaration of his Mahdism in June 1881 sparked off a relentless series of battles against the Turco-Egyptian regime that culminated in the fall of Khartoum in January 1885. Shortly afterward, al-Mahdi died before realizing his dream of carrying his Mahdist revolution beyond Sudan.

Muhammad Ahmad legitimized his Mahdism by a claim of a prophetic sanction based on a vision of the Prophet in a colloquy (*hadra*). He perceived his career as corresponding to that of the Prophet's and his mission as a universal one. He asserted that his Mahdism entailed the abolition of all juristic schools and mystical orders. His movement did not succeed in uprooting these expressions of Islam but instead led to the birth of a new politico-religious brotherhood—the Ansar (the followers of the Mahdi).

See also **Mahdi.**

BIBLIOGRAPHY

Abu Salim, Muhammad Ibrahim. *Al-Haraka l-Fikriyya fi l-Mahdiyya* (The intellectual movement under the Mahdiyya). Khartoum: Khartoum University Press, 1989.

Holt, P. M. *The Mahdist State in the Sudan, 1881–1898.* Oxford, U.K.: Clarendon Press, 1970.

Shaked, Haim. *The Life of the Sudanese Mahdi.* New Brunswick, N.J.: Transaction Books, 1978.

Mohamed Mahmoud

MUHAMMAD 'ALI, DYNASTY OF

Founded by an adventurous Turkish cotton merchant who created an autonomous Egyptian state within the Ottoman Empire, the Muhammad 'Ali dynasty lasted into the mid-twentieth century, when it was abolished by revolutionary Free Officers led by Jamal 'Abd al-Nasser.

The dynasty is named after Muhammad 'Ali (r. 1805–1849), a commander of the Ottoman force dispatched to oust Napoleon Bonaparte's army in 1801. Playing local politics shrewdly, he secured appointment as governor of Egypt in 1805. He served his sultan as loyal vassal, sending troops to re-conquer the Hijaz and to repress the Greek rebellion. At the same time, he consolidated authority over Egypt, destroying the bases of Mamluk military and economic power and seizing control of a vast amount of state land. By the 1820s he embarked on economic, military, and educational reforms, many of which presaged similar impulses in Istanbul. In 1831 Egypt invaded Syria; only European intervention prevented a drive into Anatolia. A treaty in 1840 cut back his military might and proscribed his protectionist economic policies. He did, however, retain dynastic rights to Egypt.

'Abbas (r.1848–1854) undid most of the dynast's reforms, halting conscriptions of peasants for works projects and military service. Sa'id (r. 1854–1863) sought to emulate Muhammad 'Ali, reinstituting Western-modeled educational reform and embarking upon infrastructure development, most notably granting the Suez Canal concession. Isma'il (r. 1863–1879), the first "khedive" (a special Ottoman designation for governor), inherited an enormous public debt, but continued Sa'id's reformist thrust. The debt crisis of the late 1860s led Isma'il to sell Egypt's Suez shares, institute a consultative assembly, and accept imposition of "dual control"—French and British officials to monitor Egypt's finances. His resistance to European authority, fueled by a rising nationalist movement, led to his deposition by the sultan. Tawfiq (r. 1879–1892) confronted the nationalist 'Urabi revolt that culminated, in 1882, in British occupation. His successors, 'Abbas Hilmi (r. 1892–1914) and Husayn Kamil (r. 1914–1917), ruled primarily at British behest, the latter, after Britain declared a protectorate in 1914, as sultan.

Following the 1919 nationalist revolution, Britain granted Egypt conditional independence under a constitutional monarchy. King Fuad (Fu'ad) (r. 1917–1936) retained enormous constitutional power over the newly endowed parliament, but still needed to answer to British superiors. Caught between the vise of British authority and the king's unassailable right to dissolve parliament, the "liberal experiment" quickly soured. Farouk (Faruq) (r. 1936–1952) acceded to the throne with great fanfare, a charismatic, seemingly pious, socially conscious youth who, many hoped, might stabilize the discredited order. But he quickly disappointed, becoming ultimately a caricature: the obese gambler and sordid playboy, a modern Nero. His second wife, a commoner, bore him a son, Ahmad Fu'ad, who inherited the throne under a regency when Farouk abdicated and left Egypt at the insistence of the military in July 1952. However, in June 1953 the Nasser regime abolished the monarchy, proclaiming a republic. Farouk, ever the butt of popular satire, died abroad in 1965; the officers allowed him to be buried in Egypt, although not alongside his predecessors.

See also **'Abd al-Nasser, Jamal; Modernization, Political: Authoritarianism and Democratization; Nationalism: Arab; Reform: Arab Middle East and North Africa; Revolution: Modern.**

BIBLIOGRAPHYY

Berque, Jacques. *Egypt: Imperialism and Revolution.* Translated by Jean Stewart. New York: Praeger, 1972.

Sayyid-Marsot, Afaf Lutfi al-. *Egypt in the Reign of Muhammad Ali.* Cambridge and New York: Cambridge University Press, 1984.

Joel Gordon

MUHAMMAD AL-NAFS AL-ZAKIYYA (D. 762 C.E.)

Muhammad b. 'Abdallah b. al-Hasan al-Muthanna died in 762 C.E. Due to his gentle disposition, he was known as al-Nafs al-Zakiyya, which means "the pure soul." At a gathering of the Hashimites held at al-Abwa' during the Umayyad dynasty, Muhammad's father, 'Abdallah, urged those present to accept his son as a claimant to the caliphate and the Mahdi (messiah). With the exception of Ja'far al-Sadiq, the sixth Shi'ite Imam, most of those present agreed. When the Abbasids came to power they installed Abu 'l-'Abbas (known as al-Saffah) as the new ruler, but Muhammad refused to acknowledge his authority.

With his brother Ibrahim, Muhammad instigated a revolt by seeking popular support against the new regime. The two brothers traveled extensively in Islamic lands, enlisting followers. In a desperate attempt at capturing these two renegades, al-Saffah's successor, al-Mansur, imprisoned their aged father and other family members. Since Muhammad was a descendant of the Prophet (through the Prophet's

grandson, al-Hasan), many, including the famous jurist Malik b. Anas and the 'Alids, supported his cause. Muhammad began his revolt against the caliph al-Mansur (d. 775) in Medina, where he had considerable support, while his brother Ibrahim began his revolt in Basra later on. Due to his political activism, many Zaydi Shi'ites supported Muhammad's movement. At one point Muhammad took over Mecca, anchoring his claims on descent from Fatima, daughter of the Prophet. With only three hundred men, Muhammad was killed in Medina by al-Mansur's greater forces, who were led by 'Isa b. Musa in 762. Extremist groups such as the Mughiriyya refused to accept his death, believing him to be the eschatological messiah.

See also **Ahl al-Bayt; Imamate; Mahdi; Succession.**

BIBLIOGRAPHY

Buhl, F. "Muhammad b. 'Abd Allah al-Nafs al-Zakiyya." In *Encyclopedia of Islam*, 2d ed. Edited by H. A. R. Gibb, et al. Leiden: Brill, 1960–.

Kennedy, Hugh. *The Early Abbasid Caliphate.* London: Croom Helm, 1981.

Liyakatali Takim

MUHAMMAD, ELIJAH (1897–1975)

From the 1930s until his death, Elijah Muhammad was the leader of the Nation of Islam, the most prominent African-American Muslim organization of the post–World War II era. A black migrant from Georgia who settled in Detroit and then Chicago, Muhammad became known among thousands of followers as the "Messenger of God." He spread his ideas through popular public lectures, the widely distributed *Muhammad Speaks* newspaper, and works like *The Supreme Wisdom* (1957) and *Message to the Blackman in America* (1965). His teachings combined Sunni Islamic elements with traditions of black self-determination and black closeness (the idea that blacks, like the ancient Israelites, were God's chosen people). Elijah Muhammad encouraged African Americans to convert to Islam, follow a strict moral and ethical code, and work for economic and political self-sufficiency. He also taught that blacks were the earth's original inhabitants who had become enslaved by a devilish race of white men. God, he said, had chosen him to "mentally resurrect" black people and prepare them for Judgment Day, when God would dispense with whites and reestablish a golden age of black splendor. This doctrine, called the Myth of Yacub by some outside the movement, drew criticism from many black civil rights leaders and Muslims, who deemed it un-Islamic. Elijah Muhammad's separatist Islam nevertheless found a sympathetic ear among members of the urban black working class, especially black men in prison. His emphasis on black self-determination and pride during the postwar period foreshadowed and inspired the black power movement of the 1960s and 1970s.

After his death in 1975, his son, Wallace D. (or Warith Deen) Muhammad, took over the Nation of Islam, leading the movement toward a more Sunni interpretation of Islam. But in the late 1970s, Minister Louis Farrakhan, a former aide to Elijah Muhammad, broke with the younger Muhammad, reconstituting a Nation of Islam that continued to rely on Elijah Muhammad's original teachings.

See also **American Culture and Islam; Americas, Islam in the; Farrakhan, Louis; Malcolm X; Muhammad, Warith Deen; Nation of Islam.**

BIBLIOGRAPHY

Clegg, Claude Andrew, III. *An Original Man: The Life and Times of Elijah Muhammad.* New York: St. Martin's Press, 1997.

Muhammad, Elijah. *Message to the Blackman in America.* Reprint. Newport News, Va.: United Brothers Communications Systems, 1992.

Edward E. Curtis IV

MUHAMMADIYYA (MUHAMMADIYAH)

The second largest of Indonesia's Muslim social associations, the Muhammadiyah was founded in 1912 in Yogyakarta, Java, by Ahmad Dahlan, a cloth merchant and minor court official who had studied in Mecca. The organization quickly gained additional followers among Sumatran traders. With its multiethnic urban base, the movement spread rapidly, reaching even remote towns in eastern Indonesia by the late 1920s.

The Muhammadiyah eschewed formal politics, concentrating on social welfare and religious education. In contrast to traditional Qur'anic schools (*pesantren*), Muhammadiyah *madrasa*s had age grades, modeled directly on mission schools. Curricula included science, mathematics, and geography, in addition to religious study. These emphases showed the organization's twin ambitions of urging Muslims to respond to the scientific and political challenge of the West while encouraging individual responsibility in devotion. Muhammadiyah also stressed women's education. Its women's branch, Aisyiyah, remains the largest organization of its kind in the world.

Muhammadiyah has based its success on steering clear of formal politics. The regime of Indonesian president Suharto (1966–1998) sought to nurture a conservative faction in the organization, but the mainstream leadership guarded

its independence. Although still solidly middle class, Muhammadiyah today is more intellectually diverse than at any point in history. In recent years the organization has experienced heated debates over Islamic law, women's rights, and religious tolerance.

See also **Reform: Southeast Asia.**

BIBLIOGRAPHY

Peacock, James L. *Muslim Puritans: Reformist Psychology in Southeast Asian Islam.* Berkeley and Los Angeles: University of California Press, 1978.

Robert W. Hefner

MUHAMMAD REZA SHAH PAHLEVI (1919–1980)

Muhammad Reza, son of Reza Khan, was born on 26 October 1919 and was the second and last shah of the Pahlevi dynasty. He died in exile in Cairo on 27 July 1980.

At the coronation of his father, on 25 April 1926, Muhammad Reza was invested as crown prince. On 16 September 1941, Reza Shah abdicated following the Allied invasion of Iran, and Muhammad Reza Shah succeeded to the throne. The first twelve years of his reign, between 1941 and 1953, were marked by a continuing struggle for power between the monarch and a variety of other political forces. This peaked in 1951 when opponents of the shah, led by prime minister Muhammad Mosaddeq, nationalized the oil industry. Following two years of political crisis and radicalization, the shah fled to Rome. He returned on 19 August, however, after a coup. Muhammad Reza Shah then embarked on the consolidation of a royal dictatorship, crushing all opposition. Between 1961 and 1963 he promulgated by decree a series of reforms known as the White Revolution, which included land reform and female enfranchisement. The land reform liquidated the large absentee landlords and thus had a major impact on the social structure of Iran. However, the lack of democratic freedoms continued to provoke opposition and major unrest broke out in 1963. After his exile from Iran in 1964, Ayatollah Ruhollah Khomeini assumed the leadership of the Islamic opposition to the shah.

From the time of the 1953 coup, Muhammad Reza Shah had become increasingly reliant on American support. The quadrupling of oil prices after 1973 allowed the shah to embark on a program of rapid industrialization as well as on a massive weapons' purchasing program.

Both secular and religious opposition burgeoned during the 1970s. Massive political demonstrations forced the shah to leave Iran on 16 January 1979; on 1 February 1979 Ayatollah Khomeini returned to Iran.

See also **Khomeini, Ruhollah; Modernization, Political: Authoritarianism and Democratization; Revolution: Islamic Revolution in Iran.**

BIBLIOGRAPHY

Abrahamian, Ervand. *Iran Between Two Revolutions*. Princeton, N.J.: Princeton University Press, 1982.

Stephanie Cronin

MUHAMMAD, WARITH DEEN (1933–)

Arguably the most important black Sunni Muslim leader in the history of African American Islam, Warith Deen Muhammad (b. 1933) was brought up as a member of Elijah Muhammad's "royal family." From the 1950s through the 1970s, Warith Deen served on and off as a minister in his father's Nation of Islam (NOI), but was constantly in trouble as he questioned the Islamic legitimacy of his father's teachings. Even so, when Elijah Muhammad died in 1975, Warith Deen emerged as movement leader. In the course of a few short years, he radically altered the official religious doctrines of the NOI, instructing members to observe the traditional five pillars of Islamic practice.

During this period, Warith Deen Muhammad led more African Americans toward Sunni Islam than any other person in history, before or after. He also reorganized the NOI, eventually disbanding it in favor of a decentralized national network of mosques. As Warith Deen led his followers toward Sunni Islam and away from his father's black religious separatism, however, he also insisted that African American Muslims continue to take pride in their ethnic heritage, work for improvement in the quality of black life, and interpret Sunni Islam in light of African-American historical circumstances. In 1992, Warith Deen became the first Muslim to offer the opening prayer before a session of the U.S. Senate. Now addressed as imam (leader) by thousands of followers across the country, he actively participates in interfaith dialogue and maintains strong ties to Muslim leaders both in the United States and abroad.

See also **American Culture and Islam; Farrakhan, Louis; Malcolm X; Muhammad, Elijah; Nation of Islam; United States, Islam in the.**

BIBLIOGRAPHY

Curtis, Edward E., IV. *Islam in Black America: Identity, Liberation, and Difference in African-American Islamic Thought*. Albany: State University of New York Press, 2002.

Mamiya, Lawrence H. "From Black Muslim to Bilalian: The Evolution of a Movement." *Journal for the Social Scientific Study of Religion* 23 (1982): 138–152.

Edward E. Curtis IV

MUHARRAM

The first month of the Islamic year, Muharram, is the focus of annual lamentation rituals performed especially by Shi'a Muslims in honor of Husayn b. 'Ali, the prophet Muhammad's grandson, who died in battle in 680 C.E. at Karbala (Iraq). Besieged by soldiers loyal to the caliph Yazid b. Mu'awiya, who sought to prevent Husayn from gaining political power, Husayn died on 'Ashura, the tenth day of Muharram. Family members accompanying him were killed or subjected to imprisonment and humiliation. Commemoration of the Karbala martyrs' sufferings during the yearly mourning season (from the first of Muharram to the twentieth of the month of Safar, with 'Ashura comprising the focal date) serves to help define Shi'a communal identity.

Muharram observances vary throughout the Islamic world. Iran is famous for the *ta'ziya*, a dramatic enactment of the Karbala battle. Localities in Pakistan and India stage 'Ashura processions featuring a stallion caparisoned as Zuljenah, the horse ridden into combat by Husayn. In Hyderabad, India, *matami guruhan* (Shi'a lamentation associations) sponsor the group performance of *matam* (gestures of grief ranging from rhythmic chestbeating to self-flagellation with razors and chains). *Matam* is performed in time to the chanting of *nauhas* (poems commemorating the Karbala martyrs).

In 1994 a *fatwa* by Sayyed 'Ali Khamene'i, spiritual leader of Iran, forbade the public performance of self-flagellation or other forms of bloody *matam*. This decree continues a policy promulgated by Khamenei's predecessor, the Ayatollah Ruhollah Khomeini, who advocated *taqrib* or Sunni-Shi'a rapprochement for the sake of pan-Islamic cooperation in international affairs. Sunnis have frequently condemned as un-Islamic the bloodier forms of Muharram mourning.

The most common form of Muharram ritual, however, is the *majlis al-'aza* or "lamentation gathering," where a preacher recounts the Karbala martyrs' sufferings to stimulate grief among congregants. While lamentation rituals for Husayn have been documented as early as tenth-century Baghdad, Shi'a authorities trace the history of the *majlis al-'aza* to Zaynab bint 'Ali, Husayn's sister, who was present at Karbala and who is believed to have held the first *majlis* to mourn Husayn while a captive in Yazid's palace. Traditional Shi'a belief holds that weeping for the Karbala martyrs gains mourners access to Husayn's intercession for the forgiveness

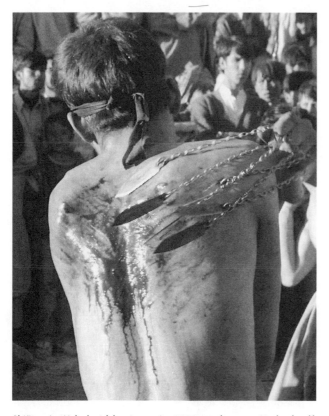

Shi'ites in Kabul, Afghanistan, in 2002 perform a ritual of self-flagellation with knives attached to chains on Ashura, the Shi'ite community's holiest day, to atone the death of Imam Husayn, the grandson of Muhammad. During the rule of the Taliban, such public celebrations of Ashura were prohibited in Afghanistan. AP/ WIDE WORLD PHOTOS

Pinault, David. *Horse of Karbala: Muslim Devotional Life in India.* New York: Palgrave, 2001.

David Pinault

MUHASIBI, AL- (781–857)

Harith ibn Asad al-Muhasibi of Baghdad was a master of Sufi ethics and the father of Sufi psychology. He is most famous for his theory of the three-part nature of the human soul. His nickname, "al-Muhasibi," refers to his practice of *muhasaba,* the critical examination of actions, motives, and spiritual states. He was an exemplar of ethical conduct and refused to allow any form of self-deception. He taught his disciples to follow reason and avoid emotionalism. His major opponent was Ahmad ibn Hanbal (d. 855). Ibn Hanbal criticized al-Muhasibi for his rationalism and his use of dialectical reasoning. He incited his followers in Baghdad to intimidate al-Muhasibi and prevent people from attending his lessons.

Al-Muhasibi's theory of the soul is contained in *al-Ri'aya li-huquq Allah wa al-qiyam biha* (How to observe and abide by the rights of God). He called his theory the "science of hearts." The "heart" is a metaphor for the soul. It includes the conscience (*sirr*), which is the spiritual center of the soul, and the *nafs,* which is the "psyche," "self," or "ego." Although the *nafs* is necessary for human existence, its desire for self-gratification undermines the spiritual nature of the soul. Using a term from the Qur'an, al-Muhasibi calls the ego-centered soul the "commanding *nafs*" (*al-nafs al-ammara*). The key to taming the "commanding *nafs*" is self-examination (*muhasaba*). Through self-examination, the "commanding *nafs*" is transformed into the "self-blaming *nafs*" (*al-nafs al-lawwama*). At this stage, one becomes aware of the damage that has been done to oneself and others by allowing the *nafs* to control one's life. But the "self-blaming *nafs*" is still ego-obsessed. Its overly critical attitude can lead to self-hatred and even suicide. Only by transcending the ego entirely is it possible to attain the third and final stage of self-awareness, the "*nafs* at peace" (*al-nafs al-mutma'inna*). In this final stage, the soul is at peace because it has transcended the human ego and is now controlled by God. This is the meaning of al-Muhasibi's aphorism, "Be God's or be nothing."

See also **Ibn Hanbal; Tasawwuf.**

Rkia E. Cornell

of sins. But recent Shi'a thinking emphasizes the political dimension of Muharram ritual as a form of communal assertiveness and revolutionary activism.

Muharram rituals are not limited to the Shi'a. In Ladakh (Jammu and Kashmir, India), where Muslims are a minority in a predominantly Buddhist region, Sunnis cooperate with the Shi'a in staging Zuljenah processions to demonstrate Islamic solidarity. In Andhra Pradesh (India), Hindus visit Shi'a shrines during Muharram. And in Darjeeling (West Bengal), where most Muslims are Sunnis, 'Ashura takes on an air of carnival, with competitions involving drumming and stickfighting.

See also **Husayn; Karbala; Ritual; Shi'a: Early; Ta'ziya (Ta'ziye).**

BIBLIOGRAPHY

Halm, Heinz. *Shi'a Islam: From Religion to Revolution.* Princeton, N.J.: Markus Wiener Publishers, 1997.

Hegland, Mary Elaine. "The Power Paradox in Muslim Women's Majales: North-West Pakistani Mourning Rituals." *Signs: Journal of Women in Culture and Society* 23 (1998): 391–428.

MUHTASIB

The term *muhtasib* has primarily been used to designate a person who has been appointed by the political power (sultan or imam) to police the enforcement of Islamic law in a particular area. In works of law, the *muhtasib* is described as being responsible for ensuring that the activities of the Muslims in an area conform with the *shariʿa*. This is particularly the case with regard to commerce and supervision of the marketplace. In later times (after 1500 C.E.), the *muhatsib* was almost exclusively responsible for ensuring that the weights and measures used in the market were fair and consistent. He alerted the judge (*qadi*) of cases of infringement, though he had the power to act without the judge's express permission. One finds the official position of *muhtasib* for towns mentioned in sources from most periods of classical Islam (from the Abbasids through the Ottomans, Safavids, and Mughals). The position appears to have disappeared in the nineteenth century, as law enforcement across the Muslim world underwent modernization. It can be argued that all Muslims should, in a sense, be *muhtasib*s, since a *muhtasib* is one who enforces "public order" (*hisba*), and because all Muslims have this responsibility under the general obligation to "command what is approved and forbid what is reprehensible" (for example Q 3:104), and the law books allow for "voluntary" *muhtasib*s to enforce public morals.

See also **Hisba; Political Organization.**

BIBLIOGRAPHY

Buckley, R. P. "The Muhtasib." *Arabica* 34 (1992): 59–117.

Robert Gleave

MUJAHIDIN

Mujahidin (mojahidin) is the plural form of the Arabic term *mujahid*, who is a person who wages jihad. According to doctrinal and historical applications of Islamic law, jihad indicates military action for the defense or expansion of Islam. While in the course of Islamic history the term *mujahidin* has been used by different groups to identify their struggles to defend Islam, the term gained global currency in the latter decades of the twentieth century after the leftist coup d'état in Afghanistan on 27 April 1978. The resistance groups first opposed the Afghan communist regime, declaring it atheist. They then turned their attention to the Soviet Union when it invaded Afghanistan on 27 December 1979. Fighting the Soviet Red Army, they collectively referred to themselves as *mujahidin* waging jihad against a communist power occupying an Islamic land.

The Afghan *mujahidin* were divided into two main groups: (1) those based in and backed by Pakistan with substantial financial and military assistance from Saudi Arabia and the United States, who mainly represented the Sunni majority; and (2) those based in and supported by Iran, representing the Shiʿite minority. The Pakistan-based group of *mujahidin* included Harakat-e Inqilab-e Islami (Islamic Revolutionary Movement), Hizb-e Islami (Party of Islam) led by Gulbuddin Hikmatyar, Hizb-e Islami led by Muhammad Yunus Khalis. Hikmatyar and Khalis initially jointly led the Hizb-e Islami, but later split the party, both retaining the same name. Itihad-e Islami (Islamic Union), Jamʿiyat-e Islami (Islamic Society), Jabha-e Nijat-e Milli-ye Afghanistan (National Liberation Front of Afghanistan), and Mahaz-e Milli-ye Islami-ye Afghanistan (National Islamic Front of Afghanistan).

In 1988, the Afghan Interim Government (AIG)—a loose alliance of the seven groups listed above—was achieved through pressure by Pakistan, Saudi Arabia, and the United States. However, various attempts to unite these and other smaller Pakistan-based *mujahidin* groups ultimately resulted in failure. In Iran, there were a multitude of *mujahidin* groups until 1989, when, owing to Iranian pressure, they united into a single party, Hizb-e Wahdat-e Islam-ye Afghanistan (Islamic Unity Party of Afghanistan).

In February 1989, the Soviet troops withdrew from Afghanistan and on 28 April 1992, the Afghan *mujahidin* finally achieved their main objective by capturing the capital, Kabul. Sibghatallah Mujaddidi, leader of Jabha-e Nijat-e Milli, was proclaimed president of the Islamic State of Afghanistan for a two-month period, to be followed by a four-month presidency of Burhan al-Din Rabbani, the leader of Jamʿiyat-e Islami. Thereafter, elections were to be held. However, Rabbani refused to leave office, barred elections, and ruled in Kabul until 27 September 1996, when a splinter *mujahidin* group, the Taliban, captured the city.

From 1992 to 1996, various *mujahidin* groups battled each other in every corner of Afghanistan. In the ever-shifting alliances and frontlines, the country was transformed into decentralized fiefdoms ruled with increasing brutality by warlords. Moreover, with the absence of a common enemy, the jihad gave way to an ethno-sectarian war. Another legacy of the Afghan *mujahidin* was the influx of foreign fighters, mainly from Pakistan and Arab states. After the *mujahidin* victory in 1992, most of these groups reorganized and became involved in places such as Algeria, Bosnia-Herzegovina, Chechnya, and Kashmir.

Beginning in 1989, Pakistan supported and organized the transfer of Afghan and Pakistani *mujahidin* groups to Kashmir, in order to have more direct control over the militants that were fighting for either the valley's independence from India or for union with Pakistan. The largest of these groups were Harakat al-Ansar (Movement of the Ansar—Helpers of prophet Muhammad in Medina), Hizb al-Mojahidin (Party of Mojahidin), and Lashkar-e Taiba (Army of Pure). The involvement of these and other *mujahidin* heightened the religious dimension of the Kashmiri conflict. By 1993, the largest and most popular Kashmiri insurgent group, the Jammu and Kashmir Liberation Front, which advocated independence and secularism for Kashmir, lost its military

With the White Mountains in the background, a mujahid stands guard in the graveyard of Achin, an Afghan village in the Nangarhar province. AP/WIDE WORLD PHOTOS

edge to the Hizb al-Mojahidin, which advocated either the establishment of an Islamic Kashmiri republic or union with Pakistan.

In the case of the Afghan resistance in the 1978–1992 period, the term *mujahidin* gained popularity, as did the groups themselves, not only in Islamic countries but also in the West. In the Islamic context, the Afghans waged a true jihad; and in Western minds, they were a liberation army fighting Soviet expansionism. Since 1992, however, the term *mujahidin* lost its religious and political currency internationally, as the Afghan *mujahidin* became associated with international terrorist figures who had once fought in their ranks, such as Usama bin Ladin. In the Kashmiri case, the groups claiming the title of *mujahidin* did not enjoy support in most Muslim countries, with the exception of Pakistan, and were seen in the West as either terrorist or rebel organizations.

See also **Political Islam; Taliban.**

BIBLIOGRAPHY

Roy, Olivier. *Islam and Resistance in Afghanistan.* Cambridge, U.K.: Cambridge University Press, 1986.

Amin Tarzi

MUJAHIDUN *See* **Mujahidin**

MULLA SADRA (C. 1572–1640)

Sadr al-Din Muhammad b. Ibrahim Shirazi, commonly known as Mulla Sadra and also given the honorific title Sadr al-muta'allihin, was born around 1572 in Shiraz, Persia, to a politically powerful and wealthy family, and he died in Basra in 1640. The most famous of the later Islamic philosophers of Persia, he carried out his early studies in Shiraz and then went to Esfahān for more advanced studies especially in the field of philosophy. There he became a student of Baha' al-Din al-Amili and Mir Muhammad Baqir Damad, the founder of the School of Esfahan. Mulla Sadra soon became a celebrated philosopher himself but because of the opposition of some religious scholars decided to leave Esfahān. He spent many years in Kahak, a village near Qom, in meditation and spiritual seclusion but finally returned to public life when the Khan School was built in Shiraz for him. He spent some three decades of the last part of his life in that city where he trained many students and wrote most of his works.

Mulla Sadra composed more than forty books, all but one in Arabic, concerning both the religious sciences and philosophy, his most famous work being *al-Asfar al-arba'a* (The four journeys). He was deeply rooted in the teachings of Ibn Sina, Suhrawardi, and Ibn al-'Arabi as well as being well-versed in the study of Qur'anic commentaries, the hadith and traditions of Shi'ite imams and Islamic theology. He created a synthesis between the purely religious thought of Islam in general, Islamic peripatetic (*mashsha'i*) philosophy, the School of Illumination (*ishraq*), and doctrinal Sufism of the School of Ibn 'Arabi. He believed that authentic *hikma* or philosophy/theosophy could only be attained by combing revealed knowledge, inner illumination, and ratiocination and he called this integral *hikma* "The transcendent philosophy/theosophy" (*al-hikma al-muta'aliyya*). His teachings soon spread throughout Persia and Muslim India and he has been without doubt the most influential Islamic philosopher of the past few centuries. He is the figure around whom the revival of Islamic philosophy has taken place during the second half of the twentieth century, especially in Persia itself.

See also **Falsafa; Ibn 'Arabi; Ibn Sina; Ishraqi School.**

BIBLIOGRAPHY

Nasr, Seyyed Hossein. *Sadr al-Dīn Shīrazī and his Transcendent Theosophy.* Tehran: Institute for Humanities and Cultural Studies 1997.

Rahman, Fazhur. *The Philosophy of Mulla Sadra.* Albany: State University Press of New York, 1976.

Seyyed Hossein Nasr

MURJI'ITES, MURJI'A

The participle *murji'* derives from *irja'*, the most profound meanings of which are "giving hope" and "postponing." The first meaning indicates that there is a hope for salvation when someone dies with faith albeit he or she has done grave sins. The second and perhaps the earliest meaning of this religiopolitical label was that the judgment about those involved in the conflict between 'Uthman, 'Ali, and al-Zubayr is "postponed" until the Last Day.

Historically, the Murji'ite sect, which is considered an extreme contrast to the Kharijite, was founded by 'Ali's grandson al-Hasan b. Muhammad b. al-Hanafiyya as a response to the fanatical Kharijite and Shi'ite sects. While Kharijites hold the view that the third caliph, 'Uthman, was a grave sinner and hence an unbeliever, and Muslims are not bound to his leadership, the Murji'ites were very much interested in the preservation of the unity of Muslim community rather than pronouncing judgment on whether or not 'Uthman and 'Ali were believers. As a consequence, Murji'ites postpone their judgment and give 'Uthman and 'Ali a temporary status of believers and accept their leadership. Any attempt to rebel against legitimate leadership is therefore unacceptable. Murji'ites also hold the view that a (grave) sinner should be punished but should not be excluded from the community, since punishment by exclusion can mean loss of security, life, or property. Another point of difference concerns the eternity of punishment. While the Kharijites strongly hold that a grave sinner is doomed in Hell forever, the Murji'ites gives the possibility of forgiveness by God's will and grace.

The Murji'ite interpretation does not belong specifically to the Shi'a or the Sunnis. Some Shi'is followed the Murji'ites in postponing their judgment of 'Uthman's and his adversaries' affairs while Sunnis adopt the Murji'ite view that no sin, other than *shirk* (idolatry or God's partnership with other than Himself) and *kufr* (infidelity), can make one an unbeliever.

See also **Kharijites, Khawarij.**

BIBLIOGRAPHY

Watt, W. Montgomery. *The Formative Period of Islamic Thought.* Edinburgh: Edinburgh University Press, 1973.

Shalahudin Kafrawi

MUSIC

While the history of music in Islam covers at least fifteen centuries, with orally transmitted repertoire and no significant notation system, its geography and distinct musical cultures include many diverse regions in the world. By necessity, this article excludes many folk musical traditions, popular musics, and other local styles; instead, it focuses on some of the universal aspects of music within the Islamic world.

The Concept of Music

While a word of Greek origin, *musiki*, was used in many theoretical works, an Arabic term, *ghina* (song), has been used also for music in secular contexts. Other terms, as well, are used for what a Westerner might call music in folk and sacred contexts—for example, *kü* is used for song or music in the Kazakh epic tradition and *ir* is used for both song and poetry in certain Turkic languages. The terms *qawwal* (one who says), and *'ashiq* (lover), are used in Pakistan and Azerbaijan, respectively, for certain types of musicians. "Singing" is never used in describing Qur'anic cantillation; instead, the term "reading" is used in both Arabic and other main languages spoken in Islam.

An article by Lois Ibsen al-Faruqi, based on a modern interpretation of historical sources, includes an illustration of a hierarchy of "sound architecture" (*handasat al-sawt*). In this hierarchy, genres are placed on continua between music and nonmusic, and legitimate and illegitimate. Consequently, "sensuous music associated with unacceptable contexts" is considered illegitimate (*haram*), and is labeled as music. Qur'anic chant (*qira'a*), other religious chants, such as the *adhan*, chanted poetry with noble themes (*shi'r*), family and celebration music (lullabies, women's songs, wedding songs, etc.), "occupational" music (caravan chants, shepherd's tunes, work songs, etc.), and military music are all considered legitimate (*halal*), and labeled as nonmusic. Then again, while vocal and instrumental improvisations, serious metered songs, instrumental music, and music related to pre-Islamic or non-Islamic origins are considered music, their legitimacy remains controversial, either forbidden or discouraged in Islamic law (al-Faruqi, 1985). Based mostly on al-Ghazali's (d. 1111) *Ihya' 'ulum al-din* (Revivification of the religious sciences), Al-Faruqi makes the case that the status of any *handasat al-sawt* genre depends on its context. Nonetheless, attitudes for this kind of labeling change in different countries. Two contrasting views may be observed in Turkey and Egypt.

In Turkey, Qur'anic recitation is considered to be music and imams, or leaders of religious services in mosques, are formally educated in music theory and practice at special state high schools and universities. As recently as 2002 the State Directorship of Religious Affairs organized a mandatory camp of intensive courses in musical theory and practice for mosque employees. However, Turkish scholars distinguish between mosque music (*cami musikisi*) and Sufi music (*Tasavvuf musikisi*) and, as in the rest of the Islamic world, musical instruments are not permitted in mosques. Many performers operate in both domains. Furthermore, some Turkish performers of Qur'anic recitation function in both religious and secular contexts. For example, Kani Karaca (b. 1930), a celebrated singer of the sacred *Ayin* of the Mevlevi (Sufi order), the Mevlid, and a Qur'anic reciter, is also recognized as an exceptional artist in the secular Ottoman classical tradition.

In Egypt, on the other hand, an ideal Qur'anic recitation is considered nonmusic. While Egyptians expect the reciter to demonstrate tasteful aesthetic skills, they also consider that the act of listening to the Qur'an (*sama'*) should not engage a musical perception because of music's association with worldly and even blasphemous irreligious contexts. Hence, in the context of Qur'anic recitation, the practice of "musical" composition is learned not through straightforward melodic exercises, but through providing a learning environment for individuals where there is no direct teaching of musical melodies.

National and local competitions of Qur'anic recitation for men, women, and children, like the *Musabaqah Tilawatil Qur'an* in Indonesia, and instructional and commercial recordings (especially in Egypt, Indonesia, Pakistan, and Turkey) help to perpetuate certain styles, and a net of artistic and spiritual critics protects the balance between the music as an enhancer of spirituality and the meaning in the text.

On the streets of Malaka, Malaysia, a Muslim musician plays a Malaysian flute. © Dave Bartruff/Corbis

Qur'anic Recitation

Two equally complex systems with specific sets of rules control most aspects of the Qur'anic recitation throughout the Islamic world. While a melodic modal system (*maqam*) helps to shape the melodic progression of a recitation (see below), the *tajwid* determines the exact pronunciation of the text.

The rules of *tajwid* have been transmitted orally generation after generation throughout the centuries. Properties of sound and rhythm are clearly articulated in the rules of *tajwid*. Some of the specific performance instructions include, for example, appropriate places for taking a breath, when to repeat a word or section, relative length of a syllable or phoneme, and so on. The degree of *tajwid*'s effect over the recitation varies in the two main styles: *murattal* and *mujawwad*.

Murattal (also known as *tartil*) is plainer and it emphasizes the meaning of the text itself. The pitch material of a *maqam* used in this style is often limited—usually within a fourth or a fifth—and elaborate melismatic contours where there is more than one musical pitch per syllable are considered inappropriate in that they obscure the meaning. Accordingly, there are no *maqam* modulations. Similar to the European recitative style, the tempo of *murattal* is relatively fast.

Since it does not demand any musical training, many practitioners of *murattal* are nonprofessionals and include both women and children. Professional woman reciters, whether they perform for a mixed audience or only females, often perform in the less ostentatious *murattal*. They are especially encouraged to recite in *murattal* since a woman's voice with elaborate melodic creations is believed to distract male listeners from the meaning of the text. On the other hand, professionals of the more elaborate *mujawwad* style are almost always men.

The *mujawwad* style—also known as *tilawa* (and more problematically as *tartil* and *tajwid*)—came out of Egypt during the first half of the twentieth century through recordings of such reciters as Shaykh Mustafa Isma'il and more notably Shaykh 'Abd al-Basit 'Abd al-Samad. Many reciters outside of Egypt emulated the *mujawwad* style from these recordings and other performances from the powerful Egyptian radio broadcasts. The *mujawwad* style gives more importance to musical composition and the emotional intensity of the melody.

Call to Prayer

Perhaps, the most familiar sound in the world of Islam is the voice of a *muezzin* (Ar., *mu'adhdhin*) reciting the *adhan*, or call to prayer. Wherever there is a mosque one may hear the *adhan* regularly five times a day from a minaret or a loudspeaker attached to the main building. People may also experience the *adhan* in other contexts: broadcast on radio or television, or from a recording on an alarm clock.

Each *adhan* is semi-improvised within a *maqam* (melodic mode) in a rather plain style. Unlike *murattal* style, certain syllables of the fixed text of the *adhan* may incite a melodic melisma within a particular *maqam*. *Muezzins* are often professionals employed by a mosque. However, they may have additional duties in the mosque. During the Ottoman Empire (1299–1918) palace *muezzins* were among the highest-paid employees.

Theory

Music, along with mathematics, astronomy, and philosophy, was one of the main scientific fields studied by the early Islamic scholars and today it remains one of the most studied art forms in the Islamic world. A number of scientific and philosophical treatises by ancient Greek scholars like Pythagoras, Plato, Aristotle, and Archimedes were translated into Arabic starting with the second and third centuries of Islam (700–800 B.C.E.). These works provided a model for later studies by Islamic scholars with their contents on cosmological associations of music, the healing affects of music, instruments, and other technical specifics such as tuning systems and melodic (*maqam*) and rhythmic modes (*iqa*).

An international congress on Arab music held in Cairo in 1932 renewed attention to many theoretical issues within the Islamic world—including Turkish and Persian—and resulted in a number of recordings by eminent musicians from the Middle East and a significant six-volume publication on music theory in French by Baron Rodolphe d'Erlanger, *La musique arabe* (1930–1959).

Melody

Theory, in general, provides a shared vocabulary of concepts and technical aspects of music for communication. Therefore, knowledge of *maqam* (melodic mode) theory has been essential for musicians' education in the art of both composition and improvisation. A *maqam* articulates a number of rules in a musical composition regardless of whether the piece is composed or improvised, the most important of which are:

pitch material (scale);

melodic progression (shape and direction);

modulations (to other *maqam*s);

and stereotypical melodic cells.

There are many *maqam*s and each *maqam* has its own set of rules. These rules are deduced from a large body of existing compositions. The number of *maqam*s used (Ar. *maqamat*, Turkish, *makamlar*, Moroccan Ar. *tubu*) varies from country to country and from one period to another; also, they may go in and out of fashion. Understanding the intricacies of *maqam* might secure a high status among musicians; in the same way, inappropriate use of a *maqam* in an improvisation, for example, could lower a musician's status significantly.

Even in the twenty-first century, musicians continue to invent new *maqam*s and compose new pieces in these complex modal entities.

Rhythm

Most early Islamic treatises included sections on the rhythmic modes (*usul* or *iqa'*). An *usul*, the counterpart of *maqam*, is a fixed rhythmic pattern and used to measure individual compositions. There may be one or more *usul*s in a given number of beats; for example, there are four known nine-beat *usul*s. Similar to the Indian rhythmic modal system *tala*, special nonlexical syllables like *dumm*, *takk*, or *tek-ka* are used to articulate *usul*s. There is often a direct correlation between *usul* and form. For example, the nine-beat *usul Evfer* is always used for the second section (*selam*) in a Mevlevi *ayin* composition; and the ten-beat *Georgina* (Turk. *Aksak Semai*) is used for the instrumental *Sama'i* (Turk. *Saz Semaisi*). Rhythmic modulation is an important compositional tool used by the composers.

Form and Genre

The suite form appears to be a significant genre in many religious, classical, and military musical traditions of the Middle East and Central Asia. The cyclical structure of these musical traditions goes back to the early centuries of Islam, and descriptions of early suite forms may be found in the writings of Islamic scholars such as Isfahani and Meraghi as early as the tenth century. A suite tradition often has a fixed body of repertoire, and shorter individual compositions are selected for performances. A specific order of pieces is determined by their rhythmic patterns (*usul*) and form.

An unmeasured solo instrumental improvisation, like Turkish and Arab *taqsim* or Persian *daramad*, appears in most suite traditions. A *taqsim* may be played at several points in a performance, for example, as an introduction to a suite in a given *maqam*, or as a transition between pieces. Although it is improvised, a *taqsim* follows the rules of the *maqam* and has a definable form. A Turkish *taksim* usually falls into three sections. The introduction shows the main pitches and other characteristics of the mode, and demonstrates the performer's mastery of a particular *makam*. The next section shows the performer's ability to modulate to other *makam*s within the rigid aesthetic rules of the tradition. Finally, the performer recapitulates and summarizes the original *makam*.

Arab *layali* and *qasida*, Turkish *gazel*, and Persian *avaz* are some of the vocal counterparts of *taqsim* that are often set to a secular poetry with additional words and other nonlexical syllables, for example, *aman*, *of*, *yar*, *yalel*, and so on.

The Moroccan Andalusian tradition also includes a quasi-improvised orchestral *taqsim*, known as *bughia*. While they follow a slow-moving specific main melody in a highly heterophonic texture, performance of *bughia* usually accommodates individual performers with some freedom to improvise. The origins of *bughia* possibly go back to a solo improvisation.

Na'at and *durak* may be shown as examples of unmeasured pre-composed genres whose text praises the prophet Mohammed. The best-known *na'at* is the *Rast Na'at-e Mevlana*, which is fixed as part of the *ayin* suite performed during the rituals of the Mevlevis, also known in the West as the Whirling Dervishes.

Some of the main Islamic suite traditions begin with a composed instrumental form performed by the entire ensemble. The *pesrev*, for example, appears in Turkish Mevlevi *ayin*, *fasil*, and military *mehter* performances. Measured in large rhythmic patterns, *pesrev*s (Ar. *bashraf*) consist of four independent sections (*hane*) and a refrain (*teslim*) following each section. The Arab *bashraf*, Moroccan Andalusian *tushia*, and Persian *pishdaramad* similarly occur at the beginning of each respective suite.

A *sama'i*, on the other hand, is the last instrumental composition of the traditional Egyptian and Syrian suite *wasla*. The basic structure of the *sama'i* is identical to the *bashraf*, that is, four sections (*hane*) with a refrain (*teslim*). The standard rhythmic pattern (*usul*) of this genre, however, is a short one, *Georgina* (3+2+2+3). In the final *hane* the meter typically modulates to *Darij* (3+3). The Turkish *fasil* and Mevlevi *ayin* also include an instrumental *semai* at the end.

Mevlevis typically use a compound musical form (*ayin*) during their rituals (*sema*), mixing the fixed *Rast na'at-e Mevlana*, several *taqsim*s, a *pesrev*, a four-section vocal composition with a text chosen from Jalaluddin Rumi's poems, instrumental interludes, various hymns, and Qur'anic recitation. A sequence of *Son pesrev* and *Son yuruk semai* is the last instrumental section played by the Mevlevi ensemble (*mutrip*). Turkish classical musicians frequently perform this particular form and certain other instrumental selections from the *ayin* form in secular concerts.

Dhikr (remembrance) is one of the most common forms performed by worshippers at Sufi gatherings of different sects. It is performed through formulized repetitions of words or short phrases in highly rhythmic specific patterns— "Allah" (God) or "*la ilaha illallah*" (There is no God but Allah), for example. Specialists or volunteers from the congregation may perform on frame drums or other percussion instruments during *dhikr*. Qur'anic recitation, hymns, and vocal improvisations with religious texts are often included into the ritual.

Education

Starting in the nineteenth century, the adoption of the Western system of musical notation in certain parts of the Islamic world changed the nature of music education in the classical genres, and, consequently, sheet music replaced memory for many in the younger generation of musicians. Conservatories and other music schools in countries like Morocco, Egypt, Turkey, and Iraq produced literate musicians with high technical skills during the twentieth century. The famous Iraqi *oud* virtuoso Munir Bashir may be given as an example.

In most Islamic countries oral transmission between the master and pupil was broadened with the advancement of the recording technologies during the twentieth century, and recordings of masters on radio, television, cassettes, compact discs, videos, and even CD-ROMs became virtual teachers for young performers. Consequently, regardless of whether it is sacred or secular, listening to the great performers remains the principal way to reach the level of mastery.

Instruments

In most locations, musical instruments are not allowed in mosques. A certain kind of inclusiveness and tolerance, on the other hand, makes it possible for a variety of musical instruments and dance to be incorporated into Sufi rituals. Most notably, the Mevlevi order, both in Turkey and Syria, features a large orchestra with classical instruments like *oud*, *ney*, and *rebab*, to name a few. The most commonly used instrument among Sufis is the drum. While the shapes and names of drums may change from one culture to another, the most common Sufi drum is a frame drum. Some peripheral countries with Muslim populations (e.g., Indonesia, Ghana), furthermore, use indigenous instruments in their Islamic rituals.

See also **Arabic Literature; Persian Language and Literature; Qur'an; Umm Kulthum; Urdu Language, Literature, and Poetry.**

BIBLIOGRAPHY

And, Metin, and Halman, Talat Sait. *Mevlana Celaleddin Rumi and the Whirling Dervishes.* Istanbul: Dost Publications, 1983.

Denny, Walter. "Music and Musicians in Islamic Art." *Asian Music* 17, no. 1 (1985): 37–68.

d'Erlanger, Baron Rodolphe. *La Musique Arabe.* Paris: Geuthner, 1930–1959.

Faruqi, Lois Ibsen al-. "Music, Musicians and Muslim Law." *Asian Music* 17, no. 1 (1985): 3–36.

Feldman, Walter Z. *Music of the Ottoman Court.* Berlin: VWB-Verlag für Wissenschaft und Bildung, 1996.

Nettl, Bruno, and Foltin, Bela. *Daramad of Chahargah: A Study in the Performance Practice of Persian Music.* Detroit: Detroit Monographs in Musicology, Number 2, 1972.

Pacholczyk, Jozef. *Sufyana Muziqi: The Classical Music of Kashmir.* Berlin: VWB-Verlag für Wissenschaft und Bildung, 1966.

Signell, Karl. *Makam Modal Practice in Turkish Art Music.* New York: Da Capo Press, 1986.

Touma, Habib Hassan. *Maqam Bayati in the Arabian Taqsim.* Berlin: International Monograph Publishers, 1975.

Wright, Owen. *The Modal System of Arab and Persian Music A. D. 1250–1300.* Oxford, U.K.: Oxford University Press. London Oriental Series, 1978.

Munir Beken

MUSLIM BROTHERHOOD *See* **Ikhwan al-Muslimin**

MUSLIM IBN AL-HAJJAJ (C. 817–875)

Muslim ibn al-Hajjaj, compiler of the second most important collection of sound hadiths, was born in Neyshabur, Persia, between 817 and 821 and died there in 875 C.E.. In order to collect hadiths (traditions), he traveled at an early age to Iraq, Egypt, the Arabian Peninsula, and Syria, where he heard traditions from well-known authorities, such as the jurist Ahmad b. Hanbal (d. 855) and Harmala, a student of the earlier legal scholar al-Shafi'i (d. 820). Of the 300,000 traditions that he is said to have amassed, only four thousand (or three thousand if one does not count the repetitions) were included in his collection, which was entitled *al-Jami' al-sahih* (The sound compendium), *al-Sahih* for short. Compared with al-Bukhari, Muslim pays meticulous attention to the

*isnad*s ("chain of transmission") for the hadiths he recorded, listing all the variant *isnad*s known to him for a particular tradition, before listing their common *matn* or text. These different *isnad*s are indicated by the Arabic letter *h* which stood for *tahwil* or *hawala*, Arabic for change. On account of this arrangement, he has been justly praised by both medieval and modern scholars; the latter in particular have found these "clusters" of *matn*s produced in this manner especially useful for the analysis of hadiths and their dating. Another important feature of Muslim's *al-Sahih* is its introduction, which deals with the subject of *'ilm al-hadith* ("the science of tradition"). The medieval sources list other works by Muslim on *fiqh* (jurisprudence) and hadith transmitters, none of which appears to be extant.

See also **Bukhari, al-; Hadith.**

BIBLIOGRAPHY

Juynboll, G. H. A. "Muslim b. al-Hadjdjadj." In *The Encyclopaedia of Islam.* New edition. Edited by H. Gibb, et al. Leiden: E. J. Brill, 1960.

Rauf, Muhammad Abdul. "Hadith Literature: The Development of the Science of *Hadith*." In Vol. 1, *Arabic Literature to the End of the Umayyad Period.* Edited by A. F. L. Beeston, et al. Cambridge, U.K.: Cambridge University Press, 1983.

Asma Afsaruddin

MUSLIM STUDENT ASSOCIATION OF NORTH AMERICA

Muslim students in universities across the United States formally inaugurated the Muslim Student Association in a national conference held in Urbana, Illinois, on 1 January 1963. The participants in this first conference represented immigrant students from all over the Muslim world. On almost every major college campus where there were Muslim students (about two hundred in all), a MSA was established as part of a network of local chapters with regional and zonal structures. The central organization was run by an executive committee, as was each local chapter, and a general national meeting was held every year in a different city.

In September 1975, the MSA established a general secretariat and a headquarters in Plainfield, Indiana. Accordingly, departments were created to oversee the dissemination of Islamic education and publications, training, public relations, finance, and administration. As members graduated, they remained active and some made the organization their life's work. By February 1977 the MSA had become the largest, best-organized, most active, financially stable, and influential American Muslim organization. It had also come to be dominated in leadership and membership by Muslim students from Southeast Asia. Since 1977 the numbers of MSAs has grown and although immigrant Muslim students from all over participate, South Asians predominate in the leadership roles.

One immediate result of the organization and influence of this group was criticism for expanding that influence to community affairs. Though students were naturally members of various communities, they had competition in the leadership of community affairs. This tension caused the emergence of the Muslim Community Association. The two groups were then organized in 1981 under an umbrella organization, The Islamic Society of North America (ISNA). Today, almost everywhere there are Muslim students there continues to exist an MSA to serve their needs on campus.

See also **Islamic Society of North America; United States, Islam in the; Youth Movements.**

Aminah Beverly McCloud

MUʿTAZILITES, MUʿTAZILA

The most prevalent tradition has it that the name Muʿtazila was used to refer to someone or a group of people who withdrew (*iʿtazala*, from which the term Muʿtazila derives) from an eighth-century circle of majority on whether a grave sinner was a believer or unbeliever. Later on, the term Muʿtazila was used to designate a school of Islamic theology that follows certain rules known as the five principles (*al-usul al-khamsa*).

This theological school is one of the most progressive schools in the history of Islamic theology and has to a high degree contributed to the development of Islamic thought. This school is theological due to its starting point that God is unquestionably regarded as the ultimate source of its worldview. However, its emphasis on the use of reason in its theological quest and its assimilation of some Greek ideas and methods of arguments with Islamic principles have contributed to a great extent to the development and flourishing of rationalism in early Islamic thought.

The seeds of Muʿtazilite views disseminated by its early figures such as Wasil b. al-ʿAttaʾ, ʿAmr b. ʿUbayd, and Abu l-Hudhayl eventually got formulated and adopted as five Muʿtazilite principles. The principle of unity (*tawhid*) suggests God's unity against any resemblance to Him. Under this principle, Muʿtazilites deny the eternity of the Qurʾan, God's attributes, and any form of anthromorphism. The principle of justice (*ʿadl*) is associated with the theory of determination (*qadar*), in which it is maintained that God is just and that human beings are free to choose and to act. The principle of promise and threats holds that God is truthful and bound in keeping His promise of heavenly reward and threat of hellfire. As He promised, for example, a great sinner will forever be in hell unless s/he repents. The principle of intermediate position (*manzila bayn al-mazilatayn*) indicates that a Muslim who does great sin is regarded as neither a believer (*muʾmin*) nor an unbeliever (*kafir*). The principle of commanding the right and forbidding the wrong (*al-amr bi al-maʿruf wa al-nahy ʿan al-munkar*) instructs every Muʿtazilite to apply this principle to the social world when he or she has the power to do it.

See also **ʿAbd al-Jabbar; Maʾmun, al-; Mihna.**

BIBLIOGRAPHY

Hourani, George F. *Islamic Rationalism: The Ethics of ʿAbd al-Jabbar.* Oxford, U.K.: Clarendon Press, 1971.

Martin, Richard C., and Woodward, Mark. *Defenders of Reason in Islam: Muʿtazilism from Early School to Modern Symbol.* Oxford, U.K.: Oneworld, 1997.

Shalahudin Kafrawi

MUTHANNA, MUHAMMAD IBN ʿABDALLAH, AL- *See* **Muhammad al-Nafs al-Zakiyya**

N

NADER SHAH AFSHAR (1688–1747)

Nader Shah Afshar was the ruler of Iran from 1736 until 1747. Born Nader-qoli Beg of the Afshar Turkmen in northeastern Iran in 1688, he rose to power by espousing the cause of Tahmasb Mirza, scion of the Safavid dynasty who had escaped from the invading Afghans. Under the name of Tahmasb-qoli Khan, Nader led an Iranian army to victory over the Afghans in 1729. In 1732 he had Tahmasb deposed and replaced by his infant son 'Abbas, with himself as regent. Having recovered the border territories occupied by Ottoman Turkey and Russia, in 1736 he engineered his own election as king, under the name of Nader Shah.

Nader signed a treaty with the Ottomans, proposing that the Iranians renounce Shi'ism (a major cause of enmity with the Turks, as champions of Sunni Islam) if the Turks agreed to recognize their Ja'fari *madhhab* (school of religious law) as a fifth rite of Sunni law. This compromise was likely seen by Nader as a stepping-stone to a larger Asiatic empire, as his enrichment of the Shi'ite shrine in his capital of Mashhad was calculated to win support at home. The Turks were unconvinced, and the religious clauses were never ratified. In 1739 Nader invaded India, defeated the Mughal army, and sacked Delhi; he returned by way of Central Asia, subduing Bukhara and Khiva. His son Reza-qoli Mirza, viceroy in Iran during the Indian campaign, was accused of ordering a failed assassination of his father, and blinded.

Exorbitant requisitions for his renewed campaigns provoked widespread rebellions. Nader became increasingly paranoid and cruelly punished all opposition, erecting towers of severed heads in his wake. His reliance on (Sunni) Afghan and Uzbek troops alienated his own (Shi'ite) Afshar and Qajar officers, who in 1747 assassinated him in his camp in Khorasan. His army disintegrated; he was succeeded briefly by a nephew, 'Adel Shah, then by his grandson Shahrokh Shah (1748–1796), but their rule did not extend much beyond Mashhad.

See also **Abbas I, Shah; Madhhab.**

BIBLIOGRAPHY

Lockhart, Laurence. *Nadir Shah: A Critical Study Based Mainly Upon Contemporary Sources*. London: Luzac, 1938.

Tucker, Ernest S. "Nadir Shah and the Ja'fari *Madhhab* Reconsidered." *Iranian Studies* 27 (1994): 163–179.

John R. Perry

NAHDLATUL ULAMA (NU)

The organization of the Nahdlatul Ulama (Revival of the Religious Scholars), or NU, was founded on 31 January 1926 as a countermovement to the increasingly successful reformist Muhammadiyah organization. NU is a mass-based socioreligious Islamic organization under the leadership of ulema, and it is the largest in Indonesia with around thirty-five million members. NU activities include the religious, social, educational, economic, and political. Its founders were ulema (called *kiyai* in Indonesia) who led rural Islamic boarding schools, *pesantren*. They represented traditionalist Muslims, those who practice Islamic mysticism (*tasawuf*; Ar. *tasawwuf*), and are not against indigenous rituals and beliefs as long as they do not contradict the normative teachings of Islam. The two most prominent founding ulema were Hasyim Asy'ari, and Abdul Wahab Chasbullah.

NU members refer to themselves as *Aswaja*: "*ahlus sunnah wal jama'a*," (Ar., ahl al-sunna wal-jama'a) people of sunna and community, who base their religious reference on the hadith, the sunna, and the *adat* (local practices, Ar., *'ada*). They follow the Shafi'i school of jurisprudence and in their interpretation of religious texts include the opinions of the great ulema in unbroken chains that reach back to the prophet Muhammad. *Pesantren* are considered the heart of

NU tradition. Here students learn the essentials of traditionalist Islam in order to maintain and spread this interpretation.

NU's history can be divided into four phases:

1. The initial years NU served as a socioreligious organization.

2. From the late 1930s until 1984 it became involved in political activities. From 1952–1971 it had its own political party and participated in the national cabinet.

3. When the Suharto government rendered all political parties ineffective with its suppressive regulations NU decided to leave politics. This was expressed in the 1984 watershed event called *kembali ke khittah*, a return to the original charter of 1926.

4. In 1998, after the fall of Suharto, NU again became involved in national politics. It initiated the National Awakening Party (PKB) while its national chair, Abdurrahman Wahid, was elected Indonesia's fourth president for a brief period (1999–2001).

The return to its socioreligious activities in 1984 not only meant withdrawal from politics, but a total refocus on education, community welfare, mission, social, and economic development. Through its new role, NU became active in guiding large numbers of Indonesian Muslims in adapting to social change and modernity. Various institutions related to NU started multilevel dialogue about issues of social justice, human rights, democracy, and the rights of women and children. This made NU an active codeveloper of a model for civil society, suitable for the Indonesian context.

Over the years, several divisions were founded within the NU structure. Among others, there are divisions for youth (Ansor), women (Muslimat NU), young women (Fatayat NU), and male and female students (IPNU and IPPNU). Apart from these divisions, NU comprises institutions for education, family affairs, agriculture, economic development, and Islamic banking. The membership of ulema and lay people is reflected in a two-tiered structure of councils that reach from the national to the local level: the *syuriah* (Ar. *shura*), the religious council, which has only ulema as members who develop and monitor the NU activities; and the Tanfidziah, which is the executive council where ulema and lay members supervise the daily affairs. It is characteristic for NU that decisions taken at the highest level are not binding for the lower levels. This is based on a tradition of the Prophet's saying that "disagreement among the ulema is a blessing from God for humanity."

See also **Southeast Asian Culture and Islam; Southeast Asia, Islam in.**

BIBLIOGRAPHY

Barton, Greg, and Fealy, Greg, eds. *Nahdlatul Ulama, Traditional Islam and Modernity in Indonesia*. Clayton, Australia: Monash Asia Institute, 1996.

Dhofier, Zamakhashari. *The Pesantren Tradition. The Role of the Kiyai in the Maintenance of Traditional Islam in Java*. Tempe, Ariz.: Program for Southeast Asian Studies, ASU, 1999.

Oepen, Manfred, and Karcher, Wolfgang, eds. *The Impact of Pesantren in Education and Community Development in Indonesia*. Jakarta: P3M, 1988.

Sciortino, Rosalia; Marcoes Natsir, Lies; and Mas'udi, Masdar. "Learning from Islam: Advocacy of Reproductive Rights in Indonesian Pesantren." *Reproductive Health Matters* no. 8 (November 1996): 86–93.

Nelly van Doorn-Harder

NA'INI, MOHAMMAD HOSAYN (1860–1936)

Mohammad Hosayn Na'ini was a leading Shi'ite scholar, theoretician of constitutionalism, and a precursor of Islamic modernism in Iran. Born into a family of scholars, Na'ini first studied with Mohammad Baqer Esfahani and Mohammad Taqi (Aqa Najafi). Then he went to Iraq where he studied with Mohammad Hasan Shirazi and Mohammad Kazim Khorasani. In Iraq, Na'ini became actively involved in the anti-British independence movement after World War I. He was arrested and expelled from Karbala and returned to Tehran in 1923. He joined the anti-Qajar forces, supported Reza Khan's accession to the throne, and maintained cordial relationship with him until his death in Najaf in 1936.

Na'ini wrote the most important treatise in support of constitutional government from a Shi'ite viewpoint; in it he presented an Islamic justification for a secular and Western model constitutional government. In *Tanbih al-umma wa tanzih al-milla dar Asas Usul-i Mashrutiyyat* (An admonishment to the [community of] believers and an exposition to the nation concerning the principles of constitutional government), Na'ini attempted to reconcile the need for an efficient government in Iran that would respect certain tenets of a democratic system of government with the need to recognize the legitimacy of the rule of the Hidden Imam, and defend the precepts of Shi'ite Islam. It is said that when Na'ini became disillusioned with the constitutional revolution, he withdrew his book and threw it into the Tigris River.

See also **Modernization, Political: Constitutionalism; Nationalism: Iranian.**

BIBLIOGRAPHY

Hairi, A. H. *Shi'ism and Constitutionalism.* Leiden: Brill, 1977.

Mohammad H. Faghfoory

NAJAF

Najaf is one of several shrine cities and a major learning center for Shi'a Muslims. Located south of Baghdad, Iraq, on a trade route between Basra and Baghdad, Najaf has existed since the reign of Harun al-Rashid. Imam 'Ali was buried here, and a shrine was built around 'Ali's tomb in 979.

The city of Najaf began as a learning center in 1056, when Shaykh al-Ta'ifa al-Tusi moved here after the Seljuks took over Baghdad. He advanced the work of his predecessors in the emerging rationalist school of Shi'ite thought. During the Ilkhanid period (thirteenth to fifteenth centuries) its prominence was reduced with the emergence of Hilla and Aleppo as centers of Shi'ite learning. In sixteenth and seventeenth centuries, Najaf, Isfahan, and Mashhad were competing over prominence as shrine cities. The rise of the Safavids in the sixteenth century and their rivalry with the Ottoman Empire for hegemony over the shrine cities escalated. Safavids ruled over the shrine cities in 1508–1533 and 1622–1638, but for political reasons maintained Isfahan and Mashhad as the most important shrine centers.

The eighteenth century was a turning point in the history of the shrine cities. First, the fall of the Safavids in Iran drove many ulema to Najaf. Secondly, the shrine cities became economically more independent of the Ottomans and the subsequent rulers of Iran, and the number of pilgrims increased. Najaf, in particular, was positively affected by the pan-Islamic policies of Sultan 'Abd al-Hamid after he came to power in 1876. Migrant Islamic scholars in Najaf gained prominence.

Around this same period, the Qajars of Iran were giving in to British and Russian colonial powers. While the Iranian religious centers were actively involved in everyday politics, centers in Iraq, such as Najaf, were not. During the late nineteenth and early twentieth centuries, Najaf was drawn into anticolonial opposition by the ulema, who responded positively to a decree by Mirza Hasan Shirazi that banned tobacco in 1891 in protest to the shah's Tobacco Concession to the British and the 1905 Constitutional Revolution in Iran which limited the power of the Qajar monarchs.

By the end of the nineteenth century, Najaf had grown to a city of 30,000 inhabitants, with a large community of learned people who came from all over the Islamic world. The formation of a patronage system, which consisted of a network of students and funding sources across political boundaries, increased the flow of funds, making it more independent of the governments. In the twentieth century, Najaf regained prominence when one of its ulema, Ayatollah Tabataba'i Yazdi (d. 1919), wrote *al-Urwa al-wuthqa*, a major work in applied Shi'ite law which reflected the contemporary social and political condition and, with Qom, once again became an important center of Shi'ite scholarship during the period from 1900 through 1979.

When the shah of Iran exiled Ayatollah Khomeini to Najaf in 1964, the city became an important political center as well. Najaf and Qom, however, were rivals for importance, as Khomeini praised Qom for being more active in the social life of the Shi'a, and chided Najaf for its relative passivity. Violent repression by Saddam Hussein during and after the Iran-Iraq War (1980–1988) forced many of the Shi'ite ulema to leave Najaf and has resulted in its eclipse as a center of Shi'ite learning.

See also **Holy Cities; Karbala; Mashhad.**

BIBLIOGRAPHY

Kazemi Moussavi, Ahmad. *Religious Authority in Shi'ite Islam: From the Office of Mufti to the Instituion of Marja.* Kuala Lumpur, Malaysia: ISTAC, 1996.

Litvak, Meir. *Shi'i Scholars of Nineteenth-century Iraq: The Ulama of Najaf and Karbala.* Cambridge: Cambridge University Press, 1998.

Mazyar Lotfalian

NAMES, ISLAMIC *See* Genealogy

NAR

Nar (from *al-nar*, Ar. "the fire") is the common designation for hell in Islam—a blazing abode where God punishes unbelievers and wrongdoers. Muslims use *nar* synonymously with *jahannam*, and they juxtapose both terms to *janna* ("garden"), the blissful home of the righteous in the hereafter. The idea of a place of punishment and suffering in the afterlife is found in many religions, but the Islamic concept is actually an outgrowth of centuries of religious reflection about the afterlife rooted in the cultures of the ancient Near East, rabbinic Judaism, early Christianity, and Zoroastrianism. Early Arabian poetic imagery contributed to its assimilation into Islamic eschatological discourse. *Nar* is also the element from which Satan was fashioned, in juxtaposition to God's light (*nur*), and the clay used in Adam's creation (Q. 38:76–77).

According to Islamic eschatological doctrine, *al-nar* is not just a natural element, but also a real place where humans experience horrendous bodily torments at the hands of angels and demonic creatures. In the Qur'an, it is described as an evil "home" or "dwelling," where wrongdoers don garments of fire, drink boiling water, eat the fruit of an infernal tree, and are dragged about by iron hooks (37:62–68, 22:19–21). This imagery complements Qur'anic discourses about the bliss of the righteous in paradise, and it was elaborated with gruesome detail in the hadith, theological tracts, and visionary literature during the Middle Ages. Abu Hamid al-Ghazali (d. 1111) wrote that in hell the damned "are thrust down upon their faces, chained and fettered, with hellfire (*nar*) above them, hellfire beneath them, hellfire on their right and hellfire on their left so that they drown in a sea of fire" (al-Ghazali, *The Remembrance of Death and the Afterlife*, p. 221). Hell was also conceived as a hierarchy of seven levels, each assigned a different name derived from the Qur'an (for example, "abyss," "blaze," and "furnace"), to which different classes of unbelievers and wrongdoers will be consigned in the afterlife. The angel Malik and his deputies, the Zabaniyya, will help administer their punishments. In some accounts, hell was portrayed as a monstrous creature with thousands of heads and mouths. Theologians debated whether the damned would suffer there for eternity, but many invoked the Qur'an (11:107, 78:23) in favor of the opinion that its torments were purgatorial, and that eventually many would be admitted to paradise.

Pious Muslims have invoked hell to promote mindfulness of God and the life of the hereafter, against the distractions of mundane existence. Sufis, however, taught that both the fear of hell and desire for paradise were distractions for wayfarers seeking intimate union with God. Some, like Jalaluddin Rumi (d. 1273), used hellfire as a metaphor for the evil inclinations of the self that can only be quelled by divine light or the water of mercy that flows from the virtuous heart. Others equated it to the burning passion of the lover that leads to annihilation of the self in God the beloved, or to the torment experienced in separation from God. Since the twentieth century, Muslim modernists have posited that both hell and paradise are psychological or spiritual states of being rather than actual places in the hereafter. Today, however, traditional understandings continue to have a compelling influence on Muslim beliefs and practices, often with politicized overtones. The Jama'at-e Islami of Bangladesh, for example, has threatened that Muslim women who fail to support this radical organization will be condemned to hell.

See also **Death; Ghazali, al-; Jahannam; Janna; Muhammad; Qur'an; Tafsir.**

BIBILIOGRAPHY

Ghazali, Abu Hamid al-. *The Remembrance of Death and the Afterlife (Kitab dhikr al-mawt wa-ma ba'dahu): Book XL of the Revival of the Religious Sciences (Ihya' 'ulum al-din).* Translated by T. J. Winter. Cambridge, U.K.: Islamic Texts Society, 1995.

Smith, Jane Idleman, and Yazbeck Haddad, Yvonne. *The Islamic Understanding of Death and Resurrection.* Albany: State University of New York Press, 1981.

Juan E. Campo

NASA'I, AL- (830–915)

Al-Nasa'i, Abu 'Abd al-Rahman Ahmad b. 'Ali b. Shu'ayb, a compiler of one of the six authoritative Sunni hadith collections, lived between 830 and 915. Unfortunately, very little is known of his early life, but like the other compilers, he was known to have traveled extensively "in search of knowledge" (Ar. *talab al-'ilm*) in order to hear traditions from the prominent traditionists of his time. He settled for a while in Egypt and then later made his way to Damascus, where he was reportedly ill-treated on account of his pro-'Alid and anti-Umayyad sentiments. Some sources suggest that the venue was instead Ramla, in Palestine. Because of his untimely death, he has been regarded as a martyr. His collection, *Kitab al-Sunan*, contains over five thousand hadiths. Unlike the other five collections, al-Nasa'i's *Sunan* does not include a chapter on the excellences of the Qur'an (Ar. *fada'il al-Qur'an*), although he composed an independent treatise on the topic. Also lacking in his *Sunan* are eschatological traditions. Al-Nasa'i is credited with nine other works, among which are a compilation of hadiths on the virtues of 'Ali and a *rijal* work that assessed the reliability of various hadith transmitters.

See also **Hadith.**

Asma Asfaruddin

NASSER, JAMAL *See* 'Abd al-Nasser, Jamal

NATIONALISM

ARAB
Nancy L. Stockdale

IRANIAN
Fakhreddin Azimi

TURKISH
A. Uner Turgay

ARAB

Ideals of Arab nationalism were extremely influential in the Middle East in the twentieth century. Emerging from nineteenth-century debates about the role of Islam in the modern world and crystallized by anti-imperialist movements after the First World War, Arab nationalists shaped the political ideologies of newly independent nations as they struggled to forge a postcolonial identity for the Middle East.

Pan-Islamic thinkers such as Jamal al-Din al-Afghani (1839–1897) and Muhammad 'Abduh (1849–1905) were early inspirations for the emergent Arab nationalist ideology. Al-Afghani despaired at the increased dominance of European empires in the Muslim world, but believed that Islamic governments could counteract Western influence if it was stripped of corruption and instilled with the values of Muslim unity, using the early caliphate as a model of success. 'Abduh, al-Afghani's most famous student, furthered his mentor's ideas with his book *Risalah al-tawhid* (A treatise on the oneness of God), asserting the compatibility of Islam with the modern world. By founding the *Salifiyya* movement and reopening the doors of *ijtihad*, 'Abduh challenged Muslims to stand up to their governments if they believed the values of Islam were being crushed. At the same time, modern technologies and Western-style reforms were acceptable if interpreted as benefiting Muslim society.

These pan-Islamic thinkers inspired others to think in more local terms. 'Abd al-Rahman al-Kawakibi (1854–1902), the author of *The Nature of Despotism* and *The Mother of Cities, Mecca*, was a Syrian journalist and student of 'Abduh who believed that the decline of the Middle East to the West was due to the Ottoman Empire and the fact that non-Arabs had taken control of the region. Because Islam was reveled to the Arabs in the Arabic language, al-Kawakibi saw the Middle East as being at its zenith when Arabs ruled. He promoted the idea that Arab leadership was perfect and argued that, if it were to be restored, the region would revive morally and politically. This became the basis of several independence movements, especially after the collapse of the Ottoman Empire at the end of the First World War.

Faced with the end of Turkish rule but the continuance of French and British rule in the Arab world, many Arab thinkers formulated programs for nationalist liberation based on ethnic identity. One of the most important was the Syrian Sati' al-Husri (1880–1968). Al-Husri wrote three influential tracts: *Arabism First, On Arab Nationalism*, and *What is Nationalism?* These pamphlets asked all Arabs—both Muslim and Christian—to unite under one state, privileging shared language and culture as the bond between them all. Al-Husri hoped that by focusing on the great past of the Arab world rather than only Islam, Christian and Muslim Arabs would join together to fight against foreign imperialism.

Fellow Syrians Michel 'Aflaq (1912–1989) and Salah al-Din al-Bitar (1911–1980) followed al-Husri's lead by merging socialist anti-imperialist thought with pan-Arabist ideals. Founders of the Ba'th ("resurrection") movement in the 1940s, 'Aflaq and al-Bitar drew on the past of the Arabs as leaders of the Islamic world and called for a revival of unity to overthrow foreign oppression and implement social justice. Two major events concurrent with the establishment of the Ba'th movement—the creation of Israel and the subsequent displacement of hundreds of thousands of Palestinians, and the emergence of a fully independent Egypt in the 1950s—catapulted the ideals of Arab nationalism into political reality.

Devastated by the losses of the Arab forces to Israel and the massive crisis of Palestinian refugees, members of the Arab League (founded in 1945) looked to Egypt to lead the Arab world to greatness. With the successful 1952 revolution against the monarchy led by Jamal 'Abd al-Nasser (1918–1970), Egypt did become the center of Arab nationalist rhetoric and action. Nasser's leadership in the nonalignment movement against the Baghdad Pact of 1954 and his successful nationalization of the Suez Canal in 1956 made the world take notice of the ideals of Arab strength and national unity. In the 1960s, the Ba'th movement came to power and ruled in Syria and Iraq through Revolutionary Command Councils.

However, the failed union between Egypt and Syria as the United Arab Republic (1958–1961), the humiliating defeat of the Arab armies against the Israelis in the war of 1967, and the split between the Ba'th regimes in Syria and Iraq underscored the real difficulties of creating a gigantic Arab super-state. Although leaders in the 1970s and 1980s tried to rally their populations behind Arab nationalist rhetoric, the Gulf War of 1991, which pitted Arab nations against each other, destroyed the dreams of Arab nationalists. This left the people of the Arab world searching for viable alternatives to the ideals that had seemed so promising earlier in the century.

See also **'Abd al-Nasser, Jamal; 'Abd al-Rahman Kawakibi; 'Abduh, Muhammad; Afghani, Jamal al-Din; Arab League; Ba'th Party; Nationalism: Iranian; Nationalism: Turkish; Pan-Arabism; Pan-Islam; Reform: Arab Middle East and North Africa.**

BIBLIOGRAPHY

Cleveland, William L. *A History of the Modern Middle East.* Boulder, Colo.: Westview Press, 1994.

Khalidi, Rashid; Anderson, Lisa; and Simon, Reeva, eds. *The Origins of Arab Nationalism.* New York: Columbia University Press, 1993.

Nancy L. Stockdale

IRANIAN

Despite the existence of various forms of primordial loyalties, a persistent sense of national consciousness or cultural distinctness was by no means absent from premodern Iran. It was sustained by a shared cultural heritage, and above all by the Persian language. From the sixteenth century it was reinforced by Shi'ism. In the nineteenth century, Iran became an arena of rivalry between imperial Russia and the British Empire and lost territory, particularly to the Russians, in two humiliating wars. The ruling Qajar dynasty tried to maintain the county's precarious independence by exploiting Anglo-Russian rivalry. The growing influence and presence of Europeans in the country created resentment, while European ideas enabled the Iranian intelligentsia to articulate their diagnosis of the country's ills in nationalist terms. They came to view meaningful national self-determination as the prerequisite of national regeneration. The burgeoning nationalism manifested itself in the Constitutional Revolution from 1905 to 1911, which signaled a crucial stage in the transformation of the country into a nation-state and sought to create a modern state structure and establish institutions that embodied the will and sovereignty of the nation.

Following the coup of 1921, which eventually established the Pahlevi dynasty, nationalism became the guiding ideology of the centralizing state and grew as a result its educational and other modernizing policies. Manifestations of the prevailing nationalism ranged from the architecture of state buildings to the attempted purification of the Persian language. In the vein of its nineteenth-century predecessors, the nationalism of the era of Reza Shah Pahlevi invoked the pre-Islamic period of Iranian history as the locus of an authentic Iranian national identity and pride.

The outbreak of the Second World War and the Allied occupation of Iran in 1941 again underlined national vulnerability and enhanced foreign influence. Toward the end of the war, Iranian resistance to the Soviet demand for an oil concession in northern Iran resulted in the refusal of the Soviet government to withdraw its forces from the country and its encouragement of autonomy movements in Iranian Azarbaijan and Kurdistan. Iranian efforts and international pressure eventually resulted in the Soviet evacuation and the collapse of the autonomy movements.

Public attention then turned to the British oil concession in Iran and the preponderant position of the Anglo-Iranian Oil Company (AIOC). The failure of negotiations to extract from the company a greater share of the oil revenues for Iran strengthened a nationalist movement, led by the veteran parliamentarian Mohammad Mosaddeq, who had spearheaded the Iranian refusal to grant an oil concession to the Soviets. The movement resulted in the nationalization of the AIOC and the premiership of Mosaddeq. Mosaddeq pursued an anti-imperialist, civic nationalism that embraced liberal democratic values and was inclusive of all Iranians, regardless of ethnicity, language, or religion. He saw the nationalization of the oil industry as a legitimate move that expressed and strengthened Iranian national sovereignty, facilitated popular self-determination, and provided the needed resources for national regeneration and modernization.

The overthrow of Mosaddeq's government through the Anglo-American sponsored coup of August 1953 dealt a severe blow to Iranian civic nationalism. Iran abandoned her neutralism and, in 1955, formally joined a pro-Western alliance. Seeking to refute the charges of dependence on Anglo-American support, the shah, Muhammad Reza Pahlevi, advocated "positive" nationalism, in contrast to what he characterized as the "negative" nationalism of Mosaddeq. However, in 1964 the issue of granting immunities to the American forces stationed in Iran was seen by the opponents of the regime as a clear affront to Iranian national dignity and sovereignty.

Like his father, Muhammad Reza Shah promoted a cultural nationalism that tended to glorify Iran's pre-Islamic past. A notable instance of this was the replacement, in March 1976, of the Islamic calendar by an imperial one. This and similar measures antagonized the religious establishment and the pious middle classes, contributing to the revolution of 1978 and 1979 and the overthrow of the monarchy.

Following the revolution, despite the declared ecumenical objectives of the emerging Islamic regime, nationalism continued to be a major force in Iran's social, political, and cultural life, as well as its foreign policy. The Iran-Iraq war of 1980 to 1988 saw the rekindling of strong nationalist sentiments, and the regime was gradually forced to come to terms with or even embrace the Iranian cultural nationalism that it had tried to suppress. Similarly, civic nationalist aspirations for popular sovereignty, political equality, and meaningful citizenship continued to grow.

See also **Iran, Islamic Republic of; Mosaddeq, Mohammad; Muhammad Reza Shah Pahlevi; Nationalism: Arab; Nationalism: Turkish; Revolution: Islamic Revolution in Iran.**

BIBLIOGRAPHY

Cottam, Richard. *Nationalism in Iran; Updated through 1978.* Pittsburgh, Penn.: University of Pittsburgh, 1979.

Kashani-Sabet, Firoozeh. *Frontier Fictions: Shaping the Iranian Nation, 1884–1946.* Princeton, N. J.: Princeton University Press, 1999.

Vaziri, Mostafa, *Iran as Imagined Nation: The Construction of National Identity.* New York: Paragon House, 1993.

Fakhreddin Azimi

TURKISH

During the nineteenth and early twentieth centuries the multiethnic, multireligious Ottoman Empire was transformed into a collection of nation-states in the Balkans and the Middle East. This was the result of social and economic developments and cultural changes brought about by internal and external forces at work in the empire. Although the reforms of the Tanzimat era (1839–1876) streamlined the empire's administrative and financial institutions and established new ones, it also inadvertently helped advance ethnic awareness.

The policies of Ottomanism pursued during the 1870s and 1880s, with the concept of citizenship replacing an individual's status as subject of the sultan, were unable to retain the loyalty of the various ethnic groups in the European provinces of the empire. After the loss of most of the Balkan territories and increasing European political and financial control of the Ottoman government's affairs, Sultan 'Abd al-Hamid II's (1876–1909) policies were affected accordingly. With the influx of Muslims into the empire, mostly from the Caucasus, and the influence of Muslim intellectuals both at home and abroad, pan-Islam replaced Ottomanism. Islam became the social and political basis of the empire, and the Sultan emphasized his role as caliph, identifying with the anti-imperialist tendencies of Islam.

The Young Turk Revolution of 1908 brought about fundamental changes. The Union and Progress Party, in charge of the newly established parliament and controlled by the Young Turks, pursued secular and—in some important areas, such as education—pro-Turkish policies. The Arab Revolt in 1916 against the Istanbul government during the First World War clearly directed the course of nationalism in the Middle East. The nationalist movements of non-Turkish Muslims, Albanians, and Arabs gave impetus to Turkish nationalism. They influenced the emergence of a Turkish nationalism with secular tendencies, which received intellectual nourishment from its chief ideologue, Ziya Gokalp (1876–1924). Gokalp took a deep interest in the history of the ancient Turks and argued that the basis of nationality was culture (*hars*). This included all feelings, judgments, and ideals, as distinct from civilization (*medeniyet*) which encompassed rational and scientific knowledge and technology. Through his poems and essays, Gokalp sought a national revival of Turkish history and language. This, along with his search for new values, led to his movement of Turkism (*Turkculuk*). Thus, he in effect underwrote the ideals of Turkish nationalism.

During the War of Independence (1919–1922), the National Pact (1919), with its territorial definitions and populist expressions, set the agenda for the formation in 1923 of the Republic of Turkey. The first two decades of the Turkish Republic were a period of political and cultural consolidation under its first president, Mustafa Kemal (Ataturk). The government relied heavily on Turkey's past to bolster national pride and integration. Kemal blamed the religious leaders for opposing the spirit of Islam, and effectively reinterpreted religion and its role in the society according to nationalist ideas. Being aware of the symbolic powers of organized institutions, the government methodically disestablished the then-existing political, legal, and educational institutions of Islam, replacing them with adaptations of Western models. Turkish nationalism substituted itself for all loyalties and values earlier expressed through religion, and thus became the ideology of the Republic.

See also **Ataturk, Mustafa Kemal; Balkans, Islam in the; Empires: Ottoman; Nur Movement; Nursi, Said; Pan-Islam; Young Ottomans; Young Turks.**

BIBLIOGRAPHY

Lewis, Bernard. *The Emergence of Modern Turkey.* 2d ed. London: Oxford University Press, 1968.

Zurcher, Erik J. *Turkey, A Modern History.* London and New York: I. B. Tauris, 1993.

A. Uner Turgay

NATION OF ISLAM

The Nation of Islam in concept was founded in the teachings of Master Fard Muhammad in 1930 with the lectures of this urban trader to the "so-called Negro" community in Detroit, Michigan. At the center of these lectures was the teaching that a large number of Africans enslaved in the Americas were Muslims and that Islam was the "true religion" of these people. With knowledge of their Islamic heritage, clean living, and a demand for freedom, justice, and equality, these Muslims would regain their humanity that had been lost in slavery. In practice, the Nation of Islam was cemented as a religious community under the leadership and guidance of the Honorable Elijah Muhammad by 1934.

Members of the Nation of Islam believe in "the One God whose proper name is Allah, in the Holy Qur'an and in the Scriptures of all the Prophets of God," according to Elijah Muhammad (*Message of the Blackman*, 1965). Initially there was a belief in a mental resurrection of the dead to which has been added the Islamic belief in the Day of Judgment. Concurrent with these beliefs the leadership aims at the reformation of the character of the African-American community. As with all Muslims, members refrain from drinking alcohol, gambling, and eating pork. Additionally, they avoid narcotics, cigarettes, slang, and profanity and use language that encourages courtesy and good manners.

Malcolm X was a member of the Nation of Islam from 1952 until his ouster in 1964. Malcolm X was known as a charismatic national spokesman for the Nation of Islam. His unauthorized comments on the assassination of President John F. Kennedy precipitated his ouster. Pilgrimage to Mecca, Saudi Arabia, inspired him to permanently leave the Nation of Islam to become an orthodox Sunni Muslim. Warith Deen Muhammad inherited the leadership of the Nation of Islam upon the death of his father, the Honorable Elijah Muhammad, in 1975. He moved the majority of the community from a black nationalist philosophy into orthodox Sunni Islam. Since that time he has become a well-respected leader in American Islam. In the 1990s Louis Farrakhan led the Nation of Islam toward stricter observance of Islamic rituals and practice. In the twenty-first century this development complements a continuing focus on the plight of African Americans.

See also **Farrakhan, Louis; Malcolm X; Muhammad, Elijah; Muhammad, Warith Deen; United States, Islam in the.**

BIBLIOGRAPHY

Muhammad, Elijah. *The Message to the Blackman*. Chicago: Muhammad's Temple No. 2, 1965.

Muhammad, Elijah. *How to Eat to Live*. Chicago: Muhammad's Temple No. 2, 1972.

Essien-Udom, E. U. *Black Nationalism*. Chicago: University of Chicago Press, 1962.

Aminah Beverly McCloud

NAWRUZ

Nawruz, literally "new day," is the Iranian holiday that celebrates the beginning of spring. Nawruz was observed in Zoroastrian Persia and has long been celebrated in areas influenced by Persian culture. Nawruz begins at the vernal equinox on the first day of Farvardin, the first month of the Iranian solar calendar, and lasts thirteen days. Renewal of home and of social ties are evident in the housecleaning that precedes Nawruz and in the visits paid to relatives and friends, in order of seniority, throughout the holiday. People wear new clothes at Nawruz, and children receive presents of money.

Central to the Nawruz celebration in Iran is the *sofreh-e haft sin*, or "cloth of the seven *s*'s"—a decorative arrangement of seven objects whose names in Persian begin with the letter *s*. These are usually sumac (*somaq*), hyacinth (*sonbol*), garlic (*sir*), vinegar (*serkeh*), apple (*sib*), sorb tree berry (*senjed*), and sprouted wheat or other greens (*sabzi*), all of which are displayed together with a mirror, candles, colored eggs, a goldfish in a bowl, and the holy book of the family that is celebrating the holiday.

Nawruz is a national Iranian holiday, celebrated by members of all religious groups, and a marker of ethnic identity among groups associated with Persian culture outside Iran. Nawruz ends with a picnic (*sizdah beh dar*—"thirteenth outside"), at which each family's *sabzi* is tossed away, preferably into running water, to take with it any lingering unhappiness of the past year.

See also **'Ibadat; Ritual; Vernacular Islam.**

BIBLIOGRAPHY

Attar, Ali. "Nawruz in Tajikistan: Ritual or Politics?" In *Post-Soviet Central Asia*. Edited by Touraj Atabaki and John O'Kane. London: Tauris Academic Studies, 1998.

Boyce, Mary. "Iranian Festivals." In *Cambridge History of Iran*. Edited by Ehsan Yarshater. Cambridge: Cambridge University Press, 1983.

Anne H. Betteridge

NAZZAM, AL- (782–C. 840)

Abu Ishaq Ibrahim b. Sayyar al-Nazzam was an early Mu'tazilite thinker. He was born in 782 c.e. and grew up in Basra, was trained by his maternal uncle Abu 'l-Hudhayl al-'Allaf, and took part in scholarly debates there in his early youth. He moved to Baghdad in the early 820s, where he received the support of the Abbasid caliphs until his death sometime between 835 and 845. He taught many Mu'tazilite scholars of the ninth century, among whom was his follower al-Jahiz.

In addition to his skills as a poet, Nazzam was interested in Greek philosophy and ancient Iranian culture. Though he had various discussions with Muslim scholars, most of his work was directed against Christians, Jews, dualists, and naturalists. He wrote many books (estimated at thirty-nine), all of which are lost with the exception of some fragments, mostly relating to scientific or philosophical issues, including a refutation of Aristotelian logic.

Nazzam disagreed with Abu 'l-Hudayl's atomist theory of physics by rejecting the existence of isolated particles within the created bodies, and their change through accidents. Changes occur in bodies, according to Nazzam, with the appearance of hidden (*kumun*) interior components by a leap of motions (*tafra*). Acting bodies are subjected to infinite divisions by their created nature (*khilqa*), though not all motions are perceptible. Nazzam did not focus on the attributes of God in his theological system. Regarding the protection of Qur'anic revelation, he developed the theory of its being prevented (*sarfa*) from challenges of unbelievers by God rather than earlier theories about the linguistic impossibility (*i'jaz*) of its being imitated. He also recommended a critical approach toward the acceptance of transmitted reports and traditions (*akhbar*). The original views of Nazzam gained support and elicited reactions both inside and outside of his school. Thus, he created an intellectual liveliness in the Muslim scholarship of that era.

See also **Kalam; Mu'tazilites; Mu'tazila.**

BIBLIOGRAPHY

Dhanani, Alnoor. *The Physical Theory of Kalam: Atoms, Space, and Void in Basrian Mu'tazili Theology*. Leiden: E. J. Brill, 1994.

Ess, Josef van. *Theology and Science: The Case of Abu Ishaq al-Nazzam*. Ann Arbor: The University of Michigan, 1978.

Frank, Richard M. *Being and Their Attributes: The Teachings of Basrian School of the Muʻtazila in the Classical Period.* Albany: State University of New York Press, 1978.

M. Sait Özervarli

NETWORKS, MUSLIM

Muslim networks, like all networks, are decentralized circuits of communication and exchange that depend on mutual trust and reciprocal need. Muslim networks are very old, dating back to the seventh century. They embrace the pre-Muslim networks of pagan Arabia, trading networks that linked a merchant named Muhammad to the citied world of Mesopotamia and beyond.

Early History

Trading networks include travel in search of knowledge, pilgrimage on behalf of faith, and proselytizing networks to spread the faith. The fourteenth-century network of the famous traveler Ibn Battuta reveals a vast Islamic world that extended from the Mediterranean Sea to the Malay Peninsula. It included Muslim polities and communities set within large clusters of non-Muslim cultures and populations, each linked to one another through port cities upon which they depended for sea trade and the transportation of both people and goods. The annual pilgrimage, or hajj, presupposed overland and sea connections to the Hijaz region on the Red Sea in western Arabia, even as pilgrimage, in turn, expanded and reinforced these same networks.

Proselytizing often occurred through Sufi orders, organized male brotherhoods that traced their roots back to the period of the prophet Muhammad and expressed Islamic loyalty through devotion to saintly persons and pursuit of inner purity. The role of Sufi orders was as inextricable from local politics as it was from transregional commerce, and nowhere is that role more evident than in the expansion of Islam from South Asia to Southeast Asia through Indian Ocean networks of trade, travel, and proselytization.

The Case of Acheh

Acheh, a port city situated at the northern tip of Sumatra astride the Strait of Malacca, exemplifies the ways in which major nodes in the various networks of the early Muslim empires worked. Acheh was the first area of modern-day Indonesia in which a Muslim kingdom was established. Marco Polo observed a Muslim king on the north coast of Sumatra in 1292, over a half-century before the oceanic voyage of Ibn Battuta landed him further to the south on the same island.

Ibn Battuta had traveled throughout the Muslim world from port cities in the Mediterranean to Arabia to India before finally arriving at Acheh in the Malay Peninsula. He found the sultan of Acheh to be an orthodox Muslim who

presided over a vast system of constant exchange and negotiation. The sultan was a Muslim networker par excellence. The wealth of his tiny court depended on tribute levied from neighboring regions, but also from the ships that used the harbor at Acheh. Later, in the sixteenth century, the sultan of Acheh fought, with initial success, against the invading Portuguese, who were using the Indian Ocean to establish their own trading network. However, he was never able to consolidate his own regional power beyond Acheh, due in part to the emergence of other like-minded Muslim sultanates in neighboring port-city states that were strewn along the vast Malay archipelago.

Later sultans of Acheh were able to benefit from expanded networks that linked them to powerful overseas Muslim allies, both in India (the Moguls) and Turkey (the Ottomans). Because he served as the common overlord of others, the prince carried the title of sultan. This was so even though the sultans never subdued the interior of the island, and even though Acheh itself was divided into many smaller districts, each governed by hereditary chiefs.

The office of sultan marks both the power and limits of Muslim networks. Its persistence from India to Indonesia demonstrates the cultural diffusion of a major Islamic political institution. Even the seal of the sultan of Acheh was ninefold, paralleling that of the Mogul emperors, and like his Mogul counterpart, the sultan of Acheh claimed to be the shadow of God on Earth. Yet the two seals applied to very different polities. While the shadow of God on earth projected the great Mogul as the semi-divine lord of a vast realm, the sultan of Acheh ruled a domain no bigger than Goa, the Portugese enclave of western India. At the same time, the ninefold Mogul seal competed with another local emblem, the fivefold seal used by the hereditary chiefs of Acheh. The latter signified the hand as a symbol of power, and meant the ability not only to project power over others, but also to protect one's own possessions and territory. By retaining both seals, the Achenese sultan sought to proclaim both his Malay and his Mogul identity as equally authoritative, yet he remained a local ruler with aspirations that far exceeded his practical resources and actual options.

The greater force of Indian Ocean networks may have been in the religious rather than the political realm. In the sultanate of Acheh, as in Mogul India, Islamic devotion was often linked to the mediating power of Muslim saints. Just as Muslim traders came to the Malay Peninsula seeking expanded markets, spiritual leaders who were identified with institutional Sufi brotherhoods came with them, but seeking different markets. These Sufi masters exemplified the appeal of the Muhammadan Way, and Islamic loyalty is often identified with them—specifically with the tomb cults that pervade Acheh. While the actual Achenese tombs are less grand than those of their precursors in Mughal India, both reflect the persistent tradition of visiting saintly tombs. And the purpose of such local pilgrimages is functionally similar in India, Indonesia, and throughout the Indian Ocean. Whatever their background or status, pilgrims came to these tombs with gifts and vows, seeking the spiritual favor of saints for material or medical relief.

Two other features of all Muslim networks are evident in the case of Acheh: internal difference and external limits. The relation of formal religious authorities (ulema) to representatives of indigenous traditions was marked by tension, negotiation, and compromise. An oft-repeated dyad pits preconversionary (pre-Muhammad) disbelief (*jahiliyya*) against divinely revealed faith (*iman/Islam*). It evokes a radical experiential break between the old and the new, the impure and the pure, the false and the true. In Southeast Asian Islam the dyad is framed as *adat* (Ar. *'ada*) and *hukum* (Ar. *hukm*), where *adat* refers to all that stands outside juridical Islam, and *hukum* means "laws," or the announced guidelines of Islamic collective life. Yet the distinction is less observed in practice than it is proclaimed in theory. For Achenese Muslims, the two polar extremes of social identity can, and did, merge. Social relations between so-called representatives of *adat*, the hereditary chiefs, and and the champions of *hukum*, the ulema, were more often marked by at least tacit politeness, and often mutual respect. Muslim networks in Acheh, as elsewhere, inscribed difference even when they celebrated transnational solidarity.

Colonial History

From the seventeenth century on a major challenge to Muslim networks came through the imposition of colonial rule. Dutch and Portuguese, then British and French commercial empires not only expanded overseas by oceanic routes, they also incorporated and then transformed the preexisting Muslim networks. As Kenneth McPherson has observed, in his essay "Port Cities as Nodal Points of Change," throughout the Indian Ocean region some ports became centers of European political, economic, and military power, while others declined or vanished. "The great European-controlled ports such as Karachi, Bombay, Madras, Calcutta, Rangoon, Penang, Singapore, and Jakarta grew at the expense of other ports in Gujarat, Bengal, southern India, the Malay Peninsula, and Java, which either declined or refocused their economies to become feeder points for these great ports or enclaves of local maritime activity."

The fate of Acheh was poignant. During the last decades of the nineteenth century, the harbor king, the sultan of Acheh, was able to keep his maritime polity cohesive by subsuming hereditary chiefs under his authority, at the same time as he waged war against the Dutch. When the Dutch finally subdued the Achenese, after more than thirty-five years of warfare, they shifted the reins of political power to Java. A bloody guerilla campaign against Indonesian forces persisted until 1956, when Acheh was recognized as an autonomous province yet made subservient to the Javanese

state. In effect, the Muslim networks of modern-day Indonesia mirror the politically centrist power of the colonial, then postcolonial state. The nodes were not equivalent; but all of the separate provinces, from Acheh to Timor, came to reflect the pre-eminence of Java, and its capital city, Jakarta.

Beyond Southeast Asia, networks of colonization and migration proliferated throughout the Muslim world, from the Indian Ocean to the shores of the Atlantic. Though decentralized, they were marked by the same transregional logic of mutual trust and reciprocal need. A notable example is the new strand of Shi'ite loyalty that emerged during the eighteenth and nineteenth centuries, at the same time as the Mogul and Safavid empires were experiencing internal revolt and foreign invasion. From Karbala and Najaf, shrine cities in the Shi'ite heartland of Iraq, to commercial centers in Iran, to princely courts in northern India, there emerged a Shi'ite network of scholarly and also familial connections. The traffic was two-way, providing material as well as spiritual benefit to all nodes on this extensive transregional circuit. While juridical scholars of Iraq and Iran received large sums from their wealthy Indian coreligionists, the scholars of India benefited from the prestige of their northern neighbors. Each of them found that the pursuit of rational sciences, along with the traditional religious sciences, not only enforced their own sense of academic prominence but also allowed them to engage European science.

Though wary of rational sciences, the Sunni world also expanded its networks of learning, through the travel and exchange of reform-minded scholars. From the Arabian Peninsula, whether the ritual heartland of the Hijaz or the strategic port cities of Yemen, to the east coast of Africa and to the Asian archipelago, Muslim reformers responded to the European colonial incursions by forming their own scholarly networks, committed to reviving and expanding the textual core of Islamic subjects. More than a few of these Sunni networks were motivated by loyalty to institutional Sufism, and to one of the most socially active of Sufi orders, the Naqshbandiyya. They promoted Islamic revitalization at all levels, and they also advocated a double jihad, militarily against European imperialism and intellectually against imitative Westernization.

Muslim Networks in the Information Age

The revolution in communications that marked the late twentieth-century global economy also transformed the nature of Muslim networks. Cassette tapes helped foster the Iranian Revolution. Satellite TV overrides governmental controls on local TV stations to beam alternative Muslim messages, including cleric talk shows, *fatwa* workshops, and a variety of Islamic entertainment to Arabic-speaking audiences. Since 1997, a major alternative to CNN-style global news has been provided through the Gulf based Al-Jazeera. CD-ROMs, too, have become popular, circulating both literary texts and visual artifacts to broad Muslim audiences.

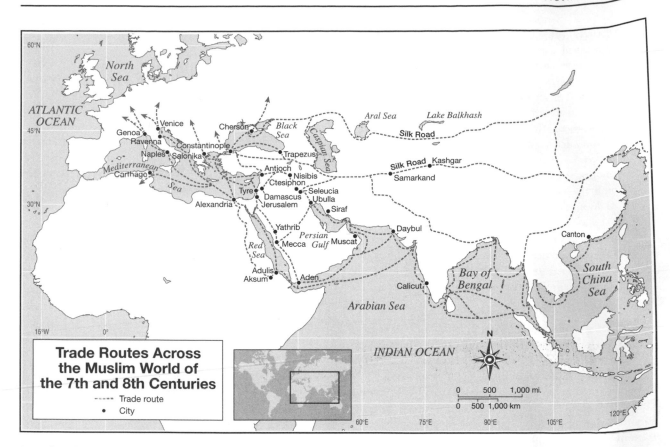

Seventh- and eighth-century trade routes. XNR Productions/Gale

Finally, there is the Internet, which offers many networking options, from chat groups to websites, and, of course, e-mail. All these options for expanded exchange and alternative authorities rely on access and speed but, even more, on the need for new criteria of trust.

These new conditions for the exchange of information have generated new kinds of networks, most notably transnational alliances of women who are working for conflict resolution, human security, and justice at the local and global levels. Since the 1980s, and particularly since the 1985 United Nations conference on women in Nairobi, networks of Muslim women have been fighting for their rights in a newly Islamizing political context where women's rights and roles are highly contested. Some of these women's networks are local, like the ones that have appeared in Pakistan, Sudan, and Algeria; others have a global reach, like the Women Living Under Muslim Laws (WLUML), whose Islamic feminist agenda is to empower women to seek their rights as observant Muslims, and it includes the exchange of information about ways to deal with gender discrimination and also transnational collaboration to reform Muslim Personal Law to make it more friendly to women.

In the current era, as in preceding phases of rapid change, networks remain pivotal yet ambivalent. The war that inaugurated the twenty-first century was the U.S.–led attack on the Taliban in Afghanistan. The administration of President George W. Bush marked terrorism as, above all, Muslim inspired, even while proclaiming that Islam itself was not to blame, just certain Muslims. Many news groups have referred to al-Qa'ida, the guerrilla organization linked to the Saudi dissident Usama bin Ladin and cofounded by the Egyptian doctor Ayman al-Zawahiri, as a terrorist network. It is terrorist because it intends to destroy Western, specifically American, targets wherever it can find them. And it is a network precisely because it is structured around nodes that communicate with one another in nonlinear space, relying on neither a hierarchical chain of command nor conventional rules of engagement. Al-Qa'ida might be best defined as a coalition of dispersed network nodes intent on waging asymmetrical warfare. Like Colombian and Mexican drug cartels, they feature small, nimble, and dispersed units capable of penetrating and disrupting, with the intent to destroy, massive structures. Often they elude pursuit and evade capture, although in the case of al-Qa'ida, its operatives kill themselves, or are killed by others, in each nodal attack on a fixed target or group.

While the case of al-Qa'ida has become compelling in the aftermath of 11 September 2001, there is another case that demonstrates the long-term organizational power of modern-day Islamic networking. The women of Afghanistan became subject of intense scrutiny after the U.S.–led invasion

October 2001. Much media footage was devoted to the oppression of veiled, secluded, and often brutalized Afghan women, yet decades before 11 September 2001 a network of Afghan women had mobilized, and also projected themselves, their history, and their cause, via the Internet. RAWA, or the Revolutionary Association of the Women of Afghanistan, predated the Internet. It was founded in 1977, even before the Soviet invasion, and it worked to defeat the Soviets but also to provide help for Afghan refugees in Pakistan. It was a network of transnational cooperation and multitiered resistance throughout the 1980s and 1990s. Now its pivotal role on behalf of Afghan women has been dramatized through its website at www.rawa.org, where RAWA advocates strive to maintain a distance both from the Taliban and their would-be successors, the Northern Alliance. RAWA, even more than al-Qaʿida, demonstrates not just the persistence but the resilience of Muslim networks as a major form of social and political organization.

Muslim networks are no longer primarily male-dominated structures. They include women and others who resist oppression and who participate in horizontal alliances that project Muslim values of justice. Above all, they seek to build structures that are at once democratic and capitalist, yet not coeval with Euro-American imperialism. While it is too early to gauge their impact, it is impossible to ignore either their novelty or their determination.

See also **Globalization; Ibn Battuta; Internet; Qaʿida, al-; Travel and Travelers.**

BIBLIOGRAPHY

Abu-Lughod, Janet L. *Before European Hegemony: The World System A.D. 1250–1350.* New York: Oxford University Press, 1991.

Andaya, Barbara Watson, and Andaya, Leonard Y. *A History of Malaysia.* London: Macmillan, 1982.

Arquilla, John, and Ronfeldt, David. "The New Rules of Engagement." *WIRED* (December, 2001): 149–151.

Dunn, Ross E. *The Adventures of Ibn Battuta.* Berkeley: University of California Press, 1989.

McPherson, Kenneth. "Port Cities as Nodal Points of Change: The Indian Ocean, 1890s–1920s." In *Modernity and Culture: From the Mediterranean to the Indian Ocean.* Edited by Leila Taraza Fawaz and C. A. Bayly. New York: Columbia University Press, 2002.

Moghadam, Val M. "Organizing Women: The New Women's Movement in Algeria." *Cultural Dynamics* 13, no. 2 (2001): 131–154

Moghadam, Val M. "Women, the Taleban, and the Politics of Public Space in Afghanistan." *Women's Studies International Forum* 25, no. 1 (2002): 1–13.

Robinson, Francis. "Ottomans-Safavids-Mughals: Shared Knowledge and Connective Systems." *Journal of Islamic Studies* 8, no. 2 (1997): 151–184.

Bruce B. Lawrence
Miriam Cooke

NIKAH

Literally the act of sexual intercourse, *nikah* is the term by which marriage is referred to in the Qurʾan. Islamic law defines *nikah* as a civil contract whose main function is to render sexual relations between a man and woman licit. Any sexual relations outside the *nikah* contract constitute the crime of *zina* (illicit sexual relations) and are subject to punishment. In practice, *nikah* is enacted in a ceremony intertwined with religious symbolism and rituals such as the recitation of *al-Fatiha*, the first verse of the Qurʾan, usually performed by religious functionaries, although Islamic law does not positively prescribe any service.

See also **Marriage.**

BIBLIOGRAPHY

Bousquet, Georges Henry. "La Conception du Nikah selon les Docteurs de la Loi Muslamane." *Revue Algèrienne.* (1948): 63–74.

El Alami, Dawoud. *Marriage Contract in Islamic Law.* London: Graham & Trotman, 1992.

Maghniyyah, Muhammad Jawad. *Marriage According to Five Schools of Islamic Law.* Tehran: Department of Transliteration and Publication, Islamic Culture and Relations Organization, 1997.

Ziba Mir-Hosseini

NIʿMATOLLAHI SUFI ORDER
See **Tasawwuf**

NIYABAT-E ʿAMMA

Niyabat-e ʿamma (Ar., *niyabat al-ʿamma*) is a term most commonly used in Imami jurisprudence to refer to the "general delegation" of religious authorities and to the Imami ulema in the absence of the imam. In early Shiʿism, there was an acceptance that the imams, when present, designated a particular individual (*naʾib*) to perform particular tasks on behalf of the imam. With the imam's absence (*ghayba*), a notion that the scholars (and more specifically the jurists) were delegated (*niyaba*), as a class, to perform certain functions normally reserved for the imam developed in the juristic writings of scholars such as al-Muhaqqiq al-Hilli (d. 1277) and his influential pupil al-ʿAllama al-Hilli (d. 1325). The delegation was eventually extended, through a series of reinterpretations of the imams' words, to refer to a "general delegation" of the scholarly class to take the place of the imam in those areas of the law where his presence is normally essential. The work of 'Ali al-Karaki (d. 1533) and al-Shahid al-Thani (d. 1588) in this area represent the earliest expressions of this doctrine. These areas of law included duties such as the distribution of the religious levies, *zakat* and *khums*, the leading of Friday prayer and, eventually, the waging of the jihad. The "general delegation" theory provided the basis for the more directly political theory of *wilayat al-faqih* (Ar., *velayat-e faqih*) developed by Ayatollah Khomeini in the 1960s and 1970s.

See also **Hilli, 'Allama al-; Hilli, Muhhaqqiq al-; Shi'a: Imami (Twelver); Ulema; Velayat-e Faqih.**

BIBLIOGRAPHY

Arjomand, Saïd Amir. *The Shadow of God and the Hidden Imam.* Albany: State University of New York Press, 1984.

Calder, Norman. "Legitimacy and Accommodation in Safavid Iran: The Juristic Theory of Muhammad Baqir al-Sabzavari." *Iran* 25 (1987): 91–105.

Robert Gleave

NIZAM AL-MULK (C.1018–1092)

Nizam al-Mulk ("good order of the kingdom") is the title by which the Seljuk wazir Hasan b. 'Ali b. Ishaq al-Tusi is most commonly known. Nizam al-Mulk rose to prominence serving Sultan Alp Arslan (1063–1072), and for much of the reign of Sultan Malik Shah (1072–1092) he was ruler in all but name. Nizam al-Mulk was an individual of many talents: administrator, patron, military man, and author, as well as a skilled and occasionally ruthless competitor in court intrigues. An ardent supporter of the Sunni ulema, he constructed and endowed a number of *madrasas* (centers for the study of Islamic law) in Iran and Iraq, which were called Nizamiyyas after him, the most famous being the Nizamiyya in Baghdad, which opened in 1067. His reasons for doing this are not explicitly known, but these institutions certainly contributed to the subsequent intellectual and political revival seen in Sunnism. In the last years of his life, Nizam al-Mulk wrote a model for princes known alternatively as the *Siyasat-nama* or *Siyar al-moluk*. This Persian-language work is noteworthy for its frank discussion of the steps necessary for an absolute ruler to administer his realm, and is sprinkled with references to philosophers and pre-Islamic kings as well as to Islamic concepts. The reforms it urged were never implemented, no doubt due to the deaths of the author and shortly thereafter its immediate intended reader, Malik Shah. Nizam al-Mulk's assassination in 1092 was linked by contemporaries (and near-contemporaries) to either the Assassins, the sultan Malik Shah, or both.

See also **Assassins; Education; Madrasa.**

BIBLIOGRAPHY

Nizam al-Mulk. *The Book of Government or Rules for Kings: The Siyasat-nama or Siyar al-Muluk of Nizam al-Mulk.* Translated by Hubert Darke. London: Routledge and Kegan Paul, 1960.

Warren C. Schultz

NIZARI

The Nizari, or more properly the Nizari Isma'ili Muslims, like other Shi'i communities, acknowledge 'Ali as imam after the Prophet. The Nizari Isma'ilis have continued to give allegiance to imams descended from 'Ali, on the basis of the principle of designation (*nass*) by the imam of the time. As of 2002, His Highness the Aga Khan, Shah Karim al-Husayni, is the forty-ninth hereditary imam.

Following the decline of the Fatimid Isma'ili dynasty and the death of Imam al-Mustansir Billah in 1094, one group of Isma'ilis continued to give allegiance to the previously designated imam, al-Nizar (hence their name), and moved their headquarters to Iran and Syria, where they established independent principalities. Though under constant threat, their centers flourished under the imams as important places of learning, international trade, and diplomacy for almost two hundred years, before being destroyed during the Mongol invasion of the thirteenth century.

Faced by new challenges of reorganization, often in the face of hostile opposition, the Nizaris gained control of several strategically located mountain centers in Iran and Syria led, respectively, by Hasan-e-Sabbah and Rashid al-din Sinan, two leading *da'is* (representatives of the imam) of the time. These provided defensible centers from where to organize a decentralized and scattered community. They were continually attacked by successive Seljuk rulers but were able to offer a strong defense from their inaccessible castles. One legend that labeled them "assassins," which was developed by their enemies and embellished by Marco Polo, became current in popular writings. However, modern scholarship has shown these stories to be largely fabrications that owed more to religious bigotry, prejudice, and sheer invention than historical reality.

During the next five centuries after the destruction of the centers in Iran in 1258, the Nizaris, though scattered and often persecuted, sustained their religious, intellectual, and community traditions in Iran, Syria, Central Asia, and the Indian subcontinent. They maintained contacts with the imam of the time living in Iran, and they further developed the Isma'ili intellectual heritage in Arabic, Persian, and the vernacular Central Asian and Indian languages that has survived in written as well as oral forms.

In the nineteenth century, the Nizari Isma'ili imamat moved from Iran to India and then to Europe. Many followers migrated in the later part of the twentieth century to Africa, Europe, America, and Canada, where they have also been joined by a small number of Nizari Isma'ilis migrating from Afghanistan, Iran, and Syria. In the early twenty-first century, this community of diverse backgrounds is found in all five continents and some thirty countries.

The imamat (office of the imam) and the heritage of Islam, as expressed within Nizari Isma'ili Shi'ism, continues to be at the heart of the modern emergence of the community. It is guided in the respective national contexts by constitutions that bring a common pattern of practice and governance, and a strong ethos of voluntarism and development in social, educational, and economic spheres. Spiritual and devotional life is maintained in the Jamaatkhana, spaces of gathering, in each major place of Isma'ili settlement, which in some cases are buildings of outstanding Muslim design and architecture.

See also **Aga Khan; Khojas; Shi'a: Isma'ili.**

BIBLIOGRAPHY

Azim, Nanji. *The Nizari Ismaili Tradition in the Indo-Pakistan Subcontinent.* New York: Caravan Books, 1978.

Jamal, Nadia Eboo. *Surviving the Mongols: Nizari Quhistani and the Continuity of Ismaili Tradition in Persia.* London: I. B. Tauris, 2002.

Azim Nanji

NURCU *See* **Nur Movement**

NUR MOVEMENT

The Nur Movement (Nurçuluk) is a Turkish Islamic movement inspired by a modern reinterpretetion of the Qur'an in the volumes *Risale-i Nur* (Epistle of light). The *risale*s (epistles) of the leader of the movement, Bediuzzaman Said Nursi (1876–1960), were first published in 1926. The Nur is not a sect but a social movement mainly because it does not have a formal structure and procedures for membership. Like a school, Nur has students. The followers of Nur constitute an Islamic community movement that can be seen as a set of effective personal networks.

The primary goal of the movement is to revitalize faith under the conditions of modernization. The movement aspires to reconcile several apparent contradictions such as those between modernity and tradition, religion and rationality, faith and science, belief and doubt, and the West and Islam. This middle ground positioning of the movement manifests itself in its vision of the ideal society, one that is a moral yet educated and scientifically competitive collectivity. The message is disseminated by its followers through an increasing use of modern technologies of mass communication. However, adherents of the Nur movement are selective in their openness to modernity. The movement is also a critique of several characteristics of modernity. Nursi's teachings challenge individualism. As Serif Mardin points out, Said Nursi's primary aim was always to "repersonalize Turkish society through the personalized stamp of the *Risale-i Nur*" (p. 12). This was an attempt to preserve strong communal ties against the individualistic tendencies of modernization.

The movement has been largely a product of the tension between Islamization and secularization, which originated in the late nineteenth century when the Young Ottomans tried to reconcile Islam and Western constitutionalism during the late Ottoman period. Said Nursi suggested compromises in order to deal with this tension under the rule of the Ottoman Empire. He challenged the division of education into three separate streams: *medrese* (Ar., *madrasa*, religious school), *tekke* (Sufi hospice), and secular education. His suggestion was the reintroduction of religious studies to secular schools. His aim was to incorporate competent ulema into the *tekke*. After the fall of the empire, Said Nursi visited the new parliament in Ankara once in 1922. Being frustrated by the cold reception and tension, he withdrew from politics for good. After the consolidation of the secular Turkish Republic in 1923, the tension between secularizing and Islamizing forces never ceased. Aiming at a radical break from the Ottoman Empire, the founding father, Ataturk, initiated a series of secularizing reforms that relegated Islam to the private sphere and de-Islamized the public sphere, (for example, the ban of the fez and veil). When the sects were banned in 1926, the Nur movement continued to expand rapidly and soon after was seen as a threat to the secular state. The pendulum swung from repression to tolerance for Islam, when a multiparty system was inititated in the 1950s.

The Nur movement remained suspicious of politics. Some followers became close to certain parties and state bureaucrats. The movement was known for its sympathy for and strong ties to the Democrat Party in the 1950s. Later, some Nur followers were associated with Necmeddin Erbakan and his religious party, National Salvation (1973–1981). However, the strong faith and national feelings mobilized by the movement did not become a part of a separate political party.

In the late 1970s and early 1980s, the political disagreements and economic differences among the followers of Nur led to fragmentation. The largest and most effective group that emerged out of Nur is the Gulen Community movement, led by Fethullah Guler. Beginning in the early 1990s, it became organized and institutionalized not only in Turkey but also internationally, particularly in the new states of

Central Asia. Although the Gulen movement inherited the nationalist and modernist orientation of Nur, it deviated from its forefathers by the engagements with the secular state, and its expansion to the international realm.

See also **Erbakan, Necmeddin; Nursi, Said; Secularization; Young Ottomans.**

BIBLIOGRAPHY

Mardin, Şerif. *Social Change and Religion in Modern Turkey.* Albany: State University of New York Press, 1989.

Berna Turam

NURI, FAZLALLAH (1843–1909)

Hajj Shaykh Fazlallah b. Mulla ʿAbbas Mazandarani Tehrani, commonly known as Fazlallah Nuri, was born in the village of Nur in Mazandaran. He was a prominent Iranian Shiʿite scholar and the *marjaʿ-e taqlid* (source of emulation) of Tehran at the turn of the twentieth century. He studied in Najaf with Mohammad Hasan Shirazi and reached the rank of *mujtahid* at a young age.

Nuri actively participated in the constitutional revolution of 1905–1906. He played a controversial role in the events of the revolution, first supporting and then turning against constitutional government. Nuri agreed with his opponents on the necessity of the rule of law and restrictions on the tyrannical power of the king. Being cognizant of the dangers of a secular constitution to Islam and the Shiʿite ulema, however, he declared constitutionalism incompatible with Islam. Instead, he advocated the *mashrutah-ye mashruʿah*, that is, a constitution based on the laws of Islam.

Nuri published his argument against constitutional government in several treatises including *Nizam nameh-ye islami* (Islamic constitution), *Tadhkirat al-ghafil wa irshad al-jahil* (A reminder to the negligent and guidance for the ignorant), and *Lawayih* (Letters) in which he argued that *mashrutah* (constitution) was against the precepts of Shiʿite Islam. He became the most outspoken critic of the constitution of 1906–1907 and the most ardent opponent of the constitutionalists. Nuri's agitation against constitutionalist forces brought him into conflict with them, who captured and finally hanged him in Tehran in July 1909.

See also **Reform: Iran; Revolution: Islamic Revolution in Iran.**

BIBLIOGRAPHY

Nuri, Fazlallah. "Two Clerical Tracts on Constitutionalism." In *Authority and Political Culture in Shiʿism*. Edited by Said A. Arjomand. Translated by Hamid Dabashi. Albany: State University of New York Press, 1988.

Mohammad H. Faghfoory

NURSI, SAID (1876–1960)

Said Nursi (also known as Bediuzzaman, or Light of the Times) was born in Bitlis in eastern Turkey. He received his early education at various religious schools in the region, mostly under the direction of the teachers who belonged to the Naqshbandi order (an orthodox Sufi order). In 1907 and 1908 in Istanbul and Salonica, he advocated the establishment of a university in Erzurum where physical sciences would be taught alongside religious topics, and supported the Young Turks's constitutional revolution.

Although he supported Mustafa Kemal (Ataturk) during the Turkish War of Independence (1919–1922), he was arrested in 1925 and exiled to Barla in the province of Isparta for his alleged participation in the Shaikh Said (Ar., Shaykh Saʿid) revolt in eastern Turkey. Here he began writing his *Risale-i Nur* (Epistle of light), the basis for the religious-intellectual movement known as Nurculuk.

Distrusted and opposed for his religious views by the Kemalist state, Said Nursi was arrested, imprisoned, and exiled to various Anatolian cities, although the accusations were never proved. During the elections of the 1950s he supported the newly formed Democratic Party. It was at this time that his major works were published in Latin script. After a brief illness he died in Urfa in southeastern Turkey. Later in the same year his grave was moved to an unknown location in Isparta.

Through his writings Said Nursi argued that religion reflects the social and human environment and that Islam could be interpreted according to the current needs of society. His *Risale-i Nur*, a commentary on the Qurʾan, explains and expounds the "truth" in the Holy Book. There he also argues that materialistic philosophy challenges Islamic ethics and the concepts of social and economic justice.

See also **Nur Movement; Young Ottomans; Young Turks.**

BIBLIOGRAPHY

Mardin, Şerif. *Religion and Social Change in Modern Turkey.* Albany: State University of New York, 1989.

A. Unal Tgay

O

ORGANIZATION OF THE ISLAMIC CONFERENCE

Since the nineteenth century, Muslim thinkers have proposed pan-Islamic ideas of uniting the Islamic community with common political, economic, and social goals. After the creation of modern independent states in the Muslim world, which were primarily governed by secularist, nationalists, and socialist ideologies, King Faysal of Saudi Arabia desired to counteract the trend of secularization by cooperating with other Muslim leaders to create the Organization of Islamic Conference (OIC). The formation of the OIC coincided with the successive military defeats in the Arab-Israeli wars and the loss of holy sites in Jerusalem like the Al-Aqsa Mosque. As a result, leaders of Islamic nations were compelled to meet in Rabat to establish the OIC in May 1971.

According to the OIC charter, the organization seeks to preserve Islamic social and economic values; promote solidarity among member states; increase cooperation in social, economic, cultural, scientific, and political areas; support international peace and security; and advance education, particularly in the fields of science and technology. In recent years the OIC evolved from a sectarian group solely focused on issues related to Muslim nations to an organization involved with global politics and U.N. global security issues, such as the Iraq-Iran war, the Persian Gulf war, the U.N.'s peacekeeping mission in Bosnia-Herzegovina, and the reconstruction of Afghanistan.

See also **Pan-Islam.**

BIBLIOGRAPHY

Ahsan, Abdullah al-. *OIC: The Organization of the Islamic Conference.* Herndon, Va.: International Institute of Islamic Thought, 1988.

Khan, Saad S. *Reasserting International Islam: A Focus on the Organization of the Islamic Conference and Other Islamic Institutions.* Karachi: Oxford University Press, 2001.

Mashet, Abdel Monem al-. *The Organization of the Islamic Conference in a Changing World.* Cairo: Friedrich-Ebert-Stiftung, 1994.

Qamar-ul Huda

ORIENTALISM

Orientalism as a field of scholarship that first emerged in the eighteenth century, when European scholars of the Enlightenment period consciously studied Asian languages and cultures to gain a richer understanding of the Middle Eastern literary and historical environment in which Judaism and, ultimately, Christianity, emerged. Some of the major French, English, and German scholars engaged in this endeavor were Armand-Pierre Caussin de Perceval (1795–1871), Ernest Renan (1823–1892), Edward W. Lane (1801–1876), Franz Bopp (1791–1867), Heinrich L. Fleischer (1801–1888), and Julian Wellhausen (1844–1918). Immediately following World War II, academic interest in Orientalism underwent a transformation, ultimately splitting out into specialized area studies across a variety of disciplines, including philology, literature, economics, political science, sociology, anthropology, gender studies, history, and religious studies. The field of Orientalism was no longer based in any one department or discipline, and this is credited to such illustrious scholars as Phillip Hitti, Gustave von Grunebaum, and Hamilton Gibb, who developed Orientalism curricula and divisions in major universities in the United States.

Edward Said's *Orientalism* (1978) was a powerful critique of the of the field, and its origins. In this volume, Said sought to illustrate how the study of Asian and Islamic cultures was connected to European imperialism and its goal of maintaining power and hegemony over non-Europeans. He argued that the Orient has historically served as a symbolic marker of European superiority and modern cultural identity. For Said, historical Orientalist literature was never interested in Islam as it is viewed and practiced by Muslims. Rather, it was an exercise in self-identity created by means of defining the "other." In other words, Said suggested that Orientalists treated others—in this case, Muslims and Asians—as objects defined not in terms of their own discourses, but solely in terms of standards and definitions imposed on them from outside. Among the influences underlying these definitions was, in Said's view, a long-standing Western concern with presenting Islam as opposed to Christianity.

In exploring the relationship of knowledge, power, and colonialism, Said is in agreement with Jean-Paul Sartre and Franz Fannon that from the time of pre-Crusader rallies, Christian writers were consumed with attacking Islam and the prophet Muhammad in order to earn legitimacy with fellow Christians. Polemical literature against Islam, like John of Damascus, concentrated on how the Prophet falsified revelation, had multiple marriages, had used violence in his lifetime, and experienced self-delusional spiritual visions. The polemical literature created a cycle of hate and promoted Islam as an evil religion with a demonically possessed prophet.

According to Said, Renaissance scholars like John Gagnier (d.1740) and Edward Pocock (c.1650) began translating Islamic sources into European languages not to enhance opportunities for crosscultural dialogue, but rather to assess the value of knowledge production in Islam. Notable scholars like Thomas Carlyle, Immanuel Kant, and Liebnitz viewed Islam as a rational and reasonable religion, but were more interested in pursuing the psychological makeup of the Muslims and learning how they went about constructing and sustaining a religious tradition. Said argued that Orientalists of the Renaissance were driven to understand Muslims only to prove that Islam was a false religion and stood in the way of truth. By targeting the deficiencies of the Prophet and of Islam, Orientalist literature was connected to evangelical purposes, used to create a sense of Christian superiority and to ultimately delegitimize the tradition of "the other": Islam.

For Said, the field of Orientalism is thus the net result of a historical vision of Islam rooted in the Christian European imagination. In the terms of this imagination, Islam could only be viewed as monolithic, scornful of human life, unchanging, uncreative, authoritarian, and intrinsically factitious.

Critics of Edward Said's work often come from the field of Middle Eastern and South Asian studies. They assert that he is unaware of contemporary methodologies and trends in scholarship. For instance, one of the major arguments against Said's *Orientalism* is that current scholars in the field are not involved with any imperialistic agenda; that they are not interested in proving the superiority of the Western culture over non-Western cultures or in enhancing the self-identity of Western culture. According to many of these critics, Said may have contributed to a historical analysis of Orientalist literature, but he is unaware of the astonishingly creative ways in which cultures and religious traditions are explored within current scholarship. They argue that he has erroneously juxtaposed a disturbing past of scholarship with the works of modern scholars, without considering the immense achievements that were accomplished in the field.

"Orientalism" is rarely used in the academy today, except for a few centers and journals that have retained the title. Instead, the field is identified by its component areas of study, such as Middle Eastern Studies, North African Studies, Iranian Studies, or South Asian Studies. In each area study, scholars employ a wide variety of interdisciplinary approaches and methodologies. For example, scholars who are trained in literature find it acceptable to incorporate gender studies, history, comparative studies, and other related forms of knowledge as part of their work. Most recently, theoretical approaches such as post-colonial theory or subaltern studies have played an important role in scholarly research.

See also **Colonialism.**

BIBLIOGRAPHY

Little, Douglas. *American Orientalism: Tthe United States and the Middle East since 1945.* Chapel Hill: University of North Carolina Press, 2002.

Said, Edward. *Orientalism.* New York: Vintage Books, 1978.

Said, Edward. *Culture and Imperialism.* New York: Knopf, 1993.

Waardenberg, Jean-Jacques. *Islam dans le miroir de l'Occident.* Paris: Mouton, 1963.

Qamar-ul Huda

P

PAKISTAN, ISLAMIC REPUBLIC OF

Pakistan secured independence on 14 August 1947 with the breakup of the British Indian Empire into two countries, India and Pakistan. The idea behind the creation of Pakistan was to provide a separate homeland for India's Muslims, who were concentrated in the eastern and western parts of the empire. The new country consisted of two parts, separated from each other by the Indian landmass; these became known as East Pakistan and West Pakistan, respectively. The two wings had different languages, cultures, and social structures. The only binding force between them was Islam and political aspirations to seek independence from Britain and separateness from the Hindu majority in India. Founders of the new states were sanguine about their ability to create common political and economic networks that would further strengthen the idea of Muslim state and nationhood.

Constitutional and democratic processes that could have formed the foundations on which the two wings might base solidarity suffered immediately after the founder of the country, Quaid-i-Azam Muhammad 'Ali Jinnah, died on 11 September 1948. His successors and the Muslim League, the party that he led, failed to pursue of his vision of a liberal, moderate, progressive democratic Pakistan. With repeated failure to develop understanding between East and West Pakistan on the questions of provincial autonomy and representation in the federal legislature and bureaucracy, constitution-making was delayed. It was only after nine years that, in 1956, the first constitution was promulgated. By that time much harm had been done to the tradition of parliamentary democracy, which Pakistan had inherited from the British colonial rule in India.

With the decline of political discipline in the political parties, their shifting alliances, and the failure to hold elections for the national legislature, the political influence of the civilian bureaucracy and the military increased. The military gained further influence because of the dispute with India over the state of Jammu and Kashmir, and Pakistan's entry into American-sponsored defense alliances: the Southeast Asia Treaty Organization (SEATO) and the Baghdad Pact (later the Central Treaty Organization, or CENTRO). After playing political games behind the scene for years, the military took direct power by declaring martial law in October 1958. General Ayub Khan introduced basic democracy, a form of local government, and a presidential constitution. His idea was that democratic participation must be guided and controlled, and that national energies must be concentrated on economic development.

Under the first military regime (1958–1969), Pakistan made substantial economic progress and achieved a high degree of modernization. During the cold war, Pakistan followed a foreign policy of alliance with the West and benefited greatly in economic and military assistance. In 1965, however, the country went to war with India over the disputed territory of Kashmir, a move which destabilized it politically and undermined its economic growth. Popular discontent and nationwide agitation against president Ayub led to a second imposition of martial law in 1969. The new military leader, General Yahya Khan, abrogated Ayub's 1962 constitution and decided to hold the first general elections on the basis of one man one vote in 1970. The mandate of this election was split between the West Pakistan and East Pakistan. The Awami League party from East Pakistan swept the elections and obtained a clear majority in the federal government. Denying the party its right to dominate led to a civil war. Military intervention by India resulted in the military defeat of Pakistan and creation of Bangladesh out of what was East Pakistan.

With this military debacle, Pakistan returned to civilian rule under Zulfikar Ali Bhutto, a populist and charismatic leader (1971–1977). He introduced socialist reforms and gave the country its first constitution to be drafted by elected representatives of the people. He faced agitation by the opposition parties in 1977 over disputed election results and was overthrown by the army chief of staff, General Zia ul Haq. General Zia promised fresh elections within ninety days, as stipulated by the 1973 constitution, and put the country back on the road to democracy. It took him eight years to do so. In the meantime, he used a controversial murder conviction to order the execution of former prime minister Bhutto. His rule for eleven years (1977–1988) was further marred by the bitter legacy of the Soviet war in Afghanistan: rising religious extremism, Islamic militancy, and political confrontation. Pakistan became an ally of the Western powers as a front-line state against Moscow's Afghan misadventure. It did better economically under Zia and developed nuclear capability during the Afghan war years.

Zia was the first ruler of Pakistan who tried zealously to Islamize the state and society, although the nation had taken the designation of "Islamic Republic" under its first constitution, in 1956. It is debatable whether this was the result of his personal religious beliefs, or if he was using religion as a source of political legitimation. Whatever the reason, Zia interpreted the movement for the creation of Pakistan in purely Islamic terms and asserted that Islamization was the best way to secure and stabilize Pakistani society. He took drastic measures for building Pakistan as an Islamic society. He introduced Islamic taxes like zakat and 'ushr, and replaced centuries-old British laws relating with Islamic penalties for offenses such as theft, robbery, adultery, and false accusation of adultery. He made the drinking of alcohol by Muslims an offence punishable by six months' imprisonment and fine of 5,000 rupees. He established a separate federal Shari'at (Islamic law) Court to hear appeals against convictions under the Islamic laws. Most of these laws and the Islamization process of the Zia regime have been controversial, but Zia's legacy in this regard lingers on.

The death of Zia in a plane crash returned the country to democracy in 1988. The elections in October of that year resulted in a divided mandate between the Pakistan Peoples Party of Benazir Bhutto and the Muslim League. Benazir became the first women prime minister of Pakistan and the first to head up a democratic government in eleven years. The Punjab, the largest province in the Pakistani federation, had a Muslim League government headed by Mian Mohammad Nawaz Sharif, a former political ally of Zia. The political confrontation between the rival political parties, and the president's willingness to use her powers to dismiss elected members of parliament, provincial assemblies, and governments at the center and in the provinces kept the country unstable. Four elected governments, two of the Pakistan Peoples Party and two of the Muslim League, were dismissed between 1988 and 1996, followed, each time, by new elections. The military continued to play a role in these dismissals from behind the scenes. Ultimately, the various political parties in the parliament closed their ranks and, in 1997, passed the thirteenth amendment to the constitution, which stripped the president of the power to dismiss future elected governments.

This collaboration between the government of Nawaz Sharif and the opposition parties didn't last very long. Sharif had a two-thirds majority in the parliament and was equipped with tremendous executive powers, and he began to act in an arbitrary manner. The opposition dubbed him as a civilian dictator. He forced a sitting president, a chief justice of the Supreme Court of Pakistan, and an army chief of staff to resign. When he removed General Pervez Musharraf from office in October 1999, the military took over power for a fourth time, through a bloodless coup. General Musharraf designated himself as the chief executive of the country, suspended the constitution, dismissed the central and provincial governments, and promised social and national reforms to return the country to a workable democracy. His coup, like previous ones, was endorsed by Pakistan's Supreme Court, but with the injunction that he would hold elections and hand over power to the elected assemblies within three years. National elections were set to be held on 10 October 2002, but Musharraf held a national referendum in April 2002 and got himself elected as president for a five-year term.

An image of the Badshadi mosque in Lahore, Pakistan, appears in the volume two color insert.

See also **Awami League; Jinnah, Muhammad 'Ali; South Asia, Islam in.**

BIBLIOGRAPHY

Afzal, M. Rafique. *Pakistan: History and Politics 1947–1971.* Karachi: Oxford University Press, 2002.

Rasul Bakhsh Rais

PAN-ARABISM

Also known as Arab nationalism, pan-Arabism is the ideology that calls for the political unity of Arab peoples and states. By consensus, Arabness is defined not by religion or geographic origin, but, as Sati' al-Husri proposed, by language. Arabs are those whose mother tongue is Arabic and who identify with the history and culture associated with it.

Although some scholars trace its origins to nineteenth-century state builders such as Muhammad 'Ali of Egypt, or religious reform movements such as the Wahhabiyya, or intellectuals such as 'Abdallah al-Nadim and 'Abd al-Rahman al-Kawakibi, pan-Arabism developed as a coherent ideology and political movement at the time of the First World War. It arose as a response to both European imperialism and to the mismanagement and pan-Turkic ideology associated with the Young Turk movement in the Ottoman Empire.

When the Hashemite-led revolt against Ottoman rule began in 1915, Sharif Husayn and his sons had managed to gain support not only in the Hijaz where they were based, but also in Syria. Husayn thought he had assurances from the British government, represented by the high commissioner in Cairo, Sir Henry McMahon, that he and his sons would govern all Arab territories freed from Turkish control. Yet, despite the efforts of Husayn's son Faysal and T. E. Lawrence at the Versailles conference, the postwar mandate system awarded Lebanon and Syria to France and Iraq and Palestine to Britain. The future of Palestine was particularly uncertain because in November 1917 the British had issued the Balfour Declaration promising favorable consideration for the creation of a Jewish homeland there. The Hashemite project for Arab unity was dealt a final blow when the Hijaz was conquered by 'Abd al-'Aziz ibn Sa'ud in 1924 and Husayn was sent into exile in Cyprus, leaving only two of his sons as rulers of British-backed monarchies: 'Abdallah in Transjordan and Faysal in Iraq.

Following the Second World War, Arab nationalism found two, initially cooperative, but later conflicting, expressions. The first was religious, as articulated by the Muslim Brotherhood (Ikhwan al-Muslimin), which saw the unity of the Arabs as the first step in pan-Islamic solidarity. The second was secular, as articulated by the Ba'th Party led by Michel 'Aflaq and later by the Nasserists. The common enemy for both was the lingering legacy of British and French imperialism in the Arab world, signified by compliant Arab elites, military bases, economic concessions, and the state of Israel.

Soon after coming to power in Egypt in July 1952, Jamal 'Abd al-Nasser began transforming Egypt into a revolutionary nucleus around which Arab unity would progress. He first crushed the religious groups that had supported the Free Officer revolt against the Egyptian monarchy and had quickly become disillusioned with his secularism. He then turned his attention to the conservative Arab monarchies.

The zenith of secular pan-Arabism came in 1958 when Egypt and Syria merged to form the United Arab Republic (UAR). Syria withdrew from the union in 1961, however, because of growing dissatisfaction with Nasser's repressive and pro-Egyptian policies. Subsequent efforts in 1963 to revive the UAR, this time with Iraqi participation following a Ba'thist coup there, proved unsuccessful.

Since the abortive UAR experiment, a number of events have allegedly marked the demise of pan-Arabism, including the crushing Israeli defeat of Arab forces in the 1967 war, Egypt's peace treaty with Israel in 1979, and Iraq's invasion of Kuwait in 1990. Yet, Arab nationalism is still very much alive rhetorically, now once again tinged with strong religious overtones, as in the manifestos of fundamentalist groups and even in the propaganda of secular dictators like Saddam Husayn, who repeatedly invoked religion to rally Arabs

during the 1991 Gulf War and in the months leading to the 2003 Iraq war that ousted him from power. More importantly, perhaps, Arab nationalism today finds institutional expression in the continued existence of the Arab League, formed in 1945, and now consisting of twenty-two members, as well as in continuing efforts to create subregional organizations, the most successful being the Gulf Cooperation Council (GCC), formed in 1981 and comprising the six Arab states that border the Persian Gulf.

See also **'Abd al-Nasser, Jamal; Arabic Language; Arab League; Ba'th Party; Ikhwan al-Muslimin; Nationalism: Arab; Pan-Islam; Pan-Turanism; Revolution: Modern.**

BIBLIOGRAPHY

Ajami, Fouad. *The Arab Predicament: Arab Political Thought and Practice Since 1967.* Cambridge, U.K.: Cambridge University Press, 1981.

Haim, Sylvia G., ed. *Arab Nationalism: An Anthology.* Berkeley: University of California Press, 1962.

Kerr, Malcolm. *The Arab Cold War: Gamal Abd al-Nasir and His Rivals, 1958–1970.* London: Oxford University Press, 1971.

Sohail H. Hashmi

PAN-ISLAM

Pan-Islam is the ideology that calls for the unity and cooperation of Muslims worldwide on the basis of their shared Islamic identity. Apart from this general description, the idea of pan-Islam has been formulated in myriad ways and used for various political ends during the nineteenth and twentieth centuries.

The term "pan-Islam" is of nineteenth-century European origin and was used primarily to describe Ottoman attempts at promoting Muslim unity to counter European imperialism. Yet, the central premise of pan-Islam, that all Muslims form a single community of believers (*umma*) that ideally should be united politically as well as spiritually, may be traced to the very origins of Islam itself. Several Qur'anic verses refer to the Muslims as constituting a single community (e.g., 2:143, 3:110). Others warn against the dangers of fragmentation and internal strife (e.g., 3:103, 105). The prophet Muhammad clearly tried to forge a sense of Muslim communal solidarity that transcended the traditional tribal loyalties of the Arabs, as in the famous example of the "Constitution of Medina," in which the migrants from Mecca and the newly converted tribes of Medina are described as "a single *umma* apart from all other men." Although the political unity of the *umma* was shattered soon after the Prophet's death, the ideal continued to linger for several centuries afterwards, as best demonstrated in the reluctance of political theorists to accept the legitimacy of multiple, simultaneous caliphs.

Numerous attempts to unite Muslims through a revival of Islamic faith may be found in Islamic history. But given the far expanse of Islamic civilization, all of these were confined geographically. Many factors converged in the nineteenth century to allow a far more universal scope for attempts to unite Muslims: the steady loss of Ottoman territories in Europe, the advance of European colonialism into Muslim states in Africa and Asia, and the spread of mass communication media. Pan-Islam developed primarily as a defense mechanism to counter the military and political advance of European powers, primarily Britain, France, and Russia. The Ottoman Empire, the largest and most centrally located Sunni state, and the guardian of the holy sites of Mecca, Medina, and Jerusalem, was best suited to exploit rising concerns with European imperialism and to initiate pan-Islamic responses.

Two men, more than any others, shaped the development of pan-Islam during the late nineteenth century: the Ottoman sultan 'Abd al-Hamid II (1842–1918) and Jamal al-Din al-Afghani (1839–1897). 'Abd al-Hamid cultivated the pan-Islamic sentiments that had emerged during the 1860s and 1870s under the impact of German and Italian unification during the reign of his predecessor, 'Abd al-'Aziz (1830–1876), and gave them the status of an official ideology. As it did for 'Abd al-'Aziz, pan-Islam provided 'Abd al-Hamid a rallying cry against both European powers and internal modernizers and critics of the sultanate.

Central to 'Abd al-Hamid's pan-Islam was the claim that the Ottoman sultan was the caliph of Islam, or at least of Sunni Islam. The Ottoman claim to the caliphate dated back centuries, but under 'Abd al-Hamid the title was asserted with far greater vigor than it had been before within the empire, and for the first time serious attempts were made to win the loyalty of Muslims beyond the Ottoman realm. Inside the empire, the sultan's pan-Islam meant the cultivation of Muslim interests over those of Christian and other non-Muslim minorities as well as increased state support for Islamic courts, schools, and religious orders. Outside the empire, a propaganda campaign was launched, using print media and emissaries or spies, to spread an image of the sultan as a pious Muslim ruler, the only one capable of effectively uniting Muslims against Christian colonizers.

'Abd al-Hamid's claims to the caliphate were challenged immediately, and the general failure of his pan-Islamic campaign partly contributed to his deposition following the Young Turk revolt of 1908. Still, the fruits of 'Abd al-Hamid's propaganda may be seen in the Indian Muslim agitation over the fate of the Ottoman caliphate following the First World War.

Jamal al-Din al-Afghani's early career emphasized the need for reform within particular Muslim countries, under the leadership of their own rulers. By the 1870s, Afghani's activism had assumed a decidedly pan-Islamic emphasis. He suggested that the only way to ameliorate the weakness of individual Muslim states was to form a bloc of semi-autonomous states, all recognizing the suzerainty of the Ottoman caliph. Afghani thus sought to combine nationalism and pan-Islam, apparently seeing no contradictions between the two.

Afghani proposed to 'Abd al-Hamid as early as the late 1870s that he be sent as an emissary to Afghanistan to rally support for the sultan's claims to the caliphate. The sultan, suspicious of Afghani's motivations, responded by encouraging him to continue his agitation from abroad but doing little to assist him. In 1892, 'Abd al-Hamid invited Afghani to settle in Istanbul. Afghani would die there four years later, disillusioned and complaining that he was a prisoner of the sultan.

Pan-Islamic appeals continued to be heard in the period before and immediately after the First World War, as in the Ottoman jihad proclamation of 1914, but increasingly they were made in the service of Turkish, Arab, or Indian Muslim nationalism. The issue that most stirred pan-Islamic loyalties was the fate of the Ottoman caliphate, particularly among the Muslims of British India. Ulema of the Deoband school led Indian Muslim opposition to the Arab revolt against the Ottomans, seeing in it a British ploy to seize control of the central Islamic lands. When Constantinople was occupied by the Allies at the end of the war, Indian nationalist leaders, chief among them the journalist Muhammad 'Ali, launched the Khilafat Movement to lobby the British government for the Ottoman caliph's retention of sovereignty over the Arabian Peninsula, Syria, Iraq, and Anatolia, the "spiritual heartland" of Islam. Meanwhile, in 1919, groups of Indian ulema organized the *hijra* (migration) of Muslims from the subcontinent to Afghanistan, arguing that Muslims could no longer remain in a territory ruled by Great Britain while it was attempting to destroy the caliphate. Approximately 18,000, mostly poor, Muslims trekked to the Afghan border, only to be denied entry by the Afghan government. Thousands lost their lives to disease and hunger in the process. By the time the Turkish Grand National Assembly abolished the Ottoman caliphate in 1924, the Khilafat agitation had already diminished because of disillusionment and internal squabbles. Hopes that a reconstituted caliphate might reinvigorate pan-Islamic sentiments died when two conferences held in 1926, one in Cairo, the other in Mecca, ended in bitter disagreements over who should assume the title. A third conference held in 1931 in Jerusalem called only for solidarity and cooperation among Muslim peoples.

Muslim solidarity and international cooperation, rather than any supranational unity, is the way pan-Islam has generally been articulated in the years since the Second World War. Even those Muslim intellectuals who challenge the legitimacy of separate Muslim nation-states according to

Islamic values do not propose any meaningful political union of Muslim states and in fact generally focus their activism on gaining control of a particular state.

The most prominent manifestation of pan-Islam today is in the host of transnational nongovernmental and intergovernmental Islamic organizations. During the 1950s, Pakistan initiated the creation of the Mu'tamar al-'Alam al-Islami, but disagreements with secular Arab governments over the organization's purpose led to its failure. During the 1960s, the campaign to create pan-Islamic organizations was revived by King Faysal of Saudi Arabia. With his backing, the Rabitat al-'Alam al-Islami was created in 1962 to provide a nongovernmental forum for the discussion and dissemination of Islamic viewpoints on issues facing Muslims around the world. In 1969, following Israel's capture of Jerusalem in the Six Day War, twenty-four Muslim states voted to form the Organization of the Islamic Conference (OIC). In 2003 the OIC consisted of fifty-seven members, and though it is frequently criticized for its ineffectiveness, it remains the most important and universal expression of pan-Islamic political aspirations since the abolition of the caliphate.

See also **Afghani, Jamal al-Din; Caliphate; Empires: Ottoman; Khilafat Movement; Organization of the Islamic Conference; Pan-Arabism; Pan-Turanism; Young Turks.**

BIBLIOGRAPHY

Khan, Saad S. *Reasserting International Islam: A Focus on the Organization of the Islamic Conference and other Islamic Institutions.* Karachi and New York: Oxford University Press, 2001.

Kramer, Martin. *Islam Assembled: The Advent of the Muslim Congresses.* New York: Columbia University Press, 1986.

Landau, Jacob. *The Politics of Pan-Islam.* Oxford, U.K.: Clarendon Press, 1990.

Sohail H. Hashmi

PAN-TURANISM

Pan-Turanism is an ideology that originated in the late nineteenth and early twentieth centuries and propagated a strong cultural attachment among all Turkic peoples. Although pan-Turanism is correlated to pan-Turkism, its adherents differ. While historically pan-Turkism was chiefly confined to the Turks living in the Ottoman Empire and its borderlands, pan-Turanism had broader pretensions. Pan-Turanism aimed at joining all Turkic peoples that claimed descent from Turan, including the Mongols. The name Turan is connected to a mythological plateau in Central Asia. In Avesta the people called Tura were represented as the enemies of the true religion, namely the people who did not accept Zoroastrianism. However, later the term Turan commonly referred to the land north of the Amu Darya River (the Oxus River of antiquity), where the non-Iranians of Central Asia and chiefly the nomadic Turkic peoples lived.

In the late nineteenth century the tsarist empire, by invading the Caucasus and Central Asia, incorporated a vast number of Turkic peoples into its realm. The Russification policy adopted by tsarist Russia in this region caused a number of local elites to promote an alternative to Russian pan-Slavism. However, their activities prior to the First World War were mainly confined to organizing all of Russia's Muslim congresses and the publication of certain periodicals such as *Yeni Fuyuzat* (New abundance) and *Shelale* (Cascade) in Baku or *Turan* in Tashkent.

The growing solidarity among Russia's Turkic peoples was welcomed in the Ottoman Empire, which was suffering from a long-lasting and humiliating decline. Among the leaders of the ruling Committee of Union and Progress in the Ottoman Empire were personalities such as Enver Pasha, who aspired to forge a Turanian empire that would bring Turkic peoples together and result in gains in the Caucasus and Central Asia. The entry of the Ottoman Empire into the First World War was partly motivated by such a desire. The Ottoman propaganda campaign in the First World War was dominated by two distinctive trends of pan-Islamism and pan-Turanism. While pan-Turanism aimed at the Turkic peoples of the Balkan peninsula, the Caucasus, northern Iran, and Central Asia, the pan-Islamist propaganda was still largely directed at the peoples of the Near and Middle East, and even as far as the Indian subcontinent. In Iran and Central Asia, with their diverse ethnic composition, the Ottomans employed a combination of pan-Turanism and pan-Islamism resulted.

With the end of the First World War and the fall of the Ottoman Empire, there were only a handful of political adventurers that still pursued pan-Turanism, among them Enver Pasha, who was killed in 1922 while fighting the Bolsheviks in Central Asia.

In the Republic of Turkey, while local nationalism with pan-Turkish allusions was tolerated and even encouraged, pan-Turanism never became a significant political trend. It was only with the disintegration of the Soviet Union in the late 1980s and early 1990s that the call for unity among the Turkic peoples was once more heard. Although this call was promoted by the cooperation pacts realized among the new independent Turkic republics of the Caucasus, Central Asia, and Turkey, the profound rivalries both on the regional as well as the international level nevertheless hampered any noteworthy achievements.

See also **Balkans, Islam in the; Central Asia, Islam in; Empires: Ottoman; Pan-Arabism; Pan-Islam.**

BIBLIOGRAPHY

Atabaki, T. "Recasting Oneself, Rejecting the Others: Pan-Turkism and Iranian Nationalism." In *Identity Politics in Central Asia and the Muslim World.* Edited by E. J. Zurcher, and W. van Schendel. London: I. B. Tauris, 2001.

Landau, J. M. *Pan-Turkism: From Irredentism to Cooperation.* London: Hurst, 1995.

Touraj Atabaki

PASDARAN

The Pasdaran (Sepah-e Pasdaran-e Enghelab-e Eslami, or Islamic Revolutionary Guards Corps) was established under a decree issued by the Ayatollah Khomeini, as leader of the Islamic revolution, on 5 May 1979. The corps of Revolutionary Guards were intended to guard the revolution and to assist the ruling clerics in the day-to-day enforcement of the government's Islamic codes and morality. The Pasdaran, as the guardians of the revolution, would counter the threat posed by either the leftist guerrillas or the officers suspected of continued loyalty to the shah. The revolution also needed to rely on a force of its own rather than borrowing the monarchic regime's tainted forces, however disorganized and undertrained such a force might be in the first years of establishment. The Pasdaran, along with its political counterpart, Crusade for Reconstruction, brought a new order to Iran. The Pasdaran and Crusade for Reconstruction had their own separate ministries in the first decade after revolution, but then they were merged with other ministries.

In time, the Pasdaran came to duplicate the police and the judiciary in terms of its functions. It even challenged the performance of the regular armed forces on the battlefield. The Pasdaran was designed as an organization that would be directly subordinate to the ruling clerics. The constitution of the Islamic Republic of Iran entrusted the regular army with guarding Iran's territorial integrity and political independence. Thus the Revolutionary Guards could only have the responsibility of guarding the revolution. Involvement in politics is a part of the Revolutionary Guards' mission to defend Islamic authority. Despite differences, the Pasdaran and the regular armed forces have cooperated on military matters.

By the end of the war between Iran and Iraq in 1986, the Pasdaran consisted of 400,000 personnel organized in battalion-size units that operated either independently or with units of the regular armed forces. In 1984 the Pasdaran acquired a small navy and elements of an air force. Until 1988, up to three million volunteers were organized under the control of the Revolutionary Guards as the Mobilization (Basij) Corps. Since the end of the war this number has decreased, as those units are used to control the internal situation or to strengthen one political faction above another

and battle to quell civil disorder. The Basij allegedly also monitor the activities of citizens, and harass or arrest women and men who violate the dress code.

The Pasdaran have maintained an intelligence branch to monitor the regime's domestic adversaries and to participate in their arrests and trials. Khomeini demonstrated his acceptance of the Revolutionary Guards' involvement in intelligence when he congratulated them on the arrest of Iranian Communist (Tudeh) leaders. Not only did the Pasardan function as an intelligence organization, both within and outside the country, but they also exerted considerable influence on government policies.

The Pasdaran have been quite active in Lebanon. By the summer of 1982, shortly after the second Israeli invasion of Lebanon, the Pasdaran had nearly one thousand personnel deployed in the predominantly Shi'ite Biqa' Valley. From their headquarters near Baalbek, the Pasdaran have provided consistent support to Islamic Amal, a breakaway faction of the mainstream Amal organization, and then Hizb Allah, which contemplate the establishment of an Islamic state in Lebanon.

See also **Iran, Islamic Republic of; Revolution: Islamic Revolution in Iran.**

BIBLIOGRAPHY

Katzman, Kenneth. *The Warriors of Islam: Iran's Revolutionary Guard.* Oxford, U.K.: Westview Press, 1993.

Majid Mohammadi

PERSIAN LANGUAGE AND LITERATURE

Persian has historically been, after Arabic, the most prestigious literary language in the Muslim world and a vehicle of cultural expression in Ottoman Turkey, Central Asia, Mogul India and, of course, Persia (greater Iran). The influence of Persian literature and Persicate culture therefore covered a wide region, from the Balkans to Bangladesh, and from the Persian Gulf to north of the Jaxartes River in Central Asia. Today Persian is the official language of Iran and Tajikistan, and one of the two official languages of Afghanistan (along with Pashto). Persian is also spoken by small residual communities in neighboring countries, such as Turkmenistan, Uzbekistan, Pakistan, the Persian Gulf states, and Iraq, as well as in newly established enclaves abroad: Persian-speaking Jewish immigrants to Israel, and the diaspora to North America, Europe, and Australia that resulted from the political upheavals and wars in Iran and Afghanistan during the 1970s and the 1980s.

Note that in recent decades the term "Farsi" has erroneously gained currency in English in place of Persian. Linguistically speaking, the nomenclatures "Farsi," "Dari," and

"Tajiki" denote varieties of Persian spoken in Iran, Afghanistan, and Tajikistan, respectively, just as one might describe English as consisting of American, Australian, and British varieties. Though distinctive regional accents and some differences in vocabulary or even grammar exist, the spoken varieties of Persian are united by a common literary and cultural heritage and are mutually understood by speakers across the Persian linguistic continuum. Nevertheless, Persian literature has been developing in distinctive and even divergent directions in modern Iran, Afghanistan, and Tajikistan since each country became a centralized nation-state. This is especially true of Tajikistan, where the written form of Persian was radically altered in the Soviet period by the adoption first of the Roman (1928) and shortly thereafter the Cyrillic (1940) script in place of the traditional Arabic script, used in Afghanistan and Iran. Tajikistan was therefore oriented toward Russian, as well as Turkic Central Asia, in its recent cultural and linguistic development, whereas Afghanistan has been in the cultural orbit of Pakistan and India, as well as the Soviet Union. The collapse of the Soviet Union in the last decade of the twentieth century, and of the Taliban in the first years of the twenty-first, along with technological innovations (such as Persian-language programs broadcast by Internet radio and satellite television across the region) have, however, brought increased opportunities for cultural interchange across the Persian speaking countries, and begun to reverse the isolation of previous decades.

Language History

Persian is classified as a member of the Iranian branch of the Indo-European family of languages. Indeed, it was partly from his knowledge of Persian and its similarity to Latin, Greek, and Sanskrit that Sir William Jones (1746–1794) postulated the existence of an Indo-European proto-language from which the modern languages of Europe, India, and Iran devolved. As such, many modern Persian words (for example, *madar*, *baradar*) share a common root with their modern German (mutter, brüder) or English (mother, brother) equivalents, and the verbal systems exhibit similar features. However, the neighboring Semitic languages, especially Aramaic and Arabic, which functioned in different eras as lingua francas of the Near and Middle East, have made an enormous impact on Persian, in terms not only of vocabulary and script, but also of literary forms.

The Persian language is divided into three historical stages: Old Persian, Middle Persian, and Persian. Old Persian survives chiefly in cuneiform inscriptions of the Achaemenid kings, written in the sixth to fourth centuries B.C.E., but it has bequeathed few if any direct literary traces to the modern language. On the other hand, a large body of literature survives in Middle Persian, much of it subsequently translated or adapted into Arabic or Persian during the Islamic period. Most of this was written in the Sassanian period (226–652 C.E.), though Zoroastrians continued to use it to write new works or compilations of a religious nature until the ninth century C.E. The larger part of surviving Middle Persian literature consists of translations or glosses on Avestan-language Zoroastrian texts, along with other Zoroastrian literature. It also includes "books of counsel" (*pand namak*), or wisdom literature providing moral or ethical precepts and advice, as in the "Wise Maxims of Bozorgmehr." Other texts include a few poems, the versification principles of which have been disputed, and "royal songs" (*srot-i khusravanik*) that were reportedly performed with musical accompaniment by well-known minstrels at the Sassanian court.

The cultural exchange with India was quite strong, as evidenced by a Middle Persian treatise on chess and a number of translations of works of Indian origin, including *Kalila wa Dimna* (from the tales of Bidpai), Barlaam and Josaphat, and the *Sindbad nameh*. The frametale structure is thus borrowed from India, but the bulk of the Middle Persian *Hazar Afsanak* ("Thousand tales"), the main source of stories for the Arabic "Thousand and One Nights" cycle (*Alf Layla wa layla*), seem to be of Persian origin.

Although spoken Persian continued to evolve grammatically into something like what we now recognize as new Persian, Zoroastrian works continued to be composed in Middle Persian until at least the ninth century, by which time the majority of Iranians had become Muslim. Many religious, literary, and scientific works written in Arabic at the same time were penned by men of Iranian, or half-Iranian parentage, including Ibn al-Muqaffa' (d. 760), translator of *Kalila wa Dimna* from Middle Persian to Arabic; the poet Abu Nuwas (d. 810), who includes a few words of Persian in his poetry; the historian and Qur'an commentator, Tabari (d. 923); and the physician Rhazes (Zakariyya al-Razi, d. 925). Indeed, many authors of the tenth through twelfth centuries who lived in Persian-speaking milieus and would have had the option to write in Persian nevertheless chose to write their most important works in Arabic. This was the case for, among others, al-Biruni, who was born in Khwarazm in 973 and died in 1051 in Ghazna; Ibn Sina (Avicenna), born near Bukhara in 980, died in Hamadan in 1037; and Mohammad al-Ghazali, of Tus, who lived from 1058 to 1111.

By the tenth century, however, some three hundred years after the Arab conquest of Persia, the spoken Persian language had re-emerged as a language of literary standing in its own right, suitable for use in discussion of science, philosophy, and religion, as well. It was now written in the Arabic alphabet, which was easier to read than the Middle Persian script, and which also derived from a Semitic alphabet, Aramaic.

Persian Poetry

The earliest Persian poetry of the Islamic period is in dialect form (*fahlaviyat*), probably based on accentual or syllable-count meters. Evidence of some prosodic experimentation and variation is discernible in the earliest recorded specimens of Persian verse, though it seems that the Persian poetry of the ninth century was already following quite different principles of versification from Middle Persian poetry, notably rhyme and quantitative metrics. Some Persian meters are borrowed from Arabic, or at least they are explained according to Arabic models by the Persian manuals of prosody and rhetoric written in the twelfth century. However, Persian poets rarely employed some very common Arabic meters (such as *tawil* and *basit*), whereas some of the frequently occurring meters in Persian poetry (such as *motaqareb* and the *roba'i* meter) seem quite uncommon in Arabic poetry of the same period. Persian poetry is furthermore fond of including a refrain (*radif*, which can be several syllables in length) after the rhyming syllable. We may conclude, therefore, that in addition to the influence of Arabic, native Persian phonology and prosody also played a distinctive role in shaping the new system of versification.

The privileged literary mode in Persian was poetry, or rhymed and metered "speech." It was composed and performed in a variety of milieus for various social functions, acquiring the greatest prestige and widest publicity through the patronage of the royal court, including sultans/shahs but also wazirs or other men of state, army commanders, and regional governors. It might also be commissioned by the landed gentry, or alternatively, circulated through Sufi networks.

Most dynasties of the Persian-speaking world considered it the duty of a civilized ruler to cultivate science and literature, and doing so increased the ruler's prestige. Some rulers even dabbled in composing poetry of their own, as a literate person was expected to be able to compose some amount of formal verse, lines of which were used as proof texts to illustrate points and conclude arguments in letters, homilies, and in conversation. Not only aspiring poets, but also secretaries and men of letters, were expected to have a huge repertoire of poetry at the tip of their tongues, and were sometimes called upon to compose extemporaneously at court. The work of successful professional poets was circulated in albums dedicated to particular patrons or particular themes. These albums would later be collected into *divans*, though often not by the poet himself. Early poetry *divans* were organized thematically, but from the sixteenth century onward they were usually divided into sections according to verse form (*qasideh*, *ghazal*, *qet'eh*, strophic poems, and *roba'i*) and then further organized alphabetically according to the final letter of the rhyme or refrain.

Themes were largely conventional, and the poets usually presented a persona rather than a personal biography, though this in no way deterred critics from reading biographical data into the poems. The imagery grew in hyperbole and complexity over the centuries, and technical virtuosity was greatly admired, so that rhetorical ornamentation could become a justification in and of itself. Metaphors, tropes, and symbols (for instance, the rose and nightingale, the bow of the beloved's eyebrow firing the arrows of his or her eyelashes, the ringlets of the beloved's hair as polo sticks sending the lover's heart skittering over the ground, and the like) were repeated from generation to generation, though subtle variation and innovations applied to the conventions have always been greatly admired. The stylistic trends have been described as evolving from heavy rhythms, rhetorical directness, and sparse use of Arabic in the tenth-century poetry, to the more mellifluous and rhetorically ornamented poetry (internal rhyme, play on words, display of Arabic erudition) associated with the flowering of the *ghazal*, and the era of the great classical poets such as Sa'di (d. 1292), Rumi (d. 1273), Hafez (d. 1390), and Jami (d. 1492). Poetry of the "Indian style" (sixteenth through eighteenth centuries) continued the focus on the *ghazal*, which became conceptually more abstract and philosophical, even *recherché*, with a distinctive taste for the subtle conceit and imagism. The neo-classical "return" of the eighteenth and nineteenth centuries rejected this trend in favor of a simpler more direct prose style, and an imitation of the past masters. This gradually gave way to the influence of European letters in the twentieth century and led to the development of a significantly new, modernist poetic.

Quatrains (*Roba'iyyat*)

The quatrain (*do-bayti*, *taraneh*, and later *roba'i*), rhyming according to the pattern *a-a-b-a* and conforming to a special meter of its own, emerged from a popular milieu to become a literary genre unto its own, the *roba'iyyat*. Roba'is can treat amorous themes or commemorate a historical occasion (such as the death of a famous person), but most famously deliver a mystical or philosophical apothegm. The eleventh-century "naked" hermit, Baba Taher, sang quatrains of human love and devotion to God in impromptu quatrains, some of which are preserved in their original Hamadani dialect form. Another poet known exclusively for *roba'i*s is Mahsati of Ganja (fl. 12th century), one of the few classical poets with a uniquely feminine voice, and a far from chaste perspective on love.

The most famous practitioner of this genre is the mathematician and astronomer 'Omar Khayyam of Nishapur (d. 1121), thanks in no small part to Edward FitzGerald's immensely successful 1859 English translation/adaptation, *The Rubaiyat of Omar Khayyam*. Khayyam acquired a posthumous reputation as a composer of *roba'iyyat* of a materialist or agnostic temperament, some of them quite blasphemous, although the actual evidence for him as author is rather flimsy. What is clear is that over the centuries, the corpus of quatrains attributed to Khayyam grew suspiciously, so that scholars in the twentieth century sought text-critical principles, to separate the forgeries from the real Khayyam. The *divans* of most subsequent poets include numerous *roba'i*s; Rumi's, for example, has nearly 2000.

Court Poetry

Panegyrics in Arabic by the great poets had conveyed prestige and authority on the Umayyad and Abbasid caliphs, so that Persian princes on the eastern edges of Persia naturally gravitated toward the practice as they began realizing their practical independence from the Abbasids. In cities like Nishapur (near modern Mashhad), Balkh (in modern Afghanistan), Samarkand, and Bukhara (in modern Uzbekistan), panegyrics in Persian were presented to the ruler or men of state on ceremonial occasions: Iranian seasonal festivals like Nawruz or Mehregan, Islamic holy days, royal investitures, victory celebrations, wine drinking parties, and the like. Poems for such occasions typically took the form of a *qasideh*, a long mono-rhyme (*a-a-b-a-c-a-d-a*), usually between 40 and 100 lines, typically beginning with an encomium on the arrival of spring, on the beloved, or on wine. This would then segue into an enumeration of the virtues and glories of the ruler, encouraging him in the process to uphold principles of generosity, forbearance and just governance.

The greatest of the early Persian poets, Rudaki (d. 940), who was also a musician, composed many narrative poems, of which precious little has survived. Many examples of his fine, thoughtful lyric poems (not yet clearly differentiated in form as *ghazal*s or *qasideh*s), in a clear and unornamented style characteristic of early Persian prose and verse, must have been performed at the court in Bukhara, for the Samanid prince Amir Nasr II (r. 914–943). In these poems, Rudaki praised the ruler and his capital, rhapsodized on the process of making wine, or meditated on the decrepitude brought by age. This latter, rather melancholy, idea afforded early poets the occasion to draw the moral that life is short, so live right. This is then interpreted in either ethical terms, to do good works (since your name, good or ill, is all that will live on), or in epicurean terms, to live happy and well (for the opportunities for pleasure are limited). The lack of appeal to the Qur'an and outwardly religious sentiment may reflect the survival of Persian religion and philosophy.

The classical form of the Persian *qasideh* was created at the court of Sultan Mahmud of Ghazna (in modern Afghanistan), who gathered a number of great poets to his court in the first half of the eleventh century. Among these were the poet laureate 'Onsori (d. 1040); Farrokhi (d. 1038), who delighted in the description of spring and the celebration of musical wine soirees; and Manuchehri (d. 1041), famous for his adaptation of classical Arabic *qasideh*s. The rival Seljuk court to the north and west also supported its poets, among them Amir Mo'ezzi (d. 1127), "prince of poets" to sultans Malik Shah and Sanjar, and Anvari (1126–c.1189), generally acknowledged as the ultimate *qasideh* poet for his erudite, ornamented yet fluid style. Panegyrical poets were richly rewarded and got to travel with the court, yet the profession could be a hazardous one. Mas'ud Sa'd Salman (d. 1121) was imprisoned for long periods on suspicion of treason; Emir Mo'ezzi was accidentally shot and seriously wounded by prince Sanjar's arrow; and Adib-e Saber was drowned by the Khwarazm shah as a spy of Sanjar.

Courts in the west of Iran also cultivated Persian poetry. In Azerbaijan, Qatran (d. 1072) wrote for numerous patrons, including a poem on the major earthquake in Tabriz in 1042, and many strophic poems. When Naser Khosrow, a poet from eastern Persia, came to Tabriz in 1046, he wrote in his fascinating travelog that Qatran was a good poet, who, however, did not fully understand Persian. This shows that, though dialectical variation must have existed, Persian was widely spoken and written by the mid-eleventh century. Khaqani of Shirvan (d. 1199) wrote *ghazal*s and panegyrics, but is best known for his elegies on the death of his son and on the ruins of a Sassanian palace. Although a declared follower of Sana'i of Ghazna in the religious/didactic themes of his verse, he incorporated Christian themes in his poetry. His mother was a convert from Nestorian Christianity, and his travels brought him into close contact with Christians in Georgia and Constantinople.

Epic Poetry

Ferdausi of Tus (near modern Mashhad) has often been credited with rescuing the Persian language from virtual extinction with his monumental work, the *Shah nameh*, or "Book of kings," begun about 975 and, dedicated in its final form to Mahmud of Ghazna, in about 1010. This hyperbolic view ignores the half-century of court poetry that preceded Ferdausi's work, including some earlier treatments of episodes from the national epic. Ferdausi himself incorporated a thousand lines from the story of Zoroaster as versified by Daqiqi (d. 981 or before) in his own work. Nevertheless, Ferdausi's *Shah nameh* would play a central role not only in Iranian national consciousness, but even in the self-identity of non-Iranian rulers, especially Turks and Mongols, who adopted Persianate culture and traditions of kingship.

Ferdausi alludes to various sources for his account of events, including a learned Zoroastrian priest and a member of the Persian landed gentry. The existence of a tradition of professional reciters orally recounting stories from the Iranian national epic in a popular (sub-literary) context has led to heated scholarly debate about possible oral sources for Ferdausi. However, Ferdausi did have an established written tradition to draw from, and appears to have studied the matter and carefully crafted his tale. Various versions of the Persian "Book of kings" (*Khoday nameh*) were already written down in Middle Persian in the sixth and seventh centuries, and several of these had been translated into Arabic in the eighth and ninth centuries, as part of the discourse of *shu'ubiyya*, or ethnic pride among non-Arabs, especially Iranians. At the initiative of Abu Mansur, a committee had translated the work from Middle Persian to Persian prose in 957.

The poem covers the mythical era of kingship in Iran, during which the rites and ceremonies of kingship were established, the demons were subdued, cooking and clothing were introduced, cultivation of the soil begun, fire was discovered, metal worked, the social castes created, and the celebration of Nawruz (the spring equinox and Iranian new year) initiated. Death enters this idyllic realm due to the hubris of the king, Jamshid, and Zahhak comes to tyrannize the land. Accursed by Satan's kiss, Zahhak has a snake growing from each of his shoulders, each of which must feed daily on the brain of an Iranian youth. Feridun eventually snatches the throne from Zahhak and restores justice, dividing his realm between his three sons before he dies. The two sons who inherit the lands to the east and west of Iran grow jealous of their brother, who has inherited the realm of Iran. They conspire to murder him, and this engenders generations of internecine conflict between Iran and her eastern neighbor, Turan.

This sets the stage for many sagas and adventures, which revolve thematically around the question of fate and free will, and the tragic forces that impel kings to conflict with their enemies, their sons and the champion warriors to whom they owe their throne. The father-son conflict usually ends poorly for the son (Rostam and Sohrab, Kay Kavus and Siyavash, Goshtasp and Esfandiyar), and the king is far less frequently wise and just (as in the tale of Kei Khosrau, in which the king abdicates and disappears) than tragically flawed or impetuous (as in the case of Kay Kavus).

The *Shah nameh* is not aware of the great Achaemenid kings Cyrus, Darius, and Xerxes, as it takes notice of the historical era only as Iran is about to be conquered by Alexander. It mostly ignores the successors of Alexander, fast-forwarding to the Sassanian rulers, whom it covers in some detail, both historical and legendary. The 50,000-line epic comes to a close with the Arab conquest of Persia, a sad fate indeed, even though Ferdausi writes as a Muslim with Shi'i loyalties.

The tremendous success of the *Shah nameh* led other authors to elaborate on portions of the epic cycle (transmitted in oral renditions by popular professional reciters) which Ferdausi either passed over in silence or did not fully develop. These focused on elaborating and embellishing the story of various champions, as in the "Book of Garshasp," written in 1066 by Asadi of Tus (also the author of an important early dictionary of Persian), about a hero even more outlandishly strong than Rostam; or the legendary history of the Iranian prophet Zoroaster, told by the Zoroastrian priest Zartosht Bahram Pazhdu in 1278. The influence of Ferdausi is apparent even in the nineteenth and twentieth centuries, in works like the *Shahanshah nameh* (The king of king's book) by Saba (1765–1823), describing a victory by the Qajar king, Fath-'Ali Shah (r. 1797–1834) over the Russians in the same archaic terms found in the *Shah nameh*; or in the verse history *Shahnameh ye haqiqat*, written by Mojrem (1871–1920) of the

leaders of the Ahl-e Haqq sect in Kurdistan. All of these, however, remained quite tangential to the main canon of Persian literature, in contrast to Ferdausi's *Shah nameh*, for which the creation of large, sumptuously illustrated manuscripts in royal ateliers became common during the Mongol period and later. In fact it was almost de rigueur for each successive Safavid monarch to commission such a royal copy, the most famous of which was the copy made for Shah Tahmasp (r. 1524–1576), which was subsequently given as a gift of state to the Ottomans, and eventually found its way to Europe and the art dealer Houghton, but has now been repatriated (at least the surviving illustrated folios) to Iran.

Romance Literature

Also spun-off from the *Shah nameh* are a number of romances, although the Persian narrative verse tradition is also fed by other sources. To have an authoritative or popular source seems to have been an important prerequisite to undertaking a narrative poem of several thousand lines (invariably in the rhyming couplet form of the *mathnavi*), which might either be commissioned by a patron, or presented to one with a dedication in the introduction in hopes of a reward. Trying one's hand at an original imaginative story could be somewhat risky under these circumstances; in any case, there were many classical stories reflecting the glorious culture of pre-Islamic Iran from which to draw inspiration. These include a poem of Parthian origins, *Vis and Ramin*, versified by Fakhr al-Din Gorgani circa 1054 for the governor of Isfahan from a Middle Persian version. It tells the story of Vis, promised in marriage before her birth to King Mobad. The latter's younger brother, Ramin, falls in love at the first sight of her, and eventually wins her over. Through the help of Vis's nurse, the pair escapes from Mobad and are eventually united as king and queen, in a saga not without similarities to that of Tristan.

Other tales of stymied love include "Varqa and Golshah," based upon an Arabic story, and versified in Persian in the *motaqareb* meter during the first decades of the eleventh century by 'Ayyuqi. This pair never unites, except through a chaste ideal love that they take with them to the grave. A similar story, both in its outcome and in its Arab origins, is Nezami's version of the star-crossed lovers Layli and Majnun, in a poem of 4,000 lines written in 1188. This tale was told and retold by subsequent Persian poets (most successfully by Maktabi of Shiraz in 1490), as well as by imitators writing in Turkish and Urdu. The retellings usually resolve the powerful psychological ambiguity in Nezami's work and rarely match his masterful ability with language. In addition to a very fine *divan* of shorter poems, Nezami (d. 1209) also authored four other long narrative *mathnavis*, including an ethico-didactic poem modeled on Sana'i, a Persian version of the Alexander romance (*Sikandar Nama*), and two poems set in the Sassanian period. The first of these is *Khosrau and Shirin*, a legend about King Khosrau Parviz (r. 590–628) and his Armenian bride, Shirin, who is loved devotedly by Farhad, who moves a mountain to attain her, but is tricked by Khosrau into thinking she is dead. The other is *Haft Paykar*, about Bahram (r. 421–439) and the seven beautiful princesses from the seven climes with whom he enjoys a variety of adventures. The five narrative poems by Nezami were often bound together in one volume and frequently illustrated. Such was Nezami's achievement that many later poets tried their hand at composing a similar quintet, following his model. This tended to limit the initiative of later poets in creating new material, but Jami (d. 1492) introduced two new stories to the traditional subjects of romance: the mystical reworking of the Joseph and Zoleikha story (very loosely based on Qur'an, sura 12), and the story of Salaman and Absal, about a Greek king who has a magician genetically engineer him a perfect son, who, however, is seduced by his beautiful nurse.

Religious and Mystical poetry

The extensive literature of imaginative poetry and prose, as well as commentaries that address various aspects of religion and spirituality is immense. All long poems, from the *Shah nameh* to romances, inevitably begin with a doxology and lines in praise of the prophet Muhammad, as well as frequently a description of his journey to heaven. Though the majority of classical Persian poets were Sunnis of the Hanafi or Shafi'i school, there are some vociferously Shi'ite poets in the early period, notably Naser Khosrow (1003–1060), an Isma'ili poet, and Qavami of Rayy (fl. 12th century).

It was the mystics, however, who created the most successful poetry of religious expression, reaching its pinnacle in the mystico-didactic poetry of the *mathnavi* form. Sana'i (d. 1135) initiated the genre with his *Hadiqat al-haqiqat*, a compendium of tales, some humorous, that were used to illustrate homilies and moral injunctions, and which focus chiefly upon control of the baser passions and correctly understanding the interior meaning of the Qur'an. Farid al-Din 'Attar (d. 1221) perfected the story-telling element of the mystical *mathnavi* genre, juxtaposing within a frame-tale structure various unrelated anecdotes and vignettes of an entertaining or inspiring nature to illustrate an overarching theme (as was also common in the European literature of the period). The best known of these include the *Elahi nameh*, in which a king and father passes life wisdom to his sons, and the *Manteq al-Tayr*, a poem of mystical psychology about a band of birds in search of their spiritual king, the mythical Simorgh, which was completed in 1177.

Modeled on these, but less thematically structured, is the "Spiritual Couplets" of Jalaluddin Rumi (1207–1273), composed piecemeal in six books through the 1260s. Its opening plaint of the reed pipe, severed from its spiritual home, remains the single most influential expression of mystical theology in Persian, perhaps in the entire Islamic world,

having been studied and taught throughout the Ottoman domains, across Iran, and into the Indian subcontinent.

The love imagery of the *ghazal*, beginning with Sana'i, was also turned into a vehicle of mystical expression. Rumi continued the project of the mystical *ghazal*, conceiving his spiritual mentor Shams (d. after 1247) as the object of love, indeed adopting the voice of his absent master in a huge body of *ghazal*s that almost always point to transcendent significance. Other poets, such as Sa'di of Shiraz (d. 1292), continued to address *ghazal*s to both amorous and mystical objects of love. This creates room for much ambiguity in the *ghazal*s of Hafez of Shiraz (d. 1390), who intertwined mystical and physical love in a sublime fashion that is difficult to unravel, and is generally regarded as the ultimate achievement in Persian lyrical poetry, though this often fails to come through in English translation, as the translators typically try to reduce him to one thing or the other. Goethe and the German Romantic poets derived much inspiration from Hafez.

Prose Genres

Continuing the Sassanian tradition of advice books, the *Qabus nameh*, written in 1082 by Kay Kavus b. Voshmgir, a local prince on the Caspian shore of Iran, provides instruction to his son in the arts of government, social graces, and the enjoyment of life. About the same time Nezam al-Molk (Ar. Nizam al-Mulk; d. 1092), after whom the first university in the Muslim world is named, composed his *Siyasat nameh* to instruct the Seljuk Turks, to whom he served as wazir, in the proper ways of Iranian kingship. Both of these charming books are written in a straightforward prose, whereas Nasr Allah Monshi's version of *Kalilah wa Dimna* (written between 1143 and 1145), which set the prose standard for later authors to match, used animal characters to convey its lessons. This volume requires more work to grasp because of its erudition and its taste for the rhetorical artifices made possible by Arabic morphology. These tales, derived ultimately (via Arabic, via Middle Persian) from the Panchatantra, were brought to then-contemporary style in 1505 by Hosein Va'ez-e Kashefi (d. 1505) as *Anvar-e Soheili*.

Along with many other such collections of tales in prose or verse, a huge body of prose literature, including the serial adventures of picaresque heroes, manuals for writers, lives of the poets, local and world histories, as well as literary anthologies, mystical disquisitions, and philosophical texts, exists in Persian, much of it delightful to read. The prose work with which Persian literature is preeminently associated is, however, the *Golestan* of Sa'di, written in 1258 and loosely organized in eight chapters by theme (kingship, dervishes, youth, contentment, and so on). Throughout it one encounters entertaining anecdotes, wittily expressed, that advocate a practical, situational ethics. It weaves together simple, unadorned prose with rhymed prose and verse to create a new, unified literary idiom that set the future standard of emulation. Frequently imitated, the *Golestan* became a textbook of

Persian language and Islamic ethics for Turkish speakers, as the many Turkish commentaries and translations of the sixteenth and subsequent centuries attest. It was also used as a textbook for Persian instruction in India, where Persian, and then Urdu, commentaries were written on it. It was also used for British students of Persian to study the language in the eighteenth and nineteenth centuries. European translations of the work had been circulating since the mid-seventeenth century and caught the attention of La Fontaine and Voltaire, among others.

Persian in India

It was under the Ghaznavids and their aggressive policy of conquest in South Asia that the first wave of Persian poets moved toward the sub-continent. Mas'ud Sa'd Salman (d. 1121) lived in Lahore, and his contemporary, Abu al-Faraj Runi, was born there. Of Indo-Turkic parentage, Emir Khusrow of Delhi (1253–1325) was a competent imitator of the quintet of Nezami and of well-received *ghazal*s. He popularized Persian poetry at the Muslim courts in India, and also among the Sufis. The poetry of Rumi and 'Eraqi (d. 1289) was also popular among South Asian Sufis. Timur enjoyed Persian books and Babur composed Persian poetry of his own. The Moguls made Persian the language of government in 1582, commissioning their court histories in Persian. Akbar (1556–1605) actively enticed a whole series of the best Persian poets of the era to come to Delhi from Iran and also encouraged translations of Hindu works to Persian. Dara Shokuh (1615–1659), son of Shahjahan, and Zib al-Nesa Makhfi (1639–1703), daughter of Aurangzib, both composed excellent Persian poems of mystical and ecumenical bent. Bidel of Patna (d. 1720) was the last major representative of the Indian style, and he remains more appreciated in Afghanistan and India than in Iran.

Urdu eventually replaced Persian as the primary literary language of South Asian Muslims, but some Urdu poets, such as Ghalib (1796–1869), also wrote in Persian, while Sir Muhammad Iqbal (1877–1938), the intellectual father of Pakistan, wrote major poems, such as his *Javid Nama*, in Persian, a more widely understood language in the Muslim world.

Modern Literature

The twentieth century saw a sea-change in Persian language and literature, as modernization, revolution, centralization and Marxist-Leninism greatly altered Tajikistan and Iran, in particular. First of all, with the advent of lithography and printing in the nineteenth century, books became more affordable, and more importantly, the appearance of newspapers created a different and wider audience for literature. For various short periods of time, the press became relatively free, and there were a number of journals published in Persian outside Iran, which made it possible to openly advocate reform or political opposition to the crown.

In Afghanistan, Mahmud Tarzi helped to introduce translations of European literature and radically new modern literary forms in his journal *Seraj al-Akhbar* (1911–1918). The Iranian poet-singer 'Aref (1882–1934) turned his back on a court career to compose populist political ballads, *ghazal*s, and song lyrics, which reached a mass audience when he sang them in concert. Reform was urged also from within the aristocratic class, many of whom learned foreign languages or studied abroad, such as Iraj Mirza (1874–1926), who held a post in the Qajar government but was noted for his biting satirical indictment of the custom of veiling of women.

Political agitation did not always turn out well. The poet Mirzadeh 'Eshqi was assassinated after satirically caricaturing Reza Shah in 1924. Abu 'l-Qasem Lahuti was obliged to flee from Tabriz in 1922, after leading an unsuccessful revolt there. He settled in Dushanbe, in the Soviet Union, where he wrote Persian poetry for a Tajiki audience, modernizing classical themes and celebrating the socialist enterprise. The fiction writer Bozorg 'Alavi also fled Iran for East Germany, as a result of his Communist Party membership. In Tajikistan, authors managed to champion the Central Asian peasants and collectives, as well as the creation of a new society, in artistically successful ways, especially Mirza Torsonzadeh (1911–1977) in poetry and Sadriddin Aini (1878–1954) in fiction.

Poets continued to compose in the traditional forms, but introduced modern themes and imagery, including descriptions of modern inventions, as in some of the poems of the literary scholar and parliamentarian, Mohammad Taqi Bahar (1880–1951). The *monazerat* (debate poems) of Parvin E'tesami (1910–1941), the first of three important women poets of the century, championed the cause of the poor and downtrodden. In Afghanistan, Khalil Allah Khalili (b. Kabul, 1909, d. Pakistan, 1987) carried on the classical tradition in a convincing modern voice.

The *ghazal* retained its thematics of love, but became slightly more personal and more modern in its sentiments, tinged with European romanticism, but developing toward a contemporary idiom, as in the poems of Simin Behbehani, who headed the Iranian Writer's Congress. Poets, however, also began to separate poetry from traditional verse. First came an effort to break down the classical meters into their constituent feet and combine these feet in new patterns. The first experiment in this direction came in the early 1920s with *Afsaneh* (Romance) by Nima Yushij (1895–1960), who developed toward free verse in the following decade. Though some poets, such as Mehdi Akhavan-e Sales (1928–1990), continued to compose in both free verse and traditional meters, the most outstanding achievements in the post–World War II era were by poets working in free verse, foremost among whom stands Ahmad Shamlu (1926–2001), whose work demonstrates a commitment and capability to uphold political and artistic values simultaneously in his best poems. Forugh Farrokhzad (1935–1967) pushed poetry toward inner authenticity by infusing it with personal experience and focusing on everyday topics, such as sexuality, sometimes from an explicitly female point of view. She was rewarded for her sincerity with public condemnation as an "immoral" woman. Her poetry, however, speaks eloquently and profoundly for itself. Meanwhile, painter and nature poet, Sohrab Sepehri (1928–1981) beautifully adapted the mystical perspective of Persian poetry to modern modes of expression.

The modernist literary idiom was entirely secular, and often political, yet allusive enough to elude the censors. Poetry played an important role in creating political symbols of freedom (dawn, day) as opposed to those of oppression (night, winter), and in inspiring revolutionary sentiment against the shah of Iran in the 1970s. Part of this process involved purging Persian poetry from its classical themes and dynamics, and creating believable characters. In prose literature, Mohammad-ʿAli Jamalzadih (1892–1997) forged a new idiom for imaginative prose literature with his short stories, as did Sadeq Hedayat (1903–1951), whose novel *The Blind Owl* (1969) remains the best known modern Persian work abroad, in part because of the author's connections with expressionist and existentialist writers in Europe, and his suicide in Paris. Jalal Al-e Ahmad (1923–1969, husband of Simin Daneshvar) wrote short stories and novels, *The School Principal* (1974) being the most interesting, but he is best known in the Muslim world for his 1962 attack on the hegemony of Western culture, *Gharbzadegi*. Several historical novels also deal with the theme of Western, especially British, imperialism in Iran: Sadeq Chubak's *Tangsir* (1963), based on a true event in southern Iran; Simin Daneshvar's *Savushun* (1990), a political love story told from the woman's point of view; and the ten-volume novel *Kelidar* (1978–1983) by Mahmoud Dowlatabadi. In the 1970s and the post-Revolution period, female prose writers have achieved popular and critical success (among them, Mahshid Amirshahi, Goli Taraqqi, and Fattaneh Hajj Sayyed Javadi). Others, like Shahrnush Parsipur and Moniru Ravanipur, succeeded in introducing magical realism to Iran.

An image of a 1650 Persian manuscript appears in the volume two color insert.

See also **Arabic Language; Arabic Literature; Biography and Hagiography; Biruni, al-; Ghazali, al-; Grammar and Lexicography; Hadith; Historical Writing; Ibn Sina; Iqbal, Muhammad; Libraries; Rumi, Jalaluddin; Tabari, al-; Urdu Language, Literature, and Poetry; Vernacular Islam.**

BIBLIOGRAPHY

Arberry, Arthur J. "Islamic Literature: Persia." In *Near Eastern Culture and Society*. Edited by T. Cuyler Young. Princeton, N.J.: Princeton University Press, 1951.

Browne, Edward G. *A Literary History of Persia*. Cambridge, U.K.: Cambridge University Press, 1951.

Canfield, Robert, ed. *Turko-Persia in Historical Perspective*. Cambridge, U.K.: Cambridge University Press, 1991.

France, Peter, ed. *The Oxford Guide to Literature in English Translation*. Oxford, U.K.: Oxford University Press, 2000.

Hanaway, William. "The Iranian Epics." In *Heroic Epic and Saga: an Introduction and Handbook to the World's Great Folk Epics*. Edited by Felix J. Oinas. Bloomington: Indiana University Press, 1978.

Kamshad, Hassan. *Modern Persian Literature*. Cambridge, U.K.: Cambridge University Press, 1966.

Karl, Jahn, ed. *History of Iranian Literature*. Dordrecht, Holland: D. Reidel, 1968.

Levy, Reuben. *An Introduction to Persian Literature*. New York: Columbia University Press, 1969.

Meisami, Julie. *Medieval Persian Court Poetry*. Princeton, N.J.: Princeton University Press, 1987.

Morrison, George; Baldick, Julian; and Shafi'i-Kadkani, Muhammad-Riza. *History of Persian Literature: From the Beginning of the Islamic Period to the Present Day*. Leiden: E. J. Brill, 1981.

Schimmel, Annemarie. *A Two-Colored Brocade: The Imagery of Persian Poetry*. Chapel Hill: University of North Carolina Press, 1992.

Yarshater, Ehsan, ed. *Persian Literature*. Albany, N.Y.: Bibliotheca Persica, 1988.

Franklin D. Lewis

PHILOSOPHY *See* **Ethics and Social Issues; Kalam; Knowledge; Science, Islam and**

PILGRIMAGE

HAJJ
Kathryn Kueny

ZIYARA
Richard C. Martin

HAJJ

The Islamic hajj refers specifically to the annual pilgrimage to Mecca, Arafat, and Mina during the second week of the Dhu l-Hijja, the final month of the Islamic lunar calendar. Called a duty of humankind to Allah in the Qurʾan (3:97), and the fifth of the five pillars of Islam, in recent years the hajj has attracted about two million Muslims annually from approximately 160 countries. All adult Muslims with proper intentions (*niya*), adequate resources, good health, and sound mind are required to perform this duty once during their lifetimes. Other pilgrimages exist in Islam, including visitations to saints' shrines (*ziyara*), but these are not officially sanctioned.

The Ka'ba, the focal point of the hajj with its heavenly black stone, was a pilgrimage site long before the time of Muhammad. Shortly before his death, Muhammad claimed this site for Islam, and determined a sequence of symbolic rituals to be performed around it by all Muslims. These rituals reenact events in the lives of Ibrahim (Abraham), the archetype for Islam as founder of monotheism (*hanifiyya*) and builder of the Ka'ba, his wife Hagar, and their son Isma'il (Ishmael). Collective and individual rites at this site not only replicate the actions of Muhammad, but also recall the sacred movements of pious biblical prophets who predate Islam.

Prior to the hajj, pilgrims undergo a ritual cleansing that separates them from their profane individual and cultural identities, and allows them to enter sacred space and time as a unified group of believers before God. Men wear a simple white garment to symbolize their unity as Muslims; women wear customary dress, which demonstrates the meeting of diverse cultures on the common holy ground of Mecca. The initial rite of the hajj (*tawaf*), which includes a sevenfold circumambulation of the Ka'ba, is followed by the "running" (*sa'y*) of pilgrims between two hills. This action recalls Hagar's frantic search for water. The apex of the hajj is the "standing" of all pilgrims on Mount Arafat from noon until sunset as they pray individually and collectively to their one God. After sundown, all spend the night at Muzdalifa before the next day's ritual performances of the "stoning" and the "sacrifice" at Mina. Both actions reenact the sacred drama of Ibrahim's attempted sacrifice of Isma'il. Pilgrims throw seven stones at a pillar representing Satan who tried to divert Ibrahim from God's command to sacrifice his son; they sacrifice to celebrate God's substitution of a ram for Isma'il. This sacrificial rite is embraced simultaneously by pilgrims and Muslims all over the world in gratitude for God's mercy. After the sacrifice, pilgrims may perform another *tawaf* and *sa'y*, and then gradually reenter profane space by cutting or shaving their hair and assuming regular dress.

The Islamic pilgrimage preserves, elevates, and reinforces collective and individual Muslim identities in a constantly changing world. Collectively, pilgrims confirm the basic tenets of Islam, including the affirmation of God's oneness, obedience to God, the necessity for a global Muslim community, and the importance of their prophetic past. Many pilgrims return to their homes with the sense they are connected to a greater, transcendent whole, a seamless religious community that surpasses economic, racial, and cultural differences. As Malcolm X pronounced in his autobiography (1990, p. 338), "The *brotherhood*! The people of all races, colors, from all over the world coming together as *one*! It has proved to me the power of the One God." In reality, distinctions among pilgrims exist, as illustrated by the vastly different services and accommodations enjoyed by those of diverse nationalities and classes. In perception, the community reflects unchallenged unity and equality.

Individually, pilgrimage acts as a rite of passage for Muslims who confront major transitions in their lives, including marriage, retirement, illness, or death. As a rite of passage, it also functions as a symbolic affirmation of faith for converts or those who are returning to or renewing their beliefs. In some societies, the hajj transforms ordinary individuals into extraordinary pious exemplars, or social elites. In parts of Egypt, those who have completed the hajj receive an elevated status close to that of a saint. As possessors of blessings (*baraka*) extracted from the holy land, returning pilgrims become saintly individuals reborn free of sin, deserving of paradise. Having successfully navigated the difficult journey to Mecca and back, pilgrims are likened to Muhammad who also made the tough trek to Jerusalem and paradise in the middle of the night. Hausa Nigerians use the pilgrimage to export local healing practices (involving spirits) into orthodox Saudi culture, for which they are greatly but clandestinely compensated. These healers return home to enjoy loftier social and economic positions as a result of their craft. In both Egyptian and Nigerian examples, the hajj accentuates local Muslim practices that challenge the orthodoxy and sense of monolithic communal unity asserted through collective ritual.

The hajj serves both as a spiritual and political arena. Nineteenth-century Muslim anti-imperialist movements were inspired by the hajj. In 1822 and 1823, Sayyid Ahmad performed the pilgrimage, and then launched a jihad against British influence in Egypt. Imam Shamil of Daghestan and Shaykh 'Abd al-Qadir of Algeria met during the hajj to discuss the French presence in North Africa and the Russians in the Causasus. Recent global controversies are played out on the pilgrimage stage, since control of the hajj is directly associated with leadership in the Islamic world. In 1935, an attempt was made to assassinate Ibn Sa'ud during the hajj, in protest of Wahhabi control of the shrines. Recent Saudi control over the hajj has bred resentment and favoritism among those billion Muslims who now have access to the hajj through the rapid air, land, and sea travel of the modern age. In 1986, when King Fahd of Saudi Arabia declared himself to be custodian of the holy sites, Iran challenged his authority by delivering sets of revolutionary sermons condemning America, Israel, and other enemies of Islam (including the Saudi government). The Libyan leader Mu'ammar al-Qaddafi bypassed Saudi authority when he invoked independent judgment (*ijtihad*) to deny the hajj as an essential pillar of Islam. In 2002, the Iraqi government provoked the Saudis to take action when they sent civilian planes to transport pilgrims to the holy land without prior notification of the United Nations Security Council, a direct violation of a 1999 agreement. Through increased media coverage of the hajj, along

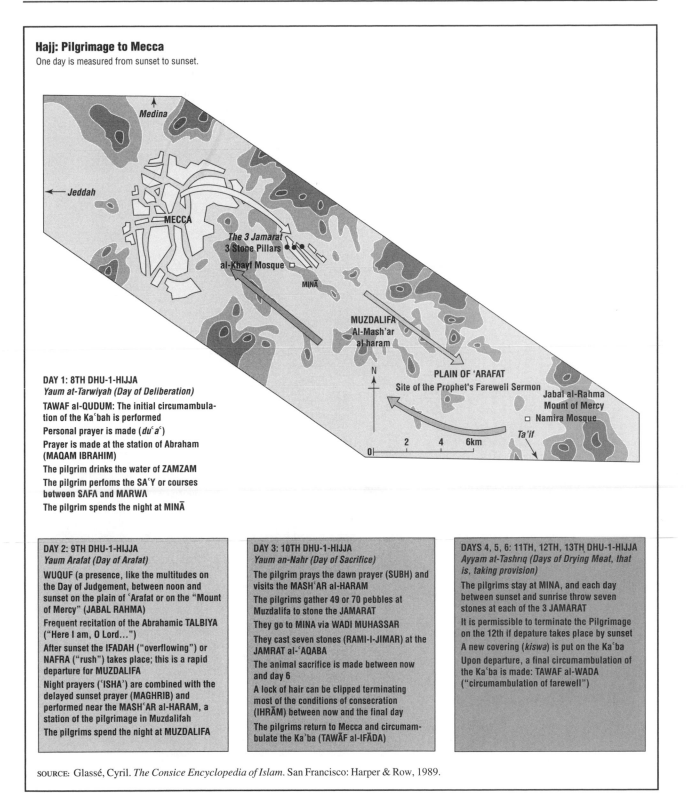

Hajj: Pilgrimage to Mecca
One day is measured from sunset to sunset.

Medina

Jeddah

MECCA

The 3 Jamarat
3 Stone Pillars

al-Khayf Mosque

MINĀ

MUZDALIFA
Al-Mash'ar
al haram

N

PLAIN OF 'ARAFAT
Site of the Prophet's Farewell Sermon

Jabal al-Rahma
Mount of Mercy
Namira Mosque

Ta'if

0   2   4   6km

DAY 1: 8TH DHU-1-HIJJA
Yaum at-Tarwiyah (Day of Deliberation)

TAWAF al-QUDUM: The initial circumambulation of the Ka'bah is performed

Personal prayer is made (*du'a'*)

Prayer is made at the station of Abraham (MAQAM IBRAHIM)

The pilgrim drinks the water of ZAMZAM

The pilgrim perfoms the SA'Y or courses between SAFA and MARWA

The pilgrim spends the night at MINĀ

DAY 2: 9TH DHU-1-HIJJA
Yaum Arafat (Day of Arafat)

WUQUF (a presence, like the multitudes on the Day of Judgement, between noon and sunset on the plain of 'Arafat or on the "Mount of Mercy" (JABAL RAHMA)

Frequent recitation of the Abrahamic TALBIYA ("Here I am, O Lord...")

After sunset the IFADAH ("overflowing") or NAFRA ("rush") takes place; this is a rapid departure for MUZDALIFA

Night prayers ('ISHA') are combined with the delayed sunset prayer (MAGHRIB) and performed near the MASH'AR al-HARAM, a station of the pilgrimage in Muzdalifah

The pilgrims spend the night at MUZDALIFA

DAY 3: 10TH DHU-1-HIJJA
Yaum an-Nahr (Day of Sacrifice)

The pilgrim prays the dawn prayer (SUBH) and visits the MASH'AR al-HARAM

The pilgrims gather 49 or 70 pebbles at Muzdalifa to stone the JAMARAT

They go to MINA via WADI MUHASSAR

They cast seven stones (RAMI-I-JIMAR) at the JAMRAT al-'AQABA

The animal sacrifice is made between now and day 6

A lock of hair can be clipped terminating most of the conditions of consecration (IHRĀM) between now and the final day

The pilgrims return to Mecca and circumambulate the Ka'ba (TAWĀF al-IFĀDA)

DAYS 4, 5, 6: 11TH, 12TH, 13TH DHU-1-HIJJA
Ayyam at-Tashriq (Days of Drying Meat, that is, taking provision)

The pilgrims stay at MINA, and each day between sunset and sunrise throw seven stones at each of the 3 JAMARAT

It is permissible to terminate the Pilgrimage on the 12th if depature takes place by sunset

A new covering (*kiswa*) is put on the Ka'ba

Upon departure, a final circumambulation of the Ka'ba is made: TAWAF al-WADA ("circumambulation of farewell")

SOURCE: Glassé, Cyril. *The Consice Encyclopedia of Islam*. San Francisco: Harper & Row, 1989.

Illustration of the pilgrim's trek to Mecca.

with computer access to the virtual hajj, these tensions among the many conflicting faces of Islam will only increase, as will efforts to make the hajj a venue for common Muslim religious identity around the world.

An image of pilgrims praying at Mount of Mercy appears in the volume two color insert.

See also **'Ibadat; Pilgrimage: Ziyara; Ritual.**

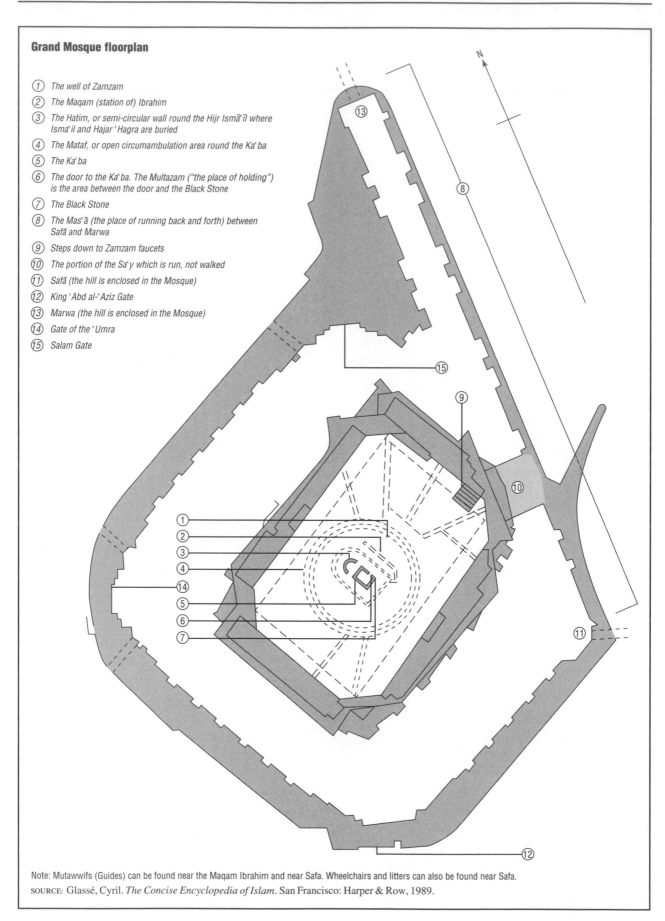

Grand Mosque floorplan

1. The well of Zamzam
2. The Maqam (station of) Ibrahim
3. The Hatim, or semi-circular wall round the Hijr Ismā'īl where Ismaʿil and Hajar ʿHagra are buried
4. The Mataf, or open circumambulation area round the Kaʿba
5. The Kaʿba
6. The door to the Kaʿba. The Multazam ("the place of holding") is the area between the door and the Black Stone
7. The Black Stone
8. The Masʿā (the place of running back and forth) between Safā and Marwa
9. Steps down to Zamzam faucets
10. The portion of the Saʿy which is run, not walked
11. Safā (the hill is enclosed in the Mosque)
12. King ʿAbd al-ʿAziz Gate
13. Marwa (the hill is enclosed in the Mosque)
14. Gate of the ʿUmra
15. Salam Gate

Note: Mutawwifs (Guides) can be found near the Maqam Ibrahim and near Safa. Wheelchairs and litters can also be found near Safa.

SOURCE: Glassé, Cyril. *The Concise Encyclopedia of Islam.* San Francisco: Harper & Row, 1989.

Floorplan of the Grand Mosque.

BIBLIOGRAPHY

Campo, Juan Eduardo. *The Other Sides of Paradise: Explorations into the Religious Meanings of Domestic Space in Islam.* Columbia: The University of South Carolina Press, 1991.

Firestone, Reuven. *Journeys into Holy Lands: The Evolution of the Abraham-Ishmael Legends in Islamic Exegesis.* Albany: State University of New York Press, 1990.

Long, D. *The Hajj Today: A Survey of Contemporary Pilgrimage to Mekkah.* Albany: State University of New York Press, 1979.

Peters, F. E. *The Hajj: The Muslim Pilgrimage to Mecca and the Holy Places.* Princeton, N.J.: Princeton University Press, 1994.

Rubin, Uri. "The Great Pilgrimage of Muhammad: Some Notes on Sura IX." *Journal of Semitic Studies* 27 (1982): 241–260.

Wolfe, Michael. *One Thousand Roads to Mecca: Ten Centuries of Travelers Writing about the Muslim Pilgrimage.* New York: Grove Press, 1997.

Young, William C. "The Kaʿba, Gender, and the Rites of Pilgrimage." *International Journal of Middle East Studies* 25 (1993): 285–300.

Kathryn Kueny

ZIYARA

In and Shiʿite Islam, the concept of *ziyara* is found in many diverse parts of the Muslim world, especially those parts for which Sufism was the main agency for the spread of Islam. The chief exception to the tolerance of *ziyara* historically is found in those regions where the Hanbali school of law has predominated. Since the eighteenth century this has been primarily in the Arabian Peninsula under the influence of Wahhabi and Salafi forms of Islamic Puritanism, which shuns all innovations in worship that were not clearly sanctioned by the Prophet.

Nonetheless, throughout most of Africa, Anatolia, as well as West, Central, South and Southeast Asia, pilgrims have visited shrines for centuries, with many local variations in architecture and ritual performance. The *mazars* are visited by pilgrims throughout the year, to seek blessing (*baraka*) from the saint buried at the shrine tomb. Often, one or two "deputies" or respected followers of the saint will be buried in the same complex. The anniversary of the death of the saint (*ʿurs*, which also means "wedding"), is the occasion of a major visitation and celebration by his devotees. For major saints *ʿurs* was an occasion for a *ziyara* marked by joyous celebration, dancing, and ritual orations.

Although many reform-minded local religious elites (ulema) have argued that visitation to Sufi shrines was an un-Islamic innovation (*bidʿa*) and thus forbidden, many others have accepted such practices as local expressions of Muslim piety. Ziyara rituals and performances often attract Christians, Hindus, and members of other religious communities who live among or near the Muslims who visit the shrines, thus making the *ziyara* a ritual negotiation of communal inclusiveness in areas where Muslims and non-Muslims live with soft boundaries between their communities. This differentiates the practice of *ziyara* from the religious duty of hajj. Yet for many Muslims over the centuries, both forms of pilgrimage have been practiced. For example, in premodern times of overland travel, pilgrims from Spain and North Africa on their way to Mecca to perform the hajj would often plan a stop in Tanta, in the Egyptian Delta, to visit the shrine of Ahmad al-Badawi (1199–1276). Although such rituals are traditional and premodern in their origins, modern urban Muslims in regions where ziyara pilgrimage is customary and deeply rooted in local practice are often seen among the pilgrims celebrating the anniversaries of these saints.

See also **Ibn Hanbal; Pilgrimage; Hajj; Saint; Tasawwuf.**

Richard C. Martin

PLURALISM

LEGAL AND ETHNO-RELIGIOUS
Irene Schneider

POLITICAL
Gudrun Krämer

LEGAL AND ETHNO-RELIGIOUS

Several Qurʾanic verses as well as hadiths seem to confirm the acceptance of ethnic and religious diversity or pluralism. One such example is found at 49:13, which reads: "O people! We have created you from a male and female; and we have made you in confederacies and tribes so that you might come to know one another. The noblest among you in the eyes of God is the most pious, for God is omniscient and well-informed." This verse offers no prejudice, but rather expresses a consciousness of difference and emphasizes that piety is more important than the birth. Ethnic pluralism, that is the existence of groups defined primarily by race, language, or other cultural, historical, and in some sense geographical criteria was thus accepted from the beginning in Islam. However, the unity of the Islamic *umma* (community of believers) was emphasized and was thought of as a kind of superstructure upon which other identities, whether tribal or ethnic, were hung.

The Spread of Islam to Other Cultures

From the time of the first conquests, Muslims spread out from the Arabian Peninsula to people who neither spoke Arabic nor could claim Arab descent. Different ethnic groups, as well as different religions, were incorporated into the new empire. The integration of people from other races and cultures did not pose great legal or religious problems, although in the first two centuries, the institution of *walaʾ*

(clienthood) was used to affiliate non-Arab Muslims to the developing Muslim society. This reflects the struggle between the pure-Arab, conquering aristocracy, who claimed ethnic and social superiority, and the Muslim converts among the conquered, who could claim neither ethnic nor familial advantage. Thus, the cohabitation of different ethnicities and races was never without problems. The idea of racial innocence and total racial (and ethnic) harmony in Islam is, in other words, a Western creation, as Bernard Lewis argues in his 1990 volume, *Race and Slavery in the Middle East*.

Accommodating Other Religious Practices

Religious pluralism, on the other hand, must be dealt with on several levels. Whereas the acceptance of the "people of the book" (comprising Muslims, Christians, and Jews) was stated from the beginning, and whereas Christians and Jews had an acknowledged (but not equal) position in the Muslim society, people belonging to other, "non-book" religions were required to convert to Islam. However, even within Islam, belief itself is not and cannot be considered monolithic. Pluralism existed in Islamic formal theology as well as in popular belief.

The common belief in Islam is based on the acknowledgment of the unity of God, and Muhammad being the prophet of God. It also requires the acknowledgment of the other four pillars of faith: prayer, fasting, pilgrimage, and the payment of alms. Those who did not accept these basic tenets were considered to be unbelievers. On the other hand, within this framework, a wide range of different forms of religiosity developed, as evidenced by the rise of the mystic orders, especially since the fifteenth century.

Theological controversies centered around several different issues, including the analysis of the concept of God, the ontological and cosmological proofs, and the politics of the application of divine rule to the community. Different theological schools came into existence, such as the Murji'a, the Qadiriyya, and the Mu'tazila. These have been complemented by diverse approaches to mystical and philosophical theology and, more recently, by a theology that reflected the confrontation with Western colonial powers.

Religious pluralism on both the normative and the social level must be looked at in a historical perspective, taking into consideration Islam's adaptation to the manifold political, economical, regional, and social conditions, and the different cultural backgrounds and separate historical developments that prevailed in the vast areas into which it spread. There is, however, a limitation to tolerance, a turning point where different beliefs must be judged as unbelief (*kufr*). Just where this turning point occurs is still under discussion today, and transgressions are still prosecuted. An example is the case of Nasr Abu Zaid (b. 1943), who was considered an unbeliever for his interpretation of the Qur'an. As punishment, he was forced to divorce his wife in 1995 (although the marriage was later reinstated).

Legal Pluralism

Islamic law can also be called pluralistic. It derives its norms, rules, and judgements from the holy texts (Qur'an, sunna), but in cases where these sources provide no clear rules, they are derived through the method of analogy (*qiyas*). Rules and judgements derived in this way were then gradually accepted through the consensus of the jurists (*ijma'*), which, however, was not institutionalized. Thus, from the beginning, there existed a wide range of acceptable legal resolutions to problems. Over time these were derived from the texts by the jurists (*fuqaha*) and laid down in the legal literature. This process of derivation was based on the independent juristic interpretation of the texts, called *ijtihad*. Codification of law only began in modern times, starting in the Ottoman Empire with the *mecelle* in 1877. The methodological tool of *ijtihad* and the pluralism of different legal norms and rules have always supplied Islamic Law with a certain flexibility.

Four major legal schools have emerged over time. These are the Maliki, Hanafi, the Shafi', and the Hanbali. In addition there are the Shi'ite schools of law, the most important of which being the school of the Twelver Shi'a. On the institutional level, this pluralism led the rulers of the Mamluk Empire, in Egypt in the thirteenth century, to create the offices of the four judges, each associated with one of the four Sunni schools of law.

Nonetheless, the application of Islamic law has always been restricted to the Muslim community, and the legal independence of the Jewish and Christian communities was accepted to a certain degree. Thus, Islamic law could be defined as a personal law and not as the law of a territory. In the Ottoman Empire, the *millet* system began as a coexistence of religious communities, each with its own administrative autonomy and jurisdiction. This system finally led to a change whereby the personal law became more territorial, ultimately becoming a law applicable to all subjects of the Ottoman Empire and not only to the Muslim community.

Legal pluralism describes the (legal) situation observed in the Islamic countries today, but it is by no means exclusive to them. From the lawyer's point of view, legal pluralism denotes a state's recognition of the existence of a multiplicity of legal sources that constitute its legislation: international treaties, customary law, religious law, and the like. From the sociological point of view, legal pluralism can be defined more broadly, to acknowledge that a plurality of sometimes interactive social fields produce norms of legitimate behavior. For Islam, the term not only recognizes the coexistence of modern, secular modern laws alongside *shari'a* norms, but also the existence of customary practice beside, or even in opposition to state law.

Throughout its history, the legal structures of Islamic society have made room not only for the coexistence of *shari'a* and *qanun* (that is, religious and secular law), but also for customary practice (*'urf*). An example of this is the so-called

"secular justice" of the *mazalim*, an institution dealing with grievances that not only is rooted deeply in the theory of Islamic constitution but which has also been practiced through centuries. The problem of accommodating multiple sources of the law, however, gained special importance under the influence of modern, secular Western law in nineteenth and twentieth centuries. In response to the growing importance of Western law in Muslim societies, a powerful political Islam arose in the 1970s that was rooted in the belief of the necessary implementation of Islamic law. Thus, Islamic law was rediscovered as a national legal tradition, and was held up in opposition to the influence of the Western law.

Kilian Bälz, a turn of the twenty-first-century legal scholar whose work has focused on the problem of the legal pluralism in Muslim society, has argued that the coexistence and relation between the modern Western law and the *shariʿa* has always been discussed in this context of influence. He has shown that in Egypt, as in many other Islamic countries, the constitution holds the principles of *shariʿa* to be the primary source of legislation. In 1994, however, Egypt's highest court defended the autonomy of the secular legal order by taking control of the interpretation of Islamic law. As Bälz reports, the court reserves to itself the right to interpret Islamic rules, and it reconstructs Islamic law on the basis of secular paradigms. This is, however, nothing new. The interpretation of *shariʿa* has historically been flexible, as can be seen in the existence of several different schools of law (*ikhtilaf*) and through the practice of *ijtihad*, which is the legal interpretation of the Qurʾan and other textual sources by jurists. Thus, Islamic legal pluralism refers not only to multiple sources of the law (religious or secular), but also to multiple interpretations of any given law.

Also important to the analysis of Islamic legal pluralism is an examination of rules, other than those enacted by the state, which govern and shape social conduct. Social norms and customary practices can in no way be considered uniform through out the lands of Islam, yet they operate within or alongside of formal legal structures. An important example of this is the *haqq al-ʿarab*, a form of conflict resolution in modern Egypt (and other Muslim countries), that operates outside of both religious and formal secular law, yet enjoys at least partial official recognition.

See also ʿAda; Hadith; Law; Qurʾan; Shariʿa; Sunna.

BIBLIOGRAPHY

Aslan, Adnan. *Religious Pluralism in Christian and Islamic Philosophy.* Richmond, U.K.: Curzon, 1998.

Bälz, Kilian. "*Shariʿa* and *Qanun* in Egyptian Law. A Systems Theory Approach to Legal Pluralism." In *Yearbook of Islamic and Middle Eastern Law*, Volume 2 (1995): 37.

Dupret, Baudoin; Berger, Maurits; and al-Zwaini, Laila. *Legal Pluralism in the Arab World.* The Hague: Kluwer Law International, 1999.

Lewis, Bernard. *Race and Slavery in the Middle East.* Oxford, U.K.: Oxford University Press, 1990.

Irene Schneider

POLITICAL

Contemporary positions as formulated by Islamic thinkers and activists can be roughly divided into two opposing views: one deeply suspicious of pluralism as menacing Muslim power and unity, the other supporting pluralism as contributing to Muslim strength and creativity. In a kind of political *tawhid* (the theological doctrine of the oneness of God), the first gives priority to the unity of the community, which figures so prominently in the Qurʾan and sunna of the Prophet. This corresponds to the concept of *ijmaʿ*, that is, the consensus of the Muslim community as expressed by its religious scholars in juridical theory (*usul al-fiqh*) to which modern authors frequently refer when trying to ground their notions in the Islamic tradition. Taken to its extremes, the emphasis on unity can imply the rejection of all divergence of opinions, or any kind of criticism or opposition to the dominant doctrines and practices, which are denounced as *fitna*, that is, a menace to, and sin against, not just the given sociopolitical system but the divinely ordained order at large. If there is only one truth, and if it can be identified without doubt or mistake, there is no room for free debate, political competition and institutionalized pluralism, for there are only two "parties" (or rather groups or communities): the party of God (*hizb allah*) and the party of the devil (*hizb al-shaytan*). Political parties represent particularistic interests at the expense of the common good (*al-maslaha al-ʿamma*), dividing and thereby weakening the community.

Quoting a well-known Qurʾanic verse (Sura 49:13) and an equally famous Prophetic saying (hadith) according to which the "diversity of opinion [*ikhtilaf*] among my community is a blessing," advocates of the alternative view point to the elements of diversity and pluralism in the religious, legal, and historical heritage of the Muslim community (including most notably the different Sunni and Shiʿite schools of law, sing, *madhhab*) as one of the very sources of its flowering, resilience, and attractiveness. Even though there is only one truth, there is no guarantee that humans will be able to find it with infallible certainty. Free debate is therefore both legitimate and necessary, and given the conditions of modern mass society, political pluralism may have to be institutionalized in political parties and associations to become effective.

However, there are clear limits to legitimate diversity and pluralism from the Islamic viewpoint: they are defined by God's law and revelation. Debate must fall short of any radical critique of religion, or its dominant interpretations, which is readily denounced as blasphemy, heresy (*kufr*) or apostasy (*ridda*). The crucial issues of religious authority and effective power of definition are largely left unaddressed. As long as the religious categories of truth and falsehood, right and wrong, licit and illicit are used to evaluate political opinions and decisions, political pluralism remains confined to what the powers-that-be define as consistent with the public order, which in its turn can be identified with prevalent understandings of religion, custom and morals.

See also **Pluralism: Legal and Ethno-Religious.**

BIBLIOGRAPHY

Krämer, Gudrun. "Islam and Pluralism." In *Political Liberalization and Democratization in the Arab World.*Vol. 1, *Theoretical Perspectives.* Edited by Rex Brynen, Bahgat Korany, and Paul Noble. Boulder. London: Lynne Riener, 1995.

Moussalli, Ahmad S. "Modern Islamic Fundamentalist Discourses on Civil Society, Pluralism and Democracy." In Vol. 1, *Civil Society in the Middle East.* Edited by Augustus Richard Norton. Leiden: Brill, 1995.

Gudrun Krämer

POETRY, LITERATURE *See* **Arabic Literature; Persian Language and Literature; Urdu Language, Literature, and Poetry**

POLITICAL ISLAM

Political Islam is the phrase used to denote a wide range of individuals and associations dedicated to the transformation of state and society so as to make them "Islamic." The term also refers to Islam conceived as a set of beliefs, a code of conduct, or a repertory of images and metaphors relevant to politics, as well as to various attempts to define an "Islamic state" or "Islamic order."

The "Islamic Trend"

Like any other term that is used to define the broad and heterogeneous "Islamic trend," such as Islamism, integralism, and even more so, fundamentalism, the term "political Islam" is problematic and contested. "Islamism," as the most comprehensive term, has the benefit of being largely value-free. It describes the fact that "Islamists" advocate the establishment of an "Islamic order" (*nizam Islami*) that is usually defined by the "application of the *shariʿa*, " that is, the implementation of Islam's divinely ordained moral and legal code regulating all human activity, including the organization of state and society. It does not indicate how they intend to establish such an order. For example, it does not specify whether they consider the use of force to be legitimate, nor does it say whether they would use, or even privilege, the political sphere in their activities. It also says nothing specific about their concept of

shariʿa, or about the precise nature of the Islamic state or system they wish to establish. While the term is mostly applied to groups and associations, including political parties, individuals can also be labeled Islamists. To the extent that Islamists engage in politics, they are part of political Islam. An alternative term, "integralism," is derived from the French, where it is more commonly used than Islamism. Both terms are, by and large, synonymous.

On the other hand, "fundamentalism" generally carries highly negative connotations, reflecting a whole set of traits and attitudes. Chief among these is a literalist, or scripturalist, reading of the normative texts (scripture or revelation; in the present case, the Qurʾan and sunna) that tends to reject all kinds of allegorical, mythical, mystical, or modernist exegesis as fundamentally wrong and illegitimate. The term also implies a common assumption that not only is there only one truth, but that the fundamentalists have a monopoly of this truth; a lack of tolerance of different opinions and interpretations flowing from this conviction; and a propensity to resort to violence if their reading of scripture and, more generally, their understanding of the faith, is challenged or threatened, be it from within the community or from without. In view of this cluster of negative attributes, it should be emphasized that a fundamentalist understanding of the faith need not be accompanied by militancy, nor does it necessarily entail political activism. In other words, fundamentalists can be either activist or quietist. If reserved for those Islamists who advocate a fundamentalist interpretation of Islam, irrespective of their stand on politics in general and violence in particular, "fundamentalism" can serve as a meaningful analytical term in an Islamic as well as in any other context.

"Political Islam" designates that particular segment of the broader Islamist trend (Ar. *al-tayyar al-islami*) that is active in the political sphere. Political Islam is not synonymous with violent, radical, or extremist Islamism, and it is not restricted to opposition groups. The spectrum ranges from advocates of an Islamic republic to sympathizers of an Islamic monarchy or a resuscitated caliphate, and from self-declared liberals to uncompromising conservatives. Some Islamists are commonly classified as moderate or pragmatic, others as radical, militant, or extremist. For practical reasons, the term is best used for organized groups, movements, and parties, keeping in mind that there may be considerable numbers of individuals who share the basic objectives and assumptions of political Islam without being affiliated to any particular group or party.

Intellectual Origins: The Salafiyya

Political Islam is one of the most conspicuous, and at the same time most controversial, phenomena of modern Muslim societies. It builds on earlier reform movements of the late nineteenth and early twentieth centuries, which in their turn took up core concerns of major reformers of the eighteenth and early nineteenth centuries. The reformers included Shah Wali Allah (1703–1762), Muhammad b. ʿAbd al-Wahhab

(1703–1792), 'Uthman Dan Fodio (c. 1754–1817), Muhammad al-Shawkani (1760–1839), and Muhammad b. 'Ali al-Sanusi (1787–1859), all of whom possessed very different assumptions, approaches, and activities. Political Islam today builds on the call to invigorate Islam through *ijtihad* (independent reasoning), while departing from the earlier reformers in several important ways. Among the reform movements of the turn of the twentieth century, the Salafiyya stands out as having had the most important intellectual influence on later generations of Islamists.

The Salafiyya movement was named after its objective to revive the spirit of the first generations of Muslims (Ar. *al-salaf al-salih*). It sought to accomplish this by recreating a vibrant Muslim society in the modern era, thereby bringing about the rebirth, or renaissance, of Islam (*al-nahda*) after centuries of weakness and decadence. The Salafiyya defined a number of themes that are still relevant to many Islamists today: that Islam constitutes the essence of Muslim identity; that it is more than the belief in God and the prophet Muhammad; that it provides for a specific way of life; and that, if properly understood, it is entirely compatible with modernity, notably modern science and the spirit of rational inquiry. However, the Salafiyya also believed that, in order for Islam to serve as the principal source of inspiration and guidance to Muslims in the modern age, it first had to be freed from the many misunderstandings and distortions that had been accumulated over the centuries.

For the Salafiyya, Islamic reform consisted of cleansing Islam of these misunderstandings and distortions. Only thus could the creative spirit of the early Muslim community be restored. This required not only dedication but also the systematic use of reason. Faith and reason do not contradict each other, but on the contrary, are mutually reinforcing. *Ijtihad*, meaning the effort to "discover" the spirit of divine law rather than blindly following the letter of traditional Islamic jurisprudence (so-called imitation, *taqlid*), provides the chief instrument of reform. Muslim jurisprudence, along with its rules and regulations, is not identical with divine law, for although God's law is infallible and unchangeable, humans—and the systems of jurisprudence that they may devise—are prone to error. Thus, the Salafiyya held that the jurists' law had to be critically revised in order to make it wholly suitable for modern life. This revision could be done by distinguishing between *shari'a* and *fiqh*.

Shari'a comprises the eternal laws and general principles that had been set down by the divine lawgiver in the Qur'an and exemplified by his prophet in the sunna. *Fiqh*, on the other hand, although based on scripture, refers to the detailed rules and regulations that were later elaborated by Muslim jurists. For the Salafiyya, the *shari'a* provides the best guidance for Muslims in the modern age, allowing them to regain the position of strength and confidence that they so gloriously occupied in earlier times, and from which they had been displaced by a triumphant West only because of its superior material power.

As an intellectual force, the Salafiyya exerted considerable influence on (Sunni) Muslim reformers from Morocco to Hadhramaut, India, Turkestan, and Java. Organizationally speaking, however, it was a weak, loosely connected group of urban scholars and intellectuals based in the major cities of Egypt, Syria, and Iraq, as well as their colleagues, friends, and family. Major figures in the movement included Jamal al-Din al-Afghani (1839–1897), Muhammad 'Abduh (1849–1905), and Rashid Rida (1865–1935). The Salafiyya made systematic use of the newly emerging press and book market, disseminating their writings over much of the Islamic world within a relatively short period of time. However, they were not linked to any formal association or party, and consequently there was no mass support for the ideas and ideals that they espoused.

Ideologues of Political Islam: al-Banna, Maududi, and Qutb

Political Islam proper came into existence after the First World War, with the emergence of organized movements that reached beyond the limited circles of Muslim scholars, writers, and journalists. The Egyptian Muslim Brotherhood was among the most influential of these movements, and its leader, Hasan al-Banna (1906–1949), became one of the best-known representatives of political Islam. Founded in 1928 in the Egyptian provincial town of Ismailiyya, the Muslim Brotherhood (*jama'at al-ikhwan al-muslimin*) grew from a rather insignificant association dedicated to moral reform into a broad-based mass movement that made a considerable impact on Egyptian society and politics. Over a period of several decades, it also expanded into several Arab countries, from Sudan to Palestine, Syria, Iraq, and Yemen. Hasan al-Banna excelled as the charismatic leader of his organization, but he was not an innovative thinker, and is mostly remembered for his activism, not for his contribution to Islamic thought.

The opposite could be said of two of the most prominent figures of political Islam of the interwar and the post-World War II period: Abu l-A'la' Maududi (1903–1979) and Sayyid Qutb (1906–1966). Both of these men were prolific writers, journalists, and to a lesser extent also political activists, the former in his native India and Pakistan, the latter in Egypt. Their major works continue to be read all over the Islamic world. Living under very different circumstances, in societies that had little in common except for having been under British colonial rule, these men nevertheless shared certain convictions concerning modern society, and they introduced certain key terms that have since become part and parcel of the Islamist vocabulary.

Perhaps foremost of these terms was their conception of sovereignty, which they attributed exclusively to God (*hakimiyya*). From His sovereign authority flows the moral and legal code that regulates human affairs. This is the *shari'a*, as it is contained in the Qur'an and sunna. Every Muslim believer is, thus, able to discover God's law by studying revelation, and is obligated to apply this law to his or her own life. From this perspective, it follows that all human attempts to create rules and laws of their own design are not only futile, but are also illegitimate. Such attempts constitute a heinous sin, for they manifest the human will to set oneself up as God's equal, if not as God's rival. Making and following laws other than the *shari'a* is therefore a sign of heresy and polytheism (*shirk*) and must be dealt with as such. For both Maududi and Qutb, contemporary Muslims had neglected their religious duties to such an extent that they had fallen back into a state of (religious) ignorance (*jahiliyya*). If this ignorance could be excused at the time before revelation, it is no longer forgivable, for all men and women are now capable of hearing the truth and obeying the Lord. Contemporary Muslims therefore are Muslims by name only. In reality, they have renounced Islam and have reverted to unbelief (*kufr*).

Both Maududi and Qutb spoke of the possibility to practice *takfir*, that is, to exclude ("nominal") Muslims from the community of believers (often described as "excommunication"). Yet they were much more reluctant than many of their followers to call for violent measures against these defective Muslims, and were similarly reluctant to propagate *takfir* and jihad against society as a whole. They did, however, declare un-Islamic any government that imposed laws and practices not exclusively based on the *shari'a* and insisted on the duty of all true Muslims to fight with all their might for the establishment of an Islamic order based on the *shari'a*.

The radical stand taken by Sayyid Qutb in the late 1950s and early 1960s is often explained by the ruthless suppression that the Muslim Brotherhood in general, and Qutb in particular, suffered at the hands of the Free Officer regime. The Free Officer movement came to power in Egypt in July 1952 and quickly turned against all potential critics and rivals, including the Muslim Brothers who had initially supported their coup. The Brotherhood likened its experience of persecution, torture, and exile to the trial and tribulations (*mihna*) suffered by such venerated figures as Ahmad b. Hanbal (780–855) at the hands of Muslim rulers in earlier times, and they left a lasting imprint on both the collective memory and the individuals concerned. Qutb's vastly influential book, *Ma'alim fi l-tariq* (Signposts), was written in prison, and Qutb himself was executed in 1966, becoming a martyr to his cause. Maududi, from whom Qutb had adopted and adapted the notions of *hakimiyya*, *jahiliyya*, and *takfir* had been fortunate enough to work under much more auspicious circumstances, for he endured no such hardships. State persecution can thus help to explain the attractiveness of militant Islamism to certain parts of the public, as evidenced by Qutb's radicalization, but Maududi's example shows that radical positions cannot be reduced to the effects of persecution.

Under Jamal 'Abd al-Nasser's regime (1952–1970), the Muslim Brotherhood was severely suppressed inside Egypt. In Syria, Iraq, and Jordan, by contrast, sister organizations were mostly able to function within the given political framework. In the 1970s, Egyptian president Anwar al-Sadat (1918–1981) revised Nasser's course in favor of a more open Egyptian political economy. After rapprochement with the United States and ultimately peace with Israel, the Muslim Brothers were able to reorganize, though they were never granted official recognition. Their past experience of violent confrontations with the government had resulted in terrible losses, and the majority of activists opted for a return to a reformist strategy. The new focus was to be on spreading the message of Islam (*da'wa*) by all possible means and in all possible arenas. The Brotherhood began to use the media and the educational system more effectively, and to engage in social and charitable work, in professional syndicates, trade unions, and other associations of "civil society." Muslim Brothers also participated in local and national elections, and for that purpose even entered into coalitions with legally recognized political parties. They did not attempt to found a political party of their own, however, even though Islamists in other parts of the Muslim world—from Morocco, Algeria, and Tunisia to Turkey, Pakistan, and Malaysia—were willing and able to do so.

The Islamic Revolution and Its Aftermath

The Islamic revolution in Iran in 1979 had an enormous impact on the Muslim world, and on Islamist activists more particularly. It seemed to prove that in spite of the Egyptian experience, a system as powerful and repressive as the Iranian monarchy could be overthrown and replaced by an Islamic republic, provided that the Islamist movement had strong leadership, an effective organization, and the support of the masses. For accomplishing this feat, the revolutionaries led by Ayatollah Ruhollah Khomeini (1902–1989) were admired well beyond Islamist circles. Still, Khomeini's theory of the "guardianship of the jurisconsultant" (*velayat-e faqih*) that vested the most qualified Shi'ite cleric with political power, remained controversial among the highest-ranking Shi'ite scholars, and entirely unacceptable to their Sunni counterparts. Islamists drew inspiration from the initial success of the Iranian revolution, hoping to follow its example in their own countries. However, with the exception of certain Shi'ite organizations like Hizb Allah in Lebanon, which initially propagated *velayat-e faqih* but later adopted different models of an "Islamic order," most Islamists generally avoided comment on the Iranian model of government, declaring it to be suited to Shi'ite traditions perhaps, but not to Sunni Islam.

In the wake of the Iranian revolution, Islamist opposition groups and movements grew more active even in those parts of the Muslim world where previously they had not been very prominent or visible. They arose or became stronger in the Maghrib, Lebanon and Palestine, Saudi Arabia, and different parts of Central and Southeast Asia. If previously there had been individuals and associations advocating an "Islamic solution" to the ills of state, culture, and society in all of these areas, they had not engaged in the same kind of organized, and often militant, activity that became the hallmark of the 1980s. Yet even after 1979, political Islam remained highly diversified in terms of ideology, strategy, and organization. At no point did there emerge an Islamist "International" capable of coordinating Islamist activities around the globe. While there clearly existed cross-links between various groups and individuals, individual groups mostly continued to operate within a regional order that was defined by the existing state boundaries.

In the 1980s, militant Islam was on the rise and receiving much attention. The assassination of Egyptian president Anwar al-Sadat in 1981; the abortive Islamic uprising in Syria in 1982; violent clashes between Islamist activists and the state authorities in Algeria, Tunisia, Libya, Pakistan, and other parts of the Islamic world; the formation of Hizb Allah and HAMAS in Lebanon and Palestine, respectively, all contributed to the impression that the Islamic world might be swept by a revolutionary tide originating in Iran. It did not happen. Even in the 1980s, militant Islamism constituted only one segment of the ever-broadening "Islamic trend." The majority of Islamists continued to follow a pragmatic path, combining energetic activities in the public sphere (da'wa) with grassroots social work as well as economic and political activities of various kinds, including local and national politics. The Islamic Salvation Front in Algeria, the Islamic Tendency Movement in Tunisia, the National Islamic Front in Sudan, the Muslim Brotherhood in Egypt, the Reform Movement in Yemen, the Salvation Party in Turkey, the Jama'at-i Islami in Pakistan, the Pan-Malayan Islamic Party (PAS) in Malaysia, and numerous other organizations advocated a pragmatic strategy of nonviolence without completely excluding the use of force where and when it was deemed necessary.

These organizations did not necessarily shrink from using pressure or even intimidation in order to implement their ideas of proper conduct. Such measures were mostly directed against women, artists, and intellectuals. At the same time, they condemned *takfir* of Muslims and armed jihad against the government. Despite serious setbacks in the 1990s, when Algeria's Islamic Salvation Front was prevented from winning an electoral majority in 1992, and Turkey's Salvation Party was forced by the military establishment to dissolve and reorganize under a different name, the pragmatic or "moderate" strategy was upheld by most Islamists throughout the final two decades of the twentieth century.

The same seemed to hold true for the aftermath of 11 September 2001. The terrorist attack revealed the existence of a new kind of transnational Islamist network that was able to recruit and operate within the Islamic world as well as outside of it. Its links to existing Islamist leaders and organizations have yet to be systematically explored. What can be said is that, within the Muslim world, and not just among Islamists, the attacks on the World Trade Center in New York City and the Pentagon in Washington, D.C., were admired by many for their sheer boldness and unprecedented effectiveness. At the same time, even radical Islamists were appalled by the loss of life, condemning the indiscriminate use of violence against innocent men and women as utterly un-Islamic.

The Islamic Alternative: Visions of an "Islamic Order"
Political Islam draws much of its strength and support from its critique of the existing power relations, blatant injustices, and rampant corruption both within the various Muslim states and societies and globally. More particularly, Islamists present Islam as the only alternative to the world's existing powers and ideologies, from capitalism to communism, and from liberalism to fascism. Since the fall of the Soviet Union, the United States and the West more generally have been identified as the most powerful external enemy of Islam. Within the Muslim world, secularism is singled out as the most dangerous internal threat to Muslim identity and authenticity, notions that have high priority on the Islamist agenda. Most of the themes and slogans put forth by Islamists have to be judged within the framework of this competition with other powers and ideologies, both within the Muslim world and beyond. With the spread and intensification of globalization, however, distinctions between internal and external trends and elements have become increasingly difficult to make.

With the exception of Iran and Afghanistan, Islamist opposition movements have not been able to overthrow the ruling regimes under which they have arisen, nor to replace such regimes with Islamic republics. The 1989 military coup in Sudan may have been staged with the help of the National Islamic Front led by Hasan al-Turabi (b.1932), but the resultant government was not controlled by the Islamists. The kingdom of Saudi Arabia, which in several respects conforms to Islamist ideas, was founded as a result of dynastic conquest, not of an Islamic revolution. In most other states with significant Muslim populations, or a Muslim majority, Islamist groups and parties have been kept under close state control and restrained as much as possible as autonomous political actors. In national elections Islamists in several instances have been able to win as much as twelve to twenty percent of the vote, but as a rule they have not been allowed to play an independent role in parliament, let alone to join the government. Turkey, Morocco, Kuwait, Yemen, and Lebanon are among the few exceptions here. The fact that Islamists outside of Iran have proved unable to stage a revolution and to capture power in the aftermath of 1979, combined with the fact that in both Iran and Afghanistan their performance fell well short of expectations, has led a number of observers to declare the "failure of political Islam."

Political Islam may well have failed, at least when politics is narrowly defined, but such a judgement completely ignores the very deep impact Islamist themes, demands, and activities have had on public debates, social behavior and legal practices all over the Muslim world and among expatriate Muslim communities. Islamist activists may have been prevented from playing an independent political role in most of their home countries, but their concerns have been adapted in various ways by the ruling elites, whether as consciously employed "Islamic" language, symbols, and imagery (using Islamic formula in their public speeches, building mosques and Islamic schools, restoring Islamic monuments, and so on), or as acts of ostentatious piety (praying in front of TV cameras, going on pilgrimage, or giving up trivial pursuits and "immoral" entertainment or alcohol) to present themselves as devout Muslims.

In a significant number of states (including Pakistan, Egypt, and Sudan, as well as individual member states of Malaysia and Nigeria), the *shariʿa*, or rather legal codes presented as such, were introduced in the course of the 1980s and 1990s. Women protesting the introduction of discriminating "Islamic" legislation in the sphere of family law were threatened by radical Islamists, including conservative ulema, and insufficiently protected by their governments. Critical intellectuals and academics were silenced and their works were either censored or banned by governments fearing Islamist challenges to their Islamic credentials. The adoption of so-called Islamic dress spread widely, even against deliberate government attempts to ban its use in schools, universities, and public administration. Religious practices from fasting to prayer and the hajj intensified in many areas and social milieus. In light of these developments, which affected the public as much as the private domains, Islamism in general and political Islam in particular have been tremendously successful.

This was possible because, contrary to widespread perceptions, Islamist ideas have not been restricted to militant opposition movements, but have been shared by a considerable portion of the broader Muslim public. With its combination of catchy slogans ("Islam is the solution," "application of the *shariʿa*," "the Qurʾan is our constitution," and the like), its commitment to social and charitable work, and its occasional application of pressure and intimidation, Islamism has appealed not just to the young, the desperate, and the uneducated, but also to many members of the urban middle class. It has found a sympathetic hearing from government officials as well as the well-educated, affluent, and widely traveled professionals, academics, and businesspeople, including active representatives of civil society. The term "political Islam" is, for practical reasons, mostly applied to organized movements, which as a rule have to work in opposition to the regimes in power, but the ideas and demands implicit in the phrase have permeated large sections of society, and have even influenced government policies, at least in the legal and social fields. Foreign policy and security affairs have been less affected by Islamist concerns, which tend to focus on Islamic solidarity, a vociferous critique of the West, and hostility to Israel. It is in domestic politics that the Islamist impact has been most deeply felt. It remains to be seen to what extent the failure of the Taliban regime in Afghanistan, and the unimpressive economic and social record of the Islamic Republic of Iran will reduce the appeal of political Islam in other parts of the world.

See also **Banna, Hasan al-; Fundamentalism; Ikhwan al-Muslimin; Islam and Islamic Law; Maududi, Abu l-Aʿlaʾ; Qutb, Sayyid; Revolution: Islamic Revolution in Iran; Salafiyya; Secularization; Shariʿa.**

BIBLIOGRAPHY

Ayubi, Nazih N. *Political Islam. Religion and Politics in the Arab World.* London and New York: Routledge,1991.

Binder, Leonard. *Islamic Liberalism. A Critique of Development Ideologies.* Chicago and London: University of Chicago Press, 1998.

Burgat, François, and Dowell, William. *The Islamic Movement in North Africa,* 2d ed. Austin: Center for Middle Eastern Studies, University of Texas, 1997.

Enayat, Hamid. *Modern Islamic Political Thought.* Austin: University of Texas Press, 1982.

Guazzone, Laura, ed. *The Islamist Dilemma. The Political Role of Islamist Movements in the Contemporary Arab World.* Reading, U.K.: Ithaca Press, 1995.

Mitchell, Richard P. *The Society of the Muslim Brothers* (1969). New York and Oxford, U.K.: Oxford University Press, 1993.

Nasr, Seyyed Vali Reza. *The Vanguard of the Islamic Revolution. The Jamaʿat-i Islami of Pakistan.* Berkeley: University of California Press, 1994.

Roy, Olivier. *The Failure of Political Islam.* Cambridge, Mass.: Harvard University Press, 1996.

Gudrun Krämer

POLITICAL ORGANIZATION

The primary model for Muslim political organization has been the early Muslim community in Medina, ruled by the prophet Muhammad, whose foundation in 622 C.E. marks the year 1 of the Muslim calendar. Rather than maintaining the segmentary system of tribal organization, it demanded that all residents submit to the authority of the Apostle of the Faith and accorded second-class status to non-Muslims. Muslims tend to evaluate all further political developments according to how closely they replicate Muhammad's precepts, example, and the life of the early community. Many political changes have occurred since then, but they have been legitimized by their congruity with Medinan precedents.

The enormous conquests of the first Muslim century created two new problems: the nature of leadership in the absence of the Prophet, and the relationship between the few Muslims and the vastly more numerous and sophisticated conquered peoples. The first problem was solved rather simply, by the institution of a monarchy (*khalifa*: "caliphate"), initially elective and subsequently hereditary. Disputes over qualifications and selection processes generated divisions in the community: Kharijites wanted to select on merit, choosing the best Muslim as leader; Shi'ites demanded a ruler from the Prophet's family who shared his charisma; while the majority Sunnis settled for whoever could maintain order in the community, by force if necessary.

The caliphs adopted many characteristics of non-Muslim monarchs but were legitimated by their claims to relationship with Muhammad and by their enforcement of the law of God. Over time the caliphs were weakened and finally eliminated (1258), but at first they were assisted, then dominated, by warlords who used the titles *emir* and *sultan*. These warlords eventually took the title of caliph for themselves. The elimination of the caliphate caused political unity to disappear, but cultural relations continued to unite the Muslim world. In the twentieth century some sultans became kings, while others were replaced by presidents and premiers. Ideologically, some Muslims see only the caliphs as legitimate political successors to Muhammad, but most believe that the politics of the community that arose immediately after Muhammad's death were not binding on future generations. Substitutes for Muhammad's religious leadership are found in the Qur'an and the Prophet's example (sunna) and their interpreters, the ulema.

The second problem, the relationship with non-Muslims, was less tractable. Political subjugation of non-Muslims was accomplished through disarmament, discriminatory taxation (*jizya*, *kharaj*), and the imposition of civil disabilities. Non-Muslims were afforded a legitimate, if secondary, status in Islamic administration; they could serve as government bureaucrats, tax farmers (private contractors for tax collection), or auxiliary troops, but could not hold primary power. If they bore arms, they were excused from *jizya*. Since most non-Muslims were accustomed to subject status in imperial systems, this was not a difficult transition for them.

Culturally, however, this order of subordination was reversed. Non-Arabs and non-Muslims, having been fully literate for centuries, even millennia, surpassed their conquerors in most fields: agricultural and craft techniques; urbanization and social stratification; cooking and building; literature, art, music, and dance; theological and legal argumentation; administration and record-keeping; royal governance; and court protocol. Three Arab achievements drew general admiration, however. These were poetry, which became the model for non-Arabic poetry as well; military prowess, at least in the

first century; and the revelation of Islam, which trumped all the rest.

The cultural assimilation of Arabs to non-Arab civilization, accompanied by resistance from purists, became an entrenched cultural pattern in Muslim society from the first. This conflict shaped the atmosphere in which political development took place. Since the purists held the high moral ground, every step toward the adoption of sophisticated governmental techniques that had not been practiced in Medina was disguised, awkwardly over-justified, and incessantly challenged.

Medieval Islamic Government

Initially, convinced Muslims were few. To achieve his conquests, the caliph 'Umar (634–644) recruited nominal converts and Christian Arabs into the army, but rewarded Muslim fighters by establishing a salary register (*diwan*) that listed combatants (plus dependents and the Prophet's relatives) in order of conversion with the earliest Muslim converts receiving the most pay. When the caliph 'Uthman (644–656) reversed this order in favor of members of the Quraysh tribe because of their administrative expertise, Islam's great civil war was ignited, leading to the split between the Sunni and Shi'ite factions. Greater administrative development was the work of the Umayyads (661–750). They adopted the Byzantine and Sasanian bureaucracies and their land and tax records, which were translated into in Arabic beginning in 697 C.E. They developed an Islamic coinage, replacing images of kings with sacred texts. They created a standing army whose commanders became provincial governors responsible for political, military, fiscal, and religious duties. As their conquests grew more extensive, they raised the caliph from tribal chief to emperor and adopted imperial court protocol and organization. The main palace official, the chamberlain or *hajib* was responsible for guarding the curtain separating the caliph from his subjects, thus regulating access to the ruler.

The revolution ushering in the Abbasid dynasty (750–945) was based in part on religious resistance to the adoption of "foreign" political practices, but such practices nevertheless continued. The Abbasids were famed for their pomp and splendor, based on the wealth of Iraq, which they made their capital region. They presided over the development of Islamic law and court systems, co-opting the ulema into the bureaucracy and imposing upon them responsibilities for urban administration and taxation, despite the ulema's own misgivings about serving secular rulers. A second governmental element, the scribes, were organized in bureaus (also called *diwan*s) headed by the wazir (prime minister). The scribes were often non-Arab and were influenced by non-Muslim culture. Pre-Islamic political thought provided models for imperial governance, and provincial scribes employed pre-Islamic forms of taxation and reporting. A scribal culture of encyclopedic knowledge and cosmopolitan politesse developed at court, conveyed in the literature of *adab*, which blended Islamic and non-Islamic influences. The third administrative element was the military. Military commanders held provincial governorships and ministerial posts, while their subordinates governed local areas.

Imperial organization, court protocol, and standardized taxation were justified in Islamic terms with quotations from the Qur'an and from the Muslim tradition as embodied in the *Kitab al-kharaj* (Book of taxation) of Abu Yusuf (d. 798). Conversion and settlement altered the early system, in which conquered non-Muslims paid taxes to the ruling Arab Muslims. As more people converted to Islam, political distinctions between Arab and non-Arab Muslims were eliminated. All Muslims, regardless of origin, paid tithe (*'ushr*) unless they acquired non-Muslims' lands. In that case, they paid the non-Muslims' higher land tax (*kharaj*). *Jizya*, initially a communal tribute, became a poll tax paid by military-age non-Muslim males in lieu of service. Non-Muslim groups retained their communal structure and personal law (administered by the clergy) but used Islamic courts for state-related purposes, although their testimony was supposedly invalid. Islamic law (*shari'a*) in its various schools (*madhhab*) systematized the interpretation of Qur'an and sunna and was administered in Islamic courts under Muslim judges (*qadis*). Royal courts (*mazalim*), administered by the ruler, adjudicated problems outside Islamic law, such as treason and governmental corruption, carrying on an ancient tradition of justice based on custom and rulers' edicts (*'urf*).

In the Abbasid period the Arab military force united by religious and tribal ties was replaced by a standing army of Khurasanian troops and a caliphal bodyguard of slave (*mamluk*, *ghulam*) soldiers, mainly of Turkish origin. At the same time, taxation became politicized, that is, the right to collect certain taxes became a political reward. This system, called *iqta'* ("division," apportionment of revenues), was soon used to reward the military forces, allowing the new military groups access to money and land and creating a new aristocracy (not quite feudal, as the new "aristocrats" had no responsibility for the lands or people from which their revenues came). *Iqta'* holders lived in the cities, patronizing culture and religion. They collected revenue in the countryside but left peasant producers to their own devices, widening the gap between urban and rural cultures.

Members of this aristocracy became provincial governors uncontrollable by Abbasid civil administration, and independent emirates soon emerged, such as the Samanids in Transoxiana (874–999). These local dynasties sent no revenues to the caliph, even if they acknowledged his nominal authority, but they copied the Abbasids' administration and slave army. In 945 C.E., even the capital, Baghdad, was captured by Shi'ite warlords, the Buyid emirs (945–1055); nearly simultaneously Cairo was taken by rival Isma'ili caliphs, the Fatimids (969–1171). The Abbasid caliph became a figurehead, dispensing legitimation for the warlords, who held the actual power. They multiplied their followers by broadening the *iqta'* system. The military bureaus of the administration expanded to manage *iqta'*s, and provincial bureaucracies developed.

The Impact of Nomad Invasions

The replacement of the Buyids by a series of nomadic Turkish and Mongol dynasties was facilitated by their adoption of Buyid-style *iqta'*s and Abbasid-style bureaucratic government. Speaking no Arabic and little Persian, the invaders replaced local *iqta'* holders with their own men, but they depended on indigenous administrators, *shari'a* courts, and local authorities to govern the realm. This pattern lasted through numerous invasions and replacements of governing regimes until the modern period.

Politics at the center became a matter of competition for the throne among members of the royal house and jostling for power and wealth among the dynasty's supporters. As the historian Ibn Khaldun observed, during and immediately after the initial takeover the ruling group was united in pursuit of conquest and control, but over time fragmentation of power and competition from other interests weakened group cohesion, permitting conquest from outside or internal takeovers. In the tug-of-war between cohesion and dissolution, centrifugal forces included hereditary devolution of office or *iqta'*, tribal disaffection, unjust treatment and consequent loss of loyalty, and neglect of irrigation or blockage of trade routes, leading to decreases in revenue. Conversely, rulers exercised control by building up revenue in their own treasuries, rewarding their followers generously, maintaining the infrastructure, putting down crime and rebellion, ensuring the proper functioning of administrative and legal systems, and supporting the symbols of religion: the caliph (until 1258), the ulema, and Islamic law. Equally important was the relationship between the regime's officials and local authorities who were respected by the common people.

Peasants, tribesmen, and city-dwellers were insulated from dynastic and court politics by a layer of local notables (*a'yan*). These men—large landholders, rich merchants, ulema, members of old elites superseded by new conquerors—acted as intermediaries between the government and the people, presenting the people's needs to the new rulers, providing information on local conditions and revenues, and interpreting royal decrees locally. The *a'yan* were connected by family, educational and sectarian commonalities, marriage relations, and patronage. Patronage also built vertical hierarchies with the people of town and village, and with members of the ruling elite.

Provincial politics was largely based upon patron-client relations passed down through generations, within which marital politics had an important part. Although women possessed no political rights in medieval Muslim society, they played a significant political role through creating family alliances, transmitting information, and preserving property within the family. In rural areas these relations were compounded by debt patronage, as large landholders and urban tax farmers loaned money, seed, and draft animals to peasant farmers, using the future crop as collateral. Tribal clientage, ever-shifting and based on power and wealth, determined nomadic politics. These relations, and the local power struggles to which they gave rise, continued independently of whoever held the capital or sat on the throne. Since they were inseparable from the revenue-producing system, they were only disturbed from above when the revenue stream was interrupted by oppression or diverted by corruption, or when the fortunes of war brought battling armies to a particular location.

The Seljuk Turks, who conquered Baghdad in 1055, ruled Iraq, Iran, and Syria for a century and dominated Asia Minor for two. Despite their origin as Central Asian tribal nomads (considered rude and barbarous by contemporaries), they wove all these disparate political elements into a single system. As Sunni Muslims, they supported the caliph and the religious establishment, unlike the Buyids and Fatimids, whose Shi'ism ran counter to the dominant religious trend.

The Seljuks also employed a professional scribal staff, which expanded as the regime split into several autonomous kingdoms. The scribal cadre's ideas on governance, derived from Abbasid and even pre-Islamic precedents, harnessed imperial and tribal ideologies and practices to an Islamic vision of governance and the creation of a just Muslim society. These ideas were expressed in the wazir Nizam al-Mulk's *Siyasat-nama* (*The Book of Governance*) and the teacher al-Ghazali's *Nasihat al-Muluk* (*Counsel for Kings*), and were made the basis of administration at all levels through dissemination to governors and officials in royal edicts. An official called *emir-e dad* presided over the *mazalim* court, dispensing justice on issues outside Islamic law. The Seljuks replaced their tribal military forces with a salaried slave bodyguard and a standing army supported by *iqta*'s, giving *iqta*' holders greater responsibility for security and prosperity on their *iqta*'s and granting military commanders important positions as governors and tutors of royal princes. They also presided over a restoration of agriculture through irrigation works, reversing temporarily the economic decline of the central Islamic lands. They recruited Sunni ulema to serve as administrators and judges, and their construction of mosques and Islamic colleges (madrasas) and expansion of pious foundations (*waqf*) gave the ulema employment and financial security.

A letter attributed to the wazir Nizam al-Mulk recommended care for irrigation systems and water sources so that blessing and abundance would not depart from the world. The wazir under the Seljuks advanced from head finance officer and bureaucrat to become a kind of co-ruler, the highest ranking of the non-Turks. He headed an administration modeled on that of the Abbasids and their successors, the Samanids and the Ghaznavids of Afghanistan (976–1186).

The Seljuks abolished the *barid*, but probably later reinstated it. Both the Abbasids and Samanids also had a bureau for the "crown lands" that went under various names (*diya, khass*). The Samanids had separate bureaus for the market inspector (*muhtasib*) and pious foundations (*awqaf*); the Seljuks developed separate bureaus for *iqta*'s (*muqaa'at*) and confiscations (*mufradat*).

The central government's administrative bureaus included a *diwan al-a'la*, bureau of the wazir; *diwan al-kharaj* or *diwan al-istifa*', finance bureau; *diwan al-insha*' or *diwan al-ughra*, correspondence bureau; *diwan al-ishraf*, bureau of inspection; and *diwan al-'ard*, bureau of the army. The Ghaznavids had a bureau for the royal household (*wikala*). The Abbasids and Samanids had a bureau for the post system (*barid*), which also encompassed a system of spies, whose job was to notify the ruler if the powerful were oppressing the weak. The chief officials besides the wazir were the treasurer (*mustawfi*) and the chamberlain, keeper of the royal household (*wakil* or *emir al-hajib*); civil bureau heads were paralleled by the heads of military contingents and guard corps. Some provinces were bureaucratically governed; others remained under their own local dynasties. The offices of provincial governor and treasurer were sometimes combined, but more often they were separated for firmer central control. The few civil officials in the province were outnumbered by the military, which was dispersed throughout the province both for security purposes and for pasturage for their horses.

The administration of the Seljuks was admired and imitated by all their successor states, from the Ayyubids of Egypt (1171–1250) to the Khwarazmshahs of Transoxiana (1150–1220). The most important imitators were the Ilkhanids (1258–1335) and the Mamluks (1250–1517).

The Mongol Ilkhanids ruled the northern Middle East from Anatolia to Iran and Central Asia. They initially exploited this territory as a reservoir of resources, but under several great Persian wazirs they adopted an organization like that of the Seljuks. Originally all officials had Mongol supervisors and all taxes were sent to Mongolia, but later the region became administratively independent from the Mongol homeland. Since its terrain would not support the Mongols' nomadic economy, *iqta*'s were assigned to the military forces. Persian, Mongol, Chinese, Armenian, and Jewish administrators kept records in Persian and drew up manuals for government secretaries that became models of bureaucratic procedure for future generations.

Although the Mongol Empire soon fragmented, the successor states preserved Ilkhanid organization on a smaller scale; Jalayirid and Akkoyunlu copies of Ilkhanid secretarial and finance manuals still exist in Turkish libraries. As for the Mamluks, their fiscal administration was unique due to the peculiarities of Nile Valley agriculture, but their secretarial and judicial organizations show Seljuk influences. They too produced influential correspondence and finance manuals, compiling traditions of the past and changes introduced by the Mamluk regime.

The Early Modern Period

Beginning in the sixteenth century, Ilkhanid and Mamluk administrative traditions were combined in the three major empires of the early modern Middle East: Ottoman (1299–1923), Safavid (1501–1732), and Mogul (1526–1857). The sixteenth century was a time of population growth, urbanization, monetarization of the economy, and technological advancement; it was also a time of political and commercial expansion and increased governmental stability. Like contemporary European countries, the Ottomans, Safavids, and Moguls expanded through conquest and trade, creating stable empires that lasted centuries rather than decades. Long-lived ruling families traded the charisma of military prowess for dynastic legitimacy, proclaiming absolute rule but actually sharing power with family members and top administrators. The palace and harem replaced the military camp as centers of power. Women became political actors in their roles as rulers' wives and mothers, and as guardians of minor heirs. Administrators and courtiers grew in influence, and rebels and rivals were co-opted and incorporated through power-sharing. Court politics became not just a struggle for power but a contest over policies.

The greatest development of bureaucratic administration came under the Ottoman *timar* system. In the late fourteenth century, *timar*s succeeded *iqta*'s as economic support for the cavalry forces. *Timar*s were individual land revenue assignments whose sizes reflected the ranks of the holders and were determined by a revenue survey held once every generation. Sultanic agents recorded all revenue sources—crops, herds, mills, fisheries, mines, manufactories, *jizya* and extraordinary levies, commercial taxes—and the names and obligations of all taxpayers. Survey results were recorded in registers of taxes assessed (*mufassal defter*s) and *timar*s allocated (*ijmal defter*s), and *timar* holders were authorized to collect only the amounts recorded in the registers, plus some fees and fines. They were also responsible for police duties in their *timar*s and could be mustered for military service during the campaigning season.

*Timar*s were reassigned regularly to prevent formation of local ties and could be revoked for transgressing the registers or local regulations (*qanun*). *Qanun*s were compilations of sultanic decrees and local customs or conditions (especially tax rates) in force when an area was conquered; over time they were modified to accord with Islamic law. They were administered locally by *qadi*s (officially appointed judges), working together with provincial governors whose soldiers enforced the judges' decisions. *Qanun* and *defter* thus governed the state's relationship with both *timar* holders and peasants, and their imposition marked an area's incorporation into the Ottoman system.

Urban areas were also surveyed, but their revenues were usually assigned to provincial governors (*beylerbey*) or district governors (*sanjakbey*), who supported their retinues from these larger allocations (*khass*). The retinues performed police and guard duties. Governors also commanded provincial or district troops on campaign. Subordinate officers received medium-sized *timar*s called *zeamet*s. The sultan's *khass* until the mid-sixteenth century comprised half of the empire's revenues and paid the expenses of the palace, harem, and janissaries and other elements of the standing army and palace guard. Collection of urban revenues such as market taxes, tolls, customs dues, and manufacturing taxes was managed by agents or farmed out to wealthy merchants or moneylenders. *Timar* records show that the military forces and administrative cadres were diverse in origin, with members from many religions and ethnicities. All were united by a common culture called "the Ottoman way," comprising religion, language, and etiquette, acquired through decades-long training in the palace, administration, or military service.

Besides organizing the *timar*s, *qanun*s regulated the palace organization from at least the era of Mehmed the Conqueror. These *qanun*s and those regarding *timar*s were updated by subsequent rulers. Suleyman the Magnificent was called "The Lawgiver" because in his reign the *qanun*s were reconciled with Islamic law and issued throughout the empire. Modifications continued into the seventeenth and eighteenth centuries, legitimized by reference to Mehmed and Suleyman. The judges administering them had a hierarchy of posts; top posts were reserved for those who had attended and taught at the best madrasas. The highest religious official (*shaykh al-Islam*), who oversaw the legal and educational hierarchies, also advised the sultan on the religious legitimacy of his decisions. He appointed preachers and guided the empire's Sunni Muslim orientation.

In the late sixteenth century, gunpowder weapons initiated a military transformation from a cavalry aristocracy to an infantry recruited from the lower classes. Recruits were paid in cash rather than land grants, and increasingly taxes were collected in cash rather than kind. They could therefore be collected by government agents or private contractors rather than cavalry members, and administration gradually became demilitarized. In other strata, too, changing recruitment patterns altered traditional relationships. Troops recruited for the campaigning season and then discharged staged a series of rebellions, the "Jalali revolts," and were defeated and co-opted only with difficulty. Janissaries stationed in the empire's cities engaged in commerce, and urban merchants were recruited into the corps. Palace cavalrymen became tax farmers, commoners and slaves became scribes, and Muslim children entered the palace school for slaves. Simultaneously, economic distress struck the empire; rapid inflation and currency devaluation played havoc with state budgets and salaries. Old ways had to change, but traditional practices still legitimated the ruler and maintained the elite. Attempting to alter too much too fast, as Osman II (1618–1622) did, risked violent resistance and deposition. Instead, devolution of power created political factions around statesmen satisfying the needs of elite groups, while sultans were reduced to arbitrating between these factions.

The dominance of the Köprülü faction after 1656 permitted administrative reform but led directly to war in 1683. Fiscal reforms in the 1690s instituted new *jizya* allotments and lifetime tax farms. These innovations improved government finances, but war revealed the empire's military inadequacy. Eighteenth-century sultans adopted policies of reform, becoming in the process leaders of their own pro-change factions. Reform, however, came in Western dress, and anti-reform factions clung to traditionalism and Ottoman patriotism. Reforms were often more successful in the provinces, as governors far from Istanbul modernized their military forces and engaged in capitalist agriculture outside imperial oversight. This conflict of interests contributed to the provinces' growing autonomy, as did an accumulation of wealth in the provinces.

The Safavid state, based on Shi'ite Islam, consisted of Turkish warriors, Persian administrators, and a bureaucratized religious hierarchy under a ruler (shah) who was also a spiritual master. The warriors, called Qizilbash, were followers of the Safavid Sufi order that conquered Iran and instituted the Shi'ite state. Defeat by the Ottomans at Chaldiran in 1514 shattered the myth of Safavid invincibility and world conquest. Over time, the shah's charismatic authority and the Qizilbash's political influence decreased, while the palace personnel and a slave army of Georgians, Circassians, and Armenians gained power. A council of officials conducted government business; law was administered by religious judges. Royal workshops produced goods for sale as well as artistic products, augmenting royal income. Provincial taxation followed traditional norms, but in provinces under direct royal control (whose number grew in the seventeenth century), the farming out of taxes to nongovernmental collectors led to overextraction and impoverishment. By the eighteenth century, military weakness permitted conquest by Afghan tribesmen who made themselves heirs of the Safavid system.

The Mughal dynasty of India was perhaps least affected by these trends. Muslims, though the rulers, were always a minority in the state, forcing emperors to balance imposition of Islamic governance against the need to conciliate Hindu officials and officers. By the 1570s Islamic-style bureaucratic administration gained prominence, but it administered less of the country's revenue than elsewhere (about 60%), and that indirectly. In the *mansabdari* system, counterpart of the *timar* system, military administrators collected land revenues to cover their expenses, but between them and the peasants stood a layer of *zamindars* (large landholders and former nobility), who administered the land itself. Islamic law courts were provided by the state, but they shared legal jurisdiction with non-Islamic village, caste, and clan councils. Imperial politics was overwhelmingly a politics of the nobility, a competition among the religious, ethnic, and factional demands of the state's powerful servants. Some rulers' unwillingness to incorporate non-Muslim elites and/or their inability to provide care and protection to productive groups alienated their loyalties and contributed to state fragmentation and British takeover. Apparently, only the Ottoman state was both powerful enough and close enough to Islamic political norms to receive the caliphal title in the nineteenth century.

See also **Caliphate; Empires: Abbasid; Empires: Byzantine; Empires: Mongol and Il-Khanid; Empires: Mogul; Empires: Ottoman; Empires: Safavid and Qajar; Empires: Sassanian; Empires: Timurid; Empires: Umayyad; Qanun; Sultanates: Delhi; Sultanates: Ghaznavid; Sultanates: Mamluk; Sultanates: Seljuk.**

BIBLIOGRAPHY

Bailey, Harold et al., eds. *The Cambridge History of Iran.* Cambridge, U.K.: Cambridge University Press, 1968–91.

Black, Antony. *The History of Islamic Political Thought: From the Prophet to the Present.* Edinburgh: Edinburgh University Press, 2001.

Ghazali, Abu Hamid Muhammad al-. *Ghazali's Book of Counsel for Kings (Nasihat al-Muluk).* Translated by F. R. C. Bagley. London: Oxford University Press, 1971.

Hodgson, Marshall G. S. *The Venture of Islam: Conscience and Faith in a World Civilization.* Chicago: University of Chicago Press, 1974.

Ibn Khaldun. *The Muqaddimah: An Introduction to History.* Edited by N. J. Dawood. Translated by Franz Rosenthal. London: Princeton/Bollingen, 1969.

Inalcik, Halil. *The Ottoman Empire: The Classical Age, 1300–1600.* Translated by Norman Itzkowitz and Colin Imber. London: Weidenfeld and Nicolson, 1973. Reprint. Orion Books/Phoenix, 1994.

Mawardi, al-. *The Ordinances of Government.* Translated by Wafaa H. Wahba. Reading, U.K.: Garnet Publishing Ltd, 1996.

Mulk, Nizam al-. *The Book of Government or Rules for Kings: The Siyar al-Muluk or Siyasat-nama.* Translated by Hubert Darke. 2d ed. London: Routledge and Kegan Paul, 1978.

Linda T. Darling

POLITICAL THOUGHT

During the premodern period, Islamic political thought found expression in a diverse group of writings such as legal compendia, theological treatises, philosophical writings, literary works on the subject of statecraft, wisdom literature, historiography, and even poetry. In the modern period, political thought may be found in some of these branches of literature, but also in separate works directly concerned with political topics, such as the nation state, government, constitutionalism, law, human rights, and the Islamic state.

The diffusion that characterizes the wide range of premodern political thinking results from many factors, two of which deserve particular mention. First, writers in the premodern period often treated aspects of politics and government not in isolation from other topics but in the context of larger subjects and a variety of intellectual disciplines. Second, the early Muslim community rapidly found itself dispersed among a culturally diverse set of peoples, and Muslims became heirs to the variegated political cultures of the larger Middle East; these cultures contributed to the shaping and expression of the range of Islamic political ideas. In the wake of the conquests, and with the formation of an Islamic imperial order, Muslim polities had at their disposal, as Aziz al-Azmeh has put it, a "floating repertoire of immensely ancient and awesomely persistent institutions, metaphors, iconographies, and propositions concerning power, and most particularly concerning power in relation to the sacred, which they welded into distinctive forms." (al-Azmeh 1997, p. 10)

The close association between religion and politics in much of the Islamic tradition, and the diversity of ways in which this association has been interpreted in Islamic history are also worthy of note. Much political thinking in the Islamic tradition takes as its point of departure the view that all sovereignty belongs to God, who alone governs the universe. (His is the "sovereignty over the heavens and the earth," as the Qur'an states repeatedly.) Many Muslim thinkers came to agree that the role of human government was to ensure that God's will, as expressed in the divine law, was enacted on earth. The ideal earthly ruler, called an imam, was a leader who ruled according to God's laws and who was consequently entitled to the loyalty and obedience of his community. While these ideals have been widely expressed, Muslims have naturally differed in their understandings of the implications of the relationship between the religious and political realms. In fact, the historical experience of Muslim societies has generated a large repertoire of political ideas, many of which assume or accommodate themselves to certain premises or coalesce around certain themes, but which collectively constitute a wide-ranging body of thought.

The Qur'an

While the Qur'an, like other scriptures, does not treat political topics in a comprehensive way, it refers in several places to power and those who exercise it. The Qur'an presents sovereignty as a divine prerogative, and all forms of earthly authority (prophetic or political) are wholly dependent on God's dispensation (see, for example, 3:26). This emphasis on the relativity of human forms of authority in relation to the divine reality is one that has left an imprint on many areas of the

Islamic tradition, into the modern period. The most frequently invoked Qur'anic passage, in discussions of political matters, is 4:59: "Obey God, obey the Prophet, and those in authority among you." This verse has been interpreted in some quarters as an injunction to obey rulers even if they are unjust, while other commentators have regarded the phrase "those in authority among you" as a reference only to holders of religious or religio-political authority. For a number of Sunni scholars, the Qur'anic phrase refers to religious scholars or ulema; in Shi'ite tradition, it refers to the imams. On the earthly plane, kingship is depicted as a great but sometimes treacherous boon that human beings are often predisposed to covet. Satan seeks to tempt Adam with the prospect of imperishable sovereignty (20:120); the Children of Israel were sometimes favored with both prophethood and kingship (for example, 5:20; 38:20); and Solomon prays for kingship (38:35). For those whom God leads astray, however, kingship is associated with overweening pride; Nimrod argues with Abraham over it (2:258), and Pharaoh boasts of his claim to the kingdom of Egypt (43:51).

Early Political Developments

Islamic political thought, as expressed in Qur'anic exegesis and elsewhere, evolved in conjunction with Muslims' historical experiences. The history of the early Muslim community is one of extraordinary political success. After facing initial adversity, the prophet Muhammad went on to unify Arabia and to create a state based largely on ties of common religious allegiance. Muhammad was the leader of this early community (the *umma*), and hence his role as God's messenger was integrally linked with his role as political head of state. The early Islamic polity, moreover, continued to grow in the decades following the Prophet's death in 632. It rapidly expanded to comprise the regions of the northern Middle East (Syria-Palestine, Egypt, Iraq, and Iran), and from there it spread across North Africa and into Spain, and eastwards into northern India. Although the pace of the expansion did not remain constant, Islamic political thought, like other branches of the Islamic tradition, was inevitably shaped by the experience of a success which seemed to validate the new dispensation and to attest divine favor towards the Muslim community. The construction on the Temple Mount in Jerusalem of the Dome of the Rock, completed under the Umayyad caliph 'Abd al-Malik in 691, suggests a striking confidence on the part of the city's rulers in the stability and endurance of the Islamic polity.

In the period immediately following the death of the Prophet in 632, issues such as the nature of political leadership and the identity of the rightful holder of political authority were much disputed. The leaders who succeeded the Prophet were addressed as Commander of the Faithful (*amir al-mu'minin*) and bore the title of caliph (*khalifa*), a term which came to be understood as meaning deputy of, or successor to, the Prophet of God. The Prophet himself had exercised both religious and political authority, the continuing conjoining of which formed the basis of the religio-political ideals of the Shi'ites. The early debates and struggles over leadership eventually crystalized in the emergence of distinct sectarian communities (generally grouped as Kharijites, Shi'ites, and, eventually, Sunnis).

The Role of the Ulema

The institution that emerged most successfully from, or in the face of, these disagreements was that of the caliphate, exercised first by a series of respected individuals who had surrounded the Prophet, and, following the conclusion of the first civil war in 661, by dynastic families: the Umayyads (661–750) and, after a revolution, the 'Abbasids (750–1258). It has been suggested that the early caliphs, including the Umayyads and early 'Abbasids, may have expected to wield not only political authority but also some degree of religious authority as part of their office. The caliphs' claims to religious authority encountered resistance, however, with the emergence of numbers of religious specialists, who came to be known collectively as the ulema (scholars) or "those possessed of religious learning" ('ilm). As the Islamic polity grew in extent and in the diversity of its population, the claim of this new intellectual elite to religious leadership and authority among the Muslims of the empire was itself contested by some individuals who held that such authority should be centralized and held by the ruler, rather than by a number of loosely associated specialists over whom the ruler had little control. An argument for limiting the power of the ulema in favor of the caliph was advanced by the Persian convert Ibn al-Muqaffa' (d. c. 756), whose apparently unsolicited warnings to the caliph al-Mansur (754–775) went unheeded and were rarely repeated so plainly in later periods. One last attempt to wrest religious authority from the ulema was made under successive caliphs in the first half of the ninth century, in the course of the *mihna*, an inquisition during which prominent religious scholars were interrogated in order to establish their adherence or lack thereof to a particular theological doctrine; this attempt too failed, and its failure marked the voluntary or involuntary ceding of religious authority to the ulema.

The scholars formulated the religious law, the *shari'a*, with only incidental reference to the state, and it was chiefly when the political power located in the institution of the caliphate could no longer be taken for granted that jurists began to address larger political questions concerning the state and government. The collectivity of the Muslim community was invested with certain duties and responsibilities that could, under certain conditions or in times of political crisis, operate regardless of, or even in opposition to, the workings of the state. One such collective (and occasionally, individual) duty is that of "commanding right and forbidding wrong" (*al-amr bil-ma'ruf wal-nahy 'an al-munkar*), a duty that in the view of many Muslims fell, ideally, to the imam, but which could also require or justify rebellion against a ruler, as well as action taken by one Muslim against another without any involvement on the part of the state.

A related area of ambivalence towards the role of the state concerns the extent of the duty of obedience. Many medieval Sunni thinkers held that obedience was incumbent on Muslims, regardless of whether the ruler was just or tyrannical, pious or irreligious, as long as such obedience did not involve the subject in transgression of the *shari'a*. In this connection, it is important to note that many scholars held themselves aloof from political power. While some of the most influential political thinkers served the state as judges and in other capacities (for example, Abu Yusuf, Ibn al-Murtada, al-Mawardi), the refusal to serve the holders of political power retained prestige and was widely regarded as morally preferable, as numerous historical incidents, anecdotes and folk tales demonstrate.

The Formation of Shi'ite, Kharijite, and Sunni Views of Political Leadership

The mainstream Shi'ite view of political leadership, subsumed in the doctrine of the imamate, regards certain Qur'anic texts and acts of the Prophet recorded in hadiths as proofs that the Prophet, contrary to most Sunni opinions, nominated as his successor his cousin and son-in-law, 'Ali. 'Ali, however, had, according to Shi'ites, been wrongfully deprived of the position that was his due, with the result that the community had fallen into error. Following 'Ali's death in 661, Shi'ites held that only descendants of 'Ali could claim the imamate. (Partly in order to distinguish between the rightful holders of authority and the actual ruling powers, Shi'ites refer to the persons whom they regard as their leaders as imams rather than as caliphs.) During the first two centuries of Islamic history, many Shi'ite groups attempted to seize power for their imams. Their efforts were largely unsuccessful (as was the case, most famously, with the challenge to Umayyad rule mounted by Husayn, a grandson of the Prophet, who was killed in 680), and Shi'ites were often ruthlessly suppressed.

In the course of the eighth century, most Shi'ites adopted a politically quietist stance, and they abandoned the attempt to establish general leadership for their imams, whom they continued to follow as leaders within their own communities. Shi'ites gradually developed a distinctive body of political ideas based on the concept of the imamate, which they came to regard as comprising both religious and political authority. Most Shi'ites belong to the Imami community, and believe that the last of their imams is now hidden, and therefore inaccessible to the vast majority of his followers. Even during the period of the presence of the imams, however, there appears to have been some dispute among Imami Shi'ites as to the extent of the imams' authority. As the work of Hossein Modarressi suggests, the power of the imams was limited not only by the adverse conditions that confronted them and their followers, but also by the view held by some of their prominent supporters that the scope of their powers should be limited in theory as well as in practice.

Gradually, however, Imami Shi'ites reached a consensus, agreeing that the role of the imamate was to provide comprehensive leadership over religious and worldly matters. Thus, under the leadership of the imam, the realms of religion and state were indistinguishable. The imam was not only the rightful political leader of the community, but he also possessed immunity from sin and error ('isma). Accordingly, he was the rightful collector and distributor of religious taxes and the only legitimate leader of jihad, and, as heir to the knowledge of the Prophet, he possessed a complete and perfect knowledge of the religious law. After the onset of the occultation in the late ninth century (when the imam became hidden), however, Imami Shi'ites could no longer turn to their imam directly, and they, like Sunnis, turned increasingly to their religious scholars for guidance in religious matters.

The Kharijites were hostile to both the Umayyad (and, later, to the 'Abbasid) and the Shi'ite positions, and held that leadership belonged to the most excellent member of the community, regardless of his genealogy or background. A few believed that the office of the imamate could be held by a woman. Most Kharijites held that the imamate was obligatory, although some, most notably the Najdiyya, did not consider an imam necessary if the community were able to function in accordance with justice without one. (Some Mu'tazilis and other thinkers similarly denied the obligatory nature of the imamate.) If the imam violated the divine law, most Kharijites held that he forfeited his legitimacy and had even lapsed into unbelief. The Kharijites continued to challenge the power of the Umayyads and the 'Abbasids for at least two centuries before those groups that survived retreated to remote areas and lived as separate, but generally quietist, communities.

The mainstream Sunni conception of the caliphate, consensus on which emerged gradually over the first four centuries of Islamic history, held that the Qur'an provided no specific injunctions regarding the leadership of the community after the Prophet's death, and (although some prominent Sunni thinkers dissented from this position) that the Prophet had left no precise instructions on the matter. According to the mainstream view, the first Muslims responded to the Prophet's death by recognizing one of their own members, Abu Bakr (d. 634), as the first caliph. He was to assume the functions of leading the Muslim community, but he was in no sense an heir to the Prophet's religious authority; he was acclaimed by the bay'a, an act by which his fellow Muslims acknowledged his leadership and pledged their allegiance. Abu Bakr was followed by three further individuals who had enjoyed close personal ties to the Prophet, after the last of whom, 'Ali, a dynastic principle was adopted with the establishment of the Umayyad caliphate.

Sunni thinkers distinguished between the caliphate of these first four "rightly guided" caliphs and later holders of the office, many of whom degraded it to kingship (mulk) and were sometimes oppressive. Yet while later Islamic leadership may not have been perfect, it remained legitimate, and the community, as a result, remained within the confines of the law. In the gradual emergence of this consensus, Sunni thinkers adopted the principles of certain earlier groups, whose first priority had been the preservation of the unity of the community; accordingly, it was preferable to accept shortcomings in the political life of the community than to risk further schism and discord.

The Political Thought of the Classical Sunni and Shi'i Jurists

Most famously among Sunni jurists, al-Mawardi (d. 1058) formulated what came to be regarded as the classical Sunni position on the caliphate. By the eleventh century, the caliphate had been weakened by its subservience to a succession of military leaders who had taken over some of its territories and established polities of their own. When al-Mawardi came to write his treatise, al-Ahkam al-sultaniyya (The ordinances of government), however, the caliphate was for the moment enjoying a certain reascendancy, which the jurist sought to enhance through his exposition of the legal status of the office. Al-Mawardi asserted that the imamate is obligatory by revelation, not by reason, and he listed seven necessary qualities for the imam: descent from Quraysh; possession of religious knowledge; probity; soundness and maturity of body and mind; and the capacity to execute the political and military duties of the office.

Of al-Mawardi's stipulated qualities, descent from Quraysh may be the most significant, since it allows for the legitimacy of all the Sunni caliphs, while it does not limit legitimacy to descent from the Prophet himself; but the same criterion excludes most other rulers, such as the Buyids, who controlled Baghdad during al-Mawardi's lifetime. At the same time, al-Mawardi argued that rule by military emirs was legitimate as long as such rulers acknowledged the authority of the caliphs and implemented Islamic law. The caliph himself was responsible for the performance of specific duties, such as the protection of religion against heterodoxy, enforcing the law and dispensing justice, executing the statutory penalties (hudud), ensuring peace in the territory of Islam and defending the realm against external enemies, the prosecution of jihad, receipt of the legal alms, and a fifth of all booty gained in combat on behalf of the community, distribution of revenue according to the law, and the appointment of reliable and trustworthy men in delegating authority.

Al-Mawardi's book, together with the identically titled work of his contemporary, Abu Ya'la b. al-Farra' (d. 1066), contributed to a gradual change in the perception of the caliphate. From the early ninth century onwards, the caliph's authority had coexisted with the reality of political fragmentation, and the office ceased to connote supreme political power. Instead, it came to assume a more symbolic role, whereby the caliphate came to represent the unity of the Muslim community regardless of the division of political power.

Almost three centuries later, following the execution in 1258 by the Mongol conqueror Hulegu of the Abbasid caliph and the establishment of the Mongol empire over much of the eastern Islamic world, the Syrian Hanbali scholar Ibn Taymiyya (d. 1328) asserted with vigor the supremacy of the *shari'a* as the means to ensure the exercise of divine sovereignty on Earth. By extension, Ibn Taymiyya declared the illegitimacy of any ruler who failed to uphold the law. In the context of the demise of the 'Abbasid caliphate and against the loss of even the symbolism of political unity, Ibn Taymiyya emphasized the ideological unity that he believed could be achieved through proper observance of the *shari'a*. His political perspective, often referred to after the title of one of his books as *al-siyasa al-shar'iyya* (government according to the religious law), has been influential among some modern thinkers.

Ibn Taymiyya sought to elevate the condition of both the state and society through upholding the law, and held that a leader who promoted increased observance of the law was owed obedience by his subjects. Ibn Taymiyya and his contemporary, Ibn Jama'a (d. 1333), who likewise spent his life in Syria and Egypt, emphasized the role of the religious scholars as counselors to the holders of political power. Furthermore, Ibn Jama'a recognized two kinds of imamate, arrived at through election and force respectively. He noted that the latter form of imamate, based on the exercise of might, was the only form that existed in his own time.

After the beginning of the imam's occultation in the late ninth century, Shi'ite jurists gradually developed a political theory in which Shi'ite scholars might assume some of the imam's responsibilities. In all likelihood, the historical imams themselves allowed some of their followers to participate in the performance of certain functions, or delegated certain tasks to individuals. The idea of deputyship to the imam was developed further in the writings of leading Imami thinkers, such as al-Shaykh al-Mufid (d. 1022), who indicated that throughout his occultation the imam remained God's proof (*hujja*) on earth, but that, during his absence, the imam could appoint a deputy or deputies.

Like many Imami jurists, al-Muhaqqiq al-Hilli (d. 1277) noted that, in the imam's absence, Shi'ites should fulfill their religious obligation of charity (*zakat*) by delivering it to a reliable jurist (*faqih*), since the latter was in possession of the necessary knowledge to ensure its proper disbursement. The same jurist, and still more notably his pupil Ibn al-Mutahhar al-Hilli (d. 1325), adopted the principle of *ijtihad*, according to which each Shi'ite jurist was obliged to undertake an investigation of the legal sources in order to reach his own conclusions in legal matters. As this practice of *ijtihad* became accepted among Shi'ites, it contributed to an increase in the authority of the Shi'ite ulema. Despite this gradual enhancement in the stature of the Imami scholars, most of them continued to emphasize the qualitative difference between the authority enjoyed by imams and prophets, to whom, on account of their immunity from sin and error, unconditional obedience was due, and that of any other leader to whom certain functions may have been delegated.

Some Imami scholars of the Usuli school, which developed in the mid-eighteenth century and became dominant by the middle of the nineteenth century, claimed that the Shi'ite scholars had in fact assumed the position of general vice-regent (*na'ib 'amm*) of the absent imam. In the Usuli view, the right to interpret Islamic law rested solely with *mujtahid*s, scholars who were recognized as qualified to exercise their independent judgment, or *ijtihad*. Ordinary Muslims were obliged to follow one eminent *mujtahid* as a model of emulation (*marja' al-taqlid*). Some scholars asserted further that the office of *marja'* represented the imam's authority not only in matters of religion, but also in worldly affairs. This idea was developed most notably by Ruhollah Khomeini (1902–1989) in the latter half of the twentieth century.

Sultans and Kings

While the classical juristic literature deals with political thought within the context of the topics of imamate and caliphate, and refers to the sultanate primarily in connection with these institutions, other branches of literary expression treat the institution of the sultanate, or kingship, in its own right. Sultans and other dynastic rulers whose power was sometimes local but sometimes very far-reaching were often the recipients of literary gifts, such as works offering advice (*nasiha[t]*) on the art of government, or "mirrors for princes," in which the ruler's duties and his subjects' needs were discussed, and the monarch's own justice was invariably praised. Occasionally, such books were commissioned by a ruler, as seems to have been the case with the famous *Siyasat-nameh* (Book of government) composed by the wazir Nizam al-Mulk (d. 1092) and presented to the Seljuq monarch, Malik-Shah (1073–1092).

In such books of advice for Muslim rulers, as indeed in many other cultural contexts, the king (or caliph) is often likened to a physician healing a body, or a shepherd guarding his flock. He is also, as in ancient Middle Eastern traditions, described as "the Shadow of God on earth." Some authors adopt the old Iranian concept of *farr*, the aura or nimbus that signifies the charisma of kingship. Most directly, these ideas and many others reached Islamic culture through the translation into Arabic of literary works composed in Middle Persian (Pahlavi) under the Sassanians (226–651). In Islamic times, authors adapted and developed many of these ancient Middle Eastern notions according to the regions and conditions in which they lived.

The understanding of kingship articulated in most works of *nasiha* rests on the premise of royal absolutism, which is closely associated with the concept of justice (*'adl*), the maintenance of which is presented as the ruler's foremost responsibility. This set of concepts is expressed clearly in the widely recorded "circle of justice," according to which the king's rule is dependent on the army, which in turn depends on wealth, which is generated through agriculture (and sometimes trade), which in turn flourishes under the king's effective exercise of his royal authority. The ruler is thus depicted as central to the preservation of the natural and social orders. The fertility and productivity of the land, and the well-being of the peasants who worked it, depended directly on the king's justice. Furthermore, royal justice was necessary to prevent the various groups within society from coalescing in such a way that any particular set of interests outweighed others. If such a process were allowed to occur, it would cause a social imbalance that was considered contrary to justice and tantamount to injustice (*zulm*).

In order to prevent such disequilibrium, it was the ruler's task, by virtue of his own position above and outside any of the social categories, to ensure that each individual remained in the place appropriate to his station. Among writers belonging to this intellectual tradition, society was often visualized in terms of a quadripartite hierarchy consisting of men of the pen, men of the sword, men of transactions, and men of agriculture, as described, for example, in the famous formulation of Nasir al-Din Tusi, 1201–1274. This model was adopted by numerous later writers, and was especially important to many Ottoman thinkers.

Such traditions of kingship came to be widely disseminated and formed a base for many kinds of courtly literature across the linguistic and cultural range of the medieval Islamic world. As this dissemination occurred, the view of royal justice expressed in this courtly literature was often linked to the upholding of the *shari'a*, and, with the establishment of Turkish and Turko-Mongol dynasties in much of the Islamic world, many of these Perso-Islamic concepts of government also became fused with Central Asian concepts.

Political Philosophy

Another important branch of premodern political thought is found in the works of the Muslim philosophers, among whom the most influential was al-Farabi (d. 950). Al-Farabi's thought was based on the common premise that it was natural for human beings to live in association with others, since on the one hand they were incapable of supplying all of their own needs and were therefore obliged to co-operate with one another, and, on the other hand, humankind was, in Aristotle's phrase, a political animal, disposed by nature to communal living. The goal of human existence, moreover, was happiness (*sa'ada*), which could only be achieved through living in a community. Communities differed in size and in type, some being "perfect" or complete, and others being

imperfect and incomplete. Happiness was best attained by living in a "virtuous polity" (*al-madina al-fadila*), which al-Farabi defined as one led by learned and excellent men, and one in which the inhabitants co-operated in striving for ultimate happiness. Human beings were connected by a chain of authority, which was based on their degree of knowledge and understanding. In this chain, each individual was in a position of both learning from and governance by those above him, and of instructing and exercising authority over those below him, down to the level of those who were fit only for service. The man who had nothing to learn from anyone was the person best suited to perform the duties of the supreme leader (*al-ra'is al-awwal*), whose purpose, according to al-Farabi, was to promote the attainment of happiness by his community.

Several of the political ideas of al-Farabi were shared and further developed by Ibn Sina (d. 1037), who himself had extensive experience in the practical workings of government and had served on several occasions as a wazir. Ibn Sina emphasized the roles of law and justice, and the need for their enforcement by a legislator and preserver of justice, as the basis for the necessary social transactions among people. In al-Andalus, Ibn Bajja (d. 1138) held that it was the ruler's responsibility to assign tasks to the inhabitants of the city, and to ensure that each man undertook the most excellent task of which he was capable. He argued furthermore that, if no virtuous polity to which a philosopher might immigrate existed, the philosopher should seclude himself from society as far as possible.

Nasir al-Din Tusi, who adopted many of the political views of al-Farabi, held that although it was the diversity among people that rendered co-operation among them possible, this co-operation could only be achieved through firm administration, without the restraining force of which, men might destroy one another. Government was necessary to ensure that each man was content with the station appropriate to him, that he received his due, and that others did not violate his rights. One of the main purposes of government, then, was to maintain order in society and to ensure the harmonious functioning of its component groups.

One of the most remarkable political theoreticians of the medieval Islamic world was Ibn Khaldun (d. 1332), who spent most of his life in North Africa and Egypt, and whose writings describe his perceptions of the historical workings of power. Ibn Khaldun shares many of the premises of earlier philosophers, and reaches the conclusion that kingship (*mulk*) is a natural and necessary human phenomenon for the regulation and restraint of human conduct. As part of his analysis of societies, Ibn Khaldun argues that ruling families whose ties of solidarity (*'asabiyya*) are strongest are best situated to impose their dominion over others in a process that gives rise to conquest and expansion. In order to create stable polities, however, it is necessary for such strength of communal ties to be conjoined with religious law, which provides a more lasting focus of communal solidarity than kinship and affiliation alone. Ibn Khaldun goes on to describe the stages through which a polity comes into existence, consolidates its power, reaches maturity, and eventually declines.

Modern Developments

Reconsiderations of the nature and responsibilities of the state have a continuous history in the Islamic world. The historical context for such reconsiderations has evolved particularly rapidly, however, over the course of the past two centuries. The vast transformations of the modern period have seen the creation in the Islamic world, as elsewhere, of modern states, in which the relationships between individuals and governments have changed dramatically from those characteristic of premodern times, and the integration of much of the Islamic world into a global economic system. Like much of the rest of the world, Muslim countries have, over the past two centuries or longer, been forced to accommodate themselves to the disproportionate power (economic, military, political, cultural) enjoyed by Western countries: the European colonial powers, the former Soviet Union, and, beginning in the latter half of the twentieth century, the United States of America.

Modern Islamic political thought thus represents the continuation of a long-standing discourse, but in circumstances that compel reckoning with the actual and theoretical aspects of Western politics. Among the many responses manifested in modern political thought, we may refer to the ideas of certain thinkers whose vision included both preservation of a redefined Muslim identity and the adoption of certain foreign institutions, such as the nation-state, democratic representation, constitutionalism, and so on; and to the ideas of thinkers who assert an Islamic form of politics that, in theory at least, is independent of Western models. The spectrum between these two poles, and the variety within them, are naturally extensive.

In the modern era, the word *dawla*, which in premodern times tended to denote a period of dynastic rule, has come to signify a state, in the sense that this concept had acquired in Europe between the sixteenth and the twentieth centuries. The term, and its referent, have come to play a central role in modern political discourse. Rifaʿa Rafiʿ al-Tahtawi (1801–1873) employed the term *watan* (corresponding to the French *patrie*) to denote the territorial aspect of the concept of the state; but he did not reject the concept of the pan-Islamic *umma*. Jamal al-Din al-Afghani (1839–1897), a highly influential commentator on political matters throughout much of the Islamic world during the nineteenth century, insisted that the Islamic religion was compatible with the exercise of human reason, and was thus compatible with the kind of scientific inquiry and technological development that had flourished in modern Europe. At the same time, al-Afghani absolutely rejected Muslim rulers' subservience to Western political power. Al-Afghani, for whom the period of the Rashidun was the period of perfected Muslim government, seems to have regarded regional nationalisms as possible steps towards the reconstitution of the Islamic *umma*. Many of the political ideas of al-Afghani were further developed in the Arab world by Muhammad ʿAbduh (1849–1905).

Among the thinkers whose ideas have been most influential in the twentieth-century Arab world are Muhammad Rashid Rida (1865–1935), who regarded al-Mawardi's work as formative to the Islamic tradition, and ʿAli ʿAbd al-Raziq (d. 1966). The twentieth-century concept of the Islamic state emerged in the context of the dismemberment of the Ottoman Empire and the abandonment of the Ottoman caliphate, which followed the formation of the modern Turkish nation-state. The final abolition of the Ottoman caliphate was briefly preceded by an interim period during which the Turkish authorities reduced the office to a purely spiritual one. Rashid Rida opposed this reduction in the role of the caliphate, and argued instead for a caliphate that combined religious and political authority and that was "a caliphate of necessity," to be situated in the Arab world. In the same era, some Indian Muslims formed the Khilafat Movement, and, along with other groups, the Khilafats took up the assertion that Islam is both a religion and a state (*al-Islam din wa dawla*). This idea shapes much of the discourse of contemporary Islamists. ʿAbd al-Raziq, on the other hand, faced strong opposition to his explicit rejection of the view that Islam necessarily combined the realms of religion and state, and argued that the institution of the caliphate was not required by religion.

The separation of state and religion, while supported by ʿAbd al-Raziq and other secularists, is rejected by Islamists, for whom Muslims' primary allegiance should be to the religious community (the *umma*) and for whom an Islamic order necessarily embraces the political as well as the personal religious realms. Hasan al-Banna (1906–1949), founder in 1928 of the Muslim Brotherhood in Egypt, emphasized the all-encompassing nature of Islam in human affairs. His intellectual successors, such as Sayyid Qutb (1906–1966), Abu l-Aʿlaʾ Maududi (1903–1979) and Ruhollah Khomeini (1902–1989), have argued that the prophet Muhammad himself combined religion and state, and that this combination established a lasting model. Sayyid Qutb, a prominent member of the Muslim Brotherhood, composed many of his most influential works while imprisoned under Jamal ʿAbd al-Nasser. Central to Sayyid Qutb's thought was the concept of neo-Jahiliyya, according to which contemporary societies, including those that were nominally Muslim, had fallen into pagan ignorance, a lapse that could only be rectified by struggle (jihad) to overturn the secular state and install in its place an Islamic order, in which human laws would give way to God-given laws. In practice, as the case of postrevolutionary Iran demonstrates, such ideas need not preclude the adoption of such principles as constitutionalism, the separation of powers, and popular sovereignty.

As India struggled for its independence from Great Britain, Maududi, founder in 1941 of the Jama'at-e Islami, opposed the forms of nationalism represented by the Indian National Congress on the one hand and by the Muslim League on the other. Instead, he argued in favor of the restoration of an Islamic order in India. Despite his opposition to the Muslim League, however, Maududi moved to the new state of Pakistan following its creation in 1947. Maududi asserted strongly the idea that Pakistan should be not merely a state for Muslims but an Islamic state. For Maududi, an Islamic state was one in which all areas of public and private life were regulated in accordance with the unchanging shari'a. His idea of the Islamic state was based on neither nationalism nor democracy. Although highly controversial in Pakistan, Maududi's books and pamphlets have been translated into many languages and are widely read throughout the Islamic world.

In the Shi'ite world, Khomeini contributed significantly to the increased emphasis on political activism in modern times through his reinterpretations of several important features of earlier Imami Shi'ite thought. For example, Shi'ites had traditionally looked to the hidden imam to establish justice on earth at the time of his eventual return; this belief had long been conducive to political quietism. Khomeini, however, took the view that Muslims need wait no longer. Instead, they could hasten the return of the imam by acting themselves to resist injustice and to establish an Islamic political order in the here and now. Furthermore, Khomeini expressed the view that the *mujtahid*s were responsible for the execution of all the religious and worldly duties that the Prophet himself had performed. These responsibilities should be exercised not through the collective body of qualified scholars but through a single jurist. This doctrine, known as "the guardianship of the jurist" (*velayat-e faqih*), remains a subject of debate among Imami scholars. In the decades since the Islamic Revolution of 1979, as a result of which Iran successfully extricated itself from Western intervention and rejected a politics conditioned by the interests of the West, a number of Iranian thinkers, such as 'Abd al-Karim Sorush, have been among the most notable contributors to a contemporary renewal and broadening of Islamic political thought along lines that emphasize individual rights and freedoms, and democracy.

See also **Caliphate; Imamate; Iran, Islamic Republic of; Law; Modernization, Political: Constitutionalism; Monarchy; Pakistan, Islamic Republic of; Political Islam; Reform: Arab Middle East and North Africa; Reform: Iran; Shi'a: Imami (Twelver); Shari'a; Succession; Ulema.**

BIBLIOGRAPHY

Arjomand, Saïd. *The Shadow of God and the Hidden Imam.* Chicago and London: University of Chicago Press, 1984.

Azmeh, Aziz al-. *Muslim Kingship. Power and the Sacred in Muslim, Christian, and Pagan Polities.* London and New York: I. B. Tauris, 1997.

Cook, Michael. *Commanding Right and Forbidding Wrong in Islamic Thought.* Cambridge, U.K.: Cambridge University Press, 2000.

Crone, Patricia, and Hinds, Martin. *God's Caliph.* Cambridge, U.K.: Cambridge University Press, 1986.

Enayat, Hamid. *Modern Islamic Political Thought.* Austin: University of Texas Press, 1982.

Lambton, A. K. S. *State and Government in Medieval Islam.* Oxford, U.K.: Oxford University Press, 1980.

Lewis, Bernard. *The Political Language of Islam.* Chicago and London: University of Chicago Press, 1988.

Madelung, Wilferd. *The Succession to Muhammad. A Study of the Early Caliphate.* Cambridge, U.K.: Cambridge University Press.

Modarressi, Hossein. *Crisis and Consolidation in the Formative Period of Shi'ite Islam.* Princeton, N.J.: The Darwin Press, 1993.

Mottahedeh, Roy P. *Loyalty and Leadership in an Early Islamic Society.* Princeton, N.J.: Princeton University Press, 1980.

Sivan, Emmanuel. *Radical Islam. Medieval Theology and Modern Politics.* New Haven, Conn.: Yale University Press, 1980.

Soroush, 'Abdolkarim. *Reason, Freedom, and Democracy in Islam: Essential Writings of 'Abdolkarim Soroush.* Translated by Mahmoud Sadri and Ahmad Sadri. New York: Oxford University Press, 2000.

Louise Marlow

POLYGAMY

Islamic law allows only men to enter more than one marriage at a time, justifying it by reference to the Qur'an (4:3, 24, 25) and the marriages of the prophet Mohammad. Although polygamy (strictly, "polygyny") has never been common in Muslim societies, in many areas it was always rare, and incidence has diminished in modern times. In the twentieth century, men's right to contract plural marriages became one of the contentious issues in debates over women's rights in Islam. Not only did the practice become stigmatized but its religious legitimacy began to be challenged by new readings of Islamic sacred texts and the introduction of notions of equity and justice in gender rights. In contrast to classical Muslim jurists, modern jurists tend to argue that interdiction of the practice, rather than its sanction, can be deduced from the Qur'an verses, and that polygamy should be allowed only in exceptional circumstances and under limited conditions. Likewise, in some Muslim countries plural marriages are either outlawed (as in Turkey and Tunisia), or the registration of such marriages is allowed only by means of a court order that either requires the first wife's consent or grants her the right to divorce (as in Jordan, Malaysia, Iran, Iraq, and

Syria). Elsewhere, especially in the Persian Gulf countries, men face no legal restrictions in contracting plural marriages. Because of social sanctions, plural marriages all over the Muslim world are often contracted in secret.

See also **Gender; Marriage.**

BIBLIOGRAPHY

Asghar, Ali. *The Rights of Women in Islam.* London: Hurst and Company, 1992.

Maghniyyah, Muhammad Jawad. *Marriage According to Five Schools of Islamic Law.* Tehran: Department of Translation and Publication, Islamic Culture and Relations Organization, 1997.

Ziba Mir-Hosseini

PRAYER, CALL TO *See* 'Ibadat

PREACHING *See* Khutba

PROPERTY

A source of conflict in the pre-Islamic Middle East, the concept of property remained controversial after the rise of Islam. From the seventh century to the modern era, Islamic rulings, opinions, and institutions designed to broaden private ownership rights coexisted with policies that undermined them. Initially, the consequent material insecurity was nothing unusual by the prevailing global standards. However, the gradual strengthening of private property rights in western Europe caused the Islamic world to sink below the standards of the day.

In the sixteenth and seventeenth centuries European travelers to the Middle East found signs of weak property rights, such as residential styles designed to conceal wealth. For their part, eighteenth- and nineteenth-century Middle Eastern visitors to the West were favorably impressed by the material security afforded to individual Europeans. Significantly, the Middle East's magnificent architectural heritage consists almost exclusively of communal structures. Had the region made early progress in broadening the scope of property rights, its surviving premodern structures would have included many private residences, as in western Europe.

Islam has influenced the evolution of ownership rights through several mechanisms, some of which operated at cross-purposes. Verse 7:128 of the Qur'an, which holds that all property belongs to God, would seem to rule out all forms of private ownership. In keeping with this implication, from the early caliphs to monarchs of the nineteenth century, successive Muslim rulers routinely confiscated uncultivated lands. Though frequently defended in Islamic terms, these expropriations also accorded with Hellenic and Persian traditions that treated the state as the ultimate owner of all land.

Like rulers everywhere, premodern Muslim rulers generally understood that threats to the material security of individuals, including confiscations and arbitrary taxation, reduced government revenue by harming incentives to produce. So Islamic history offers many examples of rulers alleviating the tax burden of a region or class of subjects with the express purpose of stimulating economic activity. However, not until modern times have there existed effective legal safeguards against state-initiated or condoned predation. A ruler urgently in need of resources to run a military campaign or overcome a political challenge could generally prey on his subjects without legal hindrance. Muslim writers of the medieval Middle East, including Maqrizi and Ibn Khaldun, observe that distressed rulers made it a habit of grabbing the visible possessions of the wealthy, including estates of the deceased. Such expropriations were often carried out under the pretext that the seized assets had been acquired illegally.

From the fact that rulers felt a need to justify their predatory acts, one may infer that subjects expected them to respect established use rights. This expectation was based partly on the principle that individuals are entitled to private ownership (*milk*). Though at odds with the principle of divine ownership, private ownership thus remained a concept recognized by Islamic law. Moreover, even as Muslim rulers pursued policies harmful to material security, Islamic courts routinely enforced individual property rights.

Another mechanism through which Islam weakened private ownership rights was grounded in *zakat*, an institution designed to prevent opportunistic taxation. Mentioned in the Qur'an and implemented by the Prophet, the *zakat* system imposed fixed tax rates that varied across income and wealth categories. For example, the rate on agricultural income was 10 percent in naturally irrigated areas but 5 percent in areas irrigated artificially. During the Prophet's lifetime, this fixity served to block attempts at radical redistribution. At the same time, it precluded the establishment of general principles for amending *zakat* rates and broadening the system's coverage. Consequently, the *zakat* system soon became outdated, allowing later rulers to impose taxes arbitrarily and opportunistically. The rate schedule of the agricultural tax known as 'ushr, though patterned after the *zakat* requirements on land, has varied greatly across time and space. In any case, this tax has often been accompanied by sundry other taxes without any basis in Islam's traditional sources of authority. In facilitating the variability of taxation, the *zakat* system unintentionally contributed to the precariousness of individual property rights.

A creative and effective response to the weakness of these rights was the *waqf* system. A *waqf* is an unincorporated trust established under Islamic law by an individual for the provision of a designated service in perpetuity. Its assets are considered sacred. From the eighth century onward, it served as an increasingly popular device to protect personal wealth by diminishing the likelihood of confiscation. Right up to modern times, Muslim rulers were much less likely to seize *waqf*-owned assets than they were to confiscate private property, for they sought to avoid developing a reputation for impiety.

Although establishing a *waqf* usually required a commitment to provide social services, it came with the privilege of appointing oneself as its *mutawalli* (trustee and manager). At some cost, therefore, a *waqf* founder was able to secure a portion of his wealth for his own and his family's benefit. If the *waqf* system became much more important to the premodern Middle Eastern economy than trusts were to the economies of western Europe, the reason is that in the Middle East private property rights were clearly weaker and, hence, the need for wealthy shelters measurably greater.

A salient characteristic of Middle Eastern history is the absence of broad movements to strengthen private property rights. It offers nothing akin to the protracted European movements that limited the economic powers of kings and queens. The very availability of the *waqf* option helps to explain this difference. It dampened collective action on the part of wealth holders likely to benefit from stronger property rights. Formal property rights arrived in the Middle East in the nineteenth century through sweeping economic reforms based largely on European models. Property rights are broadly recognized in the modern civil codes of Middle Eastern countries.

See also **Economy and Economic Institutions; Waqf.**

BIBLIOGRAPHY

Kuran, Timur. "The Provision of Public Goods under Islamic Law: Origins, Impact, and Limitations of the Waqf System." *Law and Society Review* 35 (2001): 301–357.

Mayer, A. E., ed. *Property, Social Structure, and Law in the Modern Middle East.* Albany: State University of New York Press, 1985.

Timur Kuran

PROPHETS

According to Muslim interpretation of the Qur'an, the prophet Muhammad is considered to be the "seal of the prophets," the culmination of a line of prophets stretching back through Jesus, Moses, and Abraham to Adam. Many but not all of the prophets preceding Muhammad are mentioned in the Qur'an, and later Muslim traditions attach great importance to certain beliefs and practices associated with all the prophets.

The Qur'an itself (2:136, 3:84, 4:136, 42:13) and later Muslim creeds stipulate belief in all the prophets and the books revealed to them without making distinctions among them. The *Fiqh al-akbar* (art. 8), traditionally attributed to the jurist Abu Hanifa, states that Muslims should believe that Moses and Jesus were prophets, perhaps in reference to 2:285 and 4:152. The so-called *Fiqh al-akbar II* (art. 20), the *Wasiyat Abi Hanifa* (art. 25) and the *'Aqida* of Ahmad b. Ja'far al-Tahawi (art. 5) all state the belief in the intercession of the prophets for their followers on the Day of Judgment.

Some Muslim scholars distinguish between a generic "prophet" (*nabi*) and a "messenger" or "apostle" (*rasul*), maintaining that only a select few of the many prophets were messengers, supposed to have brought a revealed book to their people. Within the Qur'an, other terms are used to refer to prophets, including "messiah" or "Christ" (*masih*) with reference exclusively to Jesus. Ibn Sa'd (d. 230) reports that the number of *rasul* including the prophet Muhammad is 315, and the total number of prophets is one thousand. Other Muslim sources list the total number of prophets as 224,000.

The stories of the prophets make up a significant portion of the Qur'an, but the Qur'an does not mention the names of all the prophets claimed by some Muslim scholars. By name there are twenty-five prophets mentioned in the Qur'an, though there are some disagreements concerning the individual identities of all these. Among those mentioned by name are: Adam (mentioned 25 times by name), Idris (1), Nah (Noah; 43), Hud (7), Salih (10), Ibrahim (Abraham; 69), Isma'il (Ishmael; 12), Ishaq (Isaac; 17), Ya'qub (Jacob; 16), Lut (Lot; 27), Yusuf (Joseph; 27), Shu'ayb (11), Ayyub (Job; 4), Dhu-l-Kifl (2), Musa (Moses; 137), Harun (Aaron; 20), Dawud (David; 16), Sulayman (Solomon; 17), Ilyas (Elijah; 1), Alisa (Elisha; 2), Yunus (Jonah; 4), Zakariyya (Zechariah; 7), Yahya (John; 5), 'Issa (Jesus; 25), and Muhammad (4).

Other passages in the Qur'an refer to prophets without mentioning names, but Muslim tradition identifies the prophets by name such as: Khidr, Ezekiel, Samuel, Jeremiah, and Daniel. In some cases, such as the case of the prophet sent to the People of the Well (25:38, 50:12) and to the People of the City mentioned in Sura Ya-Sin (36:13–29), the prophets are not identified by name in the Qur'an, and the names given to the prophets are not well known outside of Muslim exegesis. There are also important characters, mentioned by name in the Qur'an, such as Luqman and Dhu al-Qarnayn, who are not considered prophets but whose stories are nevertheless included in the later Muslim stories of the prophets.

The Qur'an mentions scriptures revealed to Abraham (53:36–37, 87:18–19), and specifies the Torah and Gospel (3:3, 3:48, 3:60, 5:43–46, 5:66), Psalms of David (4:163, 17:55), and Qur'an (12:1–3, 20:2, 27:19, 56:77–80, 76:23) as revealed books. A hadith report given on the authority of Abu Dharr states that scriptures were revealed to Adam, Seth, Idris, and Abraham in addition to the revelation of the Torah to Moses, the Psalms to David, the Gospel to Jesus, and the Qur'an to Muhammad. According to al-Tabari, the "first scriptures" mentioned in Q 20:133 and 87:18 are the scriptures revealed to Seth and Idris.

Muslim tradition also mentions the relics of prophets, some of which are venerated in shrines and are the focus of seasonal rituals. Muslims perform pilgrimages to the tombs of certain prophets such as that of Hud in the Hadramawt and Shuʿayb in Yemen. According to the Arab geographer Yaqut, the tomb of Adam is said to be in Mecca, and Muslim pilgrimages visit the tomb of Muhammad in Medina. Artifacts of the prophets are also attested such as the Ark of the Covenant, a mirror and ring that belonged to Solomon, the ring and book of Daniel, and a number of items closely associated with Muhammad including his hair and fingernails. The footprints of prophets, including Abraham, Moses, and Muhammad, are also preserved in religious institutions and museums along with articles of clothing and weapons.

In addition to the standard Qur'an commentaries that were written according to the order of the suras and verses in the Qur'an, Muslim scholars also compiled "stories of the prophets," which excerpted and commented on the large parts of the Qur'an concerned with the prophets leading up to Muhammad. These works organized the Qur'an passages in narrative order beginning with Adam and ending with Muhammad, roughly paralleling the biblical chronology of these same figures. Best known for their stories of the prophets were Thaʿlabi and Ibn Kathir, and stories of the prophets made up significant parts of universal histories such as those compiled by Tabari, Yaʿqubi, Ibn al-Athir, and in the biography of the prophet Muhammad by Ibn Ishaq.

The prophet-by-prophet and overall chronological structure of these story collections contributed to a more accessible and less piecemeal interpretation of the Qur'an. The genre of "stories of the prophets" has been more closely associated with sermons and popular Qur'an interpretation, and it is likely that some of the earliest Qur'an interpretations, like those attributed to Wahb b. Munabbih, Kaʿb al-Ahbar, and Ibn ʿAbbas, originated as sermons or stories of the prophets. Later works devoted to the stories of the prophets, especially in Persian, were richly illustrated, picturing the prophets in certain well-known scenes from the popular stories. In the Muslim world today, one of the most popular formats for presentation of the Qur'an to children is through books and videos illustrating the stories of the prophets.

Most of the prophets in the Qur'an as well as those mentioned by name in later Muslim interpretation parallel characters from the Bible and its interpretation in Jewish and Christian traditions. Muslim scholars have seen these parallels as evidence of the shared origins of these religions and their revealed scriptures, and largely embrace the diversity of the various "versions" of different stories focusing on the common veneration of certain recognized figures such as Abraham, Moses, and Jesus.

See also **Islam and Other Religions; Muhammad; Qur'an.**

BIBLIOGRAPHY

Firestone, Reuven. *Journeys in the Holy Lands: The Evolution of the Abraham-Ishmael Story in Islamic Exegesis.* Albany: State University of New York Press, 1990.

Lassner, Jacob. *Demonizing the Queen of Sheba: Boundaries of Gender and Culture in Postbiblical Judaism and Medieval Islam.* Chicago: University of Chicago Press, 1993

Newby, Gordon. *The Making of the Last Prophet: A Reconstruction of the Earliest Biography of Muhammad.* Columbia: University of South Carolina Press, 1989.

Schöck, Cornellia. *Adam im Islam: Ein Beitrag zur Ideengeschichte der Sunna.* Berlin: Klaus Schwarz, 1993.

Schwarzbaum, Haim. *Biblical and Extra-Biblical Legends in Islamic Folk-Literature.* Waldorf-Hessen: Beiträge zur Sprach- und Kulturgeschichte des Orients 30, 1982.

Tabari. *The History of al-Tabari.* Vol. 1: *From Creation to the Flood.* Translated by Franz Rosenthal. Albany: State University of New York Press, 1989. Vol. 2: *Prophets and Patriarchs.* Translated by William Brinner (1987). Vol. 3: *The Children of Israel.* Translated by William Brinner (1991). Vol. 4: *The Ancient Kingdoms.* Translated by Moshe Perlmann (1987).

Thackston, Wheeler. *The Tales of the Prophets of al-Kisaʾi.* Boston: Twayne, 1978.

Wensinck, Arent Jan. *The Muslim Creed: Its Genesis and Historical Development.* Cambridge, U.K.: Cambridge University Press, 1932.

Wheeler, Brannon. *Moses in the Qurʾan and Islamic Exegesis.* London and New York.: RoutledgeCurzon, 2002.

Wheeler, Brannon. *Prophets in the Qurʾan: An Introduction to the Qurʾan and Muslim Exegesis.* London: Continuum, 2002.

Brannon M. Wheeler

PULPIT *See* **Minbar (Mimbar)**

PURDAH

Purdah, from the Persian word for curtain, *pardah*, refers to the custom of veiling and secluding women in Islamic societies. The Arabic term is *hijab*. The custom derives from references in the Qur'an to speaking with women from behind a curtain (33:53) and to hadith enjoining modest behavior for Muslims of both sexes. *Purdah* is observed in a variety of ways, all of them involving some form of sexual segregation. In its most extreme form, women are confined to their homes; alternatively, it involves male social interaction and schooling with other males and similarly segregated social activities and schooling for females. Usually, *purdah* involves various forms of modest dress in order to keep women from being seen by unrelated males. These range from all-enveloping garments to scarves that cover the hair.

While the custom is associated with the religion of Islam, *purdah* is also a form of cultural and political symbolism. During the period of rapid modernization in the early twentieth century, many middle-class, urban Muslim women gave up the veil. In more recent times, movements of cultural pride and religious reassertion have prompted many Muslim women to don it again. *Purdah* observation varies according to region, culture, and class. In Iran, the *chador* became the emblem of the Islamic revolution, symbolic of the rejection of the West and of westernization. In Afghanistan, the all-enveloping *burqa* was required by the Taliban government, though it also provided symbolic protection for women in politically unstable situations. In Pakistan and India, Muslim women wear a variety of veil forms: the *chaddar*—a large shawl that hides the feminine form, the *burqa*—a coatlike garment with an adjustable head piece, the *dupatta*—a sheer stole that adorns the shoulders, but can be put over the hair when necessary.

Controversy exists over the meaning of renewed *purdah* observance in recent times. It can be seen as the oppressive imposition of social segregation upon women, or as a matter of choice, in which the use of the veil expresses a woman's faith and cultural identity. Indicative of this latter phenomenon is the fact that wearing a head scarf is becoming more common as Muslims migrate to non-Muslim countries.

See also **Gender; Harem; Veiling.**

BIBLIOGRAPHY

Papanek, Hanna. "Purdah: Separate Worlds and Symbolic Shelter." *Comparative Studies in Society and History* 15, no. 3 (1973): 289–325.

Shirazi, Faegheh. *The Veil Unveiled: Hijab in Modern Culture.* Gainesville: University Press of Florida, 2001.

Zuhur, Sherifa. *Revealing Reveiling: Islamist Gender Ideology in Contemporary Egypt.* Albany: State University of New York Press, 1992.

Gail Minault

Q

QADHDHAFI, MU'MAR AL- (1943–)

Mu'mar al-Qadhdhafi was the most dominant Libyan leader in the second half of the twentieth century. His childhood and political ideology were influenced by his family's tribal values, anticolonial Islam, and Arab nationalism during the upheavals of the Egyptian revolution (1952) and the Algerian anticolonial revolution (1954–1965). As the sole leader of Libya since 1969, he has changed the socioeconomic and political structures of that nation. He created and led a self-declared revolutionary state governed by an organization of popular committees and congresses with a rich oil-based rentier economy.

Qadhdhafi was born in 1943 (other sources say he was born earlier) in a tent to a poor itinerant Bedouin family that belonged to the Qadhafa tribe. In 1965, Qadhdhafi and some of his friends entered the military academy and began to recruit other officers in his revolutionary organization, the Free Unionist Officers Movement.

Qadhdhafi's ideology stresses Arab nationalism, Islam, self-determination, social justice, and denounced the corruption of the old regime. He theorizes that historical change is caused by religion and nationalism. Qadhdhafi advocates opening the gates of *ijtihad* (free reason of Islamic law) and hence accepts only the Qur'an as the main basis of Islamic law. Such views place him on the side of reformist Islamic traditions. He was also anticommunist, which brought him international recognition from the Nixon administration in the United States. After consolidating his power and crushed the opposition in 1975, Qadhdhafi began to apply his ideas, which were presented in his *Green Book* (1976, 1980). He advocated what he called the Third Universal Theory, a third way between capitalism and Marxism based on the direct democracy of popular organization of congresses and committees.

Qadhdhafi's leadership of Libya during the first decade after 1969 brought many changes to ordinary Libyans such as providing free medical care, building the infrastructure of the country, and expanding education especially for Libyan women. However, secular and Islamic opposition were repressed. Since the early 1980s, the Libyan economy has grown more dependent on oil for its revenues than it was under the old regime, and agriculture continues to decline despite large and expensive projects. Despite these mixed legacies, the Libyan revolution under Qadhdhafi's leadership is a turning point in the making of modern Libya in the twentieth century.

See also **Modernization, Political: Authoritarianism and Democratization.**

BIBLIOGRAPHY

Ahmida, Ali Abdullatif. *The Making of Modern Libya: State Formation, Colonialization, and Resistance, 1830–1932.* Albany: State University of New York Press, 1994.

Ayoub, Mahmoud M. *Islam and the Third Universal Theory: The Religious Thought of Mu'ammar al-Qadhdhafi.* London: KPI Limited, 1987.

Ali Abdullatif Ahmida

QADI (KADI, KAZI)

A *qadi* is the term for a Muslim judge who issues definitive rulings in cases brought by disputants for resolution. The word *qadi* is derived from the root word *q-d-y*, meaning "to resolve," "to settle," "to decide."

Judicial practice is seen as an extension of the function of the ruler and is thus indirectly linked to orderly governance. Muslim political theory advocates the appointment of an executive ruler (caliph/imam) as a moral obligation (*fard*) premised on religious authority. The appointment of judges is thus in keeping with the fulfillment of an obligation according to the classical Sunni legal authorities. Early Shi'ite authorities argue that the implementation of the rules of the revealed law (shari'a) is an obligation not subject to rational scrutiny (ta'abbud) and can only be fulfilled by the designated hereditary religious leader (imam) or his delegated appointees. Only those judges appointed by the legitimate political leader can be deemed to have worthy credentials as appointees to the office of judgeship.

According to the Sunni scholar al-Ghazali, the role of the judiciary (qada) is similar to the process of issuing juridical responsa (fatwa, pl. fatawa), where academic jurists offer learned opinions to questions about the moral status of practices. There is of course a crucial difference between a jurisconsult (mufti) and a judge (qadi). The former only provides information to the questioner as to what the juridical-moral status or value (hukm) of a specific act is, while the primary purpose of the latter is to apply and enforce the established rules by means of the coercive authority held by the ruler, or later devolved upon the modern state.

Across the spectrum of Muslim law schools treatises detailing the ethics of judgeship are in abundance. A high bar is set for qualification as a qadi, requiring candidates to meet an extensive list of prerequisites. The most important of these pre-requisites are that qadis should be knowledgeable of the law and its cognitive disciplines, as well as display moral rectitude as individiuals with impeccable credentials within their society. Classical Muslim authorities see an intimate link between qualification as a judge and possessing the credentials of being a reliable witness (shahada). Those who pass the test to serve as credible witnesses, also in theory qualify as having the credentials to serve as qadis.

Among the earliest judges delegated by the prophet Muhammad to serve in certain regions were the companions Mu'adh ibn Jabal, who was sent to Yemen, and 'Itab b. Usayd, who was sent to Mecca. Later successors, notably 'Umar b. Al-Khattab, gave particular attention to the development of a proto-judicial system. He appointed the famous Shurayh b. al-Harith al-Kindi (d. c. 699/700) as qadi of Kufa. Shurayh was affirmed by the caliph/imam 'Ali who held him in high esteem, provided him with a monthly stipend, even though he fired him for issuing a wrong judgment, but 'Ali also later reinstated him. 'Umar's famous letter to Abu Musa al-Ash'ari is held out as a model document that enshrines the ideals of judgeship in Islam in which he pleads for equity for all people, rich or poor, and warns against the miscarriage of justice.

Historically, the profession has been dominated by males. Most of the law schools make maleness a prerequisite for being a judge. However, in theory at least, some of the classical schools permit women to be judges, while barring them from deciding cases involving criminal penalties (hudud). However, since there is no explicit directive in the Qur'an or prophetic tradition that prevents women from holding the office of a qadi, the early juristic viewpoint on this matter reflects the social conditions of patriarchy, where the religious norm is colored by social context.

The situation in modern Muslim nation-states from the twentieth century onward is somewhat different. In many societies where a version of Islamic law is still practiced, such as family law, women do perform the role of qadis. However, the advancement of women to high levels in the profession of judgeship still remains an ongoing struggle.

According to the classical authorities, non-Muslim qadis can only have jurisdiction over fellow non-Muslims, but do not have jurisdiction over Muslim petitioners. Sunni and Shi'ite authorities do not accept the testimony of non-Muslims against Muslims. Given the parallels between judgeship and testimony, non-Muslim qadis are not viewed as qualified to give verdicts over Muslims. While these practices stem from assumptions of Islamic power and empire, this rule is often ignored in modern multireligious and multiethnic societies that include significant Muslim populations such as India, Malaysia, and Nigeria. Irrespective of Muslim majority or minority contexts, non-Muslim judges do issue binding rulings on Muslim petitioners with little objection from the traditional religious scholars (ulema).

In the premodern period qadis had jurisdiction over an entire gamut of laws ranging from administrative law, torts, and commercial law to criminal law. In several places, especially in North Africa, there were also courts of appeals. However, with the displacement of Islamic law by secular and Western legal codes in the nineteenth and twentieth centuries, the jurisdiction of the qadi is in many instances limited to family law matters; in many places the office has been abolished. On the other hand, in some countries where Islamic law has been reintroduced as the main source of law in the twentieth century, the office of the qadi has been revived.

See also **Fatwa; Law; Mufti; Religious Institutions.**

BIBLIOGRAPHY

Powers, David. "On Judicial Review in Islamic Law." *Law & Society Review* 26, no. 2 (1992): 315–341.

Tyser, C. R., et al., trans. "About a Judge and the Duties of a Judge." In *The Mejelle*. Kuala Kumpur, Malaysia: The Other Press, 2001.

'Umar al-Khassaf, Ahmad ibn, and Sadr al-Shahid, 'Abd al-'Aziz, trans. *Munir Ahmad Mughal, Adab al-Qadi: Islamic Legal and Judicial System*. Lahore: Kazi Publications, 1999.

Yaacob, Abdul Monir. "Duties of Qadis in Islamic Law." *Journal Undang-Undang IKIM, Institute of Islamic Understanding Malaysia Law Journal* 4, no. 1 (January–June 2000): 39–52.

Ebrahim Moosa

QAʿIDA, AL-

The name of the radical organization al-Qaʿida (also spelled al-Qaeda) has the literal meaning of "the foundation" or "the base." The organization arose in the last quarter of the twentieth century to oppose the military and economic intervention of non-Muslim states in predominantly Muslim lands. It came to the attention of the public in the United States and around the world on 11 September 2001, immediately following the deadly attacks on the World Trade Center in New York City and the Pentagon in Washington, D.C., that killed more than three thousand people and terrified those who witnessed the well-covered event on television. The broader association of al-Qaʿida and its leader, Usama bin Ladin, with terrorism was immediate and pervasive in media coverage and political discourse in America and elsewhere.

Al-Qaʿida was the first of the militant Islamist organizations to operate on a global scale. It did so in part by adopting many of the technologies and communications methods of the very global organization whose famous twin-tower buildings in New York it allegedly destroyed on 11 September 2001. Although a considerable amount of data on al-Qaʿida and its operatives has been gathered and published by governmental security agencies and investigative reporters, as of 2003 a thorough academic study of the organization or, more properly speaking, of the cluster of radical Muslim organizations going by the name of al-Qaʿida, had yet to be undertaken by specialists on Islam.

The ideological founder of al-Qaʿida (sometimes al-Qaʿida al-sulba: "the solid foundations") was ʿAbdallah ʿAzzam, a Palestinian born in 1941. ʿAzzam grew up under Israeli occupation of his homeland. He earned a doctorate in shariʿa studies at al-Azhar University in Cairo, after which he taught in various Middle Eastern universities. He was dismissed from his teaching post at King ʿAbd al-ʿAziz University in Saudi Arabia in 1979 for engaging in Islamist activism. He then went to Pakistan on the eve of the invasion of Afghanistan by armed forces of the Soviet Union. There he met and became a religious mentor to Usama bin Ladin, who brought to the growing anti-Soviet effort (jihad) considerable financing and experience in building the kind of infrastructure needed to conduct effective counterattacks.

In 1984 ʿAzzam and bin Ladin established the Afghan Service Bureau Front, known by its Arabic acronym M.A.K. (maktab al-khidma li-l-mujahin al-ʿarab, literally, office for services for Arab freedom fighters). Among the services they provided was keeping track of young Muslim males who joined the cause from countries around the world, particularly from Arab countries like Saudi Arabia and Egypt, and they apparently provided relief services to those who were wounded and to the families of those killed in battle. Very

soon thereafter M.A.K. began to recruit, indoctrinate, and train its volunteers in effective resistance methods, including terrorist tactics. ʿAzzam held a particularly hard-line doctrine of jihad, which, according to his understanding of the Qurʾan and sunna of the prophet Muhammad, required militant opposition to Islam's perceived enemies. This view was adopted by Usama bin Ladin, although at what point is not clear. Another important influence in the al-Qaʿida network of organizations is Ayman al-Zawahiri (1951–), an Egyptian physician who joined the radical al-Jamaʿa al-Islamiyya (Islamic Group) and affiliated with bin Ladin during the late twentieth and early twenty-first centuries.

During the Afghan war against the Soviet military, the organized resistance efforts of M.A.K. also became known as al-Qaʿida. Other names were adopted by Usama bin Ladin, such as "The Islamic Global Front for Combating Jews and Crusaders [Christians]." Indeed, such names, including al-Qaʿida, do not refer to a single organization with a single central command headquartered in a known place, but rather to a cluster or complex of organizations and movements whose affiliations and organizational structure are not yet well known or understood. In the 1980s al-Qaʿida functioned as an ally of United States against the Soviet Union, receiving covert funds through the C.I.A. When the war wound down with the defeat of the Soviets in 1988, the organization's interests expanded globally, to include other Muslim fronts that suffered non-Muslim interventions, including Chechnya, the Balkans, Central Asia, Africa, and Indonesia. This new, more global involvement included an attempt to blow up one of the towers of the World Trade center in New York (23 February 1993), simultaneous lethal bomb blasts at two U.S. embassies in east Africa (1998), an attack on the U.S.S. Cole as it came into port in the Yemen (2000), and suicidal attacks using commandeered airplanes against the World Trade Center in New York and the Pentagon in Washington, D.C., on 11 September 2001.

Many well-meaning Muslims and non-Muslims have regarded al-Qaʿida, its leaders and operatives, as beyond the pale of the Islamic faith because of the extreme and violent methods they advocate using against moderate Muslim governments and non-Muslim states. Yet it is clear that ʿAbdallah ʿAzzam, Usama bin Ladin and other leaders and mentors of al-Qaʿida regarded themselves as good Muslims, as being among the vanguard of reformers who aim to restore the true faith of the founding generations of Islam (the salaf), and as followers of a legitimate Sunni school of interpretation in Islam, the Wahhabi-Hanbali school that predominates in Saudi Arabia and elsewhere in the Gulf states. They proposed a radical Islamic response to modernism and to the constraining military and political forces of non-Muslim states and their secular agendas, basing that response on interpretations of Islam that were already circulating in the mid-twentieth century.

Chief among these interpretations are the writings of Sayyid Qutb (1906–1966), whose books and pamphlets continue to be widely read and appreciated throughout the Muslim world, even by moderate Muslims who regard their faith as greatly misunderstood by non-Muslims and under assault by secular modernity. Thus, while willful, murderous acts against innocent victims is regarded as morally reprehensible by most Muslims and non-Muslims alike, many scholars believe that the Islamic self-understanding promoted by the leadership and ranks of al-Qaʿida members must also be analyzed without the attempt to classify them as authentic or inauthentic religious beliefs. Other scholars see al-Qaʿida as a forceful response to Western imperialism during the colonial and post-colonial periods and to the rapid globalization of market capitalism and secularism since the collapse of the Soviet Union in 1989. Most scholars of Islam warn against an ill-founded tendency on the part of some religious leaders and media commentators to equate al-Qaʿida with Islam, that is, to define and grasp Islam in terms of the public manifestations of al-Qaʿida and similar radical groups.

See also **Bin Ladin, Usama; Fundamentalism; Qutb, Sayyid; Terrorism.**

BIBLIOGRAPHY

Gunaratna, Rohan. *Inside Al Qaeda: Global Network of Terror.* New York: Columbia University Press, 2002.

Richard C. Martin

QANUN

Qanun (pl. *qawanin*) is a word that apparently entered into Arabic from Greek, although according to some reports it might have been borrowed from Persian or Latin or have meant the "way to something" or its measurement in old Arabic. The word, however, has come to have broad meanings including a particular musical instrument, known simply as *al-qanun*, tax assessments, state taxes and tariffs, registers and lists, land measurements, and also rules and regulations. In modern times, *qanun* generally refers to state law, although the word is often used to signify guiding rules, customs, and principles. In both premodern and modern times, *qanun* often referred to secular laws and administrative rules, as opposed to religious laws or *shariʿa* . The word was often used in the titles of books written as early as the tenth century. The titles of some of these books included: *al-Qawanin al-sharʿiyya* (The principles of *shariʿa*), *Qawanin al-ahkam al-sharʿiyya* (The principles of Islamic law), *Tashrih al-qanun* (The explanation of the law), *Qawanin al-siyasa* (The rules of governance), *Qanun al-saʿada* (Rules of conduct and principles of happiness), *Qanun al-adab* (Rules of good character), *Qanun al-balagha* (Rules of eloquence), *Qanun fi al-tibb* (Avicenna's book on medicine), and *Qawanin al-riyada* (Principles of mathematics). All of these books were written between the tenth and fifteenth centuries, indicating that the word had passed into common Arabic usage, and was taken to mean the rules or principles of something.

From the earliest centuries of Islam and onward, the word was used in a more specialized context to refer to tax registers and lists, especially of land taxes, as in *qanun al-kharaj*, and the regulations and assessments of land taxes, as in *al-qawanin al-muqarrara*. In addition, a large number of texts written on the rules of public administration or the administration of the ruler's office were titled *qanun al-rasaʾil* and *qanun al-diwan*. In the sixteenth century, Ghiyath al-Din Khwand ʿAmir wrote *Qanun-e-Humayuni*, which recorded the rules and ordinances established by the emperor Humayun, and some of the building erected by his order.

From the Umayyad period, and especially during the Ottoman era, the word *qanun* also referred to state regulations, imperial decrees, or edicts that were based on public interest and executive discretion, instead of the jurist-based *shariʿa* law. Such regulations were considered temporal in nature, and therefore, they remained in effect as long as they were decreed by a ruler. Upon the death or removal of a ruler, such regulations had to be confirmed or continued by a successor. These regulations were not limited to the field of taxation, but often covered matters related to court procedure, commercial law, and criminal law as well. They also canonized customary practices especially for professional guilds and merchants. As far as Muslim jurists were concerned, these regulations were described as executory laws (*qawanin ʿurfiyya*) that could be mandated by public interests, but such regulations were not considered part of the divinely based *shariʿa* law. Therefore, such decrees and regulations were documented, publicized, and enforced by state functionaries, including judges, but they were not memorialized in the books of classical Islamic jurisprudence. From the perspective of Muslim jurists, the legitimacy of such regulations depended on the extent to which they served the public interest, and the interests of justice, and also to the extent they did not conflict with the jurist-made *shariʿa* law.

The degree to which consecutive Muslim governments relied on *qanun*, as executive regulations, at the expense of the jurist-based *shariʿa* law varied widely. Muslim jurists did not always oppose the imposition of administrative laws or regulations by the state, and, in fact, in tracts written on politics, jurists often acknowledged that such regulations are a functional necessity. However, since the Umayyad period, there was a pronounced tension between state functionaries and bureaucrats, and the juristic class. The jurists, as the *shariʿa* experts, were suspicious, and often defensive, toward attempts by bureaucrats to systematize and centralize the law by limiting the discretionary powers of the jurists. Nonetheless, in the period following the Mongol invasions, various dynasties resorted to increased executive lawmaking, often resulting in aggravating the tensions between the juristic class and the state.

The usage of the term *qanun*, in the sense of secular laws, became particularly pronounced in the Ottoman era (1218–1924). The Ottoman caliph Mehmed II "the Conqueror" (r. 1451–1481) promulgated his famous *qanun-nama* as a systematic codified set of laws covering various aspects of administrative law, commercial law, and criminal law. Jurists at the time were not always supportive of such attempts at centralization and codification of the laws, and often perceived it as an infringement on the integrity of the Islamic common law, as interpreted and developed by jurists. The opposition of jurists of centralized state-based laws reached a point that in 1696 Mustafa II (r. 1695–1703), by decree, forbade the use of the word *qanun* in conjunction with the word *shariʿa* . This was induced by the efforts of the jurists to make clear that state-issued *qanun* be separate and apart from *shariʿa* law.

With the age of colonialism, the jurisdiction of *shariʿa* law in most Muslim countries had become progressively restricted and, eventually, confined mostly to personal laws dealing with marriage, divorce, and inheritance. Most Muslim countries adopted a code-based system of law modeled after the French civil law system. In that respect, most Muslim countries adopted civil and criminal law codes, titled "the *qanun* of such and such." For instance, in most Arabic-speaking countries one will find the following: *al-qanun al-madani* (the civil law code), *al-qanun al-jinaʾi* (the criminal law code), *qanun al-ijraʾat* (code of legal procedures), and *al-qanun al-tujari* (the commercial code). In such countries, even in the field of personal law, where *shariʿa* still enjoys the dominant influence, matters relating to marriage, divorce, and inheritance have been codified in codes known as *qanun al-ahwal al-shakhsiyya* (the personal law code). In the modern age, state regulations or executive decrees, as opposed to codes, are often referred to as *qararat, bayanat, lawaʾih*, or *marasim*. Some Muslim countries, such as Saudi Arabia, have not adopted a civil law system, and, instead, rely on the *shariʿa* common law, and on executive decrees issued on specific matters such as banking, foreign investments, and labor and employment regulations. Although the word *qanun* today is used in a technical sense to refer to enacted codes of law, it is still used in the more expansive sense of law in general, including Islamic law.

See also **Law; Modernization, Political: Administrative, Military, and Judicial Reform; Political Organization; Shariʿa.**

BIBLIOGRAPHY

Inalcik, Halil. "Sulayman the Lawgiver and Ottoman Law." *Archivum Ottomanicum* 1 (1971).

Khaled Abou El-Fadl

QIBLA

The place toward which Muslim worshippers direct themselves for prayer, the *qibla*, has always been an important Islamic identity marker. The Kaʿba and the Holy City of Mecca play a very important role as symbolic center in several kinds of religious behavior. The *salat* (prayer) is performed with the face in the direction of Mecca; the deceased is buried lying on his right side, facing Mecca, and it is also advised to take the *qibla* into account in a positive or negative way in various other activities. Discourse about the *qibla* is often embedded in notions of power and tradition. For example, the divide among the Javanese communities in present-day Surinam and the Netherlands between East-*keblat* people and West-*keblat* are closely related to reformist versus traditionalist ideas, respectively. The traditionalist West *qeblat* people keep to their pre-diaspora Javanese customs, identity, and their original Indonesian prayer direction to the West. Reformists argue that it should be altered. Similar discussions take place elsewhere.

Recent historical research by Uri Rubin indicates that the first *qibla* the Muslims used in Mecca was the Kaʿba, in agreement with the local *hunafaʾ* (monotheists), who saw the Kaʿba as the *qibla* of Ibrahim and his son Ismaʿil. Shortly before the *hijra* to Medina, and possibly associated with the revelation of the *israʾ* (Muhammad's night journey, from Mecca to Jerusalem), the *qibla* was altered toward Jerusalem. The Meccan sanctuary became the *qibla* again in 624 C.E. (cf. Q. 2: 136ff) when an important change in Muhammad's attitude toward the Jews occurred.

See also **Devotional Life; Law; Science, Islam and.**

BIBLIOGRAPHY

Bashear, Sulayman. "Qibla Musharriqa and Early Muslim Prayer in Churches." *The Muslim World* 81, nos. 3–4 (1991): 267–282.

Ichwan, Moch. Nur. "Continuing Discourse on Keblat: Diasporic Experiences of the Surinamese Javanese Muslims in the Netherlands." *Sharqiyyāt* 11 (1999): 101–119.

King, David A., and Wensinck, Arend Jan. "Kibla." In *The Encyclopaedia of Islam*. 2d ed. Leiden: E. J. Brill, 1960–.

Rubin, Uri. "Hanifiyya and Kaʿba: An Inquiry into the Arabian Pre-Islamic Background of Dîn Ibrâhîm." *Jerusalem Studies in Arabic and Islam* 13 (1990): 94–112.

Gerard Wiegers

QOM

A provincial capital since June 1996, 140 kilometers south of Tehran, Qom is the biggest center of Shiʿite religious studies and a pilgrimage site next only to Mashhad in importance. A village before it was settled in the seventh and eighth decades of the seventh century by the Ash'aris, a Shi'ite Yemenite tribe that had migrated from Iraq due to differences with Sunni Umayyad rulers, it became, in contrast to the predominantly Sunni towns of the region, a major Shi'ite academic center in the following centuries. Many of the names of authors in al-Najashi's eleventh-century list of Shi'ite compilers, as well as those of many narrators of traditions in Shi'ite compendia of hadith, pertain to the Ash'aris of Qom (not to be confused with the Ash'ari theological school).

Qom's fame as an academy seems to have disappeared after the eleventh century, as the center of Shi'ite learning in Iran shifted to Rey and other northern towns. Although such figures as Fayz Kashani (d. 1681) and Molla Mohammad Tahir Qommi (d. 1686) lived here during the Safavid era, Qom's partial reemergence as an academy was due to the patronage of the Qajars. The presence of Mirza-ye Qommi (d. 1816), who enjoyed the patronage of Fath 'Ali Shah (1797–1834), is considered a point of departure in the history of Qom as an academy. However, a new era began with the arrival of Ayatollah Ha'eri (1859–1936) in 1921. He established the present center of learning (hawza-ye 'ilmiyya) during a period when the Qajar regime was passing away and the Pahalvi regime was taking shape. From the times of Ayatollah Borujerdi (d. 1961) onward, the hawza began its rapid growth. At the end of Reza Shah's reign the number of seminary students was about 500. It was above 6,000 in 1975, and above 23,000 in 1991, and presently students from Iran and abroad make up more than 36,000. Under the leadership of Ayatollah Khomeini, a pupil of Ayatollah Ha'eri, Qom played a key role in leading the opposition to the Pahlavi regime in the events of 1964. It was here that on 9 January 1978 the confrontation with the Shah's security forces occurred, an event that triggered off the Islamic Revolution of 1979. Qom's political importance as a spiritual and academic center of the Shi'ite clergy has grown enormously following the Islamic Revolution. From being a small town with a population of 96,499 in 1956, Qom itself has grown rapidly to become one of the major cities of Iran, with a population of 825,627 in 2000.

Qom's fame as a pilgrimage spot visited by millions from Iran and abroad is mainly due to the shrine of Fatimah the Infallible (ma'sumah) (d. 816), daughter of Musa b. Ja'far, the seventh imam. On the way to visiting her brother, Imam 'Ali b. Musa al-Reza, who was at Marv at the time, she died after a brief illness at Qom. Since then her shrine has been a pilgrimage spot, whose sacred precincts have served as a site for royal and noble mausoleums as well as a favored burial ground of the faithful since the Safavid and Qajar periods. Although the city and the shrine received some royal attention during the rule of the Buwayhid (tenth century), Seljuk (eleventh century), Qara Qoyunlu and Aq Qoyunlu (sixteenth century) regimes, the present structure dates partly from the Safavid and largely from the Qajar era. Other sites

visited for pilgrimage (ziyara) are the graves of numerous Alavite personages in and around Qom (about 400 imamzadahs, or descendents of the imams, are said to be buried in the city and surrounding hamlets). A third major attraction is the Jamkaran Mosque, located five kilometers from the city. Visited by more than an estimated ten million people annually, it is believed to have been built at the order of the Twelfth Imam. These shrines in conjunction with numerous traditions related from the imams concerning the station of Qom as a Shi'ite sanctuary and stronghold make it Iran's second holiest city after Mashhad.

See also **Mashhad; Pilgrimage: Ziyara; Revolution: Islamic Revolution in Iran.**

Rasool Ja'fariyan

QUR'AN

Muslim housewives commence cooking by reciting a verse from the Qur'an in order to ensure that more people are able to enjoy the meal. On spotting an approaching dog, Muslims will hastily read any memorized verse to deflect its possible ill-intentions. The die-hard Marxists of the Baluchistan Communist Party in Pakistan commenced their annual conference with a recitation from the Qur'an. In Cape Town, the local rugby club will organize a cover-to-cover recitation of it to celebrate its fiftieth jubilee. In California, the international Muslim homosexual organization takes its name, Al-Fatiha, from the name of the Qur'an's first chapter.

The Qur'an is memorized in small parts by virtually all Muslims, recited in the daily prayers, or rehearsed at funerals and memorial rituals, chanted at the side of the newly born, the sick, or the dying. After death it is recited to ease the passage of the departed soul into the next and to provide comfort for those left behind; as if to say "Whatever, be assured God is here; just listen to His speech!" Any inmate of a Dubai prison who memorizes it entirely can get complete remission from his or her sentence, and a memorization of each thirtieth part is rewarded by an equivalent amount off one's sentence.

An immediate end can be brought to many an argument by resorting to: "But God says . . .!" Virtually every Muslim home is adorned with some verse from it in various forms of calligraphy, as a means of both beautifying one's home and protecting it (with the inhabitants seldom knowing the meaning of the framed piece of calligraphy). Passages from it are used as amulets to protect from illness or the evil eye. A few verses containing the prayer that the Qur'an suggests Noah offered when he entered the ark are stuck on the windscreens of vehicles from Chicago to Jakarta to provide protection for the driver and passengers. Palatial mansions in many Muslim countries have the verse "This is [an outcome] of my Sustainer's bounty" (27:40) stuck on the gates or walls to ward off any evil intention. As for its inhabitants, they believe that protection is offered by pasting a few verses, known as the Verses of the Throne (*Ayat al-Kursi*), behind the front door. Written texts conform to or deviate from a language and its rules; in the case of this text, the development of the language is based on it and its rules are rooted primarily in the text.

This is the Qur'an. It fulfills many of the same functions in the lives of Muslims as the Bible does for Christians, but most importantly, it represents to Muslims what Jesus Christ represents for devout Christians or the Torah, the eternal law of God, for Jews. Similarly, the history of theological controversy about the nature of the Qur'an, which flourished from the early days of Islam until orthodoxy finally settled the issue of the "true dogma," is not unlike the early controversies about the nature of Jesus Christ and his relationship to the Father, which was finally settled for the Christian world by the Council of Nicaea in 325. In the same manner that small remnants of the dissident opinions on the nature of Christ have survived and reawakened under the impact of critical modern and postmodern thinking in Christianity, so have such opinions about the nature of the Qur'an survived in Islam.

For Muslims the Qur'an is alive and has a quasi-human personality. Muslims believe that it watches over them and will intercede with God on the Day of Judgment. The Qur'an is possessed of enormous power; "Had We bestowed this Qur'an from on high upon a mountain, you would indeed see it [the mountain] humbling itself, breaking asunder for awe of God" (59:21).

The Qur'an as Oral Discourse

The oral dimensions of the Qur'an were important in a society where poetry and the spoken or recited word were highly valued. It is also evident that the activity of committing the Qur'an or sections thereof to memory and reciting it were important parts of the religious life of the earliest Muslims, and regarded as acts of great spiritual merit. The Prophet himself would often recite from the Qur'an and at times ask others to read for him. 'Abdallah b. Mas'ud (d. 652) reported that the Prophet told him: "'Read [from] the Qur'an for me.' I [b. Mas'ud] said: 'Shall I read it for you when it was revealed unto you?' He said: 'I love listening to it from someone else.'" The overwhelming importance of the Qur'an as recited speech in contrast with it as written or read text is found in the meaning of the word Qur'an itself, in the way the earliest Muslims viewed the text, and in several verses of the Qur'an. The proper-noun sense of the term *qur'an*, as used in reference to the scripture, is that of a fundamentally oral and certainly an active ongoing reality, rather than that of a written and closed codex such as it later came to be, represented by the *masahif* (written copies, sing. *mushaf*).

From the Arabic root *qara'a* (to read), or *qarana* (to gather or collect), the word *qur'an* is used in the Qur'an in the sense of reading (17:93), recital (75:18) and a collection (75:17).

The Qur'an also describes itself as "a guide for humankind" and "a clear exposition of guidance," "a distinguisher" (25:1), "a reminder" (15:9), "ordinance in the Arabic tongue" (13:37), "a healer" (10:57), "the admonition" (10:57), "the light" (7:157), and "the truth" (17:81). From this literal meaning, it refers to a revealed oral discourse that unfolded over a period of twenty-three years as seemingly a part of God's response to the requirements of society. Only toward the end of this process is the Qur'an presented as scripture rather than a recitation or discourse. The word *qur'an* is thus used in two distinct senses: first, as the designation of a portion or portions of revelation; and, second, as the name of the entire collection of revelations to Muhammad. This twin meaning of *qur'an*, as both a collection and as a book, makes for fascinating questions about the nature of revelation. Is it a collection of divine responses to earthly events or is it a pre-existing canon according to which events must play out in order that its narratives, injunctions, and exhortations can acquire flesh and blood?

The Qur'an as Written Word

For outsiders, the Qur'an exists primarily as a literary text (*al-kitab*); for Muslims, however, it continues to function as both a written text (*mushaf*) and an oral one (*al-qur'an*), with an organic relationship existing between these two modes. Most of critical scholarship has focused on the written dimensions of the text without reflecting too carefully on its message, and has failed to appreciate that its centrality to Muslims transcends this textual form. Thus, questions are raised by critical scholars about, for example, the identity of Mary, whom the Qur'an describes as the sister of Aaron, and the seeming discrepancy between this description and one in which Mary is credited with being the mother of Jesus.

Such questions generally fail to appreciate that the Qur'an is essentially evocative to Muslims and that it is often informative through its being evocative. While exegetes would go to great lengths to resolve the difficulties presented by the portrayal of Mary as both the mother of Jesus and the sister of Aaron, the "fact" of God having stated this remains unshaken. Thus while it may not make any cognitive sense, the response of the believer downplays cognition, and comprehension, and ignores the question of which Mary is being referred to. This understanding as devotion rather than as cognition is how the believer approaches the Qur'an. In other words, comprehension can follow from the emotive and intuitive response that is evoked in the hearer and reciter rather than a study of its contents.

The Structure of the Qur'an

Modern editions of the Qur'an include a heading that provides some basic information at the beginning of each *sura* (chapter) such as its name, the number of *ayat* (verses) it contains, and whether it is regarded as having been revealed in Mecca or Medina. The Egyptian print version, the one most widely used in the Muslim world today, also suggests which verses are exceptions; that is, which verses occurring in a Medinan text were actually revealed in Mecca and vice versa. There are two major divisions in the Qur'an, *suras* (chapters) and *ajza'* (parts), and each *sura* contains a number of verses (*ayat*).

From the singular *aya* (lit. signs, indications, or wonders), *ayat* are the shortest divisions of the Qur'an and the term is usually rendered as "verses," although it may also be understood as phrases or passages. A collection of *ayat*, usually distinguishable from one another by the occurrence of rhythm, rhyme, or assonance, comprise a *sura*. However, this technical meaning of the word *aya* (or *ayat*) is not the only, or even the primary, meaning with which it is used in the Qur'an. It frequently occurs in the sense of the signs of God's presence in the universe. Muslims, however, believe that, given its miraculous and inimitable nature, the Qur'an and all of its constituent parts are signs of the presence of God in the world.

The Qur'an comprises 114 *suras*, each of which is divided into *ayat*. The word *sura* literally means row or fence, and seems to denote both a section or chapter and revelation itself. Muslims believe that the contents of the Qur'an were arranged by the Prophet in his lifetime, and that this was done annually under the guidance of the angel Gabriel. After *al-Fatiha* ("The Opening") the chapters are arranged roughly in order of descending size, beginning with *al-Baqarah* ("The Cow") and concluding with *al-Nas* ("Humankind"). These *suras* are of unequal length, the shortest, "The Fountain," consisting of three *ayat*, the longest, "The Cow," containing 286. With one exception, *al-Tawba* ("The Repentance"), all *suras* commence with "In the name of God, the Gracious, the Dispenser of Grace." This formula is known as the *basmala* and was initially used to denote the boundaries between two *suras*. Muslims suggest that the omission of the *basmala* at the head of the *surat al-Tawba* was intentional because this *sura* commences with God's disavowal of the rejecters and a declaration of war on them. Others, however, suggest that because this *sura* was revealed toward the end of the Prophet's earthly life, he simply did not have the time to insert the *basmala*.

All *suras* have names, and some are known by more than one. These names are based on diverse criteria with no obvious pattern to their naming. A number of hadith refer to specific *suras* by name, thus indicating that they were named by the Prophet. Given that this is a matter directly relating to the Qur'an, Muslims believe that it was a case where "He does not speak of his own whim," (53:3) that is, Muhammad was guided by God in this. Some have, however, suggested that these names do not belong to the Qur'an proper, but rather have been introduced by later scholars and editors for convenience of reference. Twenty-nine of the *suras* have a sequence of Arabic letters that follow immediately after the *basmala*. Known as the disjointed letters, these are meaningless in the literal sense, and their presence has intrigued both

confessional and traditional scholarship. With the exception of the second and third *suras*, they occur exclusively in *suras* belonging to the later Meccan period. There are fourteen of these disjointed letters in all, and the *suras* that contain them may have anywhere from a single letter to a cluster of five.

Another fascinating element of the Qur'an is its division into thirty equal parts, each called a *juz'* (pl. *ajza'*). These divisions are intended to facilitate the recitation of the Qur'an in a month, particularly the month of Ramadan. The *ajza'* are further divided into four neatly divided sections that are marked along the edges of the text. For reading on a daily basis, each *juz'* is divided into seven parts, called *manazil* (sing. *manzil*, lit. stage). It is significant that none of these divisions, pivotal to Muslim usage of the Qur'an, bears any relation to the meaning of the text.

The current arrangement of the Qur'an is neither chronological nor thematic. To those accustomed to reading in a linear or sequential fashion, this can prove tedious and frustrating. With the exception of story of Joseph, the Qur'an also does not have a clear narrative pattern within which its stories neatly unfold. While there is unanimity around the placement of the *ayat* within a *sura*, traditional scholars have differed as to whether the sequence of all, or only some, of the *suras* were divinely ordained. Most Muslims have accepted this arrangement although there have been a number of attempts to offer structural explanations for the way that the *suras* are laid out.

Language

Both Muslim and critical scholarship hold that the Qur'an first appeared in the Arabic language. Traditional Muslim scholarship holds that the Qur'an was written in the dialect of the Quraysh, the tribe of the Prophet, for it was also the classical language known to and understood by all the Arabs. Some Western scholars have argued that the Arabic of the Qur'an was not peculiar to any tribe, but was a kind of *hochsprache* (high speech) that was understood by all the peoples of Hijaz. Christoph Luxenberg, in his *Die Syro-Aramaische Lesart des Koran—Ein Beitrag zur Entschlusselung der Koransprache* (2000), argues that a Syriac rendition of numerous words that would normally be rendered in Arabic can provide linguistic insights on texts that scholars have had difficulty trying to understand. Through a careful process of alternately replacing obscure Qur'anic Arabic words or phrases with Syriac homonyms, changing the diacritical marks (on the assumption that they were possibly misplaced by the editors), or retranslating portions of text into Syriac, Luxenberg discovers radically different meanings for a number of texts. This method differs greatly from the established reading of the Qur'an, which is premised on the idea that it is essentially an Arabic text.

Content

The Qur'an describes its contents as an "exposition of everything, a guidance, a blessing and glad tidings for those who submit" (16:89) and declares that "no single thing have We neglected in the Book" (6:38). The Qur'an places an extraordinary emphasis on the binding relationship between faith and practice.

God. Belief in the existence of one transcendent creator and the struggle to live alongside all the implications of that belief may be said to be at the core of the Qur'an's message, and that Creator is arguably the single most important subject of the Qur'an. The Qur'an uses the word *Allah* approximately 2,500 to refer to the Transcendent. God remains free from not only the confines of biology and paternity, but also from the confines of human language. "No vision can encompass Him, whereas He encompasses all vision, for He alone is unfathomable, all-aware" (6:103). The Qur'an portrays God as a deity who stands above the religious community that serves Him and who is greater than the law. God exists in and by Himself, and any association with Him is rejected by the Qur'an. Ascribing paternity to God is abominable, as is any notion of a shared divinity. Much of the Qur'an is devoted to the praise of God; the Qur'an holds that the entire universe is engaged in extolling the praises of God.

Prophethood. The second fundamental doctrine of the Qur'an is that of the historical continuity of revelation, whereby God sent a series of messengers to every nation in order to guide them to the path of righteousness. All of these messengers came with an identical message (41:43)—that of submission to the will of God—and all of humankind is required to believe in the veracity of each one of them. The Qur'an uses two terms to denote prophethood: *rasul* (pl. *rusul*) and *nabiyy* (pl. *anbiya'*). *Rasul* seems to denote a messenger who received revelations and who actually headed his community, whereas *nabiyy* seems to denote an apostle who did not necessarily come with a new revelation or law: ". . .God elects whomsoever He will from among his Apostles. . ." (3:179). *Anbiya'* derive their authority solely from God; they cannot "bring forth a miracle other than by God's leave." Prophets are always chosen from among their own communities (7:35, 10:74 and 39:17) and are responsible only for conveying God's messages (16:35).

The Qur'an contains a number of narratives involving prophets, often told with the intention of consoling Muhammad in the face of rejection by the Quraysh and recipients of earlier revelation. The Qur'an presents these narratives as moral lessons for humankind on the consequences of disobeying God. All of the prophets referred to in the Qur'an are men. While Mary was the recipient of revelation, nowhere is there any indication that she was expected to play the socioreligious role of warner or the bearer of good tidings, or that she ever did so.

The resurrection and ultimate accountability. The Qur'an speaks repeatedly about the ultimate accountability of all human beings to God. It insists that all of life and its affairs, having originated with God are in a continuous state of purposeful reversion to a just and merciful Creator, Sustainer, and Judge. Physical death is thus not the end of life but merely evolution into another form. Human beings are placed on the earth for a predetermined period before they enter the *akhira* (hereafter).

The terms *dunya* ("the world") and *akhira* (lit. next, or last) are related both to time and space and to two moral alternatives. *Dunya* is the geographical space and the present where humankind is meant to prepare for *akhira*, yet this abode of preparation can also be good and fulfilling by itself. From the Qur'an, it would appear that there is a particular moment in time when the resurrection and judgment will begin, and that hour will commence with the sounding of the heavenly trumpet. When the resurrection begins, bodies will be reunited with their spirits and brought into the presence of God for the ultimate reckoning.

The Qur'an suggests that this resurrection is a bodily one, yet it is also a day when the earth shall be changed into nonearth (14:48). The Qur'an is explicit about two alternatives for each person in the hereafter—*janna* (paradise), or *jahannam* (hell)—and spells out the deeds that will earn one a place in the one or the other. In *Islamic Understanding of Death and Resurrection* (1981), Yvonne Haddad and Jane Smith point out that "Many of the details of the Fire, as of the Garden, are reminiscent of the New Testament; others reflect on occasions the tone of early Arabic poetry. On the whole, however, the picture afforded by the Qur'an is uniquely its own, articulated in a generally consistent and always awe-inspiring fashion."

The Qur'an, at various junctures, indicates the sins that will earn a person consignment to hell. These include lying, dishonesty, corruption, ignoring God or God's revelations, denying the resurrection, refusing to feed the poor, indulgence in opulence and ostentation, the economic exploitation of others, and social oppression. The fires of hell, however, are not the only consequence that wrongdoers will face on the Day of Judgment: "And those who earned evil, the punishment of evil is the like thereof, and abasement will cover them—they will have none to protect them from God—as if their faces had been covered with slices of dense darkness of night" (10:27). Denial of water (7:50) and of light (57:13) are also spoken of as forms of punishment for the inhabitants of hell.

Righteous conduct. The bulk of the Qur'anic message contains exhortations dealing with righteous conduct, and the consequences of following or ignoring them. These are framed within the backdrop of the all-pervading presence of God and humankind's ultimate accountability to Him. The Qur'an regards the human being as a carrier of the spirit of God and a sacred trust from Him, and that all humans are in a continuous state of journeying toward Him. This sanctity comes from humankind being the recipients of God's own spirit from the moments of humankind's creation. Returning to God entails a ceaseless struggle to prepare for the ultimate encounter. The Qur'an, while demanding that Muslims strive to fulfil all the requirements of virtuous behavior, nevertheless acknowledges that living up to such a commitment is exceptionally difficult.

The most important obligation that the Qur'an places on the believer is probably that of pursuing the pleasure of God and of desiring the ultimate encounter with Him. This is attained by cultivating a direct relationship of love with and adoration of God, as well as by leading one's life in such a way as to fulfil His commandments. In addition to setting forth the appropriate rituals, the Qur'an often speaks of the adoration of God as an important part of a Muslim's ideal life and persona. The emphasis that the Qur'an places on God as the focus and objective of a believer's life has led many a contemplative Muslim to regard the law as merely a means of facilitating closeness to God in the same way that railings may help one to climb up a flight of stairs.

Although the Qur'an cautions against excess and wasteful consumption, it nevertheless encourages a sense of joyful living. It asks believers not to impose unwarranted burdens upon themselves (5:87). The Qur'an also refers to physical cleanliness and sexual pleasure as two other dimensions of personal well-being (2:222, 30:21).

The Qur'an places great emphasis on knowledge, and the pursuit thereof, as valuable (49:9), but links the intellectual well-being of people to a profound awareness of God and justice, and emphasizes the compatibility of knowledge with faith (35:28, 58:11). The Qur'an often gives the impression that there is a certain essential body of truth, "the knowledge" (al-'ilm), that is to be acquired. In numerous other verses, though, humankind is challenged to reflect, ponder, and meditate—all qualities more closely associated to heurism and tentativeness than to certainty. Nonetheless, these qualities are usually regarded as the basis of wisdom (2:269). The Qur'anic assumption seems to be that knowledge and reflection will invariably and inevitably lead to God (39:9).

Truth. Postmodernist notions of tentativeness as a value have little place in the Qur'an, which moves from the premise that there is an absolute, single, and knowable Truth. The Qur'an speaks about the light in the singular and darknesses in the plural, making it convenient for traditional or fundamentalist scholars to claim that there is only one truth. Believers are called upon to uphold the spirit of truthfulness by staying in the company of other truthful people (9:19), and to speak the truth in the face of falsehood. Concealing the truth is prohibited (2:42) as is distorting it with falsehood (2:42). Hypocrisy is condemned in the strongest terms, and believers are enjoined to ensure that their deeds correspond to their words (61:2–3).

Social and economic relations. Notwithstanding the scriptural requirement that believers must disturb the peace whenever their silence would conceal the demons of injustice and oppression, the Qur'an also asks believers to lead lives free of pointless argumentation and quarreling (25:63). In the face of the all-pervading grace of God, the Qur'an requires believers to remain hopeful and never to despair. In fact, it describes deep pessimism as a sign of *kufr* (rejection) (12:87). A good Muslim upholds the truth and justice "and is not afraid of the reproaches of those who find fault" (5:54). The Qur'an encourages and even commands believers to lead an austere life. It is contemptuous of those who are attached to wealth beyond the requirements of one's daily subsistence. Such attachment distracts one from following the path that leads to God and provides one with an illusionary sense of eternity. The notion of sustenance being properly earned is key to the Qur'an's approach to wealth. It singles out for denunciation a number of unlawful means of acquiring money or property, including priests and monks devouring the property of people (9:34), gambling (5:90), and theft (60:12).

The Qur'an rejects all forms of sexual immodesty and speaks approvingly of only two kinds of relationship for sexual fulfillment: heterosexual marriage, or concubinage. The Qur'an also praises "… those [believers] who shun all vain activity" (23:3), and applauds those who, "when they pass by some vain activity, they pass it by with dignified [avoidance]" (25:72).

All of human life is sacred, for "verily We [God] have honored the Children of Adam" (17:70), and no one is allowed to take anyone else's life "except in truth" (6:151). This is usually interpreted to mean that killing is permissible only during a just war, in self-defense, or in retribution after due legal process within a just social system. The Qur'an holds that all of humankind is diminished by the murder of a single person (5:32). While infanticide (more specifically, female infanticide) is condemned, the Qur'an is silent on the rights of the fetus. In accordance with the social practices of pre-Islamic Arabia, the Qur'an sanctions retaliation in the case of murder and physical injury. However, it emphasizes that this must be done justly, and that the remission of the death sentence is a source of "mercy from God" (2:178).

Overt theft is condemned (60:12), as are other, more covert forms of depriving others of their property, such as depriving someone of his or her inheritance, failing to return something entrusted to one for safekeeping (4:58), and cheating when weighing goods for sale (17:35). The Qur'an is particularly vehement in its denunciation of usury. The Qur'an sanctions notions of personal property with individuals being the rightful owners thereof, but condemns individuals who seek to keep secret the extent of their wealth and to be sole arbiters of how to dispense with it.

All wealth is regarded as a trust from God. Greed is condemned and those who live their lives free from greed are regarded as "the successful ones." In contrast to those who hoard, Muslims who "spend of their wealth by night and by day, in secret and in public" are promised that they "shall have their reward with their Lord; on them shall be no fear, nor shall they grieve" (2:274). The Qur'an takes the position that "in the possessions of the wealthy there is a right due to the poor" (51:19, 70:24–15) and places great merit on giving beyond the mandatory, institutionalized wealth tax known as *zakat*. Such giving will purify one's soul, particularly if one gives away those things that are particularly dear (3:92), and does one's giving quietly (2:71). Giving to the poor can be done "day and night, in secret or in public," but it must not be followed by words of injury that make the recipient feel a sense of obligation to the benefactor.

Justice and human rights. The Qur'an takes the position that everyone is equal in the eyes of God and of the law. No human being has any inherent claim to superiority over another on the basis of lineage or race. It does, however, recognize and condone distinction, differentiation, or discrimination on the basis of gender, religion, knowledge, and piety. It is questionable whether one can really use the Qur'an as the standard to justify contemporary Islamic understandings of social equality or universal human rights. However, in the context of seventh-century Arabia, it can be viewed as having encouraged a sense of gender justice, as well as compassion toward victims of all kinds of oppression. There is a strong egalitarian trend in the Qur'an's handling of ethico-religious responsibilities, but there is an undeniable discriminatory treatment of the social and legal obligations that have to do with women. Still, on this subject the Qur'an is somewhat contradictory. Gender statements can be found that affirm gender equality, and others can be found that deny it. However, when specific injunctions are mentioned, these are generally discriminatory to women.

Justice assumes such prominence in the Qur'an that it is regarded as one of the reasons why God created the earth. The demands that the Qur'an makes upon individuals to uphold justice is extraordinary, transcending all social bonds. While justice is something that one demands for oneself, more importantly, it is something to be fulfilled for others, regardless of the cost to oneself and one's own community.

The Qur'an provides two notions that are said to govern social relations. The first is *huquq* (rights), which are defined as the obligations one owes to society, and which must be defended. The other is *ihsan*, understood to mean "generosity beyond obligation." The basic principle of rights and duties is contained in the verse "Do not wrong and be not wronged" (2:279). In social conduct this covers the need for one to be reliable and trustworthy in one's undertakings or promises (4:105, 8:27, 16:91) and economic dealings (93:1–3); to present truthful evidence in any matter or dispute (25:72); to refrain from concealing evidence (2:283), defaming others

(49:6), backbiting, and slander (49:12), hypocrisy (2:8–19), and exploiting the vulnerability of others (2:275–276).

The Qur'an also condemns more subtle forms of injury to others, for they also detract from the humanity of the perpetrator. These injuries include suspicion (49:12), mocking others or the objects of their worship (49:11), and using derogatory nicknames (49:11). These injunctions apply to everyone who participates in a society founded upon Qur'anic principles, but the Qur'an recognizes that such a society may contain religiously diverse communities within it. The Qur'an is explicit about the importance of maintaining harmonious relationships with all those who are not engaged in warfare against the Muslims (60:8), the permissibility of the food slaughtered by the people of the book, and of marriage by Muslim males to their women (5:5).

The Qur'an encourages such generally recognized virtues as expressing gratitude (22:38), showing compassion (90:17), and speaking gently (2:83). It is also explicit about the means by which Muslims can "go the extra mile," recommending that they share their wealth, care for orphans, and free their slaves. The Qur'an treats orphans, in particular, with an enormous amount of compassion. Muslims are instructed honor them (99:17–18), to treat them gently (93:9 and 4:36), to set aside wealth for the care of orphans (4:8), and to deal justly with their property (4:3). The Qur'an regards those who reject orphans as people who have rejected the faith itself (107:1–3).

There is no direct reference in the Qur'an to any notion of an Islamic state, but there are a few injunctions regarding obedience to authority. The Qur'an contains several references to the sovereignty of God, and this has been interpreted by Islamist ideologues to refer to an Islamic theocracy. The duties of the Muslim leadership include waging jihad in defense of the faith or in response to aggression, collecting and distributing *zakat*, and enacting punishment for a very limited array of sins or crimes, of which the following are mentioned: slander (24:4–9), adultery (24:2–3, 15:16), theft (5:41), robbery, treason, and armed insurrection (5:36–37), and murder and bodily mutilation (2:178–179).

Religious practices. Only three formal religious rituals or institutionalized practices receive any significant attention in the Qur'an: the formal prayers (*salat*), fasting in the month of Ramadan, and the pilgrimage to Mecca (hajj).

There are, on the other hand, numerous references in the Qur'an to prayers and its importance. Its significance can be gauged from the fact that the Qur'an outlines ways of deviating from the normal pattern of the ritual during a state of fear (2:238) or in the midst of actual physical combat during jihad (4:101). Other than in the case of illness, menstruation, or frailty, prayer is an obligation that can never be shirked. The Qur'an leaves the exact times of the prayers somewhat unclear; their times are rather fixed by interpretation of some ambiguous verses. As for the manner in which the prayer is to be conducted, the Qur'an refers only to bowing (*ruku'*) and prostration (*sujud*), and says that one should quietly recite "whatever of the Qur'an has been made easy for one" (73:20). A commitment of the mind and the heart is, of course, indispensable for prayer, and those who pray in a slothful and lazy fashion are regarded as being among the hypocrites (4:142, 9:54).

The Qur'an refers to fasting in two distinct contexts. One is the month of Ramadan, when fasting is performed as an act of worship. The other context, which is not linked to any special time or place, is when a believer feels the need to expiate a sin of or a lapse in a specific religious duty. The only objective of fasting stipulated in the Qur'an is that of acquiring *taqwa*—self-restraint arising from the awareness that one is always in the presence of God and ultimately accountable to Him. Fasting requires abstention from all food, drink, and sexual intercourse from the first sign that night is ending until just after sunset.

The hajj is obligatory for all of those of the Muslim faith who are capable of finding their way to Mecca (3:96). It occurs in the first ten days of the month of Dhu-l-Hijjah (the month of Hajj, which is twelfth month of the *Hijri* calendar). The time is specified in the Qur'an (2:189). As for the rites associated with the hajj, the Qur'an goes into somewhat greater detail for these than it does for any of the other formal acts of devotions.

Two samples of Qur'anic calligraphy appear in the volume two color insert.

See also **Allah; Calligraphy; Devotional Life; Ethics and Social Issues; Human Rights; 'Ibadat; Jahannam; Janna; Law; Mihna; Muhammad; Pilgrimage: Hajj; Prophets; Ritual.**

BIBLIOGRAPHY

Arkoun, Muhammad. *The Concept of Revelation: From the People of the Book to the Societies of the Book.* Claremont, Calif.: Claremont Graduate School, 1987.

Ayoub, Mahmud. *The Qur'an and Its Interpreters,* 2 vols. Albany: State University of New York Press, 1984.

Bell, Richard. *Introduction to the Qur'an.* Edited by Montgomery Watt. Edinburgh: Edinburgh University Press, 1970.

Burton, John. *The Collection of the Qur'an.* Cambridge, U.K.: Cambridge University Press, 1977.

Cragg, Kenneth. *The Event of the Qur'an: Islam and Its Scripture.* London: George Allen and Unwin, 1971.

Crone, Patricia, and Cook, Michael. *Hagarism: The Making of the Islamic World.* Cambridge, U.K.: Cambridge University Press, 1977.

Denffer, Ahmad von. *'Ulum al-Qur'an: An Introduction to the Sciences of the Qur'an.* Leicester, U.K.: Islamic Foundation, 1983.

Gatje, Helmut. *The Qur'an and its Exegesis, Selected Texts with Classical and Modern Muslim Interpretations.* Translated and edited by Alford T. Welch. London: Routledge and Kegan Paul, 1976.

Graham, A. William. *Divine Word and Prophetic Word in Early Islam.* The Hague and Paris: Mouton, 1977.

Izutsu, Toshihiko. *Ethico-Religious Concepts in the Qur'an.* Montreal: McGill University Press, 1966.

Jeffrey, Arthur. *The Foreign Vocabulary of the Qur'an.* Baroda, India: Oriental Institute, 1938.

Khu'i, 'Abu'l Qasim al-Musawu, al-. *The Prolegomena to the Qur'an.* Translated by A. A. Sachedina. Oxford, U.K.: Oxford University Press, 1998.

Labib, Sa'id. *The Recited Qur'an.* Princeton, N.J.: Princeton University Press, 1975.

Luxenberg, Christoph. *Die Syro-Aramaische Lesart des Koran.* Berlin: Verlag: Das Arabische Buch, 2000.

Rahman, Fazlur. *Major Themes of the Qur'an.* Minneapolis: Bibliotheca Islamica, 1989.

Sells, Michael. *Approaching the Qur'an.* Ashland, Ore.: White Cloud Press, 1999.

Smith, Jane I., and Haddad, Yvonne Y. *Islamic Understanding of Death and Resurrection.* Albany: State University of New York Press, 1981.

Smith, Wilfred Cantwell. "The True Meaning of Scripture: An Empirical Historian's Non-Reductionist Interpretation of the Qur'an." *International Journal of Middle Eastern Studies* (1980): 487–505.

Wansbrough, J. *Quranic Studies: Sources and Methods of Scriptural Interpretation.* Oxford, U.K.: Oxford University Press, 1977.

Watt, W. Montgomery. "Early Discussions About the Qur'an." *Muslim World* 60, 61 (1950): 20–39, 97–105.

Yusuf Ali, Abdullah. *The Holy Qur'an: Text, Translation, and Commentary.* New and revised ed. Washington, D.C.: Amanah Corporation, 1989.

Farid Esack

QUTB, SAYYID (1906–1966)

Sayyid Qutb was an Islamic activist and one of the principal ideologues of the Muslim Brotherhood (Ikhwan al-Muslimin). Qutb was born in a village near Asyut in Upper Egypt. He left for higher studies in Cairo around 1919 or 1920, and received a B.A. in education in 1933 from Dar al-'Ulum. The founder of the Muslim Brotherhood, Hasan al-Banna, had graduated from the same institution six years earlier and had moved the Brotherhood's headquarters to Cairo just before Qutb's graduation.

In the early part of his career, Qutb demonstrated little interest in religious activism. He focused primarily upon his work with the Ministry of Education, where he was employed from 1933 to 1951, and his literary pursuits. His early writings, consisting primarily of literary criticism and works of fiction and poetry, brought him to the attention of Egypt's cultural elite, including Taha Husayn. Later, Qutb would renounce much of his modernist views from this period.

By the late 1930s Qutb's interests were turning increasingly toward political and social concerns. He associated with a number of nationalist political parties opposed to the Egyptian monarchy and British colonialism. His first major essay along religious lines, *al-ʿAdala al-ijtimaʿiyya fiʾl-Islam* (Social justice in Islam), was published in 1949.

In 1948, perhaps to mollify his criticism, the education ministry sent Qutb to study Western methods of education, first in Washington, D.C., then in Colorado, and finally in California. He left the United States in 1950 and traveled through England, Switzerland, and Italy before returning to Egypt in 1951. Far from dissuading him from his growing activism, Qutb's sojourn in the United States and Europe only intensified and radicalized it. He was appalled by what he saw as the dominant features of Western (especially American) culture: materialism, racism, and sexual permissiveness. He also became convinced that both the United States and the Soviet Union, despite their cold war posturing, were equally unconcerned with the aspirations of Arab and Islamic countries, and prepared to exploit them for their own gains. The fact that both superpowers had supported the creation of Israel in Palestine was, for Qutb, the strongest possible confirmation of their imperialistic aims.

Qutb became actively involved with the Muslim Brotherhood immediately upon his return, although he may not have formally joined until 1953. He served as a liaison between the Brotherhood and the Free Officers who overthrew the monarchy in July 1952, perhaps expecting cooperation between the military leadership and the Brotherhood in establishing an Islamic state. When it became clear that Jamal ʿAbd al-Nasser and the military leadership intended to create a secular state, Qutb and the Brotherhood distanced themselves from the new government.

In January 1954, the government banned the Brotherhood and imprisoned many of its key figures, including Qutb, because of their increasing criticism of the regime's domestic and foreign policies. The decree was rescinded three months later. In October 1954, following an assassination attempt on Nasser by a member of the Brotherhood, Qutb was again arrested and severely tortured, despite his frail health. In July 1955 he was sentenced to fifteen years' imprisonment.

Qutb wrote the two works for which he is best known while in prison. He began his voluminous Qurʾanic commentary, *Fi zilal al-Qurʾan* (In the shade of the Qurʾan), in 1962. In 1964 his supporters published a collection of his letters under the name *Maʿalim fiʾl-tariq* (Milestones), in which he argues that jihad, entailing armed struggle, not just peaceful preaching, is necessary to overturn the corrupted state of Muslim societies (the new ignorance or neo-*jahiliyya*) and establish a true Islamic order based on God's laws (*shariʿa*).

Qutb was released from prison in December 1964, probably due to ill health. But as *Milestones'* circulation spread rapidly, he was rearrested in August 1965 and sentenced to death for sedition. Despite international appeals to spare his life, he was hanged on 29 August 1966. Since his death, his influence has steadily grown through the translation and proliferation of his work.

See also **Banna, Hasan al-; Ikhwan al-Muslimin.**

BIBLIOGRAPHY

Abu Rabiʿ, Ibrahim M. *Intellectual Origins of Islamic Resurgence in the Modern Arab World.* Albany: State University of New York Press, 1996.

Haddad, Yvonne Y. "Sayyid Qutb: Ideologue of Islamic Revival." In *Voices of Resurgent Islam.* Edited by John L. Esposito. New York: Oxford University Press, 1983.

Qutb, Sayyid. *Milestones.* Indianapolis, Ind.: American Trust Publications, 1993.

Sohail H. Hashmi

R

RABI'A OF BASRA (C. 714–801)

Rabi'a of Basra, also known as Rabi'a al-'Adawiyya, is regarded as a paradigm for Sufi women. An ascetic whose life spanned the late Umayyad and early Abbasid periods, her biographical image is a mosaic created by later writers. There are as many versions of Rabi'a's hagiographic persona as there are accounts of her. She has been portrayed as a second Mary, a miracle worker, and the originator of the concept of divine love. Hanbali writers respect her extreme asceticism and otherworldliness, and modern historians consider her the quintessential saint of Islam.

Little objective information is known about Rabi'a. She was a client of the Arab tribe of Banu 'Adi. Popular accounts state that she was sold into slavery during a drought, but her sanctity secured her freedom and she retired to a life of seclusion and celibacy, first in the desert and then on the outskirts of Basra, where she taught both male and female disciples. One of her male disciples was the jurist Sufyan al-Thawri (d. 777). Rabi'a was the culminating figure in a series of Basran female ascetics, starting with Mu'adha al-'Adawiyya (d. 719). Her teacher may have been named Hayyuna. Many stories and poems attributed to Rabi'a actually belong to her students or to other Sufi women with similar names, such as her contemporary Rabi'a al-Azdiyya of Basra, and Rabi'a bint Isma'il of Damascus (d. before 850). The Sufi biographer al-Sulami (d. 1021) portrays Rabi'a as a contemplative and rational thinker. Later writers portray her as a more emotional and legendary figure.

See also **Saint; Tasawwuf.**

BIBLIOGRAPHY

Sells, Michael A. *Early Islamic Mysticism: Sufi, Qur'an, Mi'raj, Poetic and Theological Writings.* Mahweh, N.J.: Paulist Press, 1996.

Smith, Margaret. *Rabi'a: The Life and Work of Rabi'a and Other Women Mystics in Islam.* Oxford, U.K.: One World, 1994.

Rkia E. Cornell

RAFSANJANI, 'ALI-AKBAR HASHEMI- *See* Hashemi-Rafsanjani, 'Ali-Akbar

RAHMAN, FAZLUR (1919–1988)

Fazlur Rahman was a notable scholar of Islamic philosophy and an important liberal Muslim thinker of the twentieth century. Born into a scholarly family in what is now Pakistan, he first studied Arabic at Punjab University in Lahore. He then won a scholarship that permitted him to attend Oxford University, where he received his Ph.D. in Islamic philosophy in 1949. His area of specialization was the work of Ibn Sina (Avicenna).

After spending some years teaching in the West, Rahman returned to Pakistan at the request of then–prime minister Ayyub Khan to direct the new Institute of Islamic Research. He provoked the ire of conservative Islamist movements during this volatile period, particularly with his progressive *fatwa*s and two important interpretive studies, *Islamic Metholodology in History* (1965) and *Islam* (1966), in which he tackled some of the difficult issues of historical critical understandings of revelation. In the face of such opposition, Rahman left Pakistan for the United States. He settled into a distinguished career at the University of Chicago, where he served on the faculty from 1969 until his death. He contributed further important studies, including his *Major Themes of the*

Qur'an (1980) and works on modernist thought and classical Islamic philosophy.

Overall, Fazlur Rahman's thought may be characterized as Islamic modernism in the tradition of Shah Wali Allah and Sir Sayyid Ahmad Khan. He preferred an approach that sought to recover the spirit behind Qur'anic injunctions while contextualizing the tradition as it developed historically. He encouraged a renewal of Islamic educational institutions, as can be seen in his volume titled *Islam and Modernity: Transformation of an Intellectual Tradition* (1982), and was critical of irrational or morally inconsistent elements within the Islamic tradition. He was also a critic of contemporary Muslim "neo-fundamentalisms," which he considered to be defensive and ultimately destined to wither away.

See also **Ahmad Khan, (Sir) Sayyid; Ibn Sina; Modern Thought; Wali Allah, Shah.**

BIBLIOGRAPHY

Rahman, Fazlur. *Revival and Reform in Islam: A Study of Islamic Fundamentalism.* Edited by Ebrahim Moosa. Oxford, U.K.: Oneworld Press, 2000.

Waugh, Earle H., and Denny, Frederick M. *The Shaping of an American Islamic Discourse: A Memorial to Fazlur Rahman.* Atlanta, Ga.: Scholars Press, 1998.

Marcia Hermansen

RASHID, HARUN AL- (C. 763 OR 766–809)

Harun al-Rashid (Aaron "The Rightly-Guided") was the fifth Abbasid caliph, who ruled the great Islamic empire from 786 to 809 during its zenith. A patron of learning and culture, he is known to the world through the tales of *The Arabian Nights*, which portray his court in Baghdad as a place of wealth and splendor.

Harun al-Rashid was born in 763 (or 766) in the city of al-Rayy, south of today's Tehran, the third son of the caliph Muhammad al-Mahdi ("the Well-Guided"). Harun's mother, al-Khayzuran, and his wife, Zubayda, played influential roles during his reign. Harun had eleven sons and twelve daughters; his sons al-Amin, al-Ma'mun, and al-Mu'tasim each in his turn became caliph.

Already as a teenager, Harun had led two military expeditions against the Byzantines. For his success on the battlefield, he was appointed governor of the provinces of northwest Africa (Ifriqiya), Egypt, Syria, Armenia, and Azerbaijan, although his tutor Yahya al-Barmaki was actually administrator. Harun then faced serious intrigues by his older half-brother and rival for the throne, Musa al-Hadi (Moses "the

Guide"). After their father died, al-Hadi became ruler, but he died mysteriously after only one year in power. Al-Hadi's son was forced at the point of a sword to renounce the caliphate; Harun—still in his early twenties—received the ring of the caliphate and was proclaimed caliph. Following the advice of his mother, he entrusted the administration to his Iranian tutor, Yahya al-Barmaki, and the latter's family. The Barmakides assisted Harun in controlling his political rivals and Shi'ite opponents, and in defeating major uprisings in the provinces: in Syria (796), Egypt (788, 794–795), northwest Africa (786, 794–795, 797), and the Yemen (795–804). However, the administrative body formed by the Barmakides soon became a state within the state, promoting the "Iranization" of the, until then, Arab-Islamic caliphate.

Throughout his reign, Harun personally led many military campaigns against the Byzantines and established a Muslim naval power (with raids on Cyprus in 805 and Rhodes in 807). He granted the request of the Roman emperor, Charles the Great (Charlemagne; r. 800–814), to ameliorate the conditions for European Christian visitors to Jerusalem and the Holy Land and exchanged embassies and precious gifts with him: For example, Harun sent Charles an elephant and a water-clock of curious design. In the last periods of his reign, Harun seems to have lacked the competence and energy he showed in earlier years. Deteriorated in health, Harun al-Rashid died on 24 March 809.

The picture that medieval Arabic scholarship presents of Harun is somewhat contradictory: pious, statesmanlike, and of remarkably mild countenances, on the one hand; and dissolute, incompetent, and lacking modesty in enjoying wine and other privileges claimed by the upper class, on the other. Nevertheless, the development of Islamic society benefited from Harun's enlightenment: He promoted commercial activities (as far as China), fine arts, poetry, literature, music, architecture, and the natural sciences. He reinforced law and order, secured state finances, and conducted major public construction projects. Yet, his reign marked a turning point for the Abbasid caliphate because the efficiency of administration began to decline and the political unity of the empire to disintegrate: Harun's diplomacy eventually failed to neutralize provincial dynasties and local rulers, and his decision to apportion the empire among three of his sons virtually precipitated its political decline.

See also **Caliphate; Empires: Abbasid.**

BIBLIOGRAPHY

Abbott, Nabia. *Two Queens of Baghdad. Mother and Wife of Harun al-Rashid.* Chicago: The University of Chicago Press, 1974.

Bosworth, C. E., trans. *The 'Abbasid Caliphate in Equilibrium.* The Caliphates of Musa al-Hadi and Harun al-Rashid. A.D. 785–809 / A.H. 169–193. Vol. 30 of *The History of al-Tabari.* Albany: State University of New York Press, 1989.

Clot, André. *Harun al-Rashid and the World of the Thousand and One Nights.* Trans. by J. Howe. London: Saqi Books, 1989.

El-Hibri, Tayeb. *Reinterpreting Islamic Historiography: Harun al-Rashid and the Narrative of the Abbasid Caliphate.* Cambridge, U.K.: Cambridge University Press, 1999.

Omar, Farid. "Harun al-Rashid." In *Encyclopaedia of Islam.* Edited by B. Lewis, et al. Leiden: E. J. Brill, 1971.

Sebastian Günther

RASHIDUN

The Rashidun, or *al-khulafa' al-rashidun*, the "rightly guided" caliphs, is the designation in Sunni Islam for the first four successors of the prophet Muhammad (d. 632). In their order of succession to Muhammad, these caliphs are: Abu Bakr (r. 632–634), 'Umar ibn al-Khattab (r. 634–644), 'Uthman ibn 'Affan (r. 644–656), and 'Ali ibn Abi Talib (r. 656–661).

According to the Sunni view of Islam's earliest history, the prophet Muhammad did not designate anyone to succeed him. Muhammad having been the last of God's prophets, the question, in any case, was of succession to the polity he had founded in Medina, not to his prophetical office. It was therefore left to the community to decide on his succession, and after some discussion and uncertainty a number of the Prophet's Companions elected Abu Bakr, a leading member of the community and Muhammad's father-in-law, as the first caliph. Before his death two years later (634 C.E.), Abu Bakr nominated 'Umar as his successor, a choice which, like Abu Bakr's own, was accepted by the Muslim community. For his part, 'Umar, when mortally wounded by an assassin after a reign of twelve years, left the choice of caliph to a committee of six leading figures. This committee chose 'Uthman after he pledged to follow the example of his two immediate predecessors—a guarantee that the other major contender, 'Ali, was not willing to give. The latter half of 'Uthman's reign saw strong disaffection in his capital, Medina, in the garrison towns of Kufa and Basra, and in Egypt against the policies of the caliph, who was eventually murdered in Medina by the rebels. These rebels then supported the accession of 'Ali, but he was never recognized as a legitimate caliph by the entire community of Muslims. In particular, Mu'awiya b. Abi Sufyan, the governor of Syria and a kinsman of 'Uthman, demanded that 'Ali first punish the killers of his predecessor, and a number of the Prophet's Companions, including his wife 'A'isha, made similar demands. There was dissension in 'Ali's own camp also, with some of his followers, who came to be known as the Khawarij, seceding from him on grounds that it was improper to negotiate with rebels like Mu'awiya. 'Ali was eventually murdered by one of the Khawarij, and his death, and the rise of the Umayyads to power under Mu'awiya (r. 661–680), marked the end of the Rashidun caliphate.

The events of the latter half of 'Uthman's reign and the entirety of 'Ali's disputed caliphate—known to modern scholars as the First Civil War—are remembered in Islamic religious and political history as "the *Fitna*"—a time of chaos, dissension, and tribulation. No other period in the history of Islam has been the subject of greater debate than the events of the *Fitna*. For the Sunnis, the Companions are second only to the Prophet as sources of religious guidance, and yet during the civil war they were ranged on opposite sides and bitterly fought each other. Which of the parties to the conflict was in the right, whether 'Uthman and 'Ali were legitimate caliphs, and whether someone who was a grave sinner continued to be a member of the Muslim community were questions that were to divide the Muslim community for centuries. Indeed, it is to the events of the First Civil War that the origins of the major religio-political schisms in Islam are datable.

A distinctive doctrine of those who, in the ninth century, emerged as the Sunnis was that all four of the Prophet's immediate successors were equally righteous, and that the historical sequence of their succession was also the order of their religious ranking. Agreement on this position did not come about easily. While the Khawarij did not recognize either 'Uthman or 'Ali as legitimate, and most of the Shi'a considered none but 'Ali as a true caliph and imam, many of the *ahl al-sunna* of the late eighth century, who together with the *ashab al-hadith* later emerged as the first Sunnis, themselves had reservations about the legitimacy of 'Ali's caliphate. By the time of the hadith scholar Ahmad ibn Hanbal (d. 855), many of those recognizable as early Sunnis had come to acknowledge all four of the Prophet's successors as equally righteous. It was also in the late eighth and early ninth centuries that a tradition of the Prophet, according to which the "caliphate" would last only thirty years after his death—that is, only for the duration of the reigns of his first four successors—became widely current. Though the Umayyads and the Abbasids claimed, of course, to be caliphs and were recognized as such by the Sunni religious scholars, a position such as that enshrined in the "thirty years" hadith signaled that the age of the Rashidun was to be set apart from all subsequent eras. For the Sunnis, that age has continued to be seen as a time, indeed the only time, when Islamic ideals were truly implemented. As such, invocations of the Rashidun have continued to be part of the religio-political discourse in the Sunni Islamic world to the present.

See also **Abu Bakr; 'Ali ibn Abi Talib; 'Athman ibn 'Affan; Fitna; Imam; 'Umar.**

BIBLIOGRAPHY

Ess, Josef van. "Political Ideas in Early Islamic Religious Thought." *British Journal of Middle Eastern Studies* 28 (2001): 151–164.

Hinds, Martin. *Studies in Early Islamic History.* Edited by Jere Bacharach, et al. Princeton, N.J.: The Darwin Press, 1996.

Madelung, Wilferd. *The Succession to Muhammad: A Study of the Early Caliphate.* Cambridge, U.K.: Cambridge University Press, 1997.

Tabari, al-. *The History of al-Tabari.* Vols. 10–17. Albany: State University of New York Press, 1985–1999.

Muhammad Qasim Zaman

RAWZA-KHANI

A *rawza-khani* is a Shi'ite ritual sermon recounting and mourning the seventh-century tragedy of Karbala, which was a battle in which the Prophet's grandson Husayn was martyred (in what is viewed by the Shi'a as a heroic struggle against religious tyranny and corruption). The primary catalyst in the emergence of this ritual was the appearance of Hosayn Vaez Kashifi's 1502 composition entitled *Rawzat al-shuhada'* (The garden of martyrs). *Rawza-khani*s are performed in homes, mosques, *takiya*s, *husayniya*s, religious sites, and even in the streets and bazaars of cities. The *rawza-khani* is a ritual in which a sermon is given based on a text like the *Rawzat al-shuhada'*, with a great deal of improvisation on the part of the specially trained speaker. The objective of the speaker is to move the audience to tears through his recitation of the tragic details of the Battle of Karbala. In addition to serving social, political, and psychological functions, this type of mourning ritual has been viewed by Shi'a as a means of achieving salvation. This belief is illustrated by the often-repeated Shi'ite quotation, "Anyone who cries for Husayn or causes someone to cry for Husayn shall go directly to paradise."

See also **Ta'ziya.**

BIBLIOGRAPHY

Ayoub, Mahmoud. *Redemptive Suffering in Islam: A Study of the Devotional Aspects of 'Ashura in Twelver Shi'ism.* The Hague, Netherlands: Mouton Publishers, 1978.

Schubel, Vernon James. *Religious Performance in Contemporary Islam: Shi'i Devotional Rituals in South Asia.* Columbia: University of South Carolina Press, 1993.

Kamran Aghaie

REFAH PARTISI

Refah Partisi (Welfare Party), a Turkish Islamist political party (1984–1998), was founded by Necmeddin Erbakan to replace the National Salvation Party. It was initially unpopular, but economic slowdown and political corruption attracted protest voters to it.

Refah united marginalized people around Islamic identity, morality in government, a domestic policy favoring the lower and middle classes, and a pro-Mideast/Asian and anti-Western/Israel foreign policy. After capturing Istanbul's and Ankara's mayoralties, the Refah Party won the 1995 national election with 21 percent of the vote and formed a coalition with Tansu Ciller's center-right True Path Party. This uneasy partnership achieved some domestic change and a more balanced foreign policy, but government corruption remained high.

Refah presented an alternative to mainstream parties mired in stagnation and corruption, appealing to disenfranchised small businessmen, impoverished workers, young professionals and students, women, and new export-oriented capitalists. Its Islamism sought to replace traditional Kemalism's heavy-handed secularism, statist economics, and pro-Westernism. Its religious agenda countered ethnic conflict, social dislocation, and organized crime; its Mideast agenda offered commercial profits and employment in technical fields; and its welfare plans inspired those at the bottom of the income scale. Inconsistent policies toward women and a human-rights agenda that excluded opponents frightened secularists and Kemalists. The Refah government was forced from power in 1997, and the party was closed down in February 1998.

See also **Erbakan, Necmeddin; Modernization, Political: Participation, Political Movements, and Parties.**

BIBLIOGRAPHY

Gülalp, Haldun. "Political Islam in Turkey: The Rise and Fall of the Refah Party." *Muslim World* 89 (1999): 22–41.

Howe, Marvine. *Turkey Today: A Nation Divided over Islam's Revival.* Boulder, Colo.: Westview Press, 2000.

Linda T. Darling

REFORM

ARAB MIDDLE EAST AND NORTH AFRICA
Sohail H. Hashmi

IRAN
Hossein Kamaly

MUSLIM COMMUNITIES OF THE RUSSIAN EMPIRE
Allen J. Frank

SOUTH ASIA
Ahrar Ahmad

SOUTHEAST ASIA
Mark R. Woodward

ARAB MIDDLE EAST AND NORTH AFRICA

Revivalist movements and reformist thinkers have arisen throughout Islamic history. Since the early nineteenth century, two intellectual strands have evolved among the Arabic-speaking populations of Southwest Asia and North Africa, each in its own way calling for Islamic renewal (*tajdid*) and reform (*islah*) against the status-quo traditionalists among the ulema on the one hand and Western-style secularists on the other. One of these strands is variously dubbed conservative, fundamentalist, and more recently Islamist; the other is generally known as modernist or liberal. Neither strand, it should be emphasized, advocates reform of Islamic dogma itself, which would obviously open it to charges of illicit innovation (*bid'a*). Rather, Islamic reformism is limited to correcting the interpretations and practices of Muslims, allegedly in order to better reflect the true Islam. A number of different understandings of the means and ends of reform could be accommodated within such a broad aspiration.

The Wahhabi movement that began in late eighteenth-century Arabia was the last significant reformist effort in the era before European imperialism. It erupted out of the potent mixture of the fiery religious appeal of Muhammad Ibn 'Abd al-Wahhab (1703–1792) and the political and military acumen of the Sa'ud family. Ibn 'Abd al-Wahhab called for a return to the strict monotheism (*tawhid*) that he claimed underlay the mission of the prophet Muhammad. In his view, the society around him had departed in many regards from this pure Islam, neglecting, for example, the enforcement of Islamic punishments for such things as adultery and theft and absorbing such un-Islamic practices as the building of tombs for the dead and saint worship. When the Wahhabiyya succeeded in conquering most of Arabia in the early nineteenth century, the first Saudi state set about implementing Ibn 'Abd al-Wahhab's vision of an ideal Islamic society, grounded in a strict, literal interpretation of the Qur'an and the Prophetic hadith that he considered to be authentic. Although this state was crushed by an Egyptian army in 1818, the conservative reformist message of Wahhabism spread to other Muslim areas, and its influence upon other reform movements in the late nineteenth and early twentieth century is incontrovertible.

Wahhabi forces were checked by the army of Muhammad 'Ali (c. 1769–1849), the founder of a new dynasty in Egypt and the initiator of modernization in the Arab world. Having seen the technological superiority of Napoleon's army when it invaded and occupied Egypt from 1798 to 1801, Muhammad 'Ali launched a program to reform the Egyptian military and civil administration, after becoming the Ottoman governor of the province in 1805. Educational missions were dispatched to Europe, mainly France, for scientific and technological training, beginning as early as 1809. The students returned with ideas of how to reform Egyptian politics, culture, and education as well.

The origins of modernist Muslim thought in the Arab world are often traced to Rifa'a al-Tahtawi (1801–1873). As the religious advisor traveling with an Egyptian student delegation to Paris in 1826, Tahtawi immersed himself in European history, geography, politics, literature, and science, learning French in order to do so. Upon returning to Cairo in 1831, he became Muhammad 'Ali's chief supporter among the ulema for the modernizing reforms the pasha had initiated. In his writings, Tahtawi expounded a theme that would engross later modernist thinkers: reform of Islamic law based on the needs of the modern age. To begin such legal reform, he argued, the education of the law's interpreters, the ulema, had to be overhauled. Tahtawi's most important contribution to educational reform, and his greatest influence upon later generations of reformers, was exerted through the School of Languages, of which he was appointed director in 1837. The school educated Egyptian students in European languages and translated key European texts into Arabic.

Khayr al-Din al-Tunisi (c. 1822–1890), prime minister first to the bey of Tunis and later to the Ottoman sultan, called much more directly than Tahtawi for political reforms to accompany legal and educational changes. Khayr al-Din argued that Europe's military prowess was an outgrowth of the development of effective and accountable governments. For Muslims to borrow constitutional principles from Europeans would not be innovation at all, he wrote, but merely a return to the true principles of government established by the Prophet and the rightly guided caliphs.

Despite the modernization efforts in states such as Egypt and Tunisia—limited mainly to small-scale educational and bureaucratic reforms, with no serious legal or political changes—Muslim power relative to that of Europe steadily declined during the first half of the nineteenth century, and by the century's end, Algeria, Tunisia, and Egypt had passed under direct French and British rule. The beginning of formal European imperialism produced among Arabs a more profound intellectual search for the causes of Muslim decline and the means for its reversal.

The broad term designating the movement for Islamic reform that emerged in the last decades of the nineteenth century is *Salafiyya*. Exactly when the Salafiyya movement began and who should be included among its adherents remain controversial issues. The name is derived from the phrase *salaf al-salihin*, which refers to the first three generations of Muslims and various pious figures in subsequent generations who best understood and applied the "true" Islam. Its proponents argue for a return by Muslims to the practice of these, Islam's forebears. As such, the Wahhabiyya could be and sometimes are considered a Salafi movement.

The figure most widely considered as the architect of Salafi principles, however, is Muhammad 'Abduh (1849–1905). Three basic principles underlie 'Abduh's reformism. First, he

Muslim reform and renewal movements (18th to 20th century)

Arabia
Reform teaching in Mecca and Medina
Wahhabiyya—founded by Muhammad b. ʿAbd al-Wahhab (1703–1792); allied with Ibn Saʿud to create Saudi state
Idrisiyya—founded in Mecca by Ahmad b. Idris (d. 1837)

Caucasus
Naqshbandiyya—1785–present, anti-Russian resistance

Inner Asia
Naqshbandiyya—reform-oriented Sufi tariqa leads Muslim resistance to Russia and China
New teaching, 1761–1877—offshoot of Naqshbandiya, late-eighteenth- and late-nineteenth-century resistance to Chinese rule
Khwajas and Yaʿqub Beg—holy Muslim lineage, formerly rulers of Kashgar, attempt to establish a Muslim state, defeated by China in 1878
Yunnan, 1856–1873—rebellion against Chinese rule and effort to establish a Muslim state
Usul-e jadid—Kazan, Crimean, and Bukharan intellectuals, notably Ismaʿil Gasprinskii (1851–1914), sponsor new schools, combined Muslim and Russian
    education; modernization of Muslim peoples

India

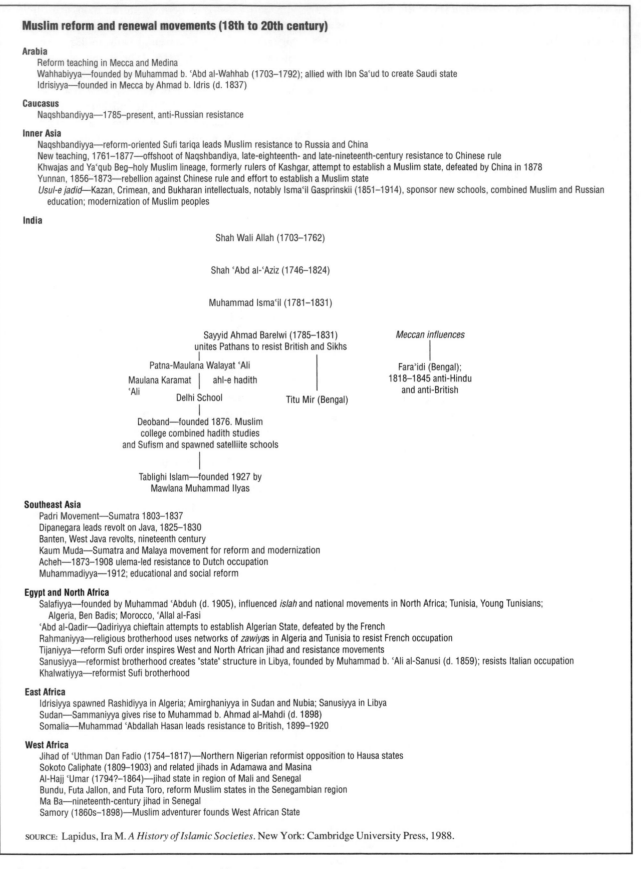

Shah Wali Allah (1703–1762)

Shah ʿAbd al-ʿAziz (1746–1824)

Muhammad Ismaʿil (1781–1831)

Sayyid Ahmad Barelwi (1785–1831)
unites Pathans to resist British and Sikhs

Meccan influences

Patna-Maulana Walayat ʿAli

Maulana Karamat   ahl-e hadith
ʿAli
     Delhi School

Titu Mir (Bengal)

Faraʾidi (Bengal);
1818–1845 anti-Hindu
and anti-British

Deoband—founded 1876. Muslim
college combined hadith studies
and Sufism and spawned satelliite schools

Tablighi Islam—founded 1927 by
Mawlana Muhammad Ilyas

Southeast Asia
Padri Movement—Sumatra 1803–1837
Dipanegara leads revolt on Java, 1825–1830
Banten, West Java revolts, nineteenth century
Kaum Muda—Sumatra and Malaya movement for reform and modernization
Acheh—1873–1908 ulema-led resistance to Dutch occupation
Muhammadiyya—1912; educational and social reform

Egypt and North Africa
Salafiyya—founded by Muhammad ʿAbduh (d. 1905), influenced *islah* and national movements in North Africa; Tunisia, Young Tunisians;
    Algeria, Ben Badis; Morocco, ʿAllal al-Fasi
ʿAbd al-Qadir—Qadiriyya chieftain attempts to establish Algerian State, defeated by the French
Rahmaniyya—religious brotherhood uses networks of *zawiya*s in Algeria and Tunisia to resist French occupation
Tijaniyya—reform Sufi order inspires West and North African jihad and resistance movements
Sanusiyya—reformist brotherhood creates "state" structure in Libya, founded by Muhammad b. ʿAli al-Sanusi (d. 1859); resists Italian occupation
Khalwatiyya—reformist Sufi brotherhood

East Africa
Idrisiyya spawned Rashidiyya in Algeria; Amirghaniyya in Sudan and Nubia; Sanusiyya in Libya
Sudan—Sammaniyya gives rise to Muhammad b. Ahmad al-Mahdi (d. 1898)
Somalia—Muhammad ʿAbdallah Hasan leads resistance to British, 1899–1920

West Africa
Jihad of ʿUthman Dan Fadio (1754–1817)—Northern Nigerian reformist opposition to Hausa states
Sokoto Caliphate (1809–1903) and related jihads in Adamawa and Masina
Al-Hajj ʿUmar (1794?–1864)—jihad state in region of Mali and Senegal
Bundu, Futa Jallon, and Futa Toro, reform Muslim states in the Senegambian region
Ma Ba—nineteenth-century jihad in Senegal
Samory (1860s–1898)—Muslim adventurer founds West African State

SOURCE: Lapidus, Ira M. *A History of Islamic Societies*. New York: Cambridge University Press, 1988.

Muslim reform and renewal movements arranged by region.

rejected predestination and the fatalism and intellectual tor-por that he believed resulted from it. Second, he emphasized the compatibility of revelation with reason. In other words, he argued that religion does not impose unduly on what reason demands as scientific or moral truths and, conversely, that human rational faculties are capable of confirming most, if not all, the spiritual truths illuminated by religion. Finally, ʿAbduh asserted a claim to renewed interpretation (*ijtihad*) of Islamic law based on the requirements of social justice (*maslaha*) of his own era.

ʿAbduh did not directly advocate a political program, implying only that Islamic principles of accountable and limited government supported the idea of liberal parliamen-tary democracy. Later reformers appealed, explicitly or implicitly, to his writings to justify their own, sometimes opposite views. The most bitter controversy erupted when ʿAli ʿAbd al-Raziq (1888–1966) published a treatise arguing that the mixture of religion and politics in the institution of the caliphate was a perversion of the Prophet's teachings and practice. Rashid Rida (1865–1935) denounced ʿAbd al-Raziq's arguments, which opened secular possibilities within Islamic political thought, as a perversion of Islamic teachings and history. Another disciple of ʿAbduh's, ʿAbd al-Rahman al-Kawakibi (c. 1849–1902), had earlier written on the need to revive the Arab caliphate as a precursor to Islamic revival worldwide.

ʿAbduh expressed his views prolifically in the pages of the journal *al-Manar*. He also tried to implement his reform program by issuing progressive *fatwa*s in his capacity as Grand Mufti of Egypt, and through his efforts at reorganiz-ing the education of Egyptian religious scholars at al-Azhar University and other institutions. Many Arab nationalists would attempt to incorporate his progressive, moderate, and flexible interpretations of Islam into their political ideologies, but generally failed to produce a true synthesis of theory and practice once independence was achieved.

ʿAbduh's reform agenda was carried on by Rashid Rida, but Rida brought to it a greater conservatism in philosophical outlook and methodology, relying primarily on Hanbali jurisprudence, whereas his mentor had advocated free bor-rowing from all Sunni schools of law. He was also much more politically oriented than ʿAbduh, seeing the institution of an Islamic state as the precursor to the application of Islamic law and the promotion of Islamic social mores. Rida thus laid the intellectual foundations for a more conservative strand of Salafi reformism, one that is associated with the Muslim Brotherhood. The reformism of Hasan al-Banna (1906–1949) and Sayyid Qutb (1906–1966), the principal ideologues of the Brotherhood, reflects Rida's influence in its advocacy of a holistic conception of Islamic state and society, where *shariʿa* regulates all spheres of life. In this regard, the Brotherhood's Salafism is similar in approach to that of the Wahhabiyya,

although their views on specific points of Qurʾanic interpre-tation and Islamic law may vary.

By the early years of the twenty-first century, Islamic reform in the Arab world remained a highly contested dis-course. In terms of political mobilization, the conservative Islamist agenda seemed to have triumphed over the liberal modernist project. Conservative reformers such as Muham-mad al-Ghazali (1917–1996) in Egypt and Hasan al-Turabi (b. 1932) in Sudan had attracted much larger public followings than their modernist counterparts. Arab modernists had thus far failed to form a mass-based organization to compete with the Muslim Brotherhood and its many, more radical off-shoots. Still, the work of such modernist intellectuals as Tariq al-Bishri and Hasan Hanafi (b. 1935) in Egypt and Muham-mad Shahrur in Syria, and the political activism of Rachid al-Ghannoushi (b. 1941) in Tunisia have demonstrated the continuing relevance and development of modernism.

See also ʿ**Abd al-Rahman Kawakibi;** ʿ**Abd al-Wahhab, Muhammad Ibn;** ʿ**Abduh, Muhammad; Banna, Hasan al-; Ghazali, Muhammad al-; Ikhwan al-Muslimin; Qutb, Sayyid; Rida, Rashid; Salafiyya; Tajdid; Turabi, Hasan al-; Wahhabiyya.**

BIBLIOGRAPHY

Binder, Leonard. *Islamic Liberalism: A Critique of Development Strategies.* Chicago: University of Chicago Press, 1988.

Hourani, Albert. *Arabic Thought in the Liberal Age, 1798–1939.* Cambridge, U.K.: Cambridge University Press, 1983.

Kerr, Malcolm H. *Islamic Reform: The Political and Legal Theories of Muhammad ʿAbduh and Rashid Rida.* Berkeley: University of California Press, 1966.

Safran, Nadav. *Egypt in Search of Political Community.* Cam-bridge, Mass.: Harvard University Press, 1961.

Sohail H. Hashmi

IRAN

The reform and reconstruction of Islamic doctrine in Iran, aimed at striking a stable balance with contemporary require-ments, exhibits important and at times idiosyncratic charac-teristics. Iran is the largest non-Arab Islamic country where the greater majority of the population adheres to Shiʿite principles. Unlike most Islamic countries, throughout West-ern colonial and imperialist expansions Iran has enjoyed unbroken, if at times fragile, native sovereignty, and this has led to a peculiar dynamic of perception and interaction with the West. The outbreak of the Islamic Revolution (1979), in a rapidly but unevenly modernizing nation-state, together with the turbulent evolution of the Iranian society ever since, further mark the Iranian experience as unique.

The roots of Islamist reform in Iran are commonly traced back to the Constitutional Revolution of 1906 to 1908.

However, for at least two generations prior to that turning point in modern Iranian history, emerging social and intellectual forces had grappled with new questions regarding Islamic, Iranian, and "progressive" identities. The enigmatic reformist Jamal al-Din Afghani (1838–1897), for example, had won a sizable following in Iran, one among whom ended up assassinating the Qajar sovereign, Naser al-Din Shah, in 1896.

Beginning in the years prior to the Constitutional Revolution, and continuing throughout the twentieth century, groups of clerics, teachers, journalists, government officials, and lay professionals attempted to flesh out a "progressive" discourse by way of molding such modern concepts as the nation (*mellat*), or a representative assembly (*majlis shura*), into historically more familiar native contexts. The discourse of Islamic reform in Iran is best understood by demarcating its pre- and postrevolutionary phases, with reference to the Islamic Revolution of 1979. In its prerevolutionary phase, the reformist discourse tended to be nativist-apologetic, maximalist, utopian, and "progressive." It also embraced, or at least condoned, militant violence as a legitimate means. Prerevolutionary reformists in Iran further called for universal Islamic union or integration, in the face of non-Muslim adversaries. The burgeoning postrevolutionary discourse, in contrast, while maintaining its "progressive" stance, exhibits eclectic-critical, minimalist, pragmatic, and pluralistic tendencies and it increasingly downplays the purported efficacy of violent tactics.

Prerevolutionary Islamic reform proceeded from the fundamental premise that Islam, as a comprehensive system, should aptly offer answers to every conceivable question of human concern, at individual and societal levels, as well as in both temporal and spiritual spheres. The discourse was maximalist in its aiming to bring an ever-expansive domain under an Islamic umbrella. Reformists, from the 1920s onward, unflinchingly formulated "nativist" Islamic solutions for issues raised by the secularizing government agenda, as well as for those put forward by Marxist activists in Iran. Reformists took on the daunting task of spelling out the proper Islamic ways for approaching a plethora of issues, from such mundane matters as personal hygiene and dietary practice to the intricate workings of the economy and international diplomacy. Pamphlets and books with formulaic titles such as "Islam and . . .," and ". . . in Islam," proliferated. As a result of its maximalist-nativist character, reformist discourse was prone to indulge in apologetics. In an effort to present a view of the Islamic tradition that was in tune with the manners of the time, reformists did not hesitate to denounce portions of it as "superstitious." Some, like the cleric Shari'at-Shangelaji (1890/2–1943), had to face ostracism, perhaps for jettisoning too much. In general, a collective penchant developed among reformists for doing away with what they deemed spurious, and for restoring the unadulterated, primordial Islam (*eslam rastin*) that transcended the vicissitudes of history. This tendency in Iran bore close kinship to the *salafiyya* movement in Egypt.

'Ali Shari'ati (1933–1977), a prolific intellectual of an unfathomable range of influence, best exemplified the utopian tendency. He not only shared in the maximalist outlook, but consciously hailed the transformation of the dormant Islamic culture into a potent ideology imparting clear-cut instructions for political struggle, as a most urgent and significant accomplishment.

The maximalist-utopian ideal, culminating in the Islamic Revolution of 1979, provided the exponents of Islamist reform, such as Mehdi Bazargan (1902–1994), Sayyed Mahmud Taleqani (d. 1979), and Morteza Mutahhari (1919–1979), with an opportunity to put into practice what they had preached for decades. The radical doctrine of "Absolute Guardianship of the Jurist" (*vilayat motlaqe faqih*), expounded by Ayatollah Khomeini, rendered absolute discretion into the hands of the religious elite, and boosted the maximalist program. A full-blown, yet ostensibly inadequate, juridical (*feqahati*) approach toward complex issues of the state alienated among others surviving pioneers of Islamist reform, such as Bazargan, who had throughout their careers vouched for a humanely tolerant view of Islam and had foreseen more inclusive methods of governance.

Beginning in 1988, the publication of a sequence of critical essays sparked new debate and led Islamist reform in Iran toward a turning point. 'Abd al-Karim Sorush (b. 1945), an academic thinker with impeccable prorevolutionary credentials, contended that Islamic doctrine lies inevitably subject to historic expansion and contraction. The body of knowledge standing outside the proper domain of "Islam," according to Sorush, inexorably influences the way questions are framed and solutions formulated within it. The recognition of a set of inalienable rights for human beings irrespective of religious affiliation, for example, should lead to a reconsideration of the primarily "duty-bound" conception of man hitherto propounded in Islamic texts. Religious texts, Sorosh contends, should be interpreted in light of the broader extrareligious context. Mohammad Mojtahed-Shabestari (b. 1936), an articulate reformist cleric, further elaborates on this hermeneutic approach, making room for alternative yet rational interpretations or "readings" of Islam. Mojtahed-Shabestari urges that true religious faith thrives on social liberty, and he earnestly criticizes the officially enforced interpretation of Islam advocated by the state in Iran.

The new discourse of Islamic reform, exemplified in the work of Soroush, and manifested in the writings of Mojtahed-Shabestari and a few others, defined a nascent group of religious intellectuals (*rowshanfekran dini*), retrospectively including in its ancestry such thinkers as Bazargan and Shari'ati. During the 1990s, a group of these religious intellectuals, sometimes referred to as the Kiyan Circle (*halqe Kiyan*), expressed their views in the important periodical *Kiyan* (officially closed down by court decree in 2000). This forum raised crucial questions with regard to Islamic reform, including issues of democratic governance, Islamic law, and faith, and probed into the fields of epistemology and ethics.

The election of Mohammad Khatami as the president of the Islamic Republic in 1997 signaled a potential triumph for postrevolutionary Islamic reformism. An advocate of religious intellectualism himself, Khatami incorporated key elements of the burgeoning discourse in his campaign slogans and called for increased social pluralism and a move toward civil society. In practice, however, theoretical as well as functional shortcomings seem to have stifled this particular promise. Nevertheless, Islamic reformism persists as an ongoing and evolving project in contemporary Iran.

Iranian reformers, more often than not, have formulated ideological or doctrinal questions in purely epistemic terms, and have shown conspicuously less concern for sociohistorical processes constituting religion in general and Islam in particular.

See also 'Abd al-Karim Sorush; Afghani, Jamal al-Din; Bazargan, Mehdi; Khomeini, Ruhollah; Mojtahed-Shabestari, Muhammad; Reform: Arab Middle East and North Africa; Reform: Muslim Communities of the Russian Empire; Reform: South Asia; Shari'ati, 'Ali.

BIBLIOGRAPHY

Boroujerdi, Mehrzad. *Iranian Intellectuals and the West.* Syracuse, N.Y.: Syracuse University Press, 1996.

Jahanbakhsh, Forouq. *Islam, Democracy and Religious Modernism in Iran, 1953–2000: From Bazargan to Soroush.* Boston: E. J. Brill, 2001.

Soroush, Abdol Karim. *Reason, Freedom, & Democracy in Islam: Essential Writings of Abdolkarim Soroush.* New York: Oxford University Press, 2000.

Taleqani, Seyed Mahmud. *Islam and Property Ownership.* Lexington, Ky.: Mazda Publishers, 1983.

Hossein Kamaly

MUSLIM COMMUNITIES OF THE RUSSIAN EMPIRE

Jadidism was an intellectual current among the Muslims of the Russian empire that emerged in the 1880s, and it remained active into the first decade of Soviet rule. Although Jadidism is commonly defined as a manifestation of Islamic reformism, it would be more correct to label it as a form of Islamic modernism. The word "Jadidism" is derived from the term *usul-e jadid*, signifying "new method," and initially first came to prominence as an educational reform movement. However, during and after the 1905 revolution the movement became increasingly politicized, and its adherents, known as *jadids*, began to articulate a political agenda increasingly

and variously influenced by pan-Turkic, pan-Islamic, and nationalist ideas. At the same time, as actors in the political life of Russia as a whole, the *jadids* were not politically unified and were to be found among several of the empire's radical, liberal, and even conservative political parties. Following the Russian Revolution (1917), *jadids* were active in the various factions engaged in the Russian Civil War, notably among the various Muslim nationalist movements, within the Socialist Revolutionary Party, and among the Bolsheviks. Following the Bolshevik victory, *jadids* became increasingly politically marginalized, as their vision of secularized Muslim communities, and their ability to effect political change, were rapidly eclipsed by revolutionary social change and secularization that became the hallmark of Soviet rule. Furthermore, their association with nationalism, pan-Turkic, and pan-Islamic ideas resulted in the complete purging of active *jadids* from political and even social life during the rule of Stalin, which ended the jadidist movement in Russia.

The ideological founder of jadidism is usually identified as Isma'il Bey Gasprinskii (1851–1914), a Crimean Tatar from the town of Bakhchesaray in the Crimea. Having studied and lived in Paris and Istanbul in the 1870s, where he came under the influence of French liberals, the Young Turks, and the pan-Islamist ideas of al-Afghani, Gasprinskii returned to the Crimea, where in 1883 he founded the newspaper *Tarjuman* (The interpreter). Until the 1905 revolution, this publication was the sole Turkic-language newspaper in the Russian empire, and a major platform for disseminating Gasprinskii's jadidist ideas. An avowed monarchist, Gasprinskii sought to unify the Turkic peoples of Russia (who constituted the vast majority of Russia's Muslim population) and facilitate their integration into the economic and civic life of imperial Russian society. To this end, Gasprinskii championed the creation of a common Turkic literary language and, most significantly, sought to reform Muslim education to make it conform more to Western models. Gasprinskii especially championed the teaching of Russian language, arithmetic, geography, and the sciences. In addition, he is credited with introducing a phonetic system of reading for pupils to learn to read faster. Gasprinskii opened the first jadidist school in Bakhchesaray in 1884.

As an educational reform movement, jadidism grew steadily from the 1880s to 1917. It was received most enthusiastically among the Tatars and Bashkirs of Russia's Volga-Ural region. The urban elites of these Muslim communities were relatively well integrated into Russian economic life, and it was precisely the Tatar urban bourgeoisie who were the most active backers of jadidist educational institutions. While jadidist schools could be found throughout the Russian Empire's Muslim regions, it was mainly brought to outlying regions by Tatar colonists. Yet jadidist schools were viewed with suspicion among traditional Muslim elites, particularly in Central Asia and Kazakhstan, but even in the Volga-Ural region as well.

*Jadid*s, including numerous graduates of *jadid* madrasas, had a substantial impact on the growth of nationalist, pan-Turkic, and pan-Islamic political activity following the 1905 revolution, especially in the emergence of Muslim nationalism. At the same time, *jadid*s also came into conflict with conservative and traditionalist elements within their own societies. This conflict between the *jadid*s and the traditionalists is often depicted as simply a conflict between "reaction and reform," but in fact was in large measure a political struggle mirroring the conflict in Russia between political conservatives and increasingly radical proponents of social and political change within the Russian Empire. In the Volga-Ural region, this conflict was characterized by a politicization of the religious debate between *jadid*s and conservatives; in Central Asia, where local adherents of jadidism were far fewer, it was even more restrictive than in Russia proper. Both native rulers and Russian administrators were openly hostile to jadidist activity.

During the period from 1905 to 1917 the jadidist movement remained ideologically heterogeneous, although many *jadid*s became increasingly secular and radicalized, as the Russian Empire drifted toward revolution. At this time, especially after 1910, many *jadid*s began making an ideological shift from Muslim nationalism to local nationalisms. This process was most evident in the Volga-Ural region, Azerbaijan, and to a lesser extent among the Kazakhs. With the outbreak of civil war following the 1917 revolution, *jadid*s played important political roles in Muslim nationalist movements, particularly in Azerbaijan, in the short-lived Idel-Ural Republic in the Volga-Ural region, and in the Qoqand Autonomy in Turkestan. Other more radical *jadid*s, who rejected nationalism in favor of class struggle, joined the Communist Party or allied themselves with the Bolsheviks. In Central Asia, Bolsheviks briefly installed local *jadid*s as the rulers of the short-lived People's Republics of Bukhara and Khorezm.

The historical legacy of jadidism remains debated both in the West and in the former Soviet Union. As Muslims, the *jadid*s were certainly the first members of imperial Russia's Muslim societies to coherently articulate a vision of secularized Muslim community integrated within the Russian Empire and, by extension, into European society. Indeed they sought to harmonize, and actually alter, Islamic culture to function within a European framework. In fact, the transition from pan-Islamic or pan-Turkic jadidism to jadidist-inspired Muslim nationalism, and even ethnic nationalism, was a relatively seamless one. Some modern Tatar nationalists, for instance, depict jadidism as a manifestation of Tatar national identity, and national genius. However, other scholars, especially those who have examined jadidism within the context of Islamic intellectual and cultural history as a whole, have depicted jadidism as a rather marginal movement within Islamic society, especially in comparison to existing traditional institutions and ideas, not only in Central Asia, but in the Volga-Ural region as well.

See also **Gasprinskii, Isma'il Bay; Reform: Arab Middle East and North Africa; Reform: Iran; Reform: South Asia.**

BIBLIOGRAPHY

Frank, Allen J. *Muslim Religious Institutions in Imperial Russia: The Islamic World of Novouzensk District and the Kazakh Inner Horde, 1780–1910.* Leiden: E. J. Brill, 2001.

Khalid, Adeeb. *The Politics of Muslim Cultural Reform: Jadidism in Central Asia.* Berkeley, Los Angeles, and London: University of California Press, 1998.

Allen J. Frank

SOUTH ASIA

Reform, in the context of South Asian Islam, can acquire two different, indeed contradictory, meanings and objectives. It can refer to the liberalizing tendencies encompassing a rational, scientific, "enlightenment" orientation to Islam, or it may signify traditionalist movements seeking to restore Islam to its more orthodox, pristine, "original" form. The first is intended to ensure the progress of Muslims in the modern world, the second to revive a glorious past. Islamic reformism in South Asia has usually struggled within this awkward dialectic.

It is noteworthy that South Asia's initial encounters with Islam were relatively benign and accommodative. When Muhammad bin Qasim landed in Sind in 712 C.E., he was instructed through a legal opinion to treat the local non-Muslims with justice. Similarly, in spite of successive waves of Muslim invasions, it was the Sufi saints (charismatic mystics) who were largely instrumental in converting the vast majority of the population to Islam through example and persuasion. And finally, while the distinctions with the Hindus were profound and obvious, the poorer classes of both communities were brought together by their poverty, agrarian existence and the syncretistic compulsions of "popular" or "folk" religion. Therefore, Hindus were seldom the dreadful "other" against whom reform movements were directed.

It is perhaps Shah Wali Allah (1703–1762) who can claim the status of being one of the first influential theologian-revivalists in the subcontinent. He belonged to the Naqshbandiya *tariqa* (a Sufi order), and represented a combination of both rationalism and traditionalism. He suggested that Muslims should practice *ijtihad* (independent reasoning) to reach conclusions relevant to the times. And while he did not subscribe to the same puritanical rigidity of his contemporary Muhammad ibn 'Abd al Wahhab of Arabia, he did criticize many un-Islamic accretions that South Asian Islam had acquired. Because of the range, eclecticism, and power of his writings, many reformists of different persuasions claim him as part of their intellectual heritage.

The gradual displacement of the Muslims from their position of privilege and authority owing to the impact of

British commercial and imperial ambitions, and the increasing fear of British intrusion into their religious practices, generated an edginess and militancy within later reformists. Anti-British sentiment was fused with ideas of religious self-preservation and purification causing Wali Allah's son to declare territories under British control as *dar-ul-harb* (land of war). Some of his followers such as Sayyid Ahmad Barelwi and Syed Ismail Shahid died in western India fighting against the Sikhs and British in 1831. In the eastern province of Bengal, other followers such as ʿHaji Shariatullah (1781–1840) and his son Dudu Mian (1819–1862) combined class and religious sensitivies to launch the *faraidi* movement (implying that which is religiously mandated), against the British indigo planters and Hindu landowners.

The aftermath of the Mutiny, or the First Indian War of Independence, in 1857, radically altered the direction of reformism in South Asia. It was felt by some that the deteriorating condition of the Muslims resulted from their sullen attitude toward the British, and their inability or unwillingness to take advantage of the opportunities for advancement that British rule provided. None perceived this more clearly, or expressed himself as emphatically, as Sir Sayyid Ahmad Khan (1817–1898). He preached loyalty to the British, promoted Western language and education to overcome Muslim backwardness, developed an exegetical rationalism in his writings on Islam, warned against the stultifying influence of the reactionary ulema (religious leaders), and called upon Muslims to stay away from Hindu political organizations. Aligarh University, which he founded in 1875, was emblematic of his approach and interests.

The Aligarh model faced challenges from scholars associated with the Firangi Mahal in Lucknow (established in the 1690s) and the theological seminary at Deoband, where classes began in 1867. Most scholars associated with these schools were opposed to the Aligarh brand of unabashed eagerness for Western knowledge, demanded greater concern for Islamic identity and heritage, bristled at the perceived subservience to the British, and sought deeper engagement with both pan-Islamist and nationalist tendencies that were gradually evolving.

In the twentieth century, Islamic reform and political activism became inextricably intertwined. It was Aligarh modernism, and its logical corollary expressed as Muslim separatism, that eventually culminated in the formation of Pakistan in 1947. It is intriguing to note that orthodox Muslim leaders like Abu l-AʿlaʾMaududi and Maulana Madani, and nationalist/populist leaders like Abul Kalam Azad, Hakim Akmal Khan, and Abd al-Ghaffar Khan, opposed the idea of Pakistan while it was a very Westernized, secular, legalistically oriented leadership (Sir Muhammad Iqbal, Liaquat ʿAli Khan, Muhammad ʿAli Jinnah) that championed it. At the time, it was assumed that Pakistan would be a home for Muslims, but not necessarily a theocratic Muslim state.

However, in independent Pakistan a tension developed between the ulema, who demanded a preeminent role for Islam in the new state, and the powerful military and bureaucratic elite who were unenthusiastic. Reform, in either modernist or orthodox directions, followed the vicissitudes of temporary political arrangements. The 1956 constitution referred to the Islamic Republic of Pakistan; the 1962 constitution dropped the word Islamic; the 1973 constitution reincorporated it in principle. The liberal Muslim Family Law Ordinance of 1961, which sought to reform marriage and divorce laws in the country, was all but gutted in the 1980s through various enactments on the punishment, inheritance, and laws of evidence relating to women. Moreover, the establishment of *shariʿa* courts to adjudicate matters according to strict Islamic principles, the declaration of Qadianis as non-Muslims, the self-conscious courtship of Arab countries through emphasizing its Islamic credentials, and the injection of a heightened sensibility about religious matters on public issues (including education and entertainment), all appeared to indicate a swing back toward traditionalist premises in the 1980s and 1990s.

The separation of Bangladesh from Pakistan in 1971 seemed to demonstrate the primacy of language and culture as more important markers for identity and destiny than religion. Initially the country adopted a determinedly indifferent posture toward religion. However, and in spite of a gradual institutionalization of democracy, political developments since the early 1980s have compelled Bangladesh to drop the word "secular" from its constitution, declare Islam to be the state religion, patronize parochial schools, and insist on outward expressions of religious zeal and commitment from its leaders.

In both countries, it is obvious that conservative religious parties do not command a large following in electoral competitions. However, it is also clear that these forces are formidable enough to drive the discourse in directions they seek. The modernist agenda—with its emphasis on women's rights, minority protections, and civil liberties—appears to face rather daunting challenges, perhaps a little more so in Pakistan than in Bangladesh.

See also **Ahmad Khan, (Sir) Sayyid; Wali Allah, Shah.**

BIBLIOGRAPHY

Ahmad, Aziz. *Islamic Modernism in India and Pakistan 1875–1964.* London: Oxford University Press, 1967.

Ahmed, Akbar. *Jinnah, Pakistan, and Islamic Identity: The Search for Saladin.* London: Routledge, 1997.

Hasan, Mushirul, ed. *Islam, Communities and the Nation: Muslim Identities in South Asia and Beyond.* Dhaka: The University Press, 1998.

Robinson, Francis. *Islam and Muslim History in South Asia.* New Delhi: Oxford University Press, 2000.

Schimmel, Annemarie. *Islam in the Indian Subcontinent.* Leiden-Koln: E. J. Brill, 1980.

Ahrar Ahmad

SOUTHEAST ASIA

In Islamic Southeast Asia the concept of "reform" is the subject of a highly contested discourse. Self-proclaimed "reformists" range from the Malaysian feminist organization Sisters in Islam, which advocates changes in Islamic family law that increase the rights and power of women, to the Indonesian Lakshar Jihad, which advocates the establishment of a conservative form of Islamic law to act as the basis of an Islamic state combining Indonesia, Malaysia, and the southern Philippines.

Reformist movements in Southeast Asia emerged in the early decades of the twentieth century as responses to British, Dutch, and American colonial rule. They were also responses to intellectual developments in the broader Muslim world. Early reformists were influenced by the writings of the Egyptian reformers Muhammad ʿAbduh and Rashid Rida and by the Wahhabi movement in Arabia. They attributed the decline of Muslim political and economic power to the impure state of early twentieth-century Islam. The rejection of Sufism and elements of popular religion—including the veneration of the tombs of saints, ritual meals, and the celebration of the birth of the prophet Muhammad—are among the hallmarks of Southeast Asian reformism. These and other aspects of popular Islam were (and are) denounced as innovation and unbelief by these reformists. In Indonesia reformists argued that the prayers of traditional Muslims were invalid because supplicants face directly west instead of northwest, which is the actual direction of Mecca.

The reformists advocated strict enforcement of *shariʿa*. They denied the authority of classical legal texts that formed the core of the curriculum in traditional Islamic schools. Like *salafiyya* reformers elsewhere, they maintained that the Qurʾan and hadith are the only allowable sources of legal decisions. This presented a major challenge to the traditional ulema. Throughout the twentieth century disputes between modernists and reformists were extremely bitter. Because of the profound implications of these religious disputes—each party describes the other as heretics bound for hell—it is unlikely that the cavernous divide between traditional and reformist communities can be closed.

Early reformists combined this religious agenda with calls for social and educational reform. They argued that the acquisition of technical and scientific knowledge is a religious obligation. The Javanese scholar Ahmad Dahlan and the Malay Tahir Jalal al-Din wrote and preached that there is an important link between the two components of the reform agenda. They taught that Islam is the religion of rationality

Megawati Sukarnoputri, front, the leader and presidential candidate of the Indonesia Democratic Party for Struggle (PDI-P) and her husband, Taufik Kimas, cast their ballots in Jakarta in 1999, in Indonesia's first free elections since 1955. Although her party won the election, she was forced to accept the position of vice-president. In 2001, President Abdurraham Wahid was forced to resign and Sukarhoputri became the president of Indonesia. AP/ WIDE WORLD PHOTOS

and that the acquisition of modern skills and knowledge is a religious duty. They also encouraged participation in the emerging modern economic system. Reformists adopted strategies similar to those of Christian missionaries. Organizations such as Muhammadiyya in Indonesia and al-Islam in Malaya established schools that combined a *salafiyya* understanding of Islam with modern (Western) subjects. They established schools for girls as well as women's and youth organizations. Muhammadiyya and other reformist organizations now maintain extensive systems of schools, universities, and hospitals. The provision of social and educational services contributed significantly to the spread of modernism, especially in urban areas.

In Indonesia, Malaysia, and Singapore a basic distinction can be drawn between reformist movements that seek to transform culture and society and those that seek to employ the political process to establish Islamic states. In the Philippines the distinction is that between those who would establish a Muslim state in the southern region and others who envision the Muslim community as a component of a pluralistic state. Muslims in southern Thailand have been influenced by Malaysian reformists and have organized to protect and expand the rights of Muslims in an overwhelmingly Buddhist society. In Southeast Asian states where Muslims are small minorities—Burma, Cambodia, and Vietnam—Islamic reformism did not emerge until after the Second World War. In these countries reformism is a religious movement of little political significance.

In the colonial era reformist movements advocating the establishment of Islamic states were subject to serious repression. Postcolonial governments have continued these policies, but have also attempted to include reformist Muslims in the political process. In Malaysia reformist political parties compete in parliamentary elections and govern in several states. In Indonesia there has been a constant tension between traditionalist Muslims, who have generally avoided political action, reformists who have attempted to establish Indonesia as an Islamic state, and other reformists, including the majority of the Muhammadiya community, who seek to build a *salafiyya*-oriented Muslim community while avoiding overt political activity. The collapse of the Suharto regime in 1998 contributed to the repoliticization of Indonesian reformism. Political parties based on reformist ideologies emerged as important voices in Indonesia's new democracy. Other, more radical, groups reject the democratic orientation of the political parties and advocate the use of force to establish a *salafiyya* state.

In Southeast Asia, and particularly in Indonesia, there have also been attempts to develop Islamic theologies emphasizing tolerance, interreligious discourse, and democratic politics. This variety of reformism differs fundamentally from earlier *salafiyya* movements. This variety of reformism began to develop in the 1980s and has come to be known as liberal Islam. In Indonesia it was initially sponsored by the government as an antidote for fundamentalism. Most of the participants in this course come from traditionalist backgrounds and are conversant with classic Arabic theological, legal, and mystical texts. The central institutional location of Islamic liberalism is the State Islamic Studies Institute. Many graduates from these programs continue their studies abroad. In the 1990s, liberalism emerged as a major force for political, social, and economic change. Liberal reformists reject the notion of an Islamic state. They are active in development-oriented NGOs (nongovernmental organizations), promote interfaith understanding and cooperation, and are advocates for human rights and gender equality. In Indonesia they played a major role in the *Reformasi* (reformation) movement that brought an end to the "New Order" regime of President Suharto.

See also **Reform: Arab Middle East and North Africa; Reform: Iran.**

BIBLIOGRAPHY

Bowen, John. *Muslims Through Discourse: Religion and Ritual in Gayo Society.* Princeton, N.J.: Princeton University Press, 1993.

Nagata, Judith. *The Reflowering of Malaysian Islam: Modern Religious Radicals and Their Roots.* Vancouver: University of British Columbia Press, 1984.

Noer, Deliar. *The Modernist Muslim Movement in Indonesia.* Ithaca, N.Y.: Cornell University Press, 1973.

Woodward, Mark, ed. *Towards a New Paradigm: Recent Developments in Indonesian Islamic Thought.* Tempe: Arizona State University, 1996.

Mark R. Woodward

OTTOMAN EMPIRE AND TURKEY

See **Empires: Ottoman; Kemal, Namik; Modernization, Political; Nur Movement; Nursi, Said; Young Ottomans.**

RELIGIOUS BELIEFS

While Islam has historically eschewed authoritative bodies for issuing creeds with the authority of an ecclesiastical order, several statements of orthodox belief have, over time, come to be recognized as defining Sunni faith (*iman*). From these creeds six central beliefs have been distilled that have come to define orthodox faith. Belief in God and his attributes, prophets, angels, sacred books, the Last Day, and predestination has, by Sunni consensus, come to define normative Islam.

Belief in God and his attributes refers to the concepts of *tawhid* (divine unity) and *sifat Allah* (the attributive characteristics of God). *Tawhid* means that God is omnipotent, that he needs no helpers, and has no partners. Associating partners with God is referred to as *shirk*, and is considered a serious sin. This concept has been extended by some Muslim thinkers to mean that submission to God's unity means the absolute adherence to God's rules, as described in the Qur'an and hadith. Failing to adhere to God's rules indicates that the individual places his or her own judgment equal to God's, and thus becomes God's associate. The attributes of God refer to God's abilities and characteristics as they are defined in the Qur'an. There are generally held to be ninety-nine characteristics that are reflected in the ninety-nine names of God.

Belief in prophets, angels, and sacred books is based on Surah 2:285. This verse equates faith with the belief that God has sent many prophets prior to Muhammad. It also indicates the larger concept that Muhammad was the end of a chain of prophetic succession beginning with Adam and continuing through the twenty-five prophets mentioned in the Qur'an.

Belief in angels is central to both the belief in prophets and in sacred books. The angel Jibril, according to Muslim tradition, conveyed the revelation from God to Muhammad and other prophets. Angels also figure prominently in a variety of beliefs, including those surrounding Munkar and Nakir, angels who interrogate the dead in their graves, and Michael, who was commissioned by God to oversee the natural world.

Muslims believe that many prophets have received sacred textual revelations similar to the Qur'an but that these revelations became corrupt over time. Thus while Christians and Jews are considered "people of the book" due to their reception of textual revelations, their religions fell into error, thus necessitating Muhammad's mission.

The Last Day refers to the belief that the world will be destroyed by God and will be followed by a Day of Resurrection on which all people will be required to account for their deeds. Those who obeyed the commands of God will go to paradise, while those who did not will go to hell. Many Muslim theologians have held that everyone will eventually be released from hell after they have suffered sufficient punishment. Some Sufis have gone so far as to include Iblis (leader of *jinn*, who rebeled against God after the creation of Adam) in this category.

Predestination means that God has total power over all of creation and therefore determines the course of all events. Paradoxically, humans have the ability to obey or disobey the commands of God. This ambiguity has never been settled fully and reached a compromise position with the concept of *kasb*, which asserts that God creates acts that humans then acquire or own, thus involving their culpability for action or inaction.

See also **Angels; Kalam.**

BIBLIOGRAPHY

Denny, Frederick Mathewson. *An Introduction to Islam.* New York: Macmillan Publishing Company, 1994.

Watt, William Montgomery. *Islamic Creeds: A Selection.* Edinburgh: Edinburgh University Press, 1994.

Wensinck, A. J. *The Muslim Creed: Its Genesis and Historical Development.* London: Frank Cass, 1965.

R. Kevin Jaques

RELIGIOUS INSTITUTIONS

Religious institutions are the visible and organized manifestations of practices and beliefs in particular social and historical contexts. Like human emotions and attitudes, religious beliefs and practices project outward onto the social and historical plan. They create identities and representations, and determine attitudes, emotions, and behavior. These manifestations and outward projections originate from beliefs and practices, but they are also limited by historical contexts. Geographical, social, and political considerations modify attitudes and practices. Religious institutions, then, take shape in relation to both religious impulses and contextual configurations. The following entry suggests some of the enduring and changing features of religious institutions in Islam in broad historical strokes.

Religious beliefs and practices have been noticeably expressed in key institutions constructed in uniquely different social and historical contexts. The caliphate as a universal political and social order was the key institution developed in the early period of Islam. This was followed by more clearly religious institutions like the school of law (*madhhab*) and Sufi order (*tariqa*). The modern period has witnessed the emergence of various forms of religious states together with the independent religious association in secular contexts.

Early Islam

The early period of Islamic history begins with the life of the prophet Muhammad and ends with the weakening of the Abbasid Empire. Following Marshall Hodgson, we can use the year 945 as a significant point in that history when the independence of the caliphate was finally shattered. A general of a regional power, the Buyids, occupied Baghdad and laid to rest the more than two hundred years of a universal political authority. The eventual failure notwithstanding, early Islam laid the foundation of the caliphate as a vital religious institution that moved and inspired Muslims. It is also an institution that has provided considerable inspiration for subsequent political and social movements in diverse cultural and historical contexts up to the present time. The caliphal order was the most important religious institution the Muslims created during this period. The word "order" is used to include the political system and ideas themselves, as well as the related notions of self, society, and others. Early Islam was a period of intense political conflicts, many of which raged particularly over the nature and shape of this political order and its related issues. At the same time, these conflicts and disagreements created opportunities for great creativity that inspired legal, theological, philosophical, and literary productions in support of one or the other conceptions of the political order.

Who must be the caliph? After the death of the prophet Muhammad in 632, one of the first questions that needed to be answered was that of his succession. Would it be someone close to him from the beginning? Would it mean the split of the Muslim community between its Meccan and Medinan followers? Or would it be someone from his family? Or would the community simply choose one among equals? In time, these political questions were answered in religious and theological terms. The history of religious ideas of early

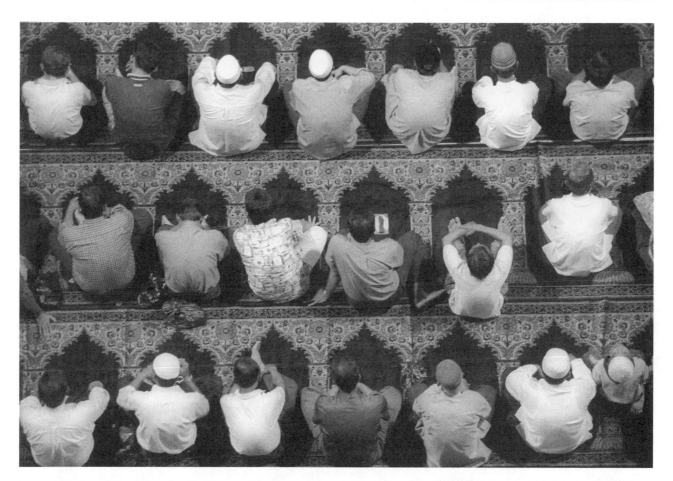

In a mosque in Jakarta, Indonesia, Muslim men listen to a sermon during Friday prayers. In Islamic nations, religious institutions have traditionally been subject to the rules of the state, but in countries where Muslims are minorities (India and the United States, for example), mosques have been able to transform themselves into more independent religious institutions. GETTY IMAGES

Islam revolves around questions and answers about the identity, nature, and authority of the caliphate.

One of the close associates of the prophet Muhammad, Abu Bakr al-Siddiq, was selected as his immediate successor in a tense political context. Soon, members of the Prophet's own clan, the Banu Hashim, and their supporters claimed that they had been deprived of rightful leadership granted by the Prophet to ʿAli, the cousin and son-in-law of the Prophet, and his legitimate successors. Thus emerged the first glimmer of a religio-political faction, the party of ʿAli (Ar. Shiʿa), that developed into a full-fledged religious and theological group within Islam. Even though it remained a minority, and the various factions were hardly unanimous on the particular descendant of ʿAli as the rightful successor, the Shiʿa produced notions of legitimate and rightful leadership for religious leadership in general. The prophetically chosen one was divinely guided, and ready to go into battle against injustice and usurpation. Such a notion of a religious leader became the cornerstone of other religious groups and political parties. Mystical schools took on the notion of direct or indirect divine assistance, and leaders of political and religious movements followed the inspiration of its revolutionary apsects. In

light of this particular discussion, such a notion of religious and political leadership is an important part of the religious institution of the caliphate of early Islam.

Another important aspect of this institution was the nature of the community and its boundaries. Shiʿite protest against the reigning caliph sowed the seeds for a degree of elitism within the community of believers. The family of the Prophet would enjoy a level of recognition and respect above ordinary believers. However, the egalitarian message of earlier biblical religions found a profound resonance in Islam as well. The first group to raise this issue on the political sphere was the Khariji, who took a position diametrically opposed to the Shiʿa. For them, the political leader was an equal in the community of believers, and open to censure and removal if he failed to live by the teachings of the Qurʾan. According to traditional Muslim historiography, the Kharijis emerged precisely during the reign of the fourth caliph, ʿAli, the first imam of the Shiʿa, when they rejected his compromising stand in war. They claimed that he had ignored a fundamental teaching of the Qurʾan by agreeing to negotiate with a usurper, and no longer deserved the allegiance of the Muslim community. The Kharijis developed another philosophy of revolution against authority. Unlike the Shi'ite ideas, it harbored a radical egalitarianism.

Standing between the Shi'a and the Khariji, other theological schools emerged to define the boundaries of Muslim identities. The first theological questions emerged directly from the issues raised by these early groups. Islamic theology, for example, asked to what extent the wrongdoing of a reigning caliph could be tolerated. From the Shi'a point of view, the absence of a rightful imam was sufficient ground for launching a revolt against the caliph, while the Kharijis declared that any person guilty of a grave sin should be deposed. Against them, the Mu'tazila argued that such a person did not automatically relinquish his faith and could not be summarily dismissed. But they said that such a person was suspended between belief and disbelief. The majority of the scholars gravitated toward a more accommodationist position, and argued that grave acts or sins by themselves do not declare a person a non-Muslim. The theological arguments were the first political arguments concerning the identity of the caliph, but it is quite clear that they contributed in no small part to the definition of a Muslim against disbelief. And the early theological debates among Muslims themselves and between Muslims and other religious groups in the Near East established the boundaries and identity of Islam and Muslims.

The identity of Muslims also raised the issue of the Arabs and Arabic. As Islam spread from Arabia and embraced many different cultures and traditions, it confronted the question of the relationship between Arabs and non-Arabs, and between Arab culture and local languages and cultures. The spread of Islamic power went hand in hand with Arabization. The first dynasty of Islam that followed the reign of 'Ali, the Umayyads, played a leading role in ensuring that the Arab nature of the conquest and its new administration were not lost. Against this hegemony of Arab authority, the Islamic impulse favored a greater sense of egalitarianism between Arabs and non-Arabs. One of the main factors that supported the Abbasid revolution (750) against the Umayyads was the alliance between Arab and non-Arab forces. The victory of the Abbasids meant the victory for universalism in the house of Islam. But the position of the Arabs and Arabic was not abandoned. The Arabic language, as the language of divine revelation par excellence, took on an elevated position in society in general and in religious scholarship in particular, and became the lingua franca of aspiring religious teachers and scholars. The genius of the Arabs lay not so much in their intrinsic ethnic worth, but on the role and eminence of the Qur'an and the teachings of the prophet Muhammad. Social movements that favored anti-Arab sentiments, like the Shu'ubiyya, remained in the society, but could never dislodge the lofty status of the Arabic language as the language of revelation. Legal, exegetical, and philological studies emphasized the indispensability of Arabic even while keeping the door open to conversions.

The boundaries of the community against outsiders were more clearly drawn, even though not always consistently applied. The caliphate was justified on the basis of a universal and expanding empire that engaged the reigning superpowers of the day. The Sassanian Empire of the Persians fell early, and the Byzantine Empire was dislodged from its territories in Palestine and North Africa. The latter remained a major adversary and target until its capital, Constantinople, fell in 1453. A condition of war between the caliphate and other political orders was accepted as the norm, even though such a norm could be temporarily regulated by treaties. The relationship with other religions followed this political norm. The expanding caliphate tolerated no polytheistic religious communities. They had to abandon their religions, and accept Islam. In contrast, Christians and Jews were recognized as People of the Book and were tolerated in the caliphate order.

But still, the caliphate was a political institution driven by the interests of those who were able to command power. Various factions of Arab tribes played a dominant role in the balance of power during the Umayyad period and the early Abbasid period, and the history and success of conquest created significant opportunities for others. The religious character of the caliphate was reinforced by the ideological claims made by various parties, from the Shi'as who declared their support for the divinely inspired leadership of the imams, to the Kharijis who lived by the letter of the Qur'an. The religious element was reinforced through the development of a religious literature on the legacy of the Prophetic period. In particular, the compilation of the Qur'an and the sayings of the Prophet and his associates provided the foundations for a religious discourse of power, authority, and community. As an institution, then, the political and religious elements of the caliphate were not so easily separated. And yet, in spite of the inseparability of the political from the religious, the production of a literary tradition provided the basis for the emergence of religious learning ('ilm) and its prestige. Those who possessed this knowledge, the ulema, were distinct from those who wielded power and from the mass of followers, even though they did not always form a distinctive institution that bound them to each other on the public plain. Sometimes one gets the impression that, in the earliest period of conquest, those who wielded brute force disdained such men of learning. But the accumulation of scholarly tradition could not be ignored in the administration of justice, the bureaucracy, and in the general legitimization of the political order itself.

In the latter half of the Ummayad and the early part of the Abbasid caliphates, the accumulation of the teachings of the Prophet and the early Muslims began in the important towns and cities such as Medina, Mecca, Kufa, and Basra. The most well known of these teachings were from prominent individuals who later came to be associated with schools of law like Abu Hanifa (d. 767), Malik b. Anas (d. 796), Muhammad b.

Idris al-Shafi'i (d. 820), and Ahmad b. Hanbal (d. 855). Their discussions on issues such as criminal justice, evidence, military warfare, and slavery provided the political and social foundations for the caliphate. At the same time, and of more lasting significance, they founded the basic framework for a religious way of life by defining and specifying the way in which to fulfill the religious duties in Islam. Theological discussions defined the boundaries of belief and membership, juridical discussions elaborated the performance of ritual practices, and mystical notions explored religious experience with the Divine.

Eventually, the apparatus of scholarship inscribed a distinct zone of authority that the caliphs and other political rulers could not access through the exercise of military means. One of the most interesting episodes in Abbasid history illustrates the limits of political authority against the authority of religious scholarship. In 833, the Abbasid caliph Ma'mun instituted an inquisition (*mihna*) to force all notable scholars to accept the doctrine of the createdness of the Qur'an as state policy. A celebrated and most popular teacher of hadith, Ahmad b. Hanbal, refused to embrace the doctrine. The state policy continued for some time after the death of Ma'mun, but was finally rescinded by al-Mutawakkil (r. 847–861). The event reinforced the authority of the religious scholars and their role in society. Some have seen in this episode the divergence of political from religious authority in Islam.

The caliphate was a religious institution created and established in early Islam. It defined a religious order of power and authority that included the meaning of the self, community, and the Other. The history of the caliphate during this period indicates that the precise details of the order were determined by the historical exigencies of internal disputes, and conflict with the Other. The beginnings of the accumulation of the teachings of the Prophet, the Qur'an, and the legacy of the earliest Muslim community provided the scholarly foundations for these conceptions, which by themselves were not always presented in one fully developed theory. In general, however, the caliphate bequeathed to Muslims the idea of a universal egalitarian community (*umma*) with a special place for the Arabic language and the family of the Prophet; an expanding political order and hegemony over Jews, Christians, and other recognized religious communities; complete dominance over polytheistic communities; and a religious authority based on knowledge of the revelations received by the prophet Muhammad.

The Middle Period

The universal caliphate faced daunting challenges from the outset, and finally collapsed as an effective political authority. The middle period refers to the time when the caliphs lost effective power to regional authorities until the modern period. One can also point to 1453 as a quasi midpoint of this period, when the Ottoman Empire conquered Constantinople and became the model of extensive, but not universal, Muslim empires until the emergence of nation-states. As challengers from religious and political groups were regular features of the caliphate, individual caliphs relied more and more on slave soldiers and generals for their personal rule and effective control. The Abbasid revolution unleashed the force of regional powers, particularly in the areas previously controlled by the Sassanian Empire. From the tenth century these regions witnessed the emergence of powerful governors and generals who wielded more power than the central government. In this same century, challenges to the universality of the institution also became apparent. A rival caliphate was established in the West by survivors of the Umayyad family who fled to North Africa and southern Spain. One of their descendants, 'Abd al-Rahman III (912–961), declared himself a caliph in 929, challenging the theory of the single political authority of Baghdad. In contrast, the Shi'a, in spite of their differences, were able to rise to prominence. The Buyids took effective control of Baghdad in 945, even though they did not completely replace the caliph with a recognized imam. But another Shi'a movement was even more ambitious. The Fatimids, with the support of Berber clans in North Africa, lay claim to the universal caliphate from Spain to India. They occupied Cairo in 969 and went on to become the largest and longest surviving political order until the 1170s, when they were defeated by the Seljuks, another group of Turkish military adventurers. The dominance of regional powers, and direct religious challenges from the Shi'a both helped to lay to rest the effective authority of the universal caliphate. The rival caliphates from both Sunni (Spanish Andalusian) and Shi'ite (Buyid and Fatimid) claims shook the institution and myth of the single universal caliphate.

The religious elements developed during the early caliphate did not completely disappear, but they were transformed in the context of these new social and political experiences. The idea of a universal community of believers (*umma*) persisted through the political breakdown of the empire, but a political unity became impossible. The place and role of the Qur'an and the prophet Muhammad reinforced this unity and this identity on social, religious, and commercial levels. Moreover, the foundation of the religious discourse during the caliphate was now employed in the production of new institutions. The juridical, theological, and mystical ideas that emerged during the late Umayyad and Abbasid periods were developed, and slowly produced institutions like the schools of law and theology, and mystical orders. It is precisely the latter institutions that were a dominant feature of the Middle Period of Islam. The caliphate gave way to more clearly definable religious institutions that expressed the emotions, attitudes, and behaviors of Muslims.

Before elaborating on the religious institutions of the legal schools (*madhhab*) and the Sufi orders (*tariqa*s), a brief note on the political situation is essential. In comparison with the caliphs, the governors and generals who wielded power in the Middle Period were less justified through religious theology. In light of the early conceptions of the caliphate, they would simply be regarded as usurpers. But scholarly articulation of the political order recognized and accepted the *realpolitick* on the ground, and provided some space and recognition for these adventurers. One of the most significant theorists to take up this task was the Baghdadian al-Mawardi (d. 1058), whose work on the caliphate has been widely acclaimed. He recognized the new realities of the political space, and tried to articulate justice as an organizing principle for public and private life. The new rulers may come to power by virtue of their strength, according to al-Mawardi, but they were duty-bound to uphold justice in their realms. The *shariʿa*, as elaborated by the religious scholars, played an important role in the administration of justice, apart from its more significant role of outlining more personal religious duties. Al-Mawardi emphasized the requirement for justice in their political behavior (*siyasa*). Such theories did not always temper the political ambitions of the men of power, but they provided a new model of political life.

In light of such a broad justification, the generals and rulers often obtained support from one of the schools of law, theology, or mystical orders. Buyid support for Shiʿite teachings was followed by a series of Sunni-inclined rulers. The Seljukid and Ayyubid rulers were prominent examples who promoted Sunni Islamic thought and life. In this period, perhaps as a result of their lesser religious roles, the generals were more inclined to shore their regimes with the support of religious tendencies. They supported the building of schools for legal and theological groups, and also embarked upon extensive architectural projects of mosques, mausoleums, and Sufi lodges. Mottahedeh's analysis has suggested that support for the religious projects was not motivated only by insecurity, or deep religious feelings and convictions. He argued that in this period the system of land grants (*iqtaʿ*) to governors and soldiers made this the most important means of acquiring and cultivating land. In this context, pious endowments (*waqf*) made by wealthy and political elites created a relatively autonomous space that escaped these land grants, and were therefore favored by wealthy patrons of religious life in general, and religious institutions in particular. Through the *waqf* then, religious practices were granted a degree of autonomy and independence in a period of often-great military conflict.

As mentioned already, Islamic juridical thought originated early during the caliphate. Shiʿite imams and other teachers started outlining rules and conditions for the performance of personal religious duties and the application of public law. During the Middle Period, the elaboration and articulation of legal theory and practices continued. But now distinct identities emerged around prominent scholars and their students. In Sunni Islam, the Middle Period witnessed the consolidation of four legal schools, linking themselves to

Abu Hanifa, Malik b. Anas, al-Shafiʿi, and Ahmad b. Hanbal. Genealogies of students linking the founders were formulated, founding texts and commentaries identified, more or less coherent theories outlined, and positions were founded against others. Makdisi has shown how the practice of commentaries and notation on earlier works played a leading role in the development of consensus within each of the schools. The schools were in no small measure supported by the foundation of the *madrasa*, a school established to teach one or another school of law. The first to introduce the *madrasa* as an institution for teaching were the Shiʿa, but it quickly became a distinct way of consolidating and promoting the teachings of Sunni schools as well. The *madrasa* did not replace the networks around individual teachers, but provided a basis for their further consolidation. In Sunni Islam, then, the four schools of law took their shape during the Middle Period. It was also this period that saw the consolidation of Shiʿism as a rival scholarly vision of Islam, as the foundation of a complete political order, or as a school of law, theology, and mysticism.

In addition to the schools of law, this period also witnessed the emergence of Sufi orders (*tariqa*s). Like the schools of law, the earliest ideas on mystical life had also emerged in the early caliphate. With the Middle Period, Sufi ideas were similarly consolidated. Compendia were compiled, biographies (or hagiographies) were collected of the early Sufis, and then, in the twelfth century, the first order was developed around the teachings of ʿAbd al-Qadir al-Jilani (d. 1166) of Baghdad. A highly respected and popular preacher, al-Jilani introduced a large number of people to the simple insights of Sufi experience. His order has become the most widespread in the Muslim world, and many others have followed it in form. The orders in general grew out of the strong relationship between a Sufi teacher and his disciple, and the additional rites prescribed to experience God through remembrance (*dhikr*).

But both legal schools and Sufi orders exemplified the chief religious institutions in this period. Both the school of law (*madhhab*) and Sufi order (*tariqa*) became complementary ways of being a Muslim in the Middle Period. Not every Muslim would belong to a Sufi order as they would adopt a school or a jurist, but Sufism became a prevalent badge of identity as well. The legal school and *tariqa* were the prominent institutions that gave shape to religious life in the Middle Period. Both assumed the presence of a political authority that supported Islamic law, even though not always very consistently. But the legal schools and the orders gave shape to the religious spheres that were created in the early caliphate.

Modern Period

The next major transformation of religious institutions occurred with the impact of Western (European) hegemony. The armies of the generals and the sultans first lost to the

Europeans on the battlefields, followed by direct occupation and widespread cultural and political influence. This latest period of Islamic history has also spawned its unique institutions, continuing from the past in some sense and inventing new features in the new political contexts.

In the central lands of Islam (the Ottoman sultanate, Iran, and Egypt) the modern period witnessed an intense conflict between the political rulers and the ulema. The former wanted to modernize the state and society as quickly as possible in order to emulate and compete with the Western powers that were defeating them on the battlefields, while the latter regarded most of these changes as a direct threat to their own positions in society and to Islam as a way of life. In the nineteenth century, individual religious scholars supported some aspects of modernization, and promoted some form of reformist interpretation of Islam. But the ulema as a class of scholars lost their unique place in the new political orders. Sometimes they were violently suppressed in the process, and the pious foundations over which they maintained control and through which they enjoyed some independence were confiscated or nationalized. In varying degrees, what emerged in the modern period was a political space occupied entirely by generals, rulers, and later politicians.

In this context, the state in Islamic society was transformed into a powerful entity that controlled all aspects of life, including religion. Religion, in this case Islam, became an instrument to bring about change and modernization, and to keep the incumbents in power. With its long history of religious politics, the new state could employ symbols and instruments to further its goals. And yet the new state was neither a continuation of the caliphate nor the military sultanates of the Middle Period. The new state accepted the rights, privileges, boundaries, and limitations of a modern state, and, like other modern states, it used religion for its particular political purposes. The new state could be a monarchy based on the prestige of the family of the Prophet (Jordan and Morocco) or a revivalist religious movement (Saudi Arabia), a socialist or capitalist one-party state (Iraq, Syria, and Egypt), or a secular republic based on universal suffrage (Turkey). In spite of their diversity, the acceptance of the modern state system, and the instrumentalization of Islam for legitimacy, united them.

In the second half of the twentieth century, most of the states witnessed opposition movements that demanded a greater degree of Islamization. But the opposing positions have not been based so much on the absence of religion in the modern states, but on their inappropriate practice and interpretation. So, the demand for an Islamic state to replace the older modern state is based on a more complete adoption of Islamic teachings in both the state and society. In particular, there is a demand that the shari'a developed by the legal schools in the Middle Period play a central and dominant role in the legal systems of the new states. But the central idea of the modern state is not rejected, and the greater degree of instrumentalization of religion in the state is not questioned. By and large, the idea of the Islamic state is a marriage between the modern state and the sultanates of the Middle Period. The modern Muslim state, advocating a greater or lesser degree of Islamization, is a unique religious institution. It is neither completely free from the influence of traditional Islamic patterns and institutions, the caliphate and the legal schools, nor from modern notions of state. So far the first and most successful of such states has been the Islamic Republic of Iran (established 1979).

But the modern period has also given rise to a different kind of religious institution in Islam. Such institutions are a product of secular states, and are most clearly noticeable in countries of minority Muslim contexts such as India, Africa south of the Sahara, and more recently Europe and America. In the secular context, religion is relatively free from direct state influence, and vice versa. In such conditions, Muslims have established anew or transformed their mosques, schools, pious endowments, and burial grounds into more independent religious institutions. The development of these institutions has been closely tied with local historical contexts, but has drawn on resources and patterns of autonomy in the Middle Period of Islam. More recently, with the emergence of new technologies of communication (the radio, Internet, and satellite), such independent institutions have proliferated. Once their role in secular pluralist societies is identified, they become easily recognized in Muslim majority countries as well. Such institutions are not always easily visible in majority Muslim states, but they play an important role in the practice of Muslims. Only the political control and monopoly of Islam in the modern state prevents their explosive proliferation.

See also **Arabic Language; Empires: Abbasid; Empires: Sassanian; Empires: Umayyad; 'Ibadat; Identity, Muslim; Islam and Islamic; Khirqah; Khutba; Masjid; Material Culture.**

BIBLIOGRAPHY

Crecelius, Daniel. "The Course of Secularization in Modern Egypt." In *Islam and Development: Religion and Sociopolitical Change.* Edited by J. L. Esposito. Syracuse, N.Y.: Syracuse University Press, 1980.

Crone, Patricia, and Hinds, Martin. *God's Caliph: Religious Authority in the First Centuries of Islam.* Cambridge, U.K.: Cambridge University Press, 1986.

Hodgson, Marshall G. S. *The Venture of Islam: Conscience and History in a World Civilization.* Chicago: University Press of Chicago, 1974.

Lapidus, Ira M. *Muslim Cities in the Later Middle Ages.* 1967. Reprint. Cambridge, U.K.: Press Syndicate of the University of Cambridge, 1984.

Makdisi, George. *The Rise of Colleges: Institutions of Learning in Islam and the West.* Edinburgh: Edinburgh University Press, 1981.

Martin, Richard C. "Public Aspects of Theology in Medieval Islam: The Role of Kalam in Conflict Definition and Resolution." *Journal for Islamic Studies* 13 (November 1993): 77–100.

Mikhail, Hanna. *Politics and Revelation: Mawardi and After.* Edinburgh: Edinburgh University Press, 1995.

Mottahedeh, Roy P. *Loyalty and Leadership in an Early Islamic Society.* Princeton, N.J.: Princeton University Press, 1980.

Starrett, Gregory. *Putting Islam to Work: Education, Politics, and Religious Transformation in Egypt.* Berkeley: University of California Press, 1998.

Zaman, Muhammad Qasim. *The Making of a Religious Discourse: An Essay in the History and Historiography of the ʿAbbasid Revolution.* Research Monograph Series, vol. 5. Islamabad: International Institute of Islamic Thought; Islamic Research Institute, 1995.

Zaman, Muhammad Qasim. *Religion and Politics Under the Early Abbasids: The Emergence of the Proto-Sunni Elite.* Leiden: E. J. Brill, 1997.

Abdulkader Tayob

REPUBLICAN BROTHERS

The Republican Brothers is a Sudanese organization advocating Islamic reformation that follows the teachings of Mahmud Muhammad Taha (d. 1985). Taha originally established a small political party advocating Sudanese independence in 1945, but following a profound religious experience in 1951, he gradually transformed the Republican Party into a reformist brotherhood. Taha called for a comprehensive rethinking of the nature of Islamic law, giving emphasis to gender equality and religious pluralism, and a new vision of what Islamic society should be. This vision came to be called "The Second Message of Islam." The Republican Brothers were not politically activist. They did not establish a political party during the eras of parliamentary politics in Sudan (1956–1958, 1964–1969, 1985–1989) and were not active in opposition to the military regimes. However, in 1983 Taha opposed the imposition of a form of Islamic law by the military regime of President Jaʿfar al-Numayri, a position for which he was executed in 1985. Although the Republican Brothers became organizationally weak following the execution of their leader, Taha's teachings gained increasing visibility among Muslims around the world. The leading representative of this school of thought is Abdullahi An-Naʾim, one of Taha's students who, as an expatriate, developed Taha's thinking further and became a prominent Muslim scholar in the field of human rights and international law.

See also **Modernity; Reform: Arab Middle East and North Africa.**

BIBLIOGRAPHY

An-Naʾim, Abdullahi Ahmed. "Introduction." In *The Second Message of Islam.* Edited by Mahmoud Mohamed Taha. Translated by Abdullahi Ahmed An-Naʾim. Syracuse, N.Y.: Syracuse University Press, 1987.

John O. Voll

REVOLUTION

CLASSICAL ISLAM
Saïd A. Arjomand

ISLAMIC REVOLUTION IN IRAN
Kristian P. Alexander

MODERN
Saïd A. Arjomand

CLASSICAL ISLAM

The concept that comes closest to revolution in early Islam is *fitna* (civil strife), used in reference to three civil wars that occurred in the first 125 years of Islamic history. The first civil war (556–561) began with the murder of the third caliph, ʿUthman, and ended after the assassination of the fourth caliph, ʿAli. Its consequence was the transfer of the caliphate to Muʿawiya, the founder of the Umayyad dynasty. The second *fitna* (680–692) began after the death of Muʿawiya and ended with the victory of the Marwanid branch of his dynasty. The third civil war began within the Umayyad dynasty, with the rebellion of Yazid III against Walid II in 744, and continued until the defeat of Marwan II and the overthrow of the Umayyads by the Abbasids in 750. The rise of the Abbasids was viewed as a new turn (*dawla*) in power. That term, *dawla*, came to mean the state as the Abbasid rule continued for centuries. Modern scholarship concurs that this change of dynasty in the mid-eighth century was of fundamental importance and generally refers to it as the Abbasid revolution.

If revolution is taken to mean a fundamental change in the political order and its social base, then the rise of Islam itself can be considered a revolution. The rise of Islam (622–632) was primarily a religious revolution that saw itself as the realization of Messianism, but it entailed a political revolution in Arabia and immediate expansion into the Roman and Persian empires. Muhammad succeeded in creating a unified community and state out of the segmentary tribal society of Arabia. He mobilized those who accepted Islam as a new monotheistic religion for "struggle (jihad) in the path of God," and unified the refractory tribes of Arabia on the basis of the acceptance of his Prophecy. Immediately upon completing the unification of Arabia after his death, his successors, the caliphs, redirected the energy the Prophet had thus mobilized, turning their attention toward the conquest of the Byzantine and Persian empires. The result of their efforts was the exportation of Islam and its gradual spread through vast conquered lands, from North Africa to Central Asia and northern India.

The subject populations of these conquered lands were converted to Islam only very gradually. Under the Umayyads (660–750), the Muslim empire remained an Arab empire. The non-Arabs who converted to Islam became the clients (*mawali*) of the Arabs, and did not have a share in political power. As the number of people in the client class grew in the second quarter of the eighth century, so did their demand for equal treatment as fellow believers in Islam. A movement with this as its aim gained momentum among the converts of Islam in Khurasan and Central Asia, whose adherents later became known as the *Murji'a*, but in fact called themselves "the people for equality."

The Shi'ite sects took advantage of the discontent among the *mawali* to form underground revolutionary organizations on behalf of different branches of the House of the Prophet, raising these as alternatives to the ruling Umayyads. These clandestine revolutionaries made messianic claims for their leaders as the Mahdi, the reviver of religion and redeemer of the world. They remained united, however, by not naming their messianic leader. Rather, he was anonymously referred to as the one to be agreed upon (*al-rida*) from the House of Muhammad.

The Shi'ites favored the House of 'Ali (the Prophet's son-in law) and were mostly active in Medina and Kufa. But the party of the House of 'Abbas (the Prophet's uncle) began proselytizing in Khurasan. The Abbasid leader, Abu Muslim, began his open rebellion in Khurasan while the Umayyad Empire was torn by an internecine civil war after a period of military overextension in North Africa. An army recruited by Abu Muslim defeated the governor of Khurasan and several Umayyad armies in Iran, and, finally, the last Umayyad caliph, Marwan II, near the river Zab in northern Mesopotamia in 750. The Khurasanian army proceeded to Kufa, brought the Abbasid family out of hiding, and proclaimed one of them, Abu 'l-'Abbas 'Abd Allah b. Muhammad, the new caliph over the objection of the Kufan revolutionary elite. The revolutionary power struggle continued under Abu 'l-'Abbas (750–754), and the real consolidation of Abbasid power took place under his brother and successor, Abu Ja'far, who later assumed the title of al-Mansur (754–775).

The first step in the consolidation of Abbasid power was the elimination of Abu Muslim, in 755. Then came Abu Ja'far's break with Shi'ism and his other former revolutionary partners. Descendants of the House of 'Ali were not only excluded from power but also persecuted. Abu Ja'far's former allies, who claimed he had in fact pledged allegiance to their

Mahdi, Muhammad b. 'Abdallah b. al-Hasan, finally rose under the latter's leadership in 762, but their rebellion was suppressed with much bloodshed.

Effects of the Abbasid Revolution

The Abbasid revolution was the social revolution of Islam, and created a more integrated polity defined in terms of Islam. The subject populations became integrated into the Abbasid Empire as Muslims in their own right, and no longer lived as disprivileged clients of the Arabs. The Abbasid caliphs embarked on an empirewide recruitment of the new political elite from the local notable families as well as the Arab tribal aristocracy, and opened their bureaucracy more widely to Iranians and Nestorian Christians. Military careers were opened to Iranian and, later, Turkish converts. Non-Arab Muslims were not only integrated into the Abbasid imperial administration and armies but also fully participated in the cultural elaboration of Islam as a universalist religion of salvation, making major contributions to the collection of the traditions of the Prophet (hadith) and the development of Islamic law, and even to the development of the Arabic language as Islam's lingua franca.

After the second civil war, which ended in 692, the caliphate had gradually been transformed from a regime of patriarchal rule over a coalition of nomadic conquerors into an imperial government employing Arab-speaking clients into its bureaucracy. This process was completed after the Abbasid revolution, and an elaborate central government emerged, divided into a number of departments (*diwan*s): a chancery, an imperial postal and inspection service, and taxation and army bureaus, each functioning under a *wazir*. Thus, like modern social revolutions, the Abbasid revolution resulted in the centralization of administration and concentration of power, inaugurating an era of caliphal absolutism.

See also **Assassins; Empires: Abbasid; Empires: Umayyad; Fitna; Shi'a: Early; Succession.**

BIBLIOGRAPHY

Humphreys, R. S. *Islamic History: A Framework of Inquiry.* Rev. ed. Princeton, N.J.: Princeton University Press.

Lapidus, I. M. *A History of Islamic Societies.* Cambridge, U.K.: Cambridge University Press, 1988.

Wellhausen, J. *The Arab Kingdom and Its Fall.* Beirut: Khayyats, 1963.

Saïd A. Arjomand

ISLAMIC REVOLUTION IN IRAN

The Iranian Revolution, which occurred between 1978 and 1979, has been called the last major revolution of the twentieth century. It marked the end of the rule of monarch Reza Shah Pahlevi and the beginning of the establishment of a theocratic state in Iran. It was urban based, meaning that

During the Iranian Revolution of 1978–1979, mass demonstrations rather than a concerted military effort brought the end of the rule of monarch Reza Shah Pahlavi. Here, with posters of the Ayatollah Khomeini (who replaced the shah after the Revolution), the Iranian army shows its solidarity with street protesters. GETTY IMAGES

many of the revolutionary groups were from the city and not peasants from the periphery. The main political instruments that brought down the shah's regime were strikes and mass demonstrations and not a concerted military action. Although the overarching ideology of the revolution was that of Shi'ite Islam cloaked in third-world sentiments, it was in actuality a multiclass coalition of widely disparate groups, from liberal nationalists to Islamic radicals, that finally overthrew the shah. The anti-shah movement was also largely detached from the international context, with little direct military or political support from outside Iran. The Iranian Revolution was so spontaneous and unexpected that it took many analysts and observers by surprise. In fact, as late as August and September of 1978, U.S. intelligence reports still indicated that opposition groups did not pose a threat to the shah's regime.

The Failure of the Pahlevi Regime

The shah's autocratic rule is widely viewed to be an important factor contributing to the rise of revolutionary action. The shah, Mohammad Reza Pahlevi, maintained total control over the Majlis (national assembly), the cabinet, the bureaucracy, and Iran's political parties. Restricted freedom, arbitrary decisions, and political repression by the Ministry of Security (known as SAVAK), as well as widespread corruption, cronyism, and bureaucratic inefficiency, are all cited by many observers as the ultimate forces that finally led to the downfall of the shah.

In addition, the Pahlevi dynasty's claim to legitimacy was irreparably damaged after the August 1953 coup, which was organized by the U.S. Central Intelligence Agency (CIA) and British intelligence, overthrew the democratically elected government of then–prime minister Mohammad Mosaddeq and reinstalled the young shah to the throne. In the mid-1970s, human rights organizations and the Western press started a campaign against violations of human rights in Iran and criticized the shah for the mistreatment of political prisoners. The administration of U.S. president Jimmy Carter sought to compel the shah to be more observant of human rights, but hoped to avoid destabilizing Iran or jeopardizing the close ties between the two countries. Responding to increasing criticism, the shah decided to permit a limited amount of public discourse. Unfortunately, the public perceived the shah's liberalization process as a sign of weakness. Further exacerbating the situation was the shah's massive modernization program (the so-called White Revolution of 1962) and his embrace of westernization, both of which alienated large parts of Iranian society. The White Revolution embodied a variety of economic and social initiatives, including land reform, public ownership of industries, enfranchisement of women, profit-sharing for workers, and a literacy corps to implement compulsory education in rural areas. However, it was opposed by landowners, who were afraid that they would lose the main source of their wealth, and by the ulema, who were alarmed by the spread of secular education and the propagation of anti-Islamic values.

Heedless of his subjects' growing dissatisfaction, the shah set forth to westernize Iranian society, patterning it along American lines. This process of the Americanization of Iranian society was undertaken with the help of American planners. Military personnel and U.S. advisors were granted legal latitude so broad as to constitute personal immunity from prosecution. The shah failed to realize that his plans for modernization, intended to foster a political environment capable of sustaining the nation's political and economic growth, neglected to recognize the importance of religion and culture in Iranian society.

The Rise of the Ayatollah

The Ayatollah Ruhollah Khomeini denounced the shah's modernization program, focusing his attacks on the new electoral law enfranchising women and the referendum that endorsed the White Revolution. He declared the new electoral law un-Islamic and the referendum unconstitutional. Khomeini called upon his followers to protest, leading to the riots that erupted in 1963, but such public demonstrations were brutally crushed by the shah. Khomeini was arrested and detained in Tehran for two months. In late 1964, when the shah extended diplomatic immunity to his American military advisors, Khomeini accused the ruler of betraying Iran and endangering Islam.

This time Khomeini was deported to Turkey, from where he subsequently moved to the holy city of Najaf, in Iraq. In his years in exile he continued to attack the shah's policies, denounced the whole institution of monarchy, confronted the religious establishment through a series of lectures condemning the ulema as apolitical, and organized his growing cadre of supporters. It was during those years that he produced his most famous handbook, *Velayat-e faqih hokumat-e Islami* (The jurist's guardianship: Islamic government), in which he argued that the shah's monarchy was incompatible with Islam and that true Muslims must strive for an Islamic

government under the leadership of the *faqih*, or Muslim jurist. In the early 1970s, Khomeini moved to Paris, which had a growing population of Iranian expatriots. There he gathered other exiled opposition leaders around him.

Two social groups were very much disaffected by the shah's rule/policies, the *bazaari*s (merchants) and the ulema. These established close ties with one another, and proved to be a formidable alliance, in which the *bazaari*s provided financial support to the ulema through the payment of tithes. In return for this financial support, the religious community provided the leadership and organizational backbone for the antigovernment alliance.

Iran's estimated 8,000 mosques provided an efficient nationwide communication network. The mosques served as centers for dissent, political organization, agitation, and sanctuary. In this context, revolutionary Shi'ite Islam was rapidly transformed into a discursive ideology that transcended class differences and social divisions and provided an effective channel of communication between dissident leaders and their followers. When the shah's minister of information planted an article in a daily newspaper attacking Khomeini and attempting to discredit him, protesting religious students in Qom staged sit-ins, which in turn led to violent repression from the shah. Some time later, several hundred demonstrators were killed during the government suppression of nonviolent protests, an event that came to be known as the "Black Friday massacre" and "Jahleh square massacre."

The deaths of the demonstrators were used to inspire a further round of protests. Mourning processions were staged to commemorate the protestors, hailing them as heroes and martyrs. Ayatollah Khomeini himself was viewed by many as the charismatic leader and provided the inspiration for the revolutionary movement. He was one of half a dozen Shi'ite *marja'-e taqlid* (source of emulation), a position that permitted him to widely publicize his views, but it was his pre-exile vehemence against the shah that garnered him his most fervent followers. Indeed, his vehement political stand against the shah, which led to his exile in 1964. Khomeini was also credited with expounding the theory of government that claimed that during the Mahdi's absence the community could only be governed by a *velayat-e faqih*. He could be the only person to execute God's will on behalf of the Hidden Imam, an agency with the mandate to rule both politically and spiritually. His conceptual reformulation of the originally quietist precept was innovative.

Postrevolutionary Government

Although antimodernization and anti-Western sentiment played an important role in the downfall of the Pahlevi dynasty, economic factors were also important. Industrial development did take place in Iran, but it proceeded very unevenly and was dependent on the state, oil revenues, and external technology. The oil sector expanded or contracted primarily in response to the world market, rather than to domestic economic needs. Partially as a result of this, Iran experienced a phase of hyperinflation, growing unemployment, a rising cost of living, and an erosion of business confidence. All of this resulted in a decline in private investment and in massive capital flight, totaling more than $100 million a month in 1975 and 1976. Strikes by oil workers and bank employees further devastated the economy of the shah's regime.

In the aftermath of the revolution, the political situation was inflamed by the struggle between secular and religious forces, by the existence of rival bases of power, and the emergence of autonomous revolutionary organizations. As the central state disintegrated, local, self-appointed committees (*komitehs*) were formed to carry out the basic tasks of security and administration. In February 1979, revolutionary tribunals staffed by religious judges were set up to pass sentence on former officials of the shah's regime, as well as on private individuals who were accused of counterrevolutionary activities. In May 1979, Khomeini ordered the formation of the *Pasdaran*, an armed force that was distinct from the regular army and deployed against opponents of the revolution. In an attempt to provide an organizational structure to the ideology of the Islamic revolution, a group of *ayatollahs* close to Khomeini formed the Islamic Republic Party (IRP) in mid-1979. The IRP sought to mobilize popular support for the Islamic Republic and to discredit the secular moderates.

The religious forces, led by Khomeini, used political maneuvering, propaganda, and terror to eliminate all opposition. The *Mujahedin-e Khalq* (an anticlerical opposition organization) were forced underground, and members of the Tudeh Party (Labor-Communist Party) and the *Fedayin-e Islam* (Devotees of Islam, a religio-political organization) were either jailed or executed. Throughout this period of consolidation, clerics and their supporters effectively eliminated the secular nationalist faction and other opponents to their rule. The chaotic postrevolutionary situation was ultimately clarified by a national referendum on the future of Iran that resulted in an overwhelming victory for Khomeini's vision of an Islamic Republic. Elections for a Constituent Assembly charged with drafting a constitution for the Islamic Republic were also won by Khomeini's supporters and further consolidated the authority of the religious forces. The resultant constitution institutionalized the principle of the *velayat-e faqih* (rule by a supreme religious leader). The constitution also created a 270-seat Majlis to write and pass new laws subject to the *faqih*'s (that is, Khomeini's) approval. The Assembly of Experts—an elected body of seventy to eighty eminent Islamic scholars—was made responsible for such high matters of state as revising the constitution and selecting a successor to the *faqih*. A twelve-member Council of Guardian, selected by the *faqih* and the Majlis, was created

An effigy of the Statue of Liberty in a demonstration in Tehran during a 2002 rally to mark the twenty-third anniversary of Iran's Islamic Revolution. Tens of thousands of Iranians gathered to protest repeated US condemnations of their country. GETTY IMAGES

to screen and, if necessary, modify all legislation issued from the Majlis before passing it on to the *faqih* for his approval, and to ensure that all candidates for Iran's newly established presidency possessed the proper Islamic credentials. It is the *faqih* and the Majlis that select the members of the council. The first presidential and legislative elections were held in early 1980, and again resulted in sweeping victories for Khomeini's handpicked candidates.

See also **Imamate; Iran, Islamic Republic of; Khomeini, Ruhollah; Majlis; Muhammad Reza Shah Pahlevi; Velayat-e Faqih.**

BIBLIOGRAPHY

Arjomand, Said Amir. *The Turban for the Crown.* Oxford: Oxford University Press, 1988.

Milani, Mohsen M. *The Making of Iran's Islamic Revolution. From Monarchy to Islamic Republic.* 2d ed. Boulder, Colo.: Westview Press, 1994.

Kristian P. Alexander

MODERN

Modern revolutions are generally viewed as part of the process of political modernization. Although marking a breakdown in the process of state-building and constituting a radical rupture with the past, they are often caused by obstacles in the path of political modernization and can result in far-reaching political transformation. The first wave of modern revolutions in the Islamic world occurred in the first decade of the twentieth century, in reaction to the suspension or frustration of the attempts at political reform.

Early-Twentieth-Century Constitutional Revolutions

Popular agitation for reform in Iran began in 1905, and forced the shah to order elections for a parliament and to grant Iran a constitution in 1906. It is therefore appropriately called the "Constitutional Revolution." The ailing Mozaffar al-Din Shah died shortly after signing the constitution at the end of December 1906. No sooner had the second part of the constitution (the Supplementary Fundamental Law) taken effect in October 1907 than serious trouble began between the constitutionalists and his successor. The Shi'ite religious leaders had been prominent in mobilizing popular agitation for the constitution, but were split when the secularizing implications of parliamentary legislation became clear to them. The young Muhammad 'Ali Shah formed an alliance with the Shi'ite traditionalists, suspended the constitution, and restored autocratic rule in 1908. Constitutional government was restored, however, after his defeat and ouster in July 1909.

The Turkish revolution of 1908 was also the result of a constitutionalist movement, this time led by the Young Turks and organized by their Committee of Union and Progress. It began with scattered revolts of military units led by army officers who belonged to the movement. They ultimately forced Sultan 'Abd al-Hamid (1842–1918) to restore the Ottoman Constitution of 1876, after a thirty-year gap. The Committee of Union and Progress won a decisive majority in the parliamentary elections of that year. In April 1909, however, the sultan instigated an abortive counterrevolutionary uprising in Istanbul among traditionalist religious students and officers who had been purged from the old army corps. This uprising, similar to the traditional counterrevolution in Iran a year earlier, ultimately failed, and the sultan was deposed in favor of his brother. The Young Turks amended the constitution and strengthened the power of parliament, and remained in power until the end of the First World War in 1918. During their tenure, however, they carried out a program of administrative reform and military modernization.

The Arab World After the Second World War

The modern revolutions of the Arab Middle East occurred after the end of the Second World War. Following the fashion of the time, especially in Latin America, military officers carried out *coups d'état* in Egypt, Syria, and Iraq in the 1950s, and in Yemen, Libya, and the Sudan in the 1960s, proclaiming them to be revolutions. These events became understood as a revolutionary wave washing across the Arab world, and were primarily motivated by Arab nationalism. Of these regime changes by the military, the two cases with the strongest claim to being considered modern revolutions are the July 1952 revolution in Egypt and the July 1958 revolution in Iraq, both of which overthrew monarchies and established republics.

Army officers were among the first groups to receive a modern, Westernized education in the Middle East. Imbued with ideas of nationalism and modernization of the state, they were considered "intellectuals in uniform" in the 1950s. In July 1952, a group of Egyptian officers of the rank of colonel or below, who called themselves the Free Officers, overthrew the ruling monarchy of the descendants of Muhammad 'Ali (1804–1841). They proclaimed a republic and named a respected army general its president. The real power, however, was in the hands of the leader of the Free Officers, Col. Jamal 'Abd al-Nasser (1918–1970), who abolished all political parties in 1953 and proscribed the Muslim Brotherhood in 1954. In its place he created the Liberation Rally, followed by the National Union in 1956, which became the Arab Socialist Union after Nasser's adoption of socialism as the ideology of the Egyptian state in 1961. Nasser immediately championed pan-Arab nationalism, which became so closely identified with him that it was sometimes called "Nasserism." He succeeded in bringing about a United Arab Republic, to which Syria, Iraq, Yemen, and Libya adhered for brief periods. The war against Israel in 1967 was primarily justified in terms of Arab nationalism, and the defeat of the Arab coalition was taken as a clear signal of its failure and of the failure of socialism as a modernizing ideology.

In July 1958, the Iraqi Free Officers overthrew the Hashimite monarchy that had been established under the British protectorate in 1921. They declared Iraq a republic, with General 'Abd al-Karim Qasim (1914–1963) as its prime minister. The revolution set in motion an intense competition for popular mobilization between the Iraqi Communist Party and the pan-Arab Ba'th Party. This competition culminated in an insurrection that brought the Ba'th party into power in February 1963, and General Qasim was executed that year.

Nationalism was the defining feature of the Egyptian and Iraqi revolutions, and it was most clearly reflected in the foreign policies of these countries. The idea of social reform was not absent, and both regimes carried out land reforms. The main impact of the respective revolutions on their economies and societies was, however, the result of the adoption of socialism and a wave of nationalizations in Egypt in 1961, and the coming to power of the Ba'th Party in Iraq in 1963.

The Iranian Experiment

The most important revolution in the twentieth-century Middle East, and the one with the greatest social and international impact, was the Islamic revolution of 1979 in Iran. Although it fits the pattern of revolution as part of the process of modernization of the state, its unique feature was the replacement of Islam for constitutionalism, nationalism, and socialism as the ideology of revolutionary transformation.

See also **Modernization, Political: Constitutionalism; Reform: Arab Middle East and North Africa; Revolution: Islamic Revolution in Iran; Young Turks.**

BIBLIOGRAPHY

Afary, J. *The Iranian Constitutional Revolution, 1906–1911.* New York: Columbia University Press, 1996.

Arjomand, S. A. *The Turban for the Crown: The Islamic Revolution in Iran.* New York: Oxford University Press, 1988.

Batatu, H. *The Old Social Classes and the Revolutionary Movements of Iraq.* Princeton, N.J.: Princeton University Press, 1978.

Godron, J. *Nasser's Blessed Moment. Egypt's Free Officers and the July Revolution.* New York: Oxford University Press, 1991.

Kansu, A. *The Revolution of 1908 in Turkey.* Leiden: E. J. Brill, 1997.

Sharabi, H. *Nationalism and Revolution in the Arab World.* New York: D. Van Nostrand Co., 1966.

Sohrabi, N. "Historicizing Revolutions: Constitutional Revolutions in the Ottoman Empire, Iran, and Russia, 1905–1908." *American Journal of Sociology* 100, no. 6 (1995): 1383–1447.

Saïd A. Arjomand

REZA SHAH (1878–1944)

Shah Reza Khan was the founder and first shah of the Pahlavi dynasty of Iran. The exact date of his birth is uncertain but has been fixed officially as 16 March 1878. He died in exile in South Africa on 26 July 1944.

Reza was born into a family of modest means in Alasht in Mazandaran, Iran, and joined the Russian-officered Iranian Cossack Brigade. In 1920 the British officer Major-General Sir Edmund Ironside organized the removal of the Russian officers and placed Reza Khan in command of the Iranian cossacks at Qazvin. From Qazvin, Reza Khan, in partnership with the pro-British journalist, Sayyed Ziya al-Din Tabataba'i, launched a coup, taking control of Tehran on 21 February 1921.

After the coup, Reza Khan received the title of Sardar-e Sipah (army commander) and in May became Minister of

War. In October 1923 he became Prime Minister. He organized the deposition of the reigning monarch, Ahmad Shah Qajar, and ascended the throne in April 1926.

Immediately after the coup, Reza Khan began the task of constructing a modern army and, using this army, he then proceeded to suppress the autonomy of the tribes and the regional magnates, later he adopted a policy of enforced sedentarization of the nomadic tribes. In the late 1920s, a number of radical, centralizing reforms were introduced, including the secularization of the judicial system, as well as a series of etatiste economic measures. In 1935, following a visit to Ataturk's Turkey, he banned female veiling.

The regime that was headed by the semiliterate Reza Shah became increasingly authoritarian and finally dictatorial. His brutality, which included the murder of many of his closest supporters, and his mania for land acquisition, through which he had become the largest landowner in the country, made his regime increasingly unpopular. He was unable to preserve his country's independence after the outbreak of the Second World War, and on 25 August 1941 British and Soviet armies invaded Iran. On 16 September he was obliged to abdicate in order to secure the succession for his son. Reza Shah went into exile in South Africa.

See also **Modernization, Political: Authoritarianism and Democratization.**

BIBLIOGRAPHY

Cronin, Stephanie. *The Army and the Creation of the Pahlavi State in Iran.* London and New York: I. B. Tauris, 1997.

Stephanie Cronin

RIBA

Of all the economic proscriptions in the Qur'an, the most controversial has been the ban on *riba*, the pre-Islamic lending practice held responsible for pushing destitute Arab borrowers into enslavement. According to some early Muslims, this ban was meant to cover all interest, regardless of form, context, or magnitude; for others, the ban's intended scope was limited to exorbitant interest charges. Although the restrictive definition triumphed, as a matter of practice the giving and taking of interest continued, at times through the use of legal ruses (*hiyal*), often more or less openly.

The latest chapter of this old controversy was ignited in the 1940s by the emergence of "Islamic economics," a school of thought that aims to purge interest from all economic operations. The accomplishments of this school include the establishment of Islamic banks in over seventy countries and the banning of interest in three of them: Pakistan, Iran, and the Sudan. Islamic banks claim that they avoid giving or taking interest, but they have found it impractical to obey their own charters. Interest is disguised under a variety of charges.

Various critics of Islamic economics, including secular economists and Islamic modernists, believe that the goal of eradicating interest is both misguided and unfeasible. Distinguishing between *riba* and ordinary interest, these critics hold that interest is indispensable to any complex economy, that competitive financial markets limit interest charges, and that bankruptcy laws now exist to protect borrowers against the horrors once produced by *riba*.

See also **Economy and Economic Institutions.**

BIBLIOGRAPHY

Chapra, M. Umer. *Towards a Just Monetary System.* Leicester, U.K.: Islamic Foundation, 1985.

Kuran, Timur. "The Economic Impact of Islamic Fundamentalism." In *Fundamentalisms and the State: Remaking Polities, Economies, and Militance.* Edited by Martin E. Marty and R. Scott Appleby. Chicago: University of Chicago Press, 1993.

Timur Kuran

RIDA, RASHID (1865–1935)

Rashid Rida was the most prominent disciple of Muhammad ʿAbduh and one of the most influential scholars and jurists of his generation. Rida was born near Tripoli, in present-day Lebanon. His early education consisted of training in traditional Islamic subjects and a brief, disenchanting exposure to the secular curriculum of the Ottoman government school in Tripoli. His reformist views began to form in 1884–1885 when he was first exposed to Jamal al-Din Afghani's and ʿAbduh's journal al-ʿUrwa al-wuthqa (The firmest grip). In 1897, Rida left Syria for Cairo to collaborate with ʿAbduh. The following year he launched al-Manar, first a weekly and then a monthly journal comprising Qurʾanic commentary (begun by ʿAbduh, continued by Rida, but never completed) and opinions on pressing legal, political, and social issues of the day. Like ʿAbduh, Rida based his reformist principles on the argument that the *shariʿa* consists of ʿibadat (worship) and muʿamalat (social relations). Human reason has little scope in the former and Muslims should adhere to the dictates of the Qurʾan and hadith. The laws governing *muʿamalat* should conform to Islamic ethics but on specific points may be continually reassessed according to changing conditions of different generations and societies. Unlike ʿAbduh, Rida narrowed the *salaf* (the "pious ancestors" as authoritative interpreters of Islamic tradition) to include only the Prophet's companions and immediate successors.

See also ʿ**Abduh, Muhammad.**

BIBLIOGRAPHY

Adams, Charles C. *Islam and Modernism in Egypt: A Study of the Modern Reform Movement Inaugurated by Muhammad ʿAbduh.* New York: Russell and Russell, 1968.

Kerr, Malcolm H. *Islamic Reform: The Political and Legal Theories of Muhammad ʿAbduh and Rashid Rida.* Berkeley: University of California Press, 1966.

Sohail H. Hashmi

RITUAL

Ritual is a term that indicates more or less fixed acts and actions that take place at certain recurrent moments and in which certain bodily gestures, words, music, and material objects may play a role.

Theories

In the past, the word ritual referred to religious ritual acts and to the rules regarding these acts. Therefore, the Roman Catholic *Rituale Romanum* (1614) and the famous Islamic work on Islamic ritual and law, the *Mukhtasar* of the Malikite scholar Khalil ibn Ishaq al-Jundi (b. c. 1374), are comparable phenomena in the sense that they both prescribe rituals. Early twentieth-century scholars of religion such as Sigmund Freud and the biologist Julian Huxley began to use the word ritual in a much broader meaning. Freud used it to describe compulsive acts and movements of neurotic patients, and Huxley for certain animal acts and behaviors. Since then there has been a tendency to use ritual in a broad sense. Hence, rituals can no longer be associated solely with the domain of religion. They play an important role in many fields of public and private life; for example, in political life, war, festivals, and feasts.

Many nineteenth-century students of religion, particularly those educated in the tradition of liberal, modern theology and later the phenomenologists of religion, tended to view ritual as merely an illustration of religious beliefs and myths. At the other end of the spectrum, scholars such as William Robertson-Smith and Émile Durkheim held the opposite view, namely that ritual is more basic than beliefs. Later scholars have tried to overcome the belief-action dichotomy by formulating notions such as habitus (learned techniques, including such basic activities as running, etc.) and discourse/discursive practice (Talal Asad) which stresses the embodied nature of beliefs or the unity of actions and beliefs. Four brief theoretical observations should be made.

1. In the course of time, rituals may *change*. In general, they tend to become more complex. Therefore, in many religions (including Islam) ritual specialists exist. These ritual specialists have different names in different parts of the world and in different religious settings. The pilgrimage to

Mecca, a very complex ritual, is guided by specialists as well.

2. The meaning of rites may be subject to *reinterpretation*. For example, according to modernist interpretations, purity rules have their background in hygiene, that is, they claim that the original meaning of these regulations has its base in conceptions of clean and dirty, thereby diminishing their religious, symbolic, meaning. For example, in traditional Islam, a menstruating woman is not *allowed* to perform the *salat* (ritual prayer) because she is ritually unclean. The modernists argue that it is *permitted* to her not to do so, on account of her being ill. Such interpretations are for obvious reasons called "medical materialism." They attempt to give a modern, "scientific" explanation.

3. In many periods of Islamic history, reformists have *criticized* ritual behavior that deviated from orthodox norms and values. This criticism is especially apparent in the orthodox reform movement of the end of the nineteenth century (Muhammad ʿAbduh [1849–1905], Muhammad Rashid Rida [1865–1935]), but we also come across it in the work of the neo-modernist Fazlur Rahman (1910–1988). He sharply criticizes forms of Sufism for teaching superstitionism, miracle mongering, tomb-worship, mass-hysteria and, of course, charlatanism (Islam, p. 246).

4. The existence of historical meanings does not mean that all participants in rituals are fully *aware of these meanings*. Muslims in the Netherlands, when asked about the meaning of shaving one's hair on the occasion of the *ʿaqiqa* ritual (see below), simply answered that it was part of their religion, or that by doing so, the hair would become thicker (Dessing, p. 30ff). In other words, rituals may drift out of meaning or acquire new meaning in changed circumstances, for example, as a result of "transplantation" to a Western country, or as result of the secularization of rituals.

Catherine Bell distinguishes six major categories of rites: rites of passage or "life crisis" rituals; calendrical or commemorative rites; rites of exchange and communion; rites of affliction; rites of feasting, fasting and festivals; and, finally, political rites. These categories will be applied here to the major Islamic rites. I have added a seventh category, rites of communication.

Rites of Communication

This type of rite mainly serves to communicate with God, *jinn* and *zar* spirits, or with deceased humans (saints, prophets). The most important example is the *salat*, or ritual prayer. According to Islam, it is a human obligation to communicate with God in prayer, or as Sura 51:56 has it: "Jinn and humans are created only to worship God." In the *salat*, the Qurʾan is to be recited as if it were revealed onto the believer's heart. The performance of the *salat* includes a number of more or less fixed bodily movements, which express core religious values. According to tradition, during the *salat* the believer speaks with his Lord. In the *salat*, there is also space for saying invocations of a personal nature, *duʿaʾ*. Prayer as well as other Islamic rituals, for example those involved in saint veneration, are in one way or the other related to notions of purity. A well-known tradition says, "Purity is half the faith." The overall term for these notions is *tahara*, which means purity.

Rites of Passage or Life Cycle Rituals

Rites of passage mark the biological and spatial transitions in human life and give them cultural meaning. Sometimes the rites occur at the same time as the biological transition themselves, but they may occur earlier or later. Important steps towards a theory of ritual structures have been made by Arnold van Gennep and Victor Turner. Van Gennep noted the threefold structure of rites of passage in the life cycle and territorial passages. Each rite of passage is marked by phases of separation, transition (the so-called liminal phase, from the Latin word *limen*, threshold), and incorporation or reaggregation.

The most important rites of passage in Muslim religious life are: the naming and birth ritual (*subuʿ*, *ʿaqiqa*), circumcision, marriage, funerary rites, and the commemorative mourning rites that follow at certain fixed periods.

Depending on the stages in life, these three stages get different values, for example, by the complexity of the rites to be performed. One example is a child's initiation ritual in Islam, which is carried out on the seventh day after birth. The rite involves three interrelated elements: sacrifice of an animal (usually a sheep, *ʿaqiqa*), the name-giving rite, and shaving the hair of the baby.

An instance of a separation rite preceding these three acts is the bathing of the child, performed in some parts of the world at the beginning of the ritual. The bath symbolizes the separation from the mother (who had kept the child near her until then) and the introduction of the child to the natural world. The naming ritual, which confers an Islamic identity (often in accordance with the Prophet's injunction to the believers to call themselves by graceful names), and expresses its membership in the community, is closely connected to the sacrifice. Shaving and sacrifice may be seen as liminal rites, whereas the festive meal that often concludes the ritual and to which the family is invited, is an aggregation ritual.

Marriage is an important social, juridical event as well as a life cycle ritual with a number of fixed elements. At many ritual occasions, including marriage rituals, a festive meal (*walima*) is held.

Performing their ablutions before their daily prayer, Muslim schoolboys wash their hands and faces. © MICHAEL S. YAMASHITA/CORBIS

Calendrical Rituals

Calendrical rituals include seasonal (often agricultural) rites and commemorative rites. They are meant to give meaningful social definitions to the passage of time. The first rites are closely connected to the changes in the seasons. The second commemorative rites recall certain important events. As is explained in the article on the *ibadat*, rituals such as the *umra* and the *hajj* are seasonal rites in origin. Because of the abolishment of the intercalation in 31 C.E., Islamic rites are no longer tied to the solar calendar, and hence no longer tied to the changes of the seasons. The determination of the new months, by sighting the new moon, acquired ritual significance, especially in connection with the beginning and end of the fast in the month of Ramadan. In Islam, the narrative component in this ritual cycle is perhaps less present than in some other religions; nevertheless it appears, for example, in a very outspoken way in the poems about the birth and life of the Prophet, which are recited at various occasions.

The ritual cycle opens with 'Ashura on 10 Muharram. 'Ashura had been a fasting day before the revelation of the Ramadan fast, and it has remained a voluntary fasting day in Sunnite Islam until the present day. For Shiite Muslims 'Ashura is the day on which the martyrdom of the grandson of the Prophet, al-Husayn, at Karbala in 680 C.E., is commemorated by emotional and at times violent mourning rituals.

On 12 Rabi' I, the third month, the birthday of the Prophet is celebrated. On 27 Rajab, the Laylat al-Mi'raj, or ascension of the Prophet to the Heavens, is celebrated. The ascension of the Prophet to Heaven via Jerusalem (Isra'-Mi'raj) is one of the great symbols of Islam that serves as a (mystical) symbol of the ascension of the believer toward God. This is when the number of daily *salat*s was fixed at five. Elements of the ritual celebration may include recitation of *Surat al-isra'* (Sura 17), followed by commentaries, singing, and the recitation of religious poems.

The popularity of the celebration of the fifteenth middle night of Sha'ban can be explained by its age-old associations with the Divine which is believed to be made on that night with regard to those who will die the next year.

The month of Ramadan is marked by the fast and by Laylat al-Qadr (27 Ramadan). On 1 Shawwal, the Day of the Breaking of the Fast ('Id al-Fitr) is celebrated.

On 10 Dhu-l-Hijja, the twelfth month of the Islamic year, *'Id al-Adha* is celebrated. This ritual marks the end of the year, but in fact it does not represent the end of the ritual cycle, since there is a clear connection between the *'id* (feast day) and the 'Ashura rituals. The pilgrimage itself can also be seen as a rite of passage, in the sense that pilgrims set out for a place "out there," from which they return with a higher religious status, that is to say, as hajjis.

Rites of Exchange and Communion

The central element in these rites is an offering (sacrifice) or a gift. Major Islamic rites that can be mentioned are the 'aqiqa and the sacrifice at the occasion of 'Id al-Adha. Moreover, sacrifice can also take place in other settings, such as possession cults (see under rites of affliction). Votive offering may also be included here. Such offerings happen at the graves of the saints.

Rites of Affliction

These rituals heal, exorcise, protect, and purify. In Islam, they occur, for example, in the context of saint veneration, where people seek healing, and in possession cults. Possession cults are marked by public and private gatherings where sacrifice, dance and trance are central elements. Those who suffer from particular mental, social or physical problems seek healing by establishing contact with the spiritual world of the *jinn* and other meta-empirical beings such as the *zar*. Other examples of (public) rites of affliction are the special *salat*s to be performed at times of drought, or the recitation of Surat Ya Sin (Sura 36) in times of distress.

Rites of Feasting, Fasting and Festivals

These rites display both the hierarchical prestige social system and the interdependence or unity of human and divine worlds. The two major "canonical" festivals are 'Id al-Fitr and 'Id al-Adha (another name for the great feast, al-'Id al-Kabir). 'Id al-Fitr marks the end of Ramadan fast. Ramadan is the sacred month par excellence. This has to do with the communal aspects of the fast, which expresses a number of basic values of the Muslim community. As various scholars have argued, fasting may extol fundamental distinctions, lauding the power of the spiritual realm, while acknowledging the subordination of the physical realm. According to popular beliefs, the devils (*shayatin*) and *jinn* are powerless, while God is nearer then than during other months. This increased religious awareness culminates in Laylat al-Qadr, when, as some people believe, the gates of heaven are opened. After the *salat al-'id*, people will pay visits to relatives, which often includes visits to the graves (*ziyarat al-qubur*).

'Id al-Adha on 10 Dhu-l-Hijja, commemorating Ibrahim's readiness to sacrifice his son, marks the end of the pilgrimage (the *hajj*). Another major festival, the Mawlid al-Nabi, grew out of the Fatimid Shiite ritual practice (11th century C.E.). Nowadays, although it is celebrated nearly everywhere (although exceptions, such as Saudi Arabia, exist), its status as a feast has nevertheless remained controversial until the present time.

In Morocco, 'Ashura is a festival honoring the dead, and during which the participants give alms, eat dried fruit, and buy toys for their children. It is marked by reversal and carnival-like rituals such as masquerades, processions, and theater (Hammoudi 1993).

Political Rituals

These rites construct, display, and promote the power of political institutions. The early history of Islamic rituals has partly been determined by their relationship to politics. For example, the *salat al-jum'a* (Friday prayers) originally had political connotations as a medium to convey messages to the body politic. Muhammad's birthday festival also came into being in highly political surroundings, that is, as a palace ritual. It was meant to enhance the position of the Fatimid ruler. It stressed his bond with the prophet Muhammad and his family in particular. By giving presents to his most faithful servants, the ruler stressed the existing hierarchy in the Fatimid state. Later in the Middle East and the Islamic West, the celebration often continued to be a court ceremony, but became a popular festival as well. The Islamic world knows numerous truly political rites, such as, for example, the celebration of the accession to the throne in Morocco, or the anniversary of the death of well-known political figures, such as (again in Morocco) that of King Muhammad V.

See also **Circumcision; Death; 'Ibadat; Khutba; Law; Marriage; Pilgrimage: Hajj.**

BIBLIOGRAPHY

Abu Zaid, Nasr. *The Qur'an: Man and God in Communication.* Leiden: Leiden University, 2000.

Antoun, Richard T. "The Social Significance of Ramadan in an Arab Village." *The Muslim World* 58 (1968): 36–42; 95–104.

Asad, Talal. *The Idea of an Anthropology of Islam.* Washington: D.C.: Georgetown University Center for Contemporary Arab Studies, 1986.

Bell, Catherine. *Ritual: Perspectives and Dimensions.* New York, Oxford: Oxford University Press, 1997.

Bowen, John R. *Muslims through Discourse: Religion and Ritual in Gayo Society.* Princeton, N.J.: Princeton University Press, 1993.

Combs-Schilling, M. E. *Sacred Performances.* Islam, Sexuality, and Sacrifice. New York: Columbia University Press, 1989.

Denny, Frederick M. "Islamic Ritual. Perspectives and Theories." In *Approaches to Islamic Studies.* Edited by R. C. Martin. Oxford, U.K.: Oneworld, 2001.

Dessing, Nathal M. *Rituals of Birth, Circumcision, Marriage, and Death among Muslims in the Netherlands.* Leuven: Peeters, 2001.

Elad, Amikam. *Medieval Jerusalem and Islamic Worship: Holy Places, Ceremonies, Pilgrimage.* Leiden: E. J. Brill, 1995.

Goitein, Shlomo Dov. "The Origin and Nature of Muslim Friday Worship." In *idem: Studies in Islamic History and Institutions.* Leiden: E. J. Brill, 1966.

Goitein, Shlomo Dov. "Ramadan, the Muslim Month of Fasting." In *idem: Studies in Islamic History and Institutions.* Leiden: E. J. Brill, 1966.

Grunebaum, Gustav E. von. *Muhammadan Festivals* (1956). London: Curzon, 1992.

Haarmann, Ulrich. "Islamic Duties in History." *The Muslim World* 68 (1978): 1–24.

Hammoudi, Abdallah. *The Victim and Its Masques: An Essay on Sacrifice and Masquerade in the Maghreb.* Chicago and London: The University of Chicago Press, 1993.

Kaptein, Nico J. G. *Muhammad's Birthday Festival: Early History in the Central Muslim Lands and Development in the Muslim West until the 10th/16th Century.* Leiden: E. J. Brill, 1993.

Peters, Francis E. *The Hajj: The Muslim Pilgrimage to Mecca and the Holy Places.* Princeton, N.J.: Princeton University Press, 1994.

Rahman, Fazlur. *Islam.* London: Weidenfeld and Nicholson, 1966.

Shinar, Pesach. "Traditional and Reformist Mawlid Celebrations." In *Studies in Memory of Gaston Wiet.* Edited by M. Rosen Ayalon. Jerusalem: Institute of Asian and African Studies, Hebrew University of Jerusalem, 1977.

Tapper, Nancy, and Tapper, Richard. "The Birth of the Prophet: Ritual and Gender in Turkish Islam." *Man, New Series* 21 (1987): 69–92.

Westermarck, Edward. *Ritual and Belief in Morocco* (1926). 2 vols. New York: University Books, 1968.

Gerard Wiegers

Thirteenth-century mystical Persian poet Jalal al-Din Mohammad-e Balkhi, above, is known as Rumi in the West, where his works have been translated widely and have come to represent a profound and tolerant vision of Islamic spirituality. He founded the Mevlani Sufi sect of the Whirling Dervishes. THE ART ARCHIVE/ DAGLI ORTI (A)

RUMI, JALALUDDIN (1207–1273)

Jalaluddin Rumi is the name by which the Persian poet Jalal al-Din Mohammad-e Balkhi is conventionally known in the West. In the Muslim world he is generally called Maulavi or Maulana (Mevlana in Turkish), meaning, respectively, "my master" or "our master," a title reflecting the veneration in which he was held by his followers, who formed the Mevlevi (*Maulaviyya*) order of dervishes around his writings and example.

Life

The hagiographical sources portray Rumi's father, Baha' al-Din-e Valad, as one of the most important Hanafi scholars and theologians of his day, placing his family origins in Balkh (near Mazar-e Sharif in modern Afghanistan), one of the four great urban centers of the eastern Iranian cultural sphere in the pre-Mongol period. When Rumi was born in 1207, however, Baha' al-Din was living in Vakhsh, a small town located in what is now Tajikistan, acting as an itinerant preacher (*va'ez*) and religious scholar. It does not appear that Baha' al-Din belonged to any established Sufi order though a small group of disciples seems to have gathered around him. Inspired by dreams, Baha' al-Din began to sign his *fatwa*s as "Sultan al-ulema" ("King of the Clerics," or scholars of religion), an unauthorized title that the local religious judge

(*qadi*) in Vakhsh would erase. The resulting conflict, which can be dated to about 1208—as well perhaps as larger questions of political instability in the region—led Baha' al-Din to move to Samarkand, where Rumi recalls living during the Khwarazamshah's siege of the city, circa 1212.

Baha' al-Din left eastern Persia (Khorasan) with much of his family by about 1216, eventually obtaining positions as preacher or teacher in provincial Anatolia, where Persian was the court language. While the family was in Karaman (Larende), Rumi's mother, Mo'mena Khatun, died, and Rumi, at the age of about seventeen, married Gauhar Khatun, with whom he had two sons, including Sultan Valad (1226–1312), who would later play an instrumental role in founding the Mevlevi order. By 1229, Baha' al-Din had been invited by Sultan 'Ala al-Din Keiqobad (r. 1219–1237) to transfer to the Seljuk capital in Konya, where he taught until his death two years later. In 1232, Baha' al-Din's protégé, Borhan al-Din Mohaqqeq, arrived from Termez to take over the leadership of the disciples. Rumi was sent to Aleppo and Damascus to be educated, and he apparently also underwent a period of retreat and fasting under Borhan al-Din's direction. By the time Borhan al-Din died in 1241, Rumi had assumed leadership of Baha' al-Din's classes and the circle of disciples in Konya.

Rumi's teaching and spiritual praxis were noticeably altered under the influence of Shams al-Din Tabrizi, an itinerant religious scholar and mystic who came to Konya in 1244. It was perhaps under Shams's influence that Rumi began composing poetry. Shams's talks (preserved in *Maqalat-e Shams-e Tabrizi*) demonstrate his strong desire to create an authentic form of spirituality that dispensed with pretensions and imitative piety. This attitude possibly detracted from Rumi's reputation as a pious preacher, even though the ostensible goal of Shams's spirituality was to closely follow the example of the prophet Muhammad. The curtailing of Rumi's teaching activities to devote more attention to Shams also led to resentment on the part of some of his disciples. Apparently in response to this situation, Shams left Konya abruptly in the spring of 1246, sending Rumi into a state of despair during which he ceased composing poetry. After about a year's absence, Sultan Valad found Shams in Syria and convinced him to return to Konya. Shams, despite a marriage to a member of Rumi's extended household, soon disappeared again (c. 1248), never again to return to Konya. Rumi searched desperately for Shams, expressing his deep sense of loss in frenetic poems (mostly *ghazals*) that cast Shams in the role of spiritual guide, and were indeed frequently spoken through the persona of Shams of Tabriz. Eventually Rumi found his own voice, after internalizing what he had learned from Shams, and even addressed other individuals, first Salah al-Din the Goldsmith (d. 1258) and then Hosam al-Din Chelebi (d. c. 1284), to whom Rumi's *Masnavi* is addressed, as spiritual mentors. Throughout his life, Rumi maintained cordial relations with several Seljuk sultans and officials, some of whom expressed their devotion and extended their patronage to him.

The Mevlevi (*Maulaviyya*) order of "whirling dervishes," founded in the last quarter of the thirteenth century through the efforts of Sultan Valad, bases itself on Rumi's poetry and his practice of "turning" to music and verse (*sama'*). Rumi's mausoleum in Konya, though now a museum, has functioned as a shrine and center of the Mevlevi order, which has been particularly influential in the history of Sufism in Anatolia, the Balkans, and the Levant. Though this order was not active in South Asia, Rumi's poetry was widely read in the subcontinent and frequently commented upon by Sufis of other orders. Rumi's poetry and teachings have continued to exert an important influence on the thinking of Islamic modernists, such as Muhammad Iqbal in Pakistan, and 'Abd al-Karim Sorush in Iran.

Works

Rumi composed his *Masnavi-ye ma'navi* (Spiritual couplets; or Couplets of true meaning), a lengthy mystical-didactic

poem of some 25,000 lines, over several years, beginning circa 1262. It consists of a series of versified anecdotes and tales, often amusing and occasionally quite ribald, varying widely in length, style, and subject matter, and rather loosely organized into six books. The *Masnavi* illustrates a practical mysticism drawing from the Persian Sufi tradition, provides a poetic commentary on the meaning of the Qur'an and hadith, and expounds Rumi's views on many of the theological cruxes of Islam. It is arguably the most widely read and frequently glossed poem in the Muslim world, from Bosnia to Bengal.

The *Divan-e kabir*, or *Kolliyat-e Shams-e Tabrizi*, collects Rumi's lyrical poems, including some 3300 *ghazals*, *qasidas*, and strophic poems, along with just under two thousand quatrains (*ruba'iyat*). These poems are characterized by an intense sense of transcendent longing or loss; a frequently conversational, though philosophically rich, style; and a captivating rhythmic musicality (many of the poems seem indeed to have been composed, and are often performed, to instrumental accompaniment). German adaptations by Friedrich Rückert of some of these poems made an impression on the German philosopher Georg Wilhelm Friedrich Hegel, and initially gave Europeans the impression that Rumi was a pantheist. Subsequently, especially after Reynold Nicholson's complete explanatory translation of the *Masnavi* into English, Rumi became synonymous in the West of a deep and tolerant Islamic spirituality. In the last quarter of the twentieth century, dozens of popular versions and "translations" of Rumi's poems appeared in English free verse, many by individuals without any knowledge of the original Persian.

Rumi's prose works include the notes recorded by his disciples during lectures, informal sermons, and classes (*Fihe ma fih*, or Discourses); seven sermons delivered on formal occasions (*Majales-e sab'a*); and a number of letters (*Maktubat*).

See also **Persian Language and Literature.**

BIBLIOGRAPHY

Chittick, William. *The Sufi Path of Love: The Spiritual Teachings of Rumi*. Albany: State University of New York Press, 1983.

Lewis, Franklin. *Rumi: Past and Present, East and West*. Oxford, U.K.: Oneworld, 2000.

Rumi, Jalaluddin. *The Mathnawí of Jalálu'ddín Rúmí*. In E. J. W. Gibb Memorial Series. Edited and translated by Reynold A. Nicholson. London: Luzac & Co., 1925–1940.

Rumi, Jalaluddin. *Discourses of Rumi*. Translated by A. J. Arberry. London: J. Murray, 1961.

Schimmel, Annemarie. *The Triumphal Sun: A Study of the Works of Jalaloddin Rumi*. Rev. ed. Albany: State University of New York Press, 1993.

Franklin D. Lewis

RUSHDIE, SALMAN (1947–)

Salman Rushdie is a novelist and critic who became a household name after his fictional work, *The Satanic Verses*, was protested by numerous Muslims and Muslim groups. Ayatollah Ruhollah Khomeini pronounced a *fatwa* (legal opinion) sentencing Rushdie to death, and as a result Rushdie was forced into hiding in England from 1989 to 1998. In later years he moved to the United States, dividing his time between Los Angeles and New York City.

Rushdie was born to Muslim parents in Bombay, India, and was educated at the Cathedral School. In 1961, he left India to attend Rugby, a prestigious boarding school in England. Rushdie then attended King's College, Cambridge, where he wrote a paper on Muhammad and the origins of Islam for part of his honors examination in history. Early literary influences on Rushdie were the *Thousand and One Nights* and the Urdu poet Faiz Ahmed Faiz, a family friend.

Rushdie's first novel, *Grimus* (1975), was a variation of the medieval Sufi poet Farid al Din 'Attar's *The Conference of the Birds*. It was a commercial failure. His second novel, *Midnight's Children* (1981), was about the lives of 1001 children born at the stroke of midnight on India's independence from Britain. This book won him critical acclaim, including the 1981 Booker Prize. However, Rushdie's satirical portrayal of Indira Gandhi resulted in a lawsuit that was resolved only after a sentence considered particularly hurtful by Gandhi was omitted from subsequent editions. His third novel, *Shame* (1983), satirized Pakistani politics and politicians, such as Zulfikar Ali Bhutto and General Zia al-Haqq, in the way that its predecessor had satirized Indian politics. Clearly, Rushdie knew much about Islam, Muslims, and South Asian politics and culture.

The Satanic Verses (1988) was Rushdie's fourth novel, and dealt with the themes of migration, of being a member of a dark-skinned minority in England, and of the multiple identities that come with being Asian in London. The main character is Gibreel Farishta, an Urdu name that translated into English as "the Angel Gabriel." Beginning with the second chapter of the book, Gibreel has a series of dreams. The first of these features a character named Mahound, who is an orphan, a businessman living in a city named Jahilia, who through revelation begins to preach a religion called "Submission." This religion is, of course, Islam. In another chapter, Gibreel has a series of encounters with an exile known simply as "the Imam," who is intended to be recognized as the Ayatollah Ruhollah Khomeini.

The book was first banned in India on 5 October 1988 at the urging of several Indian Muslim politicians. Subsequently, the book was banned in South Africa (24 November 1988), burned publicly in Bradford, England (14 January 1989), and

Novelist Salman Rushdie, above, was forced into hiding for almost a decade when in 1989 the late Ayatollah Khomeini, leader of the Iranian Revolution, issued a *fatwa* demanding Rushdie's death. Khomeini and many other conservative Muslim leaders believed Rushdie's novel *The Satanic Verses* blasphemed Islam. CHUCK KENNEDY/GETTY IMAGES

protested against in Islamabad (where six people died during a riot on 12 February 1989) and Bombay (with twelve people killed in a riot on 24 February 1989). On 14 February 1989, Khomeini pronounced his death sentence on Rushdie. While distancing itself from Khomeini's death sentence, the eleventh session of the Islamic Law Academy of the Muslim World League (held in Mecca from 10 to 26 February 1989), issued a statement declaring Rushdie an apostate and recommending that he be prosecuted in a British court, and tried in absentia under the *shari'a* laws of an Islamic country.

On the whole, North American responses were much more muted and peaceful than in other countries. To take the case of Toronto, the city with the largest population of Canada's Muslims, there was a deliberate effort made by various Muslim communities to keep the protests nonviolent. The protests in Toronto were not used for political purposes, in the same way that they were used in, for example, Iran or India, and there was even some sympathy and tolerance expressed for Rushdie.

See also **Arabic Literature; Persian Language and Literature; South Asia, Islam in; Urdu Language, Literature, and Poetry.**

BIBLIOGRAPHY

Appignanesi, Lisa, and Maitland, Sara, eds. *The Rushdie File.* London: Fourth Estate, 1989.

Clark, Roger Y. *Stranger Gods: Salman Rushdie's Other Worlds.* Montreal: McGill-Queen's University Press, 2001.

Fischer, Michael M. J., and Abedi, Mehdi. *Debating Muslims: Cultural Dialogues in Postmodernity and Tradition.* Madison: University of Wisconsin Press, 1990.

Hussain, Amir. "Misunderstandings and Hurt: How Canadians Joined Worldwide Muslim Reactions to Salman Rushdie's *The Satanic Verses.*" *Journal of the American Academy of Religion* vol. 70, no. 1 (March 2002): 1–32.

Kamali, Mohammad Hashim. *Freedom of Expression in Islam.* Cambridge, U.K.: Islamic Texts Society, 1997.

Amir Hussain

S

SADAT, ANWAR AL- (1918–1981)

The future president of Egypt, Muhammad Anwar al-Sadat, was born on 25 December 1918 in a Nile Delta town, the son of an army clerk. Sadat grew up in Cairo and entered the military academy in 1938. In the army he joined a Muslim Brotherhood cell; there he met Jamal ʿAbd al-Nasser and other future Free Officers. Patriotic, yet reckless, he contacted German agents and conspired in the murder of a pro-British pasha. Recommissioned after eventual acquittal, he regained contact with dissident officers who seized power in July 1952.

A fellow conspirator, Sadat served the Nasser regime in various capacities. Vice president in 1970, he succeeded Nasser, supported by power brokers who thought to dominate him. Instead, he purged Nasserist foes in May 1971, then threw his support to Islamist activists, releasing jailed Muslim Brothers and allowing others to return from exile. In October 1973 he initiated war against Israel, scoring a political victory that led ultimately to normal relations. In 1974 he proclaimed an "opening" to Western investment and diminution of the public sector. For several years Sadat reaped glory as "hero of the crossing," a reference to his army's initial success in breaching Israeli defenses across the Suez Canal. In November 1977, after a stunning public declaration, he traveled to Jerusalem and addressed the Israeli Knesset. The following year he accepted an invitation from American president Jimmy Carter to join Israeli prime minister Menachem Begin at Camp David. The talks paved the way for a peace treaty in 1979.

Sadat became an international celebrity, but economic troubles, anti-Israeli sentiment, a surge of intercommunal violence, and his growing aloofness shattered public optimism at home. In uncharacteristic fashion, Sadat now turned against opponents from all political tendencies, secular and religious. In September 1981 he ordered sweeping arrests of political foes. On 6 October 1981, at a parade marking his October victory, he was assassinated by Islamist extremists. Sadat remains a controversial figure at home, and a balanced assessment of him still remains impossible twenty years later.

See also **ʿAbd al-Nasser, Jamal; Reform: Arab Middle East and North Africa.**

BIBLIOGRAPHY

Beattie, Kirk J. *Egypt During the Sadat Years.* New York: Palgrave, 2000.

Joel Gordon

SADIQ, JAʿFAR AL- *See* Jaʿfar al-Sadiq

SADR

Dating from eleventh-century Transoxiana in Central Asia, by the Timurid period (fourteenth century) the *sadr* referred to the chief, government-appointed officer who oversaw the management of state and private religious endowments (*awqaf*); the appointment of mosque, madrasa, and other religious personnel; and cared for the poor, needy, and orphans. Up until the late sixteenth century, the first Safavid century, provincial *sadr*s also existed, but they were not always under the direct authority of the central-government *sadr*.

The Safavids also formalized the Timurid practice of dividing the responsibilities of the post between two figures, one overseeing the endowments bequeathed by the shah and the other those left by private individuals, with the former seemingly the preeminent figure, and gradually also divided the authority of the two along geographical lines. As befit the highly personalized nature of Safavid politics, however, one individual might hold both posts, and an individual holding another post at court might also be appointed *sadr*. The post was nearly always held by a religious scholar, a *sayyid* (descendant of the Prophet), in both Timurid and Safavid times.

BIBLIOGRAPHY

Floor, Willem. "The *Sadr* or Head of the Safavid Religious Administration, Judiciary and Endowments and Other Members of the Religious Administration." *Zeitschrift der Deutschen Morgenländischen Gesellschaft* 150 (2000): 461–500.

Andrew J. Newman

SADR, MUHAMMAD BAQIR AL- (1930–1980)

Muhammad Baqir al-Sadr was a scholar and revered figure of Shi'a in Iraq. He wrote widely on matters of Islamic economics and modern logic and philosophy. His books were bibles of Islamic modernists, Sunni and Shi'ite alike, throughout the Muslim world. Some of his works, including *Falsafatuna* (Our philosophy) and *Iqtisaduna* (Our economics), are used as textbooks in Shi'ite seminaries. Most of his writings and teaching concentrated on renewal of principles of jurisprudence in Islamic tradition. He attempted to reconcile the traditions and strictures of Islam with the ideas and practices of the West. He was one the most enlightened Shi'ite legists and inspired much devotion among the people of Iraq.

Al- Sadr's orientation was not excessively political. Nevertheless, there were many people in Iraq who were receptive to Iran's Islamic Revolution. Therefore, when Iraq's Shi'ite community began to look to al-Sadr for political leadership, and when Iran's Arabic radio broadcasts repeatedly referred to him as the "Khomeini of Iraq," he became a threat to the Iraqi regime of Saddam Hussein, whose base of support consisted of Sunni military officers and functionaries. As a consequence, both al-Sadr and his sister were executed on the orders of Iraq's president Saddam Hussein.

BIBLIOGRAPHY

Batatu, Hanna. "Iraq's Underground Shia Movements: Characters, Causes, and Prospects." *MERIP Reports: Islam and Politics* no. 102 (Jan. 1982): 3–9.

Mallat, Chibli. *The Renewal of Islamic Law: Muhammad Baqer as-Sadr, Najaf and the Shi'i International.* New York: Cambridge University Press, 1993.

Majid Mohammadi

SADR, MUSA AL- (1928–1978?)

Musa al-Sadr, who was born in Qom, Iran, was a politically active and controversial cleric. Al-Sadr arrived in Lebanon in 1959, and by 1969 he was the chairman of the Higher Shi'ite Council, which he had helped to create in that same year. Al-Sadr led and tried to transform the people of the historically quiescent Shi'ite community of Lebanon, who needed courage to stake out a claim in their fractured country. He advanced the notion of ideological Islam, and proposed that the leader in Lebanon should be an imam, much like 'Ali Shari'ati, a religious intellectual, had advocated in Iran before the Islamic revolution.

Al-Sadr was a political moderate who was considered a reformer by his followers. The title of imam was applied to only twelve individuals in the Shi'ite tradition: It was given to Musa al-Sadr and Ruhollah Khomeini, the Iranian leader, by their followers and subsequently accepted by the high-ranking clerics. Sadr disappeared in Libya while on a visit to Libya's ruler, Mu'ammar al-Qadhdhafi, in 1978. He and two companions, a cleric and a journalist, were never heard from again.

See also **Imamate; Lebanon; Political Islam; Revolution: Modern.**

BIBLIOGRAPHY

Ajami, Fouad. *The Vanished Imam: Musa al Sadr and the Shia of Lebanon.* Ithaca, N.Y.: Cornell University Press, 1986.

Majid Mohammadi

SAHARA

Once a lush and fertile environment sustaining a diversified human population, fauna, and flora, the Sahara experienced an irreversible process of desertification from 3000 B.C.E. onward. Since then, two events significantly marked the history of the Sahara: the introduction of camels, sometime after the second century, and the spread of Islam, starting in the eight century. The adoption of camels, the "vessels of the desert," revolutionized the nature of transportation in endurance, volume, and efficiency. Adherence to Islam, its philosophy, and code of law, favored the development of successful commercial and scholarly networks connecting Muslims across the Sahara desert and beyond. In time, the majority of Saharans would become Muslim.

Although Islam arrived at least two centuries earlier, the Almoravid movement in the eleventh century was the first organized attempt at religious reform in the Sahara. To be sure, the Almoravids were interested in controlling a share of the gold trade as much as they were motivated to spread their Muslim faith. From then onward, trans-Saharan trade flourished. In the first half of the fourteenth century, the ostentatious pilgrimage to Mecca of the emperor of Mali, Kankan Mansa Musa, alerted the Muslim world to the gold riches of Western Africa, and consequently would attract many more Muslim visitors to Saharan towns such as Timbuktu and Gao.

By the seventeenth century, Saharan towns were well-established markets and centers of Islamic learning. The reputations of notable scholars of Timbuktu, Walata, and Shingiti extended all the way to North Africa and the Middle East. Saharan scholars regularly organized caravans to perform the pilgrimage. They built mosques, developed libraries, and established schools. One cannot underestimate the significance of trans-Saharan trade and the development of scholarly networks to the spread of Islamic knowledge and Arabic literacy in the region. Caravaners relied on their literacy skills for correspondence, accounting, accountability, and for drawing contractual agreements, all in accordance with Islamic law.

It is no coincidence, therefore, that scholars often performed as traders and vice versa in Saharan commercial centers such as Shingiti, Tishit, Walata, Timbuktu, and Ghadames. To uphold the law, traders relied upon the services of scholars of Islamic law or judges. Moreover, until European colonization, Saharan towns tended to be governed by Muslim scholars who performed as regional judges ruling on all matters, civil, commercial, or political. These sedentary scholarly communities maintained alliances with nomadic groups who provided protection services to both town dwellers and trans-Saharan travelers.

The late nineteenth century saw the end of the great camel caravan. European conquest redirected trade toward new centers of control located along the Atlantic coast and in key colonial outposts in the interior. Consequently, the Sahara became a contested terrain and home to pockets of resistance to French, and later Moroccan, overrule. Not surprisingly, Saharans presented the greatest challenge to European conquest. This was due to the shrewdness of Muslim leaders as much as the ruggedness of the terrain. It was not until the 1930s that the French could claim control over the whole region, connecting Morocco and Algeria to their West African colonies. Later, when the Spanish relinquished their Western Saharan colony in 1975, both Morocco and Mauritania fought the Saharan independence movement, or Polisario, for claims over the contested region. To date, the fate of the Western Sahara has not been sealed, as a UN referendum is repeatedly postponed.

An image of Saharan desert landscape appears in the volume two color insert.

See also **Globalization; Networks, Muslim.**

BIBLIOGRAPHY

Hunwick, John. *Timbuktu and the Songhay Empire.* Leiden: Brill, 1999.

Levtzion, Nehemia, and Pouwels, Randall. *History of Islam in Africa.* Athens: Ohio University Press, 2000.

Levtzion, Nehemia, and Spaulding, Jay. *Medieval West Africa: Views From Arab Scholars and Merchants.* New York: Markus Wiener, 2003.

Webb, James L. A. *Desert Frontier: Ecological and Economic Change along the Western Sahel, 1600–1850.* Madison: University of Wisconsin Press, 1995.

F. Ghislaine Lydon

SAINT

Wali, the word roughly defined as "saint," which is derived from the Arabic root *w-l-y* and has a root meaning of proximity, generally is found in the construct *wali Allah*, that is, someone who is close or intimate with God. It is a designation that Muslims use to define a holy person, and can refer to overlapping categories of pious people, religious scholars, Sufis, and Shi'i imams. In English *wali* is translated variously as protégé, intimate, friend of God, or "saint." A *wali* who has power over others has *wilaya* (being a protector or intercessor) while a *wali* with *walaya* focuses on the closeness or nearness to God (being a friend of God). Both of these meanings can be harmonized with interpretations of Qur'anic usage. Except for hairsplitting grammatical discussions, popular usage conflates these meanings since one close to God has power to protect and intercede and vice versa.

The popular idea of *wali*, an heir of the Prophet, is a post-Qur'anic development whose first textual source, the writings of al-Hakim al-Tirmidhi (d. c. 910), dates to the second half of the ninth century. Tirmidhi proposed a "seal of God's friends" that was later claimed and subsequently popularized by Ibn al-'Arabi (d. 1240). This "seal" corresponds to the creedal notion of Muhammad as the final prophet or the "seal of the prophets," while assiduously subordinating *awliya'* (plural of *wali*) to prophets. The developing doctrine of *wali* accounts for non-prophetic expressions of the sacred, for example, *ilham* (non-prophetic divine inspiration) versus *wahy* (prophetic revelation) in a way that explained extraordinary phenomena without violating creedal dictates.

The contemporary theological war over legitimate religious authority, often initiated and funded by scripturalist groups such as Salafis or Wahhabis, denies that anyone can be a friend of God. Instead, they assert that all Muslims have equal access to God through the written scriptural sources of Qur'an and hadith, absolutely undercutting any possibility of intercession or of spiritual hierarchy. Presently a growing minority of Muslims shares this scripturalist perspective. They are mostly concentrated in Arabic-speaking countries and in countries like the United States, which are influenced by Salafi interpretations of Islam.

On one hand, *wali* is a socially constructed concept based upon a recognizable community consensus. Generally Muslims recognize a *wali Allah* on the basis of four overlapping sources of authority: spiritual/genealogical lineage, religious experience (spiritual traveling), acquisition of transmitted religious knowledge, and exemplary behavior in harmony with the Prophetic sunna. Hagiographic literature has established a narrative paradigm that reinforces these sources of authority in the popular imagination. On the other hand, in the Sufi environment *wali* is a technical term based on consensually verified phenomena allowing specialists to classify types of proximity to God.

In terms of religious practice, the concept of *wali* provides a basis for the development of shrine rituals at the tombs of deceased saints located throughout the Islamic world. Often at these shrines the descendants of the deceased holy person, considered to be *wali*s, act as mediating shaykhs who "pass requests to God" instead of acting as spiritual masters teaching a person how to arrive close to God through a set of contemplative practices. Although the legitimacy of these shrine rituals is strongly denied by scripturally oriented Muslims, these shrines provide meaningful religious experiences for many pious visitors. Functionally, the multivalent concept of *wali* varies historically and geographically so as to include scholars, saints, spiritual mentors, counselors, healers, and intercessors, both living and deceased.

See also **Ibn 'Arabi; Mi'raj; Silsila; Sunna; Tasawwuf; Tariqa; Ulema.**

BIBLIOGRAPHY

Buehler, Arthur F. *Sufi Heirs of the Prophet: The Indian Naqshbandiyya and the Rise of the Mediating Shaykh.* Columbia: University of South Carolina Press, 1998.

Chodkiewicz, Michel. *Seal of the Saints: Prophethood and Sainthood in the Doctrine of Ibn 'Arabi.* Cambridge, U.K.: Islamic Texts Society, 1993.

Cornell, Vincent. *Realm of the Saint: Power and Authority in Moroccan Sufism.* Austin: University of Texas Press, 1998.

Radke, Bernd, and John O'Kane. *The Concept of Sainthood in Early Islamic Mysticism.* Richmond, Surrey, U.K.: Curzon Press, 1996.

Arthur F. Buehler

SALADIN (1137 OR 1138–1193)

Salah al-Din Yusuf b. Ayyub (d. 1193), who became known in the West as Saladin, was a Kurdish warrior renowned for his victories over the Crusaders and as the founder of the Ayyubid dynasty in Egypt, Syria, and upper Iraq. Saladin's defeat of the Crusaders at the Horns of Hattin (4 July 1187) in northern Palestine led to the Muslim reconquest of Jerusalem and the near elimination of the Franks in the Levant. His success in jihad against the Crusaders was celebrated by his court biographers. Not surprisingly, Saladin's name and

example are powerful symbols in the modern Middle East. His subsequent struggles against the forces of the Third Crusade (1189–1192) and King Richard I of England became the stuff of romance in European literature, where Saladin and Richard emerge as rival chivalrous foes.

Saladin's career began in the armies of Nur al-Din b. Zangi, ruler of Aleppo and Damascus, and himself a famous counter-crusader. Saladin went to Egypt in early 1169 in a contingent of Nur al-Din's army sent to assist the Fatimid Caliphate, which in late 1168 had been attacked by Crusader forces. Saladin subsequently removed the Fatimids from power, and made himself ruler in Egypt, subservient to Nur al-Din. Upon the latter's death in 1174, Saladin moved against Nur al-Din's heirs and began to bring the Muslim cities of Syria under his command. He then used the combined resources of Egypt and Syria to attack the Crusaders. By forcibly uniting Muslim territory prior to assaulting the Franks, he followed the pattern of Nur al-Din and Zangi. The same strategy would be used by the Mamluks in their final elimination of the Latin states in 1291.

See also **Crusades.**

BIBLIOGRAPHY

Ehrenkreutz, Andrew S. *Saladin.* Albany: State University of New York Press, 1972.

Gibb, H. A. R. *The Life of Saladin.* Oxford, U.K.: Clarendon Press, 1973.

Lyons, Malcolm Cameron, and Jackson, D. E. P. *Saladin: The Politics of Holy War.* Cambridge, U.K.: Cambridge University Press, 1982.

Warren C. Schultz

SALAFIYYA

Salafiyya is the name given to those who follow the ideas and practices of the righteous ancestors (*al-salaf al-salih*). This "salafi" approach rejects later traditions and schools of thought, calling for a return to the Qur'an and the sunna as the authentic basis for Muslim life. The *salafi* approach emphasizes the application of *ijtihad* (independent, informed judgment) and rejects *taqlid* (adherence to established precedents and conformity with existing traditional interpretations and institutions).

The "righteous ancestors," or *salaf*, are usually considered to be the first three generations of Muslims, including the immediate companions of the Prophet. Because of the closeness of these *salaf* to Muhammad, later Muslims regarded the former's transmissions of the Prophet's traditions, their informed practice as believers, as having special authority.

Major figures in the definition of the *salafi* perspective and approach are Ahmad ibn Hanbal (d. 855), the founder of the Hanbali school, and Ahmad ibn Taymiyya (1263–1328).

The fundamental concern of modern *Salafiyya*, who recognize that Muslim power and influence is in decline relative to the West, is the relationship between Islam and modernity. The goal of the movement is to make Islam a dynamic force in the contemporary world. The modern *Salafiyya* invoked the classic themes: a call for a return to the Qur'an and the sunna, a rejection of the medieval authorities (*taqlid*), and an affirmation of the necessity of independent, informed thinking (*ijtihad*). In the modern context, this involved an emphasis on the compatibility of reason with revelation, and of Islam with modern science. It also entailed a call for moral social reform. However, by the end of the twentieth century, the term *Salafiyya* also came to be applied to extremist movements that advocated violent jihad against existing regimes and social orders, both Muslim and non-Muslim, and that did not adhere to a rigid and literalist understanding of the Qur'an and sunna. This new *Salafiyya* often differed from the time-honored *salafi* approach of Ibn Hanbal and Ibn Taymiyya by rejecting independent analysis (*ijtihad*).

Among those involved in the definition and establishment of the modern *Salafiyya*, the best-known are Jamal al-Din al-Afghani (1839–1897) and Muhammad 'Abduh (1849–1905). 'Abduh created the broad intellectual foundations for modern *Salafiyya*. First in exile and then as Grand Mufti of Egypt, he shaped the thinking of generations of Muslim intellectuals. The theological core was an emphasis on *tawhid*, which is the assertion of the singleness of God and the comprehensive unity of God's message. *Tawhid* was the basis for showing the compatibility of Islam with modern science and revelation with modern reason. Consistent with the earlier *Salafiyya*, 'Abduh advocated the informed, independent analysis of the Qur'an and sunna.

The new *Salafiyya* did not involve direct opposition to European imperial rule over Muslims. Rather, it saw internal Islamic reform as the first priority, and the key to the implementation of its goals was education and scholarship. 'Abduh provided the inspiration for many educational reforms and *al-Manar*, the journal published by his follower and associate, Rashid Rida (1865–1939), was read throughout the Muslim world. Following 'Abduh's death, Rashid Rida became the most visible international articulator of *Salafi* thought, becoming active in organizing Pan-Islamic congresses and, after the abolition of the Ottoman caliphate in 1924, in working for the establishment of a modern Arab caliphate. He came to view the efforts of 'Abd al-'Aziz Ibn Sa'ud to create a state in the Arabian Peninsula based on the puritanical reform traditions of the Wahhabiyya as representing an important manifestation of the reforms necessary for all Muslim societies.

Other important *Salafi*-modernist movements developed in the late nineteenth century, sometimes relatively independently and sometimes in close coordination with the group around 'Abduh. In South Asia, Sir Sayyid Ahmad Khan (1817–1898) emphasized the importance of understanding nature as a reflection of God's revelation in his teachings, and established the Mahomedan Anglo-Oriental College (which later became Aligarh Muslim University). As the Russian Empire completed its conquest of Muslim areas in the nineteenth century, another Islamic modernist movement, "Jadidism," developed there under the leadership of Isma'il Gasprinskii (1851–1914). He created a new school curriculum for Muslim children, and his journal, *Tarjuman*, was important in creating a modern, cohesive sense of identity among Muslims living in Russia.

Many movements throughout the Muslim world were directly inspired by the 'Abduh tradition, and were in communication with it. In North Africa, *Salafis* organized movements like the Association of Algerian Ulema under 'Abd al-Hamid Ibn Badis (1889–1940). *Salafi* intellectuals and organizations became important parts of Muslim life in Syria and Iraq as well, and in Egypt and many other parts of the Muslim world. In Southeast Asia, the Shi'a Imami, which became one of the largest organizations in the Muslim world, was formed in 1912 to advocate specifically *Salafi*-style reform, especially through education.

Throughout the twentieth century, individuals and groups built on and developed the modernist *Salafi* traditions in many different directions. In South Asia, the work of Muhammad Iqbal (1877–1938) provided a critical synthesis of modern and Islamic thought in his book, *The Reconstruction of Religious Thought in Islam*, and other works. At the same time, he worked for the creation of Pakistan. Some forms of nationalism were presented in *Salafi* form, as in the development of the Dustour Party in Tunisia and the drive toward liberal nationalism in Egypt in the first half of the century. Later, Mahmud Shaltut (1893–1963), as shaykh of al-Azhar University, confirmed the 'Abduh tradition at the heart of the Islamic scholarly establishment, and scholars like Fazlur Rahman (1919–1988) further developed modernist methodologies in historical and philosophical studies.

By the end of the twentieth century, the term *Salafi* came to be applied to a very different type of Islamic revivalism. When an ideology of violent jihad against existing Muslim societies and secular modernity developed, it started with a *Salafi*-style call for a return to the purity of faith exemplified by the righteous ancestors. As this message was developed by later activists, however, the emphasis was placed on militant action, rather than on intellectual effort. By the beginning of the twenty-first century, the term was widely applied to advocates of violent jihad. Terrorists like those who destroyed the World Trade Center, along with Usama bin

Ladin and his organization, al-Qaʿida, are called *Salafi*, as are militants throughout the Muslim world.

The older style of *Salafi* modernism was also significant at the beginning of the twenty-first century. The intellectual content of curricula in Islamic schools and international Islamic universities around the world reflects much of the tradition of ʿAbduh, while organizations like the Muhammadiyya in Indonesia remain a significant part of political and social life.

See also **ʿAbduh, Muhammad; Ijtihad; Muhammadiyya (Muhammadiyah); Nationalism: Arab; Wahhabiyya.**

BIBLIOGRAPHY

Hourani, Albert. *Arabic Thought in the Liberal Age, 1798–1939.* Cambridge, U.K.: Cambridge University Press, 1993.

Kurzman, Charles, ed. *Modernist Islam: A Sourcebook, 1840–1940.* New York: Oxford University Press, 2002.

Martin, Richard C.; Woodward, Mark R.; and Atmaja, Dwi S. *Defenders of Reason in Islam.* Oxford: Oneworld, 1997.

Rahman, Fazlur. *Islam and Modernity: Transformation of an Intellectual Tradition.* Chicago: University of Chicago Press, 1982.

Schulze, Reinhard. *A Modern History of the Islamic World.* New York: New York University Press. 2000.

Smith, Wilfred Cantwell. *Modern Islam in India: A Social Analysis.* Lahore: Minerva Book Shop, 1943.

Weismann, Itzchak. *Taste of Modernity: Sufism, Salafiyya, and Arabism in Late Ottoman Damascus.* Leiden: E. J. Brill, 2001.

Wiktorowicz, Quintan. *The Management of Islamic Activism: Salafis, The Muslim Brotherhood, and State Power in Jordan.* Albany: State University of New York Press. 2001.

John O. Voll

SALEH BIN ALLAWI (C. 1844–1935)

Saleh bin Allawi (Ar. Salih bin ʿAlawi) was a renowned scholar and founder of the Riyada mosque college in Lamu. He was of Yemenite origin and born in the Comoro Islands. From there he migrated to Lamu sometime between 1876 and 1885. He belonged to the Jamal al Layl Sharif lineage (one of the Sharif lineages and descendants of the Prophet), whose members have been responsible for the dissemination of Islam and its intellectual tradition in East Africa. In fact, much of Islam as it is taught and practiced in East Africa bears the stamp of Yemenite influence. Descendants of these families were born of African mothers, and this factor facilitated their easy integration into the Swahili community.

Allawi's membership in the Alawi *tariqa* (Sufi order) enabled him to side with and patronize the slaves and the poor of Lamu Island, who became the main focus of his religious efforts. Before this time religious education in Lamu was monopolized by or restricted to descendants of the Prophet and select other families. It was to the credit of Allawi both as an outsider to Lamu and as a member of the Alawi *tariqa* (that emphasized education and training of scholars) that he began to teach people previously denied this education. When he began to teach them Qurʾanic exegesis, he angered the town's elitist traditional scholars. Eventually he established his own madrasa (Islamic school) in Langoni (a district in the southern part of Lamu Island). There he taught the slaves and recent immigrants to the island. This madrasa became the famous Riyada mosque-college, which attracted students from all over East Africa, and spread his fame as a scholar and saint.

See also **Africa, Islam in; Tariqa.**

BIBLIOGRAPHY

Farsy, Shaykh Abdallah Saleh. *The Shafiʿi Ulama of East Africa.* Translated by Randall Pouwels. Madison: University of Wisconsin-Madison, 1989.

Abdin Chande

SALAH AL-DIN B. AYYUB *See* **Saladin**

SALJUQ *See* **Sultanates: Seljuk**

SANHURI, ʿABD AL-RAZZAQ, AL- *See* ʿAbd al-Razzaq al-Sanhuri

SAUDI DYNASTY

The ruling family of Saudi Arabia, the Saudi dynasty, is known as the House (*al*) of Saʿud. Founding of the dynasty is conventionally dated in 1744, when the ruler of the small oasis town Dirʿiyya (south of Riyadh), Muhammad ibn Saʿud, made an alliance with the reformist religious activist Muhammad ibn ʿAbd al-Wahhab. Muhammad ibn Saʿud accepted the strict, puritanical interpretation of Islam propounded by Muhammad ibn ʿAbd al-Wahhab as the basis for his state, and the latter pledged his support for the expansion of the former's domains. Two Saudi realms in Arabia (1744–1818, 1824–1891), destroyed by Ottoman intervention and internal strife, preceded the foundation of the current Kingdom of Saudi Arabia by ʿAbd al-ʿAziz ibn ʿAbd al-Rahman al-Saʿud (known in the West as Ibn Saud) at the outset of the twentieth century. By 1934, 'Abd al-'Aziz had expanded the kingdom to its current boundaries. He has been succeeded as ruler by a number of his thirty-six sons: Sa'ud (1953–1964), Faysal (1964–1975), Khalid (1975–1982) and Fahd (1982–present). Including the direct descendants of 'Abd al-'Aziz, the descendants of his brothers, and significant cadet branches of the family, the number of princes in the Saudi royal family is estimated now at between five and eight thousand.

F. Gregory Gause III

SAYYID

The word *sayyid* is derived from the Arabic root "to be lord over, to rule" and is commonly used to refer to a descendant of the prophet Muhammad (normally through his grandson al-Husayn), but can also, more generally, signify a holy person (also called *wali*). Descendants of the Prophet are accorded respect, particularly in Shi'ism, but also in Sunni Islam. In Shi'ism, respect is generally preserved for descendants of Fatima, the daughter of the Prophet, through her marriage to Imam 'Ali. In Twelver Shi'ism, *sayyids* gain this respect through their genealogy, including relation to one of the Twelve Imams, and many contemporary Shi'ite families claim *sayyid* status. In Zaydi Shi'ism, the leader of the community must be a descendant of the Prophet for his rule to be legitimate. In Sunni Islam, *sayyids* have certain legal privileges over non-*sayyids*. In all these branches of Islam, the privileged status of *sayyids* is perhaps most obvious in the rules concerning marriage, where a *sayyida* (female descendant) should marry only a *sayyid* to preserve the "equity" (*kafa'a*) status in the marriage. In popular religion, descendants of the Prophet in all branches of Islam are often viewed as channels for divine blessing (*baraka*). The colloquial term *sidi*, derived from *sayyid*, is used as an honorific before Muslim saints, especially in North Africa. It does not always imply that the saint is a descendant of the Prophet.

See also **Sharif.**

BIBLIOGRAPHY

Gilsenan, Michael. *Recognising Islam: Religion and Society in the Modern Middle East.* London: Croom Helm, 1982.

Robert Gleave

SCIENCE, ISLAM AND

The concept of *'ilm*, "science," has been an important one in the history of Islamicate civilization and has gone a long way to giving this civilization, and all those who participated in it

regardless of their ethnic or religious affiliation, a distinctive shape. Mention is frequently made of several sayings (hadith) of the Prophet that state "seek *'ilm*, even in China."

The Arabic term *'ilm* (pl. *'ulum*) refers more broadly to "knowledge" and its antonym is considered to be "ignorance" (*jahl*). In its various verbal forms, *'ilm* is found frequently in the Qur'an. At a fairly early date, however, the concept of *'ilm* was differentiated from that of *ma'rifa*. The latter refers to a form of knowledge derived from personal experience or intuition, whereas the former is contingent upon the observation and discovery of first principles. This is not to say, however, that all of the primary sources make a sharp distinction between these two modes of knowledge.

The concept of science in Islam is a vast subject. Historically, Arabs and Persians who were interested in explaining the natural world around them first introduced Greek scientific treatises to the Arabic-speaking world during the eighth century. From the ninth century on, scholars traveled from one end of the empire to the other, carrying books and ideas, thereby insuring what some have called the cultural and intellectual unity of the Islamic world. Since this time, countless Muslims from all over the world throughout the course of many centuries have been involved in scientific developments.

Yet, almost immediately there is a conceptual and taxonomical difficulty. How exactly is the term "Islamic science" defined? Ostensibly, "science" is a universal term that knows no linguistic or ethnic bounds; yet, the adjective "Islamic" implies a particular language by a definable group of people. Does "Islamic science," then, refer to a particular "Islamic" take on science? Or, does it refer to science done by individuals who identify themselves as Muslims? This entry assumes the latter assertion.

An equally difficult hermeneutical problem presents itself: When Arabic speakers use the term *'ilm* did they mean by it something similar to what today is called science? Because the Arabic term is not identical to the Western concept of hard science, it is often used in a number of theological and mystical contexts. For instance, early Muslim hadith criticism was known as *'ilm al-rijal* (lit., "the science of the men" who made up the chain of transmitters, or *isnad*). Despite the employment of the term *'ilm* there was nothing particularly scientific about it. Likewise, even theology (*'ilm al-kalam*) was regarded as a science with its own demonstrative method derived from first principles. These principles, however, were not derived from syllogistic reasoning, but the Qur'an. A more recent trend has fundamentalists arguing that the Qur'an predicts many important scientific discoveries, thereby validating the Qur'anic miracle for the believers.

Premodern Scientific Developments

A momentous impetus was given to the development of science in the Islamic world with the accession of the Abbasid caliphate to power and the subsequent foundation of Baghdad as its capital in 762. This resulted in a translation movement that saw, by the end of the tenth century, virtually all of the scientific and philosophical secular Greek works that were available in the Late Antique period (fourth to seventh centuries C.E.) translated into Arabic. These works included many diverse topics such as astrology, alchemy, physics, mathematics, medicine, and the various branches of philosophy. The great majority of these texts were translated from Greek into Arabic by way of Syriac. Furthermore, many of the earliest translators were Christians, many of whom were employed in the renowned *bayt al-hikma* ("House of Wisdom"). This functioned as the official institute and library for translation and research. The caliph al-Ma'mun (d. 833) sent emissaries throughout the Mediterranean world to seek out and purchase books on "ancient learning," which were subsequently brought back to Baghdad and translated into Arabic by a panel of scholars. The result was an impressive official library that included many of the most important scientific and philosophical works produced in the ancient world. These works would form the foundation for medieval science, not only in the Islamic world, but also subsequently in the Christian world.

The earliest Greek works translated into Arabic were often made for purely pragmatic reasons. This is why treatises devoted to astrology, mathematics, and alchemy represent some of the earliest scientific works in Arabic. A useful list of the treatises translated into Arabic and when and by whom can be found in the account given by the biographer of Islamic writings, Ibn al-Nadim (d. 995).

A common, though incorrect, assumption has it that the Greeks invented the sciences, the Arabs rescued them from disappearing in the "Dark Ages," and subsequently passed them untouched and uncommented upon to the Renaissance period. This ignores the fact that many people living in the Islamic world wrote commentaries to the works of important individuals such as Aristotle, Galen, and Ptolemy. The genre of the commentary was not a slavish recapitulation of a text, but often a creative way of writing about science and philosophy in the medieval period. Rather than regard commentaries as uncreative, they often allowed scholars to think about scientific matters in such a way that they could validate their claims by putting them in the mouths of ancient sages. In fact, many commentators often used ancient authors to argue the very opposite of what these ancient authors had intended in the first place. So although the Arabs worked within the parameters of science as established by the Greeks, they made many important developments in the Western scientific tradition.

Classification of the Sciences

Many of the medieval philosophers compiled various "lists of the sciences" (*ihsa' 'ulum*) and "classifications of the sciences"

(*maratib al-'ulum*). One of the most famous examples of this is the *Enumeration of the Sciences*, by al-Farabi (870–950). In the preface to this work, al-Farabi states that his intention is to give an enumeration of all the sciences of his day and provide descriptions of their themes and subject matter. He divides the sciences into those dealing with (1) language, (2) logic, (3) mathematics, (4) physics and metaphysics, and (5) political science, jurisprudence, and dialectical theology. Other lists were compiled by the Brethren of Purity (Ikhwan al-Safa'), Ibn al-Nadim, Ibn Sina (Avicenna), al-Ghazali, and Ibn Khaldun. Ghazali's list is interesting in that he divides all of the sciences into those that are either praiseworthy (*mahmuda*) or blameworthy (*madhmuma*).

Such lists, however, are by no means a medieval phenomenon. In 1980 at the Second World Conference on Muslim Education, sponsored by the King 'Abd al-'Aziz University in Jiddah and the Quaid-i Azam University in Islamabad, delegates adopted a similar list. The main difference between their enumeration and that of someone like al-Farabi was that theirs begins with the memorization of the Qur'an and ends with the practical sciences.

Highlights

Two caveats must be made at the beginning. First, the Muslims did not invent any of the sciences. Rather, as mentioned, they received texts from the Greeks (especially those of Aristotle, Ptolemy, and Euclid) and, in the process, adopted and adapted their theories as they saw fit (e.g., in order to reconcile them with monotheistic sensibilities or with new advances made in observation). Second, the term Arabic science might be better than Islamic science, because there was nothing particular religious about science, and many of the scientists spoke Arabic, even though religiously they might have been Christian or Jewish.

Muslims made many important innovations in a great majority of the sciences. In astronomy (*'ilm al-hay'a*; lit. "the science of the figure"), for example, Muslim thinkers made important advancements, following on the heels of Ptolemy, in discerning the laws governing the periodic motions of the celestial bodies. One of the most famous of the Islamic astronomers was al-Battani (Albategnius). He compiled a catalog of the stars for the year 880, in which he determined the various astronomical coefficients with renowned accuracy. He was also responsible for discovering the motion of the solar apsides. In addition, he also wrote an important introductory treatise that was used in European universities until the sixteenth century. Gradually, in order to reconcile perceived observation of the universe, Muslim thinkers, disagreeing with Aristotle, posited the existence of epicycles that revolved not around the earth, but around the various celestial spheres. This movement away from Aristotle greatly bothered the Andalusi thinkers, especially Ibn Bajja and Ibn Rushd (Averroes), who decided to remove the epicycles. This created almost as many problems as it solved. In the thirteenth century, however, at the observatory in Maragha, scientists explained the motions of the heavenly spheres as the combination of uniform circular motions. This is the model that was eventually adopted by European astronomers, such as Copernicus.

Mathematics (*'ilm al-hisab*; lit. "the science of reckoning") was, according to al-Farabi's classification, divided into seven branches. Furthermore, he divided mathematics into two types: practical (*amali*) and theoretical (*nazari*). The former is concerned with numbers as they pertain to numbered things such as tables or humans. The latter, in contrast, is concerned with numbers in the abstract, including the properties that numbers acquire when related to one another or when combined with or separated from one another. In the tenth century, Nichomachus's *Introduction* was translated from Greek into Arabic. This resulted in the acquaintance of mathematics with other subjects, such as geometry, astronomy, and music. Another important mathematician, and probably the most important Arab physicist, was Ibn al-Haytham (Alhazen; d. 1039). Among other things, he attempted, without success, to regulate the flow of the Nile. He also composed over a hundred different scientific treatises, most devoted to medicine, mathematics, and physics. Furthermore, he was responsible for establishing the theorem of the cotangent, in addition to resolving the problem of optics (the intersection of an equilateral hyperbole with a circle) that still bears his name.

In the field of medicine, probably the most important name is Ibn Sina (Avicenna; d. 1037). In his autobiography he informs us that medicine (*tibb*) was not one of the difficult sciences and he claims to have mastered it by the age of sixteen. Throughout his life he engaged in medical experiments and wrote various treatises on specific topics. He also composed a medical encyclopedia, *Qanun fi 'l-Tibb* (The canon of medicine), that became the standard textbook on the subject not only in the Islamic world, but also in the West for over five hundred years.

Mention should also be made of two disciplines that medieval scholars considered to be sciences, but which are not thought of in that way today: astrology and alchemy. Both of these sciences provided important sources for an empirical and experimental approach to nature. Whereas Aristotelianism offered an explanatory framework for understanding the physical world, astrology and astral magic supplemented this by providing explanations (and prognostications) for the phenomena of this world in the heavens. Both astrology and astral magic presupposed a thorough knowledge of mathematics and astronomy. In like manner, alchemy (*al-kimiya*) was concerned with the transmutation of base metals into precious ones. Although most often associated with the attempt to "create" gold, many regarded it as an important part of natural philosophy.

Islamic Law

Science, as is to be expected, was a very malleable term. It referred not only to those disciplines (e.g., physics, mathematics) that today are considered to be the purview of science, but also to other disciplines whose scientific veracity is rather difficult to ascertain. The Muslims had a tendency to consider every potential discipline as a science, and as a result tried to articulate first principles for them. Important in this regard is the science of law or *fiqh*. For the practitioners of *fiqh*, known as the *fuquha*, the law was a science and consisted of the proper knowledge of the Qur'an and the sunna.

In its developed form, the science of Islamic legal theory recognized a variety of sources and methods (*usul al-fiqh*) by which to derive the law. The first principle was the Qur'an, followed by the sunna which, though second in importance, provided the overwhelming majority of material from which the law was derived. The third principle is consensus (*ijma'*) of the legal scholars in the name of the entire community. The fourth principle is known as human reasoning (*qiyas*). These four principles became the means whereby legal scholars could, in their opinion, scientifically determine the legal effects of the textual sources of Islam.

The supreme Muslim science was considered to be religious law as opposed to theology as it was in the scholastic world. This had important repercussions: Because scholastic theologians also did work on logic and medicine, they contended that God could not do what was logically impossible. Islamic *fuquha*, in contrast, were not interested in deducing religious principles from reason or explaining them rationally.

Having surveyed some of the major features and trajectories of science within the orbit of Islam, the question arises: Why did Islam not carry out a scientific revolution in the same manner that the Europeans did? After all, Islam practiced the various sciences long before Europe and remained ahead of the Europeans until the thirteenth century.

The primary difference resides in the fact that, whereas European scholastics succeeded in developing the modern physical sciences, Islam created a metaphysics that was more interested in mysticism. According to the analysis suggested by John Walbridge in *The Leaven of the Ancients* (2000), this was the result of several features. First, the Muslim philosophers consistently held the position that the world existed without a temporal beginning and were thus more interested in ontological hierarchies than temporal chains of causality. As a result, they tended to speculate about metaphysics and ontology as opposed to the natural sciences. Second, Muslim theologians (*mutakallimun*) developed an extreme occasionalism that refused to bind God in any way to the natural order. At its most extreme, even a philosopher such as Ghazali, who believed in the truth of mathematics, argued that God destroyed and created the universe in every instant in accordance with His arbitrary Will. God's law, in other words, was regarded as totally arbitrary and, thus, the notion of natural law was for the most part foreign to Islam. Third, the discovery of mysticism by the Islamic philosophers (beginning with Ibn al-ʿArabi in the thirteenth century) coincided with the almost complete lack of interest in natural philosophy, especially physics and mathematics. The end result was that by the thirteenth century, philosophy increasingly was reduced to metaphysics with the primary tools of its discovery being intuition and mystical experience as opposed to deduction and scientific observation. And so it remained until the modern period when Muslims who engage in scientific discovery use, for the most part, models and paradigms developed by Europeans.

Modern Approaches

For sake of convenience, there are essentially three main trajectories. The first trajectory is that of the "fundamentalists." Many think that the Qurʾan predicts modern science. This approach is based on the assumption that the Qurʾan in its nontechnical language actually refers to modern scientific data (e.g., embryology, geology). This is impossible to verify, yet it is taken by the faithful as proof of the authenticity of their religion. A second attempt to bring science and Islam together is based on, for lack of a better term, apologetics. According to this approach, "Western" science has failed to formulate a vision of truth based on revelation; rather, it relies on the rational and secular principles as handed down by the pagan Greeks. The result is the desacralization of knowledge (cf., Nasr, Qadir). Islam, in contrast, presents a sacred worldview and it is the job of "Islamic science" to ascertain this. Proponents of this approach argue that there is such a thing as Islamic science and that it does not subscribe to the theory of evolution. Accordingly, whenever science threatens religion (e.g., evolution), the former must ultimately give way to the latter. Such a dichotomy between "Western" and "Islamic" science is, as should be clear from this entry, based on essentialism and ignores the fact that for much of its history Islamic science was, for all intents and purposes, Western science. The third and final trajectory seems to be the most mainstream; namely, the thousands of Muslim scientists throughout the globe who engage in the ongoing discovery of scientific principles by means of careful and controlled observation.

An image of a fourteenth-century yellow copper astrolabe appears in the volume two color insert.

See also **Astrology; Astronomy; Education; Falsafa; Ghazali, al-; Ibn ʿArabi; Ibn Khaldun; Ibn Sina; Ikhwan al-Safa; Law; Modernity; Qurʾan.**

BIBLIOGRAPHY

Alfarabi. "The Enumeration of the Sciences." In *Medieval Political Philosophy*. Edited by Ralph Lerner and Muhsin Mahdi. Ithaca, N.Y.: Cornell University Press, 1963.

Fakhry, Majid. *A History of Islamic Philosophy*. 2d edition. New York: Columbia University Press, 1983.

Grant, Edward. *Planets, Stars, and Orbs: The Making of the Medieval Cosmos*. Cambridge, U.K.: Cambridge University Press, 1996.

Gutas, Dimitri. *Greek Thought, Arabic Culture: The Graeco-Arabic Translation Movement in Baghdad and Early Abbasid Society*. New York and London: Routledge, 1998.

Ibn Nadim. *The Fihrist*. Edited and translated by Bayard Dodge. New York: Columbia University Press, 1970.

Ibrahim, I. A. *A Brief Illustrated Guide to Understanding Islam*. 2d edition. Houston: Darussalam, 1997.

Nasr, Seyyed Hossein. *An Introduction to Islamic Cosmological Doctrines*. Albany: State University of New York Press, 1993.

Qadir, C. A. *Philosophy and Science in the Islamic World*. London and New York: Routledge, 1988.

Rosenthal, Franz. *Science and Medicine in Islam*. Aldershot, U.K.: Variorum, 1990.

Sarton, George. *Introduction to the History of Science*. Vol. 1: *From Homer to Omar Khayyam*. Vol. 2: *From Rabbi Ben Ezra to Roger Bacon*. Baltimore: Williams and Wilkins, 1927.

Walbridge, John. *The Leaven of the Ancients: Suhrawardi and the Heritage of the Greeks*. Albany: State University of New York Press, 2000.

Aaron Hughes

SECULARISM, ISLAMIC

Islamic secularism is a movement seeking to limit the scope of religious authority, parallel to similar movements in other faith traditions. The limitation may be ideological, as in secularist movements to remove religious authority from state institutions or from social relations; or it may be experiential, as in the encroachment by consumerism and mass media on activities previously regulated by religious authority. Ideological secularism arose in the nineteenth century, when atheists such as Mirza Fath Ali Akhundzada (1812–1878) rejected Islam as inherently incompatible with modern ideals of progress. In the twentieth century, ideological secularism gained adherents among devout progressives as well. Major statements were drafted by Muhammad Husayn Naʾini (1860–1936), who warned against "religious despotism"; ʿAli ʿAbd al-Raziq (1888–1966), who argued for a separation of religious and political authority; and Nurcholish Madjid (b. 1939), who called for the "secularization" of worldly matters so as to leave the divine to God.

A generation of military leaders in the middle of the twentieth century, beginning with Mustafa Kemal Ataturk (1881–1938), forcibly secularized many Muslim societies, subjugating religious authority to increasingly intrusive lay supervision and stripping it of institutions it previously monopolized, such as courts and schools. At the same time, experiential secularism spread in the daily practices of Muslims. For example, alcohol consumption and interest-based bank accounts increased despite widespread prohibition by Islamic authorities. Nonetheless, secularism remains a taboo concept in many Muslim communities, where it is associated with atheism and Western cultural imperialism.

See also **Modernism; Modernity; Secularization.**

BIBLIOGRAPHY

Adelkhah, Fariba. *Being Modern in Iran.* New York: Columbia University Press, 2000.

Berkes, Niyazi. *The Development of Secularism in Turkey.* 2d ed. London: Hurst & Co., 1998.

Charles Kurzman

SECULARIZATION

It is often said that secularization is intimately related to the process by which the Christian West split religion from politics. The origins of this process are traced to Christ's oft-quoted words: "Render therefore unto Caesar the things which are Caesar's and unto God the things that are God's." Muslims, in contrast, have fused religion and politics in an attempt to maintain their unique cultural identity worldwide. This approach has endured a checkered history: a period of decline and external domination followed by a recent reassertion of civilizational vigor. Muslim leaders and ruling elites have been preoccupied with the exact nature of state and nation-building, the absorption of social change, and the adjustment to, or backlash against, the processes of secularization by which property, power, and prestige are passed from religious to lay control. Today, the term secularization refers to the overall process by which religious institutions have been deprived of their economic, political, and social influence.

It is important to realize, however, that the great achievements of the West in the economic, scientific, and technological realms, culminating in what is known as globalization, have spread the secular life throughout the world. The opportunities generated by enhanced higher education and mass communications have had profound impact on both women and men of the Muslim world, fostering an awareness of and a debate over new religious rethinking, public life, civil society, religious and ideological tolerance, and individual rights and responsibilities. To small but growing numbers of Muslims, human rights are the expression of the process of secularization.

The secularization process has also led to a religious revivalist backlash in both the Christian and Muslim worlds.

In the Western tradition, religious revivalist movements did not necessarily conflict with secular orientations. In the Muslim world, contrary to the expectations of the first generation of modernization theorists, there has been an upsurge in antisecular movements even in those societies long exposed to modernization (for example, Turkey). Muslim experts have argued that modernization does not have to result in secularization and that modernization is a universal concept over which no single civilization or culture has monopoly. The premise that Muslim countries will inevitably grow more secular as they are exposed to Western notions of rationality and progress is not axiomatic. The secularization process has failed to permeate all aspects of life in the Muslim world; instead, reaction to it has become a major contributor to the social and political resurgence of Islam. While a small group of leaders has adopted a Western secular worldview, the vast majority of Muslims have not adopted secular perspectives.

Islam has not experienced a reformation analogous to that of Protestantism in Western Christianity. Islamic movements have sought to purify Islam of worldly and heretical accretions by reinforcing Islamic authority over society and law. In Western Europe, the rise of the nation-state in the seventeenth century led to secularization and decreased religious influence. Muslims, instead, gave allegiance to the *umma*, the community of the faithful as defined by common adherence to faith rather than by political or ethnic boundaries. The notion of the nation-state did not take shape in Muslim thought until the late nineteenth century. Whereas in Europe the secularization process was gradual and proceeded in tandem with socioeconomic growth, in the Muslim world it was treated as an externally imposed blueprint reflecting European imperial interests. While in the Muslim world secularization preceded religious reformation, in the European case it resulted more or less from such reformation.

To understand the secularization process in the Muslim world, it is important to examine the extent to which religious institutions and norms are pervasive in all areas of life. In the majority of Muslim societies, there is not a distinct separation between religion and other aspects of people's lives. Islam is both *din wa dunya* (religion and the world). The basic conflict here is not necessarily between religion and the world, as was the case in Christian experience; rather, it is between the forces of tradition and the forces of modernity.

In the Muslim world, secularism resulted entirely from European contact and influence. Many Middle Eastern countries adopted secular legislation, inspired mostly by European models, on a wide range of civil and criminal matters. These laws are now the target of the Islamists' attack. While conceding the value of Western technology, Islamists question those values and practices associated with modernization, including materialism, consumerism, individualism, and moral laxity.

Contemporary reformists in the Muslim world vehemently resist any institutionalized control by religion over human life, arguing that such dominance fosters absolutist tendencies, destroys the existing intellectual life, and promotes less tolerant and antidemocratic forms of social and political control.

Since the 1970s, as a result of Iran's Islamic Revolution, the key question has become, if the struggle between Islamic reformists and Islamic conservatives is legal or political. Arguably the struggle between the two is both political and legal. Both reformists and conservatives have governed most Muslim countries since they gained independence from Western colonial rule. Emphasizing the separation of religion and politics, these leaders extensively secularized their legal and educational systems. Some nationalists, such as Mustafa Kemal Ataturk (Turkey, 1881–1938), Jamal 'Abd al-Nasser (Egypt, 1918–1970), and both Reza Shah (Iran, 1878–1944) and Mohammad Reza Shah (Iran, 1919–1980), adopted aggressive secularization methods and programs; others, such as Anwar al-Sadat (Egypt, 1918–1980) and Zulfaqar Ali Bhutto (Pakistan, 1928–1979), manipulated Islamic symbols and pursued a more subtle and circumspect approach to secularization.

A variety of governments—including monarchies, military dictatorships, and liberal authoritarian regimes—ruled Egypt for most of the twentieth century. They faced occasional challenges and threats from the Muslim Brotherhood and other Islamic organizations. In both Iran and Turkey, the imposition of a secular state from the top has backfired, resulting in the 1979 Islamic Revolution in Iran and by the brief takeover of political power by an Islamist prime minister in Turkey in 1996. In Algeria, nationalist rule since independence in 1962 has resulted in a bifurcated society like Egypt's. A secular society and culture for the urban bourgeoisie and intellectuals exist alongside an Islamic culture in the countryside and the urban slums. The abrogation of the 1992 electoral process, which prevented *Front Islamique du Salut* (Islamic Salvation Party or FIS) from controlling parliament, has plunged Algeria into a civil war. Secularism is now violently challenged by Islamists.

Since Pakistan's creation in 1947, that country's leaders have faced different forces vying with each other for political power. In Muslim countries where Islamists have ruled (e.g., Iran, Sudan, and Afghanistan), they have failed to find long-term solutions to many contemporary ills. In Afghanistan, the Wahhabist Taliban regime immersed the country in a civil war as well as in a foreign war as a result of the terrorist attacks of 11 September 2001.

Recent trends throughout the Muslim world point to the emergence of an intense debate over reforming Islam. Women in the Muslim world are beginning to demand greater freedom and to question the restrictive status that cultural traditions have imposed on them. Some Muslim leaders, such as the Tunisian Shaykh Rachid al-Ghannouchi, have demanded an Islamic constitution and resistance to "Westernization." Others, such as 'Abd al-Karim Sorush, an Iranian political philosopher, have called for an inward-looking approach to consider the Muslims free and responsible individuals, capable of using their independent judgments. Sorush's views are capable of revolutionizing Muslim theology and mass religiosity. Neither the lay modernism of the ruling elites nor the rejectionist populism of traditional leaders has been able to offer a sustainable course for the future of the Islamic world. Sorush's synthesis may stand as a viable alternative. The Muslim world has increasingly become the site of an emerging cultural conflict over "who" controls the process of social change as well as over "whose interests" are really served by change or resistance to it.

See also **Pakistan, Islamic Republic of; Reform: Arab Middle East and North Africa; Reform: Iran.**

BIBLIOGRAPHY

Esposito, John L. *The Islamic Threat: Myth or Reality.* 3d ed. New York: Oxford University Press, 1999.

Falk, Richard A. "The Monotheistic Religions in the Era of Globalization." *Global Dialogue* 1, no. 1 (Summer 1999): 139–148.

Filali-Ansary, Abdou. "Islam and Liberal Democracy: The Challenge of Secularization." *Journal of Democracy* 7, no. 2 (1996): 76–80.

Monshipouri, Mahmood. *Islamism, Secularism, and Human Rights in the Middle East.* Boulder, Colo.: Lynne Rienner Publishers, 1998.

Sadri, Mahmoud, and Sadri, Ahmad. "Let the Occasional Chalice Break: Abdolkarim Soroush and Islamic Liberation Theology." *The Iranian*, 26 (October 1998).

Voll, John Obert. *Islam: Continuity and Change in the Modern World.* 2d ed. Syracuse, N.Y.: Syracuse University Press, 1984.

Mahmood Monshipouri

SELJUQ *See* **Sultanates: Seljuk**

SHAFI'I, AL- (C. 767–820)

Muhammad ibn Idris al-Shafi'i, the jurisprudent, was probably born in 'Asqalan (Ashkelon) in Palestine. He was a pure Arab on both sides, and on his father's side he was a third cousin, six times removed, to the Prophet. He grew up in Mecca and northern Arabia and became renowned for his archery and Arabic as well as law. He is said to have studied under Malik ibn Anas in Medina for as long as ten years and later debated with al-Shaybani in Baghdad. He emigrated to Old Cairo about six years before his death there. Accounts vary as to how he died: of an illness; from the after-effects of a beating at the hands of aggrieved adherents of the Maliki school, one of whom he had denounced to the governor for insulting him in the course of a debate; or from a beating by adherents of the Mu'tazili theology.

Writers of the later Shafi'i school distinguish between Shafi'i's early teaching (al-qadim), in Iraq, and his later (al-jadid), in Egypt. Nine or ten short works on jurisprudence are extant, as many as half of which may be early; otherwise, the early teaching is lost except for scattered quotations. The later works that survive are the Risala (Epistle), an exposition of how to infer ordinances from the evidence of revelation; the Umm (Guidance), a large, systematic collection of ordinances; and the rest of the short works. Two large works sometimes published in his name, a substantial collection of hadith and a collection of ordinances from the Qur'an, are later extracts from known works. Other works (statements of his creed, comments on asceticism) are likely pseudonymous.

At the level of theory (usul al-fiqh), medieval Muslim commentators credit Shafi'i with reconciling the two great early approaches to discerning the law, mainly hadith and ra'y, traditionalism and rationalism. The traditionalists proposed to base Islamic law entirely on what had been transmitted from the earliest generations, especially hadith reports of what the Prophet had said and done. The rationalists allowed more play to reason and sometimes, when it came to revelation, argued for reliance on the Qur'an to the exclusion of hadith. With the traditionalists, on the one hand, Shafi'i's Risala argues for reliance on revelation before reason and for hadith as a necessary complement to the Qur'an. On the other hand, with the rationalists, it proposes a sophisticated system of manipulating the revealed texts to justify the law.

One of Shafi'i's greatest accomplishments was to systematize analogical reasoning. According to Shafi'i, the jurisprudent looks for a strictly defined condition common to known and unknown cases, concerning which there is a certain ruling from elsewhere in Qur'an or hadith. So, for example, the Qur'an expressly forbids grape wine; the reason (ma'na in Shafi'i's exposition, 'illa in the later tradition of usul al-fiqh) is that it intoxicates (not, say, that it is red or imported from Byzantine territory); date wine also intoxicates; therefore, date wine also is forbidden.

Later writers in the Shafi'i tradition argued expressly that the law had basically four sources, meaning four sorts of evidence by which the jurisprudent discerned God's will: Qur'an, hadith, consensus, and analogy. However, Lowry has shown that the Risala itself ultimately recognizes only two sources, Qur'an and hadith. For Shafi'i, analogy is just a

means toward understanding the application of Qur'an and hadith. His concept of consensus is fairly undeveloped. However, as made explicit by later tradition, consensus does not invent new ordinances but rather rests on data from the Qur'an and hadith lost to later generations but known to the Companions of the Prophet, who could scarcely have agreed unanimously without the hardest evidence.

Among modern writers, Schacht stresses an argument Shafi'i made expressly in two of the short works: that local custom, hadith from experts of the previous centuries, and common sense are always outweighed by hadith from the Prophet. (The Risala assumes without discussion that only hadith from the Prophet have weight.) Calder (1983) finds that the Risala legitimizes disagreement among jurisprudents by distinguishing between simple questions whose answers all Muslims know and abstruse questions only experts can address and whose answers even they can know only probably, not certainly. Adherents of all schools from the tenth century onwards legitimized disagreement in roughly the same way, although it is hard to say to what extent Shafi'i's arguments were what caused the theory to spread. Hallaq argues that just because it sought a middle course between traditionalism and rationalism, well in advance of majority opinion, the Risala attracted little attention until the tenth century.

The Umm as we know it manifestly includes some interpolations by later authors. Calder (1993) proposes that the Risala and the Umm (and implicitly the other extant works of Shafi'i as well) are primarily the work of later disciples writing in Shafi'i's name. Among other things, Calder argues that these works appeal to prophetic hadith (as opposed to the opinions of earlier jurisprudents) in the fashion of other works from the early tenth century, not from the early ninth. Calder's opinion has not commanded wide assent, but the question of attribution remains open.

A Shafi'i school of law was constituted when, first, Shafi'i's doctrine had been collected and organized and, second, a regular procedure had been developed for training and certifying new Shafi'i jurisprudents. The two came together with Ibn Surayj (863–918) in Baghdad. He trained his advanced students with the Mukhtasar (Epitome) of al-Muzani, Shafi'i's most important Egyptian disciple. The other surviving schools of law formed similarly over the course of the tenth century. The Shafi'i school is distinguished by the acuity of its juridical reasoning, so that writing about the theory of Islamic law was long dominated by Shafi'i jurists, although doubtless their preponderance will appear to diminish as more and more non-Shafi'i works are studied. Outside North Africa, the Shafi'i and Hanafi schools for centuries almost divided the Islamic world between them. At the end of the Middle Ages, however, the Hanafi school was favored by Turkish rulers from the Ottoman Empire to the Mogul, so the Shafi'i school is now predominant only on the edges of the Islamic world, as in Indonesia, Yemen, and East Africa.

See also **Law; Madhhab.**

BIBLIOGRAPHY

Calder, Norman. "Ikhtilâf and Ijma in Shâfi'i's Risâla." *Studia Islamica* 58 (1983): 39–47.

Calder, Norman. *Studies in Early Muslim Jurisprudence.* New York: Clarendon Press, 1993.

Hallaq, Wael B. *A History of Islamic Legal Theories.* Cambridge, U.K.: Cambridge University Press, 1997.

Khadduri, Majid, trans. *Islamic Jurisprudence: Shafi'i's Risala.* Baltimore: Johns Hopkins Press, 1961.

Lowry, Joseph Edmund. "The Legal-Theoretical Content of the Risala." Ph.D. diss., University of Pennsylvania, 1999.

Schacht, Joseph. *The Origins of Muhammadan Jurisprudence.* Oxford, U.K.: Clarendon Press, 1950.

Christopher Melchert

SHAH *See* Monarchy

SHALTUT, MAHMUD (1893–1963)

Mahmud Shaltut was an Egyptian religious scholar, jurist, and reformer of al-Azhar, the renowned center of Islamic learning in Cairo. Born in a farming village of lower Egypt, Shaltut distinguished himself as a student in the principal religious institute of Alexandria and later at al-Azhar. He became an instructor of Islamic jurisprudence (*fiqh*) at al-Azhar in 1927. The following year, the reform-minded Muhammad Mustafa al-Maraghi was appointed shaykh al-Azhar (rector), and Shaltut immediately emerged as one of his ardent supporters. When conservative opposition forced al-Maraghi out of office the following year, Shaltut continued pressing for reform. Because of his opposition, he was dismissed from al-Azhar in 1931. Upon al-Maraghi's reappointment as rector in 1935, he returned as a senior official in the faculty of Islamic law. Following service in numerous committees and conferences inside and outside of al-Azhar, Shaltut was appointed shaykh al-Azhar in 1958. During his tenure, Shaltut oversaw a modernization of the school's curriculum in theology and law, and the addition of new faculties, including medicine. His influence, however, was undermined when the Nasser government imposed direct state control over al-Azhar in 1961. The progressive bent to Shaltut's thought is best exemplified in his condemnation of Islamic sectarianism and his appointment of scholars of Shi'ite *fiqh* at al-Azhar. But on social issues such as polygyny and birth control, he adopted more conservative positions that were at odds with government reform programs.

See also **Reform: Arab Middle East and North Africa.**

BIBLIOGRAPHY

Lemke, Wolf-Dieter. *Mahmud Shaltut (1893–1963) und die Reform der Azhar.* Frankfurt: P. D. Lang, 1980.

Zebiri, Kate. *Mahmud Shaltut and Islamic Modernism.* Oxford, U.K.: Clarendon Press, 1993.

Sohail H. Hashmi

SHARI'A

Often translated as "Islamic law" the *shari'a* is better understood as the path of correct conduct that God has revealed through his messengers, particularly the prophet Muhammad. The earliest sources indicate its meaning as a "way of belief," either Muslim or non-Muslim, and it was used to translate the word *Torah* into Arabic. Jurists tend to prefer the term *fiqh* (understanding) in their books on jurisprudence, leaving *shari'a* as a general term. Intention (*niyya*) to fulfill one's duty to God is often as important as the act itself, and every action should be conceived as worshipping God.

This focus on God extended to a medieval institutionalization of the *shari'a* that limited human authority. Even today, there is no central authority for matters of Islamic law in Sunni Islam (some Shi'ites have developed authority structures), and Muslims may seek advice from a number of different authorities (*mufti*s) before making up their mind. Further, actions are assigned one of five "*shari'a* values" (*ahkam*); between required and forbidden are: recommended, indifferent, and disapproved. These valuations have led some to describe *shari'a* as ethics rather than as law. Arguably, postcolonial legal institutions have utterly changed the Muslim's relationship to *shari'a*, both by codifying the law and by replacing *shari'a* courts.

Shari'a in Western discourse has come to signify Islam as moribund or authoritarian, perhaps reflecting Christian presumptions of a distinction between law and gospel. Rhetorical use is also found among Muslim intellectuals, some of whom urge a "return" to *shari'a* focusing primarily on issues of public dress and ritual conduct, but also invoking the idea of the *shari'a* as a total way of life.

See also **Law.**

BIBLIOGRAPHY

Calder, Norman. "Shari'a." In Vol. 9, *Encyclopaedia of Islam.* Leiden: E. J. Brill, 1962.

Goldziher, Ignaz. *Introduction to Islamic Theology and Law.* Princeton, N.J.: Princeton University Press, 1981.

Weiss, Bernard. *The Spirit of Islamic Law*. Athens: University of Georgia Press, 1998.

Jonathan E. Brockopp

SHARI'ATI, 'ALI (1933–1977)

Born in 1933 in the province of Khorasan, northeast of Iran, 'Ali Shari'ati died in 1977 in London of natural causes. His intellectual disposition was formed in early adulthood through his involvement with the Center for the Propagation of Islamic Truths, an educational and advocacy institute founded by his father, and later with the movement God-Worshiping Socialists. Both organizations advocated a reformist Islam, the goal of which was to liberate religion from its "regressive" and "passive" outlook and to promote social justice. Shari'ati never received any traditional seminarian education. He earned a bachelor's degree in French from Mashad University in 1958 and received his doctorate from the Sorbonne in 1963. His residence in Paris in the early 1960s and his exposure to African anticolonial movements and their French intellectual advocates proved to be significant in the development of his Islamic worldview.

Shari'ati formulated an Islamic *Weltanschauung* in his most celebrated book *Islam-shenasi* (Islamology), published in 1969. He identified a dynamic and progressive "true Islam" of Imam 'Ali (*Alavid Shi'ism*) and distinguished it from the petrified institutionalized Islam of the clergy (*Safavid Islam*). Through a revisionist genealogy of Islamic concepts and ideas, he articulated a philosophy of history and social change that he believed would appeal to young modern Iranian intellectuals. He conceived his Islamic *Weltanschauung* as a counter hegemonic ideology against the "trinity of oppression"—the economic power of capitalism, the coercive political power of monarchy, and the cultural dominance of the *Safavid Islam*. Although Shari'ati came to be known as the ideologue of the Iranian revolution par excellence, his ideas remained marginal to the state-sanctioned interpretations of Islam in postrevolutionary Iran.

See also **Reform: Iran.**

BIBLIOGRAPHY

Rahnema, Ali. *An Islamic Utopian, A Political Biography of 'Ali Shari'ati*. London and New York: I. B. Tauris, 1998.

Behrooz Ghamari-Tabrizi

SHARIF

The word *sharif* is derived from the Arabic root "to be noble, highborn." *Sharif* is an honorific term that has a variety of meanings in Muslim usage, and the word is related in meaning to *sayyid*. *Ashraf* (the plural form of *sharif*), like *sadat* (or *sada*, the plural form of *sayyid*), are subject to special rules in Islamic law. One meaning, that of a descendant of the Prophet, is perhaps the most common, and specifically it often indicates descent through the line of al-Hasan, the Prophet's grandson. Muslim genealogists differ in their definition of *sharif* (as they do over *sayyid*). Some define *sharif* in a broad manner (including, for example, descendants of the Prophet's cousins); others are stricter, limiting the term to descendants of Muhammad through Hasan, the older son of the Prophet's daughter (Fatima) and her husband, 'Ali. The two extremes only roughly correspond to the Sunni or Shi'ite proclivities. For example, *ashraf* are prohibited from receiving the alms (*zakat*), though in Shi'ite law they are compensated by being the sole recipient of the one-fifth tax (*khums*). Some hadith portray the *ashraf* as guaranteed a place in heaven, and others exhort the community to show them respect and honor. Some commentators have argued that these stipulations are not nullified, even if the individual is a sinner. The governor of Mecca (who was always a descendant of the Prophet) was known as *al-sharif* during the Ottoman period.

See also **Sayyid.**

BIBLIOGRAPHY

Gilsenan, Michael. *Recognising Islam: Religion and Society in the Modern Middle East*. Croom Helm: London, 1982.

Robert Gleave

SHARI'AT-SHANGALAJI, REZA-QOLI (1890–1943)

A reformist Iranian theologian during the secularizing reign of Muhammad Reza Shah Pahlevi, Reza-Qoli Shari'at-Shangalaji was considered a heretic by his religious peers for his attempts to modernize and reform Islam in Iran. He supported Twelver Shi'ism: namely, the existence of free will in human beings, the infallibility of the imam, and the idea that the twelfth, or current, imam is hidden from the world and will emerge again. However, he also advocated the use of scientific thought in Islam and the pursuit of social justice, and may have been an admirer of Wahhabism, which was hostile to Shi'ism. His main suggestion, to use *ijtihad* (discussion) for the purposes of reform in order to get rid of *taqlid* (conservatism), was rejected as too secular by the religious leaders of the Iranian ulema, who were conservative and already felt under attack by Reza Shah's own secularizing and authoritarian reforms. After Reza Shah's fall from power, they reestablished control and reinstituted strict Islamic law in Iran. Shangalaji's reformist thought was subsequently declared heretical and ignored, particularly under the current, fundamentalist regime, which advocates traditional interpretations of Muslim law and opposes reform. Since his death, Shangalaji's ideas have fallen into obscurity.

See also **Muhammad Reza Shah Pahlevi; Reform: Iran; Shi'a: Imami (Twelver).**

BIBLIOGRAPHY

Richard, Y. "Shari'at Shangalaji: A Reformist Theologian of the Rida Shah Period." In *Authority and Political Culture in Shi'ism.* Edited by S. A. Arjomand. Albany: State University of New York Press, 1988.

Paula Stiles

SHAYKH AL-ISLAM

Before the rise to power of the Ottomans and Safavids, *shaykh al-Islam* (pl. *shuyukh al-Islam*) was, in general, an honorific title given to the leading scholar (or at times, spiritual Sufi master) in a particular locality. During the Ottoman and Safavid dynasties, it evolved into an official administrative position. The *shaykh al-Islam* was responsible for government control of education (through the madrasa system) and law (through the courts), and therefore, for the purposes of legitimacy, had to be a legally trained and well-respected scholar. His *fatwa* (opinion), though technically nonbinding on a judge (*qadi*), held the force of government policy. In the Ottoman Empire, the great *shaykh al-Islam* Ebus-Su'ud (Ar. Abu 'l-Su'ud, d. 1574) acted, not only as a powerful influence over the sultan in terms of policy, but also enforced the primacy of Hanafi legal doctrine within the empire. Ottoman *shuyukh al-Islam* were known as the "*Mufti*" of the empire, and while others were able to give *fatwas*, it was their legal opinions that (at least officially) were authoritative. Within the Safavid Empire, *shuyukh al-Islam* such as Mohammad Baqer Sabzawari (d. 1679) and Mohammad Baqer Majlesi (d. 1699) were renowned as scholars rather than policy makers, though they too clearly had official responsibilities which included presiding over the coronation ceremony of a new shah. The *shuyukh al-Islam* formed a network of government-appointed figures in Safavid Iran, and functioned as a means of enforcing a legal unity over a diverse and often fractious population.

The post of *shaykh al-Islam* survived in both the Ottoman Empire and Iran into the nineteenth century, though with a reduced significance. The Afshar, Zand, and Qajar dynasties of Iran certainly appointed *shuyukh al-Islam*, though these were rarely major figures within the religious establishment. In Iran, the post seems to have died out in the late nineteenth century. The *shaykh al-Islam* of the Ottoman Porte in Istanbul continued to be appointed, though there too the post was rarely held by renowned or dynamic scholars. It

was abolished, as were all the trappings of the Ottoman caliphate, in 1924.

See also **Empires: Ottoman; Empires: Safavid and Qajar.**

BIBLIOGRAPHY

Repp, R. C. *The Mufti of Istanbul.* Oxford, U.K.: Ithaca Press, 1986.

Robert Gleave

SHAYKHIYYA

Shaykhiyya was a nineteenth-century Iranian, mystical, sectarian movement within Shi'ism that was inspired by Shaykh Ahmad al-Ahsa'i, an eighteenth-century cleric who originally came from the Arabian peninsula. It was more popular with the common people, who found it more accessible and vital than its rival Shi'ite schools, Usulism and Akhbarism. It emphasized gaining gnostic knowledge through the love of God, in addition to the dry, legalistic study of the Qur'an and hadiths and rigid traditionalism advocated by the other two schools. Shaykhiyya espoused the concept that the twelfth imam (descendant of the prophet Muhammad) of Shi'ite Islam had gone into hiding from humankind and remains in "occultation" until he returns shortly before the end of the world. The "Fourth Principle" of Shaykhiyya (*rokn-e rabi'*) envisaged a "perfect Shi'a," the only person on Earth who could become aware (through mystical intuition) of the Hidden Imam while he was in occultation. Shaykh Ahmad did not claim this role for himself, but the followers of his chief successor, Sayyid Kazim Rashti, believed that Rashti was the perfect Shi'a of his time. Rashti formed much of the basic organization of Shaykiyya as a school of thought.

Shaykh Ahmad (1753–1826), one of the last great Muslim philosophers before the influx of European thought, was a gentle man of paradox who enjoyed both the patronage of the court of the Qajar Shah in Tehran and the love of the masses, yet refused an official position for fear that he might lose touch with the common people. Originally from Bahrain, he spent the last twenty years of his life in Iran. He considered himself an orthodox Shi'ite who was hostile to Sufism, yet inspired a movement that incorporated many elements of Sufi thought. Shaykh Ahmad emphasized the necessity for a religious leader to combine mystical revelation with traditional jurisprudence. His philosophy, influenced by visions of the prophet Muhammad, numerology, rigorous study of Muslim law, and the religious thought of his native Bahrain, inspired the movement that bore his name after his death. The movement was influenced heavily by its founder's fascination with myth and gnostic thought (*'irfan*). Though Ahmad was a mystic, and held many beliefs similar to the Sufis', he attacked them as anti-Shi'ite Sunnis with pantheistic tendencies and criticized them for claiming authority that only the imams should have, though the ultimate authority belonged to the prophet Muhammad. After Ahmad's death, his followers used the Sufi ideal of the Perfect Person to formulate the concept of the Perfect Shi'a. This person could be used as an authority because he had received mystical knowledge from God, in addition to his study of Muslim law. In a way, Shaykhiyya later became a form of Sufism untouched by Sunni influence, eventually inspiring Babi and Baha'ism. The Perfect Shi'a did not take precedence, however, over the imams, who were exalted to a higher degree than in the past. This reflected the chaos in eighteenth- and early nineteenth-century Shi'ism, caused by external forces, and which created an increased need for tradition and a central authority to follow. Instead, Shaykhiyya, like its founder, attempted to strike a balance between the dry legalism of pure jurisprudence and the uncontrolled (in their eyes) individualistic esotericism of the Sufis, though it did not always succeed. Two branches of Shaykhiyya have survived in Tabriz and Kerman. The activities of the Shaykhis of Kerman were suppressed under the Islamic Republic of Iran.

See also **Shi'a: Early; Shi'a: Imami (Twelver).**

BIBLIOGRAPHY

Cole, Juan R. I. "The World as Text: Cosmologies of Shaykh Ahmad al-Ahsa'i." *Studia Islamica* 80 (1994): 1–23.

Paula Stiles

SHI'A

EARLY
  Devin J. Stewart

IMAMI (TWELVER)
  David Pinault

ISMA'ILI
  Farhad Daftary

ZAYDI (FIVER)
  Robert Gleave

EARLY

The Shi'a were originally the "partisans" of 'Ali, cousin of Muhammad's cousin and husband of the Prophet's daughter, Fatima. Today, however, the label designates a number of distinct groups that have arisen over the course of Islamic history and which are united by a belief that the leader (*caliph* or *imam*) of the Muslim community (*umma*) should be a member of the Prophet's family (*ahl al-bayt*). The Shi'a include the Twelvers, second largest of all the Muslim sects (the largest being the Sunni). Other Shi'a groups include the Zaydis, Khoja Isma'ilis, and Bohra Isma'ilis, who taken together, represent more than ten percent of the world Muslim population.

The First *Fitna*

The Shi'a first formed an identifiable movement in Islamic history during the First Civil War (*fitna*), which tore the Muslim community apart between 656 and 661 c.e. According to Shi'i doctrine, 'Ali was meant to assume leadership of the community upon the Prophet's death in 632. Tradition holds that the Prophet designated his cousin as heir in a speech made at Ghadir Khumm on the way back from Muhammad's farewell pilgrimage, made shortly before his death. However, the jealousy and ambition of the Prophet's other principal Companions (Abu Bakr, 'Umar, and 'Uthman) prevented him from assuming that post. Abu Bakr was the first, serving as leader from 632 to 634. He was followed by 'Umar (634–644), and finally by 'Uthman (644–656).

Shi'ism as a movement, however, burst into full view with the assassination of 'Uthman and the ensuing civil war. 'Uthman, a member of the aristocratic Umayyah clan of Quraysh, had converted to Islam early on, marrying the Prophet's daughters Ruqayyah and Umm Kulthum. As caliph, he appointed many of his relatives to lucrative governorships in the newly conquered provinces, and was consequently widely criticized for nepotism. Disgruntled Companions, based primarily in Egypt, conspired against him and succeeded in assassinating him in Medina in 656. At this point, 'Ali was chosen as caliph, but soon met opposition from the Umayyah clan, the Prophet's widow 'A'isha, the prominent Companions Talhah and al-Zubayr, and others.

'Uthman's enemies accused him of complicity in 'Uthman's assassination, because he showed little interest in pursuing the conspirators and in fact had close ties with some of them, including his step-son Muhammad b. Abu Bakr. Protest against 'Ali sparked a major war, pitting 'Ali's supporters, who were centered in the garrison town of Kufa, in Iraq, against opposition forces based in Basra and Syria. In 656, 'Ali's forces met those of 'A'isha and her co-generals, Talha and al-Zubayr, just outside Basra, in what came to be known as the Battle of the Camel, because 'A'isha joined the fray in an armored palanquin mounted on her camel, 'Askar.

'Ali's forces were victorious. Talhah and al-Zubayr were killed, and 'A'isha was captured and returned to Medina in shame. The tide turned against 'Ali the following year, however, with the battle of Siffin in the Syrian desert. 'Ali lost this battle after his deputy bungled arbitration with the agent of Mu'awiya, the governor of Damascus. A large group of 'Ali's supporters, angered that he had submitted to arbitration, left his cause. Known as the Kharijis "deserters," they became bitter enemies of 'Ali.

'Ali retreated to Kufa, but rallied sufficiently to defeat a Khariji army at Nahrawan in 658. In 661, 'Ali fell to the blows of a Khariji assassin in Kufa. 'Ali's supporters recognized his eldest son Hasan as their leader, but Hasan soon entered into a truce with Mu'awiya and renounced his claim to the Caliphate. Thus, the First Civil War ended.

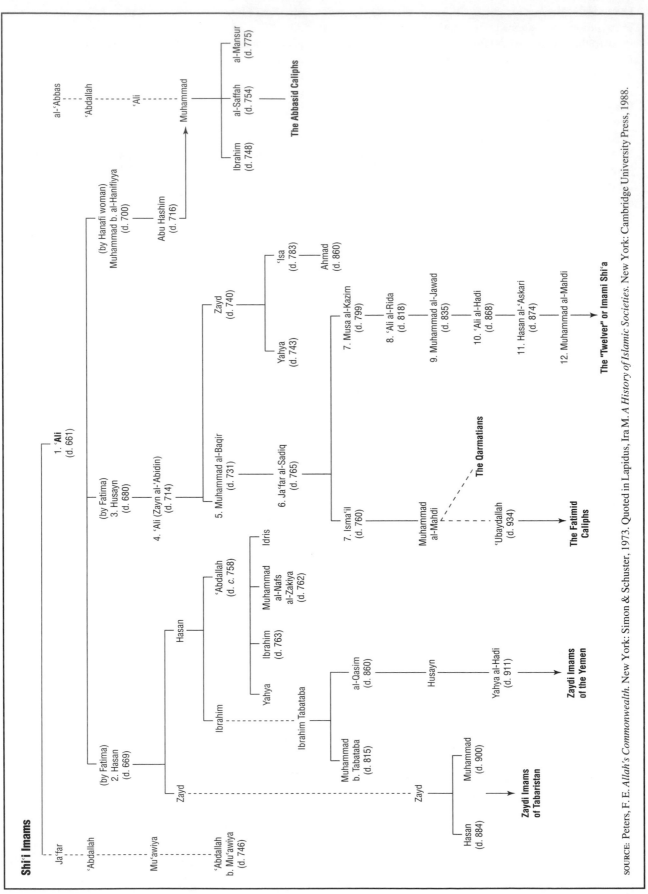

Shi'i Imams

The Abbasid Caliphs

al-Abbas ---- 'Abdallah ---- 'Ali ---- Muhammad

al-Mansur (d. 775)
al-Saffah (d. 754)
Ibrahim (d. 748)

(by Hanafi woman) Muhammad b. al-Hanifiyya (d. 700)
Abu Hashim (d. 716)

Ja'far
'Abdallah
Mu'awiya
'Abdallah b. Mu'awiya (d. 746)

1. 'Ali (d. 661)

(by Fatima) 3. Husayn (d. 680)

(by Fatima) 2. Hasan (d. 669)

4. 'Ali (Zayn al-'Abidin) (d. 714)

5. Muhammad al-Baqir (d. 731)

Zayd (d. 740)
Yahya (d. 743)
'Isa (d. 783)
Ahmad (d. 860)

6. Ja'far al-Sadiq (d. 765)

7. Musa al-Kazim (d. 799)
8. 'Ali al-Rida (d. 818)
9. Muhammad al-Jawad (d. 835)
10. 'Ali al-Hadi (d. 868)
11. Hasan al-'Askari (d. 874)
12. Muhammad al-Mahdi

The "Twelver" or Imami Shi'a

7. Isma'il (d. 760)
Muhammad al-Mahdi

The Qarmatians

'Ubaydallah (d. 934)

The Fatimid Caliphs

Hasan
Ibrahim
Zayd

'Abdallah (d. c. 758)
Idris
Muhammad al-Nafs al-Zakiya (d. 762)
Ibrahim (d. 763)
Yahya

Ibrahim Tabataba

al-Qasim (d. 860)
Husayn
Yahya al-Hadi (d. 911)

Zaydi Imams of the Yemen

Muhammad b. Tabataba (d. 815)

Zayd
Muhammad (d. 900)
Hasan (d. 884)

Zaydi Imams of Tabaristan

SOURCE: Peters, F. E. *Allah's Commonwealth.* New York: Simon & Schuster, 1973. Quoted in Lapidus, Ira M. *A History of Islamic Societies.* New York: Cambridge University Press, 1988.

Shi'a imam lineage.

Shi'a Under the Umayyads

The Muslim community was united under one regime, for Mu'awiya became caliph of the entire community by default. The capital was moved to Damascus, and when Mu'awiya designated his son Yazid as heir, the Umayyad dynasty (661–750) was established. Doctrinally, however, the Muslim community remained divided into three main groups, 'Ali's supporters (the Shi'a), enemies of 'Ali who had originally supported him but renounced their allegiance at Siffin (the Kharijis), and the main body of his opponents, the Umayyads and their supporters.

Throughout Umayyad rule, the Shi'a engaged in periodic uprisings against what they viewed as the illegitimate caliphs, revolting in the name of various members of *ahl al-bayt*. The most famous of these incidents is the revolt of Husayn, 'Ali's second son, upon the death of Mu'awiya and the accession of his son Yazid in the year 680. Husayn was summoned to Kufa to lead a revolt. He set out from Medina with a small contingent, but Umayyad forces halted him in the Iraqi desert, preventing him from reaching his supporters in Kufa. Rather than surrender, Husayn and his followers fought. Most were slaughtered, and Husayn's head was delivered to Yazid in Damascus. The martyrdom of Husayn and his followers is still retold and re-enacted by the Shi'a on 'Ashura, the tenth day of Muharram, which is the first month of the Islamic calendar.

Four years after Husayn's death, a faction among the Kufan Shi'a arose in revolt. This group became known as al-Tawwabun (the penitents), a name that reflected their dedication to the cause of Husayn and their regret they had failed to come to his aid. In 686, Mukhtar al-Thaqafi led an initially successful revolt in the name of Muhammad b. al-Hanafiyya, a son of 'Ali, holding Kufa in 686–687. In 740, Zayd, a grandson of Husayn, led a new revolt in southern Iraq, but was defeated and killed. 'Abd Allah b. Mu'awiya, a great-grandson of Muhammad's cousin Ja'far, led yet another insurrection (744–747).

Shi'a and the Abbasids

The Abbasid revolution that toppled the Umayyads in 750 began, in part, as a Shi'a movement, adopting the slogan *al-rida min al al-bayt* "the acceptable candidate from the family of the Prophet." Upon victory, a descendant of the Prophet's uncle 'Abbas assumed rule as caliph. In a clear pro-Shi'a move, the new dynasty established their capital in Iraq, first at Wasit, then at Baghdad, which was founded in 761.

The Abbasids, however, soon turned on their Shi'a allies, and eventually took over the Umayyads's role as illegitimate rulers and the nemesis of Shi'a aspirations. Muhammad al-Nafs al-Zakiyya, "the Pure Soul," led a Shi'ite revolt against the Abbasids as early as 762, and the Abbasid period would witness countless more revolts in the name of various descendants of 'Ali. Attempts at reconciliation were short-lived, the most notable being al-Ma'mun's appointment of 'Ali al-Rida, the eighth Imam of the Twelver Shi'a line, as his successor in 816.

Shi'a and Sunni: A Comparison

An untenable distinction is often made between the Sunni caliph, seen as a purely political authority, and the Shi'a imam, seen as a religious authority. In the early period, the titles imam and caliph referred, at least potentially, to the same office and authority. The goal behind the Shi'a revolts against the Umayyads and Abbasids was to depose what was considered to be the illegitimate leader of the community and to replace him with a legitimate one. Both for the Shi'a and their opponents, the Shi'ite Imam was always a potential counter-caliph. Whether chosen from the descendants of 'Ali or from another line, the caliph was held to be both a religious and political authority even by the Sunni, and was called imam as well as *sahib hadha al-amr* ("the one in charge").

In the first Islamic century, there can hardly have been any other identifiable religious authorities; jurists, theologians, and others did not gain influence until later. An indication of the caliphs' religious authority is the fact that their decisions often became enshrined in Islamic law. An example of this can be found in the "Conditions of 'Umar," restrictions on the *ahl al-dhimma* imposed by the second caliph, 'Umar b. al-Khattab (or possibly the Umayyad 'Umar b. 'Abd al-'Aziz). These "Conditions" provide the basis for many of the laws that govern the status of Jews and Christians in Islam.

Another popular misconception is that Sunnism is the original form of Islam, from which the Shi'a deviated. In the beginning, the opponents of the Shi'a were not Sunnis, properly speaking, but adherents to what might be termed Umayyad Islam. Sunni Islam is a compromise position between Shi'ite and Umayyad Islam, and could only have come into existence some time after the advent of the Abbasids. This may be seen succinctly in the Sunni phrase *al-khulafa' al-rashidun* (lit. the "rightly guided caliphs"), which indicates approval of all the first four caliphs. The Umayyads revered the first three caliphs, but 'Ali was anathema to them. They reportedly instituted a practice of cursing him from the pulpit in Friday prayer. The Shi'a, however, revered 'Ali but detested or disapproved of the first three caliphs. The Sunni approval of all four could only have developed at a much later date, as an attempt to reconcile the two opposing positions.

Rival Factions within the Shi'a Community

Conflict over leadership of the Muslim community and over succession among rival Shi'i claimants to the imamate gave rise to theological doctrines and concepts that would remain important throughout Islamic history. In the course of the eighth century the Shi'a developed the doctrines of the imam's *'isma*, meaning "infallibility" or "divine protection from sin," and *nass*, the explicit and divinely sanctioned designation of the imam by his predecessor. The *ghulat* (extremists) developed more exaggerated forms of reverence for various claimants to the imamate, including beliefs that the imam did not die but went into occultation (*ghayba*) or that he would return (*rajʿa*) as a messianic figure (*mahdi*) before the apocalypse. Others claimed that the imam shared in prophetic authority, had status equal to that of the Prophet, possessed divine qualities, or manifested divinity through divine infusion (*hulul*). Some of these extreme concepts, particularly occultation, would become standard doctrine in the main divisions of the Shiʿa in later centuries.

A second set of issues had to do with the status of the Prophet's Companions. In order to bolster the legitimacy of ʿAli, the Shiʿites used hadith reports and historical accounts concerning the first three caliphs, ʿAʾisha, and many other Companions to impugn their characters, casting them as sinners, incompetent leaders, or outright unbelievers. The Sunnis, used similar accounts to uphold the view that the Companions were all exemplary. The Shiʿite position, while certainly exaggerated over time, readily admits the seriousness of the conflicts that wracked the early Muslim community, while Sunni historiography has often endeavored to cover them up or explain them away.

A seventeenth-century fresco depicting Iman Shah Zaid is represented in the volume two color insert.

See also **Empires: Abbasid; Empires: Umayyad; Shiʿa: Imami (Twelver); Succession.**

BIBLIOGRAPHY

Amir-Moezzi, Mohammad Ali. *The Divine Guide in Early Shiʿism: The Sources of Esotericism in Islam.* Translated by David Streight. Albany: State University of New York Press, 1994.

Arjomand, Said Amir. *The Shadow of God and the Hidden Imam.* Chicago: University of Chicago Press, 1984.

Crone, Patricia, and Hinds, Martin. *God's Caliph: Religious Authority in the First Centuries of Islam.* Cambridge, U.K.: Cambridge University Press, 1986.

Donaldson, Dwight M. *The Shiʿite Religion.* London: Luzac, 1933.

Farouk, Omar. "Some Aspects of the Abbasid-Husaynid Relations during the Early Abbasid Period, 132–193/750–809 A.D." *Arabica* 22 (1975): 170–179.

Goldziher, Ignaz. *An Introduction to Islamic Theology and Law.* Translated by Anras and Ruth Hamori. Princeton, N.J.: Princeton University Press, 1984.

Halm, Heinz. *Shiʿism.* Edinburgh: Edinburgh University Press, 1991.

Hodgson, Marshall G. S. "How Did the Early Shiʿa Become Sectarian." *Journal of the American Oriental Society* 75 (1955): 1–13.

Kohlberg, Etan. "Imam and Community in the Pre-Ghayba Period." In *Authority and Political Culture.* Edited by Said Amir Arjomand. Albany: State University of New York Press, 1988.

Madelung, Wilfred. *The Succession to Muhammad: A Study of the Early Caliphate.* Cambridge, U.K.: Cambridge University Press, 1997.

Modarressi, Hossein. *Crisis and Consolidation in the Formative Period of Shiʿite Islam.* Princeton, N.J.: Princeton University Press, 1993.

Momen, Moojan. *An Introduction to Shiʿi Islam: The History and Doctrines of Twelver Shiʿism.* New Haven, Conn.: Yale University Press, 1985.

Moussavi, Ahmad Kazemi. *Religious Authority in Shiʿite Islam.* Kuala Lumpur: International Institute of Islamic Thought and Civilization, 1996.

Sachedina, Abdulaziz Abdulhussein. *Islamic Messianism: The Idea of the Mahdi in Twelver Shʿism.* Albany: State University of New York Press, 1981.

Watt, W. Montgomery. "Shiʿism Under the Umayyads." *Journal of the Royal Asiatic Society* (1960): 158–72.

Watt, W. Montgomery. *The Formative Period of Islamic Thought.* Edinburgh: Edinburgh University Press, 1973.

Devin J. Stewart

IMAMI (TWELVER)

The term Ithna ʿAshari ("Twelver") or Imami refers to the denomination of Shiʿism to which the majority of Shiʿas worldwide adhere. Characteristic of Twelver Shiʿism is recognition of the authority of twelve successive imams (spiritual leaders) who were members or descendants of *ahl al-bayt* (the prophet Muhammad's immediate family). Their authority is said to have been transmitted over time via the lineage of Muhammad's daughter Fatima and her husband, ʿAli. Also characteristic of Twelver Shiʿism is an emotional attachment to *ahl al-bayt* that manifests itself in annual rituals commemorating the battlefield death of the imam Husayn, grandson of Muhammad.

Twelver Shiʿism identifies the first imam as Muhammad's cousin and son-in-law, ʿAli b. Abi Talib. According to Shiʿa tradition, the Prophet, shortly before his own death, publicly announced the selection of ʿ Ali as his successor. But ʿAli was blocked repeatedly from power. He did not contest the election of the first three caliphs, apparently out of a desire to avoid civil war. Finally, ʿAli did obtain the caliphate and ruled for five years, only to be murdered in 661 C.E.

In Twelver Shiʿism the term *imam* indicates those members of *ahl al-bayt* who are the true spiritual leaders of the Muslim community regardless of any political recognition or lack thereof extended by the Islamic world at large. After ʿ Ali, the imamate passed to his sons, Hasan and Husayn successively.

The martyrdom of the third imam, Husayn, during the second civil war in 680 is the most decisive event in Shiʿite history. At Karbala, near the Euphrates River, he was intercepted and surrounded by forces loyal to the Umayyad caliph, Yazid. During the initial days of the month of Muharram the imam Husayn and his followers withstood siege by Yazid's army, which hoped to force the small band to surrender. Husayn chose death instead. On 'Ashura, the tenth of Muharram, Husayn was killed, his household taken captive. The train of captives, including Husayn's sister Zaynab and his son 'Ali Zayn al-'Abidin, was marched through the desert to Damascus.

Husayn's death at Karbala marks the beginning of the transformation of Shi'ism from a political movement to a distinctive religious tradition within Islam. His death is viewed by devout Shi'as as a sacrifice that benefits believers. In exchange for the suffering voluntarily undergone by Husayn and the other Karbala martyrs, God has granted them *shafa'a* (the power of intercession). Intercession is granted especially to those believers who earn *savab* (religious merit) by mourning Husayn during Muharram.

The centuries following Husayn's death saw the gradual emergence of distinctive Shi'ite communities, not only in southern Iraq, the site of the imam's martyrdom, but also in Lebanon, Syria, and parts of South Asia. To this day various localities in India and Pakistan commemorate Husayn's death with an annual "Horse of Karbala" procession. Mourners parade a riderless stallion caparisoned to represent Zuljenah, the horse ridden by Husayn at Karbala. The horse's appearance acts as a stimulus to rituals of lamentation, the performance of which earns participants *savab*.

Twelver Shi'as recognize as the fifth imam Muhammad al-Baqir (d. c. 735), the son of the fourth imam, 'Ali Zayn al-'Abidin. Like his father, al-Baqir avoided confrontation with the reigning caliphate. He promulgated the doctrine of *nass* ("designation"): guided by God, each imam designates the person who is to be his successor as spiritual leader of the Muslim community. Thus the imamate is not a matter of human choice or self-assertion. This doctrine countered the activities of al-Baqir's half-brother Zayd b. 'Ali, who attracted the support of militants impatient with al-Baqir's political passivity. Zayd led an uprising against the reigning Umayyad government in Kufa and was killed there in the fighting in 740.

The political engagement characteristic of Zaydi Shi'ism was countered by Ja'far al-Sadiq (d. 765), the sixth imam in the Twelver tradition. Like his father al-Baqir, he espoused an accommodationist attitude toward the caliphal authorities. Also like his father, he advocated the doctrine of *nass*, thereby delegitimizing rival claimants to leadership of the Shi'ite community. Some Muslim scholars trace to his imamate the doctrine of *taqiyya* ("dissimulation"), which permits Shi'as threatened with persecution to conceal their denominational identity as followers of the imams. These teachings fostered in the Imami community a political quietism that furthered their survival as a religious minority under the Sunni caliphs.

Ja'far al-Sadiq was also renowned as a scholar of law (for this reason the body of legal lore in Twelver Shi'ism is

referred to as the Ja'fari tradition). Additionally, he is credited with having further defined the qualifications for the imamate in terms of the concept of *'ilm* (knowledge). The imams are said to be the most knowledgeable of all humankind in matters pertaining to religious law, the principles governing conduct in this life and rewards and punishments in the next, and the realm of the unseen. In particular the imams' knowledge extends to scripture. They understand both the *zahir* (the external or literal meaning) and the *batin* (the hidden significance) of the Qur'an. The *batin* is accessed via *ta'wil*, an interpretive process that applies allegory and symbolism to the scriptural text.

A turning point came in Shi'ite history with the death of Hasan al-'Askari, the eleventh imam (d. 874). Skeptics in the Muslim community claimed that Hasan had died without leaving behind a son as leader of the Shi'as. But Imami doctrine asserts that Hasan did in fact have a son, named Abu al-Qasim Muhammad, and it explains the circumstance that Muhammad was unknown to his contemporaries by invoking the ancient concept of *ghayba* (occultation). To protect the twelfth imam from his persecutors, God concealed the young man from the world at large. The period from 874 to 941 is known as the Lesser Occultation. From concealment this "Hidden Imam" provided guidance to his community through a series of agents, who met with him and conveyed his directives to the world.

The period from 941 to the present day is known as the Greater Occultation. No longer are there agents who confer with the Hidden Imam directly or transmit his instructions to the faithful. Nevertheless he is alive and will return to earth one day as the Mahdi, "the rightly guided by God," when he will purge the earth of all the injustice that has stained it since the time when 'Ali, Husayn, and the other members of *ahl al-bayt* were first denied the political recognition to which they were entitled. For this reason the twelfth imam is called al-Muntazar ("the Awaited One"), for Imami Shi'ite belief looks hopefully to the Mahdi's return as the inauguration of the Day of Judgment.

Imami folklore includes tales that indicate that the twelfth imam dwells among us, invisibly present but capable of manifesting himself to individuals in moments of need. Iraqi Shi'as in the 1990s who had returned from the pilgrimage to Mecca recounted to this author stories of hajj-sightings. Elderly people who had been knocked to the ground and nearly trampled in the pilgrim-crowds told of how they had been rescued by "a tall youthful man of radiant appearance" who subsequently vanished. Surely, they argued, this had been the Hidden Imam.

The net effect of Twelver belief concerning the Mahdi was to strengthen the accommodationist attitude already prevalent among the Imami Shi'as. Desires for social justice, for radical changes in the worldly order, and for the restoration of the caliphal throne to *ahl al-bayt* were linked to the concept of *intizar*: "expectation," the passive awaiting of the Mahdi's return at the end of time.

Twelver theology underwent further elaboration with the creation of the Safavid dynasty in Iran beginning in 1501 under Shah Isma'il. This monarch established Imami Shi'ism as Iran's state religion. The Safavids clashed frequently with the neighboring empire of the Ottoman Turks, whose sultans arrogated to themselves the title of caliph, with its implications of universal Islamic sovereignty. The settlement of the caliphate in Istanbul from the sixteenth century sharpened Sunni-Shi'a tensions as a religious expression of international political rivalries.

Theological developments during the Safavid era (sixteenth-eighteenth centuries) reflected the Iranian clergy's desire to heighten adherence to Shi'ite communal identity in lands under the shah's dominion. This is reflected in the writings of the celebrated *'alim* (religious scholar) Muhammad Baqir Majlisi (d. 1698). In a work called *Bihar al-anwar* (The oceans of lights) he assembled numerous Shi'ite hadiths so as to justify the linkage of popular ritual practices with a distinctively Imami soteriology. For example, in a chapter of the *Bihar* entitled "The Ways in Which God Informed His Prophets of the Forthcoming Martyrdom of Husayn," Majlisi emphasized the predestinarian quality of the seventh-century events at Karbala.

Majlisi linked Husayn's martyrdom at Karbala with the imam's power to grant intercession in paradise to those who honor Husayn through acts of ritual commemoration. Majlisi also promoted popular veneration of Husayn and the other imams by collecting in the *Bihar* various traditions describing the twelve imams as *ma'sum* (sinless, infallible, and protected from error). In Shi'ite devotion today, the imams, together with the prophet Muhammad and his daughter Fatima, are known collectively as the "fourteen Infallibles." Their sinlessness guarantees their closeness to God in heaven as well as their ability to intercede for those on earth who remember Husayn through acts of lamentation.

Twelver Shi'ism spread in Syria during the rule of the Hamdanid dynasty in the tenth century. Aleppo became an important center of medieval Shi'ism. Another center of Shi'ite learning in the region emerged in Mamluk and Ottoman times in Jabal 'Amil in present-day Lebanon. A number of Shi'ite scholars emigrated to Iran after the establishment of the Safavid empire, but the Shi'ite community continued its life in the region and constitutes over one-third of the population of Lebanon at present.

Public rituals lamenting the Karbala martyrs are attested as early as the tenth century in Baghdad. The Safavid era, however, witnessed the elaboration of a soteriology that joined ritual mourning with Shi'ite communal identity. This is attested in a work that became increasingly popular during the reign of the Safavids, *Rawdat al-shuhada'* (The garden of the martyrs), which was written by Husayn Wa'iz al-Kashifi (d. 1504). "Paradise is awarded to anyone," argues Kashifi, "who weeps for Husayn for the following reason, that every year, when the month of Muharram comes, a multitude of the lovers of the family of the Prophet renews and makes fresh the tragedy of the martyrs."

"Lovers of the family of the Prophet": Here Kashifi defines the community of believers not in terms of doctrine but in terms of emotional disposition and ritual activity. His description suggests an important aspect of Imami Shi'ite identity. At the popular level, from the premodern era through the twenty-first century, Twelver Shi'as tend to define themselves as those Muslims who excel beyond all others in their love for the Prophet's family and for the Prophet's descendants, the imams. This affection is expressed annually in the action of *matam* (displays of grief for the Karbala martyrs).

Safavid-era ulema such as Majlisi developed a predestinarian theology of voluntary suffering, ritual commemoration, and intercession as a reward for mourners. They also campaigned vehemently and sometimes violently against Sufi shaykhs and the *tariqat* (mystical associations) that were under the direction of the Sufi masters. Twelver ulema condemned Sufism as heterodox out of a recognition that popular devotion to the shaykhs and visits to the tombs of Sufi saints threatened to compete with the forms of piety administered by the clerical hierarchy, namely, devotion to the twelve imams and pilgrimage to shrines associated with the imams.

Persecution of Sufis, however, did not preclude Sufi influence on Imami Shi'ism. Such influence can be seen in the later Safavid era with the flourishing of the "School of Isfahan," which is associated with Mulla Sadra (d. 1640). The school of Isfahan pursued the study of *Hekmat-e elahi* ("divine wisdom"), a discipline that combined formal training in Qur'anic studies and related Islamic sciences with rational philosophic inquiry and the cultivation of the direct and unmediated personal experience of divine reality. *Hekmat-e elahi* traces its origin to Shihab al-Din al-Suhrawardi (d. 1191), who in works such as *Hikmat al-ishraq* (The wisdom of illuminationist dawning) envisioned intellectual studies as the propaedeutic to mystical ascension and encounters with the sacred. In the Twelver tradition this intellectual-mystical approach to learning is linked to the term *'irfan* ("gnosis": the seeking after of experiential and participatory knowledge of the patterns governing the cosmos). The term carries political implications. With the decline of centralized governmental authority in the later Safavid and Qajar eras (eighteenth-nineteenth centuries), the ulema acquired ever more temporal power. A spiritual elitism evolved in which at least some clerics were willing to accord the highest rank to the scholar-cum-mystic: the perfected Gnostic, the theosopher-king. This illuminationist strand in Imami theology culminated in the twentieth century with the founding of Iran's Islamic Republic under Ruhollah Khomeini.

The declining power of the Safavid shahs was accompanied by the increasing importance in the public realm of the Usuli form of Shi'ite jurisprudence. One way to understand Usulism is as a refutation of traditional Imami Shi'ite attitudes toward governance. Imami theology argued that since the only legitimate government is that administered by the perfect and sinless imam, during the imam's occultation all forms of earthly government are necessarily imperfect and sinful. Many traditionalist Shi'as therefore avoided engagement with worldly politics, preferring to await the Hidden Imam's return as the Mahdi. Usuli jurisprudence, however, granted to qualified ulema the latitude to apply *ijtihad* (scripturally based independent reasoning) to every aspect of life, not only religious, but also social and political. Those scholars whose studies qualified them to exercise *ijtihad* were known as *mujtahids*.

But while elevating the exercise of rational skills among jurisprudents, Usulism restricted religious and intellectual independence among the masses. Usuli clerics insisted that the Shi'ite laity must select a living *mujtahid* as a *marja' al-taqlid* ("reference point for imitation"), a guide that one follows in legal, moral, and ritual issues. The centralizing and authoritarian tendencies implicit in Usulism were resisted by the more conservative Akhbari school of jurisprudence, which argued that Muslims should direct their *taqlid* ("imitation" or devout and unquestioning obedience) only to the imam and not to any earthly *mujtahid*. But by the late eighteenth century Usulism was clearly ascendant. Since the nineteenth century certain of the most prominent Usuli *maraji'* (plural of *marja' al-taqlid*) have received the title *na'ib al-imam* ("the Hidden Imam's deputy"), implying the jurisprudent's right to govern as the lieutenant of the twelfth imam. In recent times *na'ib al-imam* was applied most famously to the Ayatollah Khomeini after the success of Iran's 1979 Islamic Revolution. Khomeini rationalized the imamic deputy's role in society through his doctrine of *velayet-e faqih* ("the rule of the jurisconsult"): In the imam's absence, government should be in the hands of those Muslims who are most versed in Islamic law.

Preparation for the 1979 revolution involved a reinterpretation of many components of the Imami tradition. In the prerevolutionary Iran of Reza Shah Pahlevi's reign, the imam Husayn was typically regarded as a model of patient suffering, whom one lamented during Muharram and to whom one turned for *shafa'a* (intercession) and personal salvation. Such an image reflected the hierarchic and stratified social relations characteristic of Iran and other traditional Islamic societies. New interpretations in the 1960s and 1970s, however, replaced the image of Husayn-as-savior with Husayn-as-revolutionary exemplar. Such thinking is evident in the writings of 'Ali Shari'ati (d. 1977), a Sorbonne-educated intellectual who advocated the transformation of "Black Shi'ism" (associated with mourning for Husayn and the passive expectation of salvation) into "Red Shi'ism" (whereby Shari'ati invoked the color of blood to call for confrontation, revolution, and self-sacrifice in the service of society).

Not only the imam Husayn but also the revered women of *ahl al-bayt* have been subjected to reinterpretation in recent years. An example is Zaynab bt. 'Ali, Husayn's sister. Present at Karbala, she was taken prisoner by Yazid's soldiers and presented to the triumphant caliph in his Damascus court. Despite her powerlessness, she spoke out defiantly and denounced Yazid as a tyrant. Supporters of Khomeini during his struggle against the Pahlevi regime described Zeinab as a model of political activism worthy of imitation by contemporary Shi'ite women. Writing shortly after the 1979 revolution, Farah Azari, one of the founding members of the Iranian Women's Solidarity Group, stated, "[I]t was Zeinab who came to the forefront to symbolize the ideal of the modern revolutionary Muslim woman in Iran. Those enigmatic young women clad in a black chador bearing machine guns, aspire to follow Zeinab. It is not inappropriate that they have been sometimes referred to as 'the commandos of her holiness Zeinab'" (Azari 1983, p. 26).

Since Khomeini's death in 1989 contemporary Shi'ite thought in Iran has been characterized by increasing diversity and the emergence of a movement for the reformation of Shi'ism. Among recent theological developments in Imami Shi'ism is the advocacy of *taqrib* ("rapprochement"), the easing of religious clashes between Shi'as and Sunnis. In 1990 Khomeini's successor, Ayatollah Sayyed 'Ali Khamene'i, founded the *Majma' al-taqrib* ("the rapprochement association"), with the idea of establishing an international league of Sunnis and Shi'as who would be united as Muslims in the face of perceived opposition from the non-Muslim world at large.

With this goal in mind, Khamene'i has taken steps to reform a Shi'ite practice frequently denounced by Sunnis: the ritual of *zanjiri-matam*, in which mourners employ knives, razors, and chains in acts of self-flagellation to honor Husayn and the Karbala martyrs. In the 1994 Muharram season Khamene'i issued a *fatwa* forbidding acts of *matam* performed in public involving the use of weapons to shed one's own blood. Such attempts to curb "bloody" matam have met at most with very limited success. Even before Khamene'i's *fatwa*, in the 1980s an attempt to forbid Muharram self-flagellation had been made by Muhammad Husayn Fadlallah, "spiritual mentor" of the militant Lebanese group Hezbollah. But Hezbollah Shi'as in Beirut disregarded Fadlallah's prohibition. And in various localities in India and Pakistan, Shi'a *matami* (lamentation) associations continue to sponsor public *matam*-performances in which many members engage in self-flagellation. When interviewed, these mourners explained their reasons for persisting in this ritual: the wish to honor Husayn and earn religious merit, as well as the desire to assert Shi'ite communal identity in the presence of neighboring faith communities, whether Hindu, Buddhist, or Sunni Muslim. The Iranian government's program of imposing uniformity worldwide in Shi'ite ritual practice is by no means complete.

One of the most progressive Imami thinkers of the present day is 'Abd al-Karim Sorush (b. 1945). He offers a postpositivist assessment of modernity's challenge to revealed religion. While religion itself is divine in origin, Sorush argues, all human knowledge of religion is limited, indeterminate, and necessarily subject to change. No interpretation of Qur'anic scripture can ever be definitive. According to Sorush, every scriptural interpretation, no matter how authoritative the source, is fallible and can offer only an approximation of divine truth. Such indeterminacy should not be viewed with alarm. Rather, this condition is intended by God so as to encourage humans to engage in the ongoing process of ijtihad, whereby they exercise the divine gifts of intellect and independent judgment. Because of the challenge to traditional clerical authority implied by such arguments, Sorush has aroused considerable hostility among members of the governing hierarchy in Iran's Islamic Republic.

See also Taqiyya; Usuliyya.

BIBLIOGRAPHY

Arjomand, Said Amir. *The Shadow of God and the Hidden Imam*. Chicago: University of Chicago Press, 1984.

Azari, Farah, ed. *Women of Iran: The Conflict with Fundamentalist Islam*. London: Ithaca Press, 1983.

Halm, Heinz. *Shi'a Islam: From Religion to Revolution*. Princeton, N.J.: Markus Wiener Publishers, 1997.

Momen, Moojan. *An Introduction to Shi'i Islam*. New Haven, Conn.: Yale University Press, 1985.

Pinault, David. *Horse of Karbala: Muslim Devotional Life in India*. New York: Palgrave, 2001.

David Pinault

ISMA'ILI

Isma'ili Shi'a represent the second most important Shi'ite community after the Twelver (Ithna'ashari) Shi'a and are scattered in more than twenty-five countries in Asia, the Middle East, Africa, Europe, and North America. The Isma'ilis have subdivided into a number of factions and groups in the course of their complex history.

The Isma'ilis recognized a line of imams in the progeny of Isma'il, son of Imam Ja'far al-Sadiq (d. 765), hence their designation as Isma'ili. By the 870s, the Isma'ilis had organized a revolutionary movement against the Abbasid caliph in Baghdad. The aim of this religio-political movement, designated as al-da'wa al-hadiya or the "rightly guiding mission," was to install the Isma'ili imam belonging to the prophet Muhammad's family to a new caliphate ruling over the entire Muslim community. The message of the movement was disseminated by a network of da'is or missionaries in many parts of the Muslim world.

The early success of the Isma'ili movement culminated in the foundation of the Fatimid caliphate in North Africa in 909. 'Abdallah al-Mahdi (d. 934) and his successors in the Isma'ili imamate ruled as Fatimid caliphs over an important state that soon grew into an empire stretching from North Africa to Egypt, Palestine, and Syria. The Fatimid period was the "golden age" of Isma'ilism when Isma'ili thought and literature attained their summit and Isma'ilis made important contributions to Islamic civilization, especially after the seat of the Fatimid caliphate was transferred to Cairo, itself founded in 969 by the Fatimids. The early Isma'ilis developed a distinctive esoteric, gnostic system of religious thought based on a distinction between the exoteric (zahir) and esoteric (batin) aspects of the sacred scriptures as well as religious commandments and prohibitions. They also developed a cyclical view of religious history and a cosmological doctrine. The early doctrines were more fully elaborated in Fatimid times by Isma'ili da'is who were also the scholars and authors of their community. Isma'ili law was codified through the efforts of al-Qadi al-Nu'man (d. 974), the foremost jurist of the Fatimid period, and the Fatimid Isma'ilis developed distinctive institutions of learning.

The early Isma'ili movement had been rent by a schism in 899 when a faction of the community, designated as Qarmati, refused to acknowledge continuity in the Isma'ili imamate and retained an earlier belief in the Mahdiship of the seventh Isma'ili imam, Muhammad ibn Isma'il, who was expected to reappear. The Qarmatis, who did not recognize the Fatimid caliphs as their imams, founded a powerful state in Bahrayn, eastern Arabia. The Qarmati state collapsed in 1077.

The Fatimid Isma'ilis themselves experienced a major schism in 1094, on the death of al-Mustansir (1036–1094), the eighth Fatimid caliph and the eighteenth Isma'ili imam. Al-Mustansir's succession was disputed by his sons Nizar (d. 1095), the original heir-designate, and al-Musta'li (1094–1101), who was installed to the Fatimid throne through the machinations of the Fatimid wazir al-Afdal (d. 1121). As a result, the unified Isma'ili da'wa and community were split into rival Nizari and Musta'li factions. The da'wa organization in Cairo as well as the Isma'ili communities of Yaman and Gujarat, in western India, supported the claims of al-Musta'li. The Isma'ilis of Iran and adjacent lands, who were then under the leadership of Hasan Sabbah (d. 1124), upheld Nizar's right to the Isma'ili imamate.

On the death of the Fatimid caliph-imam al-Amir (1101–1130), the Musta'li Isma'ilis themselves subdivided into Hafizi and Tayyibi branches. The Hafizi Isma'ilis who recognized al-Hafiz (1130–1149) and the later Fatimid caliphs as their imams disappeared completely after the Fatimid dynasty was uprooted in 1171 by Saladin, the founder of the Ayyubid dynasty who championed the cause of Sunnism. Tayyibi Isma'ilis established their permanent stronghold in the Yemen. By the end of the sixteenth century, the Tayyibi Isma'ilis split into separate Da'udi and Sulaymani branches over the question of the rightful succession to the twenty-sixth da'i mutlaq, Da'ud b. 'Ajabshah (1567–1589). By that time, the Tayyibis of India, known locally as Bohras, had greatly outnumbered their Yemeni co-religionists. Da'udi and Sulaymani Tayyibis have followed different lines of da'is. Da'udi Bohras, accounting for the great majority of the Tayyibis, have split into a number of groupings, the largest numbering around 800,000.

Hasan Sabbah's seizure of the mountain fortress of Alamut, in northern Iran, in 1090, marked the effective foundation of what became the Nizari Isma'ili state of Iran and Syria. Thus, Nizaris acquired political prominence under Hasan and his seven successors at Alamut. In 1094, Hasan also founded the independent Nizari da'wa and severed his ties with Fatimid Egypt. The Nizari state was comprised of a network of strongholds and towns in several regions of Iran and Syria, in the midst of the Seljuk sultanate. Hasan's armed revolt against the Seljuk Turks, whose alien rule was detested by the Iranians, did not succeed, nor did the Seljuks succeed in destroying the Nizari fortress communities despite their superior military power. A stalemate, in effect, developed between the Nizaris and their various enemies until their state in Iran was destroyed by the all-conquering Mongols in 1256. The Nizaris of Syria, who had numerous military encounters with the Crusaders, and Saladin, among others, were later subdued by the Mamluks. The Iranian Nizaris elaborated their own teachings and adopted Persian, in preference to Arabic, as their religious language. They also established libraries at Alamut, the headquarters of the Nizari state and da'wa, and other mountain fortresses, also extending their patronage of learning to outside scholars.

The Nizari Isma'ilis survived the destruction of their state. Initially, for about two centuries, they remained disorganized and developed independently in scattered communities, also adopting Sufi guises to safeguard themselves against persecution. During the Anjudan revival in the post-Alamut period of their history, which lasted some two centuries from the middle of the fifteenth century, the Nizari imams emerged at Anjudan, in central Iran, and increasingly established their control over various communities of their followers, also reviving Nizari missionary and literary activities. At the same time, the Nizaris of Iran and adjacent lands retained different taqiyya or precautionary dissimulation practices of disguising themselves under the cloaks of Sufism and Twelver Shi'ism, the official religion of Safavid Iran. The Anjudan revival achieved particular success in Central Asia and South Asia, where large numbers of Hindus were converted in Sind, Gujarat, and elsewhere. The Indian Nizaris became locally known as Khojas and they developed an indigenous tradition, designated as the "Satpanth" or true path. The Nizaris of Badakhshan, now divided between Tajikistan and Afghanistan, have preserved numerous collections of Persian Isma'ili manuscripts. The Nizari Khojas, together with the Tayyibi Bohras, were among the earliest Asian communities to have settled in the nineteenth century in East Africa. In the 1970s and later, many East African Isma'ilis immigrated to the West. Under the leadership of their last two imams, Sultan Muhammad Shah, Aga Khan III (1885–1957), and Prince Karim Aga Khan IV, who in 1957 succeeded his grandfather as their forty-ninth imam, the Nizari Isma'ilis, who number several million, have entered the modern age as a progressive community with high standards of education and well-being.

See also **Da'wa; Khojas; Nizari.**

BIBLIOGRAPHY

Daftary, Farhad, ed. *Mediaeval Isma'ili History and Thought.* Cambridge, U.K.: Cambridge University Press, 1996.

Daftary, Farhad. *A Short History of the Ismailis.* Edinburgh: Edinburgh University Press, 1998.

Farhad Daftary

ZAYDI (FIVER)

The branch of Shi'ism known as the Zaydiyya owes its name to the belief in the imamate of Zayd b. 'Ali. Adherents proclaimed Zayd as imam because it was he who raised an army against Ummayad rule in an aborted uprising in 740 C.E. The Zaydis are the inheritors of that element of Shi'ism that emphasizes a willingness to challenge illegitimate political structures as a characteristic of the imam, rather than an esoteric conception of the imam as spiritual guide with a qualitatively different relationship to God than the ordinary believer. The qualities of the imam for Zaydis include a willingness and ability to assume some sort of political power, along with learning ('ilm, in the traditional, rather than esoteric sense of the word) and descent from the Prophet's cousin and son-in-law, 'Ali. It is not essential that the imam be designated by the previous imam, and there may be times when the world is entirely bereft of an imam since no descendant of 'Ali is qualified to assume the position. For some Zaydis, there may be times when there is more than one imam, each leading Islamic states in different parts of the world (though the long-term aim that these states conjoin is regularly expressed). Indeed this was the case in the tenth century, when Zaydi states existed simultaneously in Yemen and Tabaristan (on the Iranian coast of the Caspian Sea) with separate imams.

The rejection of the special qualities of the imam in Zaydi thought removes one of the elements of Shi'ism viewed as problematic by Sunni authors. This has led to a certain rapprochement between Zaydis and Sunnis, and the development of a Zaydi theological and legal tradition that intersects with the Sunni tradition more than with that of the Isma'ilis or Imamis. This rejection of the special qualities of the imam manifests itself in the common Zaydi assertion that 'Ali, Hasan, and Husayn were designated as imams, but that their designation was hidden (*nass khafi*), and could only be discovered after investigation. This exempted some of the companions of the Prophet, who had not recognized 'Ali's imamate, from blame or censure. Zaydi theologians and historians have also been less eager to criticize the caliphates of Abu Bakr (r. 632–634), 'Umar (r. 634–644), and 'Uthman (r. 644–656). The legal system, it is claimed by Zaydi scholars, owes much to Shafi'ite jurisprudence.

The theological writings of the Zaydiyya show the imprint of the Mu'tazili school. Al-Qasim b. Ibrahim al-Rassi (d.860), an early imam and supposed founder of the Zaydi legal school, set the tone for later Zaydi exploration of Mu'tazili themes with his support of standard Mu'tazili principles such as the unity of God (*tawhid*), the justice of God ('*adl*), and the promise and the threat (*al-wa'd wa'l-wa'id*). Al-Qasim's grandson, al-Hadi ila al-Haqq al-Mubin (d. 911), himself a noted theologian, founded the Zaydi state in Yemen, and a close relationship with Mu'tazilism characterized Yemeni Zaydi discourse thereafter. Other Mu'tazili principles that permeate Zaydi theological works include a belief in human free will (*qadr*), a renunciation of anthropomorphism (*tashbih*) with regard to God, and the widely cited Mu'tazili slogan *taklif ma la yutaqu*. The last of these can be interpreted as meaning that God cannot demand that his subjects (*mukallafun*) perform duties they are incapable of either doing or knowing; to do so would make God unjust. These principles were not, however, incorporated into Zaydi Islam without debate. Perhaps most notable of the dissident groups was the Mutarrifiyya, a Yemeni Zaydi movement that emerged in the eleventh century and was named after its founder Mutarrif b. Shihab (d. 1067). The Mutarrifiyya claimed to be adhering strictly to the teachings of al-Qasim b. Ibrahim in rejecting certain elements of Basran Mu'tazilism in support of some of the conclusions of the Mu'tazili school of Baghdad. In Zaydi Tabaristan, the state founded by a descendant of Zayd, al-Hasan b. Zayd (d. 888), there was also much theological and legal debate, particularly under the imamate of al-Nasir Hasan al-Utrush in the tenth century. The latter's legal doctrine was a matter of dispute among the Zaydis both during his life and after his death (in particular his doctrine that three statements of divorce announced by the husband in one session was a valid form of divorce). The intellectual history of the Zaydi school is, then, a history of debate and dispute that at times threatened the unity of the community. When the Zaydi state in Tabaristan collapsed in 1126, however, Yemen became (and remains to the present day) the undisputed home of Zaydi theology and law. The Zaydi imamate in Yemen had grown out of a loose coalition of Yemeni tribes, and the dynamics of tribal loyalty versus imamate authority are a constant theme in the history of the area.

Perhaps the most interesting figure of later Zaydi thought is Muhammad b. 'Ali al-Shawkani (d. 1834), whose learning in both Sunni and Zaydi traditions has earned him the title *mujaddid* (renewer) of the twelfth hijri century by no less a Sunni authority than Rashid Rida. Though not an imam himself, he was appointed as chief judge of the Zaydi imamate. Shawkani's exposition of *ijtihad*, and his refusal to slavishly imitate past legal authority (of either the Zaydi or Sunni schools) brought about a revivification of legal studies, the effect of which was felt well beyond the boundaries of the Zaydi state.

The Zaydi imamate in Yemen continued well into the twentieth century. This was in part due to the charismatic and dynamic imam Yahya Hamid al-Din who fought against the Ottomans (eventually negotiating for them to withdraw from the area) and took the disputed town of Badr from the Saudis. After his death in 1948, the imamate faced a number of challenges and eventually collapsed in 1962 as Yemen experienced a revolution influenced by the thought of Jamal 'Abd al-Nasser. The republicans who formed the Yemen Arab Republic, and negotiated an abortive union with Egypt, divesting the Hamid al-Din line of the imamate. This brought the end of the most long lasting Shi'ite state in the Muslim world, and although Zaydi scholars still study and teach in the highlands of Yemen, the legal tradition has become increasingly mixed with Shafi'ite law, the other major legal tradition in the area.

See also **Shafi'i, al-; Shi'a: Early; Shi'a: Imami (Twelver); Shi'a: Isma'ili.**

BIBLIOGRAPHY

Abrahamov, Binyamin. *Anthropomorphism and Interpretation in the Qur'an in the Theology of al-Qasim b. Ibrahim.* Leiden: E. J. Brill, 1996.

Madelung, Wilfred. *Religious Schools and Sects in Medieval Islam.* London: Varirum Reprints, 1985.

Robert Gleave

SHIRK

Meaning "association," the term *shirk* generally implies assigning partners or equals to God, and is considered to be the paramount sin in Islam. The central doctrine of Islam is *tawhid* (divine unity), which came to mean that God does not need nor have partners to assist Him. By contrast, Muslims base their understanding of *shirk* on three passages from the Qur'an (34:20–24, 35:40, 46:4), which advise Muslims against associating helpers or partners with God. For instance, Sura 34:20–24 establishes the non-duality of God, arguing that evil and good originate in God's creative act and that evil (the *shaytan*) has no power over creation.

Sura 34:23 has been used by some commentators to suggest that God's power is so all-encompassing that humans have no free will, and that God has predetermined who will be saved and who will be damned. The Jabriyya (compulsionists, circa eighth-to-ninth century) argued that those who advocated a free will position (the Qadariyya) held, by implication, that humans have abilities over which God has no power, in effect making humans equal to God in certain respects. This view was later modified by al-Ash'ari (d. 935), who held that God creates a range of choices from which humans have the limited ability to choose (*kasb*, literally "to acquire") at the moment of decision. In this way, God's ultimate unity is not violated and humans do not associate themselves with God's creative power.

Some contemporary Islamic revivalists have argued that the Qur'an accuses Christians and Jews of *shirk*, based on Sura 9:30, which states that "the Jews call Ezra a son of God and the Christians call Christ the son of God." Furthermore, Sura 5:72–73 accuses Christians of associating Jesus with God and contends that "if they do not desist ... a painful punishment will come upon them." Sura 2:105, however, draws a distinction between Christians and Jews, whom it refers to as *ahl al-kitab* (people of the book) and the polytheists, whom it calls the *mushrikun* (literally the "ones who associate"). The distinction is based on the idea that while Christians and Jews may be in error, they base their mistake on a corruption of earlier revelation. They, therefore, accept the basic concepts of God's true religion while interpolating certain ideas that need to be corrected for them to fully follow God's path. The *mushrikun* reject all revelation and prefer to worship their own gods in preference to the united and all-powerful God (see Sura 23:51–77).

Contemporary Islamic revivalists have also used the concept to justify attacks on non-Muslims, as well as fellow Muslims who reject revivalist ideologies. Many contemporary revivalists base their ideas on the writings of Sayyid Qutb (d. 1966), who argued that true Islam had been corrupted by pre-Islamic and extra-Islamic ideas that promoted concepts of *shirk* and interwove them with Islamic ritual and theology. According to this view, only through the violent expulsion of *shirk* concepts can true Islam flower as it did during the time of the prophet Muhammad and his Companions and successors.

See also **Allah; Arabia, Pre-Islam; Asnam; Modern Thought; Political Islam; Qutb, Sayyid.**

BIBLIOGRAPHY

Qutb, Sayyid. *Milestones*. Indianapolis: American Trust Publications, 1990.

Surty, Muhammad Ibrahim. *The Qur'anic Concept of al-Shirk (Polytheism)*. London: Ta Ha Publishers, 1990.

Watt, W. Montgomery. *Islamic Philosophy and Theology: An Extended Survey*. Edinburgh: Edinburgh University Press, 1985.

R. Kevin Jaques

SIBA'I, MUSTAFA AL- (1915–1964)

Mustafa al-Siba'i was the socialist founder of the Society of the Muslim Brothers of Syria, a branch of the Egyptian, anticolonialist organization *Ikhwan*. Unlike the original Brotherhood in Egypt, the lesser-known Syrian branch did not openly engage in terrorist activities under Siba'i and was generally regarded as following peaceful means to achieve its goals. Born in Homs, Damascus, in 1915, Siba'i went to Egypt in 1933 to study at the University of Al-Azhar, where he was influenced by the Egyptian Muslim Brotherhood. In 1949, he completed his Ph.D. dissertation, entitled "The Position of *Sunna* in Legislation." Charged with subversion by the British government in 1934 and 1940, he was eventually deported to Palestine. Siba'i questioned the economic and cultural reliance of Muslim states on either the United States or the Soviet Union, feeling that Muslims should assert their independence from Western influences. He advocated social reform based both on Marxist theories and traditional Islamic thought and strongly believed in the idea of universal Muslim solidarity. Siba'i discussed the rights of women under Islamic law in an article published in 1962. A noted author and scholar of *fiqh* and sunna, he also edited the journals *Al-Manar*, *Al-Muslimin*, and *Hadarat al-Islam*.

See also **Ikhwan al-Muslimin.**

BIBLIOGRAPHY

Salt, J. "An Islamic Scholar-Activist: Mustafa al-Siba'i in Syria, 1945–54." *Journal of Arabic, Islamic and Middle Eastern Studies* 3 (1996): 103–115.

Paula Stiles

SILSILA

Silsila, Arabic for chain, is the word commonly used to describe the spiritual genealogy of Sufi lineages, which in turn are used to legitimize the authority of Sufi shaykhs. It is assumed that both the "heart-to-heart connection" and the spiritual teaching originated with Muhammad, hence the need for a series of spiritual links constituting a "chain" that connects back to the Prophet acting as a "conduit" for divine grace from God. In many respects these sufi genealogical chains resemble hadith *isnad*s (chains of hadith transmitters).

The encompassing principle involved in both *isnad*s and *silsila*s is the personal encounter between two reliable transmitters. Generally, hadith scholars define this encounter in personal, verbal terms and for Sufis it entails a nonverbal sharing of the heart. This allows Sufi *silsila*s to have "Uwaysi links," which involve "supra-temporal" meetings of Sufis in their imaginal forms.

The earliest Sufi *silsila* traces the spiritual genealogy of Ja'far al-Khuldi (d. 959) back to the Successors. Like hadith *isnad*s, these Sufi chains were "raised" over time to connect with Companions and then to Muhammad. In many Sufi lineages disciples memorize the *silsila* of the lineage as a litany invoking divine grace or as a contemplation exercise to attract the spirits of deceased shaykhs.

See also **Khilafat Movement; Tariqa.**

BIBLIOGRAPHY

Buehler, Arthur F. *Sufi Heirs of the Prophet: The Indian Naqshbandiyya and the Rise of the Mediating Shaykh.* Columbia: University of South Carolina Press, 1998.

Trimingham, Spencer. *The Sufi Orders in Islam.* New York: Oxford University Press, 1998.

Arthur F. Buehler

SIRHINDI, SHAYKH AHMAD (1564–1624)

Shaykh Ahmad Sirhindi was born in Sirhind, a small town located two hundred kilometers northwest of Delhi. The head of a Sufi lodge as well as a competent religious scholar, he was initiated into three Sufi lineages: the Chishtiyya, the Qadiriyya, and the Suhrawardiyya. The turning point of his life came with a meeting with Muhammad Baqi billah (d. 1603), a Central Asian Naqshbandi shaykh. In three months Sirhindi returned to Sirhind with unconditional permission to transmit the teachings of the Naqshbandi lineage. Three years later Baqi billah died and Sirhindi was recognized by most of Baqi billah's disciples as the principal successor.

From this point Sirhindi elaborated a new set of Sufi doctrines and disciplines grounded in following the prophetic example (sunna) and Islamic law (shari'a). More than any other Naqshbandi since Baha'uddin, Sirhindi became the pivotal figure in India who redefined Sufism's role in society and who integrated Sufi practice into strict juristic notions of shari'a observance. Indeed, after Sirhindi's death, the Naqshbandiyya became renowned as the Naqshbandiyya-Mujaddidiyya, named after Sirhindi's title of "the renewer of the second millennium" (*mujaddid alf-e thani*). In the twentieth century selective interpretations of Sirhindi's thoughts have been utilized by Pakistani nationalists to legitimize the creation of Pakistan.

Sirhindi's notions of Islamic orthopraxy/orthodoxy and reflections on Sufi doctrine are discussed extensively in his *Maktubat* (536 Collected Letters), which have been translated from the original Persian into Arabic, Turkish (Ottoman and modern), and Urdu. Other of his writings include *Mabda' wa-ma'ad, Makashafat-e 'ayniyya, Ma'arif laduniya, Sharh-e ruba'iyat-e khwaja Baqi billah,* and *Ithbat al-nubuwwa.*

See also **Falsafa; Ibn 'Arabi; South Asia, Islam in; Tasawwuf; Wahdat-al-Wujud.**

BIBLIOGRAPHY

Friedmann, Yohanan. *Shaykh Ahmad Sirhindi: An Outline of His Thought and a Study of His Image in the Eyes of Posterity.* Montreal: McGill-Queen's University Press, 1971.

Haar, J. G. T. *Follower and Heir of the Prophet: Shaykh Ahmad Sirhindi (1564–1624) as Mystic.* Leiden: Het Oosters Instiтute, 1992.

Arthur F. Buehler

SOCIALISM

In the Arab Middle East, socialism (Arabic, *ishtirakiyya*) as an explicit political-economic ideology had a brief period of prominence in the 1960s. Policies that could be identified as socialist, however, have been much more enduring, even in countries that explicitly reject socialist ideology. If socialism is understood as government control of the major sectors of the economy, combined with a commitment to redistribution of wealth and an assurance of economic security to all citizens, then even the most "capitalist" of the Arab states in the Middle East are to some extent socialist.

Political circumstances drove early moves by Arab states in the post–World War II period to take a more controlling role in their economies. Egyptian and Iraqi military coups in the 1950s were followed by land reform measures aimed at destroying the economic base of the pillars of the old regime, the large landowners. Confiscated lands were mostly redistributed, not kept by the state, but this process brought these governments more directly into the management of the agricultural economy. Symbols of foreign economic control like the Suez Canal in Egypt and the British Petroleum concession in Iraq were nationalized in whole or in part as expressions of political independence and to provide revenue to the new regimes. While populist and nationalist in nature, such steps were not animated by explicitly socialist blueprints. They did, however, further increase government control of the economy.

The 1960s were the heyday of explicitly socialist policies in the Arab Middle East. In 1961 the United Arab Republic (Egypt) adopted the "Socialist Decrees" of 1961, in one fell swoop nationalizing most large-scale industry, all financial

Arab students occupying the Syrian embassy in London in 1963, the year the Ba'th party came to power in Syria. The Ba'th party's motto is "Unity, Freedom, and Socialism." The Ba'th party effected wide nationalization measures in Syria and, a few years later, in Iraq. GETTY IMAGES

institutions, all utilities and transportation concerns, and all foreign trade. Soviet-style "five-year plans" became the blueprint for economic development. In 1962 the Egyptian ruling party was renamed the Arab Socialist Union. In the same year an explicitly socialist party, the National Liberation Front (in French, the FLN), came to power in newly independent Algeria. The new government confiscated the agricultural and industrial assets of the departed French colonists and, rather than redistributing them, turned them into state assets. It subsequently nationalized the French companies that had developed the country's oil and natural gas reserves. In 1964 the ruling party in Tunisia added the "Socialist" sobriquet to its name as well, and adopted state planning as the way to bring about a socialist transformation of the economy. The Ba'th party (whose motto is "unity, freedom, and socialism") came to power in Syria in 1963 and Iraq in 1968, and in each state far-reaching nationalization measures were adopted. An explicitly Marxist regime took power in South Yemen in 1967 after the withdrawal of British colonialism.

The reasons behind this trend of explicit socialism in the 1960s are a mixture of intellectual fashion, foreign policy, and political opportunity. The success of the Soviet model in the 1950s, in rebuilding war-torn Russia into a superpower, was reinforced in the minds of many Arab leaders by the strong support they received from Moscow on foreign policy issues. Both Moscow and Beijing actively pushed the line that opposition to Western colonialism and neo-colonialism required a socialist orientation, and the anticolonial zeitgeist in Asia, Africa, and Latin America bolstered that notion. Undoubtedly many Arab leaders believed that "scientific" planning and state direction of the economy were the shortest path to economic development and social justice. But equally enticing to new and sometimes unsteady Arab regimes was the political power that state control over the economy placed in their hands. The state could provide jobs in its expanding bureaucracy and in state enterprises, subsidize housing and consumer goods, and direct capital toward its favored clients.

The enormous oil price increases of the 1973–1981 period had a mixed and paradoxical effect on the socialist trend in the Arab world. States with little oil, like Egypt and Tunisia, in large measure abandoned the socialist rhetoric of the 1960s in an effort to attract foreign investment and carve out a trading niche in a world where the export-led growth model had supplanted the socialist models of the 1960s. Socialist oil producers, like Algeria and Iraq, had vast new resources at their disposal to increase their control over their economies. The Libyan regime added the term "socialist" to the official name of the state in 1977. Syria, with a small amount of oil production but an ability to attract aid from other Arab oil producers and from the Soviet Union, made a few gestures in the 1970s toward a more open economy, but basically continued on the socialist economic path.

The Arab monarchies, explicit opponents of socialism on an ideological basis, during this period began to adopt policies that brought their economic profiles much closer to those of their socialist neighbors. In Saudi Arabia and the smaller Persian Gulf states, vast oil revenues allowed the governments to dominate their economies, build huge state bureaucracies, and provide a level of welfare benefits to their citizens far beyond what the socialist states could. Even in Morocco and Jordan, without oil, foreign aid and phosphate sales gave the governments the wherewithal to substantially increase their control over their economies. Differences with the "socialist" economies certainly remained. Much more of the monarchical economies remained in private hands, notably the financial sector. But the trend toward practical economic convergence was clear.

With the falling off of oil prices from the mid-1980s, the last vestiges of official socialist doctrine were for the most part abandoned in the Arab world. Algeria began to invite foreign investment; Iraq privatized (to cronies of the regime) many state assets; even in Syria the official discourse became more favorable to private sector initiatives. But while the rhetoric of the market dominated the Arab world at the turn of the new millennium, in reality the Arab states, whether formerly "socialist" or not, were having a hard time giving up the power that state control over the economy brings. The Arab states lagged far behind East Asian and Latin American states in actual privatizations and in foreign investment, outside of the energy sector. The vocabulary of socialism has disappeared, but its practices hang on, more for political than for ideological and economic reasons.

See also **Communism; Modernization, Political: Participation, Political Movements, and Parties.**

BIBLIOGRAPHY

Issawi, Charles. *An Economic History of the Middle East and North Africa.* New York: Columbia University Press, 1982.

Richards, Alan, and Waterbury, John. *A Political Economy of the Middle East.* Boulder, Colo.: Westview Press, 1996.

F. Gregory Gause III

SOUTH ASIA, ISLAM IN

South Asia is commonly known as the "Indian Subcontinent" or the "Indo-Pak Subcontinent." Its core is the landmass south of the Himalaya and Hindukush mountain ranges: the Ganges and Indus river plains and the peninsula (now the nations of India, Pakistan, and Bangladesh). Included in South Asia are the mountainous regions (Afghanistan, Nepal, Bhutan, Burma, Tibet) whose societies have been in close contact with the Indus and Ganges plains. Also in the South Asian cultural zone are islands of the Indian Ocean (Sri Lanka, Lakshadweep, Andaman, Nicobar, and the Maldives).

South Asia is a distinctive area with complex relations to other parts of Asia. The world's highest mountains separate South Asia from China, Central Asian steppes, and the Iranian plateau; yet mountain passes provided conduits for trade, religious and cultural exchange, migration, and invasion. Sea lanes connect South Asia to the "Middle Eastern" lands of the Persian Gulf and Red Sea and to islands of Indonesia and the Malay peninsula. South Asia developed complex agrarian societies, political empires, and highly developed religious systems (from local cults to Brahmanical Hinduism, Buddhism, and Jainism).

Islam in South Asia

These geographic boundaries and connections shaped the growth of Muslim communities in South Asia, which contains a diversity of Muslim groups. Muslims in South Asia include all major sectarian groups and different legal schools, and speak many regional languages. If the populations of India, Pakistan, and Bangladesh are combined, the South Asian core area has the highest population of Muslims globally.

Early Muslims in South Asia

Commerce, conquest, and conversion led to the growth of Muslim communities in South Asia. Maritime commerce first established a Muslim presence in South Asia. The western coast of South Asia had intimate commercial and political relations with the "Middle East" long before the time of Muhammad (died 632 C.E.). The southwest of Malabar (from *Ma'bar*, Arabic for "place of crossing," now Kerala) housed merchants and settlers from pre-Islamic Arab, Jewish, and Christian communities.

The advent of Islam transformed Arab settlers into Muslim settlers. At first, this may not have dramatically changed their relation with rulers or local populations. Arab merchants married local women and were recognized as a distinct caste with high status. Muslim Arab traders built mosques and acted as overseas commercial agents of local rulers and political advisors. Tamil-speaking Muslims on the southern tip of the peninsula are known as *Marakkayar*, meaning "sailors" (possibly derived from Arabic *Markab* or ship).

Arabic literacy raised the status of Muslim Arabs in Malabar, as the Islamic empire in the Middle East and the Iranian plateau established Arabic as the commercial lingua franca in the Indian Ocean basin. Children of Arab merchants and South Asian women were raised Muslim, creating the nucleus for a more indigenous Muslim community; in addition Hindu

In Bhopal, India, Muslims in the streets surrounding the Taj al Masjid mosque offer prayers on the final day of the Tablighi Ijtema religious gathering, in which thousands of Muslims from over forty countries took part. © AFP/CORBIS

rulers appointed children to Arab families to learn techniques of the seafaring trade. According to legend, a Hindu ruler converted to Islam during Muhammad's lifetime and traveled to Medina, leaving his Hindu descendants to rule by delegation from the disappeared "Muslim king." This legend provided a mythic explanation of the cooperative relationship between Hindu kings and Arab-Muslim trade communities.

The Conquest of Sindh (711–997 C.E.)
Unlike Malabar, the northwest coast was not hospitable to Arab and Persian merchant settlers. The Hindu communities of Sindh and Gujarat were already engaged in maritime trade; Arab settlements were competition, not complement. As the Islamic community expanded into an empire in the seventh century, it conquered the Sassanid empire and absorbed the Iranian potential to dominate the Indian Ocean basin.

The Umayyad dynasty initiated diplomatic and commercial relations with Sri Lanka and the Indonesian archipelago, coming into conflict with Hindu rulers in Sindh over pirates' interference in sea routes. Sindhi rulers failed to control piracy (or perhaps profited by it). In 711, when Sindhi pirates captured a ship bound from Sri Lanka to the Umayyad ruler with royal gifts, the Arab-Islamic empire mounted a naval expedition that conquered Sindh.

The expedition leader, Muhammad ibn Qasim, established the first Arab-Islamic polity in South Asia. Sectarian feuds in Sindh facilitated conquest; Mahayana Buddhists struggled for political supremacy against Brahmanical Hindus, and may have colluded with Arab Muslims in order to displace them. Muhammad ibn Qasim extended *dhimmi* status to Brahmanical Hindus and Buddhists: the first example in Islamic history of "protected religious community" applied to groups not mentioned in the Qur'an. Despite this, Arab rulers justified their conquest of Sindh with a call for conversion to Islam. There is no evidence of a sustained effort to convert local populations (as in the Umayyad empire as a whole). After conquest, Brahmanical temples functioned and Hindu communities administered revenue collection.

The Arab conquerors founded Mansura as a garrison and the capital city (from approximately 730). Multan became the second Islamic urban center, though it had been a major city and Hindu temple site before the Arab conquest. After the Abbasid empire transferred the caliphal capital to Baghdad, cultural, religious, and scientific contact between South Asians and Muslims in the central Islamic lands increased.

Political strife in the central Islamic lands affected Sindh. As the Fatimids established a revolutionary counter-caliphate at Cairo, Isma'ili missionaries (*da'is*) in Sindh engineered a coup. Sunnis were driven underground and Sindh became a satellite of Fatimid rule. Isma'ili missionaries drew equivalence between Islamic beliefs and those of native populations to facilitate conversion and gain support beyond urban centers. Allah was pictured as equivalent to Brahma, while Adam was an incarnation or *avatar* of Shiva and 'Ali was an *avatar* of Vishnu. Beyond political strategy, this syncretic theology promoted the idea that Hindu theism was compatible with or equivalent to Islam.

The Ghaznavid Sultanate (997–1175 C.E.)
Initial contact between Islam and South Asia came via sea routes, but more sustained contact came through land routes. During the Abbasid period Central Asia, Khurasan, and Afghanistan became important regions of the Islamic empire. When Abbasid rule became weak, Turkic slave-soldiers (mamluks) governing outlying territories asserted independence as sultans, beginning with the sultanate of Ghazna in 962. With its capital of Ghazayn (in Afghanistan), the sultanate bridged the land routes between the Iran plateau and South Asia.

Mahmud of Ghazna ruled this sultanate from 998–1030, creating a Turkic aristocracy with Persian court rituals and strong loyalty to Sunni sectarianism. He expanded westward into Khurasan and eastward into Punjab, establishing Lahore as a frontier garrison town and important center of Islamic scholarship. Mahmud patronized Abu Rayhan al-Biruni, a scholar who authored a study of the religions and sciences of South Asia (*Kitab al-Hind*).

Mahmud participated in larger political and religious rivalries. He invaded Sindh, opposing the Isma'ili Fatimid presence there. He raided far into the Ganges plain; political chronicles attribute to him a policy of plundering the wealth of Hindu temples. Historians argue over the extent of his plunder and whether iconoclastic desecration was a religious justification for military campaigns. All agree, however, that plunder funded westward campaigns rather than ruling South Asia beyond Lahore.

Sufi organizations began to move into Ghaznavid-controlled territories and acted as missionaries for Sunni allegiance. Suhrawardi Sufis were active in opposing the Isma'ili presence: These include Baha'uddin Zakariya, who created a devotional center in Multan; Sayyid Jalal Bukhari in Uchh; and Ali Hujwiri (known as Data Ganj Bakhsh) in Lahore. Sufis continued the Isma'ili effort to convert South Asians to Islam by preaching, teaching, and healing.

The Sultanates of Delhi (1175–1526 C.E.)

Ghaznavid rule allowed further Turkic slave-soldier regimes to invade. In 1175, Muhammad ibn Sam invaded from Afghanistan into Punjab. Unlike the Ghaznavids, he conquered Delhi and set up a lasting administration in the South Asian heartland. This administration, known as the sultanate of Delhi, was ruled by a succession of slave-soldier regimes: Ghuri (1193–1290), Khalji (1290–1320), Tughluq (1320–1398), Sayyid (1414–1450), and Lodi (1451–1526).

Despite rapid dynastic change, these sultans created a stable political structure. In their rhetoric, "Islam" meant the political dominance of the Sunni Turkic and Afghan elite. This rhetoric (preserved in coinage, monumental architecture, and historical chronicles) should not obscure the fact that local Muslim communities were growing outside state control. Hindu kings (rajas) who fought against the Turkic dynasties employed South Asian Muslims as soldiers, just as Hindu soldiers fought with the Turkic armies. Political conflict between Turkic sultans and Hindu rajas was not a clash between two religions or two incompatible civilizations despite claims of colonial-era and contemporary nationalist histories.

The Delhi sultanates introduced new forms of political administration (the iqta' or jagirdari system), military organization, architecture, coinage, and patronage of literature and music. These last two cultural spheres involved syncretic creativity between Hindus and Muslims. The system of North Indian (Hindustani) classical music was shaped by Muslim innovations through court patronage; Amir Khosrow (died 1325), an innovator in Hindustani music, was involved in Sufism and court life.

The Delhi sultanate expanded across the Ganges plain to Bengal, and southward to Rajasthan and Gujarat, encompassing the Deccan region of peninsular South Asia in 1310 C.E. The Delhi sultans' profound military success was against Mongol incursions, turning South Asia into a haven for Islamic rule while Iran, Iraq, and Syria were devastated.

Because of this continuity, Muslim artisans, intellectuals, and religious leaders immigrated to South Asia, causing Sufism, Islamic scholarship, and literary and fine arts to flourish. Official structure of the administration included religious leaders: A shaykh al-Islam, who was the most authoritative Islamic scholar in each city or region, presided over qadis, who acted as judges and notaries drawn from the ranks of scholars trained in jurisprudence (fiqh) and theology (usul al-din). Although the sultans of Delhi favored the Shafi'i school of law, most South Asian Muslims adhered to the Hanafi school (as did Turkic peoples in Central Asia). Muslims of the southern coasts like Malabar continued to follow the Shafi'i school.

Religious life outside state control was vibrant. Sufis established mosques and hospices (khanaqa or jama'at-khana) in smaller towns as devotional, educational, and charitable centers. Discourses of Sufi masters introduced new intellectual disciplines and scholarly knowledge. The Chishti Sufi, Nizam al-Din Awliya' (died 1325 C.E.), was one of the first in South Asia to debate religious topics through constant reference to prophetic hadith. Although state officials and Sufi leaders debated issues of religious practice, they were not diametrically opposed. Especially outside the capital, tacit cooperation between qadis and Sufi leaders was the norm.

Regional Islamic Kingdoms (1338–1687 C.E.)

The Delhi sultanate became weak in the mid-fourteenth century; governors asserted independence, creating regional Islamic dynasties. The Ilyas Shahi dynasty built a kingdom in Bengal from 1342 with its capital at Lakhnawti, while the Bahmani dynasty threw off Delhi's rule in the Deccan in 1347. Thereafter, the Deccan split into five small Islamic states: Golkonda, Khandesh, Bijapur, Ahmadnagar, and Berar. In 1401 in Gujarat, the Zafar Shahi dynasty created its local capital at Ahmadabad. These smaller Islamicate dynasties created distinctive regional Islamic societies and literature in local languages beyond Persian.

Regional dynasties justified independence from Delhi by patronizing local Sufi leaders or adopting Shi'ite loyalties. In Gujarat, the Zafar Shahi dynasty built the tomb of Shaykh Ahmad Khattu, after whom they named Ahmadabad. In the Deccan, the Bahmani dynasty built a tomb for the Chishti Shaykh, Muhammad Hussayni Gesu Daraz, at Gulbarga. The Faruqi dynasty of Kandesh named their capital Burhanpur after the Chishti Sufi master, Burhan al-Din Gharib. These Sufi leaders migrated from Delhi as central power of the Delhi sultanate broke down. Some of the Deccani dynasties were Shi'a and fostered cultural and commercial relationships with Iran.

This centrifugal process accelerated when Timur (Tamerlane) invaded South Asia and sacked Delhi in 1389. Timur did not occupy Delhi, but a chieftain of Chaghatai

Marriage

A candid photo from the wedding ceremony of a Muslim couple in Karachi, Pakistan. © *Charles Lenars/Corbis*

Southeast Asian Culture and Islam

Wayang, a traditional shadow play, on a wooden stage in Kota Baharu, Malaysia. In Indonesia, shadow play puppeteers, along with other specialists such as healers, spirit mediums, shamans, and midwives, combine ancient local religious customs with Islamic elements. © *Goh Chai Hin/Corbis*

Miracles

From the *Fine flower of histories (Zubdat al-Tawarikh)* by Luqman (1583), a depiction of the legend of the Seven Sleepers of Ephesus, referred to in the Qur'an (18:9–31) as the Companions of the Cave. The Qur'an states that the young men, having publicly declared their belief and faith in God, hid from persecution in the cave where God put them and their dog to sleep for 309 years. *The Art Archive/Turkish and Islamic Art Museum Istanbul/Dagli Orti*

Mi'raj

A 1583 Turkish painting depicts Muhammad's vision of Ascension or mi'raj. In most versions of the night journey and ascension narrative, Muhammad is asleep in Mecca, awakened by angels, and borne to Jerusalem by the magical creature Buraq. In Jerusalem, Muhammad prays in the Temple with Abraham, Moses, and Jesus, before being accompanied to heaven by the angel Gabriel (Jibril). *The Art Archive/Turkish and Islamic Art Museum Istanbul/Harper Collins Publishers*

South Asia, Islam in
A late-eighteenth-century depiction of the Mogul Emperor Shah Jahan (1592–1666). Shah Jahan ruled from 1628 to 1658 and helped push Mogul rule as far east as Burma. *The Art Archive/Victoria and Albert Museum London/Sally Chappell*

Pakistan, Islamic Republic of
The Badshahi Mosque (1674) in Lahore, Pakistan. When the British relinquished control of the Indian subcontinent on August 14, 1947, Pakistan (including what is now Bangladesh) achieved independence as a separate homeland for Muslims apart from India's Hindu majority. *© Arvind Garg/Corbis*

Pilgrimage: Hajj
On a rocky hill known as the Mountain of Mercy (*Jabal al-Rahma*), near the holy city of Mecca, approximately two million pilgrims gather at the site of Muhammad's last sermon fourteen centuries ago. *AP/Wide World Photos*

Qur'an
Qur'an, with sura headings in Naskhi script. The Qur'an contains 114 suras or chapters, arranged by length, thus the text as a whole does not have a clear narrative pattern. It is also divided into thirty equal parts for reading over the course of a month. *The Art Archive/Private Collection/Eileen Tweedy*

Qur'an
A man in Chuinguetti, Mauritania, holding an old copy of the Qur'an. Muslims believe the Qur'an to be the divine revelations of God, and it is therefore unalterable and untranslatable. Muslim prayers require worshippers to recite verses of the Qur'an, such as the Fatiha (the opening sura) as well as other chapters. Muslim children learn to recite the short chapters at an early age and are taught their meaning and context from family members and teachers. © *Nik Wheeler/Corbis*

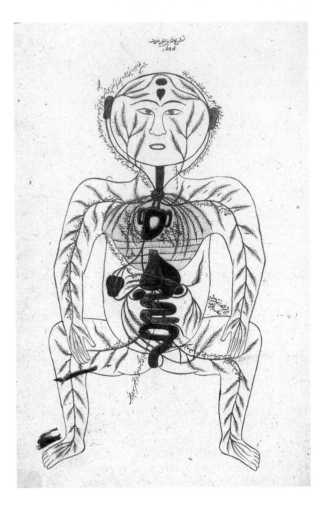

Medicine
Anatomical drawing of the body showing the heart, arteries, liver, and intestines from the 1390 *Tashrih-e badan-e insan* (Anatomy of the human body) by Mansur ibn Muhammad ibn Ilyas al-Balkhi. *The Art Archive/British Library*

Science, Islam and
A yellow copper astrolabe from the fourteenth century. This medieval instrument was used to measure the height of stars from the horizon. *The Art Archive/National Museum Damascus Syria/Dagli Orti*

Shi'a, Early
This Safavid fresco from the seventeenth century depicts Imam Shah Zayd (presumably Zayd b. 'Ali) preaching during the seventh-century schism within Islam. © *SEF/Art Resource, NY*

Persian Language and Literature
A Persian manuscript dating from 1650. Though the Arabic language is the most prestigious and commonly used language in Islam, by the tenth century the Persian language re-emerged, after a period of disuse, as suitable for discussion of science, arts, and philosophy. Persian prose literature encompasses a huge number of texts, from serial picaresque adventures to world histories and philosophical and mystical treatises. *The Art Archive/Museum of Islamic Art Cairo/Dagli Orti*

Sahara
The Taghit oasis of the Sahara Desert. This oasis exists to the west of the Grand Erg Occidental, the second largest cluster of sand dunes in Algeria. © *Jose Fuste Raga/Corbis*

Travel and Travelers
Part of a Catalan map of southern Spain and North Africa depicting king Mansa Musi of Mali and a Saharan merchant, by Abraham Cresques, circa 1375. By the time of the Empire of Mali (circa 1200–1400 C.E.), parts of Mali's ruling class had adopted Islam, although earlier, local religions persisted as well. *The Art Archive*

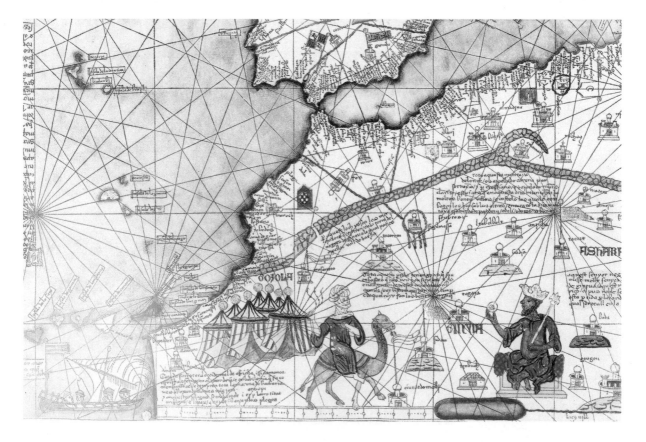

Turks who claimed descent from Timur did. Zahir al-Din Muhammad Babur, a Turkic warlord from the Ferghana Valley (now Tajikistan), invaded South Asia to rebuild his fortune until he could reconquer Ferghana, defeating Ibrahim Lodi, the last ruler of the Delhi sultanate, in 1526.

The Mogul Timurid Empire (1526–1857 C.E.)

Babur died five years after his conquest of Delhi, yet his descendants build the largest and strongest agrarian empire of the early modern world. His son, Humayun (ruled 1530–1556), consolidated Mogul rule against Afghan nobles. Military remnants of the Lodi regime rallied under the leadership of Sher Shah Suri, an Afghan leader in Bihar. Sher Shah Suri defeated Humayun's armies in 1540, drove the Moguls into exile in Safavid Iran, and reestablished the Delhi sultanate under a new Suri dynasty. The Safavid ruler, Shah Isma'il, supported Humayun who reinvaded South Asia in 1555, defeated the Suri regime, and established Mogul rule. Humayun began conquering regional dynasties in Bengal and Gujarat.

Jalal al-Din Akbar (ruled 1556–1605 C.E.) continued this expansion, giving Mogul rule stability and ideological maturity. Akbar conquered Rajputana, Sindh, and Kashmir. Later Mogul rulers Nur al-Din Jahangir (ruled 1605–1627), Shah Jahan (1628–1658), and Aurangzeb (1658–1689) pushed Mogul rule southward into the Deccan and eastward into Sikkim and Burma.

The Mogul empire succeeded because of some unique administrative features. The army and court moved with the emperor on a circuit of urban fortress-cities like Lahore and Agra, and tent-cities in the provinces. This mobility facilitated central rule and tax collection. An elaborate system of promotions in court and military kept administrators dependent on following centralized policy. Assignments for administration and tax collection were routinely rotated, preventing governors from building independent power. From the time of Akbar, the Mogul ruling class absorbed Rajput (Hindu) warlords through promotion and marriage. The Mogul empire was ideologically open to sharing power with Hindu elites and Ithna 'Ashari (Twelver) Shi'ite nobles, diffusing the insistance on Sunni and Turkic supremacy that had sustained the Delhi sultanate.

Religious Life in the Mogul Empire

To manage the multiethnic and multireligious court elite, Akbar elevated the emperor into a divinely guided figure (through an eclectic blending of Sufi, Mahdawi, and Shi'ite ideas). Courtiers experimented with a new cult of devotion to the emperor, the *Din-e Ilahi* or Universal Religion of God. Shahjahan and later emperors discontinued it and restored traditional Islamic titles and symbols. Islamic scholars and Sufis argued that Akbar's experiment was heretical, but in reality, once Rajput and Shi'ite nobles integrated into court life, the cult was no longer needed.

Chaghatai Turkish was the native tongue of Mogul royal family, but Persian was the language of court chronicles, secular poetry, and Sufi devotional literature. Cooperation and intermarriage between Muslim and Rajput Hindu elites created new syncretic possibilities in literature. Urdu, the language of the army camp, formed with Hindawi grammar absorbing vocabulary from Persian and Turkish and became the common language of the Gangetic plain and a literary language complementing Persian. Sufis innovated in devotional literature in vernacular Indic languages. Shah Hussayn (1539–1599) expanded Sufi poetry in Punjabi. Sayyid Sultan (late sixteenth century) composed the *Nabibhanmsa*, a mythic retelling of the prophet Muhammad's life, in Bengali. Such vernacular literatures bridged the gap between elite Persian poetry and folk traditions, drawing equivalencies between Islamic theological concepts and local Indic images.

Vernacular compositions reveal increasing conversion of local South Asians to Islam. Castes of artisans (like weavers) joined Muslim communities, giving rise to syncretic and iconoclastic religious leaders like Kabir of Banares (1440–1518). While many Sufis advocated the inviolability of the *shari'a*, the Mogul era witnessed a rise of Sufis who ignored or disparaged Islamic communal norms. New Sufi communities came to prominence in the Mogul era; the Shattari around Muhammad Ghawth Gwaliori (1501–1562) and the Sabiri-Chishti around 'Abd al-Quddus Gangohi (died 1537) explored yogic exercises and images that were common to Hindus and Muslims. The Mogul elite cultivated ties to Sufi communities, and some Mogul nobles were outspoken "unifiers" (*muwahhid*) who believed that Islamic and Hindu theology were compatible rather than contradictory. Prince Dara Shikoh argued the ultimate identity of Hindu and Islamic theological concepts. The Mogul court patronized Persian translations of the Upanishads, Ramayana, and Mahabharata.

In contrast, this relaxation of communal boundaries inspired Muslim reformers who called for a return to the *shari'a*. Naqshbandi Sufis, like Baqi Billah (died 1603) and his disciple, Ahmad Sirhindi (1562–1624), tried to influence Mogul nobles. However, reformers came from many communities. In Ahmadabad, 'Ali Muttaqi (1480–1575) strove to reform Sufism and advocated the centrality of the Prophet's example. His follower, 'Abd al-Haqq Dihlawi (1551–1642), established a reformist madrasa in Delhi in friendly competition with the Naqshbandis. Even earlier, Sayyid Muhammad Jawnpuri (1443–1505) led a reform movement by declaring himself the Mahdi. The Mahdawi movement was a Sunna-inspired reform movement that conflicted with Sunni elites and led to violent conflicts in Gujarat, where it was especially strong.

Reformers gained popularity under the emperor Aurangzeb. Naqshbandis like Shah Wali Allah (1703–1762) strove to integrate Sufism with study of the Qur'an, hadith, and Islamic law to strengthen allegiance to *shari'a* among South Asia Muslims. He urged Muslims to avoid sectarian extremes and blind adherence to legal schools by reviving independent legal reasoning (*ijtihad*). Two of his grandsons, 'Abd al-Qadir (d. 1813) and Rafi al-Din (d. 1818), translated the Qur'an into Urdu.

British Dominance and Muslim Reaction

After the death of Aurangzeb in 1707, weaker Mogul rulers could not hold the empire together. Local powers grew in strength: Sikhs in Punjab, Marathas in the Deccan, and Shi'ite nobles in Lucknow and Hyderabad. Later Mogul rulers grew so weak that the Safavid emperor, Nadir Shah, sacked Delhi in 1739. The Afghan ruler, Ahmad Shah Abdali Durrani, plundered it again in 1761.

Chaos in the Mogul capital facilitated European expansion in South Asia. The British East India Company (EIC) grew from a trading post to a regional military power based at Calcutta. By 1765, the EIC's governor general had assumed the title of Diwan of Bengal with rights of taxation and fiscal administration. Though a nominal "vassal" of the Mogul emperor, the EIC began military and commercial expansion into Bihar and Orissa. The British acted as mercenaries and political advisors to surrounding Muslim rulers, such as the Nawab of Awadh (Oudh). Orientalist scholars in the EIC, like William Jones and Charles Hamilton, translated Persian and Arabic texts into English. After the "Permanent Settlement" of land-ownership regulations in 1793, the EIC administered Islamic law to Muslims in the territories it controlled, and synthesized Islamic and British legal norms in Anglo-Muhammadan Law.

By 1840, the British controlled most Mogul dominions directly or indirectly. After conquering the Sikh kingdom in 1849, the British integrated the local rulers under their control. When the EIC deposed the Nawab of Oudh in 1856, Muslim and Hindu soldiers in the EIC army revolted in the first Anglo-Indian war (called the Sepoy Mutiny). Rebel soldiers and nobles rallied around the Mogul emperor, Bahadur Shah II. A proclamation issued in his name read, "In this age the people of Hindustan, both Hindus and Muslims, are being ruined under the tyranny and oppression of the infidel and treacherous English. It is therefore the bounded duty of all wealthy people of India to stake their lives and property for the well being of the public." By 1857, the EIC army reconquered Delhi and executed or exiled the Mogul royal family, and EIC rights were transferred to the British crown.

Some Muslim leaders opposed British expansion and tried to restore Islamic rule militarily. Sayyid Ahmad Barelwi (1786–1831), a Sufi leader and soldier, declared South Asia to no longer be Dar al-Islam (realm of Islamic rule). He allied with Wali Allah's family and was *ghayr muqallad* (independent in legal and ritual rulings), abandoning conformity with the Hanafi legal school. Organizing his followers into a militia, he waged a struggle (that he called jihad) against the Sikh kingdom, and was killed in 1831. Hajji Shari'atullah (1780–1839) organized a similar movement among peasants in Bengal, known as Fara'idi (The Obligatory Duties). He declared Bengal to no longer be Dar al-Islam since the British ruled it through landlords. He urged Bengali Muslims to reform and conform more closely to the sunna of Muhammad, which he identified with the Arabian practices of Mecca. His son politicized the movement, attacking Hindu landlords, resisting British taxation, and subverting Anglo-Muhammadan courts. Many Islamic leaders participated in the 1857 rebellion, like the Sabiri-Chishti leader, Hajji 'Imdadullah (1817–1899). Under threat of arrest, he lived in exile in Mecca while guiding disciples in South Asia who founded the Deoband Academy (see below).

Other Islamic leaders did not oppose British colonization after the war of 1857. Sayyid Ahmad Khan (1817–1898) founded the Muhammadan Anglo-Oriental College (now Aligarh Muslim University). To the British, he demonstrated the loyalty of Muslim educated classes; with Muslim elites, he urged cooperation with Christians, politically and theologically. Through the journal *Tahdhib al-akhlaq* (The refinement of morals), he sought to reconcile rationalism, science, and Islamic theology while promoting the education of Muslim women. More conservative Islamic scholars founded a competing school, Dar al-'Ulum (known as the Deoband Academy), in 1960 to preserve Islamic law and education after the destruction of Mogul patronage.

Political modernists like Jamal al-Din Afghani (1838–1897) and Muhammad Iqbal (1876–1938) criticized both the Aligarh movement's acceptance of colonialism and the Deoband movement's traditionalism. They agitated for cultural revival and political self-rule for Muslims in South Asia through "nationalism" and "Pan-Islamism." Exemplary of this movement, Amir 'Ali's *Spirit of Islam* presented Islam as a more "liberal" civilizing force than European Christianity. Epic poems of Altaf Husayn Hali ("The ebb and flow of Islam" in 1879) and Iqbal ("Complaint and answer" in 1909) popularized these sentiments in Urdu. Islamic modernists blamed "despotic" Mogul rule, Sufi mysticism, and "effeminate" Persian culture for the political weakness of South Asian Islam.

With the First World War, these sentiments crystalized in an anticolonial movement. South Asian Muslim elites protested when Britain imposed the Treaty of Sevres on Ottoman Turkey in 1920. The Khilafat movement aimed to preserve the authority of the caliph in Turkey, spreading anti-British sentiment and inviting Muslim leaders into Gandhi's "Non-Cooperation Movement." The Jam'iyat-e 'Ulama-e Hind (JUH), the Indian Congress of Islamic Scholars, formed to support the Khilafat movement. Students and

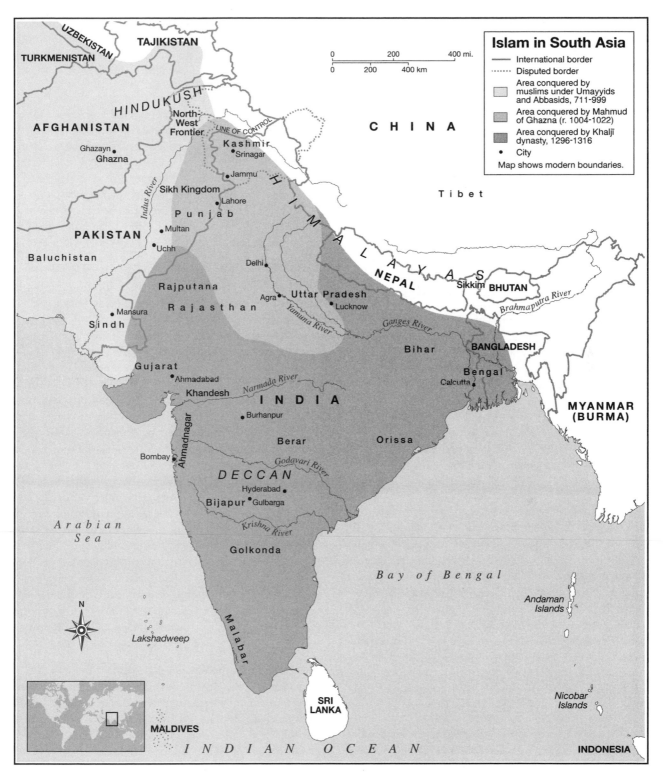

Islam in South Asia

— International border
····· Disputed border
☐ Area conquered by muslims under Umayyids and Abbasids, 711-999
☐ Area conquered by Mahmud of Ghazna (r. 1004-1022)
☐ Area conquered by Khaljī dynasty, 1296-1316
• City
Map shows modern boundaries.

Muslim dynasties in South Asia. XNR Productions/Gale

faculty withdrew from Aligarh Muslim University and founded a "nationalist" Muslim University, Jami'a Milliya Islamiya.

Islamic anticolonial activity was split between two groups. The first group felt Muslims had to join Hindus, Sikhs, and other South Asians to oppose British domination and create a "secular" and multireligious nation. They can be called "Islamic integrationists" (they have been traditionally labeled "Islamic Nationalists"). These include 'Abd al-Ghaffar Khan (1890–1988), a Pashto-speaking educator in the North West Frontier Province who led the nonviolent Khudai Khidmatgar movement ("Servants of God") and Abul Kalam Azad (known as Maulana Azad, 1888–1958), an Urdu-speaking theologian and journalist from Calcutta. Such leaders cooperated with Gandhi and Nehru in the activities of the Indian National Congress (INC).

The second group felt Muslims should form an exclusive community based on religious identity and communal ethics, and that Muslims could not coexist in an independent nation with a Hindu-majority. They can be called "Islamic exclusivists" (they have traditionally been labeled "Islamic Communalists"). This group included leaders of the Muslim League, a political party organized in 1906 by landholding Muslims to seek concessions from the British. Muhammad 'Ali Jinnah reorganized the League in 1936 to stand provincial elections, rivaling the INC. In 1940 the Muslim League declared that a constitutional government for Independent India was not possible, demanding that Muslim-majority provinces be formed into "autonomous and sovereign" states.

Partition and Independence of India and Pakistan

British policies placed Muslims and Hindus into two separate and irreconcilable "communal" groups. British histories and ethnographies since the eighteenth century portrayed these groups in racial terms as opposites. After 1857, British policy suppressed upper-class Muslim communities while promoting Hindus who embraced colonial education and bureaucracy. The colonial acquiescence to parliamentary representation for South Asians in 1937 raised questions of "proportional representation" and quotas, polarizing communal relations between Muslims and Hindus.

The British administration experimented with partition to organize colonial subjects by communal identity. In 1905, the administration tried to partition Bengal into Eastern "Hindu-majority" and Western "Muslim-majority" portions, sparking riots and resistance. As the anticolonial movement gained momentum after 1917, the British used concern over rights of "minority" communities to stall discussions of impending independence. The Muslim League at first advocated that Muslim-majority provinces become autonomous regions within a federal government of independent India. Later, the League advocated the "two-nation" solution: British India would be partitioned and Muslim-majority provinces would form the separate state of Pakistan.

Despite opposition by the INC and some Islamic leaders, partition became a political reality in 1947. Partition uprooted millions as Sikhs and Hindus fled Muslim-majority areas of the Punjab and Sindh, while Muslims in Hindu-majority areas of Punjab, Uttar Pradesh, Bihar, and Bengal experienced a similar displacement. Communal riots erupted on both sides, resulting in countless murders, looting, and destruction of property.

Partition did not solve the political complexities of South Asia's multireligious population. Many Muslims refused or were unable to move to Pakistan, including those loyal to the INC's "secular" democracy, those more rooted in their local community than in Islamic nationalism, or those without economic resources to move. Muslims remain the largest religious minority in independent India.

In 1947, Pakistan began as one nation with two noncontiguous territories. Its western territory included West Punjab, Sindh, Baluchistan, Kashmir, and North-West Frontier; its eastern territory included East Bengal. The Awami League, a political party stressing language and cultural distinctiveness of Bengali Pakistanis, succeeded in democratic elections in 1970 and pressed for Bengali autonomy. West Pakistan leaders stalled implementation of the election results, leading to a civil war in 1971. The Indian military intervened, allowing former East Pakistan independence as Bangladesh.

Partition created geopolitical crises, such as in Kashmir. The British ruled most of South Asia directly, but ruled many regions indirectly through 570 "princely states." The largest was Kashmir where a Hindu prince, the Dogra of Kashmir, governed a 75 percent Muslim population. He negotiated for autonomy, but faced an ultimatum to choose between India or Pakistan. A Muslim Kashmiri leader, Shaykh Muhammad 'Abdallah (born 1905), demanded democratic representation, made acute by a Muslim peasants' insurrection. In reaction, the Dogra declared Kashmir annexed to India without a popular referendum with his majority-Muslim population. The Pakistani government saw this as a betrayal of the principle of partition, while the Indian government saw it as legal annexation of integral territory. Military stalemate created a "line of control," with Pakistan occupying one-third of Kashmir and India occupying two-thirds, which includes the heavily populated valleys of Srinagar and Jammu. The "line of control" exists up until the present, though both nations claim the entire territory. The United Nations mandated a popular referendum about Indian annexation, but the Indian government has never executed this. Since the 1980s, some Kashmiri Muslims have resisted Indian military occupation through civil disobedience and violence.

Religious Communalism and Radicalism

India built a multireligious and multiethnic democratic state. However, communalist Hindu forces advocate a Hindu India in which Muslims (and other religious minorities) would be excluded from full citizenship. A member of the paramilitary Rashtriya Swayamsevak Sangh (RSS) assassinated Mahatma Gandhi in 1948, claiming that he "capitulated" to Muslim concerns. Leaders who sympathized with the RSS ruled Maharastra, furthering Hindu communal politics. The Bharata Janata Party (BJP) organized a national party combining Hindu communalist ideology (commonly called "Hindutva"), neo-liberal capitalist economics, and opposition to the INC.

To capture power in parliament, the BJP raised a controversy, claiming that the Babri Mosque was built (in the sixteenth century) over the site of a destroyed Hindu temple at the birthplace of Rama at Ayodya. Calling for destroying the mosque and rebuilding the temple, the BJP came to national power. A coalition of Hindu communalist organizations demolished the Babri Mosque in 1993, leading to communalist riots in Bombay and other urban centers. Hindu communalist militancy (and Hindu middle-class support of it) compromises the promise of democratic citizenship for all religious minorities and threatens the life and welfare of Indian Muslims in particular.

Muslims in South Asia have also formed communalist organizations. The Tablighi Jama'at or "Missionary Party" is a communalist religious movement that is largely apolitical. Maulana Muhammad Ilyas (died 1944) began a missionary movement to properly "Islamize" Indian Muslims, in reaction to Hindu missionary movements, like the Arya Samaj, that viewed them as "lapsed Hindus" who must re-convert (*shuddhi*) to "Hinduism." The movement advocated religious revival and abandoning participation in "secular" projects like modern education and critical inquiry into religious tradition. It has become international, one of the largest Islamic organizations worldwide.

The journalist turned political theologian, Abu l-A'la' Maududi (died 1979), organized the Jama'at-e Islami as a radical political party to forge Pakistan into an Islamic state. The party has not succeeded in parliamentary elections, but formulates "Islamist" ideology. The Jama'at spread internationally to Bangladesh, Britain, and North America. Along with al-Ikhwan al-Muslimun in Egypt, the Jama'at is the oldest and most institutionalized radical political association calling for Islamic revolution in postcolonial nation states. Both the Jama'at-e Islami and Tablighi Jama'at question the legitimacy of the parliamentary democratic governments of Pakistan and Bangladesh, especially since the election of women as prime ministers (Benazir Bhutto in Pakistan and Khalida Zia in Bangladesh).

A reproduction of a painting captures Mogul emperor Shah Jahan on a peacock throne in the volume two color insert.

See also **South Asian Culture and Islam.**

BIBLIOGRAPHY

Ahmad, Aziz. *Studies in Islamic Culture in the Indian Environment.* Oxford, U.K.: Oxford University Press, 1964.

Eaton, Richard. *The Rise of Islam on the Bengal 1204–1760.* Berkeley: University of California Press, 1993.

Eaton, Richard. "Temple Destruction and Indo-Muslim States." In *Beyond Hindu and Turk: Rethinking Religious Identities in Islamicate South Asia.* Edited by Bruce Lawrence and David Gilmartin. Gainsville: University of Florida Press, 2000.

Ernst, Carl. *Eternal Garden: Mysticism, History and Politics at a South Asian Sufi Center.* Albany: State University of New York Press, 1992.

Friedmann, Yohanan. *Shaykh Ahmad Sirhindi.* New York: Oxford University Press, 2000.

Gopal, Ram. *Islam, Hindutva, and Congress Quest.* Delhi: Reliance Publishing House, 1998.

Habib, Mohammad, and Nizami, Khaliq Ahmad. *A Comprehensive History of India: the Delhi Sultanat (A.D. 1260–1526).* Delhi: People's Publishing House, 1970.

Hermansen, Marcia. *The Conclusive Argument from God: Shah Waliullah's Hujjat Allah al-Baligha.* Leiden: E. J. Brill, 1996.

Kugle, Scott. "Framed, Blamed and Renamed: The Recasting of Islamic Jurisprudence in Colonial South Asia." *Modern Asian Studies* 35, no. 2 (2001): 257–313.

Lawrence, Bruce. *Notes from a Distant Flute: The Existent Literature of Pre-Mughal Indian Sufism.* Tehran: Imperial Iranian Academy of Philosophy, 1978.

Lelyveld, David. *Aligarh's First Generation: Muslim Solidarity in British India.* Princeton, N.J.: Princeton University Press, 1978.

Maclean, Derryl. *Religion and Society in Arab Sind.* Leiden: E. J. Brill, 1989.

Metcalf, Barbara. *Islamic Revival in British India: Deoband, 1860–1900.* Princeton, N.J.: Princeton University Press, 1982.

Minault, Gail. *The Khilafat Movement: Religious Symbolism and Political Mobilzation in India.* New York: Columbia University Press, 1982.

Nasr, Seyyed Vali Reza. *Mawdudi and the Making of Islamic Revivalism.* New York: Oxford University Press, 1996.

Richards, John. *The Mughal Empire.* New Delhi: Cambridge University Press, 1993.

Robinson, Francis. *Separatism Among Indian Muslims: the Politics of the United Provinces Muslims, 1860–1923.* Cambridge, U.K.: Cambridge University Press, 1974.

Schimmel, Annemarie. *Islam in the Indian Subcontinment.* Leiden: E. J. Brill, 1980.

Shackle, Christopher, and Majeed, Javed. *Hali's Musaddas: The Flow and Ebb of Islam.* Delhi: Oxford University Press, 1997.

Smith, Wilfred Cantwell. *Modern Islam in India: A Social Analysis.* London: Victor Gollancz, 1946.

Troll, Christian. *Sayyid Ahmad Khan: A Reinterpretation of Muslim Theology.* Karachi: Oxford University Press, 1978.

Scott A. Kugle

SOUTH ASIAN CULTURE AND ISLAM

When the Muslims arrived, South Asia had already cradled two great religions, Buddhism and Hinduism, and was divided into culturally distinct areas by differences in terrain, climate, ethnicity, religion, and social background. Apart from the Arabic, Persian, Turkish, and Urdu introduced by the Muslims, there were already a vast number of existing languages, all of which cut across religious barriers, and Muslim contributions to the various extant literatures were, and are, substantial. Although there were some cities, society was still predominantly rural and agricultural, and religion played an important role in people's lives. Even today, many social customs are rooted in ancient Hindu practices, for example the hereditary caste system, which Islam appropriated rather than threw away.

Islam's Entry and Early Conversions

Arab Muslim mercantile interest in western India began in the seventh century, predating the conquest of Sind (in what is now Pakistan) by Muhammad b. Qasim in 712. Qasim executed opposing soldiers, but spared the traders, artisans, and ordinary people, and wrought minimal changes in the social and administrative structures of Sind. He also struck a deal with the Brahmins, the priestly high caste of Hindus, co-opting them as partners in the administration, exempting them from paying the poll tax imposed on non-Muslims and ensuring their right to worship freely. Temples, such as the famous sun-temple in Multan, were important to the early Muslim rulers as a source of revenue, as they could collect the pilgrims' donations.

As Turks and Afghans after Qasim established small, Muslim-ruled enclaves in the northwest of India, Arab and Persian mercantile communities flourished along the western coast. The merchants were honored and protected by local Rashtrakuta kings (eighth to tenth century), intermarried with lower-caste Hindus, spoke Malayalam, and dressed like the Hindu military caste. However, Muslims and lower castes were excluded from the social life of upper-caste Hindus.

Muslim kings up to the eighteenth century ruled over a vast majority of non-Muslims, largely Hindus, but including Buddhists, Jains, and indigenous tribes. They wisely followed a policy of conquest and reconciliation; conversion was not prioritized because it meant less revenue. The fact that the Muslims of South Asia have remained a minority suggests that the vast majority of Indians did not seek conversion. While the Brahmins resisted change, it was within the lower castes that most conversions took place. Yet the advantages to converts were minimal, because their post-conversion lifestyle did not differ much from that which they practiced as Hindus.

The Effects of Caste and Culture

At the partition of India in 1947, following almost two hundred years of British rule, the country was divided along communal lines. At that point Bengal and Punjab, the two foremost agricultural provinces, had the largest number of Muslims. The converts in these areas were from indigenous groups who had never been fully integrated into a strong Hindu social system, and even after conversion had been distanced from the centers of Muslim political power. Caste remained operative in Muslim society in India, where families

of foreign extraction (Arabs, Turks, Afghans, and Persians) were considered nobility, lived in cities, and maintained exclusiveness. They spoke first Persian and later Urdu, a new language combining Hindi syntax with Persian and Arabic vocabulary. The seed for a separate state for the Bengalis of East Pakistan was sown when there was a move from the West to impose Urdu as the state language. The cultural divide between the two wings, separated by a thousand miles of Indian territory, and an economic disparity rooted in oppression and exploitation, led to civil war and the emergence of Bangladesh in 1971.

Next in the social hierarchy of Muslim times were upper-caste Hindu converts, such as the Rajputs. After them came the artisans and "clean" castes, with the "unclean" occupational castes occupying the lowest rung. (Caste is still important in arranging marriages.) Local officials learned to speak and dress like the Muslim ruling classes, and gradual intermarriage with the local population led to Muslim adoption of indigenous food and customs. The Muslim and Hindu aristocrats kept their women secluded behind *purdah* (curtains) in separate apartments, whereas women of the artisan and cultivating classes had relatively more freedom, probably because of the economic necessity of working with men. Marriage customs and rituals also cut across religions. Although not sanctioned by traditional Muslim law, dowry, a Hindu custom by which the bride's father must give money to the couple, was widely practiced among Muslims (it remains so, today), and has resulted in much violence against women.

The practices of Islam and Hinduism influenced each other; Muslim mystics (*sufis*) and holy men (*pirs*) showed this influence the most. Their mystical doctrines centered around union with God through love. Highly unorthodox, they were nonetheless often revered by Hindus as well, and their tombs became pilgrimage sites for people of all religions, a phenomenon particular to South Asia. In many rural areas such charismatic men took part in clearing forests, introducing agriculture, settling populations, and effecting large-scale conversion.

Interactions with Folk and Indigenous Religions

In the fifteenth century Sufism resonated with popular Bhakti devotional movements in Hinduism, whose leaders attacked institutionalized religion, disregarded caste, and taught in the vernacular languages. Kabir (1440–1518) and Nanak (1469–1539), both of Punjab, were two of the most significant contributors to the Bhakti movement, and both assimilated Muslim ideas. They taught devotion and love devoid of ritual framework, and aimed at a reordering of society along egalitarian lines. Their followers are known as the Kabirpanthis and Sikhs, respectively.

Among the Muslims, interesting developments took place within the Nizari branch of the Shi'ite Isma'ili community. Their most successful leader in Sind, Sadr al-Din (fifteenth century), is considered to be the first author of the literary genre of *Das avatar* (The tenth incarnation), an amazing blend of Islamic and Hindu ideas, in which ʿAli and the prophet Muhammad are acknowledged as incarnations of the Hindu gods Vishnu and Brahma.

At the popular level there were folk religions of indigenous origin, like the cults of Panch Pir (five holy men) and Satya Pir (the true holy man), in which various beliefs and practices were assimilated. Religious reform movements of the eighteenth to twentieth centuries, led by returnees from Mecca, disputed the Indian influences on local Muslims, and aimed to instill in the masses a commitment to "pure" Islam. Descendants of Shah Wali Allah Dehlawi (1703–1762), perhaps the greatest Indian theologian, spearheaded this movement; and the later Deobandis and *Ahl-i hadith* opposed the excessive veneration of saints and tomb worship. Shah Wali Allah translated the Qurʾan into Persian that it might be more widely understood, and his grandsons made an Urdu translation. Later, Haji Shariʿatullah (1781–1840) of Bengal also made it his mission to correct the Islam of the Bengali peasantry. His movement was known as the Faraʾiziyya (Ar. Faraʾidiyya), laying emphasis on the *faraʾid*, or Muslim religious duties. Bengal had well-developed local religious traditions, including the veneration of local saints, because of a dearth of orthodox Sunni Islamic writings in Bengali.

Language and the Arts

At the advent of Muslim rule, Sanskrit was limited to Hindu texts, while Buddhist and Jain texts used Prakrit. The new Indic vernaculars (Hindi, Bengali, Kashmiri, Punjabi, Rajasthani, Marathi, Gujrati, Oriya, Sindhi, and Assamese), which grew out of the Prakrit and the Apabhramsa stages of Sanskrit, received a tremendous boost from the Muslims, who preferred the newer languages over Sanskrit and Prakrit.

Arabic enjoyed prestige as the language of the Qurʾan, and was used mostly for religious scholarship, historiography and for translating scientific books on astronomy, medicine, and arithmetic for the West Asian market. Turkish flourished briefly as a literary language under the early Mughal emperors, but was replaced by Persian. Muslims were the most influential writers in the Indic languages of Kashmiri, Sindhi, and Punjabi, and the writing of Indo-Iranian languages Baluchi and Pashto was exclusively done by Muslims. In Bengal, Muslim sultans patronized the translations of Sanskrit classics into Bengali, and Muslims like Syed Sultan (sixteenth century), Dawlat Qazi, and Alaol (seventeenth century) were well-known writers in Bengali.

In the heartland of northern India, Amir Khosrow (1253–1325) mainly composed poetry in Persian, but also wrote in the Awadhi dialect of Hindi. During the sixteenth and seventeenth centuries the Muslim contribution to mystic (both Sufi and Bhakti) poetry in several dialects and languages was considerable. The so called "Indian style" of Persian poetry peaked during the reign of the Moguls (Fayzi, ʿUrfi, Naziri, Zuhuri, Kalim); the greatest exponent being

ʿAbdul Qadir Bedil (b. 1644) of Uzbek descent. Well acquainted with Indian religions and philosophy, and influenced by Sufis, he was skeptical of all dogma. Persian remained the official language of Muslim India until 1835.

Due to the disapproval of dance and theatre by orthodox Muslim scholars, which stemmed from concerns over the portrayal of the human image, performing arts were regarded with extreme caution. Nevertheless, a form of passion play developed, especially in areas of Shiʿite concentration, enacting the tragedy of Karbala when Husayn's (the Prophet's grandson) family was killed in battle. In spite of the orthodoxy, Kathak dancing, born of a marriage of Hindu and Muslim cultures and enacting the love story of Radha and Krishna, flourished in the Mughal courts in the seventeenth century. *Ghazal*s, short lyrical poems in Urdu set to music; *Marsiya*, songs on the tragedy of Karbala; and *qawwali*, songs celebrating the life of the Prophet or a Sufi saint, became popular during this period, and remain so today.

In India, the most dramatic impact of the Muslims was on the visual arts. Because of the orthodox Muslim aversion to the representation of living beings, non-figural art, such as calligraphy, and vegetal and geometric designs in both architecture and painting are preferred. Once settled, Muslim sultans started commissioning religious and secular manuscripts in the various Persian Islamic styles, replacing palm leaf with paper. Thus, the Indo-Persian style of painting developed, reflecting Indian styles as well as individual rulers' tastes. The *Nʿimat-nama* (Book of recipes) was done in this style for the Sultan of Malwa in the sixteenth century. It can be seen today in the India Office Library in London.

Two Persian masters, Mir Sayyid ʿAli and Khwaja ʿAbd al-Samad, founded the Mughal School of painting in the sixteenth century. The atelier, composed of mostly Hindu artists, illustrated both Persian and Indian histories and romances; for example the *Dastan-e Amir Hamza* (Stories of Amir Hamza), part of which is in the Metropolitan Museum of Art, New York. The compositions, fine line, and architectural detailing were Persian influences, while the vigorous movement and bold color were indigenous. Contemporaneous with the Mughal school was the Rajput style, the subject matter of which was almost exclusively Hindu. The interplay between these two artistic styles depended on the contact between the Mughal and Rajput rulers—political, cultural, and marital, or simply the movement of artists from the Mughal court. These traditional styles of painting were revived in the early twentieth century by the stalwarts of the Bengal School, who wished to make Indian artists aware of their own heritage.

Architectural Influences

In architecture, the Indian temple, with its sculpture-encrusted walls and ceilings and dark interior housing an image of a deity, with entry restricted to the Brahmin priest, radically differed from the mosque of the Muslims, which was open, large enough for congregational prayer, and contained no imagery. Yet the new Muslim architecture became eclectic, capitalizing on the ancient Indian traditions, and introducing new forms brought from West Asia; for example, the voussoired arch (composed of wedge-shaped constituent pieces). Muslim building activity passed through three stages. The first was short and violent, when the new rulers politically appropriated temples by destroying them. In the second, material from destroyed sites was used to build mosques and tombs. Finally, once they settled, Muslims prepared their own building materials for individual structures, and used salvaged material only rarely.

As in painting, provincial architectural styles developed in the independent sultanates as the rulers assimilated the local culture. Elegance of style depended on indigenous traditions, terrain, climate, and available materials. This accounts for the enormous difference between the brick and terracotta mosques of Bengal (Mosque at Bagha, 1523), the wooden mosques with spires in Kashmir (Friday Mosque, Srinagar, 1385, 1402, and 1674), and the stone-built mosques of Gujarat, the interiors of which have marked temple features (Ahmed Shah's Mosque, Ahmedabad, 1411).

The Mogul style, which started in the imperial capitals of Delhi, Agra, and Fatehpur Sikri in the sixteenth century, and which is marked by the spectacular architecture of Humayun's tomb, Delhi (1571), the Jami Mosque of Fatehpur Sikri (1574), and the Tajmahal, Agra (1643), diffused to the provinces as they increased. The universal Mogul style can be recognized everywhere, but there were special features in every provincial context that were rooted in the vernacular tradition. For example, in Bengal, where there was no marble, the brick surface was plastered, lime coated, and polished to a gleam.

Although European styles took over during British rule, the Mogul style resurfaced again in the late nineteenth century, when the Indo-Saracenic style became popular for the official British buildings. It was an architecture of facades, with a traditionally Indian exterior favoring the Mogul arch and dome masking a European interior. Examples of this style include the Law Courts in Madras, built between 1888 and 1892. This linkage to the Mughals and to India's past was useful to the British in establishing legitimacy for their rule.

See also **Hinduism and Islam; South Asia, Islam in; Urdu Language, Literature, and Poetry.**

BIBLIOGRAPHY

Asher, Catherine B. *The New Cambridge History of India.* Vol. 4: *Architecture of Mughal India.* Cambridge, U.K.: Cambridge University Press, 1992.

Beach, Milo C. *The New Cambridge History of India.* Vol. 3: *Mughal and Rajput Painting.* Cambridge, U.K.: Cambridge University Press, 1992.

Dallapiccola, Anna Libera, and Lallemant, Stephanie Zingel-Ave, eds. *Islam and Indian Regions.* Stuttgart: Franz Steiner Verlag, 1993.

Eaton, Richard M. *Sufis of Bijapur 1300–1700: Social Roles of Sufis in Medieval India.* Princeton, N.J.: Princeton University Press, 1978.

Eaton, Richard M.. *Essays on Islam and Indian History.* New Delhi: Oxford University Press, 2000.

Hasan, Perween. "The Indian Subcontinent." In *The Mosque.* Edited by Martin Frishman and Hasan-Uddin Khan. London: Thames and Hudson, 1994.

Schimmel, Annemarie. *Islam in the Indian Subcontinent.* Leiden: E. J. Brill, 1980.

Tarachand, M. A. *Influence of Islam on Indian Culture.* Allahabad: The Indian Press (Publications) Private Ltd., 1963.

Wink, Andre. *The Making of the Indo-Islamic World.* Vols. 1 and 2. New Delhi: Oxford University Press, 1999.

Perween Hasan

SOUTHEAST ASIA, ISLAM IN

Island Southeast Asia, that is, the Malay world, has one of the heaviest concentrations of Muslim peoples on earth. This "Muslim archipelago" encompasses Malaysia (around 55% of 22 million people are Muslim), Indonesia (87% of 200 million), Brunei (68% of 330,700), and the Philippines, where Muslims are concentrated in the western and central parts of the Mindanao island and the Sulu archipelago (4 to 7% of 74 million).

The Era of Islamization

Islam was first brought to the "lands below the winds" around the eighth century by Arab Muslim traders. Not until the thirteenth century did the process of society-wide Islamization start with the kingdom of Aceh in northern Sumatra, situated at what used to be Indonesia's gateway to India and the Middle East. In the next one hundred years, local communities of Muslims sprang up in port towns.

Between the fifteenth and the seventeenth century Islamic kingdoms replaced the Hindu-Buddhist states and Islam spread rapidly throughout the Malay world due to intense commercial activity. Muslim merchants, religious scholars, and mystics, West Indians from Gujarat and Malabar, and Arabs from Hadramaut carried the message of Islam with them along the main trade routes. Islamic sultanates encroached on the power of the Hindu-Buddhist empires. The most formidable one of Majapahit on Java collapsed in 1525 and was replaced by the Muslim dynasty of Mataram. Islam was both a religion and an ideology of rule. The prevailing model was "*raja*-centered": When local rulers (*raja*s, later sultans) embraced Islam, their subjects followed, accepting them as worldly and spiritual leaders. Islam provided the theocratic and political base for the Islamic sultanates of the Malayan peninsula, Sumatra, Java, the southern Philippines, and Borneo. The flourishing commerce led to cultural innovation comparable to Europe's Renaissance while Islam created a sense of shared identity among the peoples living throughout the archipelago.

The Islam received was pluralistic and mostly tolerant of other religious traditions. Cultural influences from the Hindu-Buddhist era were tolerated or incorporated into Islamic rituals. In certain pockets of the area (the north and northeast coasts of Java) a legalistic Islamic tradition prevailed. Existing religious traditions facilitated the reception of mystical Sufi practices. Seeking unity with God through meditation was part of Hindu-Buddhist religious beliefs. Inspired by the works of the great Islamic scholar al-Ghazali, a tradition of Islamic learning emerged that combined *fiqh* (jurisprudence), *kalam* (philosophy), and Sufism.

The Era of Colonialism

Island Southeast Asia was the major source of spices and other natural resources that Europeans sought to control. In 1511 the commercial empire of Melaka fell to the Portuguese. In the 1570s, Spain began colonizing the Philippines with the three Muslim principalities of Sulu, Maguindanao, and Buayan. The Dutch started trade missions to Indonesia's spice islands in the seventeenth century, gradually colonizing Indonesia. By 1841, British rule started in Malaysia while Brunei became a British protectorate (1888).

Initially, European colonization changed the outward-looking, vibrant profile of Islam during the age of commerce into an inward-looking conservatism. Islam became regulated by colonial rules, bureaucratized, and suppressed. The Dutch tried to deny Indonesian Islam by ignoring its deep roots in society, stressing local traditions and European law instead. Local custom (*adat*, Ar. '*adat*) was made the basis of laws for the indigenous population. Personal matters normally regulated by the Islamic *shari*'*a*, such as marriage, divorce, inheritance, and almsgiving, were under the jurisdiction of *adat* laws. Recourse to Islamic law was only allowed when the rules overlapped the *adat*.

The British curtailed the political role of Malay sultans but allowed them a degree of authority as heads of religion in their states. They misrepresented Islam by incorporating within it local traditions yet left the application of Islamic law to the sultans.

By the 1570s, Spanish incursions halted the Islamization process in the islands of the Philippines. The colonizers called the Muslims in the Philippines Moros (because they had the same religion as the Moors of Spain). For over four centuries the Moros tried to defend their Islamic identity in the "Moro Wars" against the colonial forces of Spain and the

United States. Moros could not identify themselves with the majority of Christian Filipinos but failed to be excluded from the Philippine state when it gained independence in 1946.

During the colonial era, Sunni Islam of the Shafi'ite school continued to grow in Southeast Asia. Rural Islamic boarding schools called *pesantren* became the heart of orthodox Islam in Indonesia where students studied religious subjects combined with mystical practices.

Contact between the area and the heartlands of Islam in the Middle East grew after the Suez canal opened in 1869. The growing number of pilgrims making the Hajj to Mecca led to deepened Islamic learning and a growing tendency toward Islamic orthodoxy. Teachers of Islam and Arabic studied for years with *shaykh*s (sheikhs) in Mecca and upon return contributed to the reform of Sufism and orthodox Islam.

At the beginning of the twentieth century, Islam became a rallying banner to resist colonialism. Mild successes of Christian missions caused a decline of confidence in Islamic authorities. Resistance arose among reform-seeking Muslims and among the ulema who led the traditional *pesantren*. The first Islamic reform movements started in the nineteenth century in Sumatra. Reformist ideas were brought to Indonesia by religious teachers returning from the hajj and via journals published in Singapore and Egypt. Reformists urged Muslims to return to a simple lifestyle, renew the moral basis of Islam, return to the original scripture, and purify Islam from unlawful innovations. Inspired by the teachings of the famous Egyptian Islamic scholar Muhammad 'Abduh, they advocated an accommodation with modern thought and technology. In 1912, Indonesian reformers strengthened their movement by creating Muhammadiyah. This social-religious organization aimed at purifying Islam from indigenous and Sufi practices. It built schools that combined an Islamic and secular curriculum for the majority of Muslims who did not have access to the Dutch school systems. The movement was unique in its concern for women who were trained as preachers for women. The traditionalist Muslims based at the *pesantren* furthered Muslim piety through activities in the mosques and by bringing local village rituals in conformity with Islam. In 1926, these ulema grouped together in the Nahdlatul Ulama movement (NU).

In Malaysia, the reform movement drew educated, urban Muslims who gathered around journalistic enterprises. A student of Muhammad 'Abduh founded the periodical *al-Iman* in 1906 to spread the reformist message. Hindered by the British colonial regime and opposed by traditionalists and Malay secular elites, reformism in Malaysia remained less diverse and socially effective than its counterpart in Indonesia.

The Era of Independence

Indonesia. Upon gaining independence, the newly formed nation-states had to redefine the position of Islam in their

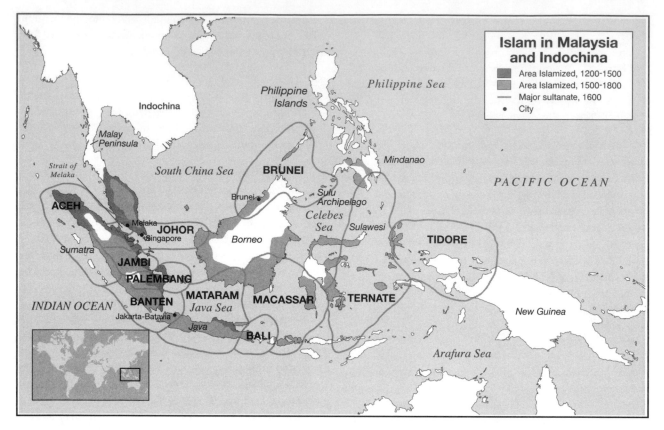

Islam in Malaysia and Indochina

- **Area Islamized, 1200–1500**
- **Area Islamized, 1500–1800**
- Major sultanate, 1600
- • City

Islam in Malaysia and Indochina. XNR PRODUCTIONS/GALE

governments. Indonesia chose a nonconfessional government over an Islamic state in order to unite some six thousand inhabited islands that hold a variety of cultures and religions. The founding fathers promoted the state ideology of Pancasila, the concept of unity in plurality—one God worshiped in separate ways by Muslims, Christians, Hindus, and Buddhists. Muslim aspirations to an Islamic state regularly led to uprisings in Sumatra, West Java, and Sulawesi. The Suharto regime (1966–1998) curbed the political power of Islam. The state established a ministry of religion to monitor religious matters such as the hajj, religious education, and the judicial administration. In 1973 the government tried to introduce a marriage bill that would give precedence to civil authority in cases of marriage and divorce, rather than to the religious Muslim courts. The bill was modified when Muslim leaders protested vigorously.

Leading intellectuals such as Nurcholish Madjid and Abdurrahman Wahid advocated focusing on a "cultural" Islam as opposed to a "political" Islam. The goal was Muslim renewal —spiritual, intellectual, and economic. This led to a strong revival of Indonesian Islam during the 1980s, and the Suharto government realized that Islam was becoming a force to reckon with. Non-Muslims started to worry when in 1990 the government established the Indonesian Muslim Intellectuals' Association (ICMI) to promote Islamization of state and society.

Differences of opinions among Indonesian Muslims still run along the spectrum of reformist Muhammadiyah and traditionalist NU. Reformists wish to purify Islam from all indigenous culture. They consider Islamic scripture to be complete and self-sufficient, and support the use of *ijtihad* (independent reasoning) and personal study. At the conservative end of the reformist spectrum are those who are against religious pluralism and who lobby for an Islamic state. After independence the Masyumi political party represented reformist aspirations in the national government of President Sukarno (1945–1965). One of their concerns was the growing communist movement. They were banned after rebellions in Sumatra and Sulawesi demanding Islamization of the state. When political aspirations were denied to all Muslims, in 1967, theologically conservative ex-Masyumi reformists formed Dewan Dakwah Islamiyah Indonesia (DDII), an organization for Muslim proselytization.

NU is the umbrella for Muslims tolerant of local culture that does not interfere with Islamic teachings. They stress the study of *fiqh* because it espouses the views of generations of scholars starting from the prophet Muhammad. They only exercise *ijtihad* in the context of this historic body of teachings, preferring *taqlid*, following traditional opinions. The political aspirations of its ulema were represented by the NU party until the Suharto government forced all Islamic parties to unite into one government-supervised Islamic party, the

In Bangkok, Thai Muslim women attend a prayer for peace one week before the start of Ramadan. GETTY IMAGES

Partei Persatuan Pembangunan (Party for Unity and Development, or PPP). When the Suharto government demanded that all mass organizations affirm Pancasila as their ideology, the NU dropped its political aspirations and focused on religious, social, and economic development instead. This shift away from politics has resulted in increased piety among Indonesian Muslims and a steady strengthening of a democratic-minded civil society.

After Suharto stepped down in May 1998, the structure that repressed religion and society collapsed. Political parties representing Muslims of various affiliations were set up, religious organizations were free to have Islam as their sole constitution, and Muslims are fully represented in the democratically elected Parliament. Freedom of religion also led to the emergence of extreme groups such as Lashkar Jihad in 2000 that called for holy war against the Christian population in the Malaccan islands.

Malaysia and Brunei. In 1946, conservative, nationalist Malaysians aspiring for independence formed the United Malay Nationalist Organization (UMNO). In 1955 the Pan-Malayan Islamic Party (Partai Islam Se-Malaysia, PAS) registered to press the establishment of an Islamic state in British

Malaysia. When in 1957 Malaysia became independent, UMNO was committed to a secularist vision of the new nation. Challenged by PAS, UMNO became more committed to Islam as Malaysia's religion. After the 1969 clashes with the Chinese population, "Malayness" came to be defined in terms of the three pillars: Muslim religion (*agama*), Malay language, or *bahasa* (not English, Chinese, or Indian), and the government of the sultans (*raja*). The Malay rulers of each state serve as guardians of Islamic religion and Malay custom. The constitution requires Malaysians (55% of the population) to be Muslim. Islam and Malayness are identified with political dominance. Islam is coordinated through the state, rather than through independent socio-religious organizations as is the case in Indonesia. Being Malay permits access to affirmative action programs that are part of the New Economic Policy (NEP), which was created to allow Malaysians to compete with the wealthy Chinese population. The goal is to transform Malaysia into an industrialized nation by the year 2020.

During the 1970s the revivalist Dakwah (Ar. *da'wa*) movement emerged among urban, middle-class youth organizations that faced the influences of modernization and globalization. It reiterated the reformist themes, seeking to implement Islam as a holistic way of life in society through religious renewal. It made Islam the main pillar of society and challenged the state led by prime minister Mahathir Mohamed to adopt its own Islamization strategy to "out-Islamicize" the opposition. The result was the Islamization of government bodies, the arts, the press, and institutes for learning. The Malay population became more devoutly Islamic. PAS continued its demands for an Islamic state and managed to implement *shari'a* in the state of Kelantan. Through the new ethnic definition, increased Islamization, and economic benefit, the Malay community has been transformed in what is called the "new Malay."

In Brunei Islam is the national religion. The wealthy country is ruled by an Islamic monarchy, the original *raja*-centered model. The sultan, Hassanal Bolkiah (r. 1968–), is head of the faith and responsible for upholding the Islamic way of life. One of the main issues in Brunei public religious life is the disagreement between those who advocate a theocratic Islamic state, and those who are secularly oriented.

Philippines. Philippine Muslims, the Moros, live in the only Christian-dominated country in Southeast Asia. Moros do not identify themselves as Filipinos and have been marginalized within the institution of the nation-state. Since the 1950s Moro Islam has witnessed a revival in Islamic piety. Moro Muslims have received assistance to build mosques and educate religious leaders from other Muslim countries. Marginalization and the increasing influx of Christian Filipino immigrants into the Muslim regions gave rise to armed secession movements. The most popularly supported of these movements is the Moro National Liberation Front (MNLF).

Its actions caused the Filipino government to implement affirmative action programs for the benefit of the Moros such as building religious schools, and scholarships for Moro students. The administration of Corazon Aquino (1986–1992) granted autonomy to four provinces in Mindinao. Armed struggle continues in the twenty-first century with groups such as the extremist Abu Sayyaf pressing its claim for independence.

See also **Muhammadiyya (Muhammadiyah); Nahdlatul Ulama (NU); Reform: South Asia; Southeast Asian Culture and Islam.**

BIBLIOGRAPHY

Andaya, B. Watson, and Andaya, L. Y. *A History of Malaysia*, 2d ed. Honolulu: University of Hawaii Press, 2001.

Barton, G., and Fealy, G., eds. *Nahdlatul Ulama, Traditional Islam and Modernity in Indonesia*. Clayton, VIC, Australia: Monash Asia Institute, 1996.

Hefner, R. *Civil Islam. Muslims and Democratization in Indonesia*. Princeton, N.J., and Oxford, UK: Princeton University Press, 2000.

Hefner, R., and Horvatich, P., eds. *Islam in an Era of Nation-States. Politics and Religious Renewal in Muslim Southeast Asia*. Honolulu: University of Hawaii Press, 1997.

Leake, David. *Brunei: The Modern Southeast-Asian Islamic Sultanate*. Jefferson, N.C.: McFarland, 1989.

Majul, C. A. *Muslims in the Philippines*. Diliman, Quezon City: The University of the Philippines Press, 1999.

McKenna, T. M. "Muslim Rulers and Rebels." In *Everyday Politics and Armed Separatism in the Southern Philippines*. Berkeley and Los Angeles: The University of California Press, 1998.

Muzaffar, Chandra. *Islamic Resurgence in Malaysia*. Petaling Jaya, Indonesia: Fajar Bakti, 1987.

Nagata, Judith. *The Reflowering of Malaysian Islam*. Vancouver: University of British Columbia Press, 1984.

Woodward, Mark R. *Islam in Java: Normative Piety and Mysticism in the Sultanate of Yogyakarta*. Tucson, Ariz.: Association for Asian Studies, 1989.

Woodward, Mark R., ed. *Toward a New Paradigm. Recent Developments in Indonesian Islamic Thought*. Tempe: Arizona State University Program for Southeast Asian Studies, 1996.

Nelly van Doorn-Harder

SOUTHEAST ASIAN CULTURE AND ISLAM

The rich tradition of Islam in Southeast Asia is characterized by a variety of local practices and beliefs. Unifying this colorful spectrum are the basic precepts of Islam, the Malay language, and sets of shared cultural characteristics, many of which are shaped by pre-Islamic cultural systems. Concepts of power and spirituality, respect for ancestors, belief in spirits, and the local understanding of gender relations owe much to the pre-Islamic beliefs. Key concepts of pre-Islamic ethics are fused with Islamic ethical teachings. Southeast Asians stress concepts such as the maintenance of social and religious harmony (*rukun*), respect toward those whose position in society demands it, and sincerity in one's actions (*ikhlas*).

Islam, however, is not just a veneer painted over Hindu-Buddhist notions. Islam became vibrant by accommodating core elements of the traditions present in the area at the time of Islamization through patterns of interpenetration and local variation. Over time, acceptance was increasingly measured against the scale of compatibility with Islamic teachings. How far Islam should coincide with Arab culture became a recurrent topic of debate.

When considering elements of culture and Islam in the region, the past and the present, the local and the global, intersect. There are many stages of commitment to normative Islam in local expressions of Islam. Nowadays, local cultures are also changing rapidly under the influence of modernization and globalization. With increasingly higher levels of education and knowledge of Western and Arab culture transmitted via the modern media, rituals held sacred for centuries can fade within one generation. Reformists altogether condemn indigenous rituals deemed inconsistent with Islam. "Purifying the faith" has been their rallying cry since the beginning of the twentieth century. Traditionalist Muslims incorporated local rituals, purging them of beliefs or practices forbidden by Islam. This entry discusses some of the main ideas that have governed religious rituals practiced by indigenous Southeast Asian Muslims, and the debates and interpretations generated by these practices.

Hierarchy and Power

Pre-Islamic understandings of hierarchy and power shape many cultural practices. In many places the king was the defender of the faithful and the mystical anchor of the religious community. Power is considered a quality that can be obtained through inheritance or by divine favor. Many became Muslim when the king accepted Islam. The king, and later the sultan, protected this power by performing ceremonies and rituals and by possessing certain artifacts that were said to be laden with mystical power, such as the *kris*, a dagger that was a symbol of manhood, honor, and ethnic identity. Religious and worldly power are preferably combined with various mystical powers (*kasekten*). Power is stratified according to rank and generation: elders are higher than juniors, and aristocrats are higher than commoners. Peoples (and spirits) live in a more or less clearly defined hierarchical structure. This hierarchy is expressed during important festivities. Before marriage the bride and groom will ask forgiveness for wrongs done against the parents. During the 'Id al-Fitri feast that completes Ramadan, Indonesians honor those ranking above them in a ritual called *halal bi-halal* when they visit them, in the family, the neighborhood, or their work, to show respect, seek reconciliation, and preserve or restore harmonious relations.

Some sultans, for example on Java, still organize large traditional celebrations such as the Sekaten and the Gerebeg. The Sekaten is a month-long fair held prior to the Mawlid al-Nabi (Prophet's birthday), one of the most popular feasts in Southeast Asia. This festivity used to be the prime tool of conversion to Islam: Peasants coming from the surrounding villages were moved to pronounce the shahada, thus nominally converting to Islam. The Gerebeg is a parade between the sultan's palace and a nearby mosque where a mount of fruits laden with blessings from the sultan's palace is divided among the people.

A variety of specialists from the earlier traditions (many of them called *dukun*) became incorporated in Islam. Among them are healers, spirit mediums, shamans, specialists in certain agricultural rituals, and midwives. They combine Islamic and customary or *adat* ceremonies, using incense, offerings to spirits, and prayers. They preserve their spiritual power by fasting, ascetic practices, and communication with guardian spirits. Many consider the spirits to be unacceptable to Islam. Their prayers contain Islamic elements and start with the invocation of *Bismillah al-Rahman al-Rahim* (In the name of God, the Compassionate, the most Merciful). Shadow-play puppeteers (*dalang*) belong to these specialists. They preserve one of the most popular art forms in Southeast Asia, the *wayang* plays, performing the Javanese versions of Indian epics of the Ramayana and the Mahabharata. To many these plays convey the picture of a proper social and spiritual order. *Dalangs* are of high moral character and spiritual potency. Part of their potency is the word; their voice expresses the realm of the inner or mystical world. Traditions were invented to defend some of these practices by crediting early Muslim saints with creating them. Indonesians believe that nine holy men, *wali songo*, converted its population. The first *wali songo*, Sunan Kalijaga, is said to have invented the shadow plays.

Slametan/Kenduri: Meals of Blessing

A meal called *slametan* on Java and *kenduri* in other parts of Indonesia and Malaysia is a meal of blessing that forms the central rite of popular religion. The purpose for holding a *slametan* is to obtain *slamet*: well-being, safety, social and spiritual harmony. The meal is held for a variety of events ranging from pregnancy and birth, circumcision, marriage, life crises and death, and occasions such as starting a long trip, finishing a house, or to resolve a dispute. *Slametan* are subject to a wide range of interpretations. Some believe they please the spirits of deceased ancestors (*roh*), or local spirits (*jinn*) who are sometimes given special dishes called *sajen* (offerings). Foods served at the meal have ritual meanings and are presented in symbolic arrangements of four, seven, or forty-four. Some believe that the use of incense facilitates communication with ancestral spirits. Prayers said during the *slametan* are a mix of Arabic and local language. When held in orthodox Muslim families, only Qur'anic verses are used and the participants refrain from speech or symbolic acts that refer to spirits. Many Islamic feast days and life-cycle rituals are celebrated with a *slametan*. The framework for interpreting the *slametan* depends on the Islamic or indigenous orientation of the participants.

Ancestors and Caring for the Dead

Many in Southeast Asia consider death a transition. In order to help the deceased on their way in the afterlife special *slametan* (called *sedekah* for the Arabic *sadaqa*, alms) are held at certain intervals after death: on the first, third, seventh, fortieth, and one hundredth day, followed by one year, two years, and a thousand days. Combined with the meal are recitations from the Qur'an in the forms of praise, prayers, *dhikr* or *tahlil* (repetitions of "there is no god but God"), and requests for forgiveness. The foods, in combination with the prayers, help to ask the deceased for forgiveness for outstanding offenses and create merit transferable to the dead that will aid the spirit's passage from the world of the living to the afterlife.

Remembering the dead prior to important events is crucial. Often people gather at the graves for prayer and cleaning. Especially at the beginning and end of Ramadan, people will visit the graves in masses to include those who passed on in the spiritual and physical purification during the month of fasting.

Spiritual Authority

The Islamic equivalent of the charismatic person endowed with spiritual potency are the Muslim saints (*wali*) who are remembered and honored by traditionalist Muslims. In this same tradition the *kiyai*s, leaders of Islamic boarding schools called *pesantren*, are considered links in a chain of sacred knowledge that reaches back to the prophet Muhammad. They are not only religious, but also social and political leaders. Spiritual and physical power are linked together when students are trained in fasting, meditation (*dhikr*), and martial arts (*pencak silat*). Developing *ikhlas*, an inner attitude of resignation that moves a person to do good deeds for the sake of good and not for self-promotion, is part of this training.

Academic study in the *pesantren* concentrates on Qur'an, Arabic, and *fiqh* (jurisprudence). Part of the curriculum used to be, and in some places still is, the practice of mysticism (*tasawwuf*) and asceticism. Some *pesantren* became centers for mystical orders (*tarekat* from Ar., *tariqa*). Mysticism here was

The Masjid Raya, in the city of Medan in North Sumatra, was built in 1906 by Sultan Makmum al-Rasyid. Adapting elements of Andalusian Moorish architecture, the mosque and the nearby Maimoon Palace are part of the legacy of the Deli Sultan, that was founded in 1630. © STEPHEN G. DONALDSON

closely connected to legal Islamic learning. Certain Sufi groups in Malaysia practice meditation combined with trance dancers. Some practice special veneration for their leaders. At times Messianic figures gain followings in their quest for a just and prosperous society.

Similar to the Sufi *shaykh*, a *kiyai* passes his charisma and position on to the son who is deemed most fit. After a spiritually potent *kiyai* has passed away, his students will visit his grave once a week in order to bring the "gift" of praise (*tahlilan*), and Qur'an recitation. The popular practice of visiting graves of saints (*ziyara*) to perform rituals of prayer, praise, and meditation is shaped by the idea that their exemplary religious life brings some persons closer to God after death than others, which qualifies them to become intermediates for the living. Graves are found all over Lara; the most powerful of these are those of the *wali songo*. Some graves are believed potent enough that visiting them a certain number of times is considered equal to performing the hajj to Mecca. Graves shape a sacred landscape filled with male and female saints, teachers, kings, and princes. Reformist and legalistically minded Muslims have long vehemently opposed *ziyara*. In Malaysia, the reformist Dakwah movement has reduced the practice of *ziyara*, especially in urban areas, although local villagers continue to perform cherished rituals.

Speech

Recitation of Arabic verses from the Qur'an is considered a powerful medium for healing, protection, to have a wish fulfilled, or to gain power. The words by themselves are purifying and uplifting. Many do not necessarily understand their meaning. When in 1998 Indonesia fell into a massive economic crisis with ensuing social unrest, mass prayers during *dhikr* meetings called *istighosah* were held all over the country to strengthen and heal the nation. Those who learn the Qur'an by heart are obliged to guard the text the rest of their life. Forgetting will be their gravest sin. During the month of Ramadan, the use of holy words is intensified through *tarawih* prayers at night and nightly readings of the entire Qur'an, or nightly recitation of one-thirtieth of the Qur'an. Beliefs in the power of speech are inspired by the Sufi intellectual tradition that identifies material reality as emanating from God. This means that powerful speech can change this reality. Words from the Qur'an are believed to have healing qualities when used in amulets or mantras. In Malaysia, shamans use Islamic stories, images, and texts to heal sickness caused by spirit possession. Spirits are identified as the *jinn* that are mentioned in the Qur'an. Imbalance or impurity within the body also causes disease that can be healed by the pronunciation of formula.

Literature

Apart from Qur'anic texts, a large body of Islam-inspired writings, poetry, and prose developed in the Malay language. The writings that reacted to Islamic mysticism became some of the richest in the world. The most famous are the seventeenth-century works of Hamzah Pansuri, Nuruddin ar-Raniri, and Samsuddin al-Sumatrani. Hamzah Pansuri created a form of written poetry called *syair* that became a major vehicle for Sufi poetry and that has inspired Malay poetry up to the present period. Ar-Raniri defended orthodox mysticism using the works of al-Ghazali. Tales (*hikayat*) about the Prophet and his Companions became a popular genre of writing. Poems and tales are meant to be sung and recited. Students in *pesantren* still chant the *Barzanji* (poetic eulogy) several times a week in honor of the prophet Muhammad.

Local genres of semi-Islamic literature are the chronicles (*babad*) that were composed in the courts of the early sultans to establish their Islamic legitimacy. Certain Javanese *babad* describe the sultan as a saint who has the power to fly.

After independence an Islamic literature developed that espouses Islamic values. Especially in Malaysia, edifying novels became popular. Contemporary Indonesian writings by writers like Emha Ainun Nadjib explore the relationship between the individual and God. Young activists have started to use the novel as a medium to teach concepts such as human rights to students in the *pesantren* and other Islamic schools.

Women

Especially in Indonesia, women share the power of the word. Many women have memorized the Qur'an to become a *hafidha* and go on to become finalists in the national Qur'an reciting contests. In the past, international competition was not possible since contestants from other Muslim countries were only men. Nowadays women are allowed to compete in certain Muslim countries. Women also teach in the *pesantren* and make up more than half of the judges in Islamic *Syari'a* (Ar. *shari'a*) courts.

Islam and *Adat*

Southeast Asian societies have developed local legal codes or practices called *adat*. This code existed and in many places still exists alongside the *Syari'a*. *Adat* complemented the Islamic law in many matters of tradition and custom. The two law systems collide regularly in evaluating the same problems: how to divide an estate, what position to assign to women. In general, *adat* allowed women a position equal to that of men. Orthodox Muslims took offense to these rules, for example, in the division of an estate where *adat* grants the woman a share equal to that of her male relatives. *Syari'a* law

applies the Islamic rule that gives only half a man's share. Through the activities of orthodox and Reformist Muslims, the tendency now is to stress *Syari'a* rather than *adat*.

An image of a pupeteer at work appears in the volume two color insert.

See also 'Ada; 'Ibadat; Southeast Asia, Islam in.

BIBLIOGRAPHY

Beatty, Andrew. *Varieties of Javanese Religion. An Anthropological Account.* Cambridge, U.K.: Cambridge University Press, 1999.

Bowen, John, R. *Muslims through Discourse: Religion and Ritual in Gayo Society.* Princeton, N.J.: Princeton University Press, 1993.

Geertz, Clifford. *The Religion of Java* (1960). Chicago and London: The University of Chicago Press, 1976.

Hefner, Robert, W. *Hindu Javanese. Tengger Tradition and Islam.* Princeton, N.J.: Princeton University Press, 1985.

Ibrahim, Ahmad; Siddique, Sharon; and Hussain, Yasmin, eds. *Readings on Islam in Southeast Asia.* Singapore: Institute of Southeast Asian Studies, 1985.

Keeler, Ward. *Javanese Shadow Plays, Javanese Selfs.* Princeton, N.J.: Princeton University Press, 1987.

Laderman, Carol. *Taming the Wind of Desire: Psychology, Medicine, and Aesthetics in Malay Shamanistic Performance.* Berkeley: University of California Press, 1991.

Siegel, James. *The Rope of God.* Berkeley: University of California Press, 1969.

Van Doorn-Harder, Nelly, and de Jong, Kees. "The Pilgrimage to Tembayat." In *The Muslim World* 91, nos. 3 and 4 (Fall 2001).

Nelly van Doorn-Harder

SUCCESSION

The issue of succession—the assumption by a person of political or other institutional authority previously possessed by another—entered Islam with the death of the prophet Muhammad and has been a subject of continuous debate ever since. Simply put, Sunni Muslims believe that the Prophet's religious authority died with him, that his political authority passed to a succession of caliphs initially selected on the basis of consensus and merit, and that the institution of the caliphate rapidly declined into hereditary monarchy and ultimately military usurpation. Shi'ites believe that both the Prophet's religious and political authority remained united in a hereditary line of imams, that his dying wishes were subverted and suppressed by Sunnis, and that the caliphal succession has never been legitimate. Recently, scholars have increasingly questioned the traditional Muslim view of both the theory and the practice of caliphal succession. Some have argued that the historical record is obscure on even the most crucial points, and that in any case what can be gleaned from it suggests that divine absolutism, primogeniture, and forcible seizure of power were present from the beginning. Others have stressed the contributions of pre-Islamic Middle Eastern political traditions— particularly that of Persian/Zoroastrian divine absolutism—to the development of Islamic political theory. Whatever the exact course of events, it is clear that "the classical theory of the caliphate" as formulated by al-Mawardi (d. 1058) was the culmination of an ongoing process of interaction between the Islamic religious and political establishments. Subsequently, Muslim thinkers who strove to preserve an Islamic component in political succession were forced into increasingly distressing compromises by such cataclysms as the Mongol destruction of the Baghdad caliphate, the advent of secular dynastic rule in most Muslim lands, and the increasing intervention in Middle Eastern politics by European imperialism. After the dismantling of the Ottoman Empire following the First World War, most governments in Muslim lands adopted modern secular principles of political legitimacy, although by the end of the twentieth century, popular support for the reinstatement of Islamic principles and practices of political succession was increasing.

Etymology of Khalifa

The original significance of the Arabic verb for "to succeed," kh-l-f—from which is derived the word for caliph (khalifa)— is irretrievably buried beneath ancient and impenetrable layers of usage. It occurs in Akkadian meaning "to slip into or put on [especially clothes]" and in Hebrew meaning "to succeed, replace or pass away." Dictionaries of early South Arabic give one occurrence of the word khalifa with the quasi-political meaning of "viceroy" in a fourth-century South Arabic inscription, but also give meanings as diverse as "suit of clothes," "gate of a city," and—happily confirming a popular conception about Arabic etymology—"pregnant camel." It is a sign of the ambiguity of the meaning of the word that, although in both Arabic and Hebrew the first form of the root commonly denotes succession in time, place, or function, it has come in the former to be applied to the thing succeeding and in the latter to the thing succeeded. Lane's *Arabic-English Lexicon* gives the primary meaning of the verb khalafa as "he came after, followed, succeeded, or remained after, another, or another that had perished and died." Of the 127 instances of the root kh-l-f in the Qur'an, most have specialized meanings related only distantly to the first form meaning of "to come behind or after." As demonstrated by al-Qadi, the array of meanings encompassed by kh-l-f and its derivatives is closely paralleled by the array of meanings encompassed by b-d-l, which can mean both "to exchange" and "to be exchanged" and is used by the Qur'an in contexts closely analogous to those in which it uses kh-l-f. The near identity of these two roots is echoed today in the use by modern Arabic and Hebrew of badla and khalifah, respectively, to denote "suit"—that is, change of clothes.

The Term "Khalifa" in the Qur'an

The etymological significance of the word khalifa in the Qur'an is less obscure than its pre-Qur'anic usage because the Qur'an has been an object of philological exegesis since very early after its appearance. The two plural forms khulafa' and khala'if occur seven times between them in the Qur'an, and in all cases are said by commentators to denote tribes or peoples who, despite the warnings of their apostles, disobeyed God's will and were consequently wiped off the face of the earth by Him. Most commentators similarly treat the two occurrences of the singular khalifa as referring to the classic Qur'anic theme of a succession of peoples governing the earth, rather than the succession of individual rulers governing peoples. However, a handful of interpretations of Qur'an 2:30— "When your Lord said to the angels: I am about to put a successor (khalifa) on the earth, they said: Will You place on it one who will do harm on it and will shed blood ..."— interpret the word khalifa as a reference to Adam as an individual rather than the Children of Adam as a collective. The scarcity and lateness of commentators who ascribe to the word khalifa the connotation of an individual person with a political office have suggested to some scholars that the connection between the Qur'an's term khalifa and the office of caliphate was not made "before the end of the Umayyad period or the early decades of Abbasid rule" (al-Qadi, "The Term Khalifa"). To others it implied that the idea of a connection was in the air but played down by early commentators "anxious to avoid approving the Umayyad caliphs' use of the verse about Adam to enhance their own dignity" (Watt 1971, p. 567).

Umayyad Succession

The role of religion in the Umayyads' justification of their succession to the caliphate has itself undergone substantial revision by scholars—a revision that parallels revisionist views of the progress of both empire and theocracy in the early Islamic state generally. The Umayyads' use of the title khalifat Allah—"Caliph of God" (denoting a direct connection to the Divine) as opposed to "Caliph of the Apostle of God" (denoting succession to Muhammad as political leader of the umma)— belies the conventional picture of the entire Umayyad period as an interval of secular kingship between the perfect theocracy of the Rashidun and the less perfect theocracy of the Abbasids. 'Umar II's reprise of Abu Bakr's humble declaration that "I am not khalifat Allah" was the exception rather than the rule. The sources abound in evidence of a concerted effort by Umayyad court poets and scribes to augment the initial Umayyad claim to the caliphate as avengers of the blood of 'Uthman with the claim that they had been installed in their position by God. Crone and Hinds rely heavily on this court poetry to reverse the traditional view of the emergence of divine absolutism in Islam. They argue that the

'Abd al-Hamid (1842–1918) was the sultan of Turkey from 1876 to 1909. Towards the end of the nineteenth century the Ottoman sultan 'Abd al-Hamid tried to counter national separatism among Muslim ethnic minorities in the Empire by pushing the idea that the Ottoman sultans were legitimate successors to the caliphate on the basis of dubious claim that the last descendant of the Abbasid caliphs in Mamluk, Cairo, had transferred the caliphate to Selim III upon his conquest of Egypt in 1517. © BAIN COLL/CORBIS

theocratic Shi'ite-type conception of the imamate was the original one and that from the very first, caliphs aspired to as much, if not more, religious authority than the Prophet. It can be plausibly argued either that the interpretation of the title *khalifat Allah* by the Umayyads constituted "the first formulated 'theory' of the caliphate in Islamic history" (al-Qadi, "The Religious Foundation of Late Umayyad Ideology and Practice") or that the Umayyads "had still not decided to transfer the concept of 'Caliph of God' from the sphere of court flattery and rhetorical salutation into the sphere of law" (Barthold).

Early Islamic Sectarianism and Caliphal Succession

If the precise etymology of the caliphal title and the exact nature of the ideological basis on which the Umayyads justified their succession are matters of speculation, the fact that the air was thick with theological ferment surrounding the issue of political succession in the *umma* throughout the Umayyad period is not. Sectarianism in any religion often has thinly disguised political roots, but because of Islam's status as a state religion from its inception, the political roots of early Islamic sectarianism are not disguised at all. The three broad non-Shi'ite sectarian subdivisions of the earliest period—Kharijite, Qadarite, and Murji'ite—all contained parallel theological and political components—that is to say, doctrinal positions on sin that very closely allied with conceptions of legitimate political succession. The Kharijite doctrine that any sin renders the sinner an apostate had its political reflection in their position that any injustice on the part of the caliph renders his succession invalid. The Qadarite doctrine that humans possess control over (*qadar*) and therefore responsibility for their actions had its political reflection in their position that the legitimacy of the caliph's succession depended on his dispensing equitable justice to the ruled. The Murji'ite doctrine that judgment of any sinner must be deferred to God had its political reflection in their view that the legitimacy of caliphal succession was the concern of God rather than men. While Kharijite anarchism and Qadarite activism were persecuted under the Umayyads, Murji'ite quietism seems to have been the political ideology of choice for the silent majority during the Umayyad caliphate. In contrast to the supposed period of Rashidun harmony during which no fewer than three of the first four caliphs were felled by assassins, not one of the Umayyad caliphs–with the sole exception of the battlefield death of Sulayman b 'Abd al-Malik—ended his term of office for any reason other than death by natural causes until al-Walid II was edged out by Yazid III in 744 after the Abbasid revolution had already begun.

Hadiths About Caliphal Succession

It is against this background of political and theological ferment that hadith statements about caliphal succession attributed to the Prophet must be evaluated. In contrast to the dearth of explicit statements in the Qur'an about legitimate political succession, hadith literature has many explicit references to the caliphate as a political office. Many of these hadiths use the terms imam or emir rather than *khalifa* in some or all variants, leaving open the possibility that they might have been initially uttered by the Prophet in reference to following the leader of the communal prayer and obeying the commanders of early military expedition, and were later reinterpreted—willfully or not, and with or without substitution of the word *khalifa*—as allusions to a political institution that did not exist prior to the Prophet's death. Those hadiths which refer unambiguously to the caliphate reflect debates about the political succession in Islam going on among early Muslim intellectuals who wrote down the record of the Prophet's utterances and the history of the early exemplary Rashidun (rightly guided) caliphate centuries after the fact. A vast majority of approved hadiths about caliphal succession fall into the quietist Muji'ite rather than the radical Kharijite or activist Qadarite category.

The question of whether the caliph's full title was properly *khalifat Rasul Allah*, ("the successor of the Apostle of God"), with the connotation of succeeding the Prophet in his temporal function as defender of the faith, or *khalifat Allah* ("the successor of God"), with the connotation of being appointed by and having a direct connection with God Himself, was also a much-vexed and obscure issue of early Islamic political discourse. The uneasiness of Sunni orthodoxy with the latter title and its accompanying conception of the caliph as possessor of the type of divine charisma claimed for the Shi'ite imams is reflected by the widely circulated stories about the first caliph Abu Bakr's insistence on being called *khalifat Rasul Allah* rather than *khalifat Allah*. The second caliph 'Umar rejected both *khalifat Allah* as applying only to King David and *khalifat Rasul Allah* as applying only to Abu Bakr and decided that the correct title was "Caliph of the Caliph of the Apostle of God." In view of the potential of this title for cumbersome recursiveness, 'Umar opted for *amir al-mu'minin* ("Commander of the Faithful"), a title that continued to have a rarified status even after the title *khalifa* became debased in the late Middle Ages through widespread usage by many different rulers of widely varying power and piety.

Caliphal Succession Under the Abbasids

As is attested to by the survival of hadith expressing some of their views in the standard Sunni collections, aspects of the Khariji, Qadari, and Murji'ite approaches all fell within the boundaries of what later became the Sunni discourse on the legitimacy of caliphal succession. But it was slogans borrowed from 'Alid groups later consigned by the heresiologists to the moderate but nonetheless heretical fringes of Shi'ism that swept the Abbasids into office. The Abbasids borrowed three planks from the 'Alid platform. First of all, they claimed the right to caliphal succession as members of the house of Muhammad (*ahl al-bayt*) by virtue of their eponymous ancestor's having been the uncle of the Prophet. Secondly, they claimed to be the beneficiaries of *nass*—designation by virtue of the father of the first Abbasid caliph's having had the imami charisma transferred to him by the son of Muhammad b. al-Hanafiyya, the reluctant figurehead of the revolt of al-Mukhtar which had first put both the *mawali* constituency and their 'Alid ideology on the Islamic political map. Thirdly, they claimed to be rightful caliphs by virtue of being the members of the family of Muhammad (*Al Muhammad*) most capable of achieving power. The first two of these claims were shaky to say the least. While it is true that in terms of genealogy al-'Abbas was on the right side of the 'Abd Manaf family tree relative to Umayya, he had not even converted to Islam during Muhammad's lifetime, and was certainly not the relative of the Prophet whom the 'Alids had in mind when they chanted the slogan "most pleasing of the house of Muhammad." The alleged transfer of imami charisma to the father of al-Saffah by the son of Ibn al-Hanafiyya had all the plausibility of the Donation of Constantine employed a half century later to justify papal dominion in Western Europe. The third justification of the Abbasid succession—that the Abbasids were the members of the family of the Prophet most

capable of achieving power—was rendered unassailable by the successful result of the Abbasid revolution.

The early Abbasid era, in addition to being the golden age of the Baghdad caliphate, was also the period during which the embryonic Sunni Islam defined its approach to legitimate caliphal succession—frequently in opposition to the vision of the reigning caliph. The view favored by the caliphs is represented by the *Risala fi al-Sahaba* of Ibn al-Muqaffa' (d. 756), which advises the caliph al-Mansur (r. 754–775) to aspire to be something like the high priest of Islam and act as the final arbiter on points of Islamic law. The view favored by the "proto-Sunni" ulema was represented by the *qadi* (judge) Abu Yusuf, who in his *Kitab al-Kharaj* advises the caliph Harun al-Rashid (r. 786–809) to subordinate his will to the stricture of the book and the sunna like any other Muslim. The issue was decided by the outcome of the *mihna*, or "Islamic Inquisition" (833–847), during which Ahmad b. Hanbal's (d. 855) heroic opposition to the caliphal government's efforts to enforce adherence to the Mu'tazilite doctrine of the createdness of the Qur'an upheld the ascendance of the book and the sunna over the will of the caliph of the day. This triumph of the emerging Sunni approach to caliphal legitimacy resulted in the dispersal of religious authority away from a central governing body and toward multiple schools of law and a decentralized clerical authority. In retrospect, this separation between Islam and the state insured that Islam would avoid the fate of Zoroastrianism, the official religion of Iraq-based, Middle East-wide, divine-absolutist Sassanian Empire to which the Abbasid caliph was successor, and develop into a supranational world religion that was able to survive the demise of the first Islamic state.

The Classical Theory of the Caliphate

It is one of the oft-noted paradoxes of Islamic intellectual history that the theory of caliphal succession was explicitly formulated just at the time when the institution of the caliphate was declining into political insignificance. But it is precisely in weakness that political institutions are in need of theoretical bolstering. The fullest expression of the classical theory of the caliphate was articulated by al-Mawardi (d. 1058), whose *Ahkam al-sultaniyya* (Rules of sovereign power) defines the relationship between the caliph's spiritual and temporal duties, noting that the "imamate is established for the succession of prophecy in the preservation of the religion (*din*) and the administration of the world (*dunya*)."

The necessity of the caliphate as a collective religious duty (*fard kifaya*) upon the Islamic community is demonstrated through such *shari'a* evidence as hadiths enjoining obedience to the imams, the *ijma'* (consensus) of the community about establishing an imam. Traces of the polemic against Shi'ism that conditioned the formulation of the embryonic theories of caliphal succession of al-Mawardi's predecessors—for example, the Ash'arite theologians al-Baqillani (d. 1013) and al-Baghdadi (d. 1037)—surface only rarely in al-Mawardi's exposition. The awkward position into which Sunni theorists of the caliphate were squeezed by the need to defend the historical record of the caliphate, on the one hand, and the need to oppose Shi'ite theocratic conceptions of political succession, on the other is illustrated by al-Mawardi's insistence that, while the caliph should be selected by election, rather than appointment, and this election can be accomplished by a single elector—this last provision justifying what became the most common mode of succession, appointment by a caliph of his son as heir. Al-Mawardi is careful to refer to this mode of succession as 'ahd ("investiture") rather than with the Shi'ite term nass ("designation"). Similarly, the principle of imamat al-mafdul ("the imamate of the less qualified") does double duty for al-Mawardi. It serves as a rejection of the Kharijite stance that as soon as a better qualified candidate appeared he must replace a less qualified sitting caliph no matter how much civil disturbance this might cause; it also counters Shi'ite claims that the successions of the first three caliphs were illegitimate because 'Ali—who even by most Sunni accounts was a more qualified candidate than 'Uthman—was passed over. For all his willingness to compromise on the person of the caliph, al-Mawardi strives at every point to uphold the sanctity of the caliphal succession itself. Despite the many principles of caliphal succession that he draws by analogy with shari'a contracts, al-Mawardi stresses that the caliphal bay'a is "a public interest whose consequences go beyond that of private contracts" (al-Mawardi, al-Akham al-sultaniyya, p. 9).

As the caliphate progressively declined into powerlessness and caliphal succession eventually became the plaything of the sultan of the moment, al-Mawardi's successors were forced into a progressively more realistic accommodation with historical actuality. Al-Ghazali (d. 1111), for example, adds to election and investiture by the preceding caliph a third mode of succession: investiture by a man of power (rajul dhu shawka). As he reluctantly concedes: "Government in these days is a consequence solely of military power, and whosoever he may be to whom the possessor of military power gives his allegiance, that person is the caliph." (Al-Ghazali, Ihya' 'ulum al-din)

Succession after the Caliphate

After the Mongol conquests obliterated the Baghdad caliphate, the terms in which men of religion evaluated the legitimacy of political succession diverged still further from al-Mawardi's "classical" theory. Two different approaches to a world without a caliph are represented by Ibn Taymiyya (d. 1328) and al-Taftazani (d. 1389). Ibn Taymiyya's theory of the caliphate can best be characterized as a revival of Kharijite positions. He abandons the Quraysh lineage requirement, the imamate of the less qualified, and even the necessity of the caliphate itself. Ibn Taymiyya seems to regard excessive stress on the importance of even the Sunni imamate as a Shi'ite-like heresy and is as antipathetic to Sunni consensus as to imami charisma

as a religious principle of legitimate political succession. For Ibn Taymiyya, good Islamic government is any state in which emirs and ulema collaborate in the interests of Islam.

Al-Taftazani is far less sanguine about the removal of the caliphate from the political legitimacy equation, and is far less ready than Ibn Taymiyya to accept the political fragmentation of the Middle Period (c. 1000–1500) as a permanent feature of the Islamic world. Al-Taftazani's views on the caliphate were referred to frequently by proponents of the revival of the caliphate in the late nineteenth and early twentieth centuries. His Sharh was used as a textbook at al-Azhar, and both his Maturidi rationalism and his frequent references to the salaf al-salih ("upright predecessors") appealed to the reformist Salafi movement of the nineteenth century that touted original Islam as the true religion of reason and enlightenment. By contrast, the favoritism toward Hanafism and eventual revival of caliphal universalism by the Ottoman sultans banished Ibn Taymiyya's Hanbali puritanism to the margins, where it became associated with groups on the religious fringe, such as the Wahhabis. However, after the failure of the caliphal revival efforts of the 1920s, Ibn Taymiyya's tactical retreat to "Islamism-in-one-country" got a second look from groups like the Muslim Brotherhood (Ikhwan al-Muslimin) that worked for Islamic renewal from the ground up instead of from the top down.

In the meantime, in addition to eradicating the Baghdad caliphate, the Mongols also brought to the Islamic world a theory of dynastic succession in which God chose the ruler of the world directly, without the agency of the umma, and demonstrated His choice not through the consensus of scholars but through the outcome of military struggles. This made the subject of legitimate political succession less a matter for prescription by men of religion and more a matter for description by historians. The most prominent of these was Ibn Khaldun, "the world's first sociologist," who viewed the succession of political sovereignty as driven by 'asabiyya—or the ruling dynasty's group cohesion. Indeed, he interprets the restriction by previous theorists of the caliphate to the house of Quraysh not as deriving from hadith text but rather as from the fact that Quraysh was in possession of the 'asabiyya of the moment during the period of Islamic origins. Although Ibn Khaldun is more of a historian than a religious scholar, his views on the relationship of religion to political succession were often quoted by later ulema because of his general prestige. In particular, his portrayal of the Quraysh lineage requirement as a practical rather than doctrinal consideration was much cited by proponents of non-Quraysh candidates for the caliphate.

Dynastic succession displaced caliphal legitimacy as a political principle in the Islamic world from the Mongols through the period of the early modern Timurid, Safavid, and Ottoman empires. Toward the end of the nineteenth century the Ottoman sultan 'Abd al-Hamid II tried to counter national separatism among Muslim ethnic minorities in the empire by pushing the idea that the Ottoman sultans were legitimate successors to the caliphate on the basis of a dubious claim that the last descendant of the Abbasid caliphs in Mamluk Cairo had transferred the caliphate to Selim III upon his conquest of Egypt in 1517. Immediately following the defeat of the Ottoman Empire in 1918, several efforts to revive the caliphate as a governing body of the world Muslim community garnered support among Islamic liberals and pan-Islamists. By then it was too late, however, European hegemony having imposed on the Middle East principles of political succession that had neither religious roots nor cultural resonance in the Islamic world. By the end of the twentieth century this had provoked an Islamist reaction whose vision of political legitimacy has far more in common with historically marginal fringe Islamic political movements than with traditional mainstream views of caliphal succession.

See also **Abu Bakr; Caliphate; Empires: Abbasid; Empires: Umayyad; Islam and Other Religions; Tasawwuf; 'Umar.**

BIBLIOGRAPHY

Barthold, V. V. "Caliph and Sultan." *Islamic Quarterly* 7 (1963): 117–138.

Binder, Leonard. "al-Ghazali's Theory of Islamic Government." *The Muslim World* 45 (1955): 229–241.

Crone, Patricia, and Hinds, Martin. *God's Caliph: Religious Authority in the First Five Centuries of Islam.* Cambridge, U.K.: Cambridge University Press, 1986.

Gibb, H. A. R. "al-Mawardi's Theory of the Khilafah." *Islamic Culture* 11 (1937): 291–302.

Goitein, S. D. "A Turning Point in the History of the Muslim State." In his *Studies in Islamic History and Institutions.* Leiden: E. J. Brill, 1968.

Ibn Khaldun. *al-Muqaddima.* Beirut: Dar al-Kitab al-Lubnani, 1961.

Ibn al-Muqaffa', 'Abdallah. *al-Risala fi al-Sahaba.* In *Conseilleur du Calife.* Edited and translated by Charles Pellat. Paris: G. P. Maisonneuve, 1972.

Lambton, A. K. S. *State and Government in Medieval Islam: An Introduction to the Study of Islamic Political Theory.* London: Oxford University Press, 1981.

Margoliouth, D. S. "The Sense of the Title Khalifah." *Oriental Studies Presented to Edward G. Brown.* Edited by T. W. Arnold and R. A. Nicholson. Cambridge, U.K.: Cambridge University Press, 1922.

Qadi, Wadad al-. "The Term 'Khalifa' in Early Exegetical Literature." *Die Welt des Islams* 28 (1988): 392–411.

Qadi, Wadad al-. "Religious Foundation of Late Umayyad Ideology and Practice." In *Religious Knowledge and Political Power.* Edited by Manuela Martin et al. Madrid: Consejo Superior de Investigaciones Cientificas, 1993.

Watt, W. Montgomery. *God's Caliph: Qur'anic Interpretations and Umayyad Claims.* Edinburgh: Edinburgh University Press, 1971.

Mark Wegner

SUFISM *See* **Tasawwuf**

SUHRAWARDI, AL- (C. 1154–1191)

Shihab al-Din Yahya b. Amirak Suhrawardi was a philosopher and mystic whose Neoplatonic "Illuminationist" school was a major influence on later Islamic philosophy, especially in Iran and India. Suhrawardi was born and educated in northwestern Iran and as a young man was an adherent of the Peripatetic philosophy of Avicenna. His mystical experiences and a famous dream of Aristotle convinced him of the inadequacy of this philosophy and made him a Platonist. The key elements in his new system were a reliance on intuition as a basic tool of philosophy, the closely related theory of knowledge later called knowledge by presence, and an insistence on the reality of the Platonic Forms conceived as immaterial intelligences. The most important statement of his mature doctrine was his book *Hikmat al-Ishraq* (*The philosophy of illumination*), in which he attacked certain Peripatetic doctrines and expounded his system in the form of a metaphysics of light.

Though Suhrawardi wrote his major works in Arabic, he also wrote in Persian. His short philosophical allegories, written in a simple and elegant style, are still considered masterpieces of early Persian prose.

In 1183 he attracted the attention of the young al-Malik al-Zahir, the governor of Aleppo, and for a time enjoyed an ascendancy over the prince that aroused the jealousy of religious scholars and alarmed the prince's father, the great Saladin, who was facing the threat of the Third Crusade. It seems likely that Saladin was alarmed by the political implications of Suhrawardi's philosophy, which called for a mystical philosopher-king and which resembled the view of the Ismailis, whom Saladin had suppressed in Egypt and Syria. Suhrawardi was put to death at Saladin's orders, probably in 1191.

Though Suhrawardi's philosophy has always been influential in the Islamic East, it was almost unknown in the West until it was popularized by the French Orientalist Henry Corbin, who interpreted Suhrawardi as an Iranian "theosopher" committed to the revival of ancient Iranian thought. Though Corbin's view remains influential, it has been challenged by those who view Suhrawardi as a Neoplatonist whose project was primarily philosophical.

See also **Falsafa; Ishraqi School; Tasawwuf.**

BIBLIOGRAPHY

Aminrazavi, Mehdi. *Suhrawardi and the School of Illumination.* Richmond, Surrey, U.K.: Curzon, 1996.

Suhrawardi, Shihab al-Din. *The Philosophy of Illumination.* Edited and Translated by John Walbridge and Hossein Ziai. Provo, Utah: Brigham Young Univesity Press, 1999.

Walbridge, John. *The Leaven of the Ancients: Suhrawardi and the Heritage of the Greeks.* Albany: State University of New York Press, 2000.

John Walbridge

SUKAYNA (671–737)

Sukayna was the nickname (*laqab*) of the granddaughter of Fatima (the daughter of the Prophet) and 'Ali bin Abi Talib. Her full name is variously given as Umayma (according to al-Kalbi) or Amina (according to al-Isbahani) bint Husayn. Her mother was al-Rabab bint Imri' al-Qays al-Kalbiyya, a poet, whose father was the reputed military leader of the Kalb.

Having lost both her father and husband ('Abdallah b. al-Hazan b. Abi Talib) at Karbala, Sukayna moved to Medina, where she acquired a taste for intellectual matters from her mother. In 686 C.E. she married Mus'ab b. al-Zubayr (d. 691 C.E.), who was killed fighting for his brother, 'Abdallah, the acknowledged caliph in Medina and Iraq. Then, after a couple of marriages which ended in divorce, she finally wed Zayd b. 'Umar, the grandson of 'Uthman b. 'Affan. She died as his widow at the age of sixty-seven.

A member of the *ahl al-bayt* (family of the Prophet), Sukayna nevertheless had the reputation of a *barza*, a woman who is never veiled, entertains men at home, and is recognized for her judgment and sound reasoning. Her bold integrity was expressed politically in her opposition to the Umayyads, and socially, in her marriage contracts, wherein she insisted on her freedom from marital control and demanded the monogamy of her intended husband. Though it was to a hairstyle—*al-turra al-Sukayniyya*—that she gave her name, Sukayna was, importantly, a lover of the arts: According to Abu Zinad (d. 757), Jarir (d. 728) and Farazdaq (d. 727) were two famous poets whose skills she encouraged, and Ibn Surayj (d. 744), one of the great singers of the Hijazi School, considered himself her protege, and set many of her verses to music.

See also **Ahl al-Bayt; Law.**

BIBLIOGRAPHY

Mernissi, Fatima. *The Veil and the Male Elite: A Feminist Interpretation of Women's Rights in Islam.* Translated by Mary Jo Lakeland. Reading, Mass.: Addison Wesley Publishing Co., 1991.

Sanni, Amidu. "Women Critics in Arabic Literary Tradition with Particular Reference to Sukayna bt. al-Husayn." *British Society for Middle Eastern Studies* (July 1991): 358–366.

Rizwi Faizer

SULTAN *See* **Monarchy**

SULTANATES

AYYUBID
Carole Hillenbrand

DELHI
Iqtidar Alam Khan

GHAZNAVID
Walid A. Saleh

MAMLUK
Warren C. Schultz

MODERN
Hassan Mwakimako

SELJUK
Saïd Amir Arjomand

AYYUBID

The Ayyubids were the family dynasty of Saladin (Salah al-Din), the famous Kurdish Muslim hero of the Crusades. The dynasty is normally dated from Saladin's career onward (c. 1169), but is named after Saladin's father, Ayyub. In their heyday, the Ayyubids ruled Egypt, Syria, Palestine, the Jazira (a region to the north of Baghdad and extending into Syria), and Yemen. Their rule may be divided into three major phases: Saladin's career, his prominent successors, and the dynasty's decline.

Ayyub and his brother Shirkuh came from Dwin in Armenia and served the Turkish warlords Zengi and his son, Nur al-Din, Saladin's two great predecessors in the Muslim "Counter-Crusade." Saladin accompanied Shirkuh on three expeditions to Egypt in the 1160s. After Shirkuh's death in 1169, Saladin took control in Egypt in the name of Nur al-Din and reestablished Sunni Islam there. However, a rift began to develop between Saladin and his master, Nur al-Din. This rift was prevented from developing into open warfare only by the death of the latter in 1174. That same year Saladin sent his brother Turanshah to conquer Yemen.

Much of Saladin's first decade as an independent ruler, from about 1174 to 1184, was devoted to subjugating his Muslim opponents and creating a secure power base in Egypt and Syria for himself and his family. In 1187 he achieved a decisive victory against the Crusaders at the battle of Hattin and reconquered Jerusalem for Islam. The Third Crusade, launched in response to this loss, ended in 1192 in truce and stalemate. Saladin died the following year. Despite his undoubted successes, he nonetheless failed to rid the Levant of the Crusaders.

Saladin did not envisage the development of a centralized state. He bequeathed a divided empire among his relations, giving his sons the three principalities centered on Damascus, Aleppo, and Cairo. In the ensuing power struggle, Saladin's brother, al-ʿAdil, a seasoned politician, rather than Saladin's sons, emerged triumphant by 1202 and reorganized Saladin's inheritance in favor of his own sons. This kind of inter-clan struggle was deep-rooted. Yet, despite the fragmented nature of the Ayyubid confederation, three rulers, al-ʿAdil (1202–1218), al-Kamil (1218–1238), and al-ʿAli Ayyub (1240–1249), managed to exercise overarching control. The succession of rulers in Aleppo remained among Saladin's direct descendants. Other principalities were set up in Transjordan and Mesopotamia. Two of these, and Mesopotamia, survived beyond the year 1250.

In 1218, the Fifth Crusade arrived in Egypt but made little impact. That year al-ʿAdil died and was succeeded by his son, al-Kamil, who in the treaty of Jaffa (February 1229) gave Jerusalem back to Frederick II, Holy Roman Emperor and king of Germany. However, al-Kamil retained a Muslim enclave in Jerusalem, including the Aqsa Mosque, the Dome of the Rock, and a corridor from Jerusalem to the coast. The pious on both sides were horrified at this diplomatic maneuver.

The death of al-Kamil in 1238 ushered in a turbulent period. His son, al-ʿAli Ayyub, emerged as the new sultan with the help of the Khwarazmians, displaced troops from Central Asia who had fled the approaching the Mongols. In 1244 the Khwarazmians sacked Jerusalem, to widespread condemnation. The Ayyubid dynasty was terminated in 1250 in a coup instigated by the sultan's own slave troops, the Mamluks, who raised one of their number to the rank of sultan. At the same time a new crusade, launched against Egypt under the French king Louix IX, was defeated by the Mamluks.

The unique focus of jihad during Saladin's time was the reconquest of Jerusalem. This goal had faded by the thirteenth century. With the Crusaders, the Ayyubids often practiced *détente* and they were criticized, even in their own time, for their lukewarm prosecution of jihad. During the Ayyubid period the remaining Crusader states became fully integrated as local Levantine polities. The Ayyubids made treaties and truces with them and sometimes, as at al-Harbiyya (1244), fought alongside them against fellow Muslims. Trade was important for the Ayyubids. They were afraid of further crusades being launched from Europe, which would disrupt their lucrative arrangements with the Italian maritime states.

Despite their religious reverence for Jerusalem, the Ayyubid dynasty never chose it as a capital, preferring Cairo or Damascus. During the Fifth Crusade in 1219, al-Muʿazzam, who, like other Ayyubids, had beautified the Holy City, dismantled its fortifications lest it should fall into Crusader hands again. This action, justified as sorrowful necessity by al-Muʿazzam, provoked widespread condemnation among the local Muslim population. Worse was to come when al-Kamil, plagued by inter-familial strife, and anxious to deflect another crusade, ceded Jerusalem to Frederick II. The Holy City remained a pawn on the Levantine chessboard, coming back under the control of the Ayyubids in 1239 and then handed back to the Crusaders five years later, then being sacked in 1244 by the Khwarazmians and returning to Muslim control.

In other respects, the Ayyubids were keen to prove their Sunni credentials, building religious monuments in Jerusalem, Damascus, Cairo, and elsewhere and choosing grandiose jihad titulature on their correspondence, coins, and monumental inscriptions. They founded no less than sixty-three religious colleges in Damascus alone (the Ayyubids were Shafiʿis or Hanafis). They welcomed Sufis, for whom they founded cloisters (*khanqah*s).

The Ayyubids's relationship with the Baghdad caliphate was complex. Like earlier military dynasties that had usurped power, the Ayyubids sought legitimization from the caliph in Baghdad. Caliphal ambassadors mediated in inter-Ayyubid disputes, and the caliph al-Nasir (d. 1225) created around himself a network of spiritual alliances with Muslim rulers, including the Ayyubids. Such symbolic links did not remove mutual suspicion, however. Both sides feared each other's expansionist aims and denied each other military support.

Saladin inherited eastern governmental traditions brought to Syria by the Seljuks. In Egypt continuity also existed between Fatimid and Ayyubid practice, especially in taxation. This process is mirrored in the career of Qadi al-Fadil, a Sunni Muslim who had served the Fatimid government in Cairo but later became Saladin's head of chancery. The Ayyubids expanded the existing system of *iqtaʿ* (land given to army officers in exchange for military and administrative duties) to the benefit of their kinsmen and commanders. Armed with the revenues of Egypt, Saladin built up a strong army which included his own contingents (*ʿaskar*s) as well as *iqtaʿ* holders, vassals, and auxiliary forces. The Ayyubid armies were composed of Kurds and Turks, with the latter predominating. The recruitment of slave soldiers (*mamluk*s),

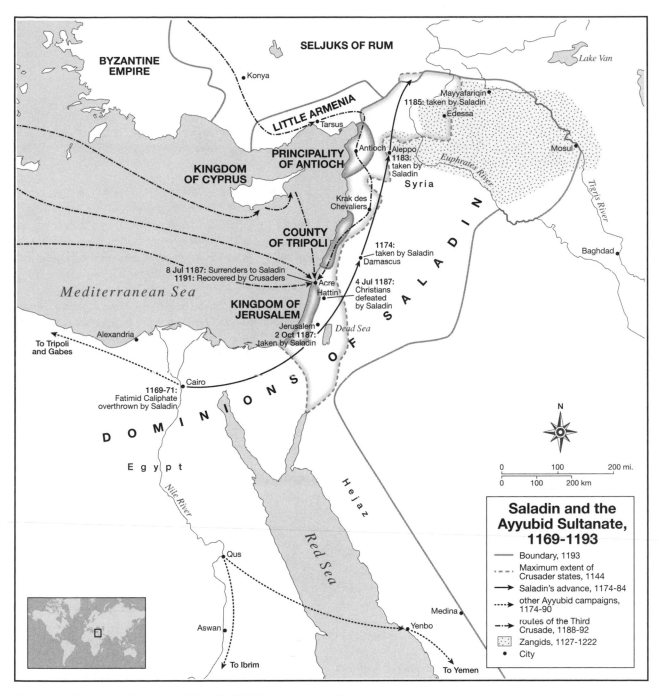

Saladin and the Ayyubid Sultanate 1169–1193. XNR Productions, Inc./Gale

always a feature of Ayyubid military policy, intensified under al-ʿAli Ayyub. This able ruler began to centralize his administration in Cairo, thus foreshadowing the policies of the Ayyubids's successors, the Mamluks.

Apart from Saladin's brief attempt to build a navy, the Ayyubids were not interested in fighting the Crusaders at sea. They did not construct castles in the Crusader manner, preferring instead to build or strengthen city fortifications and erect citadels, as in Cairo and Aleppo. The fragmented nature of Ayyubid power led to a proliferation of small courts

based on individual cities, such as Cairo and Damascus. Here the Ayyubid princes patronized the arts. Some, such as al-Amjad Bahramshah and Abul-Fida of Hama, were themselves men of letters; others (Saladin, al-ʿAdil, and al-Kamil) were exceptionally able rulers.

Two key characteristics of Ayyubid policy were already evident in Saladin's time: the promotion of Sunni Islam and the need to rule a united Syro-Egyptian polity. Saladin had acquired great prestige by abolishing the two hundred-year-old Ishmaʿili Shiʿite caliphate of Cairo. The key Ayyubid principalities were Cairo and Damascus; when these were united under one ruler, equilibrium and stability prevailed.

It is important to view the Ayyubids not only in relation to the Crusaders but also within their wider Islamic context, where they had to contend with other neighboring states. Among these were the powerful Anatolian Seljuks, the Artuqids and the Zengids in the Jazira, and the Caucasian Christian kingdoms. Traditionally, the Ayyubids have been cast as opportunistic, self-serving politicians, but their survival depended on local Levantine solidarity. In times of crisis or external aggression the Ayyubids would ally with their close neighbors, whoever they were, to defend their territory.

See also **Cairo; Caliphate; Crusades; Education; Saladin; Sultanates: Delhi; Sultanates: Ghaznavid; Sultanates: Mamluk; Sultanates: Modern; Sultanates: Seljuk.**

Carole Hillenbrand

DELHI

The Ghorian prince Shahab al-Din (who assumed the title of Mu'izz al-Din Muhammad on becoming the sultan in 1202) conquered extensive territories in North India up to Bengal during the years 1175 to 1206. His Turkish slave Qutb al-Din Aibek became an independent ruler following his death in 1206. Aibak was succeeded by his slave Iltutmish (1211–1236), who, after having established himself at Delhi, received diploma of investiture as the "Sultan of India" from the Abbasid caliph. The Delhi sultanate thus formed was ruled over by the Turkish slaves down to 1290; by Iltutmish's descendants until 1266, and by Ghiyas al-Din Balban (1266–1286) and his offspring subsequently. Later, during the period 1290 to 1412, it was ruled over successively by two non-Turkish dynasties, the Khaljis (1290–1320) and Tughlaqs (1320–1412). The sultanate underwent great expansion during the reign of 'Ala' al-Din Khalji (1296–1316), under whom Gujarat was annexed, and the southern states down to Tamil Nadu were subjugated. By the time of Muhammad Tughluq (1325–1351), all the major South Indian states had been annexed. However, before his death a large number of provinces had seceded, forming independent principalities such as the Bahmanis in the Deccan. Timur's invasion in 1398 weakened the sultanate irretrievably; thenceforth it ceased to be a pan-Indian entity.

Shahab al-Din's original principality, Ghor, comprised the Afghan province of the same name located in the zone more exposed to Iranian culture. It was organized on a clan and family basis; the royal office was confined to the Shansbani clan while the military commanders (*pahalwanan*) were of the Kharmil and Salar clans. The troopers were recruited from among the inhabitants of Ghor and those of the lowlands (*garmsir*) in the Hilmand valley. After the occupation of Ghazni by the Ghorians in 1173 and 1174, the Ghaznavide tradition of governance identified with a corps of Turkish slaves and a system of temporary land assignments (*iqta*) was incorporated in the Ghorian state structure. These institutions combined with Ghaurian control over the sources of horse supply, and their greater expertise in mounted archery and use of crossbows may explain the sweep and rapidity of their conquests in India. The Delhi sultanate's success in checking the Mongols had much to do with the efficacy of its military organization identified with the *iqta* system. 'Ala-al-Din Khalji's measures of price control and assessment of a land-tax by measurement (*wafa-e biswa*) also greatly enlarged the sultanate's fiscal resources.

Structure of Delhi Sultanate

During the thirteenth century, the sultans' nobility consisted of two main segments: the Persian-speaking Tajiks and the Turkish slaves. The latter were more influential; many of the high military positions and assignments were held by Turkish nobles of slave origin known as the forty (*chahalgani*). Balban's reign witnessed the eclipse of the forty. There emerged a new set of nobles many of whom, like Khaljis, were not necessarily of Turkish origin. There was also a perceptible tendency toward accommodating within the ruling elite Indian and Mongol converts to Islam as well as some of the Hindu warrior elements (*rawats*) having a long tradition of military service. Ziya Barani's perception of the rise of the "low born" appears to be a reflection of this tendency, which became quite strong during Muhammad Tughlaq's reign (1325–1351).

Once they received land tax at the rate of one-half of the produce, the sultans did not disturb the rights of the non-Muslims on the lands they tilled. Down to Firoz Shah Tughlaq's accession (1351), no attempt was made to impose *jizya*—a tax on the person rather than on the land, usually on non-Muslims—on any section of the non-Muslims, though the land tax itself was often called *khiraj-o-jizya*. Again, the Hindu chiefs (*rays* and *ranas*) were left in possession of their principalities in lieu of annual tribute; some of them were even recruited as the officers of the sultan's government. Similarly, the village headmen (*khuts* and *muqaddams*) were incorporated into the machinery of revenue collection. 'Ala al-Din Khalji is reported to have prevented them from shifting the burden of their share of land tax to the ordinary peasants.

Economic and Cultural Impact

The state patronage in the Delhi sultanate was distributed among deserving members of the Islamic elite by the head of the ecclesiastical affairs (*sadr al-sudur*), who also acted as chief judge (*qadi-e mumalik*). He enforced the orthodox law through a network of local courts.

The establishment of Delhi sultanate coincided with the coming to India of new skills and crafts such as the manufacture of paper, the arcuate technique in buildings, and the spinning wheel. The sultanate was marked by an urban revival and commercial expansion. Both Delhi and Daulatabad (in the south) were exceptionally large cities by the standards of the time.

The sultanate gave rise not only to a large Muslim population but also to the implantation of a culture revolving round the Persian language. As the noted poet Amir Khosrow (d.1325) showed, the Muslim stream began to merge with the traditional Indian to create a genuinely composite culture. This was reflected in the realm of architecture where the two merged, to create not only the Qutb Minar at Delhi, but a number of other splendid monuments as well. The Sufic schools interacted with the Yogic, and played their part in bringing about the later monotheistic movements of Kabir and Nanak.

See also **Sultanates: Ghaznavid; Sultanates: Mamluk; Sultanates: Seljuk.**

BIBLIOGRAPHY

Habib, Irfan. "Formation of the Sultanate Ruling Class of the 13th Century." In Vol. 1, *Medieval India*. Edited by Irfan Habib. Delhi: Oxford University Press, 1992

Jackson, Peter. *The Delhi Sultanate: A Political and Military History*. Cambridge, U.K.: Cambridge University Press, 1999.

Iqtidar Alam Khan

GHAZNAVID

The Ghaznavids were a Turkish slave-soldier dynasty (*mamluk* or *ghulam*) who ruled a sultanate that rose to dominance in eastern Iran, central Afghanistan, and modern-day Pakistan during the eleventh and twelfth centuries C.E. Though on the periphery of the Muslim world at the time, this sultanate was to play a major role in the formation of Persian literature and the opening of India for Muslim control. Motives aside, the Ghaznavids were great patrons of arts and literature, and their courts were magnets for a large number of poets, artists, and scholars. The Persian national epic, the *Shah-nameh*, was dedicated by Firdawsi (940–1025) to Sultan Mahmud (r. 998–1030). Even more than the Samanid dynasty that preceded them, the Ghaznavids brought a huge realm under the control of a single dynasty that made Persian the primary language of communication, both officially, as the language of the chancery, and artistically, as the preferred language of panegyrics addressed to the sultans. Moreover, Iranians would start writing their histories now in Persian, a move of momentous cultural significance. Arabic continued to enjoy the primary position as the language of science, and religion, yet Persian now stood on its own and soon would come to replace Arabic in most fields.

The founder of the dynasty was Sebuktigin (r. 977–997), a Turkish commander in the semi-independent city of Ghazna. Though part of the Samanid state, Ghazna was governed by army generals who ten years earlier had rebelled against the central authority. Sebuktigin managed to consolidate his rule in Afghanistan and was able to defeat the Hindushahis princes, wresting from them the Kabul river basin and the Panjab plains. Meanwhile, the Samanid emirs, under severe pressure from Turkish invaders from the inner Asian Steppes, had to turn to Sebuktigin and his son Mahmud, who was already the commander of the Samanid army. Having saved the Samanids, Mahmud came to inherit most of their domains, bringing their rule to an end.

Through a life of continuous military campaigning, Mahmud (r. 998–1030) built a vast empire; by the time of his death he had united eastern Iran and the southern parts of the Oxus River, Khwarazm, northern Iran, Afghanistan, and northern India. The army that conquered this realm was made up of professional Turkish slave-soldiers who were bought and trained for the purpose of fighting. Its core was the *ghulam-e saray*, an elite palace guard. Alongside this core was a wider force of Turkish slave-soldiers. The Ghaznavids, in turn, employed other auxiliary soldiers, such as Iranians, Arabs, and Hindus. In its campaigns in India, the Ghaznavid army was augmented by *ghazi*s, or volunteer Muslim paramilitary groups. In many respects, the story of the Ghaznavids prefigures the story of the Ottoman Empire: each at the periphery of the Muslim world, each made up of a Turkish core, and both staunchly orthodox in their ideology.

This expanding military sultanate was, however, in the long run impossible to maintain. It would be dealt a crushing defeat soon after it reached its zenith. Mahmud, busy campaigning in India, where looting Buddhist monasteries had become a very profitable enterprise, failed to realize the danger posed by the advancing Seljuq Turkish tribes. His son Mas'ud (r. 1030–1041) was no match to the challenge when the moment arrived. The battle of Dandanqan (1040) in Khorasan was so decisive that the Ghaznavid Sultan, having been forced to abandon all of the northern parts of his empire, was even contemplating deserting Ghazna. This being a military empire, the soldiers soon killed their discredited sultan.

The battle of Dandanqan signaled a turning point in the history of the Ghaznavids. Mawdud (r. 1041–1048), the new sultan, would work on consolidating what was left of the empire, which meant an expansion toward the Indian subcontinent. First Ghazna and then Lahore would be made the capital cities of what was now the first important Indian Muslim sultanate. Less is known about the remaining one hundred and fifty years of the dynasty than is known about the earlier phase, since far fewer sources are preserved, but this should not skew a present-day assessment of the historical significance of the later Ghaznavids. By turning their energy to northern India, they made possible the Islamization and conquest of large parts of India by later Muslim invaders. Their courts remained centers of literary and cultural activity, producing such important works as the Persian translation of the classic in statecraft, *Kalila va Dimna*, and the poetry of Mas'ud Sa'd Salman. In 1186 the Ghurids brought this dynasty to an end.

The Ghaznavids were fortunate to be immortalized by the adoration and admiration that was showered on Mahmud and later sultans by poets, ulema, and ideologues. Their rise to power would become exemplary in the mirror-of-princes literature. Moreover, Mahmud and his page Ayaz would become the ideal lovers for the Sufis, who sang of their love in their poetry. Some modern Indian Muslims would revive the memory of Mahmud as a Muslim Indian hero.

See also **Persian Language and Literature; Sultanates: Seljuk.**

BIBLIOGRAPHY

Bosworth, Clifford Edmund. *The Ghaznavids: Their Empire in Afghanistan and Eastern Iran 994–1040.* Edinburgh: Edinburgh University Press, 1963.

Bosworth, Clifford Edmund. *The Later Ghaznavids: Splendour and Decay, The Dynasty in Afghanistan and Northern India 1040–1186.* Edinburgh: Edinburgh University Press, 1977.

Walid A. Saleh

MAMLUK

The Mamluk Sultanate of Egypt and Syria (1250–1517) had its origins in the recruitment of military slaves (Arabic *mamluk*, literally "owned") by the Ayyubid sultan of Egypt, al-Malik al-Salih (d. 1249). By this time, military slavery was a well-established institution in the Islamic world. Young males from outside the Islamic world would be purchased as slaves, transported to the city of the purchaser, converted to Islam, and trained in the techniques of war. Upon reaching adulthood and usual manumission, they would form—it was hoped—a loyal military force, without ties to the local population. In the turbulent period after al-Salih's death (during a Crusader invasion of Egypt), al-Salih's Mamluks murdered his son and heir Turanshah. Over the ensuing decade they took steps to rule in their own name. By the time these Mamluks defeated the invading Mongols at 'Ayn Jalut in Palestine in 1260, they controlled the Nile valley and much of the Syro-Palestinian littoral. Under the early sultans, most notably Baybars (1260–1277) and Qalawun (1279–1290), the Mamluks eventually eliminated the last of the Crusader states and kept the Mongol Il-Khans at bay. The Mamluk regime remained a major regional power until it was conquered by the Ottoman Sultan Selim I in 1517.

The Mamluk Sultanate is commonly divided into two periods. The contemporary sources base this division on the ethnicity of the leading Mamluks. During the first period, which ended in 1382, the majority of the sultans were Turks from the Kipchak steppe. During the second period (1382–1517), most of the sultans were ethnic Circassians. The utility of this division is limited. Moreover, the labels Bahri and Burji, frequently applied to the same twofold periodization, are of later invention and should be avoided as they do not hold up to scrutiny.

The Mamluks of al-Salih established a ruling system in which only Mamluks were supposed to participate. The sultan was to be a *primus inter pares*, atop a hierarchy of graduated ranks and responsibilities. As both the sultan and leading Mamluk emirs would purchase Mamluks of their own, the jockeying for power and influence among the resulting factions was often quite intense and complex. A typical Mamluk career might begin in the ranks, and then progress through the grades of Emir of ten (number of Mamluks in his retinue), Emir of forty, and Emir of one hundred. In addition to these promotions, a Mamluk might receive positions in the military-political administration, from posts as governors of small towns or larger cities to commander of the army or even vice sultan. Salaries for the lower ranks would consist of cash payments. As his rank increased, a Mamluk would count on receiving an *iqta'*, or right of revenue, from agricultural districts of varying size and wealth. Cadastral surveys were carried out early in the Mamluk sultanate to aid in the process of revenue inventory and *iqta'* distribution.

As freeborn Muslims, the sons of Mamluks were excluded from the system. This was the ideal. In actuality, upon reaching the sultanate many Mamluks attempted to pass the office on to their sons. While we thus see apparent "dynasties" of sultans from the same lineage—the most famous being that descended from al-Malik al-Nasir Muhammad ibn Qalawun (third reign, 1309–1340)—most of these sultans were in fact puppets, controlled by the senior Mamluk emirs who were maneuvering to take the throne themselves. Many of the sons of Mamluks, known collectively as *awlad al-nas* ("sons of the people," that is, of those who matter), pursued careers in other endeavors.

Fueled by the agricultural richness of Egypt and sitting astride the lucrative trade routes linking the Mediterranean region to the Indian Ocean and points east, the cities of the Mamluk sultanate were centers of commerce, art, and learning. The Mamluk sultans recognized and supported all four Sunni schools of law, and appointed (and demoted) chief *qadis* (judges) at their discretion. The patronage of leading Mamluks resulted in the construction of many mosques, madrasas, Sufi *khanqas* (hospice), and other structures. Mamluk financial support for the building and upkeep of these institutions was often codified in endowment deeds (*waqfs*). These would typically provide for the salaries of the clerics who taught there and the religious functionaries who staffed the buildings, underwrite the living expenses of students, and support other charitable activities. One repercussion of this active religio-educational environment was the production of a large number of written works in many genres. Today those same texts provide a wealth of primary source material for scholars interested in Mamluk history, culture, and society.

See also **Sultanates: Delhi; Sultanates: Ghaznavid; Sultanates: Seljuk.**

Battle of Cairo, 1798. Murad Bey's Mamluk army lost control of Egypt to the French, led by Napoleon Bonaparte. © HISTORICAL PICTURE ARCHIVE/CORBIS

BIBLIOGRAPHY

Ayalon, David. *Studies on the Mamluks of Egypt (1250–1517)*. London: Variorum Reprints, 1977.

Ayalon, David. *The Mamluk Military Society*. London: Variorum Reprints, 1979.

Ayalon, David. *Islam and the Abode of War: Military Slaves and Islamic Adversaries*. London: Variorum Reprints, 1994.

Holt, P. M. *The Age of the Crusades: The Near East from Eleventh Century to 1517*. London: Longman, 1986.

Irwin, Robert. *The Middle East in the Middle Ages: The Early Mamluk Sultanate 1250–1382*. Carbondale: Southern Illinois University Press, 1986.

Petry, Carl F., ed. *The Cambridge History of Egypt,* Vol. 1: *Islamic Egypt, 640–1517*. Cambridge, U.K.: Cambridge University Press, 1998.

Raymond, André. *Cairo*. Translated by Willard Wood. Cambridge, Mass.: Harvard University Press, 2000.

Warren C. Schultz

MODERN

Sultan is a Near-Eastern term that connotes a variant form of Muslim governors emerging out of the Ottoman, Umayyad, and Abbasid practices of ruleship, power, and authority over Muslim societies. *Sultanate* implies a Muslim polity precluding the caliphal states. The Islamic political doctrine lays emphasis on the *umma*, whose internal organization was secured and defined by a common acceptance of and submission to the *shariʿa* and the temporary head of the community, the caliph or the sultan, who are religious leaders, representatives of the communities, and sometimes referred to as the successors of the Prophet, (*khalifat rasul Allah*), or commanders of the faithful (*amir al-muʾminin*), but subordinate to the law.

Muslims believe in the divine origins of government. Authority emanates from God and the *shariʿa* established the principles or roots of religion (*usul al-din*). Islamic law is immutable. The Islamic political theory assumes absence of legislative powers by humans and the state, but the state and rulers are expected to carry out the law. To disobey a law is to infringe on a rule of the social order. As such, it is an act of religious disobedience, a sin (*fisq*), involving a religious penalty. Consequently, the Islamic theory of government views man as *khalifat rasul Allah* and produced idealistic forms of government based on lineage illustrative of Max Weber's sultanism, which refers to Middle Eastern Muslim rulers who dominate their society through the establishment and development of administrations and military forces as purely personal instruments of the sultans. Sultanates are, therefore, geographical and political units that characterize Muslim power embodied in patronage, nepotism and cronyism. Nevertheless, not all regimes headed by a sultan were in fact "sultanism" in Weber's definition. Other scholarship refutes this view especially in the case of the Ottoman Empire, which had a political system that was much more bureaucratic, based on objective rules rather than being rapacious and despotic. Ottoman historian Halil Inalcik applied sultanism to the Ottoman Empire without ascribing negative connotations, thus minimizing its anti-Islamic tinge.

Nineteenth to twenty-first century sultanates in Islamic communities are construed as polities based on personal rulership, where loyalty to the ruler is motivated not by embodying an ideology, or charismatic qualities, but by a mixture of fear and rewards to collaborators. Sultans exercise power at their own discretion and are unencumbered by rules, usually subverting bureaucratic administration by arbitrary personal decrees. Those who administer sultanates are chosen by the ruler, and may include family members, friends, or individuals who submit themselves to the ruler. Some sultanates are modern, but are nevertheless characterized by the weakness of their legal legitimacy.

Twentieth-century examples of Muslim sultanates include the sultanate of Oman located on the southeastern Arabian Peninsula. Ruled on Ibadhi principles by the Al-Busaidi dynasty, the Ibadhis initially believed that the *umma* had priority over the ruler and could function without the superior authority because people could themselves apply the *shariʿa*. The Yarubi dynasty changed this with succession based on preference for members of current ruling families over claims of outsiders. The sultanate emerged in 1791 when Ahmad b. Saʿid al-Busaʿidi seized control of Muscat from his brother Imam Said b. Ahmad and informally recognized a single ruling family, assuming the title of *sayyid* or sultan.

In 1840, Sayyid Saʿid b. Sultan b. Saʿid al-Busaʿidi (1791–1856) acceded to the throne after the death of his father, Sayyid Sultan b. Ahmad. He moved his capital from Muscat to Zanzibar and established the sultanate of Zanzibar, which ruled the towns and settlements along the eastern coast of Africa through the nineteenth century. From the close of the seventeenth century, Zanzibar and its territories formed part of the Oman sultanate, then a powerful maritime regime. Sayyid Saʿid's death in 1856 led to a succession dispute between his sons and division of the sultanate between the Muscat branch and the African dominions. European influences weakened the sultanate of Zanzibar, which became a British protectorate in 1890. In 1898 the minor Sayyid ʿAli II ruled under a British regent.

During the late nineteenth century, the sultanate of Zanzibar experienced severe racial tensions between the predominantly African population, Arab landowners, and Indian trading interests, which eventually escalated into open conflict. Reforms followed thereafter, including preparations to terminate the British protectorate when the sultanate became an independent constitutional monarchy. In 1964, the African populations revolted against Sultan Jamshid b. ʿAbdullah (b. 1929) and led Zanzibar to join mainland Tanganyika to form the Republic of Tanzania, thus ending one of Africa's Muslim sultanates. While Sultan Jamshid was deposed the Oman branch has continued with Sultan Qaboos b. Saʿid (b. 1940) as the head. Other petty sultanates in the eastern coast of Africa include the Pate sultanate founded by Nabhani Arabs around 1205. Around 1858 former rulers of Pate founded the sultanate of Witu, which became a German protectorate in 1885 and a British protectorate in 1890.

The Sokoto sultanate is a West African Islamic empire established by a Fulani cleric named ʿUthman dan Fodio (1754–1817). By 1812 his jihads had conquered most Hausa states of northern Nigeria. As the territory of the sultanate extended, it was divided in 1817 into the emirate of Gwandu and the sultanate of Sokoto, each being overlord to a number of tributary emirates. The sultan of Sokoto remained overlord of the empire. Dan Fodio was succeeded by his son Muhammad Bello (1781–1837). In 1885 the empire was conquered by the British but the sultans survived through indirect rule. In the nineteenth and twentieth centuries subjects of the sultanate held important portfolios in Nigeria including the first premier of Northern Nigeria, Ahmadu Bello, and Shehu Shagari (b. 1925), the first executive president of Nigeria (1979–1983). In 2002, the sultan of Sokoto was Muhammad Maccibo ibn Abubakar (b. 1948).

The sultanate of Brunei is located on the northern coast of the island of Borneo, in eastern Asia. Its people are Malay with Chinese and Indian minorities and a variety of indigenous communities such as the Dayaks, Iban, and Kelabit. Chinese annals of the sixth and seventh centuries indicate early Islamic influences, as evidenced by Jawi, a script derived from Arabic that had been in use as the written language before 1370. The late fourteenth century saw a widespread conversion to Islam in Brunei as Sultan Muhammad Shah, formerly Awang Alak Betatar, embraced Islam and became the first Muslim ruler around 1371. Islam spread rapidly when Sharif ʿAli from Taʾif, a descendant of the Prophet's grandson Husayn, became sultan (Seri Sultan Berkat) succeeding his father-in-law, Sultan Ahmad. From the sixteenth through nineteenth centuries Brunei was a powerful state ruling over the northern part of Borneo and the adjacent chain of islands. Its power declined when it became a British protectorate in 1888 and a British dependency in 1905. In 1959, Sultan ʿUmar ʿAli Saifuddin III, who had nominal authority, promulgated the first constitution. In 1963 Brunei declined to join the Federation of Malaysia. In October 1967, Sultan ʿUmar ʿAli Saifuddin Saʿadul Khairi Waddin abdicated in favor of his eldest son, Sultan Haji Hassanatul

Bolkiah Mu'izzidin Waddaulah (b. 1946), who was coronated in August 1968. In 1979, a treaty was signed with the British, and Brunei became an independent sovereign state in January 1984. In 1991 Sultan Bolkiah introduced an ideology called Malay Muslim Monarchy that represented the monarchy as a defender of Islam.

See also **Caliphate; Monarchy; Succession.**

BIBLIOGRAPHY

Binder, Leonard. "Al-Ghazali's Theory of Islamic Governments." *The Muslim World* 45, no. 3 (1955): 209–325.

Chehabi, H. E., and Linz, Juan J. *Sultanistic Regimes.* Baltimore and London: The John Hopkins University Press, 1955.

Guenther, Roth, and Wittich, Claus, eds., *Max Weber, Economy and Society: An Outline of Interpretive Sociology.* Berkeley: University of California Press, 1978.

Haim, Gerber. *State Society and Law in Islam: Ottoman Law in Comparative Perspective.* Albany: State University of New York Press, 1994.

Huntington, Samuel P. *The Third Wave: Democratization in the Later Twentieth Century.* Norman: University of Oklahoma Press, 1991.

Inalcik, Halil. "Comments on 'Sultanism': Max Weber Typification of the Ottoman Polity." *Princeton Papers in Near Eastern Studies* 1 (1992): 49–72.

Hassan Mwakimako

SELJUK

The Seljuk Sultanate was the first empire built by a Turkish nomadic tribe from Central Asia. In 1040, the Seljuks, who belonged to the Oghuz Turks, decisively defeated the Ghaznavid Sultan Mas'ud under the leadership of two brothers, Tughril Beg and Chagri Beg. They went on to establish an empire in Iran that soon extended to Mesopotamia, where Tughril captured Baghdad in 1055 and assumed the titles of sultan and shahanshah (shah of shahs). His nephew and successor, Alp Arslan (1063–1072), defeated and captured the Byzantine emperor in the battle of Manzikert (Malazgird) and opened Anatolia to Turkish migration. His son, Malekshah (1072–1092), completed the conquest of Syria in 1084. The empire thus extended from the Oxus to the Mediterranean. It is known as the empire of the Great Seljuks, and remained unified for some half a century.

The architect of this unity was Nizam al-Mulk (d. 1092), the great wazir of Alp Arslan and Malekshah. Nizam al-Mulk unified the centralized administrative systems of the Ghaznavids in eastern Iran and the Buyids in western Iran and Iraq. In the western regions, he took over the system of land assignments in exchange for military and administrative service known as *iqta'*. In the east, where the conquering

armies had been recruited among the Turks, large land-grants were made to the members of the Seljuk family as appanages, which, before long, were also referred to as *iqta'*.

Nizam al-Mulk also built an extensive network of colleges (madrasas) throughout the empire. These became known as the Nizamiyyas after him, and were devoted to the teaching of orthodox traditions, law, and theology. He appointed many of the professors himself, including the great Muslim thinker, Abu Hamid Muhammad al-Ghazali (d. 1111), who taught at the Nizamiyya college of Baghdad for a number of years. The Seljuk sultans and the women of the ruling household endowed similar colleges throughout the empire. The aim of Nizam al-Mulk's educational reform, which was somewhat controversially referred to as "the Sunni restoration," was to curb the influence of revolutionary Isma'ili Shi'ism, which emanated from the Fatimid Empire in Egypt, the fortresses in northern Iranian mountains and the Isma'ili clandestine cells in the cities.

There can, however, be no doubt about the long-term impact of the colleges on the pattern of learning and subsequent development of Sunni Islam. Isma'ili militants assassinated both Nizam al-Mulk and Malekshah in the same year, 1092, which marked the end the unified empire. The Seljuks remained in power, and the sons and grandsons of Nizam al-Mulk remained prominent among their wazirs.

The disintegration of the Seljuk Empire did not result from revolutionary Isma'ili Shi'ism, but rather from the Turkish tribal practice of dividing the kingdom as the patrimony of the ruler among his male heirs. In other words, the Seljuks, like the Timurids and a number of other Turko-Mongolian dynasties, failed to solve the problem of succession without the division of the empire, and in the twelfth century the territory had become fragmented into a large number of principalities. Malekshah's sons fought among themselves. One of them, Sultan Sanjar (1097–1157), became a powerful ruler in the East, but the disintegration of the empire elsewhere set in irreversibly. This fragmentation was facilitated by the practice of granting large *iqta's*, which alienated provinces from central control, and even more by another Turkish institution: rule by the *atabeg*, who was the tutor of a minor prince, but who would often marry his ward's mother.

Important Atabeg dynasties came into being in Azerbaijan, Syria, northern Mesopotamia, and Fars, while different branches of the Seljuks ruled in Kerman and in Anatolia. Many of the Atabeg dynasties survived the death of the last mainline Seljuk sultan, Tughril III, in 1194. The courts of these local dynasties became centers of culture, and continued to support new institutions of Islamic learning, the madrasas, through endowments. The kingdom of the Seljuk of Rum (Anatolia) flourished in the thirteenth century, after the Mongol invasion, when their court received a large

Sultan Hani Caravanserai Portal in Aksaray, Turkey, of the Anatolian Seljuk style. The Seljuks' empire arose in the eleventh century, and ultimately included Iran, Mesopotamia, Turkey, and Syria. © VANNI ARCHIVE/CORBIS

number of learned refugees, such as the great poet and mystic, Jalaludin Rumi (d. 1273), and his father, who fled from Iran to escape the advance of the Mongols.

The women of the Seljuk ruling house were very powerful, owing to the continuation of the Turkish nomadic custom. They were active in courtly politics, and acted as patrons of religion and learning. Many of them had their own wazirs even under the Great Seljuk sultans. Their power increased further as queen mothers under the *atabeg* system after the fragmentation of the Seljuk territories, and a few of them ruled in their own right after the death of their husbands, as did Zahida Khatun, who ruled Fars in southern Iran for over twenty years in the mid-twelfth century.

See also **Sultanates: Ghaznavid; Nizam al-Mulk.**

BIBLIOGRAPHY

Boyle, J. A., ed. *The Cambridge History of Iran*, Vol. 5: *The Saljuq and Mongol Periods.* Cambridge, U.K.: Cambridge University Press, 1968.

Saïd Amir Arjomand

SUNNA

Sunna refers, in common usage, to the normative example of the prophet Muhammad, as recorded in traditions (hadith) about his speech, his actions, his acquiescence to the words and actions of others, and his personal characteristics. This close identification of sunna with Muhammad, and with authentic hadith reports originating with the Companions of the Prophet, has prevailed since the ninth century. Earlier sources, however, reflect a more flexible use of the term.

The noun "sunna" (pl. sunan) is related to the Arabic verb *sanna* and refers to a normative practice ordained or instituted by a specific person. The argument that sunna refers more generally to group norms or tribal customs is based on a false etymology, which takes sunna to refer to a smooth or well-worn track, implying in a social context the established or "well-trodden" custom of a tribe or group. In fact the ancient Arab idea of sunna is necessarily associated with a particular person responsible for establishing that sunna. "Every people has a sunna," according to a celebrated Arab poet, "and a progenitor of that sunna." Such sunna can be good or bad.

The same poet boasts that his ancestors left nothing bad in the way of sunna, and early Muslim traditions warn against following the bad sunna of the pre-Islamic Arabs.

Bad sunna is also a concern of the Qur'an, where the word appears in two contrasting expressions: *sunnat al-awalin*, the sunna of the ancients, which incurs the judgment of God; and *sunnat Allah*, the sunna of God, according to which He metes out judgment. The Qur'an thus contrasts ancestral norms to the norms of God, according to which the ancestral sunna will be judged. The Qur'an never explicitly associates sunna with Muhammad, although the notion may be considered implicit in the repeated Qur'anic command to obey God and His Prophet.

Early Muslim Uses of the Term

It was natural, given Muhammad's prominence and the Qur'anic command to obey him, that early Muslims began to consider the Prophet a source of sunna. Ideas about prophetic sunna among the earliest Muslims differed significantly from later usage, however. First, the association of sunna with Muhammad was not exclusive. The first four caliphs in particular, and the Companions of the Prophet in general, were also sources for sunna. The caliph 'Umar, for instance, asserted his freedom with regard to the appointment of a successor on the basis of conflicting precedents: Muhammad did not appoint a successor, whereas Abu Bakr did. Hence, for 'Umar, either course of action was sunna. Similarly, 'Ali reports that Muhammad and Abu Bakr both applied forty lashes as a penalty for drinking wine, while 'Umar applied eighty. In the words of the tradition, "All this is sunna."

For those who circulated such traditions, Muhammad's sunna was one sunna among many, and in principle held no higher status than the sunna of Abu Bakr or 'Umar. This association of sunna with prominent leaders other than the Prophet continued among Shi'ite Muslims, for whom the Shi'ite imams became sources of sunna. The second difference between early understandings of sunna and those that came later was that, in early Muslim usage, sunna was not yet closely identified with hadith. Early theological treatises and historical reports show a clear dissociation of the two ideas. Sunna was often invoked as a general principle of justice or right conduct, without any reference to specific hadith reports. Even more significantly, some of the earliest Muslim legal writings are virtually hadith free. Malik b. Anas (d. 795), author of the *Muwatta'*, the earliest extant manual of Islamic law, appeals to sunna but treats the existing practice of the Muslims of Medina as a more reliable source of that sunna than hadith.

During the lifetime of the great jurist Muhammad b. Idris al-Shafi'i (d. 820) these early, flexible ideas of sunna still persisted, but they were under challenge. In his polemical writings Shafi'i records a contest to define sunna involving three parties: speculative theologians, the *ahl al-kalam*, who distrusted hadith reports and argued that to follow the prophetic sunna simply meant to follow the Qur'an; scholars of Islamic law, the *ahl al-ra'y*, who acknowledged the authority of prophetic sunna in theory, but resisted its exclusive identification with hadith and relied on other sources as well; and traditionists, the *ashab al-hadith*, represented by al-Shafi'i, who argued that sunna could only be known from reliable hadith reports traced back to the Companions of the Prophet.

Sunna as Revelation

The traditionist argument championed by al-Shafi'i ultimately won the day, a triumph reflected in the elevation of sunna to the status of revelation (*wahy*). According to one hadith report that reflects the traditionist point of view, "Gabriel used to descend to the Prophet with sunna just as he descended with the Qur'an." This and many similar traditions reflect the early, pre-dogmatic form of a doctrine that would later be spelled out explicitly: that the Qur'an represents recited revelation (*wahy matlu*) whereas sunna is unrecited revelation (*wahy ghayr matlu*). The two manifestations of revelation differ in form and function—the words of the Qur'an are themselves of divine provenance and the Qur'an is recited in ritual worship—but the Qur'an and sunna do not differ in substance. Both are revealed by God and are equally authoritative sources of guidance. This doctrine bears a striking similarity to the doctrine in rabbinic Judaism of a dual Torah, one part written, one part orally transmitted by the rabbis, but both originating with Moses at Mount Sinai. The authority of sunna was further reinforced by the doctrine of *'isma*—the assertion that, as Prophet, Muhammad was protected by God from error.

In practice the relation of the Qur'an to sunna came to be expressed in the maxim, "the Qur'an has more need of the sunna than the sunna has of the Qur'an." As al-Shafi'i argued, the Qur'an gives general commands, whereas the sunna specifies the exact intent and application of those commands. Without sunna, Muslims would know, for example, that they should perform ritual worship, *salat*, but they would be in the dark about precisely when, how, or how often to do so. Moreover, the sunna provides the historical context essential for interpretation of the Qur'an by means of the "occasions of revelation," or *asbab al-nuzul*.

The dependence of Qur'an on sunna, and the primacy of the latter, is further illustrated in discussions of abrogation (*naskh*). Most legal scholars agreed that prophetic sunna had in certain cases abrogated, that is, replaced, earlier revelations, whether in the Qur'an or in a prior sunna. "There is no dispute," writes the great medieval theologian al-Ghazali (d. 1111), "that the Prophet did not abrogate the Qur'an on his own initiative. He did it in response to inspiration. God does the actual abrogating, operating through the medium of his Prophet." Information about which commands abrogate and which are abrogated can only be known, of course, by means of sunna.

Sunna and Hadith

The primacy and authority of sunna as a form of revelation, as the authoritative commentary on the Qur'an and as an independent source of guidance, was thus established in principle. In practice, however, knowledge of sunna required sifting authentic traditions from the voluminous, diverse, and forgery-ridden mass of hadith reports. The chief tool for this sifting was examination of the *isnad*, a hadith report's formal chain of transmission. Hadith specialists evaluated the *isnad* on two criteria: the reliability of the individuals who transmitted the tradition, and continuity within the chain of transmission.

When those alleged to have transmitted a tradition met the highest standards of character, memory, and reliability, and when each transmitter could be shown to have been in sufficient proximity with the next to have plausibly passed on the report, then the tradition could be considered sound (*sahih*). Traditions judged less reliable were classified as fair (*hasan*), weak (*da'if*), or fabricated (*mawdu'*). A huge literature grew up around this process, including massive biographical dictionaries, collections of hadith, and manuals of hadith criticism. The process of sifting hadith culminated in the tenth century with the compilation of the great collections of *sahih* hadith, especially the six "canonical" collections, the most celebrated of which are those of Muhammad b. Isma'il al-Bukhari (d. 870) and Muslim b. al-Hajjaj (d. 874). From the tenth century onward, the canonical collections of hadith, especially the collections of Bukhari and Muslim, became virtually synonymous with sunna, exerting a profound and pervasive impact on Islamic culture.

The Influence of Sunna on Islamic Law and Piety

The triumph of hadith had an especially deep impact on the theory and method of Islamic law. The traditionist thesis exerted extraordinary pressure to document every legal opinion with generous citations of hadith, hence the tendency for hadith reports to proliferate and for chains of transmission to grow backwards. The impact of hadith on the actual content of the law was mitigated, however, in a variety of ways. Acceptance of a hadith report as embodying authentic sunna did not necessarily assure its legal application. Jurists commonly distinguished, for example, between the personal habits and preferences of the Prophet (*al-sunna al-'adiyya*) and actions related to his Prophetic mission (*sunnat al-huda*). The former gave rise, at best, to recommended actions, while the latter were legally binding. This distinction is reflected in a tradition that recounts an occasion on which Muhammad gave bad advice to some date farmers. When confronted with the unfortunate results he replied, "I am only human. If I command something related to religion, then obey, but if I order you to do something on the basis of my own opinion, then I am only a human being." Among the schools of Islamic law, only the Zahiris, who were extreme literalists, insisted that the sunna in its entirety was legally applicable.

From the perspective of Muslim piety, however, the sunna of the Prophet as reflected in authenticated hadith reports was to be imitated in all its particulars. Thus al-Ghazali instructs Muslims that "the key to joy is following the sunna and imitating the Prophet in all his comings and goings, words and deeds, extending to his manner of eating, rising, sleeping, and speaking." The term sunna also came to be used more generally in any claim to represent the authentic and original practice of the Muslim community. The opposite of sunna in this sense is *bid'a*, or innovation. Thus Sunni Muslims distinguished themselves from Shi'ites and claimed to represent the authentic legacy of the Prophet by adopting the label *ahl al-sunna wa'l jama'a*, people of the sunna and of the community. It is also in this sense that reformist Muslims have from time to time called for a revival of the sunna as remedy for the ills of their time. Such appeals have been especially associated with scholars of the Hanbali school of law, most notably the school's founder, Ahmad b. Hanbal (d. 855), and its most celebrated medieval jurist, Taqi al-Din Ibn Taymiyya (d. 1328), whose intellectual legacy has continued to modern times.

Modern Controversies

A call to revive the sunna (*ihya' al-sunna*) became a particular focus of eighteenth-century reformers like Shah Wali Allah of India and Muhammad al-Shawkani of Yemen, who appealed to sunna to critique existing religious practices and received legal doctrine. This pattern of sunna-based reform continued in the nineteenth and twentieth centuries, especially among certain Indian Muslims who called themselves the *Ahl-e Hadith* (people of the hadith) as well as among the *salafi* reformers of Egypt and Syria. At the same time that these reformers were emphasizing the centrality of sunna as a means of reviving Islam, however, others began to challenge its authority for the same purpose.

Modern challenges to the authority of sunna have had two points of focus. First, a number of Muslims have argued that the hadith reports from which sunna is derived are unreliable. Nineteenth-century modernists Sayyid Ahmad Khan (d. 1898) of India and Muhammad 'Abduh (d. 1905) of Egypt were among the first to openly express doubts about the reliability of hadith, partly under the influence of European hadith criticism. Beginning in the twentieth century some Muslims, most notably Mahmud Abu Rayya and Ghulam Ahmad Parwez (d. 1985), came to reject hadith altogether, arguing that oral transmission, rampant forgery, and the late recording of hadith reports in writing make it impossible to sort authentic hadith from the mass of forgeries. Second, some Muslims have argued that even if the details of Muhammad's life could be known with certainty, not all of his words and deeds are meant to be followed. Secularists, like Chiragh 'Ali (1844–1895) and 'Ali 'Abd al-Raziq (1888–1966), argued that Muhammad's authority was limited to spiritual matters only. A small number of Qur'an-only Muslims, the so-called *Ahl-e Qur'an* (people of the Qur'an) of Pakistan as well as individual scholars like Parwez, contend that Muhammad's only legacy is the Qur'an. Even some revivalist Muslims, notably Abu l-A'la' Maududi (1903–1979), a fierce defender of sunna in theory, limit the scope of sunna by distinguishing between Muhammad's actions as an ordinary man and his actions as a Prophet.

These challenges to sunna have provoked vigorous polemics in defense of its authority from conservative scholars. Consequently sunna has become the single most important focus of controversy in modern Muslim discussions of religious authority.

See also **Bid'a; Hadith; Law; Modern Thought; Muhammad; Qur'an; Religious Institutions.**

BIBLIOGRAPHY

Adams, Charles J. "The Authority of Prophetic *Hadith* in the Eyes of Some Modern Muslims." In *Essays on Islamic Civilization Presented to Niyazi Berkes.* Edited by Donald P. Little. Leiden: Brill, 1976.

Bravmann, M. M. *The Spiritual Background of Early Islam: Studies in Ancient Arab Concepts.* Leiden: Brill, 1972.

Brown, Daniel. *Rethinking Tradition in Modern Islamic Thought.* Cambridge, U.K.: Cambridge University Press, 1996.

Burton, John. "Notes toward a Fresh Perspective on the Islamic *Sunna*." *British Society of Middle Eastern Studies Bulletin.* 11 (1984): 3–17.

Burton, John. *An Introduction to Hadith.* Edinburgh: Edinburgh University Press, 1994.

Crone, Patricia, and Hinds, Martin. *God's Caliph: Religious Authority in the First Centuries of Islam.* Cambridge, U.K.: Cambridge University Press, 1996.

Dutton, Yasin. *The Origins of Islamic Law.* Richmond, U.K.: Curzon Press, 1999.

Goldziher, Ignaz. *Muslim Studies.* Translated by C. R. Barber and S. M. Stern. Albany: State University of New York Press, 1967.

Graham, William. *Divine Word and Prophetic Word in Early Islam: A Reconsideration of the Sources with Special Reference to the Divine Saying or Hadith Qudsi.* The Hague: Mouton, 1977.

Juynboll, G. H. A. *The Authenticity of Tradition Literature: Discussions in Modern Egypt.* Leiden: Brill, 1969.

Juynboll, G. H. A. "Some New Ideas on the Development of *Sunna* as a Technical Term in Early Islam." *Jerusalem Studies in Arabic and Islam* 10 (1987): 97–118.

Rahman, Fazlur. *Islamic Methodology in History.* Karachi: Central Institute of Islamic Research, 1965.

Schacht, Joseph. *The Origins of Muhammadan Jurisprudence.* Oxford, U.K.: Oxford University Press, 1950.

Shafi'i, Muhammad b. Idris al-. *Islamic Jurisprudence: Shafi'i's Risala.* Translated by Majid Khaduri. Baltimore: Johns Hopkins Press, 1961.

Yusuf, S. M. *An Essay on Sunnah.* Lahore: Institute of Islamic Culture, 1966.

Daniel W. Brown

SUNNI *See* Shi'a; Succession; Sunna

SUYUTI, AL- (1445–1505)

Al-Suyuti was an Egyptian scholar best known for his prolific writings on prophetic tradition (hadith), Islamic jurisprudence (*fiqh*), Qur'anic studies, Arabic language, and related subjects. The son of a minor religious scholar, he was trained in the Sunni religious disciplines, and held several endowed academic positions in Cairo. Convinced that he alone was truly learned in an age of scholarly decline, he compiled a series of works intended to preserve the fundamentals of classical Sunni scholarship for posterity. His sense of his own superiority and his quickness to denigrate others' abilities provoked his colleagues, and he was embroiled in numerous scholarly disputes. His claims to be qualified to give independent legal opinions (*ijtihad*) and to be the reviver of Islamic knowledge at the beginning of the sixteenth century were highly controversial. Al-Suyuti's relationship with the Mamluk sultans who ruled Egypt was also an uneasy one, since he firmly believed that the religious scholars (ulema), as guardians of God's law, should be the supreme authorities in the state. Toward the end of his life, frustrated and disheartened, al-Suyuti relinquished his public posts and sought consolation in mysticism (*tasawwuf*). He continued to write, leaving at his death over 550 books and treatises on a wide range of subjects. Several works are still in use as valuable references. Some modern scholars have dismissed him as a mere compiler, a judgment that underrates his scholarly contributions, especially in the fields of jurisprudence, prophetic tradition, and Arabic language.

See also **Arabic Language; Hadith; Ijtihad; Tasawwuf.**

BIBLIOGRAPHY

Garcin, Jean-Claude. "Histoire, opposition politique et piétisme traditionaliste dans le Husn al-muhadarat de Suyuti." *Annales Islamologiques* 7 (1967): 33–90.

Sartain, Elizabeth M. *Jalal al-din al-Suyuti.* Cambridge, U.K.: Cambridge University Press, 1975.

E. M. Sartain

T

TABARI, AL- (839–923)

Muhammad b. Jarir al-Tabari was an important jurisprudent, Qur'an commentator, and historian (in descending order among tenth-century Muslims; in ascending order among modern scholars). Born in Amul, Tabaristan (by the Caspian Sea), Tabari memorized the Qur'an at eight and left home to study under more distant masters at twelve. He finally settled in Baghdad, always mainly supported by remittances from his landowning family in Tabaristan.

In theology, he advocated the moderate Sunni tendency, accepting such tenets as the uncreatedness of the Qur'an (against the Mu'tazila, among others) and recognition of 'Ali as fourth caliph and fourth-best Companion (against the Shi'a) but arguing rationally in their defense. Likewise, he inferred the law chiefly from the prophetic sunna but gave reason considerable freedom to manipulate the revealed texts. Extremist Sunnis were sufficiently offended to blockade his house near the end of his life.

Tabari's jurisprudential works were massive, and during the tenth century, a Jariri school of law vied with the Shafi'i, Hanafi, and other schools for the attention of Sunni Muslims; however, the Jariri school then died out, and most of the works are now lost. His massive Qur'an commentary was the first to deal systematically with every verse in succession. Tabari quotes many alternative interpretations from past authorities but he normally gives his own preference at the end, often appealing to grammar to establish the meaning. The author's voice is most faintly heard in his world history, likewise a succession of quotations; however, the grand scheme that emerges agrees with what else is known of Tabari's theology.

See also **Historical Writing; Qur'an.**

BIBLIOGRAPHY

Gilliot, Claude. *Exégèse, langue et théologie en Islam—L'Exégèse de Tabarî.* Paris: J. Vrin, 1990.

Rosenthal, Franz. *The History of al-Tabari*, Vol. 1: *General Introduction and From the Creation to the Flood.* Albany: State University of New York Press, 1989.

Christopher Melchert

TABLIGHI JAMA'AT

The Tablighi Jama'at ("the society for inviting or conveying") may be the most widespread movement of Islamic *da'wa* ("call," "proselytism") in the world today. Annual congregations held in Tablighi centers in Raiwind (Pakistan) and Tungi (Bangladesh) are said to include perhaps two million participants each. Dewsbury (U.K.) serves as a center for Islamic education and *tabligh* activity in Europe. Its annual meeting attracts several thousand participants, as do annual meetings held in North America. Overall leadership is based at the Banglewali Masjid at Nizam al-Din in New Delhi, India, where the movement began.

The 1920s were a period of violent religious competition in northern India, spurred by the beginnings of mass politics. Muslims in Mewat, southwest of Delhi, were a particular target of Hindu "reconversion" movements. Maulana Muhammad Ilyas (1885–1944), the movement's founder, first encountered humble Mewati laborers in Delhi. He quickly realized the limitations of mere schooling in influencing them, and instead initiated a method of practical learning, encouraging even the uneducated to remove themselves from their environment and preach to others. *Tabligh*, he argued, was incumbent not only on the learned but on every Muslim.

The movement requires no bureaucracy and no paid staff. It depends on small groups or cells (*jama'at*s) of perhaps ten men, financing themselves, going out door-to-door and speaking in mosques. Participants ideally volunteer one day a week, one three-day period a month, one forty-day period a year, and one four-month tour at least once in a lifetime. Women do *tabligh* within their own circles and gather regularly for instruction with other women; they accompany a traveling *jama'at* only if it includes one of their male relatives. Tablighis follow and teach "Six Points:" the attestation of faith (*kalima*), canonical prayer (*salat*), knowledge and ritual remembrance of Allah (*'ilm o zikr*), respect toward all Muslims (*ikram-e Muslim*), sincerity (*ikhlas-e niyyat*), and volunteering time for *tabligh* (*tafrigh-e waqt*). Writings by Maulana Muhammad Zakariyya Kandhlawi (1897–1982), based on hadith and known as the *Tablighi nisab* (The tabligh curriculum) or *Faza'il-e a'mal* (The merits of practice), serve as the movement's vade mecum. Mutual consultation (*mashwara*) is a fundamental principle in allocating responsibilities and making decisions.

Partition spurred new centers in Pakistan and served as a fillip to the movement in places like Mewat, which saw virulent anti-Muslim devastation. Maulana Muhammad Yusuf (1917–1965), who succeeded his father as emir of the movement in 1944, toured actively throughout the subcontinent. The Jama'at's activities increasingly spread to Southeast Asia, Africa, Europe, and North America.

During Maulana In'amu'l Hasan's leadership (1965–1995) worldwide activity increased dramatically, dependent in part on the growth of an Indo-Pakistani diaspora. This continued under the leadership of the council, which succeeded him. The movement more recently has taken root among North African immigrants to France and Belgium, as well as among Southeast Asian Muslims. Followers of the "Barelwi" school, who see Tablighis as Deobandis, as well as modernists, and state-oriented Islamist parties like the Jama'at-e Islami, who reject Tablighi withdrawal from social and political activism, are their primary opponents. These latter critics deplore the narrowness of Tabligh teachings. The Tablighi Jama'at's stance has, however, allowed it to operate without government suspicion across many countries.

See also **South Asia, Islam in; Traditionalism.**

BIBLIOGRAPHY

Haq, M. Anwarul. *The Faith Movement of Mawlana Muhammad Ilyas.* London: George Allen, 1972.

Masud, Muhammad Khalid, ed. *Travellers in Faith: Studies of the Tablighi Jamaat as a Transnational Islamic Movement for Faith Renewal.* Leiden: Brill, 2000.

Metcalf, Barbara D. "Living Hadith in the Tablighi Jama'at." *Journal of Asian Studies* 52, no. 3: 584–608.

Muhammad Zakariyya Kandhlawi, Maulana. *Teachings of Islam.* New Delhi: Isha'at-e-Islam, 1960.

Barbara D. Metcalf

TAFSIR

Tafsir refers to Qur'anic exegesis. *Tafsir* claims to "clarify" the divine word, which serves to make the text "speak" to current social, moral, legal, doctrinal, and political conditions. Through their interpretive strategies, exegetes have struggled to make the Qur'anic text more accessible to believers, and more applicable to changing environments.

Origins

The emergence of the word *tafsir* as both a process and a literary genre is unclear. The word *tafsir* appears only once in the Qur'an (25:33), suggesting that no formal science of interpretation was established early in the Islamic tradition. Traditionally, *tafsir* can be traced back to Muhammad. However, within hadith collections, only a small amount of *tafsir* is ascribed to the Prophet; much of the early exegesis is attributed to one of his companions, 'Abdallah ibn 'Abbas. During the first three centuries of Islam, the words *ta'wil* and *tafsir* were used interchangeably to mean "interpretation of the Qur'an," and many authors employed either one of these terms (or none at all) to describe their exegetical enterprises. For example, Ibn Ishaq (d. 768), in his biography of the Prophet (*Sirat rasul Allah*), surrounds his citings of scripture with contextual detail, which serves to explain many vague, ahistorical Qur'anic passages; however, his activity was never formalized or labeled as *tafsir*. Other early exegetical works focus on explicating legal issues or theological rhetoric, such as Muqatil ibn Sulayman's (d. 804) *Tafsir khams mi'a aya min al-Qur'an*, and Ibn Qutayba's (d. 889) *Ta'wil mushkil al-Qur'an* (respectively), but again, each author uses a different term to describe his activities. After the tenth century, a gradual distinction was drawn between *ta'wil*, which came to refer to exegesis based upon reason or personal opinion, and *tafsir*, which relied on hadith reports going back to Muhammad and his early companions. Throughout history, individual *tafsir* works emphasize either opinion or tradition, but sometimes rely on both.

With the rapid expansion of Islam, problems arose in non-Arabic speaking communities with regard to the Qur'an and its translation and interpretation, which called for more formalized exegetical commentary that extended beyond the words of Muhammad or his companions. During the time of the successors, schools of *tafsir* evolved within distinct geographical regions: Mecca, Medina, and Iraq, along with their corresponding exegetical "specialists" (*mufassirun*). The justification for the development of *tafsir* schools rests on Qur'an 3:5–6, which lays out two categories of Qur'anic verses: clear (*muhkamat*) and unclear (*mutashabihat*). The role of the exegete (*mufassir*) is to reiterate what is already "clear" and to clarify what is "unclear." Much debate arose concerning what passages fell into either of these categories, as well as to what extent finite human reason could be relied upon to make such determinations. The resolution of this debate served to shape *tafsir* works (and continues to do so) on into the twenty-first century.

Typology

Generally, *tafsir* works emphasized four types of issues that required systematized interpretive efforts: linguistic, juristic, historical, and theological. Linguistic efforts focus on the meaning of a word, where to put in punctuation and pauses, the case endings of words, or the rhetorical presentation of information: Why are entire sentences or phrases repeated again and again? A juristic accent stresses what is to be taken as the general or specific application of a command, or what verses were to be abrogated by others. Questions of abrogation (*naskh*) rely heavily on those *tafsir* that deal specifically with the occasions of the revelation (*asbab al-nuzul*), that is, those *tafsir* that embed ahistoric Qur'anic passages within a progressive timeline. Without the exegetical efforts that contextualize specific Qur'anic passages, the legal tradition, in particular the theory of abrogation, would have no firm basis from which to operate. Theologically oriented *tafsir* engage such problems as predestination versus free will, the nature of God, or the infallibility of the prophets. Many *tafsir* works revolve around a single issue; others are composite in nature.

Tafsir studies can be divided roughly into six groups based on discrete literary and methodological features: classical, mystical, sensual, Shi'ite, modern, and fundamentalist. Classical *tafsir* emerges with full force in the fourth century of Islam, typified by the work of Abu Ja'far Muhammad b. Jarir al-Tabari (d. 923), whose *Jami' al-bayan 'an ta'wil ay al-Qur'an* (The collection of the explanation of the interpretation of the Qur'an) presents a seemingly objective collection of hadith reports that originated with the Prophet and his Companions. Other classical exegetes include Mahmud ibn 'Umar al-Zamakhshari (d. 1144), who looked to Arabic poetry as a valuable source for his linguistic and literary interpretation of the Qur'an. His work engages both the rhetorical and theological aspects of Qur'anic exegesis. Fakhr al-Din Razi (d. 1210) surveys a whole range of debates in his commentary, in particular the differences between the Ash'ari and the Mu'tazili theologians. The Mu'tazalis, for example, argued that irrational passages could be interpreted to make sense through metaphorical (*ta'wil*) interpretation. Other exegetes defend the legal views of one school of law or another in their works, such as Ibn al-Jawzi (d. 1200), who supports the Hanbali tradition, or Abu 'Abdallah al-Qurtubi (d. 1273), who backs the Malikis. In these examples, commentaries further a variety of theological, legal, or political agendas through formal explication of Qur'anic passages.

Mystical (Sufi) *tafsir* favors allegorical interpretation of scripture. Sufi exegetes suggest there are two possible readings of the Qur'an: the literal (*zahir*), and the allegorical (*batin*). They are most interested in allegorical readings, which often counter growing orthodox interpretations. Generally, Sufis are concerned with establishing an intimate relationship with the divine, and look to those Qur'anic verses that reveal his hidden nature in gnostic fashion. These inner meanings of scripture are accessible only to those who grasp it through intuitive knowledge (gnosis), rather than the intellect (grammatical, rhetorical, legal, and discursive interpretation). Sufi exegesis privileges seemingly random verses in the Qur'an rather than presenting a symbolic reading of the entire work. Oftentimes Sufi interpretations extract a single sentence from the Qur'an, give it an allegorical reading, and then use that reading to decipher a whole pattern of nontextual symbols through which the inner nature of God is revealed. The relationship between the sign and the signified is not always apparent to the non-Sufi reader, who may expect a more systematized set of interpretative strategies. For example, Qur'anic references to Muhammad's "night journey" (*al-isra'*;17:1), a journey that is taken quite literally by classical exegetes, is treated metaphorically by Sufis, who cast it as a model for one's ascent along the Sufi path that requires a stripping away of the self so only the divine remains. Sufis understand the anthropomorphic statement in the Qur'an about God seating himself upon his throne (7:54) to mean God metaphorically setting himself over the heart of Muhammad. Some of the well-known collections of Sufi *tafsir* include Sahl ibn 'Abdallah al-Tustari's (d. 986) *Tafsir al-Tustari* (Exegesis of al-Tustari) and Muhyi al-Din ibn al-'Arabi's (d. 1240) *Tafsir Ibn al-'Arabi* (Exegesis of Ibn al-'Arabi).

Sufis further interpret the Qur'an through their emphasis on the recitation of certain Qur'anic passages (*dhikr*), and their calligraphic art. Generally, Qur'anic recitation makes a written text a living text (for Sufis and non-Sufis). The words themselves do not lie static on the page, but rather resound in everyday existence, collapsing ordinary time into sacred time: the moment when God first uttered his revelation to the Prophet; when mystics directly encounter their God. And, just as the mystic finds hidden meanings within the written word, so too does he see the calligraphic form of particular words allowing for deeper reflection upon the dual meanings of their shapes and sounds. The calligraphic form of "Muhammad" or "Husayn" allows one to reflect not just on the word that signifies the person, but on the person's true qualities and intimate relationship with the divine. These oral and visual forms of *tafsir* serve to extend the written document into the realm of direct sensual experience.

Shi'ite *tafsir* rose in parallel with its Sunni counterparts. Shi'ites are primarily concerned with establishing a line of divinely ordained, infallible leaders (imams) who stem from the Prophet's family, starting with 'Ali, who was the first in a series of twelve. Shi'ites, like Sufis, rely heavily on the distinction between literal and allegorical readings of the Qur'an to support their understanding that the concept of the imam (along with the necessity of blood descent for true leaders of the Islamic community) is rooted in and validated by the Qur'an. For example, the cryptic Qur'anic statement that likens a good word to a good tree (14:24) is understood by Shi'ites to refer specifically to the Prophet and his family. Contrarily, a corrupt word likened to a corrupt tree (14:26) points to the immoral Umayyads, whom Shi'ites view as usurpers of their rightful leadership. As is the case with Sufis, the connection between the sign and the signified is not readily apparent to those who do not accept Shi'ite theology. In their interpretive efforts, the Shi'a move beyond symbolic interpretations to favor textual variants of the Qur'an that validate their imamate doctrine, including one reference where Sunnis read "*umma*" (community), and Shi'a read "*a'imma*" (imami leaders). Some of the major Shi'ite *tafsir* include Abu Jafar al-Tusi's (d. 1067) *al-Tibyan fi tafsir al-Qur'an* (The explanation in interpretation of the Qur'an), and Abu al-Tabarsi's (d. 1153) *Majma' al-bayan li-'ulum al-Qur'an* (The collection of the explanation of the sciences of the Qur'an).

Modern *tafsir* refers to twentieth-century interpretation. The aim of modern *tafsir* is to understand the Qur'an in light of reason, rather than tradition; to strip the Qur'an of any traces of superstition or legend; and to use the Qur'an as a source to justify its own claims. Generally, modern exegetes try to make the text more readily accessible to the common person who faces the challenges of modernity in a post-colonial environment where past tradition no longer seems applicable to current concerns. Modern *tafsir* works differ from classical works in that they no longer focus on issues of grammar, rhetoric, law, or theology, but privilege more immediate social, political, moral, and economic concerns of the day. However, they are similar in that they strive to make the divine word more accessible to those who believe. A major modern work is Muhammad 'Abduh's (d. 1905) "*Tafsir al-manar*" (The beacon of interpretation), which calls for a rational approach to applying the Qur'an to modern dilemmas. 'Abduh elaborates on the Qur'anic passage that suggests the taking of four wives is really an impossibility, due to the fact that a man could never treat them all equally (4:129), and argues that such polygamous relationships cause harm to spouses and children. Modernists like 'Abdu locate the moral core of the text, and then use their rational capabilities to extend that general moral injunction to a variety of modern issues.

Future Trends

The study of fundamentalist *tafsir* is still in its early stages. Many fundamentalists interpret the Qur'an according to their own political and theological agendas, with little regard for traditional modes of systematic exegesis. For example, in *Fi zilal al-Qur'an* (In the shadow of the Qur'an), Sayyid Qutb (d. 1960), spokesperson for the Egyptian Muslim Brotherhood, denies the established Islamic tradition that jihad is a defensive act of war, and determines that jihad is incumbent upon all Muslims as they abolish corrupt political and religious regimes. In the early twenty-first century, Usama bin Ladin also bypasses the traditional understanding of jihad by reinterpreting the definition of a defensive attack to include the mere occupancy of sacred Muslim lands by foreign powers, or the sheer presence of anti-Islamic values in those

lands, such as promiscuity or usury. Like many modernists, bin Ladin searches for the general intent of the Qur'an—as opposed to traditional statements—and then seeks to apply that general intent to specific political and religious crises. For example, bin Ladin bypasses traditional theories of abrogation of an earlier by a later verse to select and privilege those Qur'anic verses that most closely support his military goals, in particular verses that urge believers to slay idolaters (9:5) and to smite the necks of disbelievers (47:4). Unnamed members of al-Qa'ida describe the hijackings of the planes that destroyed the World Trade Center in New York City on 11 September 2001 as a kind of sacrificial ritual sanctioned by the Qur'an. In each of these examples, the fundamentalist exegete discards tradition in favor of his own personal charisma, which ultimately gives him the authority to "interpret the Qur'an by the Qur'an."

In each type of *tafsir*, the Qur'an is made eternally pliable to offer numerous interpretative solutions to Muslims as they confront changing political, economic, doctrinal, moral, and scientific conditions.

See also **Calligraphy; Law; Muhammad; Qur'an.**

BIBLIOGRAPHY

Ayoub, Mahmoud M. *The Qur'an and Its Interpreters.* Albany: State University of New York Press, 1992.

Baljon, J. M. S. *Modern Muslim Koran Interpretation, 1180–1960.* Leiden: Brill, 1961.

Brown, Daniel. "The Triumph of Scripturalism: The Doctrine of *Naskh* and its Modern Critics." In *The Shaping of an American Islamic Discourse: A Memorial to Fazlur Rahman.* Edited by Earle H. Waugh and Frederick M. Denny. Atlanta: Scholars Press, 1998.

Gatje, Helmut. *The Qur'an and Its Exegesis: Selected Texts with Classical and Modern Muslim Interpretations.* Translated and Edited by Alford T. Welch. Berkeley: University of California Press, 1976.

Madigan, Daniel A. *The Qur'an's Self-Image: Writing and Aauthority in Islam's Scripture.* Princeton, N.J.: Princeton University Press, 2001.

Rahman, Fazlur. *Islam and Modernity: Transformation of an Intellectual Tradition.* Chicago: The University of Chicago Press, 1982.

Rippin, Andrew. "Literary Analysis of the *Qur'an, Tafsir,* and *Sira*: The Methodologies of John Wansbrough." In *Approaches to Islam in Religious Studies.* Edited by Richard C. Martin. Tucson: University of Arizona Press, 1985.

Rippin, Andrew. *Approaches to the History of the Interpretation of the Qur'an.* Oxford, U.K.: Clarendon Press, 1988.

Rippin, Andrew. "Present Status of *Tafsir* Studies." *Muslim World* 72 (1982): 224–238.

Kathryn Kueny

TAHA HUSAYN (HUSSEIN) *See*
Husayn, Taha

TAHMASP I, SHAH (1514–1576)

Tahmasp I, born on 22 February 1514, was the eldest son of Shah Isma'il. He succeeded his father to the throne in 1524 and ruled Iran until his death on 14 May 1576. His fifty-two-year reign was marked by religious consolidation and battles with rival Uzbeks and Ottomans.

Tahmasp came to power at age ten, at which time Qizilbash (Turkoman tribesmen) forces took control of Iran for the first decade of his rule. The Qizilbash were not united, however, and the situation deteriorated into civil war in 1526. By 1533, Tahmasp reasserted his sovereignty, having executed the main Qizilbash chief who was effectively ruling the country. By this time, rival Ottomans and Uzbeks had taken advantage of Iran's weak position, gaining territory from the Safavids. Nevertheless, the Safavids held on, fighting numerous defensive wars on two fronts. As a result of the Ottoman threat to the capital city of Tabriz, Tahmasp moved the capital to the city of Qazvin in 1555.

Tahmasp's reign witnessed a flowering of the arts, in particular the arts of the book, best exemplified by a magnificent *Shah-nameh* (Book of kings), commissioned in 1522 and containing some 250 outstanding miniature paintings. Tahmasp was a man of great piety, and his long reign was of great importance for the spread and consolidation of Twelver Shi'ism in Iran.

See also **Empires: Safavid and Qajar.**

BIBLIOGRAPHY

Savory, Roger. *Iran under the Safavids.* Cambridge, U.K.: Cambridge University Press, 1980.

Sholeh A. Quinn

TAJDID

Tajdid is the Arabic term for "renewal." In formal Muslim discussions, this term refers to conscious efforts to bring about the renewal of religious faith and practice, emphasizing strict adherence to the prescriptions of the Qur'an and the precedents of the prophet Muhammad. The foundation for this usage is a widely accepted tradition in which Muhammad is reported to have said, "God will send to this *umma* [the Muslim community] at the head of each century those who will renew its faith for it." Persons engaged in this activity of renewal are called *mujaddid*s.

Although there have been disagreements over the details, and over which Muslim leaders were deserving of the title of *mujaddid*, the basic understanding of the importance of renewal has been remarkably constant throughout Islamic history. In the course of the history of the human community of Muslims, Muslims recognize that the actual faith and practice of the people sometimes departed from the ideal defined by the Qur'an and the model of the Prophet. Muslims believe that the prophet Muhammad is the final Messenger of God so that in those times when Muslims have not lived up to the Islamic ideal, the community does not need a new prophet, it needs renewal. This mode of response to historical change is most important among Sunni Muslims. Within the Shi'ite traditions, there is greater emphasis on messianic styles of religious resurgence, with an important theme being the coming of the anticipated Mahdi, or rightly-guided leader whose appearance will be part of the events leading to the final establishment of God's rule of justice.

The approaches of leaders of renewal have usually emphasized certain common themes. The first was the call for the return to the Qur'an and the sunna (traditions of the Prophet). This often involved condemnation of practices that were identified as illegitimate innovations and departures from the Islamic ideal. This was not a simple conservative perspective since it involved a rejection of at least some aspects of existing conditions. As a result, a common second element in movements of renewal is the call for exercising informed independent judgment (*ijtihad*) and a rejection of the practice of simply following the judgments and interpretations of previous teachers (*taqlid*). The debates between the advocates of the two positions, *ijtihad* and *taqlid*, form a major part of the intellectual history of movements of renewal in Islamic history.

A number of major figures in Islamic history are usually identified as having been *mujaddid*s in their era. Among the most important of these are Abu Hamid al-Ghazali (d. 1111 C.E.), a teacher who brought together mystical and legal dimensions of Islamic faith, Ahmad ibn Taymiyya (d. 1327), a scholar whose ideas inspired later puritanical movements of renewal, and Shah Wali Allah of Delhi (d. 1763), whose teachings on socio-moral reconstruction provide foundations for most major modern Islamic movements in South Asia. A special figure in the line of renewers is Ahmad Sirhindi (d. 1624), who was called the "Mujaddid of the Second Millennium" because he lived at the end of the first thousand years of the Islamic era. Sirhindi was a leader of a reform-oriented Sufi brotherhood, the Naqshbandiyya, in India. His branch of that order became known as the Mujaddidi. It later played important roles in activist reform in Central Asia and the Middle East and organized resistance to European expansion in areas like the Caucasus.

In the modern period, concepts and movements of *tajdid* take many different forms. Many movements have their intellectual origins in the teachings of Muhammad ibn ʿAbd al-Wahhab (d. 1792), who joined with a chieftain in central Arabia, Muhammad ibn Saud (d. 1765), to create a political system and movement of puritanical renewal. In its strictness and uncompromising approach to what it defined as innovations, the Wahhabi movement came to be seen as the prototypical militant style of Islamic renewal. By the late twentieth century, even militant movements that had no direct connections with the actual Wahhabi tradition came to be called "Wahhabi."

Modern movements that emphasized the importance of the intellectual dimensions of renewal through *ijtihad* became important by the late nineteenth century. A leading personality in this was the Egyptian scholar Muhammad ʿAbduh (d. 1905), who served as Grand Mufti of Egypt. ʿAbduh emphasized the compatibility of reason and revelation in Islam. *Al-Manar*, the journal reflecting his teachings, was read by intellectuals throughout the Muslim world at the beginning of the twentieth century. Other conscious movements of intellectual renewal developed in the Russian Empire under Ismaʿil Gasprinskii, in India with Sir Sayyid Ahmad Khan, and elsewhere.

Throughout the twentieth century, the movements of rationalist renewal continued. However, they were overshadowed by Muslim movements advocating broader programs of social and political Islamization. The Muslim Brotherhood, established in Egypt by Hasan al-Banna in 1928, and the Jamaʿat-e Islami, established in South Asia by Abu l-Aʿlaʾ Maududi (d. 1979) in 1941, became the most visible examples of modern-style renewal movements. These movements presented programs for creating Islamic states and societies in the modern world. Although for a time they were overshadowed by secular nationalist and radical leftist movements, by the 1980s the movements of Islamic resurgence were the most visible opposition movements in many countries, and often they set the agenda for the Islamization of political discourse throughout the Muslim world. Intellectuals within these movements, like Hasan al-Turabi, who led the Muslim Brotherhood in Sudan for most of the final third of the twentieth century, wrote about the necessity for *tajdid* in rethinking all of the fundamentals of political, social, and legal structures in the Muslim world.

By the late twentieth century, many of the more visible militant Muslim groups, like al-Qaʿida, were concentrating on issues of power and jihad rather than *ijtihad*. The broad tradition of renewal in Islam continued in new forms, among the militants and also among scholars who continued the process of reexamining the sources in order to present ways of having renewed Islamic life in the contemporary world.

See also **Ijtihad; Reform: Arab Middle East and North Africa; Reform: South Asia; Taqlid.**

BIBLIOGRAPHY

Brown, Daniel. *Rethinking Tradition in Modern Islamic Thought.* Cambridge, U.K.: Cambridge University Press, 1996.

Voll, John O. "Renewal and Reform in Islamic History: *Tajdid* and *Islah.*" In *Voices of Resurgent Islam.* Edited by John L. Esposito. New York: Oxford University Press, 1983.

John O. Voll

TALIBAN

The word *taliban* derives from the Persian plural form of the Arabic word *talib*, meaning "seeker" or "student." As a general term, *taliban*, or its Arabic equivalents *tullab* or *talaba*, alludes to students from madrasas (religious schools) dedicated to theological studies of Islam. After 1994, however, Da Afghanistan da Talibano Islami Tahrik (The Afghan Islamic Movement of Taliban), or "Taliban," was known internationally as the name chosen by a *mujahidin* splinter group that eventually dominated the civil war in Afghanistan.

The rise of the Taliban as a military force is debated. Their supporters maintained that the movement surfaced in Kandahar to enforce public safety and order in reaction to the looting and harassment of the local population by other *mujahidin* groups. Their opponents viewed the Taliban as a creation of Pakistan's Interservices Intelligence (ISI) in order to gain indirect control of Afghanistan and unhindered access to Central Asia.

In any case, the Taliban, with direct Pakistani military and diplomatic support and financial backing from Saudi Arabia and the United Arab Emirates (UAE), emerged as the dominant military force that gradually came to rule about 85 percent of Afghanistan by 1999 (the remainder of the country was controlled by an anti-Taliban alliance under the leadership of Ahmad Shah Masʿud). Comprised of former *mujahidin* belonging mostly to the Pashtun ethnic majority, the group first emerged in Kandahar in 1994. The original leaders and members claimed to be students from religious schools run by Pakistan's Jamʿiyat-e ʿUlama-e Islam (JUI).

The Taliban gained international notice on 3 November 1994, when the group freed a convoy of Pakistani trucks commandeered by a local Afghan *mujahidin* group. Two days later, the Taliban captured Kandahar, and in September 1995, the western city of Herat. The Taliban seized the capital, Kabul, on 27 September 1996, ousting the ruling *mujahidin* government of President Burhan al-Din Rabbani.

Initially, the Taliban claimed that its goal was to rid the country from factionalism and the rule of warlords. However, on 3 April 1996, Mulla Muhammad ʿOmar Mujahid proclaimed himself Emir al-Muʾminin (Commander of the Faithful), thus becoming the Emir (ruler) of Afghanistan. Taking

A young girl peers out among a group of Afghan women wearing the Burqa covering at a Red Cross distribution center in Kabul in 1996, when the ruling Taliban forced women to cover themselves completely in public, and banned women from schools and workplaces. AP/WIDE WORLD PHOTOS

advantage of inter-Uzbek rivalries in northern Afghanistan, in May 1997, the Taliban captured Mazar-i-Sharif, the last significant Afghan city not under its control. This victory brought the Taliban recognition from Pakistan, Saudi Arabia, and the UAE as the legitimate rulers of Afghanistan. Although defeated in a subsequent battle, with heavy losses to their ranks (including some 250 Pakistani casualties), the Taliban recaptured Mazar-i-Sharif and then seized the Hazarah stronghold of Bamiyan in 1998 and 1999. This consolidation of power changed the internal structure of the Taliban movement from loose pockets of fighters led by a consultative council in which Mulla 'Omar was primus inter pares, into an theocratic regime increasingly ruled with secrecy and terror as a means of control, with no leader accessible to the people. As rulers, the Taliban sought the creation of what the movement believed to be pure Islamic rule according to the *shariʿa* (Islamic law).

From its appearance on the Afghan political scene until its capture of Kabul, the Taliban were viewed by some sectors of the Afghan population as a means of restoring order. This view was also shared by certain foreign powers, including the United States, which tacitly welcomed the Taliban capture of Kabul. However, while securing the territories under its control, the Taliban proved to be yet another destabilizing group of warriors whose methods included ethnically targeted mass murder of unarmed civilians (in the northern and central parts of Afghanistan) as well as the total blockade of

food supplies (to the Bamiyan region). What triggered international condemnation of the Taliban, though, was their maltreatment of women, who were banned from attending schools, holding jobs, venturing outside of their homes unless accompanied by a male relative, and being treated by male physicians. The Taliban also placed restrictions on foreign female aid workers helping Afghan women.

Signs of the Taliban's eventual international isolation began to show in 1998. With pressure from women's rights groups, the absence of international investment, and the Taliban's double-dealings with rival pipeline projects, the U.S. oil company Unocal pulled out of a major business deal that would have facilitated the construction of a gas pipeline from Turkmenistan to Pakistan through Afghanistan, a project planned by Unocal and a Saudi company, Delta Oil.

In August 1998, in retaliation for the bombings of two U.S. embassies in Africa by affiliates of Usama bin Ladin and the Taliban's refusal to surrender him, the United States launched cruise missile attacks on suspected terrorist camps in Afghanistan and spearheaded an international effort to isolate the Taliban through unilateral and U.N. sanctions.

In addition, the Taliban's drug production and trafficking activities brought international scorn. In 2001 the United Nations acknowledged Taliban efforts to reduce the production of narcotics, the first such recognition since their assumption of power in 1994. However, these efforts did not gain the movement much international sympathy, as its radicalization intensified. In March 2001, Mulla 'Omar ordered the destruction of all idols in the country, including two 1,500-year-old colossal Buddha statues in Bamiyan. Two months later, in a decree that brought international outrage, the Taliban ordered all non-Muslim Afghans to wear distinctive yellow patches.

The policies of the Taliban affecting women and religious minorities, its destruction of ancient Buddha statues, and the banning of music, television, photography, and traditional Afghan games such as kite flying were carried out under an innovative form of the *shariʿa*, combining Pashtun tribal codes and a radical form of Islamic teaching propagated by some of the graduates of the Dar al-ʿUlum (House of Sciences) *madrasa* in Deoband, India, who later became members of JIU and other radical Islamic movements in Pakistan. The presence of radical Arabs encamped in Afghanistan led by Usama bin Ladin also galvanized this development. While some Taliban members genuinely believed their rule was based in Islam, others appeared to use Islam as a justification for absolute "divine" power. The policies of the Taliban have given birth to the term "Talibanization," referring to this new form of radical Islam.

The 11 September 2001 suicide bombings of the World Trade Center in New York City and the Pentagon in Washington, D.C., were immediately attributed to Usama bin

Ladin. Because the group of Arab and other Muslim fighters he headed, known as al-Qaʿida, had operated in Afghanistan with the knowledge and protection of the Taliban government, a U.S.-led war of retaliation led to the destruction of the Taliban government and the routing of al-Qaʿida forces from Afghanistan. In early December 2001, the leaders of both the Taliban and al-Qaʿida escaped and fled into the mountains of eastern Afghanistan or into Pakistan.

As of early Spring 2003, the Taliban had begun regrouping and instigating frequent, low-level attacks against Afghan and U.S.-led anti-terror coalition forces in the south and southeastern regions of Afghanistan, along the border with Pakistan. Many Taliban members were believed to be sheltered in the southwestern region of Pakistan and assisted by sympathetic individuals and groups there. The whereabouts of top Taliban leaders, including Mulla ʿOmar, remained unknown. However propaganda distributed by the group in Afghanistan claimed that he continued to lead the Taliban.

See also **Mojahidin; Qaʿida, al-; Political Islam.**

BIBLIOGRAPHY

Marsden, Peter. *The Taliban: War and Religion in Afghanistan (Politics in Contemporary Asia)*. London: Zed Books, 2002.

Matinuddin, Kamal. *The Taliban Phenomenon: Afghanistan 1994–1997*. Karachi: Oxford University Press, 1999.

Rashid, Ahmed. *Taliban: Militant Islam, Oil and Fundamentalism in Central Asia*. London: Yale University Press, 2000.

Amin Tarzi
Kimberly McCloud

TANZIMAT

The Tanzimat (meaning reorganization, reordering) was a reform period in the Ottoman Empire lasting from 1839 to 1871. Its aims were modernization, centralization, increasing revenue, and forestalling fragmentation and conquest. Its main agents were the influential grand wazirs Mustafa Resit Pasa (1800–1858) and his protégés, Fuat (1815–1869) and ʿAli (1815–1871). Sultan Mahmud II's 1826 destruction of the old janissary military corps, which resisted change and deposed those who advocated change, and the introduction of Western-language education paved the way for these reforms.

The 1839 Imperial Rescript (*Hatt-i Serif*) of Gülhane guaranteed security and equal justice to all subjects, regardless of religion. He also proposed reforms in taxation and military conscription and created a lawmaking body. A new class of modern-educated men staffed a reorganized bureaucracy and military, and standardized provincial government and taxes. The Crimean War (1853–1856) interrupted progress, but at its end a new reform rescript (*Hatt-i Hümayun*, 1856) reiterated and expanded earlier reforms. Councils of State, Justice, Education, and Reform were established at various points in time, charged with the task of overseeing the process. Provincial councils were also established, including representatives of different religious and social groups.

Tax reforms were insufficient to prevent bankruptcy (1876), but communications and education gradually improved, and a new lawcode (*Mecelle*) was prepared, which codified Islamic law in the Western style. Reforms were stringently applied, leading to complaints of tyranny. The Young Ottomans proposed a constitutional government, but were suppressed by the absolute monarchy of ʿAbd al-Hamid II. Technical modernization continued, but political liberalization was postponed until the twentieth century.

See also **Empires: Ottoman; Modernization, Political: Administrative, Military, and Judicial Reform; Young Turks.**

BIBLIOGRAPHY

Lewis, Bernard. *The Emergence of Modern Turkey*. Oxford: Oxford University Press, 1961.

Shaw, Stanford J., and Shaw, Ezel Kural. *History of the Ottoman Empire and Modern Turkey*, Vol. II: *Reform, Revolution, and Republic: The Rise of Modern Turkey, 1808–1975*. Cambridge: Cambridge University Press, 1977.

Linda T. Darling

TAQIYYA

Often translated as "dissimulation," the word *taqiyya* is etymologically linked to piety and devotion. In Twelver Shiʿite thought it has come to refer to the tactic employed by the imams (and recommended to the Shiʿites) of hiding one's beliefs when faced with oppression. Normally, a Muslim is expected to declare his belief, so to deny it is a grave sin (*kabira*). However, according to tradition, the Shiʿite imams were faced with oppression from the Sunni majority, and in order to preserve the well-being of both their followers and themselves, they dissimulated. Outwardly they would conform to Sunni belief and practice; inwardly they would remain Shiʿite. When the Abbasid caliph al-Mansur embarked on a campaign against the supporters of the sixth imam, Jaʿfar, the imam is said to have encouraged the Shiʿa to dissimulate in order to save themselves. The doctrine was based upon a certain interpretation of the Qurʾanic verse 16:106, where the wrath of God is said to await the apostate "except those who are compelled while their hearts are firm in faith." This exceptive clause is interpreted in Shiʿite Qurʾanic commentaries as referring to "those who are forced to practice *taqiyya*."

Taqiyya, within the Shiʿite tradition, can be seen as a balance to *shahada*—the willingness to expose oneself to danger in the cause of truth. While Imam Ja'far recommended *taqiyya*, the example of Imam Husayn seems to encourage self-sacrifice in the face of oppression. Shi'ite theologians and jurists have debated long and hard about when one should be willing to face martyrdom, and when one may resort to *taqiyya*. There has not emerged a unanimous orthodox position or teaching on this point, though the factors to be considered include the magnitude of the evil perpetrated by the oppressor and the estimated risk to oneself, one's family, and the community of believers. The different tactics have been employed at different times in Shi'ite history. The Shi'a in the Ottoman empire, living under Sunni rule, were encouraged by some Shi'ite ulema to perform *taqiyya*. At the beginning of the revolutionary movement in modern Iran, on the other hand, martyrdom was seen as a virtue, and *taqiyya* was discouraged by some ulema.

In Shi'ite law, *taqiyya* was employed as an explanation of why at times the reports from the imams contradict each other. The occurrence of contradictions was explained by designating one of the reports (hadiths or *khabar*s) as being generated by "*taqiyya*." While for most jurists and hadith scholars, reports were evaluated on the basis of the chain of authorities, *taqiyya* served as an alternative means of rejecting a report as inauthentic (or rather, as an inauthentic source of law). This, in turn, gave rise to extensive debates about how to recognize a *taqiyya* report, and whether one receives punishment in the hereafter if one follows one, and thereby transgresses the law. Among the means of recognizing a *taqiyya* report was a direct comparison with Sunni doctrine. If one of the contradictory reports agreed with Sunni doctrine, then it was clearly a *taqiyya* report. The imam was obviously agreeing with the Sunnis to avoid persecution of himself or his community.

See also **Shi'a: Imami (Twelver).**

BIBLIOGRAPHY

Gleave, Robert. "Silence, Obscurity and Contradiction in Revelation." In *Inevitable Doubt*. Edited by Robert Gleave. Leiden: E. J. Brill, 2000.

Kohlberg, Etan. "Some Imami-Shi'a Views on *Taqiyya*." *Journal of the American Oriental Society* 95 (1975): 395–402.

Robert Gleave

TAQLID

The term *taqlid* refers to the "following" or "imitation" of a legal expert by a nonexpert. In Sunni Muslim law, in both its classical and modern manifestations, *taqlid* is generally viewed negatively. *Taqlid* is the activity that the legally unaccomplished (called *muqallid* or *'ammi*) are forced to perform. As they have no legal qualifications, they must merely obey the interpretation of the law put forward by the *mujtahid*. *Taqlid* in the Sunni tradition was, however, not always used with negative connotations. The theory of *ijtihad* developed within the Sunni tradition, with grades of *ijtihad* from absolute *ijtihad* (*ijtihad mutlaq*) to *ijtihad* within the school (*al-ijtihad fi'l-madhhab*) to partial *ijtihad*. A more sophisticated theory of *taqlid* accompanied these developments. A scholar might be viewed as *muqallid* to the founding imam of the *madhhab* (since a jurist would not normally claim that his *ijtihad* was superior to that of the imam), but was a *mujtahid* with regard to jurists of lesser rank within the school. *Taqlid* was, therefore, a recognition of the importance of the *madhhab* tradition as both a legal identity and as setting the broad parameters within which a jurist might operate.

Within the Imami Shi'ite tradition, such a nuanced definition of *taqlid* did not, on the whole, emerge. The Imamis had no founding imam whose *ijtihad* had to be viewed as superior, because the imams in Twelver Shi'ism were sinless (*ma'sum*). The imams did not need to perform *ijtihad* to find a ruling, since they were granted a complete knowledge of the law by God. *Taqlid* to anyone other than the imam does not form a feature of early Shi'ite jurisprudence. However, as Shi'ite jurists realized that the *ghayba* was to be a prolonged absence of the imam, a theory of *ijtihad* did emerge in embryonic form in the work of al-Muhaqqiq al-Hilli (d. 1277), and was fully developed in the writings of his pupil, al-'Allama al-Hilli (d. 1325). The result was an acceptance that an ordinary Shi'ite Muslim was forced to perform *taqlid* to a *mujtahid*. For the believer, with no access to the imam himself, the rulings of the *mujtahid* were all that was necessary to obey the law. In effect, *taqlid* of the *mujtahid*, even when the *mujtahid*'s rulings were mistaken, was sufficient to guarantee full obedience to the law of God.

This theory was one of the ideological foundations of the authority of the scholarly class in Shi'ism, and led, in part, to a heightened respect for the ulema in Shi'ite communities in comparison with that found in the Sunni world. *Mujtahid*s gained authority and prestige by the number of *muqallid*s they attracted. Since the ulema were, for much of Shi'ite history, unaligned with any governmental structure, the *mujtahid*s were, in effect, building up an independent power base. This power base of *muqallid*s could be (and was) used to mobilize opposition to government measures in the largely Shi'ite country of Iran. Indeed, the theory of *taqlid* enabled a number of *mujtahid*s to call for the opposition to the shah, which eventually led to the Iranian revolution of 1979.

See also **Ijtihad; Madhhab; Marja' al-Taqlid; Muhtasib; Shi'a: Imami (Twelver).**

BIBLIOGRAPHY

Arjomand, S. A. "The Muqaddas al-Ardalili on *Taqlid*." In *Authority and Political Culture in Shi'ism*. Albany: State University of New York Press, 1988.

Clarke, L. "The Shi'i Construction of *Taqlid*." *Journal of Islamic Studies* 12, no. 1 (2001): 40–64.

Hallaq, W. "Was the Gate of *Ijtihad* Closed?" *IJMES* 16 (1984): 3–41.

Robert Gleave

TARIQA

Tariqa is an Arabic term for the spiritual path, especially in the sense of a method of spiritual practice, often embodied in a social organization and tradition known as a Sufi order.

Tariqa has the etymological sense of way or path, and along with its near twin, *tariq*, it is used as a generic term for the way or path to God in the mystical writings of the Sufis. Despite the existence of numerous different traditions of Sufi practice and organization, it is common for Sufi teachers to point out that there is only one spiritual path that encompasses all of these different variations. At the same time, it is frequently asserted that there are as many paths to God as there are human souls. It is difficult to translate this kind of spiritual ideal into any definitive enumeration of Sufi orders as sociological entities.

Early History

The early Sufi movement as it developed in the first centuries of the Muslim era was characterized by informal association of like-minded individuals. But as Sufi communities gradually coalesced, Sufi leaders increasingly were associated with residential hospices (Ar., *ribat* or *zawiya*; Pers., *khanqa*), an institution first developed in Iran by a puritanical religious movement known as the Karramiyya. The followers of Abu Ishaq al-Kazaruni (d. 1033) established their own hospices in southern Persia and in coastal trading towns of the Indian Ocean. Abu Sa'id ibn Abu 'l-Khayr (d. 1049) established a center for Sufis in eastern Iran, with codes of conduct for the guidance of novices. Newly arrived Muslim rulers such as the Seljuk Turks found it attractive to sponsor the construction and upkeep of such hospices, along with academies (madrasas) for the teaching of the Islamic religious sciences. These hospices typically were places dedicated to prayer, study of the Qur'an, meditation, and communal meals, where travelers and the needy were welcome. Sufi masters would impart instruction and advice to their students and to visitors.

Some hospices like the Sa'id al-Su'ada' in Cairo (founded by Saladin in 1173) depended entirely on royal patronage. Other hospices had a broad clientele among the artisan classes, from which many of the Sufi masters came. The hospice of Ruzbihan Baqli (d. 1209) was built in Shiraz in 1165 by stonemasons among his followers. Yet the need of political leaders for religious legitimation put pressure on the new Sufi institutions to become part of the state patronage apparatus, typically through accepting endowment with land-tax income. Thus by 1281, the Mongol rulers of Iran set up an endowment for the previously independent hospice established by Ruzbihan, in this way linking its fortunes with the state. In India, the residences of Sufi masters of the Chishti order were typically one large room where everyone lived and pursued their discipline, unlike the multiple private cells of hospices in Syria and Iran. These "meeting houses" (*jama'at khana*s) tended to be supported, at least initially, by voluntary donations rather than fixed land income. In Turkey the hospices were known as *tekkes*. Because of hospitality regulations that required feeding and lodging guests for a limited time, the Sufi hospices became centers where members of different levels of society interacted with the Sufi master.

It was only in the twelfth and thirteenth centuries that a significant number of outstanding Sufi masters lent their names to groups constituting individual spiritual methods or "ways" (*tariqa*s). It was also common to characterize each way as a "chain" (*silsila*), with masters and disciples constituting the links. Names of Sufi orders ending in the Arabic feminine form (*-iyya*), such as Naqshbandiyya, are short hand for "the Naqshbandi way or chain" (*al-tariqa al-Naqshbandiyya, al-silsila al-Naqshbandiyya*). These chains were plotted backward in time to end ultimately with the prophet Muhammad as the final human figure; some chains are duly depicted as continuing with the angel Gabriel and God as the ultimate sources. Nearly all of these chains reach Muhammad via his son-in-law and cousin 'Ali. A notable exception is the Naqshbandi order, which reaches the Prophet via Abu Bakr instead (although the Naqshbandi lineage includes other early Shi'ite imams). A complication in the notion of the chain as a historical lineage results from the phenomenon of transhistorical or Uwaysi initiation (named after Uways al-Qarani, a contemporary disciple of the prophet Muhammad in spite of never having met him). On this basis, many Sufis have been initiated by eminent saints of the past or by the immortal prophet al-Khidr (Per., Khizr), and this transcendental relationship also falls into the category of a Sufi order. Another challenge to our understanding of Sufi institutions is the presence of deliberately deviant wanderers such as the Qalandars, who criticized the established Sufi orders even as they adopted the charismatic roles of Sufi teachers.

While it is convenient to refer to these organizations as "orders," with an implicit analogy to the monastic orders of Christianity (Franciscans, Dominicans, etc.), the comparison is inexact. Sufi orders are much less centrally organized than their Christian counterparts, and they have a more fluid hierarchical structure, which is formulated in terms of different types of initiations. Complicating the situation is the phenomenon of multiple initiation, observable at least since the fourteenth century, through which individual Sufis could receive instruction in the methods of various orders while maintaining a primary allegiance to only one. Sufi orders are

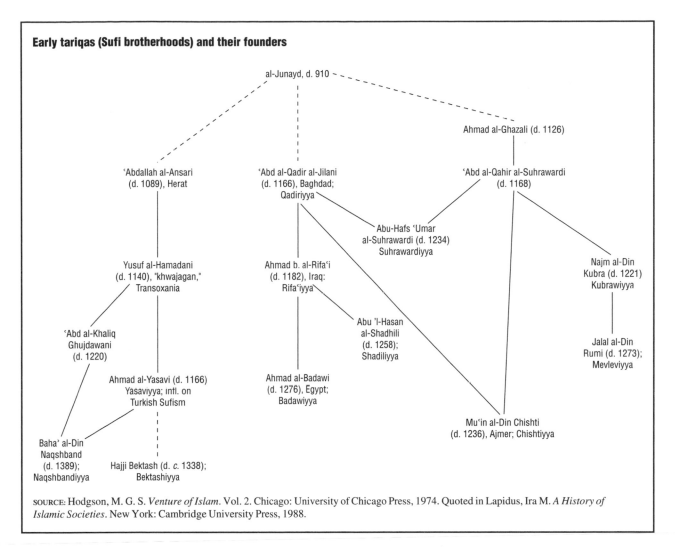

Early tariqas (Sufi brotherhoods) and their founders

al-Junayd, d. 910

Ahmad al-Ghazali (d. 1126)

'Abdallah al-Ansari
(d. 1089), Herat

'Abd al-Qadir al-Jilani
(d. 1166), Baghdad;
Qadiriyya

'Abd al-Qahir al-Suhrawardi
(d. 1168)

Abu-Hafs 'Umar
al-Suhrawardi (d. 1234)
Suhrawardiyya

Najm al-Din
Kubra (d. 1221)
Kubrawiyya

Yusuf al-Hamadani
(d. 1140), "khwajagan,"
Transoxania

Ahmad b. al-Rifa'i
(d. 1182), Iraq:
Rifa'iyya

'Abd al-Khaliq
Ghujdawani
(d. 1220)

Abu 'l-Hasan
al-Shadhili
(d. 1258);
Shadiliyya

Jalal al-Din
Rumi (d. 1273);
Mevleviyya

Ahmad al-Yasavi (d. 1166)
Yasaviyya; infl. on
Turkish Sufism

Ahmad al-Badawi
(d. 1276), Egypt;
Badawiyya

Baha' al-Din
Naqshband
(d. 1389);
Naqshbandiyya

Hajji Bektash (d. c. 1338);
Bektashiyya

Mu'in al-Din Chishti
(d. 1236), Ajmer; Chishtiyya

SOURCE: Hodgson, M. G. S. *Venture of Islam.* Vol. 2. Chicago: University of Chicago Press, 1974. Quoted in Lapidus, Ira M. *A History of Islamic Societies.* New York: Cambridge University Press, 1988.

Genealogy and origins from 600 until 1200.

not inherently driven by competing and exclusive ideologies, although competition in the sociopolitical arena is certainly not unknown. The majority of Sufi orders have a Sunni orientation, although Shi'ite orders exist as well, particularly in Iran, but Sufis have been associated with all of the major Islamic legal schools. Although it is commonly asserted that the Sufi orders played an important role in spreading Islam on a popular level, there is little historical evidence that premodern Sufi leaders took any interest in seeking the conversion of non-Muslims.

The major social impact of the Sufi orders in terms of religion was to popularize the spiritual practices of the Sufis on a mass scale. The interior orientation of the informal movement of early Sufism became available to a much wider public through participation in shrine rituals, the circulation of hagiographies, and the dispensing of various degrees of instruction in *dhikr* recitation and meditation. Elaborate initiation rituals developed, in which the master's presentation of articles such as a dervish cloak, hat, or staff would

signify the disciple's entrance into the order; special procedures governed the initiation of women disciples, though masters were typically male. A frequent feature of initiation was the requirement that the disciple copy out by hand the genealogical "tree" of the order, which would link the disciple to the entire chain of masters going back to the Prophet.

The tombs of many Sufi saints were usually erected at or near their homes. Under Islamic law, the ownership and maintenance of these tombs fell to family members, who may or may not have had spiritual qualifications. In subsequent generations, the devotion of many pilgrims thus created a class of hereditary custodians who were in charge of the finances and operations of the tomb-shrines, which could be combined with a functioning hospice where the teachings of a Sufi order took place, or with other institutions such as mosques or madrasas. Increasingly, however, the Sufi tomb came to be an independent institution, in some cases functioning as the center of massive pilgrimage at the annual festival of the saint; these festivals were variously termed the saint's birthday (*mawlid*) in the Mediterranean region, or "wedding" (*'urs*) in Iran and India, in the latter case symbolically celebrating the death anniversary as the "wedding" of the saint's soul with God. The tombs of especially popular saints eventually were surrounded with royal burial grounds, where kings and members of the nobility would erect their own tombs, to acquire a borrowed holiness or to benefit in the afterlife from the pious exercises of pilgrims to the nearby saints. Examples of this kind of necropolis include the Sufi shrines of Khuldabad and Gulbarga in the Indian Deccan, Tatta in Pakistan, and the various graveyards of Cairo. Since many founders and important figures of the Sufi orders are buried in such shrines, the history of the orders cannot be separated from the phenomenon of pilgrimage to these tombs.

Periodization of Pre-Modern Sufi Orders

The standard view of the history of Sufi orders advanced by Trimingham suggests that the Sufi *tariqa* orders enjoyed their "golden age" in the thirteenth century. Trimingham viewed the institutionalization of Sufi orders in the fifteenth century, in the form of organizations (*ta'ifa*s), as a "decline" from original spirituality into sterile ritual and vulgarization. This Orientalist perspective on the Sufi orders, with its background in the Protestant rejection of Catholic tradition and ritual, unfortunately does not adequately represent the later history of Sufism. While the existing scholarly literature on Sufism largely focuses on what is often called its "classical" phase, the ramification of Sufi orders in Muslim countries in the later so-called period of decline was extensive, and the literary and social impact of these more recent developments remains largely unexplored. The "golden age" view of Sufism is also shared by modern Muslim reformists and fundamentalists, who are extremely critical of modern and contemporary Sufism, although they may concede that long-dead Sufi masters of the past were pious Muslims. As Carl Ernst and Bruce Lawrence have argued, however, neither of these ideological views of Sufi history does justice to the self-conscious efforts of later Sufi teachers to give life to Sufi teachings in their own time.

Some of the Sufi orders, such as the Qadiriyya (named after 'Abd al-Qadir al-Jilani, d. 1166), are spread throughout Islamic lands from North Africa to Southeast Asia. Others are more regional in scope, like the Shadhiliyya in North Africa (named after Abu 'l-Hasan al-Shadhili, d. 1258), or the Chishtiyya in South Asia (named after Mu'in al-Din Chishti, d. 1236). Particular orders are known for distinctive practices, such as the loud *dhikr* recitation of the Rifa'iyya, in contrast to the silent *dhikr* favored by the Naqshbandiyya. Some orders, including the Chishtiyya and the Mevleviyya (the latter being known to Europeans as the "whirling dervishes"), have integrated music and even dance into their practice, while other orders resolutely shun these activities as distractions to spiritual training. Sometimes Sufi leaders, such as the early Chishti masters, tried to keep political power at arm's length, and they advised their followers to refuse offers of land

endowment. Some Sufi masters would demonstrate their disdain of the world by refusing to entertain rulers or visit them at court.

On the other hand, certain orders have a history of close association with political power; the Suhrawardiyya and the Naqshbandiyya in India and Iran felt it was important to influence rulers in the proper religious direction, and the Bektashiyya had strong links to the elite Ottoman troops known as the janissaries. The Safawiyya, once a moderate Sunni order based at Ardebil, became widespread among Turkish tribes on the Persian-Ottoman frontier, and it emerged with a strongly Shi'ite and messianic character to become the basis for the Safavid empire that ruled Iran from the sixteenth through the eighteenth century. During the period of nineteenth-century colonialism, when much of the Islamic world fell under European domination, Sufi institutions played varied roles. Hereditary custodians of Sufi shrines in places like the Indian Punjab were treated as important local landlords by colonial officials, and they became further entrenched as political leaders due to British patronage; ironically, the cooperation of these Sufi leaders became essential in later independence movements directed against British control. Similarly, the Senegalese order known as the Muridiyya became heavily involved in peanut farming as a result of being favored by French colonial authorities, and they have emerged in the postcolonial order as a prominent social and religious institution. With the overthrow of traditional elites by European conquest, Sufi orders in some regions remained the only surviving Islamic social structures, and they furnished the principal leadership for anticolonial struggles in places such as Algeria ('Abd al-Qadir), Libya (the Sanusiyya), the Caucasus (Shaykh Shamil), and China. French administrators in North Africa viewed Sufi orders with suspicion, and colonial scholars produced studies of the Sufi orders designed to predict their possible resistance to or cooperation with official policies.

Post-Colonial Era

In the postcolonial period, Sufi orders and institutions have an ambiguous political position, which is inevitably determined in relation to the nation-state. Governments in many Muslim countries have inherited the centralized bureaucratic organization of their colonial predecessors, which sometimes themselves go back to precolonial bureaucracies. In countries like Egypt and Pakistan, efforts have been made to subject the orders and shrines to governmental control. Nonetheless, many of the largest and liveliest Sufi organizations, such as the Burhaniyya in Egypt, flourish without official recognition. Officials frequently appear at Sufi festivals and attempt to direct popular reverence for saints into legitimation of their regimes, and governments also attempt to control the large amount of donations attracted to the shrines. State sponsorship of Sufi festivals also aims to enroll support against fundamentalist groups critical of the government, and to redirect reverence for saints in a nationalist direction.

Contemporary fundamentalist movements attack Sufism with a virulence sometimes even more intense than that which is reserved for anti-Western diatribes. Reformers frequently denounce pilgrimage to Sufi tombs as an idolatry that treats humans on the level of God, and they reject the notion that saints are able to intercede with God on behalf of ordinary believers. Sufi orders have been illegal in Turkey since the 1920s, when Mustafa Kemal Ataturk secularized the Turkish state. The public performance of the Sufi rituals such as the "whirling dervish" dance of the Mevleviyya, and the *dhikr* of the Istanbul Qadiriyya, is tolerated only as a cultural activity, which is exported abroad through touring companies and sound recordings; the tomb of the great Sufi poet Jalaluddin Rumi (1207–1273), which many visitors treat as a shrine, is officially regarded as a museum. This reformist critique of Sufi practice has been internalized in some Sufi circles, such as the Sabiri Chishti tradition associated with the Deoband academy in India; leaders of this group, such as Ashraf ʿAli Thanvi (1863–1943), have been highly critical of traditional Sufi practices such as listening to music and visiting the tombs of saints. Certain Ottoman thinkers from Sufi backgrounds (Bediuzzaman Saʿid Nursi [1876–1960], Kenʿan Rifai [1867–1950]) rejected life in the hospice and insisted on living in the world, and they interpreted Sufi theorists like Ibn al-ʿArabi (1165–1240) and Rumi in terms of modern thought and science. Modernist secular thinkers and Muslim countries have also been critical of Sufism, but for different reasons. To authors like Muhammad Iqbal (1877–1933) in South Asia and Ahmad Kasravi (1890–1946) in Iran, institutional Sufism was the source of fatalism, passivity, and civilizational decline. Sufi advocates such as the Barelwi school in South Asia, and the Naqshbandis led by Shaykh Hisham Kabbani (b. 1945), have responded to these reformist critiques with polemics and apologetics of their own, defending Sufi practices as authentic and even necessary according to Islamic principles. In response to the modernist critique, Sufi theorists have asserted that science ultimately seeks what Sufism alone can offer, and they have adopted the language of psychology and modern technology.

Sufi activities are not publicly tolerated in Saudi Arabia and Iran, since Sufi leaders and tomb cults would constitute an unacceptable alternative spiritual authority to the regnant religious orthodoxy in either case. Still, it is remarkable that the founders of certain fundamentalist movements, such as Hasan al-Banna (1906–1949) of the Muslim Brotherhood in Egypt, and Abu l-ʿAlaʾ Maududi (1903–1979) of the Jamaʿat-e Islami in India, were exposed to Sufi orders in their youth, and they seem to have adapted certain organizational techniques and leadership styles from Sufism; the main difference is that these movements substitute political ideology for Sufi spirituality, in order to become mass parties in the modern political arena. Another movement that has branched off from Sufism in a hostile fashion is the pietistic Tablighi Jamaʿat, founded in India and with immense followings in many Muslim countries; although it derives from a branch of the Chishtiyya and still respects the early Sufi saints, this movement considers contemporary Sufi practice to be illegitimate and attempts to dissuade people from pursuing it.

Contemporary Orders

In recent years, Sufi orders have extended their reach into Europe and the Americas, and today branches of orders from India, Iran, Africa, and Turkey are actively attracting adherents in major urban centers in many Western countries. Some orders have also expanded into other Asian and African countries where they were never previously found. Certain groups derived from Sufi orders, such as the International Association of Sufism derived from the teachings of Hazrat Inayat Khan (1882–1927), have only tenuous associations with Islam; they present Sufism as a mystical universal religion that may be pursued through dancing and chanting, without requiring the practice of ritual prayer or other duties of Islamic law. Other groups have more explicit relations with Islamic tradition, including even insistence on the clothing and customs of the order's country of origin. Sufism is taking on some aspects of modern American and European culture, such as joint participation of men and women in contexts where gender separation was the norm in many premodern Muslim societies; several American Sufi groups even have female leaders, something quite rare in the traditional societies where Sufism has flourished. At the same time, Sufism in Europe and America strives to preserve some of the distinctive rituals and institutions of traditional Sufism—the tomb of Sri Lankan Sufi master Bawa Muhaiyuddin near Philadelphia has already become a place of pilgrimage.

Perhaps the most remarkable aspect of Sufism in the nineteenth and twentieth centuries has been the publicizing of a previously esoteric system of teaching through modern communications media. Today, Sufi orders and shrines produce a continual stream of publications aimed at a variety of followers from the ordinary devotee to the scholar. Evidence suggests that Sufi orders, along with governments, were among the first users of print in Muslim countries in the nineteenth century. Not only traditional treatises on Sufi metaphysics and practice, but also new genres like periodicals and novels, became vehicles for the expression of Sufi thought in multiple languages. Other technologies, such as the audio cassette (especially for music), and now the Internet, have been extremely effective in disseminating Sufi ideas and culture to broad audiences. In short, the Sufi orders have employed the technologies and ideologies of modernity even as they have been forced to respond to them.

See also **Dhikr; Khirqah; Pilgrimage: Ziyara; Tasawwuf.**

BIBLIOGRAPHY

De Jong, Fred, and Radtke, Berndt, eds. *Islamic Mysticism Contested: Thirteen Centuries of Controversies & Polemics.*

Islamic History and Civilization: Studies and Texts, 29. Leiden: Brill, 1999.

Ernst, Carl W. *Guide to Sufism*. Boston: Shambhala Publications, 1997.

Ernst, Carl W., and Lawrence, Bruce. *Sufi Martyrs of Love: Chishti Sufism in South Asia and Beyond*. New York: Palgrave Press, 2002.

Friedlander, Shems. *The Whirling Dervishes: Being an Account of the Sufi Order Known as the Mevlevis and its Founder the Poet and Mystic Mevlana Jalalu''ddin Rumi*. Albany: State University of New York Press, 1992.

Gramlich, Richard. *Die schiitischen Derwischorden Persiens*. Wiesbaden, Germany: Steiner, 1965–1981.

Hoffman, Valerie J. *Sufism, Mystics, and Saints in Modern Egypt*. Columbia: University of South Carolina Press, 1995.

Karamustafa, Ahmet T. *God's Unruly Friends: Dervish Groups in the Islamic Middle Period 1200–1550*. Salt Lake City: University of Utah Press, 1999.

Lifchez, R. *The Dervish Lodge: Architecture, Art, and Sufism in Ottoman Turkey*. Berkeley: University of California Press, 1992.

O'Fahey, R. S. *Enigmatic Saint: Ahmad ibn Idris and the Idrisi Tradition*. London: Hurst & Co., 1990.

Popovic, Alexandre, and Veinstein, Gilles, eds. *Les voies d'Allah: Les ordres mystiques dans le monde musulman des origines à aujourd'hui*. Paris : Fayard, 1996.

Schimmel, Annemarie. *Mystical Dimensions of Islam*. Chapel Hill: University of North Carolina Press, 1975.

Trimingham, J. Spencer. *The Sufi Orders in Islam*. London: Oxford University Press, 1971.

Zarcone, Thierry; Işin, Ekrem; and Buehler, Arthur, eds. *Journal of the History of Sufism*. Vols. 1–2: *The Qâdiriyya Order*. Istanbul: Simurg Press, 2000.

Carl W. Ernst

TASAWWUF

Tasawwuf is an Arabic term for the process of realizing ethical and spiritual ideals; meaning literally "becoming a Sufi," *tasawwuf* is generally translated as Sufism.

The etymologies for the term Sufi are various. The primary obvious meaning of the term comes from *suf*, "wool," the traditional ascetic garment of prophets and saints in the Near East. The term has also been connected to *safa'*, "purity," or *safwa*, "the chosen ones," emphasizing the psychological dimension of purifying the heart and the role of divine grace in choosing the saintly. Another etymology links Sufi with *suffa* or bench, referring to a group of poor Muslims contemporaneous with the prophet Muhammad, known as the People of the Bench, signifying a community of shared

poverty. The ideal qualities evoked by these derivations are the key to the concept of *tasawwuf* as formulated by authors of the tenth century, such as Sulami (d. 1021). While acknowledging that that the term Sufi was not current at the time of the Prophet, Sufi theorists maintained that this specialization in spirituality arose in parallel with other disciplines such as Islamic law and Qur'anic exegesis. But the heart of Sufism, they maintained, lay in the ideal qualities of the prophet Muhammad and his association with his followers. Definitions of Sufism described ethical and spiritual goals and functioned as teaching tools to open up the possibilities of the soul. In practice, the term Sufi was often reserved for ideal usage, and many other terms described particular spiritual qualities and functions, such as poverty (*faqir*, *darvish*), knowledge (*'alim*, *'arif*), mastery (*shaykh*, *pir*), and so on.

Orientalist scholarship introduced the term Sufism to European languages at the end of the eighteenth century. Prior to that time, European travelers had brought back accounts of exotic religious behavior by Oriental dervishes and the miscellaneous Indian ascetics called fakirs, who were considered important only when their social organization posed a problem for European colonialism. The discovery of Persian Sufi poetry, filled with references to love and wine, allowed Europeans to imagine Sufis as freethinking mystics who had little to do with Islam. The "-ism" formation of the word (originally "Sufi-ism") reveals that "Sufism" was a part of the Enlightenment catalog of ideologies and belief systems, and frequently it was equated with private mysticism, pantheism, and the doctrine that humanity can become divine. Scholars such as Sir William Jones (d. 1794) and Sir John Malcolm (d. 1833) advanced the thesis that Sufism derived from Hindu yoga, Greek philosophy, or Buddhism. This concept of the non-Islamic character of Sufism has been widely accepted in Euro-American scholarship ever since, despite (or perhaps because of) its disconnection with the Islamic tradition, in which *tasawwuf* and its social implementations have played a central role. Thus, in terms of its origin, the introduction of the term Sufism into European languages may be regarded as a classic example of Orientalist misinformation, insofar as Sufism was regarded primarily as a radical intellectual doctrine at variance with what was thought of as the sterile monotheism of Islam. Nevertheless, as a word firmly ingrained in the vocabulary of modernity, Sufism can usefully serve as an outsider's term for a wide range of social, cultural, political, and religious phenomena associated with Sufis, including popular practices and movements that might be in tension with normative definitions of Sufism.

Origins and Early History

The Qur'an itself may be taken as a major source of Sufism. The experience of revelation that descended upon the prophet Muhammad left its mark in numerous passages testifying to the creative power of God and to the cosmic horizons of spiritual experience. God in the Qur'an is described both in terms of overwhelming transcendence and immanent presence. In particular, the ascension (*mi'raj*) of the prophet Muhammad to Paradise, as elaborated upon from brief references in the Qur'an (17:1–2, 53:1–18), provided a template for the movement of the soul toward an encounter with the Creator. While it was commonly accepted that the Prophet's ascension was accomplished in the body, for Sufis this opened up the possibility of an internal spiritual ascension. The notion of special knowledge available to particularly favored servants of God, particularly as illustrated in the story of Moses and al-Khidr (18:60–82), provided a model for the relationship between inner knowledge of the soul and outward knowledge of the law. Another major theme adopted by Sufis was the primordial covenant (7:172) between God and humanity, which established the relationship with God that the Sufi disciplines sought to preserve and restore. A broad range of Qur'anic terms for the different faculties of the soul and the emotions furnished a basis for a highly complex mystical psychology.

The earliest figures claimed by the Sufi movement include the prophet Muhammad and his chief companions; their oaths of allegiance to Muhammad became the model for the master-disciple relationship in Sufism. Muhammad's meditation in a cave on Mount Hira outside Mecca was seen as the basis for Sufi practices of seclusion and retreat. In an extension of the authority of the Prophet as enshrined in hadith accounts, Sufis regarded the model of the Prophet as the basis for spiritual experience as well as legal and ethical norms. While there is debate about the authenticity of much of the classical hadith corpus, many hadith sayings favored by Sufis describe the cosmic authority of Muhammad as the first being created by God, and in many other ways these sayings establish the possibility of imitating divine qualities. Veneration of the prophet Muhammad, both for his own qualities and in his role as intercessor for all humanity, became the keynote of Sufi piety as it diffused through Muslim society on a popular basis.

Among the early successors to the Prophet, the later Sufi movement singled out as forerunners ascetics like al-Hasan al-Basri (d. 728), who was renowned for preaching the vanity of this world and warning of punishment in the next. By the end of the eighth century, small groups of like-minded individuals, particularly in northeastern Iran and in Iraq, had begun to formulate a vocabulary of interior spiritual experience, based in good part on the Qur'an and the emerging Islamic religious sciences. Intensive and protracted prayer (including not only the five obligatory ritual prayers daily, but also five supererogatory or "extra credit" prayers) and meditation on the meanings of the Qur'an were notable features of early Sufi practice. The sometimes stark asceticism of early Sufis, with its rejection of the corrupt world, came to be tempered by the quest to find God through love. This emphasis on an intimate and even passionate relationship

with God is associated particularly with the outstanding early woman Sufi, Rabi'a of Basra (d. 801). Other early Sufis contributed to the development of an extensive psychological analysis of spiritual states, as a natural result of prolonged meditative retreats. Socially speaking, many of the early Sufis came from lower-class artisan and craftsman origins. Their piety often included deliberate critique of the excesses of wealth and power generated by the rapid conquests of the early Arab empire. Major early figures in the Sufi movement included Dhu al-Nun of Egypt (d. 859), the ecstatic Abu Yazid al-Bistami in Iran (d. 874), the early metaphysician al-Hakim al-Tirmidhi (d. 910) in Nishapur, and the sober psychologist and legal scholar Junayd of Baghdad (d. 910).

Although religious criticism of Sufi practices and doctrines started to occur as early as the late ninth century, it is particularly in the case of al-Hallaj (executed in 922) that tensions between Sufism and the legal establishment became apparent. Although the trial of al-Hallaj was a confusing mix of politics and crypto-Shi'ism, in hagiographical sources it became mythologized as a confrontation between radical mysticism and conservative Islamic law. Sufi writers adapted to this crisis by insisting upon adherence to the norms and disciplines of Islamic religious scholarship, while at the same time cultivating an esoteric language and style appropriate to the discussion of subtle interior experiences. Early Sufi writers such as Sarraj (d. 988), Ansari (d. 1089), and Qushayri (d. 1072) emphasized Sufism as the "knowledge of realities," inseparable from yet far beyond the knowledge of Islamic law and scripture. Many of these writers also declared their loyalties to established legal schools or the Ash'ari school of theology.

The institutional spread of Sufism was accomplished through the "ways" or Sufi orders, which increasingly from the eleventh century offered the prospect of spiritual community organized around charismatic teachers whose authority derived from a lineage going back to the prophet Muhammad himself. Under the patronage of dynasties like the Seljuks, who also supported religious academies in their quest for legitimacy, Sufi lodges eventually spread throughout the Middle East, South and Central Asia, North Africa and Spain, and southeastern Europe. While dedicated membership in Sufi orders remained confined to an elite, mass participation in the reverence for saints at their tombs has been a typical feature in Muslim societies until today.

Major Figures and Doctrines

The central role of Sufism in premodern Muslim societies is perhaps best typified by the intellectual career of Abu Hamid al-Ghazali (d. 1111). Having become the foremost theologian at the Nizamiyya academy in Baghdad at a very youthful age, he underwent a spiritual crisis chronicled in his autobiographical *Deliverance from Error*. Systematically questioning everything, he interrogated the four chief intellectual options available in his day: dialectical theology, Greco-Arabic philosophy as interpreted by Ibn Sina, Isma'ili esotericism, and Sufism. He regarded theology as a severely limited discipline, and philosophy as tainted by metaphysical arrogance, while the Isma'ilis were dismissed as authoritarians with a fallacious understanding of religion and morality. This left the Sufis as the only custodians of knowledge that transcends the limits of reason; Ghazali's conclusion was that Sufism, properly understood, was the surest guide to the spiritual ideals deriving from the Qur'an and the Prophet. While Ghazali programmatically separated Sufism from theology, philosophy, and Shi'ism, in fact the subsequent history of Sufism could not be separated from these three streams of Islamic thought. Ghazali assumed that Sufis would be based in an authentic tradition of Islamic law, and it was in fact normal for Sufis to profess whichever school of law was current in their region (Hanafi in South and Central Asia and the Ottoman lands, Shafi'i in Persia and the eastern Mediterranean, Maliki in North Africa and Spain, and Hanbali sporadically in Khurasan and Egypt). Ghazali's massive synthesis, *Giving Life to the Sciences of Religion*, connected basic Islamic ritual and religious texts and practices with the interiorization of Sufi piety in a way that was accessible to Muslim intellectuals trained in the madrasa legal tradition. The intellectual integration of Sufism with the Islamic religious sciences typified many Muslim societies up to the age of European colonialism. In other writings, Ghazali was also critical of antinomian tendencies and unconventional practices found in Sufi circles. These deliberately nonconformist trends were also inevitably a part of the Sufi ambience.

The pervasive role of Sufism is demonstrated by countless biographical works in Arabic, Persian, and other languages, recounting the virtues and exemplary religious lives of the Sufi saints. Many of these biographical traditions about Sufis are also enmeshed in the history of Islamic religious scholarship and dynastic political history. Although it is difficult to select a handful of representative figures out of the innumerable possibilities, it would be impossible to leave out the great Andalusian Sufi, Ibn al-'Arabi (d. 1240). Perhaps more than any other, Ibn al-'Arabi illustrated the fusion of ethical and psychological mysticism with powerful metaphysical analysis, all in the context of Islamic law and the Qur'an. His teachings on human perfection, the manifestation of divine attributes in creation, the divine names, imagination, and the nature of existence were expressed through a series of difficult but extremely popular Arabic writings, including the voluminous encyclopedia *The Meccan Openings*, and the succinct treatise on prophecy and mysticism, *Bezels of Wisdom*. The latter work has attracted over one hundred commentaries, in Arabic, Persian, and Turkish, in countries ranging from the Balkans to South Asia. Ibn al-'Arabi also elaborated upon the doctrine of sainthood, which in Islamic contexts derives from authority and intimacy conferred by God rather than from sanctity as recognized in official Christian doctrines of sainthood. In particular, Ibn al-'Arabi described in detail the invisible hierarchy of saints who control the destiny of the world; he also expressed, sometimes in enigmatic code, his own role as one of the chief figures of this hierarchy.

Although polemical opponents as well as modern scholars have criticized Ibn al-'Arabi for identifying God with creation and nullifying Islamic law, works of recent scholars like Michel Chodkiewicz and William Chittick have demonstrated both Ibn al-'Arabi's metaphysical complexity and his strong engagement with the *shari'a*. The phrase most commonly used to describe the teachings of Ibn al-'Arabi, "oneness of existence" (*wahdat al-wujud*), never occurs in his writings; it vastly oversimplifies his doctrines, which are better described as demonstrating the dialectical tension between the different modes of existence in terms of divine attributes. Nevertheless, there have been many critiques directed at Ibn al-'Arabi over the centuries, accusing him of flagrant heresy. Ironically, the best-known of his critics, the Hanbali legal scholar and controversialist Ibn Taymiyya (d. 1328), was himself a Sufi and a member of the Qadiri order.

Another major Sufi figure was the great Persian poet Jalaluddin Rumi (d. 1273). Trained as a theologian with a Sufi background, Rumi unleashed his spiritual talent after encountering the enigmatic dervish Shams-i Tabriz. His collection of lyrical poems, named after Shams, is the largest body of such poetry by any Persian poet of the last millennium. His great poetic epic, *Masnavi-ye ma'navi* (Spiritual couplets), is a vast repository of Sufi teaching through stories and images. The Sufi order established by his descendants in Anatolia, known as the Mevleviyya, have become famous to foreign observers as the "whirling dervishes," due to their characteristic turning meditative dance. Rumi's writings, which have been immensely popular from Southeast Europe to India, portrayed divine beauty and mercy through unforgettable and vivid imagery, easily memorized and popularized in musical performance. Today Rumi's poetry enjoys a new vogue in English translation by American poets Robert Bly and Coleman Barks.

Despite Ghazali's earlier objections to philosophy, Sufi teachings in their metaphysical form overlapped with both the terminology and the doctrines of Aristotelian and Neoplatonic philosophy as interpreted in the Arabic tradition. Although Sufis aimed at a knowledge that transcended intellect, it was inevitable that philosophical categories would be used to put Sufism into cosmological and metaphysical perspective. Figures such as Shihab al-Din Yahya al-Suhrawardi (executed in 1191) combined a critical revision of the metaphysics, logic, and psychology of Ibn Sina (Avicenna, d. 1037) with an identification of being as light. His "Illuminationist" (*ishraqi*) philosophy, expressed both in logical treatises and in Platonic fables in Arabic and Persian, drew upon Sufi mystical experience as an important source of knowledge. Although

Men in Oman participate in a Sufi dhikr performance where they repeat the name of God and his attributes or engage in a call and response in praise of God and the prophet Muhammad. The beating of the drums, the swaying body movements, and the repetition of the chants can lead to trances or states of ecstasy among Sufis. HULTON ARCHIVE/GETTY IMAGES

Ibn al-ʿArabi was not a philosopher, and Suhrawardi was not really a Sufi, the shared quest for understanding the relationship between God and the world allowed Sufism and philosophy both to play roles in the intellectual tradition of later Muslim societies.

Likewise, although Ghazali had made clear his objections to Shiʿism in its Ismaʿili form, it is also apparent that Sufism cannot be separated from Shiʿism either. The recognition of the Shiʿite imams as spiritual leaders possessing authority and intimacy with God (*walaya*) is closely related to the rise of the spiritual master and the concept of sainthood in early Sufism. Sufi lineages either include ʿAli or some of the later imams in their spiritual genealogies, and the imams of Twelver Shiʿism

are deeply revered in Sufi circles. While the majority of Sufi scholars have been affiliated with Sunni legal schools, some Sufi orders (Niʿmatallahi, Khaksar) have had a Twelver Shiʿite orientation. Certainly there have been Shiʿite theologians who have rejected the claims of Sunni saints, and the Safavid dynasty suppressed organized Sufism in Iran after seizing power in the early sixteenth century and making Shiʿism the state religion. As a result, formal Sufi orders in Iran have had a precarious existence or even gone underground under threat from militant Shiʿism. Nevertheless, philosophical Sufism (*ʿirfan*) has remained an important aspect of the advanced curriculum in Iran. Philosophers of the Safavid period, such as Mulla Sadra (d. 1640), drew upon

Ibn Sina, Ibn al-'Arabi, Suhrawardi, as well as Sufi and Shi'ite themes.

Ranging further afield, Sufi theorists in India and China to some extent adopted aspects of those cultures. Sufis in India were aware of yogic practices, including breath control and other psychophysical techniques. Knowledge of hatha yoga was disseminated through a single text known as *The Pearl of Nectar* (*Amrtakunda*), which was translated into Arabic, Persian, Turkish, and Urdu with a heavy dose of Islamizing tendencies. Sufi masters of the Chishti and Shattari orders adopted certain yogic meditations into their repertoire through this channel. Similarly, when the Chinese Sufi Wang Daiyu (d. 1658) translated Persian Sufi works by Jami and others into classical Chinese, he employed a neo-Confucian vocabulary and cosmology that made the works virtually indistinguishable from the productions of Chinese literati.

Alongside these main currents of Sufi thought, one can also distinguish a kind of anti-structure in a series of movements that were deliberately unconventional. Psychologically the mood was set in the concept of self-blame (*malama*), which called for incurring shame before the public as a discipline for the ego. While the early self-blamers among the Sufis were not supposed to infringe on religiously forbidden territory, the dropout dervishes of the Qalandar movements (including Abdals, Haydaris, Malangs, and Madaris) rejected institutional Sufism as a betrayal of independent spirituality. Shunning respectability, maintaining a bizarre appearance, and indulging in intoxicants, these eccentrics led civil disturbances in Delhi and even organized peasant rebellions against Ottoman rulers. They still may be seen on the fringes of Muslim societies as a kind of spiritual underground.

Practices

Aside from the obligatory daily prayers and supererogatory ones, the most important Sufi practice is undoubtedly the recollection of God (*dhikr*) by recitation of Arabic names of God as found in the Qur'an. This recitation, which could be either silent or spoken aloud, typically drew from lists of ninety-nine names of God (it being understood that the one-hundredth name was "the greatest name" of God, known only to the elect). As with the supererogatory prayers, *dhikr* aimed at interiorizing the Qur'an and its contents, in order to obtain closeness to God. As meditations, these practices aimed to empty the heart of anything but God and to begin to establish the qualities of the divine in the human being. Treatises like *The Key to Salvation* by Ibn 'Ata' Allah of Alexandria (d. 1309) described in detail the psychological and existential results to be obtained from multiple repetitions of particular names of God. The parallelism between repetition of the divine names and Islamic theology is significant; in Ash'ari theology, the divine names are the attributes of God, and are the faculties through which the divine essence interacts with the created world. Recitation of the divine names

thus reinforced the Islamic cosmology of Sufism. The mystical psychology that accompanied these practices articulated different levels of the heart and soul, which are further differentiated in terms of multiple spiritual states (*ahwal*) and stations (*maqamat*) that have been charted out in varying degrees of detail.

While *dhikr* recitation may originally have been restricted to adepts undertaking retreat from the world, as a kind of group chanting this practice can also be accessible to people on a broad popular scale. Simple chanting of phrases like "there is no god but God" (*la ilaha illa allah*) did not only express the fundamental negation and affirmation of Islamic theology, but also made it possible for a wider public to adopt the practices of Sufism. One of the advantages of *dhikr* was that it could be practiced by anyone, regardless of age, sex, or ritual purity, at any time. Under the direction of a master, Sufi disciples typically are instructed to recite *dhikr* formulas selected in accordance with the needs of the individual, based on the different qualities of particular divine names.

The tombs of Sufi leaders, especially those associated with major orders, played an important role in the public development of Sufism. On a popular level, these tombs were commonly connected to lodges or hospices maintaining open kitchens where all visitors were welcome. Major festivals were held not only for standard Islamic holidays but also in particular for dates honoring the prophet Muhammad and the Sufi saints. While the birthday of the Prophet was a popular observance in many places, the death-anniversary of the saint was also a focus of attention. The practice of pilgrimage (*ziyara*) to the tombs of saints was generally considered to be beneficial, but was especially valued at the anniversary of the moment when the saint was joined with God; all this assumes the saint's ability to intercede with God on behalf of pilgrims. At major shrines like Tanta in Egypt, or Ajmer in India, hundreds of thousands of pilgrims may congregate for days at the annual festival, with many distinctive local rituals and performances. Over the past two centuries, with the rise of the Wahhabis in Arabia and kindred Salafi reform movements elsewhere, there has been extensive criticism of pilgrimage to tombs and the notion of saintly intercession, all of which is considered to be sheer idolatry. Although in Saudi Arabia the tomb of practically every Sufi saint and family member of the Prophet has been destroyed, elsewhere pilgrimage to saints' tombs continues to be popular.

Other widely encountered forms of Sufi practice are music and poetry, which take on different regional forms in accordance with local traditions. Although conservative Islamic legal tradition has been wary of musical instruments as innovations not present during the time of the Prophet, the rich and sophisticated musical traditions of Iran, India, Andalusia, and Turkey have furnished irresistible and highly developed forms for the communication of Sufi teachings, particularly when combined with poetry. Sufis in fact speak mostly of "listening" (sama'), emphasizing the spiritual role of the listener far more than that of the musical performer, and the focus is upon the words of poems that may or may not be accompanied by musical instruments. Early Sufi poetry in Arabic and Persian is frequently indistinguishable in form and content from secular love and wine poetry emanating from the courts. The difference is that Sufi listeners would refer libertine images and daring expressions to the passionate relationship with God or the Sufi master. Leading Sufi poets like the Egyptian Ibn al-Farid (d. 1235) made mystical verse into an art form of great density and subtlety; for centuries, pilgrims to his shrine recited his poems at his annual festival. In Persian, multiple genres ranging from the quatrain (ruba'i) to the lyric (ghazal) and the ode (qasida), along with the epic couplet (masnavi), were cultivated by poets in Sufi lodges as well as by court poets with Sufi leanings. Particularly famous poets in Persian include Rumi, 'Attar (d. 1220), Hafiz (d. 1389), and Jami (d. 1492).

Poetic literature developed in many regional languages, sometimes using language and themes derived from Arabic and Persian models, but frequently employing rhyme, meter, and subject matter of local origin. The Indian subcontinent offered many local languages to Sufi poets, who freely explored the resources of Hindi, Bengali, Gujarati, Tamil, and Kashmiri. Writers like the Chishti poet Muhammad Jayasi (d. 1542) used Hindu figures from Rajput epics to convey Sufi themes. Turkish became a vehicle both in the simple verse of Yunus Emre (d. 1321) and in the sophisticated Ottoman poetry of figures like Shaykh Ghalib (d. 1799). Other major languages employed by Sufi include Malay, Swahili, Berber, and Hausa.

Contemporary Manifestations and Situation

The changes wrought by European colonial expansion in Asia and Africa, and by globalization in the postcolonial period, have had major effects on Muslim societies. The overthrow of local elites by foreign invaders removed traditional sources of patronage for Sufi orders and shrines. Under the suspicious eyes of European colonial administrators, hereditary administrators of Sufi shrines in India became integrated into landholding classes, while the extended networks of Sufi orders furnished some of the only centers of resistance against European military aggression, as in the Caucasus, North Africa, and Central Asia. Sufi responses to colonialism thus ranged from accommodation to confrontation. As with traditional religious scholars, so too for Sufis it was necessary to come to terms with new roles dictated by the technological and ideological transformations of modernity.

One of the first notable features of modern capitalism and technology introduced into Muslim countries by colonial regimes in the nineteenth century was Arabic script printing, whether in movable type or lithography. Printing, along with the expansion of literacy by colonial regimes, not only facilitated the workings of administration for the government, but also permitted the dissemination of formal religious knowledge among Muslims on a scale never before attempted. On one hand, the replacement of manuscript culture with identical printed books doubtless encouraged the scriptural authoritarianism that arose with Salafi reform movements. On the other hand, Sufi orders, with their large guaranteed markets, were major patrons of printing. The spread of previously esoteric Sufi texts to a broad reading public amounted to a publication of the secret. Postcolonial governments, modern universities, and academic societies also sponsored the printing of books related to Sufism. Parallel with the printing phenomenon is the rise of audio recordings of Sufi music distributed on global scale, initially for ethnomusicological audiences, but more recently for popular world music and fusion recordings. Major recording artists with Sufi connections include Pakistani singer Nusrat Fateh 'Ali Khan (1948–1997) and Senegalese musician Youssou N'Dour (b. 1959).

As Sufism became publicized on global scale, likewise major ideological shifts occurred in Muslim countries, through which the term Islam increasingly became a symbol of anticolonial identity. Salafi reform movements, often described as fundamentalist, opposed Sufism as a non-Islamic innovation based on idolatrous worship of saints. Just as European Orientalists detached Sufism from Islam, now Muslim fundamentalists came to the same conclusion. Sufism has now become a position to be defended or criticized in terms of ideological constructions of Islam. In the most recent forms of representation of Sufism, Internet advertising paradigms and polemics have become the norm. Transnational Sufi movements, with the help of technically educated members in Europe, North America, or South Africa, maintain websites both for informing the public and for maintaining connections for a virtual community. Some Sufi websites also engage in extensive polemics against fundamentalists, who are often dismissed with labels such as Najdi (Wahhabi).

Through encounters with colonial missionaries and through migration to Europe and America, Sufis have become engaged with non-Islamic religious traditions in various ways. Some Sufi teachers, such as Hazrat Inayat Khan (d. 1927), decided to present Sufism to Europeans and Americans as a universal mystical teaching with no essential connection to Islam. The traditional Sufi emphasis on universality provided a conceptual basis for this ecumenism, although non-Muslim membership in Sufi orders had been decidedly rare prior to the twentieth century. Now there are significant numbers of self-professed Sufis in Europe and America who do not consider themselves Muslims. At the same time, other Sufi movements from Iran, Turkey, and West Africa include varying degrees of emphasis on Islamic identity and traditional custom. The relationship between Sufism and Islam is thus debated and contested both in its traditional homelands and in its new locations.

Another recent shift of emphasis in Sufism concerns women's public participation in Sufi activities and what may be called feminist interpretations of Sufism. American women are now trained to perform the Mevlevi turning dance in public ceremonies, and to take on the role of *shaykha* or female spiritual leader. While such prominence of women was not unknown in traditional Muslim societies, global changes in the roles of women are bringing women to the fore in Sufi organizations to a remarkable extent, in countries like Turkey and Pakistan as well as in America and Europe.

As with religious matters everywhere, Sufism in the end is governed by the state. The dervish orders in Turkey were outlawed by decree of Mustafa Kemal Ataturk in 1925 as part of official secularism, and the revival of the Mevlevi "whirling dervish" performance was permitted only on condition that it be a nonreligious activity, destined especially for foreign tourists. Sufi groups in Iran keep a very low profile under the watchful eyes of the Islamic regime. Sufism in the former Soviet republics, like most other religious activities, was practically extinguished under Soviet rule, although some informal networks survived. The Sufi-oriented Darul Arqam movement in Malaysia was banned in 1994 for its political activities. A Lebanese Sufi group of African origin, the Ahbash movement, promotes a program of religious pluralism and peace within the framework of the secular state. Government bureaucracies closely control Sufi shrines in Egypt and Pakistan, both because of the extensive revenue gathered at the shrines and to monitor the large crowds that attend.

Despite the vicissitudes of foreign invasion, the collapse of traditional social structures, the imposition of European education and culture, and the rise of the secular nation-state, Sufism in many different local forms persists and survives both among illiterate members of the lower class and among urban elites. Whether defended in traditional languages as part of classical Islamic culture or attacked as a non-Islamic heresy, Sufism still forms part of the symbolic capital of majority Muslim countries. As a form of religious practice spread to Europe and America by transnational migration and through the global marketplace, Sufism is seen both as an eclectic form of New Age spirituality and as the mystical essence of Islam. The globalizing fortunes of Sufism over the past two centuries are one more indication why it is no longer possible to speak meaningfully of a separate Muslim world.

See also **Arabic Literature; Ash'arites, Ash'aira; Basri, Hasan al-; Ghazali, al-; Hallaj, al-; Ibn 'Arabi; Ibn Sina; Ibn Taymiyya; Jami'; Madrasa; Muhammad; Mulla Sadra; Rabi'a of Basra; Persian Language and Literature; Pilgrimage: Ziyara; Rumi, Jalaluddin; Shi'a: Imami (Twelver); Suhrawardi, al-; Tariqa; Urdu Language, Literature, and Poetry.**

BIBLIOGRAPHY

Addas, Claude. *Quest for the Red Sulphur: the Life of Ibn 'Arabi.* Translated by Peter Kingsley. Cambridge, U.K.: Islamic Texts Society, 1993.

Chittick, William C. *The Sufi Path of Knowledge: Ibn al-'Arabi's Metaphysics of Imagination.* Albany: State University of New York Press, 1989.

Chittick, William C. *Sufism: A Short Introduction.* Oxford, U.K.: Oneworld Publications, 2000.

Chodkiewicz, Michel. *An Ocean Without Shore: Ibn 'Arabi, the Book and the Law.* Albany: State University of New York Press, 1993.

Corbin, Henry. *Creative Imagination in the Sufism of Ibn 'Arabi.* Princeton, N.J.: Princeton University Press, 1969.

Ernst, Carl W. *Ruzbihan Baqli: Mysticism and the Rhetoric of Sainthood in Persian Sufism.* Richmond, U.K.: Curzon Press, 1996.

Ernst, Carl W. *Guide to Sufism.* Boston: Shambhala Publications, 1997.

Ernst, Carl W. *Teachings of Sufism.* Boston: Shambhala Publications, 1999.

Ewing, Katherine Pratt. *Arguing Sainthood: Modernity, Psychoanalysis, and Islam.* Durham, N.C.: Duke University Press, 1997.

Homerin, Th. Emil. *Umar Ibn Al-Farid: Sufi Verse, Saintly Life.* New York: Paulist Press, 2001.

Hujwiri, 'Ali. *The Kashf al-mahjub, The Oldest Persian Treatise on Sufiism.* Translated by R. A. Nicholson. Leiden and London: Luzac, 1911.

Knysh, Alexander D. *Islamic Mysticism: A Short History.* Leiden: Brill, 2000.

Lewis, Franklin. *Rumi: Past and Present, East and West.* London: Oneworld Publications, 2000.

Massignon, Louis. *Essay on the Origins of the Technical Language of Islamic Mysticism.* South Bend, Ind.: University of Notre Dame Press, 1998.

Razi, Najm al-Din. *The Path of God's Bondsmen.* Translated Hamid Algar. New York: Delmar, 1982.

Schimmel, Annemarie. *Mystical Dimensions of Islam.* Chapel Hill: University of North Carolina Press, 1975.

Schimmel, Annemarie. *As Through a Veil: Mystical Poetry in Islam.* New York: Columbia University Press, 1982.

Sells, Michael Anthony. *Early Islamic Mysticism: Sufi, Qur'an, Mi'raj, Poetic and Theological Writings.* New York: Paulist Press, 1996.

Sulami, Muhammad ibn al-Husayn. *Early Sufi Women: Dhikr an-Niswa al-Muta'abbidat as-Sufiyyat.* Translated by Rkia Cornell. Louisville, Ky.: Fons Vitae, 2000.

Werbner, Pnina, and Basu, Helene, eds. *Embodying Charisma: Modernity, Locality, and Performance of Emotion in Sufi Cults.* London and New York: Routledge, 1998.

Carl W. Ernst

TA'ZIYA (TA'ZIYEH)

Ta'ziya is an Islamic Shi'ite ritual performed mainly in Iran. The Arabic term *ta'ziya* (Per., Ta'ziyeh) means to mourn or to offer one's condolences for a death. It is also sometimes called *ta'ziya khani*, or *shabih khani*. The term *ta'ziya* has been used primarily in Iran to refer to a Shi'ite religious ritual consisting of a theatrical re-enactment of the tragic seventh-century Battle of Karbala. This historic battle was fought between the followers of prophet Muhammad's grandson Husayn and the troops of the second Umayyad caliph Yazid. While *ta'ziya* performance rituals have been mostly restricted to Iran, the Shi'a of South Asia and Iraq use the term *ta'ziya* to refer to a model or replica of Husayn's tomb, which they use in their ritual processions, after which they are ritually discarded.

The Battle of Karbala

Accounts of the Battle of Karbala can be summarized as follows. In the year 680 C.E., Husayn, who was also the third imam of the Shi'a, was killed in the desert of southern Iraq along with over seventy of his family and close friends by troops loyal to the caliph Yazid. The women and children were taken prisoner and paraded in various cities, adding to the humiliation, but also providing opportunities for these women, particularly Husayn's sister Zaynab, to speak out publicly against Yazid. Yazid is portrayed by the Shi'a as notoriously corrupt, immoral, and oppressive. Hence, Husayn's rebellion and subsequent martyrdom is understood by the Shi'a as an epic struggle between good and evil. For the Shi'a this event has served as a vindication of the Shi'ite cause in the face of Sunni criticism, as well as constituting the central event in their understanding of human history.

Historical Development

Following the battle itself, popular elegies of the martyrs were composed. However, the earliest reliable account of the performance of public mourning rituals was recorded in 963 C.E. during the reign of Mu'izz al-Dawla, the Buyid ruler of southern Iran and Iraq. When the Safavid dynasty came to power in Iran a new type of ritual called *rawza-khani* emerged, consisting mainly of a ritual sermon recounting and mourning the tragedy of Karbala. This ritual was based on texts like Husayn Va'ez Kashfi's 1502 composition entitled *Rawzat al-shuhada'* (The garden of martyrs). Kashfi's text was a synthesis of a long line of historical accounts of Karbala by religious scholars.

By the time the Qajar dynasty took power in Iran in 1796, the *rawza-khani* ritual had evolved into the much more elaborate ritual called *shabih-khani* or *ta'ziya*. The *ta'ziya*, an elaborate theatrical performance of the Karbala story based on the same narratives used in the *rawza-khani*, involved a large cast of professional and amateur actors, a director, a staging area, costumes, and props.

Qajar Patronage

The heyday of *ta'ziya* was the Qajar era (1796–1925). The most elaborate example of Qajar patronage of *ta'ziya* was the Takiya Dawlat, which was built in Tehran in 1873 by the order of the Iranian monarch Naser al-Din Shah. This *takiya* was built on a very grand scale. Nevertheless, it was in most ways a typical *takiya*. It consisted of a large circular amphitheater with several entrances surrounding a large open area; a tent was used as a roof. Its primary purpose was to provide a staging area for the most elaborate *ta'ziya* performances. Lady Sheil, a European traveler, resident in Tehran in 1856, gives a brief account of the *ta'ziya* performance in the Takiya Dawlat in 1856, concluding, "It is a sight in no small degree curious to witness an assemblage of several thousand persons plunged in deep sorrow, giving vent to their sorrow" (p. 127).

Modern Trends

Following the fall of the Qajar dynasty in the early twentieth century, the *ta'ziya* slowly declined until it was mostly abandoned in the large cities in the 1930s and 1940s. However, *ta'ziyas* have continued to exist in Iran on a smaller scale throughout the twentieth century, especially in traditional sectors. There were two reasons for this relative decline. The first Pahlavi king, Reza Shah, outlawed the *ta'ziya*. More importantly, as Iranian society changed modernized elites became less interested in sponsoring such traditional ritual events. Scholars of literature and drama as well as government agencies attempted to preserve this theatrical tradition in the 1970s, and again in the 1980s and 1990s. However, unlike the Qajar period, which was the heyday of the *ta'ziya* ritual, the dominant public rituals since the 1930s have been the *Muharram* processions, and various forms of the *rawza khani*.

See also **Hosayniyya; Rawza-Khani; Taqiyya.**

BIBLIOGRAPHY

Chelkowski, Peter, ed. *Ta'ziyeh: Ritual and Drama in Iran.* New York: New York University Press, 1979.

Hegland, Mary Elaine. "The Majales-Shi'a Women's Rituals of Mourning in Northwest Pakistan." In *A Mixed Blessing: Gender and Religious Fundamentalism Cross Culturally.* Edited by Judy Brink and Joan Mencher. New York and London: Routledge, 1997.

Pelly, Sir Lewis. "The Miracle Play of Hasan and Husayn." *Collected from Oral Traditions.* London: Wm. H. Allen and Co., 1879.

Kamran Aghaie

TERRORISM

Terrorism is one of today's most contested terms. It is widely used polemically to delegitimate both state-sponsored violence as well as counter-state insurgencies. Although there is as yet no scholarly consensus in defining and theorizing about the subject, there is some agreement that terrorism involves the threat and actual use of violence against civilians to bring about political, social, and economic change. During the late twentieth century, political elites, state intelligence agencies, the establishment media, and an array of experts (qualified and unqualified) began to use the term to describe the militant tactics of various movements and organizations, none more than those connected with Islam. The subject is considerably more complicated, however.

Origins and Meanings of the Term

The origin of the word "terror" in Latin-derived languages is the French *terreur*, which assumed its modern meaning in the context of the French Revolution. Following the overthrow of the monarchy in 1789, the new government established its laws and its authority through a "reign of terror," which inspired in the population a constant fear of arrest and execution. In this context, *terrorisme* was understood as fear created by the state, or government rule through the specter of violence. This definition also applies to the totalitarian states of the twentieth century. More contemporarily, however, terrorism has become synonymous with violence perpetrated by non-state actors.

In Arabic, the term *irhab* is commonly used today as the equivalent for "terrorism," its meanings largely affected by the use of the latter term in Western languages, particularly English and French. *Irhab*, derived from *arhaba* ("to frighten," "to strike with fear," or "to terrify"), never appears in the Qur'an, though its imperfect verbal form occurs once. The Qur'an states, "Against them make ready your strength to the utmost of your power, including steeds of war, *to terrify* (*yurhibuna*) thereby the enemies of God, your enemies, and others whom you do not know, but God knows" (8:60). The historical context for this command is that of the early battles of Muhammad and his followers against their Meccan enemies; it has had limited use subsequently in the context of discourses on jihad. Other variations of the same root appearing in the Qur'an refer to humanity's awe of God, particularly as an appellation for Christian monks (*ruhban*). Since the 1980s, *irhab* has been widely used in Arabic political rhetoric to condemn Israel's use of military force. Egyptian political elites and government-controlled media usually use the term to describe violence committed by anti-state Islamist groups.

More Recent Usages

After the Second World War, movements countering colonialism and imperialism grew in strength and influence in Africa, Asia, and Latin America. In the Middle East (for example, Israel/Palestine, Egypt, Algeria, and Iran), nationalist and Islamic movements engaged in active and, at times, violent opposition to Western powers and the emergent client regimes they supported. Then, as now, the means of resistance differed within and among the many groups at work, regardless of whether or not this resistance was articulated in terms of national struggle and liberation, as with many early resistance movements, or in religious terms through the concept of jihad, a concept that acquired greater salience in the 1970s. At that time, revisionist formulations of classical Islamic jihad doctrine by Islamist ideologues such as Abu l-A'la' al-Maududi (1903–1979) and Sayyid Qutb (1903–1966) were adapted by radical Islamic groups to legitimate the use of violence, first against agents of secular, pro-Western nation-states, and subsequently against civilian populations.

Groups as diverse as the European anarchists, Viet Cong, Irish Republican Army, Nicaraguan Sandinistas, and Nelson Mandela's African National Congress have been branded with the terrorist label. In Middle Eastern contexts, terrorism has been used generically to characterize incidents of violence such as the attacks by Jewish guerillas against the British during the Mandate Period; the 1972 killings of Israeli Olympic athletes in Munich at the hands of Palestinian Liberation Organization gunmen; violence committed by agents of the Islamic Republic of Iran at home and abroad since 1979; the assassination of Egyptian president Anwar Sadat by the Jihad group in 1981; the 1983 bombing of a United States Marine barracks in Beirut and the kidnappings of westerners in Lebanon; the Islamist insurgency against the Algerian government since the mid-1990s; and attacks against Israeli forces and civilians. While anti-Soviet Muslim combatants in Afghanistan received moral, economic, and military support from the United States from 1979 to 1988 as "freedom fighters" (a loose translation of *mujahidin*), spin-off organizations such as al-Qa'ida and the Taliban have come to epitomize what many now call terrorism.

In the wake of the 11 September 2001 attacks on the World Trade Center and the Pentagon, the administration of George W. Bush placed the war against terrorism, known officially as Operation Enduring Freedom, at the top of its foreign and domestic political agendas. This new anti-terrorism policy led to large-scale military actions in Afghanistan and Iraq, as well as implementation of stringent security measures in the United States, including mass deportations, detentions, and curtailment of the civil rights of immigrants and visitors to the country—especially those coming from the Middle East, South Asia, and Southeast Asia and who may be Muslims.

The way in which the international community—including Western and Arab states—interpreted these events has had a profound effect on how terrorism is identified today. The incidents described above reflect many different contexts and many different kinds of violence. What links them analytically is that various actors have described each as terrorist activity. When attempting to identify terrorism, however, the term's broad use offers little guidance in describing or understanding a particular situation.

Defining Terrorism Today

How we define "terrorism" creates the intellectual framework that delimits the explanations available to us in working to understand an event or series of events. Most states, and much of the international community, now define terrorism as the use of force by non-state actors, a definition that focuses analytic attention on the violence of resistance at the expense of attention to violence perpetrated by the state. The analytic and conceptual shift in the meaning of terrorism in the last decades of the twentieth century has had important consequences. Rather than focusing on the causes that lead to violent resistance, discussions of terrorism are often limited to questions about the legitimate use of force to eliminate it.

Brought into greater relief, the modern meaning of terrorism comes out of the use of violence to justify and preserve a regime of law, relations of power, or, more broadly, a way of life. While all states use violence to protect the authority of the law and the state itself, those using violence to resist state authority do so in order to undermine that authority. Both kinds of violence aim at a similar end: creating and maintaining a system that orders the world. In fact, when seen in a broader context, state terror and non-state terror legitimize each other, marginalizing alternatives to that violence.

Defining terrorism in terms of "essential meanings" of Islam—or of any religious tradition—provides little help in understanding how violence functions. Violence is not particular to a specific religion, or to religion in general, or to a particular kind of socio-political organization, though it is indelibly part of both. The term "terrorism" used to describe any and all violent activity unsanctioned by a sovereign state or by international authority is insufficient to arrive at a nuanced understanding of events. As a result, the term "terrorism" should be limited to a heuristic role, and should not be used as an explanatory tool in analyzing specific incidents of violence or patterns of violence.

See also **bin Ladin, Usama; Conflict and Violence; HAMAS; Intifada; Qa'ida, al-; Taliban.**

BIBLIOGRAPHY

Crenshaw, Martha, ed. *Terrorism in Context.* University Park: Pennsylvania State University Press, 1995.

Esposito, John L. *Unholy War: Terror in the Name of Islam.* Oxford and New York: Oxford University Press, 2002.

Falk, Richard. *The Great Terror War.* New York: Olive Branch Press, 2003.

Juergensmeyer, Mark. *Terror in the Mind of God: The Global Rise of Religious Violence.* Berkeley: University of California Press, 2000.

Walzer, Michael. *Just and Unjust War.* New York: Basic Books, 1977.

Juan Eduardo Campo
Caleb Elfenbein

THAQAFI, MUKHTAR AL-
(C. 622–687)

Mukhtar b. Abi 'Ubayd al-Thaqafi took over Kufa (in Iraq) for a year and a half during the Second Civil War (*fitna*, set off by the murder of Husayn in 680), as the Zubayrids and Marwanids struggled for control of the empire in succession to the Sufyanid branch of the Umayyad caliphs. Mukhtar initially supported the Zubayrids but later, in 685, he deposed their governor of Kufa in the name of Muhammad b. al-Hanafiyya (d. 700), son of 'Ali by a concubine of the Hanafi tribe. When Mukhtar sent an armed force to Medina, the Zubayrids released Muhammad b. al-Hanafiyya, who, however, declined to join Mukhtar in Kufa. In 686, he defeated a Marwanid army from Syria, but soon after, the Zubayrids of Basra defeated his army and beleaguered him in the citadel of Kufa. After perhaps six months, Mukhtar was killed in battle. Four years later, the Zubayrids themselves were driven out of Iraq by the Marwanids, who refounded the Umayyad dynasty on the principle of vigorous direction from Syria.

Mukhtar's history is difficult to make out because of the vagaries of transmission between his time and that of our sources in the ninth century. The difficulty is further aggravated because numerous politico-religious factions have had an interest in dissociating themselves from him. It does seem, however, that non-Arab converts were prominent among his soldiers and that some elements of his program were taken up by later radical Shi'ites, including the early Abbasids, while other elements, such as the concept of a *mahdi*, or a reformer who appears at the end of time, attracted later Sunnis. The distinctive religious tinge of Mukhtar's reign, although now difficult to identify with certainty, helped provoke the Marwanids to Islamize their administration.

See also **Muhammad al-Nafs al-Zakiyya; Shi'a: Early; Succession.**

BIBLIOGRAPHY

Dixon, 'Abd al-Ameer 'Abd. *The Umayyad Caliphate 65–86/ 684–705: A Political Study.* London: Luzac and Company, 1974.

Hawting, G. R. *The First Dynasty of Islam. The Umayyad Caliphate AD 661–750.* Carbondale and Edwardsville: Southern Illinois University Press, 1987.

Christopher Melchert

THEOLOGY *See* Disputation; Kalam; Law

TITLES, ISLAMIC *See* Sayyid; Sharif; Shaykh al-Islam

TIMBUKTU

During the early medieval period, Timbuktu was a seasonal camp of Berber nomadic tribes as they took their livestock to the Niger River during the dry season. It became a semi-permanent settlement in the twelfth century. By the fifteenth century, the settlement had become one of the most famous intellectual and commercial cities of the African continent. Salt and gold were among the precious products sought after in Timbuktu. Merchants and scholars from North Africa visited or settled in there during the second half of the fourteenth century. A number of universities were established in Timbuktu from the fifteenth century onwards. Notable among them are the following: Sankore, which was established by Sanhaja Berbers; Djingerey Bey; and the Oratory of Sidi Yahya. Their course offerings included the study of the Qur²an, the hadith, law, theology, rhetoric, logic, prosody, and Arabic grammar. The universities of Timbuktu maintained close contact with other universities in North Africa and Egypt. They offered the same topics and recognized each other's degrees.

The two major sources of the political history of the medieval Western Sudan are the *Ta²rikh al-Sudan* (History of the Black people) and the *Ta²rikh al-Fattash* (History of the researcher) were written by Timbuktu scholars: ²Abd al-Rahman al-Sa²di and Mahmud Ka²ti, respectively. During the 1990s, the al-Furqan Islamic Heritage Foundation published catalogues of thousands of manuscripts in Arabic or Ajami located in the libraries and private collections of Timbuktu. These manuscripts include scholarly works and other documents, providing crucial information on the religious social, economic, and political history of the region.

See also **Africa, Islam in; Kunti, Mukhtar al-.**

BIBLIOGRAPHY

Hiskett, Mervyn. *The Development of Islam in West Africa*. London and New York: Longman, 1984.

Hunwick, John. *Timbuktu and the Songhai Empire: Al-Sa²di's Tarikh al-Sudan down to 1613 and Other Contemporary Documents*. Leiden : Brill, 1999.

Ousmane Kane

TOUBA

The city of Touba is located in the region of Diourbel in Senegal, West Africa. It is the second largest city in Senegal and (in 2001) had approximately one quarter of a million inhabitants. The city was established in 1887 by Ahmad Bamba, the founder of the Muridiyya (Mouride) brotherhood (*tariqa*), as the headquarters for his new brotherhood. According to tradition, the location was revealed to him by the angel Gabriel while he was seated praying. The French, fearful of an uprising against their regime, did not permit Ahmad Bamba to live in Touba but he continued to see it as a holy site and the center of his brotherhood. Succeeding caliphs would either live in Touba or have a principal home there.

Before his death in 1927 Ahmad Bamba began the construction of the great mosque in Touba, which is today the largest mosque in Senegal. The founder's mausoleum is in Touba as are several religious and Arabic schools, libraries, historical sites, and tombs of other Muridiyya leaders. The city is home to the annual Muridiyya festival, the Magal. The date of the Magal marks the exile of Ahmad Bamba to Gabon, symbolizing his suffering and resistance to the French colonial authorities. Hundreds of thousands of disciples make the pilgrimage every year to pray at the founder's tomb and to celebrate their religion. Especially during the immediate pre- and post-independence periods, when Muriddiyya caliphs played a large role in the political process of Senegal, Touba was a major seat of political as well as religious power.

See also **Africa, Islam in; Bamba, Ahmad; Tariqa.**

BIBLIOGRAPHY

Coulon, Christian. "The Grand Magal in Touba; A Religious Festival of the Mouride Brotherhood in Senegal." *African Affairs* 98 , no. 391 (April 1999): 195–210.

Ross, Eric. "Touba: A Spiritual Metropolis in the Modern World." *Canadian Journal of African Studies* 29 , no. 2 (1995): 222–259.

Lucy Creevey

TRADITIONALISM

The term *traditionalism* is commonly used to describe the early Islamic movement that coalesced around the ideas of Ahmad Ibn Hanbal (d. 855) during the *mihna* (inquisition, c. 833–847). Traditionalism indicates the loose configuration of scholars who rejected the rationalist interpretation of Islamic theology proposed by the Mu'tazili school of thought. Traditionalists were also known as the *Hashwiyya* (promoters of farce) by their rationalist opponents who argued that there was little scholarly depth to traditionalist ideas. Central to traditionalism was the rejection of the doctrine of the created Qur'an, which held, contrary to traditionalist views, that the Qur'an was not eternal and was revealed ad hoc in response to specific crises in the life of the prophet Muhammad. Traditionalism, however, should not be confused with the term "traditionists," which more narrowly describes scholars engaged in the development and promotion of hadith literature as a major component of Islamic theology and law (the *muhaddithun*). While it is true that most traditionalists were traditionists (i.e., proponents of hadith), not all *muhaddithun* agreed with the anti-rationalist tendency of the group that came to embrace Ibn Hanbal. In contemporary discussions of Islam, the term *traditionalism* has come to refer to Islamic revivalists (so-called fundamentalists) due to their links to Ibn Hanbal through the writings of Ibn Taymiyya (d. 1328). However, modern traditionalism has little similarity to the ideas that gave rise to anti-rationalist groups in early Islam. Contemporary traditionalism is loosely based on the idea that all individuals have the faculties of reason necessary, when combined with piety and a reading knowledge of Arabic, to discern on their own the will of God, an idea that would have been anathema to Ibn Hanbal and early traditionalist thought.

See also **Hadith; Ibn Hanbal; Ibn Taymiyya; Mihna.**

BIBLIOGRAPHY

Hallaq, Wael. *A History of Islamic Legal Theories: An Introduction to Sunni Usul al-Fiqh.* Cambridge, U.K.: Cambridge University Press, 1997.

Lawrence, Bruce. *Defenders of God: The Fundamentalist Revolt Against the Modern Age.* San Francisco: Harper and Row, 1989.

Makdisi, George. "Ash'ari and Ash'arites in Islamic Religious History." *Studia Islamica* 17 (1962): 37–80; 18 (1963): 19–39.

R. Kevin Jaques

TRANSLATION

Scholars working under the sponsorship of Muslim patrons undertook the translation of works on Greek philosophy and scientific learning and transmitted them to the West. An early and particularly fertile center for translation was Jundi-Shapur in Khuzistan, southeast of Baghdad. There the Bukhtishu', a family of physicians at the court of the caliph, became energetic translators of Greek works on medical matters. Hunayn ibn Ishaq (808–873), based in Baghdad, translated the medical as well as ethical and philosophical works of Galen, which were preserved in Arabic long after the originals were lost. Arabic translations preserved the works of other Greek writers, such as Euclid, Rufus of Ephesus, Nicolaus of Damascus, Porphyry, and Proclus. Hunayn bequeathed his translation legacy to his son, Ishaq ibn Hunayn (d. 910). Hunayn and his school created a genuine home in the Arabic language for a rich repertoire of new ideas and concepts. Most of the major translators were Christian, with the possible exception of a Jewish scholar named Marsajawayh, who translated from the Syriac, and Thabit b. Qurrah (c. 834–901), a Sabian from Harran.

Translation was almost entirely devoted to scientific, medical, and philosophical works. Philosophical texts were paraphrased and included commentaries for Arabic students. Simplified adaptations of the works of Plato and Aristotle were known in Arabic. Another area of great intellectual interest was Neo-Platonism, particularly the works of the Egyptian Plotinus (c. 200–269 C.E.), and of his disciple Porphyry (233–301).

Yet it would be wrong to overemphasize the impact of Greek ideas on Islam's religious life and culture. Only a small circle of educated elites was shaped by the influence of Greek intellectual ideas. The Qur'an survived the critical Greek encounter to endure as the great devotional and missionary text of the religion, conveying the sounds and tones of the original sacred Arabic of Scripture to multitudes of adherents down the centuries and scattered well beyond the Arab heartlands.

Mission and Translation

In the course of its worldwide expansion and cross-cultural transmission, Islam has maintained a remarkable consistency in promoting the nontranslatable status of the Qur'an. That may account in part for the relative unity of faith and practice among Muslims who are otherwise characterized by an extraordinary diversity of race, language, culture, and social status. Without an institutional central authority to enforce doctrine and to adjudicate the affairs of believers, Islam has nevertheless continued to enjoy a degree of solidarity that is belied by its organizational decentralization. It happens that only a minority of the world's one billion Muslims is Arab in language and culture, yet for all Muslims the Holy Qur'an in the original Arabic is divine oracle. Rather than impede the spread of Islam, this fact has been the basis of the appeal of the religion in societies even beyond the Arab heartland. The language of scripture has been a major force in establishing boundaries and shaping identity for new communities in Islam.

The Qur'an bears witness to its own unique and manifest status as Arabic speech (12: 1–3; 16: 105; 41: 41–42), a celestial discourse designed for repeated recitation "whereat shiver the skins of those who fear their Lord; then their skins and their hearts soften to the remembrance of God" (39: 23). The Qur'an as the "essence of divine speech" is sublime and wise guidance for the faithful, and is preserved in its Arabicness with God as such (43: 3).

The transmission of Islam has been accompanied by adaptations in local practice and understanding, and, accordingly, the Qur'an has been appropriated to reflect new situations, whether as divine oracle, rule book, breviary, vade mecum, periapt, or as universal template. There being no rival versions of the Qur'an, Muslims possess in their scripture a single and unvarying standard of faith and devotion, and a tangible symbol of the oneness of the *umma* (community of believers). Through Islam's worldwide expansion the Arabic of scripture became, according to H. A. R. Gibb, "a world language and the common literary medium of all Muslim peoples" (1974, p. 37).

Although proficiency in the language of Scripture is the preserve of a small circle of specialists, nevertheless the task of learning the holy book by rote memorization is the sacred duty of all Muslims, scholar and sundry alike, because only that way may Muslims observe the obligatory five daily periods of worship known as *salat*. Even though there are translations of the Qur'an, they are invalid for *salat* for which the sacred Arabic has been instituted as a prerequisite, a rule that gives translations no canonical merit in the central religious rites.

A potent connection exists between the Arabic script and Islam's sacrosanct view of language. One tradition speaks of the human face as God's image, of language as the mark of humanity, and the twenty-eight letters of the Arabic script as containing the essence of that contained in language: the mysteries of God, humanity, and eternity. Echoes of such reverence for the sacred Arabic can be found in mosque calligraphy composed of Qur'anic verses and the names of God, the Prophet, the *shahada* (profession of faith), and the early caliphs. Calligraphic art has spread widely, and with it an iconographic reverence for the sacred script. Muslim devotions involve rhythmic chanting (*tartil*) of the Qur'an.

The widespread iconographic reverence for the language and script of the Qur'an led travelers in the far regions of the Islamic world to comment on the prominence given to study of the Qur'an and to its use in canonical worship. Thus did Ibn Battuta recount how Muslim Africans were punctilious in mosque attendance and zealous in learning the Qur'an, testifying that parents "put their children in chains if they show any backwardness in memorizing it, and they are not set free until they have it by heart." Dr. Edward Wilmot Blyden (1832–1912), a pan-African visionary of West Indian origin, made a close study of Islam and Muslim life, noting that even at the margins of the Muslim world the untranslated Qur'an held a particularly high position. He said he saw evidence of the Holy Book exerting a powerful influence on nonliterate populations, providing a ground of unity for the disparate tribes and a sentiment of loyalty that promoted a sense of common identity. The words of the sacred book, he testified, were held in the greatest reverence and esteem. Although for many Muslim Africans the words of the Arabic Qur'an were little understood, they possessed still great beauty and music, a subtle and indefinable charm "incomprehensible to those not acquainted with the language in which the Koran was written."

Translation, Reform, and Revolution

The tradition of orthopraxy that a uniform Qur'an promoted, and that was important where caliphal authority was weak or unknown, was difficult to maintain among acephalous Muslim populations such as existed in North Africa. For more than three centuries after the introduction of Islam, the Berbers there remained poorly instructed in the faith and remained, therefore, susceptible to splintering and heresy. To remedy such defects, the Almoravid movement, launched in 1056, sought to assemble the dispersed Berber tribes under Islamic rule in forms that were frankly outlandish: the Qur'an and the sunna, for example, were discounted as too demanding for the simple and ignorant, their place now taken by a culture of strict discipline on the masses and unquestioning obedience to the leader. Religious illiteracy became even more conspicuous from the high expectations raised by Almoravid power.

The illiteracy aggravated the moral delinquency belonging with the fictitious nature of power, and that finally provoked a reaction. An idea had been growing steadily that it was necessary to extend to the Berber tribesmen the unifying dividends that the Ash'arite revolution had achieved in the eastern provinces of the caliphate. By making use of reason to defend revelation, Ash'arism repositioned Muslim intellectual life after its encounter with Greek ideas by stressing God's omnipotence (*qadar*) and by rejecting the naturalist inferences of anthropomorphism (*tajsim*).

Transferred to North Africa, these Ash'arite ideas would have a major impact on religion, state, and society. In the circumstances of political fragmentation and religious syncretism that characterized North Africa in the eleventh century, a movement of reaction and revolution erupted to channel pent up forces through a political outlet under a charismatic leader. This leader was Ibn Tumart (d. 1130), founder of the militant Almohad (*al-muwahhidun*) counter-revolution against the lackadaisical Almoravids.

Ibn Tumart assumed power and had the Qur'an translated into his native Berber; he ordered the call to prayers (*adhan*) to be given in Berber; the Friday sermon (*khutba*) likewise was delivered in his mother tongue; and he required the clerics, the ulema, to know and function in that language. He arranged for his own theological writings to be circulated in Berber as well as Arabic. Such translation activity stimulated sentiments of local nationalism, though it conflicted with Ibn Tumart's own aims of integrating Berber Islam into the unified Ash'arite and Ghazalian tradition that he so much admired. Undertaking his ambitious translation enterprise as a facet of the changes he wished to see introduced in Muslim North Africa, Ibn Tumart ended by producing a variation so colorful and so rare as to amount to a serious rupture with Qur'an and sunna.

The nationalist impulse of language reform and religious renewal converged again much later, during the Ottoman Empire. By the late nineteenth century this linguistic nationalism was gaining a foothold within and without. Students from the empire returned from their studies in European universities with a heightened sense of national identity. Works on Turkish language and grammar, some the result of European Orientalist scholarship, were coming into general circulation. Works in European languages, particularly French, were translated into Turkish. Hungarian and Polish refugees, many of whom converted to Islam, wrote in French and Turkish. Russian Turks brought a strong sense of national identity, infusing the Turkish language with a sense of historical destiny. These impulses coalesced into the Turkish Society, founded in Istanbul in 1908. The society was dedicated to objectives that were scholarly as well as cultural, including the advancement of language and literature. As part of its aggressive program of secularization, the new political authorities set about reforming religious life and practice. In 1929 Arabic and Persian were abolished as subjects of instruction in schools to facilitate the teaching and spread of Turkish. A reorganization of religious schools and mosques was undertaken, with the requirement that the language of worship be Turkish, and that all prayers and sermons be in the national language, and not Arabic. Measures were adopted to translate the Qur'an and the hadith into Turkish, with money voted for the scheme in 1932. In that year for the first time the *adhan* resounded from minarets in Turkish.

Beginning in 1928 with the adoption of a new Latin alphabet to replace Arabic, a vigorous, if at times overenthusiastic, language reform program was undertaken. The Turkish language was purged of its Arabic and Persian borrowings and grammatical features to bring it closer to national aspirations. Although some of the excesses of this linguistic purge were later reversed, the language reforms achieved the goal of closing a crucial gap between written and spoken Turkish, giving birth to a new sense of national identity. The attempts to carry the translation efforts into the mosque failed because of clerical opposition. A similar fate befell attempts in India to translate the Islamic canonical rites into Hindi, in that case also for reasons of trying to bring Islam into line with the national sentiment.

Translation and Cross-Cultural Consolidation

These large-scale national reforms aimed at shifting people's devotion to the sacred script and language are testimony to the enduring influence of the Qur'an on the habits and customs of Muslim peoples. Yet a different impulse has worked in translation to fashion in people a sense of identity and to provide boundary markers. This is the case, for example, with Swahili in East Africa and Hausa and Fulfulde

in West Africa. Swahili verse and prose literature have functioned to impress on the fabric of popular life images of Islam drawn from the Arabic classics: accounts of the Prophet in popular praise songs; studies of the origins of the Islamic state; stories of the caliphs and the Prophet's companions; devotional literature tied to the religious calendar; exegetical works expounding the Qur'an; and manuals designed for exchange and study in shops, markets, and private homes. Swahili has thus worked in favor of Islam's penetration into coastal and transient populations of East Africa.

Hausa verse and prose have had a comparable effect on the Hausa people of Nigeria and beyond. Early in the nineteenth century an era of revolution and reform produced an environment conducive to the large-scale use of written Hausa in Arabic script. That in turn inspired a corresponding pan-Islamic sensibility among scholars. Writers in Hausa appealed to the Arabic classics, including the literature produced during the Abbasid caliphate, to reform local practice and to implement the religious canon. The reformers drew upon the Qur'an, the hadith, the history, and the legal and biographical traditions to create structures and institutions in their part of the Muslim world, and the gains they made became a permanent part of the life of the people.

For its part, Fulfulde enjoyed a long and distinguished role as the language of instruction, catechism, and exegesis in Qur'an school and beyond. The educational syllabus was based on a four-stage process: introducing the Arabic alphabet (*jangugol*), writing (*windugol*), Scriptural exegesis in Fulfulde (*firugol*), and higher studies (*fennu*; Ar., *'ilm awfaq*). Religious catechism was conducted in Fulfulde. All this linguistic activity laced Fulbe national feeling with a heightened sense of Islamic exceptionalism. Beginning with the reforms of Karamokho Alfa of Futa Jallon in 1727, and 'Uthman dan Fodio of northern Nigeria in 1804, the Fulbe became energetic sponsors of reform in West African Islam and the self-acclaimed defenders of Sunni orthodoxy. Under Fulbe hegemony, the language issue acquired a central status: the accommodationists among the local Muslim clerics were decried as *'ulama' al-su'*, the "venal clerics," and charged with allowing scriptural standards to slip and political corruption to spread. Literacy in Arabic, however limited, became a criterion of reform and renewal. Such limited literacy represented precious intellectual capital in marginal Muslim societies, and the Fulbe reformers deployed it to great effect. Literate clerics, accordingly, became the vanguard of change in state and society.

It is not the case, however, that all literate clerics adopted the path of militancy from their privileged position as masters of Arabic. An outstanding example are the Jakhanke Muslim clerics of Senegambia who, as a matter of principle, have, from medieval times, rejected jihad as well as political co-option, and have instead adopted the methods of peaceful persuasion in their role as educational specialists. They have introduced the Arabic of scripture and tradition in their schools by means of local languages, adapting the grammatical concepts and special vocabulary of the Qur'an to local usage. They created in West Africa a culture of religious and political moderation in spite of a bruising era of confrontation under an anticlerical French colonial administration. At the hands of the pacific clerics, translation assured the renewal of Islam and its continuing vitality as a pillar of civil society without the compromise of armed intervention or state enforcement.

See also **Arabic Language; Ibn Battuta; Persian Language and Literature; Qur'an; Science, Islam and.**

BIBLIOGRAPHY

Battuta, Ibn. *Travels in Asia and Africa, 1325–1354.* Edited and translated by H. A. R. Gibb. London: Routledge and Kegan Paul, 1983.

Gibb, H. A. R. *Arabic Literature: An Introduction.* London: Oxford University Press, 1974.

Grunebaum, G. E. von. *Classical Islam, A History 600–1228.* London: George Allen & Unwin, 1970.

Hayes, John R., ed. *The Genius of Arab Civilization: Source of Renaissance.* 1976. Reprint. Oxford, U.K.: Phaidon, 1978.

Lewis, Bernard. *The Emergence of Modern Turkey.* Oxford, U.K.: Oxford University Press, 1968.

Nasr, S. H. *Islamic Science: An Illustrated Study.* London: World of Islam Festival Publishing Company Ltd., 1976.

O'Leary, De Lacy. *How Greek Science Passed to the Arabs.* London: Routledge and Kegan Paul, 1948.

Rosenthal, Franz. *The Classical Heritage in Islam.* London: Routledge and Kegan Paul, 1975.

Sanneh, Lamin. *The Crown and the Turban: Muslims and West African Pluralism.* Denver, Colo.: Westview Press, 1997.

Ullmann, Manfred. *Islamic Medicine.* Edinburgh: Edinburgh University Press, 1978.

Walzer, Richard. *Greek into Arabic: Essays in Islamic Philosophy.* Cambridge, Mass.: Harvard University Press, 1962.

Lamin Sanneh

TRAVEL AND TRAVELERS

Travel has been a part of the Islamic culture from the beginning. The obligation of every Muslim, once in a lifetime, to make the pilgrimage, or hajj, to Mecca and Medina was an early and significant reason for much of the travel.

Before air transport the greater the distance one needed to travel on the hajj the more the journey tended to become a grand study tour of the greater mosques and madrasas of the Muslim heartland. It was an opportunity for the traveler to acquire knowledge.

The expansion of Islam beyond its early borders meant that such a pilgrimage invariably required long-distance travel. The conversion of the local population to Islam necessitated travel for both new converts and for those proselytizing. This expansion resulted not only from war, but also through commerce as traveling merchants established trading posts farther away from Islam's original center.

The most fundamental values of Islam have tended to encourage a high degree of social mobility and to free movement of individuals from one city and region to another. Travel was promoted through Islamic culture and put great emphasis on egalitarian behavior in social relations based on the ideal of a community allegiance to one God.

Travel was made easy by the dynamics of social life centered on an egalitarian, contractual, and relatively free play of relations among individuals striving to conform to Islamic moral standards. Wherever an individual traveled, pursued a career, or bought and sold goods, the same social and moral dictates of Islam largely applied. The language common to early Islam, Arabic, ensured another unifying characteristic.

The pattern of travel and migration of adherents to Islam all but ensured a persistent dispersion of architects, writers, craftsmen, legal scholars, scribes, Sufi divines, and theologians outward from the older centers of Islam to the new frontiers of Muslim activity.

The members of the cultural elite maintained during traveling a close tie with the greater cities of the central part of the Islamic lands. They created, thereby, not only a scattering of literate and skilled Muslims across several continents, but an integrated, growing, self-replenishing network of cultural communication.

A great interest in knowledge and learning has been a common thread of Islam from its earliest days. Travel solely in search of knowledge has been an integral part of the intellectual life of the Islamic world. The scholarly class was an extraordinarily mobile group, who circulated incessantly from one city and country to another, studying with renowned professors, leading diplomatic missions, and taking up posts in mosques and government chanceries.

Scholars from the more remote part of the Islamic world traveled to the countries considered central to Islam in search of civilized models, higher knowledge, and learned companionship.

The need for travel and interest in it created an equal need for knowledge of geography and navigation both on land and sea. As a consequence the *rihla*, or book of travels, emerged. The genre recounted for the reader the journey to Mecca with information and entertainment of religious sites on the route.

A copy of a Catalan map showing North Africa appears in the volume two color insert.

See also **Biruni, al-; Ibn Battuta; Ibn Khaldun; Pilgrimage: Hajj.**

BIBLIOGRAPHY

Eickelman, Dale F., and Piscatori, James, eds. *Muslim Travellers: Pilgrimage, Migration, and the Religious Imagination.* Berkeley and Los Angeles: University of California Press, 1990.

Thyge C. Bro

TRIBE

The English word *tribe* is an ambivalent term that is used indiscriminately to refer to a wide variety of social groupings that range from small, preliterate, and relatively isolated communities in the Amazon jungles of South America to large, powerful confederacies whose chiefs are members of the national political elite such as the case of the Bakhtiyari of southwest Iran. In what follows, the concepts of "tribe"and "tribalism" are discussed in the specific context of the Middle East.

The Arabic term for tribe is *qabila* (pl. *qaba'il*). The word *qabila* is mentioned in the Qur'an: " O mankind: we have created you from a male and a female and made you into peoples and tribes [*qaba'il*] that you may know each other" (49:13). In its most common usage, *qabila* refers to a named group of people who share an ideology of common descent in the male line, claim a common geographical territory, and are politically united under the leadership of a chief, called a *shaykh* in Arabic, or *khan* in Persian and Turkish. As such, the concept of "tribe" and "tribalism" is used to simultaneously indicate a personal and group identity, a form of social organization, and a distinct political structure.

As a source of personal and group identity, tribal affiliation can be analogous to ethnicity albeit on a more limited scale; it confers a distinct identity on its members, binding them together in a distinct moral code expressed most commonly in the idiom of honor, courage, and personal autonomy. Tribal identity, based on ties of kinship (real or fictitious), is further reinforced by the common practice of close endogamy that favors the marriage of a man to his father's brother's daughter. Among Arabic speakers, intratribal bonds and group cohesion are expressed in the idiom of *'asabiyya*, or group solidarity, based on blood ties and common descent.

Tribal systems of sociopolitical organization are also based on the ideology of common descent from a founding ancestor; some pastoral nomads, like the Bedouins of the Arabian and Syrian deserts, keep elaborate genealogies that serve to organize the different segments of the tribe in a network of mutual rights and responsibilities. Typically, the smallest tribal segment is the household made up of one or more patrilineally related families; a number of such households make up the next ascending segment, or lineage. Among the Bedouins, this level of organization is known as *fakhd*; members of a *fakhd* or lineage usually lay claim to a common grazing territory, brand their herds with the same symbol, and are collectively liable to pay blood money in the case of a murder committed by one of their memebrs. A number of related lineages are grouped into the next all-encompassing level of the tribe, or *qabila*; in some parts of the Arabic-speaking Middle East, this level is also referred to as *'ashira*. The tribe is thus the largest named unit of incorporation constructed on a genealogical framework. While today tribes serve mainly as reference groups for related lineages, in the past they played an important role in the political life of the region. Each tribe united behind a paramount chief who acted as a military commander in intertribal warfare. Tribal members typically share a strong sense of common heritage that goes beyond that of common descent. They tend to speak one dialect, dress in a distinctive style, and have their own customs and traditions.

Tribes have a long and complicated history in the Middle East; unlike the case for other parts of the world, tribes did not disappear with the formation of nation-states in the region. In fact, the historical coexistence of state and tribe lends a unique texture to Middle Eastern human geography. Beginning with the Islamic conquest in the seventh century (itself carried out by Arab tribal forces) tribes and tribal confederacies have played a key role in the creation and disintegration of several Islamic imperial dynasties such as the Abbasids, the Ottomans, and the Qajars. Equally significant were the many tribes who managed to maintain their autonomy in defiance of state rule. This was the case with the Bedouin tribes of Arabia, the Kurds of the Zagros mountains, and the large tribal confederacies of Iran like the Bakhtiyari and the Qashqa'i.

In the mountain and desert areas of Kurdistan, the Arabian Peninsula, and Iran, tribally organized confederacies managed to escape the reach of the state and maintain their independence well into the twentieth century. Following the breakup of the Ottoman Empire after the First World War and the arrival of European colonial powers in the region, the role of tribes in the newly formed nation-states assumed a new significance. In their effort to stem anticolonial and nationalist movements in the region, colonial powers encouraged tribal separatism by promoting tribal identities and reinforcing the authority of tribal leaders. This policy of "divide and rule" came to an end after the Second World War, which marked the end of colonialism in the region. Seeking to promote national unity, the policy of the newly independent governments aimed at integrating the tribes into the nation-state. In cases of pastoral nomadic tribes such as the Bedouins of Arabia and the Qashqa'i of Iran, this took the form of forced sedentarization, taxation, and conscription into the national army.

Today all over the Middle East, tribes have ceased to be important political units capable of challenging the power of the central governments. Tribal leaders have been generally co-opted or were absorbed into the national elite. But while their political role has been generally undermined, tribes and tribalism remain an important component of Middle Eastern cultural landscape. Supplanted by nationalist and Islamist ideologies, tribalism as an ideology has not disappeared. Tribal identity and tribal ties continue to be an important source for self-reference and social organization for many people in the region.

See also **'Asabiyya; Bedouin; Ethnicity.**

BIBLIOGRAPHY

Bates, Daniel G., and Rassam, Amal. *Peoples and Cultures of the Middle East.* Upper Saddle River, N.J.: Prentice-Hall, Inc., 2001.

Khoury, Philip S., and Kostiner, Joseph, eds. *Tribes and State Formation in the Middle East.* Berkeley and Los Angeles: University of California Press, 1990.

Amal Rassam

TURABI, HASAN AL- (1932–)

Hasan al-Turabi is a Sudanese political leader and Islamist intellectual. Al-Turabi's family was well known and had a recognized tradition of piety. Al-Turabi's father was one of the first Sudanese to be trained as a judge in the British system of administering Islamic law in Sudan, and Hasan received a traditional Islamic education from his father along with his modern education in the government-supported system. In secondary school and then at the University of Khartoum, al-Turabi became active in the small, Islamically oriented student groups. He studied in London and received a doctorate from the Sorbonne. He returned to Sudan in 1964, in time to be a visible participant in the October Revolution that overthrew the military regime of Ibrahim 'Abboud.

In the second period of civilian parliamentary politics in Sudan (1964–1969), al-Turabi led the Sudanese Muslim Brotherhood (established in the 1950s) into an important place in Sudanese politics. It was not a mass party but was well organized among students and professionals, and was able to give prominence in Sudanese politics to issues of Islamic identity. The Brotherhood continued this role in changing political contexts. Al-Turabi's Brotherhood was the core of the Islamic Charter Front in the 1960s, and then became part of the opposition to the military regime established by Ja'far al-Numayri in 1969. In the late 1970s, al-Turabi participated

in the national reconciliation process and became a significant force in the Islamization policies initiated by Numayri. Although al-Turabi did not have a direct role in drafting "the September Laws" of 1983 that imposed a version of Islamic law on Sudan, he and his group gained prominence in the new context. When Numayri was overthrown in 1985, al-Turabi reorganized the Brotherhood as the National Islamic Front (NIF), which emerged as the third largest party in the new parliamentary system. NIF was able to prevent the repeal of the September Laws and kept Islamic issues in the forefront of the Sudanese political agenda.

Al-Turabi's role was transformed in 1989, when a military coup led by Hasan 'Umar Bashir established an Islamist-style military regime in which al-Turabi was the ideological mentor. Throughout the 1990s, the Bashir-Turabi alliance attempted to create a new political system. The regime engaged in severe violations of human rights and the civil war between the central government and the southern region intensified as a result of military intransigence and the NIF's agenda of Islamizing the whole country. In 1998 and 1999, Bashir relieved al-Turabi of all official posts and al-Turabi became a marginal force in Sudanese politics.

During the 1970s and 1980s, al-Turabi's ideas became widely known in the Muslim world. He called for significant renewal of the whole structure of Islamic legal thought and developed important concepts of Islamic democracy. His writings on the importance of gender equality in Islam were controversial but gained him a reputation as an Islamic liberal activist. However, the failures of the NIF regime in the 1990s and its excesses in blocking human rights reforms meant that al-Turabi's international visibility and reputation declined by the end of the twentieth century.

BIBLIOGRAPHY

Affendi, Abdelwahab el-. *Turabi's Revolution: Islam and Power in Sudan.* London: Grey Seal, 1991.

Esposito, John L., and Voll, John O. *Makers of Contemporary Islam.* New York: Oxford University Press, 2001.

Hamdi, Mohamed Elhachmi. *The Making of an Islamic Political Leader.* Boulder, Colo.: Westview, 1999.

John O. Voll

TUSI, MUHAMMAD IBN AL-HASAN (SHAYKH AL-TA'IFA) (995–1067)

Muhammad b. Hasan al-Tusi (d. 1067), who was given the honorific "Shaykh of the sect" (shaykh al-ta'ifa), was an important Imami Shi'ite thinker of the early period. He hailed from Tus in Khorasan, but made his name in Baghdad. His work represents both of the two main trends in early

Twelver Shi'ism: rationalism and hadith study. His commentary on the Qur'an (*tafsir*), *al-Tibyan*, exemplifies this trend as both styles of argumentation are employed to explain the meaning of each Qur'anic verse. His hadith works, the most famous being *al-Tahdhib* and *al-Istibsar*, are more than mere collections, but are also detailed expositions of the legal employment of the traditions of the imams. His work in law proper was similarly sophisticated, particularly his *'Uddat al-usul* (a work in the principles of jurisprudence) and *al-Mabsut* (one of his many works of law). Tusi also wrote theological works, in which arguments in the Mu'tazilite style were used alongside more text-based justification for the imamate. His activities in bibliography and biography enabled the discipline of biography (*'ilm al-rijal*) to develop into a sophisticated science in Twelver Shi'ism. His prolific output as a scholar can, in part, be explained by the criticism of the Twelver tradition by Sunni intellectuals—that they lacked a sufficient corpus of respectable writings. Tusi's response was to compile and collate works of great importance.

BIBLIOGRAPHY

Stewart, Devin J. *Islamic Legal Orthodoxy: Shiite Responses to the Sunni Legal System.* Salt Lake City: University of Utah Press, 1998.

Robert Gleave

TUSI, NASIR AL-DIN (1201–1274)

Nasir al-Din Tusi, Abu Ja'far Muhammad b. Muhammad b. al-Hasan, was a Shi'ite philosopher, theologian, astronomer, mathematician, and political advisor. Tusi was born in Tus, in northeastern Iran, and died in Baghdad, in present-day Iraq. A man of astounding intellectual breadth, he witnessed the transfer of power in the Islamic world to the Mongols. Beginning his career as a court astronomer to the Isma'ili governor Nasir al-Din Abi Mansur at Sertakht, he continued to work for the Isma'ilis at various Iranian fortresses, including Quhistan, until he transferred to the Isma'ili castle at Alamut, where he remained until joining the Mongol Hulagu's entourage as a political advisor in 1247. Subsequent to the Mongol victory over Baghdad (1257), he was encouraged by Hulagu to found an observatory at Maragha in Azerbaijan, equipped with the best instruments, some constructed for the first time. His courtly duties included supervision of *waqf* estates, a position that he retained under the Mongol leader Abaqa, until Tusi's death in 1274. Two critical issues concerning his religious persuasion and political stance remain the subject of scholarly and ideological debate: one, whether he was an Isma'ili Shi'ite by choice or by employment; and two, whether his involvement in the fall of Alamut and Baghdad, respectively, entailed treachery or prudence. G. M. Wickens, for instance, in his introduction to *The Nasirean Ethics* holds the view that Tusi's alignment with the Mongols "made possible the continuance in new and flourishing forms of Islamic learning, law and civilization," a point that underscores Tusi's political acumen under difficult circumstances. Although over one hundred books are attributed to Tusi, only a handful have survived. Apart from his many scientific works, his noteworthy texts include the *Hall mushkilat al-Isharat*, a commentary on Ibn Sina's *al-Isharat* as well as a refutation of Fakhr al-Din al-Razi's *Muhassal*; an ethical treatise titled the *Akhlaq-e Nasiri*, which evinces the influence of Ibn Miskawaih; the Isma'ili-inspired works *Tasawwurat* (also known as *Rawdat al-taslim*) and the autobiographical *Sayr wa Suluk*; the Twelver-Shi'ite *kalam* or theological works *Tajrid al-'aqa'id* and *Qawa'id al-'Aqa'id*; and a mystical work titled *Awsaf al-Ashraf*. An original and innovative thinker, his works continue to merit attention.

See also **Falsafa; Khojas.**

Zayn R. Kassam

U

ULEMA

Literally "those who have knowledge" or "those who know" (singular *ʿalim*, plural *ʿulama*). The term is most widely used to refer to the scholarly class of Muslim societies, whose main occupation is the study of the texts that make up the Islamic Tradition (religious sciences such as Qurʾan, hadith, Qurʾanic commentary, jurisprudence, and theology, but also the applied sciences such as medicine, biology, astronomy, and mathematics). Members of the ulema class have also been called upon to act as advisors to rulers, or as *qadis* (judges) implementing the law (*shariʿa*) within Muslim societies. The authority of the ulema class in defining right doctrine and right practice within Islam has been immense in Muslim history.

In the early period (7th–9th centuries C.E.), a separate class of scholars concerned with the elaboration of knowledge (*ʿilm*) took some time to develop. Most historians date the emergence of a scholarly class to the early years of the Umayyad period, when Islamic doctrine was much debated. Debates concerning the constituent elements of faith (*iman*), or predestination (*qadr*), as well as the transmission of hadith (from the Prophet or other notable figures) and legal doctrine (*fiqh*) were the principal intellectual concerns of the emerging scholarly class. Many of the ulema also, it appears, participated in the opposition movements to the Umayyad caliphate. Some viewed them as deviating from true Islam in their leadership of the Muslim empire, and wished to put forward a more sophisticated religio-intellectual criticism of the Umayyads. It was, however, in the Abbasid period that the ulema began to gain both political influence and popular respect, as Abbasid caliphs and their wazirs sponsored institutional schools in which scholars could develop the intellectual foundations of Islam. It was early in this period that the ulema, with the support of some caliphs, became interested in the Greek tradition of philosophy and science, and works in languages other than Arabic began to be translated. These translations mark the beginnings of the incorporation of the applied sciences into the curriculum of learning, to complement the religious sciences, in which the ulema were already considered expert.

Once established, the ulema class became a fundamental element of Muslim societies. The expansion of the Muslim world, incorporating many different cultures and traditions, did not obviate the need for a scholarly class whose primary functions were to maintain the intellectual tradition and provide religious and scientific guidance to the population. Their fortunes waxed and waned depending on the receptivity of the dynasties to religious influence, but the vast majority of Muslim societies, both past and present, have included a class of scholars, usually given the generic name ulema.

The authority of the ulema in matters of doctrine and law has been definitive. The ulema themselves, though, have been divided on many issues, and hence should not be viewed as a unified group with common aims and intentions. An example of this division can be seen in the famous Inquisition, (*mihna*) from 829 onwards, when one group of scholars (the Muʿtazilis) persuaded the Abbasid caliph to persecute (and declare as heretics) scholars who did not adhere to the doctrine of "the created Qurʾan."

The authority and respect demanded by the ulema has usually been justified on the simple basis of a practical division of labor. Not all members of society have the time, the skills, or the inclination to dedicate their lives to the study necessary to determine right doctrine and practice. Hence, it is argued, a class of society that dedicates itself to this task should be instituted, and since these matters affect each individual's fate (both in this world and in the afterlife), the guidance of this class is of paramount importance. In the area of legal matters, this attitude was enshrined in the theory of *taqlid*, whereby the Muslim community is divided between scholars and those who follow the rulings of the scholars (typically called the *muqallid*s).

Apart from this practical justification for the ulema's authority, scholars also turned to the Qur'an. Q. 4:59 states "Obey God, the Prophet and those in authority amongst you." Many Sunni scholars argued that "those in authority" probably refers to the ulema (some also included the political rulers in the category). Similarly, Q. 16:43: "Ask the people of remembrance if you do not know" was interpreted by Sunni scholars as exhorting the people to submit in matters of knowledge to the ulema. There were also convenient hadiths, traced back to the prophet Muhammad, which could be used to establish the ulema's status. For example, the well-known words attributed to the Prophet, "The ulema are the inheritors of the Prophets," was interpreted as implying that in religious authority, the ulema were given the responsibility of announcing the message of Islam to the community.

Although there were many scholars whose individual charismatic power is well attested, their authority was ultimately based on learning. The ulema deserved this respect, not because of lineage, or familial connections, or even because of individual piety and religiosity. Rather, the ulema were due respect because of they had undergone a particular type of training and education that elevated their understanding of religious matters above the ordinary populace. It was on this basis that the institution of the ulema became an indispensable part of Muslim culture.

In Muslim history, however, the respect due to the ulema did not translate into political power. Most scholars who wrote on the relationship between political power and religious authority accepted that the ulema were advisors who aided the ruler in the maintenance of the religion. Al-Ghazali (d. 1111), for example, argued that the sultan should "exercise coercive power and have authority because the sultan is the representative of God," whereas the ulema were appointed by the sultan and given the responsibility of enacting the law. This theory of the dependence of the ulema upon the ruler for their practical authority in society reflected the relationship of the Sunni ulema with political power in historical terms. During the Ottoman Empire the ulema became an increasingly structured class of society, headed by the mufti, who advised the sultan on both religious and political issues, headed the judiciary, and controlled the religious education system in the empire. The situation was not dissimilar in the Indian Mogul Empire.

Al-Ghazali's influential formulation of the sultan-ulema relationship can be informatively contrasted with the views of Shi'ite groups. Some Shi'ite groups, particularly the Isma'ilis in the medieval period, saw religious authority and political power conjoined in an individual, who was given the title imam. The need for a class of religious scholars who advised the imam was reduced, since the imam was, himself, blessed in a mystical manner with knowledge of doctrinal and legal matters. Twelver Shi'ites also placed an imam at the apex of the ideal political system, but believed that the imam had gone into hiding (ghayba). Since there was no ideal political leader other than this missing imam, Twelver Shi'ites were greatly concerned with the issue of community authority. A theory of "delegation" (niyaba) was therefore needed. The Twelver Shi'ites recognized a succession of Twelve Imams after the death of the Prophet. Only the first of these, Imam 'Ali, had succeeded in gaining political power, and the last of these had gone into hiding. Reports from a number of these Twelve Imams were interpreted to indicate that the imams had delegated leadership of the community to the ulema in the absence of the Imam.

In works of fiqh, one sees a gradual expansion of the ulema's role in areas that, in early Twelver Shi'ism, were seen as the prerogative of the Imam. This position faced a serious challenge when the Safavid mystical order came to power in Iran in 1501. The first Safavid Shah, Isma'il, declared Twelver Shi'ism to be the state religion. Jurists either devised means whereby the shah might be considered a legitimate ruler, despite the absence of the true ruler (the imam) or they rejected association with the Safavids and maintained the ultimate authority of the ulema.

The debate over the role of the ulema in the life of the Muslim community has become more acute in the modern period. In Twelver Shi'ism, Ayatollah Ruhollah Khomeini argued that the ulema should rule the Muslim community until the return of the Hidden Imam, a theory he had the opportunity to put into practice following the Islamic Revolution in Iran in 1979. In the modern Sunni Muslim world, on the other hand, one can recognize a variety of trends. Many Sunni Muslim governments have used members of the ulema to brand their government as religious in a manner reminiscent of the medieval period. In the revivalist movements, however, one sees a reaction against the ulema, who often are characterized as obscurantist and pedantic, worrying about matters of religious technicalities, rather than the more important issues of preserving Muslim identity in the face of non-Muslim imperialism. The popularist commentaries on the Qur'an of, for example, Sayyid Qutb or Abu l-A'la' Maududi, represent a rejection of the ulemas and an exhortation to "the people" to approach the divine text without the encumbrance of the scholarly tradition of learning.

This rejection of the ulema's authority in matters of religion is likely to increase as literacy and the availability of foundational texts of Islam become more widespread in the Muslim world. In some Muslim countries, however, one sees the re-emergence of the ulema as active political agents, working for change. Two examples of this are Saudi Arabia and Morocco. In the recent past, Saudi ulema have challenged the concentration of power in the person of the king and his royal family. Attempts continue to be made to diffuse this power to a larger body, within which the ulema would play a larger role. In Morocco, legal scholars such as Muhammad 'Allal al-Fasi have been at the forefront of the modernization of Islamic law. Al-Fasi and others are responsible for the production of an intellectual movement in which the *shariʿa* is considered more responsive to the needs of a society changing under the influence of new technology and science. The ulema have, then, at different times been loathed and loved by the political establishment. However, their participation in the institutions of power remains an essential component of any Muslim political system wishing to call itself "Islamic."

See also **Knowledge; Law; Madrasa; Qadi (Kadi, Kazi); Shariʿa; Shiʿa: Imami (Twelver); Shiʿa: Ismaʿili; Succession.**

BIBLIOGRAPHY

Ephrat, Daphna. *A Learned Society in Transition: The Sunni Ulama of Eleventh Century Baghdad.* Albany: State University of New York Press, 2000.

Makdisi, George. *Religion Law and Learning in Classical Islam.* Hampshire, U.K.: Variorum Reprints, 1991.

Momen, Moojan. *Introduction to Shiʿite Islam.* New Haven, Conn.: Yale University Press, 1985.

Robert Gleave

ʿUMAR (C. 581–644)

ʿUmar b. al-Khattab al-ʿAdawi al-Qurashi, an early Meccan companion of the prophet Muhammad, became the Prophet's second successor and is usually viewed as having done much to establish the foundations of the caliphal state. At first opposed to Islam, ʿUmar embraced it circa 615 in a reversal cherished and dramatized by tradition. Like Abu Bakr, with whom he was closely associated, ʿUmar married a daughter of the Prophet in 625. Because of his strong personality, a motif frequently noted in the sources, he gained considerable influence. At the death of the Prophet in 632, he helped Abu Bakr to be elected as successor, and Abu Bakr in turn appointed ʿUmar to succeed him two years later.

On taking office, ʿUmar placed the new caliphal state on firmer footing. He assumed the new title of Commander of the Believers (*amir al-muʾminin*), thus making clear his superior authority. He continued the campaign started by Abu Bakr to expand the caliphate outside of Arabia. Under his rule, Syria (636), Iraq (637), Egypt (639–642), and western Iran (641–643) all came under Muslim rule, a transformation that greatly altered the nature of the state. Internally, he organized the state over a much larger area, founded new

cities, and distributed offices more widely among the various Arabian tribes, thereby moving away from Abu Bakr's favoritism for the Quraysh.

See also **Caliphate; Law; Succession.**

BIBLIOGRAPHY

Kennedy, Hugh. *The Prophet and the Age of the Caliphates: The Islamic Near East from the Sixth to the Eleventh Century.* London: Longman, 1986.

Madelung, Wilfred. *The Succession to Muhammad: A Study of the Early Caliphate.* Cambridge, U.K.: Cambridge University Press, 1997.

Khalid Yahya Blankinship

UMAYYID *See* **Empires: Umayyad; Muʿawiya**

UMMA

The term *umma* is an Arabic word. It was used sixty-two times in the Qurʾan, in both the Meccan and Medinan periods. Its most common meaning is that of a group of people or a community, and it also refers to a religious community or a group of people who follow God's guidance. Most usages of *umma* in the Qurʾan, however, are not related to the community of prophet Muhammad.

The concept of a community of believers (*umma*) took shape during the Prophet's lifetime, first in Mecca then in Medina. In Mecca, the small group of the Prophet's followers shared certain common beliefs, values, and practices associated with the new religion, Islam, and gradually came to be differentiated from the rest of the Meccans. Meccan families were split; some followed the traditional religion of Mecca (paganism) while others followed the new religion. Religious affiliation became more important than family relationship or tribal membership. When the Prophet and his small group of followers fled Mecca to Medina, they formed, with the Muslims of Medina, a distinct community (*umma*) as opposed to, for instance, the Jewish community there. By the time of the Prophet's death in 632 C.E., his followers, known as "believers" or Muslims, had a distinct identity. The early struggle of this community with non-Muslims, either in the general Arab rebellion (632–633) against Muslim rule from Medina, or, after that, with the Byzantine and Sassanid empires in the wars of conquest, led to a sharper view of what the Muslim *umma* was; that is, it was based on belief in one

God, in the prophethood of Muhammad, and in a supranational brotherhood.

Although some scholars have attempted to identify *umma* with ethnicity, the understanding of *umma* in the Prophet's time, and particularly in the post-prophetic period, became divorced from ethnic identity but remained firmly bound to the religious identity of Islam. In early Islam, this religious *umma* coincided with the political *umma*: Muslims united under one ruler during the periods of the Prophet, the Rashidun caliphs, the Umayyads, and the early Abbasids. However, this united political body became fragmented by the emergence of a series of separate political communities among Muslims from the beginning of the ninth century onward. Despite this, the concept of *umma* as a common brotherhood of all Muslims based on the two key ideas of shared beliefs and equality has remained an ideal to which Muslims generally aspire.

In the twentieth century, nationalism became an important force in Muslim lands, following on the history of fragmentation. In the same period, and despite debate as to its "islamicity," the nation-state model was adopted by Muslims, particularly after the abolition of the last, but at the time largely symbolic, Ottoman caliphate in 1924. There remains, however, significant unease among some Muslims as to where their primary loyalty lies: with the nation-state or with Islam, particularly where the objectives of the two do not necessarily agree. What is emerging is a view that the nation-state is a political reality that is here to stay but that effort must be made to ensure that Muslim nation-states as well as minorities across the globe are brought closer to each other within the framework of the religious *umma*. Instances of this are the creation of supra-national institutions such as the Organization of Islamic Conference and its subsidiaries, formed to promote political and economic cooperation. More importantly, the concept and ideal of *umma* are strengthened by common teachings and by religious institutions such as pilgrimage (*hajj*), an annual gathering of Muslims in Mecca. While these may bring the Muslim nations closer together, there are also divisive forces at work, represented in ideological, ethnic, linguistic and cultural differences.

See also **'Ibadat; Modern Thought.**

BIBLIOGRAPHY

Ahsan, Abdullah al-. *Ummah or Nation? Identity Crisis in Contemporary Muslim Society.* Leicester, U.K.: Islamic Foundation, 1992.

Ali, Muhammad Mumtaz. *The Concepts of Islamic Ummah & Shariah.* Selangor, Malyasia: Pelanduk Publications, 1992.

Black, Antony. *The History of Islamic Political Thought: from the Prophet to the Present.* Edinburgh: Edinburgh University Press, 2001.

Abdullah Saeed

UMM KULTHUM (1904?–1975)

An accomplished and famous Egyptian singer, Umm Kulthum's career extended over fifty years. Born to a poor village family in the Egyptian delta, Umm Kulthum learned to sing Muslim devotional songs by imitating her father, the imam of the village mosque who sang for local occasions. She began to perform with her father, who dressed her as a boy to avoid the opprobrium of presenting his daughter on public stages.

In the early 1920s, the family moved to Cairo to work in the lucrative world of performance and recording. At first Umm Kulthum appeared markedly rural and lower class compared to the more sophisticated actresses and singers of the day. However, her strong voice attracted the attention of poet Ahmad Rami who wrote lyrics for her and taught her poetry. She adjusted her appearance and repertory and, by the late 1920s, commanded a busy schedule in major venues and one of the best recording contracts in the Middle East.

Between 1935 and 1946, she made six musical films. As the Egyptian economy worsened in the 1930s and the problems of imperialist European domination persisted, Umm Kulthum altered her repertory from escapist, romantic lyrics, to the terse, localized colloquial poetry of Bayram al-Tunisi set to music by Zakariya Ahmad. With this, she rooted her performance in the sounds and meanings of local Egyptian words and music. With Islamism growing as an alternative to Westernization in the 1940s, she sang complicated religious and political *qasa'id* (sing. *qasida*, a centuries-old sophisticated poetic genre) by Ahmad Shawqi set to music by Riyad al-Sunbati.

In the 1950s, she recorded numerous songs in support of the 'Abd al-Nasser government and became linked with Egypt's charismatic president as an ambassador of Egyptian culture. In 1964, she joined forces with long-time rival Muhammad 'Abd al-Wahhab, producing ten new songs marked by 'Abd al-Wahhab's characteristic "modernity" and the historically Arab performance style of Umm Kulthum.

After the Egyptian defeat in the war with Israel in 1967, Umm Kulthum toured the Arab world giving concerts to raise funds to replenish the Egyptian treasury. She became a near-mythical figure, drawing together Egyptians and Arabs from different social classes and regions. Her legacy springs from her compelling renditions of fine poetry, her musical skill, and her uncanny ability to connect with her audience.

See also **Music.**

BIBLIOGRAPHY

Braune, Gabriele. *Umm Kultum, ein Zeitalter der Musik in Ägypten: die moderne ägyptische Musik des 20. Jahrhunderts.* Frankfurt-am-Main: P. Lang, 1994.

Danielson, Virginia. *"The Voice of Egypt": Umm Kulthum, Arabic Song, and Egyptian Society in the Twentieth Century.* Chicago: University of Chicago Press, 1997.

Virginia Danielson

UNITED STATES, ISLAM IN

Many scholars believe that Islam is the fastest growing religion in the United States. While debates continue about how many Muslims actually live in the country—estimates range from 2 to 8 million persons—there is no dispute over the fact that, due both to conversion and immigration, the number is on the rise. In addition, over twelve hundred mosques now operate across the United States in small towns, suburban locations, and inner cities. American Muslims are like a microcosm of the Islamic world; they are diverse by race, class, ethnicity, linguistic group, and national origin. African Americans, perhaps the largest racial or ethnic group of Muslims in America, may account for 25 to 40 percent of the total population. South Asian Muslims, who trace their roots to India, Pakistan, and Bangladesh, represent approximately 30 percent. The third largest ethnic group of Muslims in the United States traces its roots to the Arab world, including countries in both the Middle East and North Africa. This group may total approximately 25 percent of all Muslims in the United States. The United States is also home to thousands of Turkish, Iranian, Central Asian, Southeast Asian (especially Malaysian and Indonesian), southeastern European (especially Bosnian), West African, and white and Latino American Muslims.

In addition to possessing great racial and ethnic diversity, Muslims in the United States can be characterized as a religiously diverse population as well. Muslims in the United States engage in a wide array of Islamic practices and adhere to differing schools of Islamic thought and interpretation. The vast majority of Muslims, including African Americans, identify themselves as Sunni, those who follow the sunna, or the traditions of the prophet Muhammad. Some American Muslims also call themselves Sufis, meaning that they seek intimate and closer ties to God by traveling one of the mystical paths of Islam. Still others are Shiʿite Muslims, persons whose Islamic practice pays special attention to the role of the prophet Muhammad's family in leading the community of believers. Finally, there are Muslims that do not fit easily under any of these labels, choosing to follow interpretations of Islam that are considered unorthodox, if not heretical by most Muslims—one famous example is the Nation of Islam led by Minister Louis Farrakhan.

History
From the 1600s until the abolition of legal slavery in 1865, West African Muslims were brought as slaves to the British North American colonies and later the United States. Perhaps 10 percent or more of all slaves in the Americas were Muslim, depending on what times and places are being considered. The number of Muslim slaves in the Americas may have increased even more during the early 1800s, after the West African Muslim leader ʿUthman dan Fadio (c. 1754–1817) successfully waged a campaign to Islamize much of the region. Though the importation of foreign slaves to the United States was officially banned in 1808, many U.S. residents violated the law, continuing to import slaves, including Muslims.

Despite the documented presence of Muslim slaves in the United States, however, there is little direct evidence that the practice of Islam was widespread among slaves in North America. In many cases, slave owners attempted to control slaves more easily by separating families and others who shared ethnic and linguistic ties. Though this assault did not translate into the elimination of African culture, including Islam, it did often lead to the recasting of certain customs, beliefs, and practices into different and often synthetic cultural forms. Some slaves adapted certain Muslim traditions, like facing toward Mecca in prayer, to their practice of Christianity. A few others, like the famous ʿUmar ibn Sayyid (1770–1864), a North Carolina slave who was literate in Arabic, eventually relinquished key elements of their Muslim identities, publicly converting to Christianity. Tellingly, the Muslims about whom the most is known generally lived in parts of the American South that had relatively large, isolated slave communities—places like the Sea Islands of Georgia where African Islamic traditions stood a better chance of being preserved and passed on.

Thus, by the end of the Civil War, there seem to have been very few practicing Muslims in the United States. Beginning in the 1870s, however, large numbers of Muslims once again came to the shores of the New World. From 1875 until the First World War, and then again from the 1920s until the Second World War, tens of thousands of Muslims from the Ottoman Empire, especially Arabs from greater Syria, traveled to the United States seeking economic opportunity. These Muslims made their homes in places as far flung as Quincy, Massachusetts, and Cedar Rapids, Iowa, whose Muslim community eventually established the Mother Mosque of North America, one of the oldest continuously operating Muslim communities in the United States. By 1920, hundreds of Muslims from both Anatolia and the Balkans had also created their own chapter of the Red Crescent (the Muslim equivalent of the Red Cross) in Detroit, Michigan, and had obtained a cemetery where fellow Muslims could be buried according to Islamic law. Many of these Muslims became peddlers, grocers, and unskilled laborers. Some eventually found jobs as farmers and factory workers, especially in the burgeoning automobile industry in Detroit. These Muslims also practiced various forms of Islam. They not only identified themselves as Sunnis and Shiʿa, but also as Druze, a

In New York City, a Muslim street vendor observes the daily prayer ritual. GETTY IMAGES

Syrian and Lebanese group that had long ago separated from the Shi'a; as Bektashi Sufis, a community made up mainly of Albanians; and as Mevlevis, the so-called whirling dervishes.

During the 1920s and 1930s, the number of Muslims in the United States also grew as hundreds, if not thousands, of African Americans converted, or as some African-American Muslims would put it, reverted to Islam. These conversions occurred in the context of the Great Migration, the movement of over a million and a half persons from the rural South to the more industrialized, urban North throughout the first half of the twentieth century. Attempting to escape racism and economic oppression, black migrants often worked and lived near immigrant Muslims who were also in search of new opportunities in cities like Detroit; St. Louis, Missouri; Pittsburgh, Pennsylvania; Newark, New Jersey; and Chicago, Illinois. African Americans became part of a dynamic cultural milieu, where people from every part of the globe were coming in contact with each other, confronting each other's differences and exchanging both goods and ideas.

This period also witnessed one of the first serious Muslim attempts to convert Americans to Islam. The Ahmadiyya movement, considered heretical by many other Muslims, was the first Muslim group to mass-distribute English translations of the Qur'an, hoping to make the holy book more accessible to those who could not read it in Arabic. Beginning in the 1920s, they also published the *Muslim Sunrise*, a

newspaper that contained information about the movement and the rudimentary practices of Sunni Islam, especially daily prayer, almsgiving, and fasting during the month of Ramadan. The Ahmadiyya focused many of their missionary efforts on African Americans. The head missionary, Muhammad Sadiq, promoted Islam as a religion of freedom and equality, often criticizing white Christianity's links with slavery and the destruction of African culture. This was an attractive message and hundreds of African Americans, like P. Nathaniel Johnson of St. Louis, Missouri, converted to Islam. By the mid-1920s, Johnson had become Shaykh Ahmad Din and was leading a multiracial community of Ahmadiyya Muslims in the Gateway City.

African Americans also formed their own Islamic groups during the 1920s and 1930s. Some of these groups, like the Moorish Science Temple, merely adopted certain Islamic names and symbols to create new African-American Islamic traditions. While many scholars have dated the origins of this movement to 1913, the Federal Bureau of Investigation believed that it began sometime in the 1920s, probably in Chicago, Illinois. Adapting certain Islamic symbols from the black Shriners (an African American fraternal organization that stressed racial cooperation and self-improvement), movement founder Noble Drew Ali (1886–1929) taught that American blacks were actually members of the Moorish nation whose original religion was Islam. His *Holy Koran of the Moorish Science Temple* (1927), a sacred text that had no direct connection to the Qur'an revealed to Muhammad in the seventh century C.E., stressed the importance of morality, industry, and group solidarity, and promised that the practice of Moorish Science was the key to both earthly and divine salvation for persons of African descent.

Some other groups established by African-American Muslims, however, embraced more traditional Islamic practices, placing greater emphasis on the five pillars of Islam and on the Qur'an. Among these communities, many of which can trace their origins to the 1930s, were the First Cleveland Mosque, led by African-American convert Wali Akram (d. 1994); the Adenu Allahe Universal Arabic Association in Buffalo, New York; and Jabul Arabiyya, a Muslim communal farm also located in upstate New York. Most historians have tended to ignore these Sunni African-American Muslim groups, largely because their scholarly gaze has focused on the more controversial Nation of Islam.

In the early 1930s, W. D. Fard, a mysterious immigrant peddler probably of Turkish or Iranian origin, founded the Nation of Islam in the Detroit metropolitan area. By 1934, he had disappeared, leaving Elijah Poole (1897–1975), an African-American migrant from Georgia, to continue his legacy. Poole, who had since become Elijah Muhammad, echoed the claims of Noble Drew Ali, arguing that Islam was the original religion of the "Blackman." He said that Fard was God in the flesh and that he, Elijah Muhammad, was God's Messenger, sent to resurrect black people from the dead—a teaching that violated many of the most basic tenets of Sunni Islamic traditions. An advocate of black separatism, Elijah Muhammad also emphasized black economic and political independence from whites, the building of moral character, and the practice of his unique Islam as solutions to the social and economic challenges facing black America. It was not until after the Second World War, however, that his teachings garnered national attention, due largely to the successful missionary work of the articulate, fiery, and handsome Malcolm X (1925–1965), who had become a follower of Elijah Muhammad while in prison.

During the postwar period, the face of American Islam was also transformed by a new wave of Muslim immigration from overseas. These Muslims included Palestinians who had become refugees after the creation of the State of Israel in 1948 and Egyptian citizens who had been dispossessed after Jamal 'Abd al-Nasser's revolution in 1952. Sometimes, they made contact with older generations of Muslim immigrants, who by this time were beginning to organize national networks like the Federation of Islamic Associations in the United States and Canada, a group of more than twenty mosques that began operations in 1952. Other times, however, these new immigrants challenged what they saw as the unhealthy assimilation of Muslims into American culture. The most active critics of such behavior were often foreign students in American universities. They had arrived from newly independent countries in Africa and Asia where Islamic activists arose to challenge political regimes that stressed nationalist and socialist rather than Islamic identities. In 1963, some of these students formed the Muslim Student Association, which would eventually become one of the largest Muslim organizations in the United States.

In fact, it is clear that by the 1960s, a global Islamic revival was underway, and Islam in the United States was deeply affected by it. Many Islamic revivalists stressed the universality of Islam, arguing that Muslims should reject divisions along lines of race, language, or nationality and work toward more unity in the Muslim *umma*, or worldwide community of believers. The revival, which also called for a return to strict interpretation of the Qur'an and the hadith, attracted African American Muslims, as well. In places like the Islamic Mission to America in Brooklyn, New York, for example, one could find a multiethnic and multiracial crowd of Muslims engaging the ideas of Egyptian activist Sayyid Qutb (1906–1966), whose writings were being circulated all over the globe. During the same period, some African American Muslim revivalists, like members of the Darul Islam movement, intentionally separated themselves from mainstream society, hoping to recalibrate the rhythms of their lives in accordance with Islamic law. Others, like Malcolm X, embraced Sunni religious practices, but insisted on the need to struggle simultaneously for black political liberation.

In the meantime, more and more Muslim immigrants were making their homes in the United States. In 1965, President Lyndon B. Johnson signed a new immigration law, inviting large numbers of non-Europeans, including Asians and Africans, to join the American nation. Many of the Muslim immigrants were professionals with South Asian roots and became successful doctors, engineers, and academicians in cities and towns throughout the United States. Others were from Africa, Europe, other parts of Asia, and even Central and South America; they represented over sixty different countries in all. Like Muslim immigrants before them, they subscribed to a variety of Islamic practices. Among just the Shi'ite immigrants, for example, there were many Twelvers (the largest group of Shi'ite Muslims in the world) and Isma'ilis, a smaller community that is itself divided into subgroups.

Sufism, the mystical branch of Islam, also grew during this period. While there had been Sufis in the United States for some time, a larger number of white Americans began to join various Sufi groups or to follow various Sufi masters in the 1960s and 1970s. Some of these Sufi converts did not call themselves Muslims and did not practice the five pillars of Islam. Others, however, insisted on adherence to foundational Islamic practices. By the beginning of the new millennium, Sufi Islam in the United States was a multiethnic and cross-class phenomenon. And American Muslims were members of a number of different Sufi groups, including the

Tijaniyya, Naqshbandiyya, Qadiriyya, Bektashis, Shadhiliyya, Ishraqiyya, Sufi Order International, and numerous independent Sufi communities in cities and even small college towns like Carbondale, Illinois. In addition, there were pan-Sufi organizations, like the Sufi Women Organization, which encouraged female Sufis to organize for social change among Muslims and society in general.

The post-1965 period of American Islamic history was also shaped by important transformations in African-American Islam. The number of independent African-American Muslim groups continued to increase as did the number of individual converts—especially in prisons, where Muslim individuals and groups, of all ethnic and religious stripes, reached out to male inmates. But perhaps the most important event of this period was the death of Elijah Muhammad in 1975. After inheriting the leadership of the Nation of Islam, Wallace D. Muhammad (b. 1933, a.k.a. Warith Deen Muhammad), one of Elijah's sons, dramatically altered the religious nature of the movement. Rejecting the most controversial elements of his father's teachings, including those about the divinity of W. D. Fard and the inherent evil of the white race, Wallace D. Muhammad (now known as W. D. Mohammed) emphasized the importance of Sunni Islamic practices, including daily prayer, the pilgrimage to Mecca, and fasting during Ramadan. He even changed the name of the organization from the Nation of Islam to the World Community of al-Islam in the West, and eventually, the American Muslim Mission. Though thousands of members followed the leader through what he called the "Second Resurrection," Minister Louis Farrakhan (b. 1933) criticized these deviations from Elijah Muhammad's teachings. By the late 1970s, he had reconstituted a version of the old Nation of Islam, which he still leads as of the time of this writing.

Discrimination and Prejudice

From the beginning of Islamic history in North America, Muslims have lived in an environment often dominated by curiosity, suspicion, fear, and even hatred of Islam and Muslims. Anti-Muslim prejudice has several roots, including a thousand-year-old European Christian bias against Islam and nineteenth-century American racism and xenophobia. In the last half of the twentieth century, however, these prejudices have been amplified by several events, many of which involve the foreign policy of the U.S. government. During the cold war against the Soviet Union, for example, the United States generally sided with Israel in its disputes with Soviet-backed Arab Muslim neighbors, prompting many Americans to believe that Arabs and Muslims were the "enemy." During the 1973 oil embargo of the United States by OPEC (Organization of Petroleum Exporting Countries) nations, who were protesting U.S. military support of Israel, many Americans became resentful of Arabs and Muslims more generally. Political cartoonists regularly drew racist images of the stupid, but dangerous, "Arab shaykhs" who controlled the world's

oil supplies. In 1979, American-Islamic relations were further strained when revolutionaries overthrew the U.S.-backed shah of Iran and then held dozens of Americans hostage for over a year. Direct American military involvement in the Lebanese Civil War (1982), the Persian Gulf War (1991), and the War in Iraq (2003) only added to these tensions.

In the aftermath of the 11 September 2001 terrorist attacks on the World Trade Center and the Pentagon, however, some Americans began to question the deeply embedded prejudices against Muslims in American culture. Americans of many faiths offered support to their Muslim neighbors, visited a mosque for the first time, and attended large interfaith prayer services. Many understood that though the terrorists may have been Muslim, they did not act on behalf of Islam. Other Americans, however, continued to argue that Islam itself was a threat. Muslims faced discrimination on airplanes and in employment. And in some instances, Muslim property and Muslim persons were physically attacked. In addition, negative portrayals of Muslims continued to appear in the popular media and in books written by a few academic critics. Muslim organizations in the United States responded quickly to the events of 11 September 2001 by unequivocally condemning the attacks, offering support for victims, increasing their outreach efforts, and working to protect Muslims in the United States against any further backlash.

Gender

Of all issues discussed in the American media regarding Muslims, gender is one of the most popular. The status of women in Islam is a symbol of particular importance for Muslims and non-Muslims alike, often used as a poetic stand-in for larger arguments about society, politics, economics, and religion. Muslim women in the United States face a variety of challenges, including discrimination from several sources: non-Muslims who regard them as the "oppressed women of Islam"; male family members and religious leaders who act in sexist ways; and a society that has not delivered on its promises of equality of economic and educational opportunity to women in general, especially women of color.

American Muslim women themselves disagree about how to face these challenges, but virtually no practicing Muslim woman would argue that Islam is an inherently sexist religion. Echoing what other conservative Americans would call "family values," some Muslim women maintain that the Qur'an directs men and women to operate in separate spheres—the man in the public world of the workplace and the woman in the private world of the home. Men and women are equal, they say, but they are also fundamentally different. Others, like African American Muslim and Qur'anic scholar Amina Wadud (b. 1952), argue that while there may be differences between men and women, women's roles should not be

In 2001 Imam Sa'd al-Kassas speaks to other Muslims during their weekly service in New Jersey. AP/WIDE WORLD PHOTOS

restricted to the private sphere. The Qur'an guarantees equality between the sexes, Wadud argues, and it does not prescribe one right way of being a man or a woman.

Regarding the controversial issue of the *hijab*, or the headscarf, some Muslim women claim that wearing the veil is unnecessary and that modesty of the heart is what matters. Some cover their heads only when making their prayers. Some say that they would like to cover, but are afraid of the discrimination that they would face from non-Muslims. Still others consistently cover whenever outside their homes or in the presence of men who are not relatives. Likewise, Muslim women disagree over the issue of polygyny. Some argue that having up to four wives is a Qur'anic right given to men, as long as these wives are treated equally; others say the practice was meant to be temporary or that the Qur'an itself virtually bans polygyny when it warns against treating one's wives unjustly (4:3).

Several factors influence Muslims' views of gender, including their ethnic, racial, class, linguistic, and generational identities. Children of first-generation immigrants, for example, sometimes challenge what they regard as the sexist views of their parents and grandparents. In so doing, they often make a distinction between the patriarchal culture of the old country and what they say is the true, egalitarian Islam of the Qur'an and the hadith. On the contrary, some female converts to Islam, including white Christian women who marry Muslim men, defend what they identify as the traditional relationship between husbands and wives in Islam, arguing that Islam is liberating precisely because it elevates their status as wives and mothers.

Islamic Organizations

There are dozens of political, religious, economic, and cultural organizations that focus on issues of interest to Muslims in the United States. The largest is the Islamic Society of North America (ISNA), an umbrella organization formed by members of the Muslim Student Association in 1982. Over three hundred mosques are associated with ISNA, whose headquarters are located in Plainfield, Indiana. The organization holds a popular annual conference during the first weekend in September in which Muslims network, discuss concerns of the day, and even meet future mates. In addition, it publishes the magazine *Islamic Horizons*, offers workshops on Islam for teachers, and maintains an active website. Perhaps the second largest Muslim organization in the country is the American Society of Muslims (ASM), a loose configuration of predominately African American mosques that recognize W. D. Mohammed as their leader. Publisher of the *Muslim Journal*, the ASM also offers an annual conference, oversees the broadcast of Imam Mohammed over the radio, and encourages followers to attend his many public addresses, which often draw thousands of listeners.

Many smaller Muslim organizations focus their energies on more specific concerns. For example, the Council for American-Islamic Relations defends the civil rights of Muslims, educates other Americans about Islam, and encourages Muslim participation in national politics. The Association of Muslim Social Scientists helps Muslim professionals, educators, and academics develop and share Islamic perspectives on contemporary issues. And the Fiqh Council of North America, a group of Muslim legal scholars, regularly offers counsel to Muslim individuals and local communities regarding everything from business contracts to haircuts. New groups continue to be formed every day—one recent example is al-Fatiha, an organization that offers support to gay, lesbian, bisexual, and transgendered Muslims.

Education and Outreach

There are probably more than two hundred full-time Islamic schools for children in the United States, and most mosques offer some sort of weekend school for both children and adults. The full-time schools are located mainly in cities and suburbs with large Muslim populations. Most of them offer primary education programs. Their curricula include state-mandated subjects like reading and math in addition to Islamic studies and Arabic classes. Perhaps one-quarter of these, called Sister Clara Muhammad Schools, are associated with the community of W. D. Mohammed. Originally part of Elijah Muhammad's Nation of Islam, these now-Sunni Islamic African American schools are named in honor of the wife of Elijah Muhammad, who played a key role in the Nation of Islam's survival during the early years of the movement. Located mainly in inner cities, these schools offer an alternative to African American parents, both Muslim and non-Muslim, who view their public schools as troubled, if not failing.

Many Muslim parents argue that the public school system has too many drawbacks, including the dangers of drugs, dating, and an unhealthy consumerist culture. They hope that Islamic schools will help their children develop Islamic values and behaviors. Interestingly, what is defined as "Islamic" is itself a subject of debate within Muslim schools. While some schools attempt to enforce gender segregation among their students, others actively defend the practice of encouraging responsible interaction among boys and girls, not only during class but also during social activities. In addition, some Muslim parents fear that the creation of Islamic schools will only make the integration of Muslims into mainstream American culture more difficult. Muslim children have been known to argue that their absence from the public schools is a missed opportunity to explain their Islamic religious convictions to their non-Muslim classmates.

Most mosques in the United States also engage in a number of outreach activities. Members share their faith experiences with non-Muslims, visit a school or church to talk about Islam, contact the media, and welcome visitors to the mosque. Though their activities have gone largely unnoticed by major media outlets, many Muslim leaders have also played prominent roles in interfaith dialogue in the United States. W. D. Mohammed, for example, has become well known among some Roman Catholics for his work with the Focolare movement. Maher Hathout (b. 1936), a leader of the Muslim Public Affairs Council in southern California, has held interfaith dialogues with both Jewish and Christian leaders. And Imam Elahi of the Islamic House of Wisdom in Dearborn, Michigan, has even organized an interfaith celebration of Thanksgiving Day.

Leadership

It is often said that there is no pope in Islam. Indeed, since the death of the prophet Muhammad, Muslims have never agreed on one central authority in religious or secular matters. In the United States, Islamic leadership is arguably even more fluid, due to the diversity of American Muslim communities, their relatively short history in North America, and constitutional guarantees of religious freedom. Furthermore, there are many different kinds of Muslim religious leaders in the United States, including Sufi masters, Muslim academics and educators, Islamic legal advisers, the heads of various Muslim organizations and movements, and the imams or presidents of local mosques.

In many parts of the Islamic world, an imam is simply a male who leads the communal prayers on Friday. In the United States, however, an imam can play several different roles in the community. In most African American mosques, the imam operates in both spiritual and administrative capacities, like many Protestant ministers. In predominantly immigrant mosques, however, the imam is more likely to be a spiritual leader who answers to an executive committee or board of directors that is composed of men and women from the local community. Furthermore, many mosque leaders, whether called president or imam, work on a volunteer or part-time basis, requiring them to seek employment outside the mosque. While most of them have completed studies at the college level or above, less than half have any kind of formal Islamic education. Muslim women are generally barred from serving as imams, although some do become mosque presidents—for instance, when rifle fire pierced the stain-glassed windows of her Toledo, Ohio, mosque after 11 September 2001, Chereffe Kadri led two thousand people, both Muslim and non-Muslim, in prayer as they literally joined hands around the building, asking for God's protection.

Muslim Identity

Muslims in the United States constantly debate the issue of identity, engaging the question of what it means to be a Muslim from a number of different angles. One of these is the relationship between Muslims and the state. For decades, some Muslims have proudly embraced their identity as American citizens, even patriots. Others, however, have sought to distance themselves from American culture and especially American foreign policy. During the Gulf War, for example, W. D. Mohammed supported the coalition against Iraq, arguing that it was desirable, from an Islamic point of view, to expel the Iraqi army from Kuwait; but Minister Louis Farrakhan joined some prominent Sunni Muslim figures in denouncing the presence of American troops on Islamic lands.

There have been similar divisions in the attempt to find an answer to the question of how Muslims should function in a non-Islamic country, a nation that sometimes seems quite hostile to Muslims themselves. Should Muslims run for political office? Should they serve in the military? How much should Muslims interact with non-Muslims and in what capacities? The need for answers only increased in the wake of 11 September 2001and the war in Iraq as many American Muslims attempted to show support for America while simultaneously questioning American foreign policy toward various Muslim countries. Some Muslim organizations in the United States, like the Tabligh Jama'at, worry that Muslims will become corrupted by participating more fully in American culture, which they see as un-Islamic. Similarly, Hizb Tahrir, or the Liberation Party, argues that the United States is *dar al-kufr* (the realm of disbelief), advising Muslims to work for the reconstitution of the Islamic caliphate, which was abolished in 1924 by Turkish leader Mustafa Kemal Ataturk. Most Muslim groups, however, advocate full participation in American public life. These include both the Islamic Society of North America and W. D. Mohammed's Muslim American Society in addition to the American Muslim Council and the Council for American-Islamic Relations.

Muslims in the United States also continue to debate the place of racial and ethnic difference within their own communities. Most Muslims, including African American Muslims, affirm the idea that Islam is a creed or way of life universally applicable to all, regardless of race, ethnicity, gender, class, or any other sociological category. Most also espouse Islamic notions of racial equality and categorically denounce racism. Many African American Muslims argue, however, that the reality of racial divisions in American Islam contradicts these

ideals. They complain that immigrants often take condescending attitudes toward them, especially in deciding who gets to determine what the "real" Islam is. There are also serious linguistic, ethnic, class, and religious differences among Muslim immigrants themselves. These differences often come to the fore when immigrants form cultural centers along linguistic lines, separating themselves into groups, respectively, of Urdu, Persian, or Arabic speakers. Some Muslims defend such activity by arguing that the Qur'an encourages ethnic and racial diversity (49:13). Some African American Muslims also assert that cultural autonomy and a sense of racial pride are especially important in their struggles for black liberation. But other groups, like the Islamic Center of Southern California (ICSC), work actively to create inter-ethnic and interracial American Muslim communities, often linking the future growth of American Islam to the diminution of racial divisions among American Muslims.

There is, in the end, little unity over the question of Islamic identity and many other issues of concern to Muslims in the United States. Such disagreements, while sometimes seen as problematic by Muslims themselves, reflect the diversity of American Islam. That diversity—the many faces and voices and manifestations of Islam in the United States—is an inextricable part of its growth.

See also **Farrakhan, Louis; Gender; Islamic Society of North America; Malcolm X; Muhammad, Elijah; Muhammad, Warith Deen; Muslim Student Association of North America; Nation of Islam.**

BIBLIOGRAPHY

Austin, Allan D. *African Muslims in Antebellum America: Transatlantic Stories and Spiritual Struggles.* New York: Routledge, 1997.

Bagby, Ihsan; Perl, Paul M.; and Froehle, Bryan T. *The Mosque in America: A National Portrait.* Washington, D.C.: Council of American-Islamic Relations, 2001.

Curtis IV, Edward E. *Islam in Black America: Identity, Liberation, and Difference in African-American Islamic Thought.* Albany.: State University of New York Press, 2002.

Dannin, Robert. *Black Pilgrimage to Islam.* New York: Oxford University Press, 2002.

Eck, Diana L. *A New Religious America: How a "Christian Country" Has Become the World's Most Religiously Diverse Nation.* New York: HarperSanFrancisco, 2001.

Haddad, Yvonne Yazbeck, ed. *Muslims in the West: From Sojourners to Citizens.* New York: Oxford University Press, 2002.

Haddad, Yvonne Yazbeck; and Smith, Jane Idleman, eds. *Muslim Communities in North America.* Albany: State University of New York Press, 1994.

Haddad, Yvonne Yazbeck; and Esposito, John L. *Muslims on the Americanization Path?* New York: Oxford University Press, 2000.

McAlister, Melani. *Epic Encounters: Culture, Media, and U.S. Interests in the Middle East, 1945–2000.* Berkeley: University of California Press, 2001.

McCloud, Aminah Beverly. *African American Islam.* New York: Routledge, 1995.

Smith, Jane I. *Islam in America.* New York: Columbia University Press, 1999.

Turner, Richard Brent. *Islam in the African-American Experience.* Bloomington: Indiana University Press, 1997.

Wadud, Amina. *Qur'an and Woman: Rereading the Sacred Text from a Woman's Perspective.* New York: Oxford University Press, 1999.

Edward E. Curtis IV

URDU LANGUAGE, LITERATURE, AND POETRY

Urdu is a language whose exceptionally complex linguistic and cultural history reflects the special position of Islam in the Indian subcontinent of South Asia. While linguistically related to Bengali, Hindi, Punjabi, and the other languages of the Indo-Aryan family (whose classical representative is Sanskrit), Urdu is distinguished by the very high proportion of Perso-Arabic elements in its vocabulary. This Islamic cultural orientation is also reflected in its written form, which uses the Perso-Arabic script with appropriate modifications to mark distinctive Indic features such as retroflex and aspirated consonants.

While its origins elude precise definition, Urdu clearly began in medieval times from a mixture of the local Indian dialects of the Delhi region with the Persian spoken by the Muslim conquerors whose armies rapidly spread the new lingua franca across the subcontinent. Since Persian continued to be the preferred administrative and cultural language of the Delhi sultanate and the Mughal empire, it was only with the collapse of unitary Muslim political authority in the eighteenth century that Urdu came to be cultivated in northern India as a literary language for a courtly poetry that constitutes the classical heritage of Urdu literature.

From the early nineteenth century, when British colonial rule was extended across northern India, Urdu came increasingly to be used also as a written prose language. British policy itself favored the development of Urdu as an official bureaucratic medium, and Muslim writers took ample advantage of the opportunities provided by the colonial state for the production of textbooks, newspapers, and very varied prose writings. It is from this early modern period, when British India was the scene of the most intense debates about the definition of Islam in the modern world, that Urdu became a language of Islamic expression second only in international importance to Arabic.

Throughout the twentieth century Urdu successfully retained this role as an Islamic language while also developing as the medium of a modern secular literature much influenced by English. As an administrative and educational language, however, Urdu has progressively lost ground to modern standard Hindi, the rival Sanskritized language promoted as a replacement for Urdu by Hindu nationalists. Since independence from British rule in 1947, Urdu has thus increasingly become marginalized in its Indian homeland and identified with Pakistan. Although spoken there as a mother tongue only by Muslim immigrants from India and their descendants, Urdu is the official language of Pakistan, where languages like Punjabi, Sindhi, or Pashto have limited regional status only. As such, Urdu has been carried by the Pakistani diaspora to many other parts of the world, including the Middle East, Europe, and North America.

Classical Urdu Poetry

Persian poetry was for many centuries one of the major arts to be cultivated across the eastern Islamic world. The patronage of the great Mughal emperors encouraged a further development of Persian poetry in sixteenth- and seventeenth-century India by both immigrant and native-born poets. While their works were formally cast in the long established traditional poetic genres, some novelty of expression came from their development of the new baroque manner called the "Indian style" (*sabk-e hindi*).

The eighteenth-century switch from Persian to Urdu as the preferred language of courtly poetry in northern India had been linguistically foreshadowed by the preclassical Urdu poetry produced in the southern Muslim kingdoms of the Deccan. But the living tradition of classical Urdu poetry is identified with the period when the empire had collapsed under the twin pressures of external invasions and internal struggles into several successor states, notably the court of the Navvab-Vazirs of Avadh in Lucknow and that of the politically shadowy later Mughals in Delhi, both of which were maintained as puppet kingdoms by the British until the mid-nineteenth century.

The carefully cultivated conscious rivalry between the "schools" of Delhi and Lucknow now seems less significant than the common features of classical Urdu poetry, which is both the direct heir to the immense artistic heritage of Persian poetry (itself now linguistically inaccessible to most South Asian Muslims) and the chief vehicle for the public and private literary expression of an elite society facing major political and cultural challenges. Most of the poetic genres are of the well-known Persian types, and are similarly based on rhyming verses composed in the usual Persian meters, typically ending with the incorporation of the poet's pen name (*takhallus*) in the final signature verse. By far the most popular genre is the *ghazal*, the ubiquitous short lyric whose cultivated formal rhetoric readily allows its expressions of private feeling to achieve widespread public outreach through

An Afghan refugee child writes in Urdu in a school in Pakistan. While Urdu was used widely as a written prose language under British colonial rule on the Indian subcontinent, its usage has decreased in India and it is now much more identified with Pakistan. AP/WIDE WORLD PHOTOS

recitation and musical performance as well as written dissemination. The two great classical masters of the Urdu *ghazal* are generally acknowledged to be the very prolific Mir Taqi Mir (c.1722–1810), who is known for the poignancy of his direct expression of the sufferings of love, and the Delhi poet Ghalib (1797–1869), whose slim collection (*divan*) of *ghazal*s is an iconic masterpiece combining refinement of sentiment with the ironic intellectualism of the "Indian style."

Of the longer public genres of Persian poetry, the narrative *masnavi* was more successfully cultivated in Urdu during its pre-classical phase in the Deccan. Although Mir himself wrote a number of striking short *masnavi*s on contemporary romantic subjects, it is his versatile and innovative contemporary Sauda (1713–1781) whose poetry addresses the greatest variety of public themes, using the formal ode (*qasida*) as well as various strophic forms to compose not only elaborately rhetorical eulogies and satires but also a number of striking elegies on the cultural and political devastation of Delhi in the mid-eighteenth century. In the *qasida* Sauda is later matched only by Zauq (1790–1854), the great rival of Ghalib for the favor of Bahadur Shah II Zafar (1775–1862), the last Mogul "emperor" whose sad fate at the hands of the British has helped to assure a special status for his own elegiac *ghazal*s.

While the Lucknow poets are in general considered less notable for their thematic range than for their cultivation of a formal Persianizing elegance, the Shiʿa allegiance of the rulers of the Avadh kingdom encouraged the magnificent flowering of the strophic *marsiyya*, the innovative Urdu genre that deployed the full resources of the "Indian style" for the elegiac celebration of the sufferings of Karbala celebrated in the annual rituals of Muharram, and whose two great masters are Anis (1801–1874) and Dabir (1803–1875).

Modern Urdu Literature

While the transition from the classical to the modern period can be sharply marked by the annexation of Avadh by the British in 1856 and the destruction of much of Delhi that followed their ruthless suppression of the Great Revolt of 1857, there was also naturally much overlap between the two. Under the patronage of other Indian Muslim rulers, some poets were able to continue working in the classical style, like Ghalib's younger relative Dagh (1831–1905) who perfected a mastery of the light *ghazal* designed for singing by courtesan artistes.

On the other hand, many of the developments most characteristic of later nineteenth-century Urdu literature such as the increasing importance of prose and of explicitly

Islamic writing had already begun before 1857, not least because of the emergence of an Urdu publishing industry based on the lithographic reproduction of professionally calligraphed texts. It was through this means that a wider public was found, for instance, for such early masterpieces of Urdu prose as Ghalib's elegantly informal letters.

It was, however, after the cultural watershed of 1857, when the Muslims of India had to confront the reality of the definitive loss of their political power, that the new trends associated with the early modernity of the colonial period became firmly established. Some writers of the later nineteenth century were provoked into formulating new styles of literary response to the acute sense of cultural loss caused by the political changes of the period. Two of the most notable of these were Muhammad Husain Azad (1834–1910), whose *Ab-e Hayat* (1881) is a pioneering history of Urdu poetry lovingly reconstructed around his revered master Zauq, and the maverick Muhammad Hadi Rusva (1858–1931), whose *Umrao Jan Ada* (1899) remains the most appealing of Urdu novels with its wonderful evocation of the life of a courtesan in the old Lucknow.

For other writers of the period, new kinds of Islamic ideology were as important as the new genres opened up by the example of English, which now increasingly came to supplant Persian as the model for Urdu prose styles and genres. This was particularly the case with the talented group of writers associated with the Aligarh movement inspired by the modernist interpretation of Islam promulgated by the great reformer Sir Sayyid Ahmad Khan (1818–1898), himself a vigorous and prolific exponent of a forcefully stripped-down Urdu prose style. The leading poet of the Aligarh movement was Altaf Husain Hali (1837–1914), whose long *Musaddas* of 1879 (revised in 1886) is the greatest poem of the period. Inspired by what he had read of Wordsworth's poetic ideals, Hali used a quite new style, that he called "natural poetry" and that consciously dispensed with most of the familiar Persianizing rhetoric, first to evoke the lost glories of Islam under the Arabs, then to embark on a savage critique of the failings of contemporary Islam in India. In prose, a similarly reformist message is conveyed with greater stylistic subtlety, if smaller artistic impact, in the moralistic novels of Nazir Ahmad (1836–1912).

Poetry, however, continued to be the favored medium of expression among the next generation of Urdu writers, which is dominated by Muhammad Iqbal (1879–1938). It was Iqbal's achievement to combine his own uplifting call for a Muslim renascence, looking to contemporary European philosophy as well as to an individual reinterpretation of certain Sufi ideas, with a hugely powerful poetic voice that drew anew upon the full resources of a rich Persian vocabulary to reinvigorate Urdu poetic diction after the successful challenge of Hali's "natural poetry" had undermined the appeal of traditional styles. A grandiloquent master both of the

philosophical *ghazal* and of the new kind of thematic poem (called *nazm* in Urdu), Iqbal is rightly remembered in South Asia for his Urdu poetry rather than the longer Persian *masnavis* on which his international reputation tends to be based. Although Iqbal continues to be the object of an inflated official cult in Pakistan as the ideological founder of the nation, his power directly to inspire, whether as a thinker or as a poet, has long been supplanted by the numerous writers of very different types who have subsequently flourished in Urdu.

As an Islamic ideologue, the most influential Urdu prose writer of the later twentieth century was certainly Sayyid Abu l-A'la' Maududi (1903–1979), the founder of the Jama'at-e Islami, while the Urdu poetry of the post-Iqbalian period came quickly to be dominated by Faiz Ahmad Faiz (1911–1984), whose combination of an idealistic socialism with a unique ability to intermingle the style of English romantic poetry with graceful references of Ghalib has ensured his continuing ability to inspire new generations of poetic followers in the *ghazal* and the *nazm*.

Modern Urdu narrative prose is less ambiguously based on the example of English genres and styles. While a few novelists, notably Qurratulain Haidar (b. 1928) and 'Abdullah Husain (b. 1936), have been able to establish serious reputations on the basis of major works, it is the short story that has generally proved to be the most successful genre. Following on the earlier example of the Urdu-Hindi writer Prem Chand (1880–1936), whose short fiction was inspired by Gandhian ideals, the new school of self-proclaimed Progressive Writers that emerged in the 1930s (and with which Faiz was associated) looked rather to socialist realism. By far the most successful of these short-story writers was Sa'adat Hasan Manto (1912–1955), some of whose most memorable stories were inspired by the tragedies of the Partition of 1947, and his overall achievement in the genre has yet to be fully matched by later writers in Pakistan. But several memorable collections of short stories, variously combining genuinely modernist formal experimentation with troubled articulations of a modern Pakistani Muslim cultural identity, have been produced by such leading exponents as the emigre Intizar Husain (b. 1933) with his continual reflections on the loss of an Indian Shi'i cultural heritage, or Mazhar ul Islam (b. 1949) with his attempts to integrate the local Sufi heritage embodied in the regional languages of Pakistan with a bleakly romantic individualism.

See also **Pakistan, Islamic Republic of; South Asia, Islam in; South Asian Culture and Islam.**

BIBLIOGRAPHY

Faiz, Faiz Ahmad. *Poems by Faiz.* Translated by Victor G. Kiernan. London: Allen and Unwin, 1971.

Matthews, D. J.; Shackle, C.; and Husain, Shahrukh. *Urdu Literature.* London: Urdu Markaz, 1985.

Matthews, D. J., trans. and ed. *Iqbal: A Selection of the Urdu Verse.* London: School of Oriental and African Studies, 1993.

Russell, Ralph, and Islam, Khurshidul. *Three Mughal Poets.* Cambridge, Mass.: Harvard University Press, 1968.

Russell, Ralph, and Islam, Khurshidul. *Ghalib, 1797–1869,* Vol. I: *Life and Letters.* Cambridge, Mass.: Harvard University Press, 1969.

Sadiq, Muhammad. *A History of Urdu Literature,* 2d ed. New Delhi: Oxford University Press, 1984.

Christopher Shackle

USULIYYA

The term "usuliyya" applies to those who adhere to the principles in law that, in Twelver Shi'ism, came specifically to mean the principles of jurisprudence (*usul al-fiqh*). The notion of principles was at first imbued with the theological doctrines of the Mu'tazila in the works of al-Shaykh al-Mufid (d. 1022) and his students, al-Sharif al-Murtada (d. 1044) and al-Shaykh al-Tusi (d. 1067), who exposed the imami conception of *usul al-fiqh*. However, the methodology for extrapolating legal norms (*ahkam*) from the sources had not yet been thoroughly incorporated into jurisprudence to the extent seen in later periods. The ulema of the tenth and eleventh centuries viewed themselves more as rational-theological jurists rather than as followers of the Usuli tradition.

After Tusi, Shi'ite jurisprudence stagnated for a century and a half, during which Sunni law flourished more creatively. Ibn Hazm (d. 1064), an Andalusian of the Zahirite school, presented an unusual combination of theology, linguistics, logic, and epistemology in his *al-Ihkam*. He defends logic and reasoning on the grounds that all thinking, even "the tradition," should be verified by reason. A contemporary of Ibn Hazm was Imam al-Haramayn al-Juwayni (d. 1085) who combined a strong Ash'arite tendency with a certain measure of logic and rationalist epistemology in the introduction to his *usul* work *al-Burhan*.

One of Juwayni's students, Abu Hamid Ghazali (d. 1111), gave a new structure to Islamic legal methodology that inspired Shi'ite Usulis. In *al-Mustasfa*, he proposed a horizontal scope for *usul al-fiqh* which differed from the hierarchical classification of the sources of legal knowledge as initiated by al-Shafi'i. Ghazali's approach to *usul al-fiqh* impressed such subsequent Sunni legal authors as Sayf al-Din al-Amidi (d. 1233) and Ibn al-Hajib (d. 1248). These scholars focused on the method of drawing out legal norms rather than on the categorization of the legal sources, as pre-Ghazali authors had done. Amidi dedicated a chapter to syllogism under the title of *istidlal* (evidentiary proof; 1967, 104–120),

including his brief epistemo-theological introductory remarks whose elaboration he presented in another work *Abkar al-anwar*. Amidi defined *istidlal* in its specific sense, as syllogistic reasoning which is not necessarily based on the four classical Islamic legal sources.

The Shi'ite school of Hilla, which flourished in the thirteenth and fourteenth centuries, did not disregard the rationalist Usuli achievements of its Sunni counterparts. This school historically begins with Ibn Idris al-Hilli (d. 1202) who, benefiting from the growing rationalist tendency among the Twelvers, made a more detailed exposition of Shi'ite jurisprudence in his *al-Sara'ir*. In refuting the traditionalists, Ibn Idris negates the validity of isolate traditions, and explicitly identifies the human rational faculty (*'aql*) as the fourth source of law in deducing legal norms.

The Usuli doctrinal movement truly began with al-Muhaqqiq al-Hilli (d. 1277), who was the first to open a chapter of *ijtihad* and *qiyas* (analogy) in Shi'ite jurisprudence. Like Ghazali, Muhaqqiq defines *ijtihad* in such a way that, by making a distinction between the speculative component (*zann*) on the one hand, and *qiyas* and unrestricted reasoning on the other, *ijtihad* is legitimized on the basis of valid *zann*. He challenges Mufid on the question of *qiyas* by claiming that the *ratio legis* (*'illa*) in certain kinds of *qiyas* are discernible and may be applied to new cases under the pretext of *tanqih al-minat* (scrutiny of criterion). It is noteworthy that the initiation of *ijtihad* is regarded as the major source of dynamism in Shi'ite law since the thirteenth century, when the claim of "closure of the gate of *ijtihad*" began to circulate in the Sunni milieu. Moreover, Muhaqqiq tried to redefine the Shi'ite conception of *'aql* by restricting it to three applications: (i) verbal inferences such as the tone (*lahn*) of religious discourse, (ii) what is implied in God's address (*fahwa al-khitab*), and (iii) the reason for the address (*dalil al-khitab*). Only the second is considered to be referring to the human conception of good and evil.

Muhaqqiq's nephew, al-'Allama al-Hilli (d. 1327), advanced this Usuli position by not only upholding *ijtihad*, but also by distinguishing the status of the *mujtahid* as a necessary office for Shi'ism. From the vantage point of knowledge of jurisprudence, he divided the community into two groups: *mujtahid*s and their followers. In his *Tahdhib*, 'Allama legitimized two kinds of *qiyas*: i) *al-mansus al-'illa* in which the *leges ratio* is designated in the Qur'an and Sunna, and ii) *al-hukm fil-far' aqwa*, wherein the minor case has more applicability to law than its premise.

By the middle of the Safavid era (the seventeenth century), the Usuli trend suffered a temporary setback due to the Akhbari (traditionalist) resurgence that seriously challenged the Usuli way of resorting to *qiyas* and *ijtihad* instead of relying on the imams' traditions. The founder of the neo-traditionalist trend was Mulla Muhammad Amin Astarabadi

(d. 1626), who had been educated by Usuli masters. Astarabadi succeeded in turning Akhbarism into a legal school with distinct methods of jurisprudence. Among his formulas was the principle of "customary certainty" (al-yaqin al-ʿadi or al-qatʿ al-ʿadi), which proposed that the Shiʿites should content themselves with "the general certainty" (al-qatʿ al-ijmali) that the contents of imams' traditions convey to them. According to Astarabadi, these traditions are compiled in the four canonical collections of Shiʿite traditions as well as other early Shiʿite compilations.

The Usuli methodology found a new momentum in the Shiʿite seminaries during the second half of eighteenth century, when the leading Akhbari-oriented jurist of the shrine cities of the ʿAtabat, Shaykh Yusuf al-Bahrani (d. 1772), incorporated the key elements of Usuli principles, including the ijtihad, in his comprehensive work on Shiʿite law, al-Hadaʾiq al-Nadiraʾ. Bahrani, moreover, allowed his Usuli opponent Baqir al-Bihbihani (d. 1791) to flourish in the ʿAtabat by encouraging his own students to attend Bihbihani's lectures, and still more, by assigning Bihbihani to lead the funeral prayer at his death.

Bahrani's goal, which was to reduce the differences between the two parties, was viewed as having been defeated by later Usulis, since they awarded Bihbihani victory over the Akhbaris. Enjoying his family connections and ability to support his students, Bihbihani succeeded in re-establishing Usulism in the shrine cities. However, he wrote more polemical treatises such as Risalat al-ijtihad wal-akhbar, rather than works on Usuli legal methodology. Despite Bahrani's aspiration, the Usuli-Akhbari conflict continued, and eventually climaxed into personal refutations and even bloody clashes between supporters of the two groups during the nineteenth century.

The re-establishment of the Usuli position not only increased the authority of the ulema, but also placed the doctrine of ijtihad and taqlid at the heart of the Shiʿite juristic structure upon which the subsequent institution of marjaʿ al-taqlid had to be built. The juridical office of marjaʿ al-taqlid appeared as an independent institution when the Usuli ulema of the ʿAtabat began to acknowledge the superiority of one or several senior mujtahids in expounding legal opinions, and in some cases in pronouncing final and binding verdicts.

The institution was manifested more completely when Shaykh Muhammad Hasan Isfahani was singled out as the sole supreme mujtahid in Najaf in 1846, and he formally took charge of paying the stipends of the students of other seminaries in the shrine cities of the ʿAtabat. In view of the considerable socio-political roles performed in the modern period by this institution and by the ulema in general, it is suggested that the consolidation of the independent Shiʿite "hierocracy" resulted in a duality within the structure of authority during the Qajar reign in Iran.

Another consequence of Usuli dominance was the reformulation of the doctrine of juristic mandate (velayat-e faqih) with a methodical argumentation. The idea of the juristic mandate still contained at its heart the concept of the imam as deputy, but it came to include as well an acknowledgement of the legitimacy of qualified jurists to succeed the all-embracing authority of the imam, due to the work of an Usuli jurist of the Qajar court, Molla Ahmad Naraqi. The executive force of this doctrine is taqlid or the unquestioned mass following.

Concurrent with the increase of the mujtahid's social prestige, the Usuli legal methodology reached another peak with Shaykh Murtada Ansari (d. 1864), who shifted the emphasis of the contents of usul al-fiqh from the semantics of the Qurʾan and traditions to what he termed "the rational practical principles" (al-usul al-ʿamaliyya). Ansari defended the use of syllogism in legal methodology, and he applied it in parts of his work. Ansari rejected the application of "juristic mandate" beyond religious matters, but he advocated the necessity of a mujtahid for approbation of Muslim actions. Ansari's discourses were compiled and circulated among Shiʿa in the form of the juridical manual (risala-ye ʿamaliyya) that were issued by the supreme exemplar of the community.

The notion of unquestioned following taqlid was further corroborated by Sayyed Mohammad Kazem Yazdi (d. 1919), who maintained that the actions of Muslims would be void without emulating a mujtahid. Yazdi set the problem of taqlid as the opening issue of Shiʿite law. The last bolster of taqlid, in its Usuli context, was made by Ayatollah Khomeini (d. 1989). He claimed that the object of taqlid was not limited to sheer "following," but was intended to mean complete obedience to the qualified jurist's commands.

The centrality of taqlid in some of the Usuli works should not be taken to mean that the Usulism of the contemporary era was actually reduced to taqlid and its corollary ijtihad to enhance the mandate of jurists; but rather that several genuine attempts were made to present the Shiʿite Usuliyya in its best methodical form. The most successful work in this vein belongs to Shaykh Mohammad Reza Mozaffar (d. 1963), who dedicated half of his book to discussions of "rational entailments" and "the practical principles." He expounded the Shiʿite conceptions of "independent rational inducements" (al-mustiqillat al-ʿaqliyya), rational proofs, and the presumption of continuity of the past.

BIBLIOGRAPHY

Arjomad, Said Amir, ed. *Authority and Political Culture in Shiʿism.* Albany: State University of New York Press, 1988.

Kazemi Moussavi, Ahmad. *Religious Authority in Shiʿite Islam.* Kuala Lumpur: ISTAC, 1996.

Ahmad Kazemi Moussavi

'UTHMAN DAN FODIO (1754–1817)

'Uthman dan Fodio was a religious scholar and the founder of the Islamic empire of Sokoto in present-day northern Nigeria.

'Uthman dan Fodio was born in Maratta in the Hausa kingdom of Gobir. He studied the Qur'an with his father, and other Islamic sciences such as *fiqh* and hadith with a number of scholars of the region. Through Shaykh Jibril b. 'Umar he was initiated into the Qadiriyya Sufi brotherhood. After completing his education in circa 1774, he started to teach and preach in Gobir. His preaching brought him into a conflict with the political establishment in Gobir that, although claiming to be Muslim, was still committed to a policy of accommodation with respect to the non-Muslim majority of the population. In 1804, this conflict led to a military confrontation between the *jama'a* (community) of 'Uthman dan Fodio and the King of Gobir. In the subsequent jihad the *jama'a* of Uthman dan Fodio was able not only to defeat the King of Gobir in 1808, but also to conquer almost all other Hausa states and to establish an empire that was ruled by religious scholars and defined as an Islamic state, the so-called "Sokoto caliphate." 'Uthman dan Fodio became *emir al-mu'minin* (the title "commander of the faithful" taken by the second caliph, 'Umar) of this empire and was able to exert great influence on neighboring jihad movements, in particular those in Bornu (from 1808) and Masina (1818). Dan Fodio was also author of more than one hundred scholarly works that were to influence decisively the intellectual, religious, and political development of Islam in the Sokoto empire as well as other parts of West Africa such as the Masina imamate. His most influential works are probably those he wrote to legitimize the jihad, on the necessity of *hijra* (emigrating to establish a Muslim community), on reviving the sunna and quelling innovation, and on the distinction between Muslim rule and the rule by nonbelievers.

See also **Africa, Islam in; Caliphate; Kano.**

BIBLIOGRAPHY

Hiskett, Mervyn. *The Sword of Truth. The Life and Times of the Shehu Usuman dan Fodio*. New York: Oxford University Press, 1967.

Last, Murray. *The Sokoto Caliphate*. London: Longman, 1967.

Roman Loimeier

'UTHMAN IBN 'AFFAN (R. 644–656)

'Uthman b. 'Affan, a wealthy merchant of the Qurayshi tribe who was noted for his elegant dress, supported Muhammad when he first began preaching in Mecca. He converted to Islam and married Muhammad's daughter Ruqayya, with whom he emigrated to Abyssinia. Soon after they rejoined the Muslims in Medina, Ruqayya died during the Battle of Badr and Muhammad gave him Umm Kulthum, another of his daughters, in marriage.

On the death of 'Umar b. al-Khattab, 'Uthman was elected the third caliph by a council of six, including 'Uthman, 'Ali, and 'Abd al-Rahman b. 'Awf. Noticeably, the Ansar (the Medinan companions of the Prophet), had no representation in the council, a detail which helped 'Uthman defeat 'Ali.

'Uthman is credited with establishing the canonical version of the Qur'an during his caliphate. He handed the pages of Qur'an, left by 'Umar in the care of his daughter Hafsa (a widow of the Prophet), to Zayd b. Thabit (one of the scribes of the Prophet), and ordered him to compile it in the dialect of the Quraysh. Three other Quraysh were selected to help Zayd in this effort. Finally, a copy was deposited in all the administrative centers of the caliphate, and the destruction of all other Qur'ans ordered.

'Uthman was resented for appointing his irresponsible relatives as governors of Kufa, Basra, and Egypt. Dissension came to a head when the rebels, having been promised reforms, intercepted a message, supposedly from 'Uthman to the governor of Egypt, ordering their execution. They promptly returned to 'Uthman's home and despite 'Uthman's denial, killed him. This event is known as *Yawm al-Dar*.

See also **Caliphate; Fitna; Khutba; Religious Institutions; Shi'a: Early; Succession.**

BIBLIOGRAPHY

Hinds, Martin, "The Murder of the Caliph 'Uthman." *Journal of Middle East Studies* 3 (1972): 450–469.

Madelung, Wilfred. *The Succession of Muhammad*. Cambridge, U.K.: Cambridge University Press, 1997.

Motzki, Harald. "The Collection of the Qur'an." *Der Islam*, 78 (2001): 1–34.

Rizwi Faizer

V

VEILING

The word for veiling, *hijab*, is derived from the root *h-j-b*. Its verbal form *hajaba* means to veil, to seclude, to screen. The complex phenomenon of *hijab* is generally translated into the English as *veil* with its correlate seclusion.

The term *hijab* or veil is not used in the Qur'an to refer to an article of clothing for women or men, rather it refers to a spatial curtain that divides or provides privacy. The Qur'an instructs the male believers (Muslims) that when they ask of anything from the wives of the prophet Muhammad to do so from behind a *hijab*, a curtain that creates a visual barrier between the two sexes (33:53). The observance of this *hijab* is the responsibility of the men and not the wives of the Prophet.

In later Muslim societies this instruction specific to the wives of the Prophet was generalized, leading to the segregation of Muslim men and women not related to each other through family ties. It created a social and political division between public male space and private female space with the effect of a political, social, economic, and psychological disenfranchisement of the women. The gender-segregated space has also provided an intimate homosocial context conducive to deep bonds between members of the same gender and inimical to bonds and commitments across genders, including heterosexual relations.

Although the term for dress or garment in the Qur'an is *libas*, *hijab* has come to mean the headgear and outer garment of Muslim women. *Libas* is used both literally to refer to physical/material dress and adornments and figuratively as a covering of human shortcomings and vulnerabilities. (16:14; 35:12; 18:31; 44:53; 22:23; 35:33).

In the Qur'an the righteousness or *taqwa* of *libas* is modesty. It is the correct balance between the function of *libas* as protection and as ornamentation. Modesty concerns both men's and women's gaze, gait, garments, and genitalia. The specific articles and aspects of clothing that are mentioned with regard to women only are *jilbab*, a loose outer clothing or cloak, and *khimar* or scarf. When in the company of men, women are asked to raise their *khimar* (scarves) over the necklines of their shirts (24:31). When in public women are asked to draw their *jilbab* (cloaks) over them so they may be identified as respectable women and not be harmed (33:59). These Qur'ic verses do not mention any parts of the women's body. No body parts of either men or women are mentioned in the modesty verses except the genitalia, which are to be guarded (24:30–31). Guidelines for covering of the entire body except for the hands, the feet, and the face, are found in texts of *fiqh* and hadith that are developed later.

Early in the twentieth century the tradition of veiling among Muslim women created controversy. Different ideologies and attitudes, whether in Western countries or on the part of Muslims influenced by the West, challenged the practice. Regimes in a few Muslim countries have legislated the veil on or off Muslim women. In most Muslim countries where Muslim women have the freedom of choice, some, especially in the modern urban centers, have discontinued the practice of veiling. Some of those who had discarded the veil have returned to it. But this modern return to the *hijab* actually gives many women access to public spaces and jobs instead of secluding them. For many Muslim women, due to a complex of personal belief, social reinforcement, and public self-image, the use of the *hijab* is an integral part of their being in the world and an outward expression of their inward faith that dictates modesty and chastity.

Beginning with the twentieth century, Western perceptions also underwent change with regard to the image of the veiled Muslim woman. Originally perceived as being submissive or oppressed, some Muslim women are now being viewed as being an embodied threat to Western culture. The custom of Muslim women to publicly cover themselves with garments that completely hide their body and hair creates a mystique regarding the wearer and challenges Western modernity and feminism.

Western perceptions of a stereotypical harem with trapped, seductively veiled women were played out in the erotic imagery of early twentieth-century films and paintings.

This misrepresentation of Islam persisted until the sudden decolonization of French Algeria. The dramatic events of the Algerian war (1954–1962) marked a turning point in Western perceptions of Islamic women when heavily veiled Muslim female militants utilized their garments for the concealment of weapons. The use of veiling by Muslim women now had politically sinister connotations of danger, fanaticism, and terrorism. In the West veiled Muslim women now may be seen both as oppressed and dangerous.

In the case of the woman who veils her face, gaze-reversal is implied; instead of being scrutinized herself she is free to gaze upon men without their knowledge, a perception that thus may cause another degree of discomfort.

Any analysis of appearance must be viewed within the totality of the social environment. The Western analysis of its gaze on Muslim women is not capable of representing the reality of the lived experience for each individual woman. The Western and modern Muslim view of Islam and of women has changed over the last hundred years or so. Whether the *hijab* liberates or oppresses or is simply a part of one's everyday clothing is not an issue that can be easily answered because of the complexity of each individual situation.

See also **Clothing; Gender; Harem; Law; Purdah.**

BIBLIOGRAPHY

El-Guindi, F. *Veil. Modesty, Privacy and Resistance.* Oxford U.K.: Oxford International Publishers Ltd., 1999.

Hussain, F., ed. *Muslim Women.* New York: St Martin's Press Inc., 1984.

Mernissi, F. *The Veil and the Male Elite. A Feminist Interpretation of Women's Rights in Islam.* Translated by Mary Jo Lakeland. Reading, Mass.: Addison-Wesley Publishing Company, Inc. 1991.

Watson, H. "Women and the Veil: Personal Responses to Global Process." In *Islam, Globalization and Postmodernity.* Edited by A. Ahmed and H. Donnan London: Routledge, 1994.

Ghazala Anwar
Liz McKay

VELAYAT-E FAQIH

Velayat-e faqih (Ar., *wilayat al-faqih*), literally "the authority of the jurist," refers to a development in the Imami Shi'ite theory of scholarly authority. The term *velayat* in Shi'ism was normally associated with devotion to, and obedience of, the imams, and consequently was a defining aspect of Shi'ism generally. Imami Shi'ite jurists, over time, developed a theory whereby the obedience due to the imams, particularly in matters of law, was channeled through the jurists (sing. *faqih*, pl. *fuqaha*), who acted as representatives of the imam during the occultation (*ghayba*). Until the nineteenth century, this was phrased in terms of a general delegation (Per., niyabat-e 'amma, Ar., niyaba 'amma) of the jurists. In the early nineteenth century, the scholar Ahmad al-Naraqi (d. 1829) was probably the first to describe this obedience in terms of *velayat-e*, signifying a further expansion of the authority of the jurists during the *ghayba*.

The *velayat* of the jurist (*velayat-e faqih*) was not, at first, viewed as entirely replacing the political and legal role of the imam by Imami jurists, and there were jurists (such as Murtada al-Ansari [d. 1864]) who viewed the idea of *velayat-e faqih* with some suspicion. The concept remained undeveloped in legal works, though the idea of the legal authority of the jurist was developed in other areas. This all changed with the work of the Iranian scholar Ruhollah Khomeini. In his lectures, he proposed a political theory in which a *faqih* took on political leadership, replacing existing forms of government with Islamic government. The jurist who was to rule was conceived not as the most learned (*a'lam*), but as one who had the political skills to gain (and maintain) power. If a *faqih* was able to do this, Khomeini argued, all other jurists were duty-bound to support his rule. This theory Khomeini termed *velayat-e faqih*, thereby making a link between his political ideas and Imami traditional jurisprudence.

At first, Khomeini's ideas were debated on a theoretical level. However, in 1979 Khomeini was propelled into power on a wave of public opposition to the rule of the shah. On his return to Iran from exile, Khomeini set about putting his political theory into practice. In the referendum of March 1979, the Iranian population voted for the establishment of an Islamic republic. In October 1979, a constitution was adopted that included the famous article 5, stating that during the occultation "the *wilaya* and leadership of the *umma* devolve upon the just and pious *faqih*." This *faqih* was Khomeini. The principle of *velayat-e faqih* was, then, enshrined in the constitution which theoretically gave the *faqih* power, though, in a concession to democratic principles, the *faqih* was to share power with the (popularly elected) president and parliament (*majlis*). After Khomeini's death in 1989, the constitution was amended in order that his chosen successor, 'Ali Khamane'i, might take over this position. Since then there have been vigorous (and, as yet, unresolved) debates in Iran over the relative jurisdictions of the *faqih*, the president, and the *majlis*.

See also **Hukuma al-Islamiyya, al- (Islamic Government); Shi'a: Imami (Twelver).**

BIBLIOGRAPHY

Ende, Werner, and Brunner, Ranier, eds. *The Twelver Shia in Modern Times. Religious Culture and Political Culture.* Leiden and Boston: E. J. Brill, 2001.

Robert Gleave

VERNACULAR ISLAM

The central Islamic tenet of *tawhid*, the essential oneness and unity of God, contributes to a self-conception and representation of Islam as a universal and singular religious tradition. The idea of singularity is reinforced by the *shahada*, or witness ("There is no god but God. Muhammad is the Messenger of God"), and shared ritual practice obligatory for all Muslims (*'ibadat*) in Arabic, often called the Five Pillars in English. This ideology of singularity is based upon the authority of the Qur'an and hadith. The fact that one can hear nearly identical Arabic recitation of the Qur'an in New Delhi, Jakarta, and Detroit, that South Asian, African, Arab, and Indonesian Muslims perform similar ablution rituals before they attend Friday prayers together in London or New Delhi, or that pilgrims from all over the globe gather at Mecca for the hajj are visible manifestations of a tradition shared across geographic and social boundaries of difference.

Muslims, however, live in particular cultures, locales, and geographies that influence their practice and create local knowledge and variation. Knowledge and practice particular to a locality can be identified as vernacular Islam. In linguistics, the vernacular is associated with the language or dialect spoken in a particular geographic location; it is the common everyday language of ordinary people in a given locality. The vernacular may be juxtaposed to a language that is shared across geographic boundaries or locales. A. K. Ramanujan has distinguished, in the Indian context, the vernacular regional language as the mother tongue in contrast to the pan-Indian, literary language of Sanskrit, which he calls the father tongue. For Islam, Arabic is the father tongue that is known, at least for Qur'anic recitation purposes, across the globe; but Muslims speak numerous languages and dialects in everyday interactions, sermons, and rituals.

Scholars of Islam have distinguished many local practices, confined to specific cultural contexts, from pan-regional (universal) Muslim practice and belief by calling the former elements of "folk Islam" or "popular Islam." If "folk" is used simply to refer to practices that are local or nontextual, the term is an accurate descriptor. However, in both lay and academic usage, the term often connotes a hierarchy of practice and belief in which "folk Islam" is at the low end. Frequently, educated Muslims who have been exposed to

Muslim practice in multiple cultural and geographic contexts, and are keenly aware of an ideal of a "universal" Islam that may be seemingly threatened by this diversity, refer to these practices as cultural rather than religious and therefore not "real" Islam. The term "vernacular Islam" is less value-laden than "folk Islam" and more easily inclusive of both textual and nontextual traditions. To understand Islam in practice, scholars need to pay attention to the various levels of interaction between vernacular and universal practices.

The practice of Islam may take regional shape and vernacular expression on multiple levels. For example, in some regions, women are not allowed to pray in the mosque (Pakistan, India, Morocco, for example), while in other countries (the Arab world, Malaysia, the United States, Canada, England), women do pray in the mosque, although each mosque varies in the architectural design for the separation of men and women in prayer. Another tangible regional/cultural, vernacular expression of Islam is found in the levels and style of women's head coverings and the meanings and historical and political motivations for these. Prior to the revolution in 1979, many Iranian women adopted the veil (chador) to protest the rule of the shah; veiling was both a religious and political act. Since the revolution, women have been forced to veil and are under the surveillance of religious police. In the secular state of Turkey, where Muslims are nevertheless a majority, women are forbidden to wear head coverings in government buildings; in the Islamic state of Saudi Arabia, where the Wahhabi tradition that interprets Islamic law very literally is dominant, women are not permitted to go out in public without veiling and all public buildings and work spaces are gender segregated. In other contexts, the practice of female veiling may become more prevalent as the influence of "Islamization" becomes greater, such as in Egypt, where, for example, Bedouin women have begun to adopt a "standard" style of veiling as they become more educated in state-supported schools (Abu-Lughod).

The vernacular expression of Islam also varies according to whether or not the culture is one of immigrants. For example, the diversity of ethnicities represented in many American mosques affects worshipers' experience and practices, which differ significantly from those of Muslims living in more ethnically homogeneous cultures. Muslims living in multiethnic communities often begin to draw distinctions between culture and religion. Those practices limited to specific regional contexts may be labeled as culture, or as religious practice interpreted through and influenced by culture. An example of such practices is the wedding ritual of decorating the bride. While many Indian and Pakistani Muslims may say that the ritual application of turmeric paste on the new bride's skin is a Muslim practice, it is not prescribed in the Qur'an or hadith and non-Asian Muslims do not practice this ritual. There are other practices, such as the sacrifice of an animal at the Feast of the Sacrifice, which are mandated in the Qur'an, but whose implementation may be interpreted differently in various cultural contexts. One reason for vernacular expressions of a shared sacrificial practice may be something as "secular" as governmental public health regulations, which in American cities may differ significantly from cities in the Philippines, India, or Indonesia.

Veneration of Saints

References to "folk Islam" are most often associated with specific kinds of vernacular practices—in particular, visitations (*ziyarat*) to the graves of local holy men or saints and associated performance and healing traditions. In Morocco the cult of saints is called maraboutism. The majority of these saints are Sufi teachers, guides, or masters (*pir, shaykh*), who may be part of a lineage of authority within specific Sufi orders (*tariqa*), or they may be independent of an order. These saints are "friends of God" (*awliya' Allah*) who embody particular spiritual powers (*barakat*) that may result in their ability to perform miracles. Many Muslims believe that even after death, the *barakat* of the saint is accessible, and miracles may be performed at his grave site; for believers, the saint is still alive and close to God and may serve as an intermediary between worshiper and God. Women may visit the grave to ask for fertility, for the health of a child, or resolution of a marriage negotiation; men may ask for business success or success in an exam. Others visit the grave for general well-being, without a specific request, or simply to honor the saint, who may be one's teacher, teacher's teacher, or founder of the Sufi lineage to which one belongs. The presence of these shrines sacralizes the land itself; they are local or regional, vernacular sites of power. In many Muslim cultures, the annual death anniversary of the saint is celebrated in grand fashion at his tomb, with large processions of pilgrims carrying flags, musicians, and new cloth grave coverings that are gifted by the pilgrims. The anniversary is called an *'urs* (literally, wedding), as the saint is not considered to have died, but to have simply left his worldly body and joined God. Dreams are a common idiom through which Sufi saints, both living and dead, communicate to their disciples.

Most Muslims worshipping at a saint's grave site (called *dargah* in South Asia; Ar. *qabr*) would draw a clear distinction between honoring a saint and asking for his intervention and performance of miracles, and worshiping the saint, which would be *shirk* (idolatry or blasphemy through assignation of partners to God). However, because the practice of worship at the tomb of a saint can be so easily misconstrued as worship of the saint (making offerings of flowers, incense, elaborately decorated cloths, etc. at the grave, and taking back some of these offerings as embodiments of the *barakat* of the saint), many Muslim modernists and fundamentalists label this practice as superstition, a cultural practice adopted from other religious traditions rather than from Islam itself, or outright *shirk*. Even if the critics of saint veneration accept that the saint is not being worshiped, they may critique the practice as placing an unnecessary intermediary between God and the worshiper.

The controversy over the veneration of saints and worship at their tombs takes different forms and magnitude depending on local religious, cultural, and political circumstances and contexts. For example, according to Katherine Ewing, in Pakistan (where Muslims are a majority, living under a Muslim state) certain movements (Ahl-e Hadith, Ahmadiyya, Jama'at-e Islami) have attempted to eliminate saint veneration and practices around the institution of the *pir*; and public discourse is filled with debate about what is the correct practice of Islam. Similarly, John Bowen describes a vigorous debate in Indonesia over what constitutes proper Islamic practice, including whether or not rituals of farming, healing, and casting spells are acceptable. In India, while educated Muslims may denounce veneration of the *pir*, the level of public debate over these practices is much less vigorous than it appears to be in Muslim states such as Indonesia and Pakistan. Furthermore, many educated Muslims who criticize such "folk" practices as visiting the shrine of a saint to ask for miraculous intervention, may themselves access such practices when their own family members are ill, infertile, or otherwise in distress. These practices are not limited to rural contexts or nonliterate participants.

Religious Healing

Veneration of saints and local pilgrimage to their shrines are often associated with religious healing traditions that address illnesses caused by intervention by spiritual forces (including evil eyes, jinn, spirits of the dead, and ghosts) into the physical human world. Many *pir*s are both teachers and healers. Their healing practices are based on the assumption that illnesses or troubles caused by spiritual forces must be counteracted by spiritual force. One method of diagnosis of a patient's problem is called, in Urdu, *abjad ka phal kholna* (literally, opening the mystery of the numbers). According to these Sufi traditions, every Arabic letter is associated with a particular numerical value. The numerical value of the letters in the patient's name is determined by the healer and then that of the patient's mother. These are added, along with the numerical value of the lunar day of the month. The total is divided by three or four (the four directions or the three worlds) until a single digit remains, which determines what kind of force is causing the illness. Other diagnostic rituals may include "reading" the ways in which a lemon shrivels over time, dreaming by the *pir*, visions obtained through trance, or reflection in a surface of oil and kohl. The most common prescription against spiritual forces that have caused illness is the written word of God; that is, amulets, on which are written the various names of God, his angels, and Qur'anic verses, are given to patients to wear as protection, to dip in water to drink, to burn, bury, or hang from a doorsill. The physical manifestation of the very word of God is inherently powerful; it may call back a lost child, deflect a neighbor's or spouse's argumentative words, soothe a child's high fever, or serve as a literal shield against the evil eye. Pilgrimages to shrines of saints and given periods of time to be spent there may also be prescribed by the *pir*.

See also **Arabic Language; Persian Language and Literature; Urdu Language, Literature, and Poetry.**

BIBLIOGRAPHY

Abu-Lughod, Lila. *Writing Women's Worlds: Bedouin Stories.* Berkeley: University of California Press, 1993.

Bowen, John. *Muslims Through Discourse.* Princeton, N.J.: Princeton University Press, 1993.

Bowen, John. *Religions in Practice: An Approach to the Anthropology of Religion.* Boston: Allyn & Bacon, 2002

Eaton, Richard M. *The Rise of Islam and the Bengal Frontier, 1204–1760.* New Delhi: Oxford University Press, 1994.

Eickelman, Dale. *Moroccan Islam: Tradition and Society in a Pilgrimage Center.* Austin: University of Texas Press, 1976.

Ewing, Katherine. *Arguing Sainthood: Modernity, Psychoanalysis, and Islam.* Durham, N.C.: Duke University Press, 1997.

Fluehr-Lobban, Carolyn. *Islamic Society in Practice.* Gainesville: University of Florida, 1994.

Geertz, Clifford. *Islam Observed.* New Haven, Conn.: Yale University Press, 1968.

Hoffman, Valerie. *Sufism, Mystics, and Saints in Modern Egypt.* Columbia: University of South Carolina, 1995.

Loeffler, Reinhold. *Islam in Practice: Religious Beliefs in a Persian Village.* Albany: State University of New York Press, 1988.

Joyce Burkhalter Flueckiger

VIZIER *See* **Wazir**

W

WAHDAT AL-WUJUD

Wahdat al-wujud, which means "oneness of being" or "unity of existence," is a controversial expression closely associated with the name of Ibn al-ʿArabi (d. 1240), even though he did not employ it in his writings. It seems to have been ascribed to him for the first time in the polemics of Ibn Taymiyya (d. 1328). Through modern times, critics, defenders, and Western scholars have offered widely different interpretations of its meaning; in "Rûmî and *Wahdat al-wujûd*" (1994), William Chittick has analyzed seven of these.

Taken individually, the two words are among the most discussed in Sufism, philosophy, and *kalam* (theology). *Wahda* or "oneness" is asserted in *tawhid,* the first principle of Islamic faith. *Wujud*—being or existence—is taken by many authors as the preferred designation for God's very reality. All Muslims agree that God's very reality is one. Controversy arises because the word *wujud* is also employed for the "existence" of things and the world. According to critics, *wahdat al-wujud* allows for no distinction between the existence of God and that of the world. Defenders point out that Ibn al-ʿArabi and his followers offer a subtle metaphysics following the line of the Ashʿarite formula: "The attributes are neither God nor other than God." God's "signs" (*ayat*) and "traces" (*athar*)—the creatures—are neither the same as God nor different from him, because God must be understood as both absent and present, both transcendent and immanent. Understood correctly, *wahdat al-wujud* elucidates the delicate balance that needs to be maintained between these two perspectives.

See also **Falsafa; Ibn al-ʿArabi; Sirhindi, Shaykh Ahmad; Tasawwuf.**

BIBLIOGRAPHY

Chittick, William C. "Rûmî and *Wahdat al-wujûd.*" In *Poetry and Mysticism in Islam: The Heritage of Rumi.* Edited by Amin Banani, Richard Hovannisian, and Georges Sabagh. Cambridge, U.K.: Cambridge University Press, 1994.

Knysh, Alexander D. *Ibn ʿArabi in the Later Islamic Tradition: The Making of a Polemical Image in Medieval Islam.* Albany: State University of New York Press, 1999.

William C. Chittick

WAHHABIYYA

The Wahhabiyya is a conservative reform movement launched in eighteenth-century Arabia by Muhammad b. ʿAbd al-Wahhab (1703–1792). It provided the ideological basis for the military conquest of the Arabian peninsula that had been undertaken by the Saʿud family, first in the late eighteenth and early nineteenth centuries, and then again in the early twentieth century. Wahhabism is the creed upon which the kingdom of Saudi Arabia was founded, and it has influenced Islamic movements worldwide.

Muhammad b. ʿAbd al-Wahhab began to preach a puritanical form of Islam during the 1740s in the small settlements of the Najd, the arid province of north central Arabia. His basic teachings are found in a small treatise titled *Kitab al-tawhid* (Book of unity), and from it his followers took the name Muwahiddun (Unitarians). His Muslim opponents, along with Westerners, initially used the term "Wahhabiyya" and its anglicized form, "Wahhabism," as derogatory references to what was depicted as a fanatical sectarian movement. To this day, the term is often used pejoratively by critics of the movement.

Ibn ʿAbd al-Wahhab wanted to restore the pristine Islam of the Qurʾan and the Prophet by cleansing it of all innovations (*bidʿa*) that challenged strict monotheism. Foremost among these was the cult of saints, which had developed over the centuries among both Sunnis and Shiʿites. Such popular practices as pilgrimages to the tombs of saints, beseeching the dead for intercession with God, asking blessings upon saints following the ritual prayer, and the construction of domed mausoleums for pious personalities were strongly condemned as *shirk*, or associating divinity to beings other than God.

Among the "innovations" condemned by Ibn 'Abd al-Wahhab was the centuries-long heritage of jurisprudence (*fiqh*) that coalesced into four Sunni schools of law and the many schools of Shi'ism. The Wahhabiyya considered themselves the true Sunnis and acknowledged their affinity to the Hanbali legal tradition. Yet they rejected all jurisprudence that in their opinion did not adhere strictly to the letter of the Qur'an and the hadith, even that of Ibn Hanbal (780–855) and his students. Consequently, Ibn 'Abd al-Wahhab, along with other Muslim reformers of the eighteenth century, such as Shah Wali Allah (1703–1762) in India, was one of the most important proponents of independent legal judgment (*ijtihad*) of his time. His *ijtihad*, however, was of a very conservative type, aimed at enforcing a literal reading of the Qur'an and hadith, especially in such matters as the punishment for adultery, theft, drunkenness, and failure to follow religious obligations like daily prayers and fasting during Ramadan.

Having been expelled from the first two towns in which he preached, Ibn 'Abd al-Wahhab settled around 1744 in Dir'iyya, an oasis controlled by Muhammad b. Sa'ud (r. 1746–1765). The religious teacher and tribal chieftain concluded a pact by which Ibn Sa'ud pledged to give military support for the propagation and enforcement of Ibn 'Abd al-Wahhab's teachings. The alliance was cemented by Ibn Sa'ud's marriage to the daughter of Ibn 'Abd al-Wahhab, the beginning of frequent intermarriage between the two families that continues to the present. Ibn 'Abd al-Wahhab's sons would also participate actively alongside the Sa'ud family in the military expansion of the movement.

By 1747, Ibn Sa'ud was at war with the neighboring ruler of Riyadh, a conflict that would continue for nearly thirty years. Conquest of territory was followed by the establishment of a fort and mosque, where Wahhabi preachers and judges were settled to propagate Ibn 'Abd al-Wahhab's teachings. Control over the entire Najd was achieved by 1780 under the leadership of Muhammad b. Sa'ud's son, 'Abd al-'Aziz.

Following the death of Ibn 'Abd al-Wahhab in 1792, the movement advanced east toward the Persian Gulf and north into Iraq. In 1802, Wahhabi tribesmen sacked the Shi'ite shrine city of Karbala, severely damaging a number of religious buildings, including the gold-domed tomb of the Prophet's grandson, Husayn. To avenge this destruction, a Shi'ite from Karbala, who had infiltrated the Wahhabi camp as a convert, killed 'Abd al-'Aziz in November 1803.

Under Sa'ud, 'Abd al-'Aziz's son and successor, the Wahhabis advanced upon the Hijaz. In 1803, they entered Mecca after the city was abandoned by its Ottoman garrison, and quickly moved to purge the sanctuary of the Ka'ba of any offending ornamentation. Medina was not taken until the

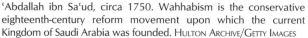

'Abdallah ibn Sa'ud, circa 1750. Wahhabism is the conservative eighteenth-century reform movement upon which the current Kingdom of Saudi Arabia was founded. HULTON ARCHIVE/GETTY IMAGES

following year, when a Wahhabi force marched into the city and proceeded to level the gravestones of those members of the Prophet's family and companions who are buried in the cemetery adjacent to the Prophet's tomb.

By 1811, the Wahhabi domain extended over much of the Arabian Peninsula and north into Syria. The movement was checked only when the Ottoman sultan authorized the governor of Egypt, Muhammad 'Ali (c. 1769–1849), to crush it. The Turco-Egyptian forces succeeded in taking Medina in 1812 and Mecca the following year. In the Najd, however, Wahhabi forces fought fiercely until the death of Sa'ud in May 1814. Sa'ud's successor, 'Abdallah, tried to negotiate a settlement with Muhammad 'Ali, but in September 1818 was forced to surrender the capital of Dir'iyya and was later executed in Istanbul.

The Wahhabi state was restored in the new capital of Riyadh under Turki, a cousin of Sa'ud's, following the departure of Egyptian troops from the Najd in 1822. By the time of

Turki's death in 1834, most of the tribes in northeastern Arabia acknowledged Wahhabi rule. A power struggle within Wahhabism began after Turki's death, when the Rashid clan of Ha'il began increasingly to challenge Sa'udi control. In 1891, Muhammad b. Rashid (r. 1872–1897) won a decisive victory over the Sa'udis and occupied Riyadh as the head of the Sa'ud family, 'Abd al-Rahman (r. 1889–1902), fled to Kuwait.

The Sa'ud clan, now led by the young son of 'Abd al-Rahman, 'Abd al-'Aziz (1880–1953), reclaimed control of Riyadh in 1902. In 1912 'Abd al-'Aziz founded the first of the agricultural colonies known as *dar al-hijra* (abode of migration). These colonies would produce the Ikhwan, a group of devoted Wahhabi loyalists who were prepared to fight for the Sa'ud family at short notice. The Wahhabi expansion in Arabia was curtailed under British pressures during the First World War, but immediately afterward 'Abd al-'Aziz began to advance beyond the Najd. The Hijaz was conquered by the end of 1925.

Wahhabi doctrines have governed much of the legal and cultural life of the kingdom of Saudi Arabia since its founding in 1932, even though followers of Wahhabism may be a minority within the country. A Supreme Council of Ulema advises and oversees the government on the application of Islamic law (*shari'a*), which from the period of Ibn 'Abd al-Wahhab has been based largely on Hanbali jurisprudence. While legal reform has taken place in certain areas—slavery and concubinage were officially outlawed in 1962, for example—the ulema have resisted reform in such fields as personal, economic, and penal law. The courts enforce a largely unwritten legal code that permits capital punishment for murder, rape, drug smuggling and adultery, amputation of the hands for theft, and flogging for drunkenness. The *mutawwa'in*, a sort of religious police officially charged with "commanding the right and forbidding the wrong," enforce Wahhabi societal mores, including "modest dress" for both sexes and a ban on public displays by Muslims or non-Muslims of heterodox religious beliefs.

The rapid modernization of Saudi society has often led to clashes between the Sa'udi family and clerical establishment and the most zealous Wahhabi loyalists. The first major crisis came in the late 1920s, when 'Abd al-'Aziz crushed his own Ikhwan militias when they revolted against some of his modernization efforts. Later, dissident ulema challenged the government over such matters as the introduction of radios, television, and automobiles into the country. Social reforms involving greater rights for women have provoked particularly severe reactions. The opening up of higher education to women in the 1970s led to riots in some cities; and at the start of the twenty-first century, women were still unable to drive their own automobiles, despite domestic pressure to lift this ban. In 1992, more than one hundred scholars circulated a petition criticizing the government for, among other things, not adhering strictly to *shari'a* and for wasting billions of dollars of the country's wealth. By 2003, the presence of American military bases in the kingdom had become the major source of conflict between Wahhabi activists and the royal family. Although the government has not taken any concerted steps to shut down or curb private Wahhabi organizations, it has jailed or exiled a number of dissident scholars and activists.

Saudi Arabia's tremendous oil wealth has made possible the dissemination of Wahhabi ideas and influence throughout the world, through religious propaganda and financial assistance to mosques and schools. During the Afghan war against the Soviet Union, many wealthy Saudis financed charities that educated and cared for Afghan refugees in Pakistan. The religious schools (*madrasas*) where poor Afghan boys were educated produced the foot soldiers for the Taliban, who seized control of much of Afghanistan during the 1990s and established a state grounded in Wahhabi doctrine. One wealthy Saudi, Usama bin Ladin, personally directed the recruitment, training, and fighting of Arabs coming to Afghanistan to wage jihad against Soviet occupiers. This was the basis for the terrorist organization that developed in the 1990s into al-Qa'ida. Wahhabi groups in Saudi Arabia, Kuwait, and other Gulf emirates are allegedly funding other militant and terrorist organizations in such diverse parts of the Muslim world as Algeria, Sudan, Palestine, Chechnya, Kashmir, and the Philippines.

BIBLIOGRAPHY

Lacey, Robert. *The Kingdom*. New York: Harcourt Brace Jovanovich, 1982.

Layish, Aharon. "Saudi Arabian Legal Reform as a Mechanism to Moderate Wahhabi Doctrine." *Journal of the American Oriental Society* 107, no. 2 (April-June 1987): 279–292.

Philby, Harry St. John Bridger. *Arabia*. New York: Charles Scribner's Sons, 1930.

Sohail H. Hashmi

WAJIB AL-WUJUD

The concept of *wajib al-wujud* (necessary existence) is the most central aspect of Ibn Sina's (980–1037) philosophy and the one on which his cosmology rests. In subsequent Islamic thought, *wajib al-wujud* is synonymous with "God."

Ibn Sina distinguishes between the necessary, the possible, and the impossible. The necessary is that whose nonexistence is impossible. The possible is that whose existence or nonexistence is not impossible. The impossible is that whose existence is impossible. Thus, the necessary existence of a thing always belongs to that thing. This necessity of existence is manifest either through the thing itself or through something else. A thing whose existence is necessary through itself cannot be necessary through something else. The converse is true. A thing whose necessity of existence is through something else cannot be necessary through itself. The name of the latter type is "possible in itself, necessary through another."

What is possible in itself may not exist. But if it exists, it does so through an external cause that necessitates its existence. Since the chain of causes cannot be infinite, it must stop with a thing whose existence is necessary through that thing itself and not through another.

This first cause must be necessary in all respects. For if it had an aspect that was possible in itself, then there would be need for something prior to it that could bring it into existence, and so on.

Based on the fact that the first or uncaused cause is necessary in all respects, Ibn Sina argues in ways beyond this brief discussion, that, among other things, the first cause is also as follows. One, that is, nothing can share in it. Thus, it cannot have any differentiating characteristic (as rationality is for humanity), species (as humanity is for animality), or genus (as animality is for humanity). Therefore, it is indivisible in discourse and, hence, indefinable. For a definition is a discourse divided into genus, species, and difference.

Wajib al-wujud, also called, among other things, the first, the first mover, the first manager, the principle of all, the creator and Allah, is a desired intellect that knows itself and knows other things in a universal manner inasmuch as it is their principle.

Ibn Sina's concept of *wajib al-wujud* had a great influence on later Islamic and Christian thought (see, for, example, the third Way of the five Thomistic proofs of God's existence).

See also **Falsafa; Ibn Sina.**

BIBLIOGRAPHY

Hourani, George F. "Ibn Sina on the Necessary and Possible Existence." *Philosophical Forum* 4 (1972): 74–86.

Ibn Sina. *Al-Najat.* Edited by Majid Fakhry. Beirut: Dar al-Afaq al-Jadida, 1985.

Shams C. Inati

WALI *See* **Saint**

WALI ALLAH, SHAH (1703–1762)

Shah Wali Allah was the most prominent Muslim intellectual of eighteenth-century India and a prolific writer on a wide range of Islamic topics in Arabic and Persian. The fact that his writings are often characterized by a historical, systematic approach coupled with an attempt to explain and mediate divisive tendencies leads him to be considered a precursor to modernist/liberal Islamic thought.

From an early age his father, Shah 'Abd al-Rahim, trained him both in Islamic studies and Naqshbandiyya Sufism. In 1731, Wali Allah left India to perform the pilgrimage to Mecca and Medina, where he stayed for some fourteen months. His most important and influential work, *Hujjat Allah al-baligha*, in which he aimed to restore the Islamic sciences through the study of the hadith, was composed in Arabic sometime during the decade after his return to India.

After Shah Wali Allah's death in 1762, his teachings were carried on by his descendants, in particular his sons, Shah 'Abd al-'Aziz (d. 1823) and Shah Rafi' al-Din (d. 1818), and his grandson Shah Isma'il Shahid (d. 1831). Shah 'Abd al-'Aziz was a noted scholar and teacher with a wide circle of pupils, some of whom are linked directly with the establishment of the Deoband madrasa.

South Asian Muslims with an anti-Sufi, puritan outlook such as the Ahl-e Hadith, and even the followers of Maulana Maududi, find in Shah Wali Allah's return to the fundamentals of *shari'a* and political rejection of alien influences a precursor to their own reformist beliefs. Another group of his successors, best exemplified by his closest disciple and cousin, Muhammad 'Ashiq (1773), seems to have pursued Wali Allah's mystical inclinations.

See also **Deoband; South Asia, Islam in; Tasawwuf.**

BIBLIOGRAPHY

Baljon, J. M. S. *Religion and Thought of Shah Wali Allah.* Leiden: E. J. Brill, 1986.

Hermansen, Marcia K., trans. *The Conclusive Argument from God: Shah Wali Allah of Delhi's Hujjat Allah al-Baligha.* Leiden: E. J. Brill, 1996.

Marcia Hermansen

WAQF

The common textbook definition of *waqf* (pl. *awqaf*) as a "charitable and religious trust" only partly conveys the much richer history of these institutions. *Awqaf* always had familial and political dimensions along with, as well inseparable from, the purely pious ones. These dedications did provide ways of organizing welfare and piety, but also ways of passing from one generation to the next wealth as well as the social power that wealth insured. Most endowments mixed private and public dimensions.

In technical terms, a *waqf* depends on the "stopping" (one basic meaning of the Arabic root verb, *waqafa*) of some piece of property. An owner surrenders his/her rights of possession to God. The house or field or garden so dedicated should never again pass to a human owner—unless replaced with something of equal value. The person making the dedication (the *waqif*) retains two important powers. He can distribute the income of the *waqf* in any way that does not violate Islamic sensibilities (a *waqf* to support a tavern would be bad): therefore, donors as well as their near relations can receive the income from such a trust. Also, the dedicator appoints a trustee (*mutawalli*) who administers the income of the *waqf*. Donors are free to appoint as *mutawallis* themselves, their children, and grandchildren.

Although permanent, in theory, the historical record shows that most *awqaf* were fragile. The earliest engraved announcement of a *waqf* so far discovered emerged from a heap of rubble in Palestine. As the economic, social, and political needs of people whose livelihoods depended on endowments changed over time, succeeding generations inevitably altered the terms of the trusts until they ceased to resemble their founders' dictates concerning the disposition of real property and its income. For example, in postcaliphal states such as Mamluk Egypt, rulers sometimes seized endowments established by their predecessors and set about recreating them to suit a different understanding of their own epoch's religio-political needs. Colonial regimes and the nationalist states that succeeded them followed the practice of "Islamic" states by renewing and reconstituting endowments.

Muslim endowments acquired a kind of dual status in almost every region of the Dar al-Islam. On the one hand, their status according to scholars of *shari'a/fiqh* (the terms badly translated as Islamic law) was a constant source of debate although they generally agreed that *awqaf* should be permanent. On the other hand, the institutions themselves continually evolved to suit the economic, social, as well as political circumstances of particular times and places. Of the four *madhahib* of the contemporary Muslim world, the Hanifite seems to have the most elaborate doctrines concerning endowments.

In a brilliant study of the shrine (*Mazhar-e Sharif*) of Hazrat 'Ali in what is now Afghanistan, Robert McChesney has traced a series of *awqaf* over a period of four hundred years. Custodians (*mutawallis*) were the central figures in Mazhar-e Sharif's *waqf* complex. A few families managed to pass the guardians' office along a direct line of descent. Such continuity merely deepened a particular group's commitment to the Mazhar. Custodians of 'Ali's shrine concentrated on the management of a vast irrigation project watering the fields dedicated to this holy place. McChesney shows that over time the valuable canals fell into disrepair. The total amount of land under cultivation declined. Even so, the value of the produce from the shrine's lands remained considerable.

Managing relations with the power holders attracted by that wealth was a second task falling to the overseers. In this case, describing the history of a particular *waqf* gives insights into the ways that political organizations shift. At Mazhar-e Sharif, shrewd management brought a relatively smooth transition from the period of Uzbek domination to the era of Pushtun ascendency marked by the creation of Afghanistan.

Several important studies by Carl Petry are founded on information provided by the *awqaf* connected to the Mamluks of Egypt and their families. Sultans and great emirs founded mosques and theological seminaries (*madrasas*). Since their sons were not likely to inherit any political power, endowments provided the only economic future the dependents of Mamluks could have. Therefore, women featured prominently in the *awqaf* of Mamluk Egypt.

The history of Mamluk women and their *awqaf* find analogies in the rest of the Muslim world. Women founded and managed many of their own endowments. Females in the early modern Dar al Islam probably had more economic and social power than they possessed in more recent times.

Mamluks had a peculiar place in medieval Egypt. They were of foreign birth. They were Central Asians or from the Caucasus Mountains: Turks, Circassians, and the occasional Mongol. As martial artists, they differed in almost all social ways from the Arabic-speaking peasants of the Nile basin. Their status as warrior-slaves was not inheritable. Therefore, many high-ranking Mamluks planned the economic and social futures of their families, especially that of their womenfolk, with *awqaf*. Their wives and offspring could receive stipends guaranteed by endowments' incomes. Egyptian religious scholars (ulema) also figured in the Mamluk way of *waqf* making. As educated members of the Arabic-speaking majority, ulema were often go-betweens representing the rulers to their subjects. Scholars were, therefore, a favorite choice when appointing custodians.

Other studies of single places in periods of transition can yield insights into the political as well as the social operations of *awqaf*. Miriam Hoexter's study of the endowments managed by ulema of Algiers city in the late seventeenth and early eighteenth centuries establishes a model for analytical social dimensions of endowments. Most of the trusts in her study were actually founded, under the Hanifi rite, in the interests of the donors' own families. But the urban population of Algiers suffered from violence that had both internal and external origins. When creating a *waqf*, the poor of the Holy Cities of Mecca and Medina were often the residual beneficiaries of the income. The scholars of Algiers city honestly managed those endowments. Almost every year for nearly a century, they managed to forward a tidy sum in coin to poor Algerians living out their lives in Mecca or Medina.

Colonial regimes often thought of themselves as preserving and reforming Muslim institutions. Gregory Kozlowski describes some of the ways in which colonial governors in India not only changed the character of specific endowed establishments, but shaped all subsequent views, Muslim and non-Muslim alike, concerning the legal status of *awqaf*. Because imperial regimes shaped the characters of the independent states that succeeded them, attitudes that were colonial in origin have exerted some power on the present day Muslim nation-states. In particular, colonial and post-colonial regimes tended to suppress any *awqaf* primarily dedicated to the founders' families. The second trend was to have a state-controlled bureacracy administer all public dedications. Government-controlled endowments were sometimes the core of one or another officially endorsed versions of Islam.

In the years since 1950, old trends of the history of endowments have continued. Particular institutions are still fragile and depend upon watchful managers. Circumstances of the moment still shape Muslim philanthropy. HAMAS began its life as a charitable trust for Palestinians. Much of its work continues to be feeding the poor or tending to the sick and wounded. New kinds of *waqf* that have a global focus have emerged as a prosletyzing tool for Saudis and Iranians. Others with a less confrontational approach dedicate themselves to such noble tasks as preserving Islam's architectural heritage. Though their institutional shape may alter, *awqaf* will be a feature of Muslim life in the years to come.

See also **Economy and Economic Institutions; HAMAS; Law.**

BIBLIOGRAPHY

Hoexter, Miriam. *Endowments, Rulers and Community: Waqf al-haramayn in Ottoman Algiers.* Leiden: E. J. Brill, 1998.

Kozlowski, Gregory C. *Muslim Endowments and Society in British India.* Cambridge, U.K.: Cambridge University Press, 1985.

McChesney, Robert D. *Waqf in Central Asia: Four Hundred Years in the History of a Muslim Shrine, 1480–1889.* Princeton, N.J.: Princeton University Press, 1991.

Petry, Carl F. *Protectors or Praetorians? The Last Mamluk Sultans and Egypt's Waning as a Great Power.* Albany: State University of New York Press, 1994.

Gregory C. Kozlowski

WAZIFA

A *wazifa*, or pension, refers to a payment made to members of the religious institution in Iran. The term was employed by Persian and Arab writers with a variety of meanings including task, duty, and office. But the term had a special meaning exclusive to the administrative system of Iran, which differs from the other Muslim administrative systems. The multiple meanings of *wazifa* explain why information on it is found in such a diversity of sources.

Apart from the allusions to *wazifa* that are found in chronicles and biographical dictionaries, information on its meaning as a pension for the members of the religious institution in Iran is found in Safavid administration sources.

Wazifa was a state stipend given to deserving individuals or institutions, invariably religious in nature. In principle the stipend was attached to a function. For example, in late Safavid times in Iran, all leading members of the religious establishment received a *wazifa*, which was paid out of the state treasury or royal endowments. Another kind of *wazifa* was paid to Armenian religious leaders from the income of the Armenian Christian churches.

After the fall of the Safavid state, the payment of the *wazifa* by the state was discontinued. When the Qajar dynasty came to power in Iran, the state paid greater attention to religious leaders, and resumed the payment of the *wazifa* to them.

See also **Political Organization.**

BIBLIOGRAPHY

Floor, Willem. *A Fiscal History of Iran in the Safavid and Qajar Periods 1500–1929.* New York: Bibliotica Persica Press, 1999.

Mansur Sefatgol

WAZIR

In medieval Muslim society, the *wazir* (Per., vazir) was the prime minister who administered the central government for the caliph. The term *wazir* occurs in the Qur'an once (25:35), where it has the meaning of "helper"—a meaning that is loosely applied to political assistants in the early Umayyad period (661–750). The Islamic office of *wazir* developed in the early Abbasid Age (750–1258), probably during the reign of Caliph al-Mahdi (775–785). Historians believe the office evolved out of the administrative functions of the chief scribal secretary (*katib*) whose duties, functions, and authority were well established under the Byzantine and Sassanian governments that fell in part or in total, respectively, to Muslim rule in the seventh century. Thus, some of the earliest figures to serve in this important and powerful post in Baghdad and other capitals of government established by the Abbasid caliphs were chief secretaries trained under non-Muslim governments who converted to Islam and continued to apply their skills under the new Muslim rulers.

A famous line of early *wazir*s came from the Barmakid family, originally affiliated with a Buddhist temple in Balkh (Bactria) in Central Asia. A patriarch of the Barmakid family,

Khalid ibn Barmak, joined the Abbasid revolution against the Umayyad caliphate in the mid-eighth century, and he and his son and descendants served as *wazir*s to Abbasid caliphs for the next few decades. The main duty of the *wazir* was to run the government for the caliph on a day-to-day basis. As the complexity and size of the central government grew in the eighth century and thereafter, so did the duties and executive power of the *wazir*. Included among these duties was supervision over several subdivisions of administrative government (sing. *wizara*), such as the military, treasury, and post. The actual power of the *wazir* began to diminish in the late ninth century, when military warlords in Central Asia (many of whom accepted Islam) seized control of the Islamic lands beyond Baghdad and its immediate surroundings in Iraq. In later times the term *wazir* came also to mean an advisor to a ruler.

See also **Caliphate; Empires: Abbasid; Empires: Umayyad.**

Richard C. Martin

WEST, CONCEPT OF IN ISLAM

Muslim awareness of the region called "the West" reflects the changing historical nature of the West itself over the centuries. In the early centuries of Islamic history, Muslims knew of the existence of lands and peoples north of the Mediterranean, but they were identified primarily in ethnic and geographical terms and described as primitive. By the time of the Crusades (the twelfth and thirteenth centuries), the most common term used by Muslims for Western Europeans was *al-ifranj* or "Franks." This term implied a Christian and foreign identity and a relatively barbarian lifestyle.

In the early modern era there was a growing awareness of European societies. However, there was not a single generic cultural concept—like "the West"—that Muslims regularly used for European societies, although there was recognition that Europeans (often still "Franks") were Christians and therefore unbelievers. Until the nineteenth century, whatever identifying labels were used, Muslim conceptualizations of the West involved a sense of peoples and regions that were ignorant infidels and inferior to the civilization of Islam.

The situation changed dramatically in the nineteenth century. As European states expanded control over much of the Muslim world, Muslims' visions of the West were filtered through the lens of experiencing European imperialism. The West became identified with modernity. Muslim reformers sought European advisors and models as a part of their efforts to modernize society. There was recognition of the greater material prosperity of European societies and of the stronger military power of European states when compared with Muslim societies.

By the late nineteenth century there was a growing conceptualization of Western Europe as an entity. Earlier Muslim reformers had worked simply to adopt European techniques and ideas within their own societies but by late in the century, some Muslim intellectuals, like Jamal al-Din al-Afghani (d. 1897), began to argue that Muslim thought and societies could be modernized without having to become culturally European and that there were distinctive differences between Christian-based European civilization and Muslim civilization. As this conceptualization developed, many Muslims began to define "the West" as a materialist civilization, as distinguished from the spiritually strong "Eastern" civilizations like Islam.

During the first half of the twentieth century, for many Muslims, the West became the model for reform and material development. Mustafa Kemal Ataturk's vision of transformation of Turkey during the 1920s, for example, was explicitly based on a concept of the West as a model. These concepts of the West tended to be liberal in mode but by the middle of the twentieth century the West also became a source for radical programs of societal transformation. Although radical Arab socialist movements like the Ba'ath in Syria made some symbolic gestures to Muslim identity, their programs of socialist revolution involved concepts of the West that reflected Marxist and other Western radical ideologies.

By the 1960s, many Muslims began to have new concepts of the West. Influenced by major crises of Western civilization like the two world wars and the Great Depression, Western self-criticism, and Muslims' own sense of self-assertion following the decline of Western imperialism, many Muslims were more willing to be critical of the Western model, even in terms of material dimensions of life. The fixation with copying Western models was seen as weakening Muslim society, and an influential Iranian intellectual, Jalal Al-i Ahmad, called it the disease of being intoxicated by the West (*gharbzadeghi*). New movements of Islamic resurgence began to be explicitly anti-Western in both political and cultural terms, while arguing that modern Western technology and science were still important for Muslims. This new type of position was already clearly articulated in the mid-1960s by the Egyptian militant ideologue, Sayyid Qutb (executed in 1966), in his book *Milestones*. Just as the concept of the success of the West was an important part of the logic of Muslim modernizing reformers in the nineteenth and early twentieth centuries, the concept of the failure of the West was an important part of the ideological logic of the late twentieth-century Islamic resurgence.

Late in the twentieth century a new concept of the West developed among some Muslims. As Muslim minority communities became significant parts of Western societies, European and U.S. Muslims began to identify themselves as authentically "Western" as well as Muslim. Scholars like

Tariq Ramadan argued forcefully for the effective existence of a legitimate "European Islam." At the beginning of the twenty-first century, a new concept of the West as a location for truly Islamic life was emerging along with the more traditional concepts of the West as somehow being in opposition to, and completely different from, Islam.

See also **Crusades; European Culture and Islam; Islam and Other Religions.**

BIBLIOGRAPHY

Ahmad, Jalal Al-e. *Gharbzadeghi (Weststruckness).* Translated by John Green and Ahmad Alizadeh. Costa Mesa, Calif.: Mazda Publishers, 1997.

Haddad, Yvonne Yazbeck, and Smith, Jane I., eds. *Muslim Minorities in the West: Visible and Invisible.* Walnut Creek, Calif: Altamira Press, 2002.

Hourani, Albert. *Arabic Thought in the Liberal Age, 1798–1939.* Cambridge, U.K.: Cambridge University Press, 1983.

Lewis, Bernard. *The Muslim Discovery of Europe.* New York: Norton, 1982.

Voll, John O. "Islamic Renewal and the 'Failure of the West.'" In *Religious Resurgence.* Edited by Richard Antoun and Mary Elaine Hegland. Syracuse, N.Y.: Syracuse University Press, 1987.

Von Laue, Theodore H. *The World Revolution of Westernization: The Twentieth Century in Global Perspective.* New York: Oxford University Press, 1987.

John O. Voll

WOMEN, PUBLIC ROLES OF

There are religious and historical considerations concerning the inclusion of Muslim women in the public sphere. The Qur'an addresses women as individuals who are responsible for their moral individuality. It states that no individual, regardless of sex, will be forced to bear hardship beyond his or her capacity (2:233, 2:286); that each person is responsible for his/her own account (6:164, 40:17, 20.15); and that any good deed returns to the one who performs it (2:272).

Qur'anic Examples

The Qur'an further associates the call for women's individual piety with communal participation in public good, as indicated in verse 33:53. This verse invites human beings to display their individual and communal virtues for the public good. It also establishes a common obligation for both men and women to endow themselves with the ethical qualities, such as chastity, truthfulness, and patience, which work at both personal and communal levels.

Whereas the Qur'an provides the general principles governing a women's participation in public life, concrete examples of how they actually participated can also be found in the early history of Islamic civilization. Muslim women in early Islam had numerous public roles in such different fields as the economy, education, religion, and the military. For example, Khadija b. Khuwaylid (d. 619), the Prophet's first wife, was renowned among the Quraysh for her business acumen.

During wartime, Muslim women participated in the military. Muhammad used to bring his wives to the battlefields. 'A'isha b. Abu Bakr (d. 678) accompanied the Prophet to the wars and learned many military skills, such as initiating prewar negotiations between combatants, conducting, and ending wars. It should come as no surprise that Muhammad's contemporaries and companions entrusted her military ability to restore justice and the communal good. At the Battle of the Camel, in 656, she led a force of 13,000 soldiers against the caliph 'Ali (d. 661) after he failed to punish the murderer of 'Uthman (d. 656). Muslim history is replete with the tales of many other Muslim women warriors, such as Husayba (of the Battle of Uhud, in 625), Umm 'Umara (of the Battle of 'Uqraba, in 634), al-Khansa' (of the Battle of Qadisiyya, in 636), and Hind bint 'Utba and Huwayra (of the Battle of Yarmuk, in 637).

Women have also played important roles in the field of religious knowledge. 'A'isha was one of the most authoritative sources in the transmission of the prophetic tradition. Hafsa, another Prophet's wife, preserved the original collection of the Qur'an. And Fatima, the Prophet's youngest daughter, played an equally important role in the transmission of the Prophetic tradition within the eminent Shi'ite circles.

Medieval Times

Religious scholarship and outstanding personal devotion in life allowed these and other early Muslim women to insert themselves into the male-dominated public sphere. Rabi'a al-'Adawiyya (d. 801) was famous for her mystical pursuits. Sayyida Nafisa (d. 824), a female descendant of the Prophet, was respected for her piety and knowledge. Al-Qushayri's wife, the daughter of his master Abu 'Ali al-Daqqaq, was renowned for her transmission of hadith as well as for her piety.

In the medieval period, Muslim women achieved less public participation. Compared to the previous generations, only a few Muslim women were well known for transmitting prophetic traditions. Among them were Khadija bint Muhammad (d. 1389), Bay Khatun (d. 1391), and Khadija bint 'Ali (d. 1468). Women's participation also became less and less visible as their roles were subject to the general codification of Islamic law. The jurists generally agreed that the most honorable roles for women were those of wife, mother, and capable household manager. Less valued but acceptable was the role of religious teacher. The most inappropriate role for women, however, was generally held to be that of a judge or a head of the state. Nonetheless, jurists' opinions varied greatly on female leadership, and Abu Hanifa (d. 767) and Ibn Jarir al-Tabari believed that women could be appointed judges.

Benazir Bhutto, above, was Prime Minister of Pakistan from 1988–1990 and 1993–1996. AP/WIDE WORLD PHOTOS

The legal assertion of a gender-based division of societal roles excluded women from much of the public sphere, resulting in their seclusion within the private sphere. This exclusion coincided with the misogynistic assumption that women's participation in public life invites evil and creates social disorder for society, largely because of the temptation they pose to men.

Modern Movements

The influx of modernity to the Muslim world has changed the faith of many Muslim women. Opportunities for Muslim women to receive education and get involved in nation building have multiplied. By early 1900, women had become more socially and politically active. Egyptian women, such as Huda Sha'rawi (1879–1947) and Malak Hifni Nassef (1886–1918), were among the first generation of Muslim women to promote education for women and discuss the possibility that aspects of Western life might be appropriate. The call for educating women was heard as far away as Indonesia. There, men's political activist groups were quickly joined by women's organizations, which provided collaboration and support. For instance, the Muhammadiya ("Way of Muhammad," founded in 1912) had a women's counterpart in the A'isyiah ("way of 'A'isha," founded in 1917). Similarly, the women's counterpart to the Persatuan Islam (Islamic Union, 1923) was the Persatuan Islam Istri (1936), and

women supporting the male-only Nahdlatul Ulama ("Rise of Religious Scholars," 1926) formed the N.U. Muslimat (1946).

The trend toward globalization presents ever-greater opportunities for Muslim women to engage in public life. More women find that public participation provides them with an avenue for self-expression and an opportunity to become affluent, whereas others are driven into the public sphere by necessity. Muslim women have availed themselves of the opportunity to contribute to the public good in a variety of ways, such as religious teachers, lawyers, doctors, teachers, farmers, laborers, and politicians. Some Muslim women have become the heads of Muslim states, for example Benazir Bhutto of Pakistan (prime minister, 1988–1990 and 1993–1996), Megawati Sukarnoputri of Indonesia (elected president in 2001), Shaykh Hasina Wajed of Bangladesh (elected prime minister in 1996), and Tansu Ciller of Turkey (prime minister, 1993–1995).

Although women have achieved important advances in the public sphere, the idealization of the proper Muslim woman as a mother and a wife has never died. Islamists, both male and female, continue to disseminate this idea in order to counter ideas of women's roles that they see as having been imported from the West. Zaynab al-Ghazali (b. 1918), the founder of Islamic Women's Association, set forth a critique against women who modeled themselves on the Western ways of life and images, even taking to task her own early mentor, Huda Sha'rawi.

Embedded in Islamist movements throughout the Muslim world is the ideal image of a veiled wife and mother as the pillar of social order and family. Some such movements praise women's roles as mothers and wives, but still permit them to engage in public life if need drives them to do so; others confine women to their own households, denying them more public roles, as in the case of the Taliban.

See also **Feminism; Gender; Law.**

BIBLIOGRAPHY

Ahmed, Leila. *Women and Gender in Islam: Historical Roots of a Modern Debate.* New Haven, Conn.: Yale University Press, 1992.

Hibri, Azizah Y al-. "An Introduction to Muslim Women's Rights." In *Windows of Faith: Muslim Women Scholar-Activists in North America.* Edited by Gisela Webb. Syracuse, N.Y.: Syracuse University Press, 2000.

Mernissi, Fatima. *The Veil and Male Elite: A Feminist Interpretation of Women's Rights in Islam.* Translated by Mary Jo Lakeland. New York: Addison-Wesley Publishing, 1991.

Roded, Ruth. *Women in Islam and the Middle East: A Reader.* New York: Taurus, 1999.

Etin Anwar

Y

YAHYA BIN 'ABDALLAH RAMIYA (1856–1931)

Yahya bin 'Abdallah Ramiya was born named Mundu, in eastern Congo, in 1856. He became a house slave of Shaykh 'Amr bin Sulayman al-Lemki (d. 1901) at the age of eight, embraced Islam, and became a successful merchant, plantation owner, Sufi shaykh, and colonial administrator. Owing to the endogamous nature of the 'Ibadi sect to which Ramiya's master adhered, he became a Sunni. His religious studies began at the age of thirty, and he completed the Qur'an under Sharif 'Abdallah bin 'Alawi al-Jamal al-Layl around 1889. He continued studying jurisprudence (*fiqh*), mysticism (*tasawwuf*), exegesis (*tafsir*), theology (*tawhid*), and logic (*mantiq*) under Shaykh Abu Bakr bin Taha al-Jabri, matriculating around 1900.

In 1911, Shaykh Ramiya received an *Ijaza* (certificate of instruction) from Shaykh Muhammad bin Husayn al-Lughani, became a khalifa of the Qadiriyya Sufi order, and was selected the shaykh of Bagamoyo after the death in 1910 of his master, Shaykh Muhammad Ma'aruf bin Shaykh Ahmad bin Abu Bakr. Shaykh Ramiya established the Maulid in Bagamoyo, to celebrate the Prophet's birthday. This ritual became the most popular Muslim celebration on mainland Tanganyika during the colonial period, equaled by that held at the Riyadha Mosque in Lamu. In 1916, he was appointed *Liwali* (district governor) of Bagamoyo, making this former slave an influential personality throughout East Africa. He died on May 1931 and was succeeded both materially and spiritually by his son, Shaykh Muhammad Ramiya.

See also **Africa, Islam in; Tariqa.**

BIBLIOGRAPHY

Cruise O'Brien, Donal Brian, ed. *Charisma and Brotherhood in African Islam*. Oxford: Clarendon Press, 1988.

Nimtz August, H. *Islam and Politics in East Africa: the Sufi Order in Tanzania*. Minneapolis: University of Minnesota Press, 1980.

Hassan Mwakimako

YOUNG OTTOMANS

A movement committed to constitutional reform in the Ottoman Empire, the Young Ottomans were influential between 1860 and 1876. After 1865 they were the leading critics of the Ottoman state. They used the press to create public opinion and introduced political concepts such as nationalism, patriotism, and parliamentarianism into the Ottoman debates. They developed the first constitutionalist ideology in the Ottoman Empire. Civil and official leaders of the society embraced them.

From the beginning of the seventeenth century, the Ottoman Empire gradually fell behind the emerging West. Discovery of America altered the economics of gold. Europe slowly became a bigger gold holder while the Ottoman Empire began to lose its buying power. This was reflected in its tax policies that made its subjects uncomfortable and later rebellious. As Europe grew richer, it entered an era of technological development that was reflected in its military and especially in its fleet power. European colonialism took off when the Ottoman Empire became less comfortable with its institutions of government. The growth of Europe, inevitably, happened at the expense of the only non-European imperial power. Ottomans slowly lost their control of trade routes, and gave privileges to European traders in order to be able to keep them in their markets. Borrowing from the European bankers to keep the state intact was a short-term solution, which hastened the bankruptcy of the Ottomans. Modernization became an issue as the need for a better military power to fight the Europeans rose during the eighteenth century, and the entire nineteenth century was an attempt to reach an Eastern style social-military-modernity. This shaped the politics of the Middle East to the date.

After losing many of its social estates in the eighteenth century, the empire started to reform itself. At the beginning of the nineteenth century these reforms were intensified, and after 1839, with the proclamation of the Hatt-i Şerif of Gülhane (The Rescript of the Rose Chamber), the period of Tanzimat (Reformation) started. Hatt-i Şerif recognized equal rights for Muslims and non-Muslims alike, promised security of life, and administrative, educational, and economic reforms. Another document, the Hatt-i Hümayun (The Imperial Edict) of 1856, reasserted the equal rights of non-Muslims and Muslim Ottoman subjects alike. This edict also triggered some negative responses among Muslims. In 1859, the so-called Kuleli Conspiracy took place when a religious leader led a riot to which young officers and clerics also gave support. Evidently, the Tanzimat generated political and cultural conflicts for it changed the *millet* (protected religious communities) structures. Secular, ethnic, and nationalist ideals began to mobilize Ottoman subjects, first non-Muslims, then Muslims.

The Young Ottomans represented the first sound Muslim intellectual response to the Tanzimat. It was initiated by Ibrahim Şinasi (1824–1871), a young Ottoman bureaucrat, and a protege of Mustafa Reşit Paşa, director of the Army Arsenal (Tophane). Şinasi entered the Arsenal and rose within the bureaucracy. He was sent to Europe by Reşit for further education. In Paris he attended the literary soirées of Ernest Renan and Lamartine. In 1855, he was a leading Tanzimat bureaucrat but his high profile threatened some of his colleagues. As a result of internal conflicts, he was never allowed to hold a significant position. He was especially disliked by 'Ali Paşa, the grand wazir. After 1860, Şinasi became involved in literature. He started his own paper *Tasvir-i efkar* (Description of Ideas, 1861–1870), which later became the news organ of the Young Ottomans. In 1864, he asked for a government post and was refused by 'Ali Paşa one last time. He went into exile in Paris, leaving *Tasvir-i efkar* to Namik Kemal (1840–1888), a member of his circle.

The intellectuals who became associated with Şinasi and his paper were critics of the government. They accused 'Ali and Fuat Paşas of using Tanzimat to establish the autocratic rule of elite bureaucrats, of undermining Islam and Ottoman culture, and of not defending the empire against the influences of the Western powers. In 1865, six men formed a secret group called the Patriotic Alliance, to criticize 'Ali Paşa and act against him. Most of these men were former employees of the Translation Bureau of the Porte, and were thus exposed to international developments. They shared a common knowledge of European civilization and concern over the dissolution of the Ottoman Empire. Their names were Mehmet Bey, Nuri Bey, Reşat Bey, Namik Kemal, Ayatollah Bey, and Refik Bey.

As the alliance grew, three intellectuals became its leading figures: Namik Kemal, Ziya Paşa (1825–1880), and 'Ali Suavi. Under their guidance the Young Ottomans used *Tasvir-i efkar* to communicate their ideas. Eventually, they were censored and in 1867 Kemal and Ziya had to escape to Europe. They continued to communicate their work through foreign post offices that were outside the scope of official Ottoman censorship. In Europe, the Young Ottomans formed an opposition movement, based in London and Paris. An Ottoman-Egyptian prince, Mustafa Fazil, who tried to use the movement to pressure the Ottoman government for his own ends, sponsored them. Mustafa Fazil had also helped Ibrahim Şinasi, in 1861, with the establishment of *Tasvir-i efkar*.

Later 'Ali Suavi also went to exile. Suavi represented the more Islamic reaction to the Tanzimat and it was essentially after his arrival that the Young Ottomans became aware of their differences. Kemal and Ziya's understanding of parliament and democracy had little resemblance to 'Ali's conception of these institutions. Their newspaper, called *Hurriyet* (Freedom), was closed due to the conflicts among the leaders of the movement. In 1870, most of the Young Ottomans returned to the Ottoman Empire and continued to express their ideas. They were subjected to further censorship and exile.

Although the Young Ottomans were liberals, they were often conservative in their criticism of Tanzimat leaders like 'Ali Paşa. They believed the reforms undermined Muslim and Ottoman identity. They admired European nations and parliamentary systems, but they argued that the Ottoman Empire was different from the European countries. They accepted that the subjects of the empire were heterogeneous, varying in race, religion, and language. For the future of the Ottoman state, they argued, it was necessary to implement a constitution, a parliament, and Ottomanism, an ideology that combined Ottoman culture and Islam with modern nationalism. In their view a parliament would provide a political forum where these differences could be consolidated and government policies developed. Participation in such a system would generate a feeling of belonging and emphasize the concept of *vatan* (fatherland). Some of the Young Ottomans argued that the entire *millet* system had to be abolished in order to allow a full expression of Ottomanism.

Ironically, 'Ali Paşa and Fuat Paşa were modernizers too. They belonged to the same generation of reformists as the Young Ottomans but they believed that reforms had to be achieved through a strong, centralized state. In their view, representative government would delay modernization and undermine the power of the state.

In part, it was the Young Ottomans who inspired the civilian and military officials who dethroned Sultan Abdulaziz in 1876. In the same year, the first constitution and the first parliament were introduced in the Ottoman Empire, under Sultan Abd al-Hamid II (Ar., 'Abd al-Hamid II). These developments can also be attributed to the influences of the

Young Ottomans, who saw to it that the first constitution of the empire emphasized Ottomanism as its ideological basis.

Among the leaders of the Young Ottomans, Namik Kemal proved to be the most influential. Later generations, and especially the Young Turks who emerged after 1889, embraced his image and his fervent patriotism.

See also **Pan-Islam; Reform: Arab Middle East and North Africa.**

BIBLIOGRAPHY

Mardin, Serif. *The Genesis of Young Ottoman Thought*. Princeton, N.J.: Princeton University Press, 1962.

Shaw, Stanford J., and Shaw, Ezel Kural. *History of the Ottoman Empire and Modern Turkey*, Vol. II: *Reform, Revolution, and Republic: The Rise of Modern Turkey, 1808–1975*. London: Cambridge University Press, 1977.

Murat C. Mengüç

YOUNG TURKS

Young Turks is the term generally applied to the opposition to the Ottoman sultan Abdulhamit II's rule (Ar., 'Abd al-Hamid, 1876–1908). Although the foundations of the movement can be traced back to 1889, it only became politically active prior to the Young Turk Revolution in 1908. Its members at the time forced the reinstatement of the constitution and the parliament after thirty years of autocracy. Between 1908 and 1918 it was the Young Turks who governed the Ottoman Empire.

The Young Turks belonged to the generation following that of the Young Ottomans, whose legacy was the constitutional era inaugurated in December 1876. But when in February 1878 Sultan Abdulhamit II dissolved the parliament and embarked on absolute rule, an opposition slowly began to form underground. In 1889 a group of students from the imperial Medical School formed an alliance called the Association for the Union of Ottomans. By 1895 they had changed their name to the Committee for Union and Progress (CUP). The CUP was mostly active in Europe and Egypt. Its members came from diverse backgrounds, ethnically and professionally. Due to Abdulhamit's autocratic rule, many educated Turks, Greeks, Kurds, Arabs, Albanians, and Armenians came to support the idea of Ottomanism, a nineteenth-century ideology that combined Ottoman culture and Islam with modern nationalism. In 1902 the First Congress of Ottoman Liberals was held in Paris where the opposition to the sultan came into the open.

In 1906 some military officers and government officials formed another group called the Ottoman Freedom Society,

in Salonika. They joined the CUP in 1907 and because of their reputation for action these men became the ruling faction. From then on the new coalition was named the Committee for Progress and Union (CPU). In the same year, between 27 and 29 December, the Second Congress of Ottoman Liberals met in Paris and resolved to topple Abdülhamit II from power.

By the spring of 1908 those CPU members who had served in the Ottoman army in Macedonia began to act more openly. They reacted to Abdülhamit's efforts to discipline and spy on their activities by assassinating inspectors and others loyal to the sultan. In July, Adjunct Major Ahmed Niyazi Bey and later Enver Bey renounced their loyalty to the sultan and took their troops into the mountains to engage in guerilla activity. Later, the special military commander sent to take control of the Macedonian army was assassinated by a CUP member. The CPU further pressured the sultan with a series of telegrams threatening to occupy the capital if the constitution were not reinstated. In July 1908, Abdülhamit felt obliged to reinstitute the 1876 constitution, inaugurating the second constitutional era, also known as the Young Turks' revolution.

The event was celebrated by every ethnic group that stood to acquire greater security. Yet when the parliament began meeting, the division among the Young Turks's supporters became clear. Two major factions were identified: unionists CPU and the liberals. The unionists favored a strong centralized state to achieve modernization and progress. The liberals wanted a decentralized and autonomous polity benefiting non-Muslim and non-Turkish groups. The multireligious and multinational population of the empire eventually forced the Young Turks to adopt a middle way, which has been called Ottomanism. Meanwhile, Turkist and Islamist thinkers were still involved in the government.

In April 1909 an insurrection led by an Islamist organization made it clear that Muslim influences were strong among the unionists. But in 1912 a military coup brought the liberals into power. Meanwhile the demographics of the empire were changing: the Ottoman army had suffered repeated defeats in the Balkans, and during its last withdrawal from 1911 to 1913, the empire lost almost all of its remaining European lands and one-quarter of its population. The unionists took advantage of the political turmoil and in January 1913 took over the government once and for all. By June, they had eliminated the liberal opposition.

Throughout World War I, with the deportation and ethnic cleansing of Armenians and the arrival of Turkish people from the Balkans and Caucasus, the empire population became increasingly Muslim-Turkish and Arab. The unionists started to rely more on religion. Their pan-Islamism was often aimed at appeasing Arab constituencies who were displeased with the empire.

In the prewar period, both the Turkish and the Arab nationalists were intent on forming a solid nationalist ideology. Under the CPU, official and popular sentiment started to embrace Turkish nationalism. The Turkish Hearth (Türk Ocagi), founded after March 1912, was a side organization of the CPU whose original duty was to advocate Islamism and Ottomanism. But they were also trying to convince Turkish people that the only way for the empire to survive was to embrace Turkish nationalism. The Turkish Hearth was also responsible for propagating the use of Turkish instead of other languages. Under CPU pressure, government officials increased the use of Turkish in government administration, and as the religious schools and courts came under state control, Turkish started to predominate. The immigrating Caucasian and eastern European Turks participated in these developments, and a project to unite all the Turks, or all the Turanian people, began.

After 1914 the notion of Arab independence emerged, along with the possibility of the Ottoman Empire's fall and the inevitability of subsequent foreign hegemony. Many such ideas were current in Beirut, Damascus, and Basra, where the independence movements in the Balkans had already been noted and the Young Turks had been active. Triggered by an alliance between Sharif Husayn of Mecca and the British, in 1916, the Arab Revolt started the separation of Arab lands from the Ottoman Empire.

During World War I, the Ottoman Empire proved incapable of fighting on a scale equal to the European forces. The end of the war in 1918 also signaled the end of the Young Turks era. After the ensuing war for independence, the new Turkish republic was formed, owing much of its social infrastructure to the Young Turks. Although under the CPU the state ideology remained Ottomanist and Islamist, the emergence of non-Turkish Muslim nationalist movements among the Balkan and Arab populations strongly influenced Turkish intellectuals and statesmen. The major intellectual development of the Young Turks era was Turkish nationalism. The secular ideas of Young Turks leaders like Ziya Gökalp found popular support long after the CPU.

See also **Modernization, Political: Administrative, Military, and Judicial Reform; Revolution: Modern; Young Ottomans.**

BIBLIOGRAPHY

Ahmad, Feroz. *The Young Turks: The Committee for Union and Progress in Turkish Politics, 1908–1914.* London: Oxford University Press, 1969.

Hanioglu, H. Sukru. *Preparation for a Revolution: The Young Turks, 1902–1908.* New York: Oxford University Press, 2001.

Kayali, Hasan. *Arabs and Young Turks: Ottomanism, Arabism, and Islam in the Ottoman Empire.* Berkeley: University of California Press, 1997.

Lewis, Bernard. *The Emergence of Modern Turkey.* New York: Oxford University Press, 1961.

Murat C. Mengüç

YOUTH MOVEMENTS

Youth typically refers to the ages fifteen to twenty-four or eleven to twenty-nine. Analysts view youths as intellectually idealistic, psychologically impatient, practically inexperienced, socially liberal, and politically radical. Since they often lack a socially defined position in society, they tend to demand more far-reaching changes in society than their elders. Youth movements also bear these characteristics.

Although youth movements are modern phenomena, youths' collective involvement in politics is not new to the Middle Eastern societies. The *futuwwa* brotherhoods in medieval periods consisted of semireligious, voluntary, urban, youth organizations engaged in acts of chivalry (*javan-mardi*) protecting the less fortunate, supporting public causes, and at times acting in parallel with official security forces. Though not always viewed positively or engaged in benevolent acts, the *futuwwa* groups represent early forms of collective action by youths in Muslim societies. These youth organizations imposed strict ethical standards on their members and required strong group loyalty.

Youth movements in the Middle East emerge in the context of politics or popular culture. Youths express themselves through sports, music, and dress. Because most Middle Eastern states are undemocratic, officials have considered the rise of independent social movements a threat to political stability. Any issue that captures youths' attention, even if nonpolitical in nature, takes on a political character, and state officials respond accordingly, exerting control and resorting to repression.

The region's youth movements are usually connected to broader changes under way in society, especially political and cultural developments. Influenced by such developments, these movements in turn intensify the broader changes. For instance, in 1908, drawing young members of the military, a liberal opposition movement known as the Young Turks forced the Ottoman sultan, 'Abd al-Hamid II (r. 1876–1909), to restore the constitution and parliament that he had suspended in 1878. Youths were also energetic partners in most anticolonial struggles. In Iran, young people, especially university students, were an important force in the push to nationalize the oil industry in the early 1950s. Nowhere have youths' struggles been more intense and persistent as in the Israeli-occupied Palestinian territories, where they have borne the burden of two major uprisings, the *Intifada* (1987–1988) and *Al-Aqsa Intifada* (2000–2002). Youths also fought most fervently during the Iran-Iraq war (1980–1988) and in the war that resulted in the withdrawal of the Israeli military from south Lebanon in May 2000. In the 1970s and 1980s, both leftist and Islamic associations grew in countries as far apart as Egypt and Pakistan, polarizing university campuses.

Having little stake in the status quo, young people join opposition groups hoping to create an "ideal society." Both governments and their oppositions exploit youth's abundant idealism and impassioned activism. Because oral traditions are prevalent in Muslim societies, religious and political leaders use their speaking skills to establish credibility, cultivate charisma, and recruit and mobilize followers, particularly youths. In the late 1950 Egypt, Jamal 'Abd al-Nasser's (1918–1970) powerful lectures drew youth support for his policy of Arab unity. During the 1970s, 'Ali Shari'ati's (1933–1977) oratory won over Iranian youths to his radical Islamic ideology. In the 1980s and 1990s, 'Abd al-Karim Sorush's (b. 1945) deft use of language has similarly appealed to Iranian youths in the Islamic Republic, who sympathize with his liberal Islamic ideology. Often, religious leaders attract youths to their political causes through mosques or underground networks, as the Egyptian Muslim Brotherhood (al-Ikhwan al-Muslimin), founded in 1928, and the Iranian Fedaiyan-e Islam, created in 1945, have shown.

In societies marked by limited upward political and economic mobility, student movements enable youths to crack the system and open up spaces for participation in the politics. Many nationalist leaders began their political socialization in student organizations. Realizing this fact, governments also try to recruit students to their administrations. In the early 1970s, the shah of Iran, Muhammad Reza Pahlevi (1919–1980), undermined the growing power of the Confederation of the Iranian Students in the United States and Europe by luring its leaders to lucrative government posts. The Saudi and Kuwaiti governments have likewise co-opted their young opposition and with greater success than the shah.

The correlation between the emergence of youth movements and economic decline is not strong in the Middle East. Since most youth movements are sociocultural and political, they have arisen during both economic prosperity and decline. In the 1970s, a guerilla movement emerged in Iran as the oil export boom brought new wealth. During the mid-1990s, proreform students formed a movement, reacting to the last decade's political developments rather than to poor economic conditions. The relationship between youth movements and the Iranian state has been discontinuous. When in late 1940s, Mohammad Mosaddeq (1880–1967), then elected prime minister, launched a campaign to end the British control of the Iranian oil industry, students backed both his stance as well as his antimonarchy efforts. However, once the CIA-supported coup ended Mosaddeq's government in 1953, restoring the monarchy, the student movement opposed the shah's rule by using both violent and nonviolent tactics.

In the political arena, the locus of Middle Eastern youth movements is often universities. Where allowed, political organizations and parties establish subsidiaries in universities for recruitment and mobilization. Where outlawed, opposition groups still operate on campuses underground for political agitation and recruitment. In the absence of serious political parties in many societies, student movements become the principal advocates of ideological and political trends in society and a vanguard of change. In the 1980s and 1990s, a host of sociological variables has contributed to the rising expectations among the youth and created fertile grounds for youth activism. In 1998, 40 percent of the Middle Eastern population was under fifteen years old, as opposed to one-fifth for the developed world. The general decline in oil prices around the world, coupled with increasing population, has led to economic decline in the Middle East. Unemployment, aggravated by the increase in the rate of rural-urban migration and urbanization, has led to disenchantment among the youth making further demands for education, social freedom, jobs, housing, and resources for establishing a family. These factors have delivered frustrated youth to extremist ideologies, especially Islamic fundamentalism. The 1990s has witnessed massive recruitment among the youth by Islamic radicals like HAMAS in Palestine, Hezbollah in Lebanon, the Jama'a Islamiyya in Egypt, the Mobilization (Basij) Forces in Iran, and al-Qa'ida in Afghanistan.

The most interesting demographic change has been a sharp increase in the number of young women in Middle Eastern universities outnumbering men in a number of fields. In the second decade of the revolution in Iran, more females studied in various fields, despite official restrictions. In Syria, Turkey, Jordan, and Iraq, the governments encouraged female participation in most aspects of social and political life. Among the Persian Gulf countries, Kuwait, Yemen, and Oman have developed policies promoting female education and social participation, but except in Kuwait, success has been generally slow and limited.

The dominant features of student movements in the region are radicalism, intellectual idealism, anti-authoritarianism, anti-imperialism, anti-Americanism, and nationalism. The scope of these movements is national and the respective state apparati are their targets of attack. Iran's student movement exemplifies these characteristics the best. A close look at this movement will demonstrate the dynamics and diversity of the student movement in the region.

The Student Movement in Iran

Before mass protests erupted against the Pahlevi regime in 1978, the Iranian student movement splintered into Islamic, liberal, and Marxist factions. The secular or non-Islamic associations, the strongest and largest groups, had ties to the guerrilla movement operating outside of universities. The Muslim associations comprised a small segment of the student movement and had loose contacts with Ayatollah Ruhollah

Khomeini (1902–1989) and the Freedom Movement of Iran. All these associations cooperated to topple the regime. During the shah's final years, students initiated the process that culminated in revolution. Student poetry readings, lecture series, and political forums were catalysts in a chain of events that crippled the old regime. In 1977, when demonstrations against the shah became widespread, the student associations recruited many members, organized numerous rallies in major cities, and became supporters of Khomeini's call for the shah's departure.

Once the revolution succeeded, students expanded their activities, joined revolutionary forces, and occupied numerous properties belonging to the fleeing former officials. By the time Khomeini returned to Iran, student associations had established de facto headquarters for their respective groups in universities. Faced with the tasks of institution and state building, the clerics considered student demands as obstacles to the consolidation of their power, using the Muslim Student Organization as an instrument to challenge its secular counterparts.

On 4 November 1979, after an earlier attempt by the Marxist organization, the Iranian Fedaiyan Organization, a Muslim student group engaged in the boldest and most consequential act in the history of student activism in Iran: the seizure of the U.S. Embassy and the holding of American diplomats as hostages for 444 days. Khomeini endorsed the takeover, capitalizing on this event to undermine opposition to his new theocracy. In 1980, the secular student organizations were effectively outlawed and their members physically attacked by the religious vigilantes. Muslim student associations identified and helped to arrest non-Islamic students, sabotaging their political and cultural activities. This was the first time ever that elements of the Iranian student movement turned against each other. Later, Khomeini ordered universities closed until purged of un-Islamic elements and the grounds laid for their Islamization. He created the Council for Cultural Revolution to review faculty and students' activities as well as university programs. Many activist students and faculty members were fired or arrested for their affiliations with political groups.

When universities reopened two years later, leftist, nationalist, secular, and opposition students and professors were gone, with new Islamic and ideological criteria defined for admission and recruitment. Female students were barred from studying certain disciplines. In addition to meeting educational criteria, students had to show commitment to Islamic values and have an untainted moral history. Until Khomeini's death in 1989, these restrictions remained in force, although students and the faculty had devised mechanisms of resistance.

In the 1980s, numerous Muslim associations were formed at colleges. New admission quotas for war veterans and the armed forces' families enabled these associations to grow.

These associations encouraged student participation in government rallies, reported on antigovernment activities and faculty criticisms of the state ideology, and implemented state gender policies by monitoring male-female interactions on campus. In short, the student movement, formerly an active, independent, creative, and antiestablishment force, was transformed into a watchdog of the state, alienating most students who feared religious vigilantism and spying by the government. These associations lost their appeal among students who felt increasingly apathetic and disenchanted. Although these associations' members were closely affiliated with the regime and some occupied government positions, conservatives still suspected some students whose nonconformity and radical outlook they found troubling. Conservative religious organizations established parallel Islamic student associations in the universities to discourage unfavorable and unpredictable activities by others.

Sociological and political factors during the revolution's second decade inspired another momentous rise in student and youth activism. According to the Secretariat of the Supreme Council of the Youth, of 60,055,488 total population in 1997, 40.4 percent, or 24,248,768, were eleven to twenty-nine years old—a 37.3 percent increase since 1987 and more than 104.7 percent growth since 1977. With the doubling of the population between 1978 and 1996, the number of institutions of higher education increased as well. Alienation, disillusion, and frustration among youths intensified. Islamic vigilantes constantly interfered in youths' and women's lives, compelling them to obey strict religious codes of behavior.

After 1988, Iran's clerical establishment split into two major factions. With the decline of the Islamic leftists' fortunes during the 1989 to 1996 period, the student organizations lost their influence within the government. Many of its influential members began careers in political journalism. Radical individuals who had served in high-ranking positions during Khomeini's rule were isolated and pushed to the background. President Mohammad Khatami's election in 1997 breathed new life into the student movement. An unprecedented coalition of dissatisfied youths and women, politically isolated supporters of the Islamic left, and other segments of the public voted for Khatami. A new chapter in student activism had begun.

New student organizations emerged, and activists challenged the conservative faction's authority within the Islamic Republic. Reacting to broad support for Khatami in universities, the conservatives introduced measures to depoliticize students and asserted more control over their organizations. All these measures failed, ironically reinvigorating student activism. As the conservatives blocked Khatami's reformist policies, students marched in his support. As student demonstrations against the judiciary and the conservative faction multiplied, one of the protests, on 8 July 1999, led to a deadly

The Thai Muslim Student Association protesting in front of the Government House in Bangkok in September 2001. © REUTERS NEWMEDIA INC./CORBIS

attack on a student dormitory in Tehran by Islamic vigilantes and the police. This attack provoked three days of student uprisings in Tehran and several other cities in that month.

After these uprisings, the government cracked down on the students, leaving them alienated, agitated, and restless as they looked for any opportunity to express their frustrations. Protests spilled over from the universities to the soccer fields, cinemas, and music concerts. Disturbances in various cities following the loss of an international soccer game by the national soccer team in 2001 highlighted widespread discontent with the status quo. In November 2002, students started a series of mass protests at a death sentence passed against Hashem Aghajari, a reformist university professor, for alleged blasphemous remarks about clerics in Iran. In early June 2003, students began a new round of protests in commemoration of an attack on a student dormitory on 9 July 1999. Most of these irregular and spontaneous protests have lacked a clearly articulated political agenda. The government's systematic efforts to weaken the student movement have led youths to become more spontaneous and momentum-driven. Most protests have begun as friendly gatherings rather than as a result of any organization or planning. In fact,

the ruling clerics have successfully crushed these protests, despite their persistence, because the students lack organization, goals, and leadership. At the end of February 2003, the students' Office for Consolidating Unity finally expressed its disillusionment with President Khatami by withdrawing its support for the reformist camp in the local elections. A number of student organizations have emerged since, demanding an end to theocracy and the establishment of a secular government based on the principles enshrined in the Universal Declaration of Human Rights.

Conclusion

During the 1990s, youths in the Middle Eastern countries, especially Iran, have shown a strong desire for Western cultural icons, music, and arts, as they reject the imposition of undemocratic, traditional, and strict policies on their lives. Part of this desire for more freedom is due to the limitations imposed by the states. However, part of it is a demonstration effect: The communications revolution and globalization of local regional economies have stimulated youth's attraction to a material lifestyle as well as to the cultural norms and political freedoms typically identified with Western societies. Government authorities have resorted to various means to limit these demands: In Saudi Arabia, Kuwait, Iraq, Syria, and Yemen, state-sponsored programs are designed to respond to the youths' demands by creating synthetic opportunities where nonoffensive and nonpolitical forums are created for releasing youthful energy. While sport has been a successful means for this purpose, cultural and social programs have had little success in tempering these energies. The Iranian government has often resorted to moral campaigns against vice, publicly arresting and flogging violators, thus furthering youth's anger against the government. Interestingly, the appeal of the West contradicts the rejection of the same culture during the Iranian revolution two decades ago. Coupled with the sociological factors discussed earlier, these developments will surely give a new impetus to student activism in the years to come.

See also **Futuwwa; HAMAS; Ikhwan al-Muslimin; Khomeini, Ruhollah; Muslim Student Association of North America; Qaʿida, al-.**

BIBLIOGRAPHY

Mahdi, Ali Akbar. "The Student Movement in the Islamic Republic of Iran." *Journal of Iranian Research and Analysis* 15, no. 2 (November 1999): 5–32.

Matin Asgari, Afshin. *Iranian Student Opposition to the Shah.* Costa Mesa, Calif.: Mazda Publisher, 2001.

Meijer, Roel, ed. *Alienation or Integration of Arab Youth: Between Family, State and Street.* Richmond, U.K.: Curzon Press, 2000.

Ali Akbar Mahdi

YUSUF ALI, ʿABDULLAH (1872–1953)

Author of the most widely read English translation of the Qurʾan, ʿAbdullah Yusuf Ali presents a unique figure in Islamic modernism at the turn of the twentieth century.

Yusuf Ali was the son of a police officer of Gujarati parentage. With communal Muslim schooling in Bombay, he looked beyond his Bohra Shʿite origins and was extremely concerned about the fate of Muslims in British India and beyond. But he was very successful in achieving the highest rank in British schooling. He earned a scholarship at Cambridge, and after graduation won a place in India's civil service. Yusuf Ali honored these two traditions, British and Muslim Indian, with equal vigor. For his devotion to the British cause in the First World War, he was awarded the title of Commander of the British Empire. He was called upon to represent loyal British Muslims against pan-Islamic tendencies in India. Yet, he was still respected by Muslims like Muhammad Iqbal, who called upon him to head a Muslim school.

Yusuf Ali, however, was more than an anglophile and communal Muslim. His translation of the Qurʾan represents the kernel of his ideas on Islam, mysticism, and progress. In addition, he wrote a number of pamphlets and articles on Islamic issues in which he took a critical stance on both Sir Sayyid Ahmad Khan and Sir Muhammad Iqbal. His was a vision of Islam that stood on an equal footing with other religions, just as he viewed Indian Muslims on an equal footing with the family of nations.

In the closing years of the twentieth century, Muslims revisited the legacy of Yusuf Ali's widely read translation. Perturbed by the modernist and mystical tendencies in his translation, Islamist groups have tried to expurgate his commentary of so-called unorthodox leanings.

See also **Qurʾan; Translation.**

BIBLIOGRAPHY

Sherif, M. A., *Searching for Solace: A Biography of Abdullah Yusuf Ali, Interpreter of the Qurʾan.* Islam in South Asia Series. Islamabad: Islamic Research Institute, 2000.

Yusuf Ali, Abdullah. *The Holy Qurʾan.* Lahore: Sh. Muhammad Ashraf, 1934.

Abdulkader Tayob

Z

ZAND, KARIM KHAN
(c. 1705–1779)

Karim Khan Zand was the ruler of western Iran from 1751 until 1779. A chieftain of the minor tribe of the Zand, of the Lakk branch of the Lors, Karim Khan led his contingent from the debacle of Nader Shah's army in 1747 back to their inner-Zagros mountain ranges. In alliance with ʿAli Mardan Khan of the Bakhtyari, he established a puppet Safavid shah in Isfahan and consolidated the southwest under their rule. In 1751 he overthrew ʿAli Mardan, and subsequently defeated several other contestants for regional power among Afghan, Afshar, and Qajar leaders. By 1765 he had emerged as de facto ruler of the whole of Iran except Khorasan, with his capital at Shiraz.

Karim did not assume the title of shah, even when the putative Safavid king predeceased him, but ruled as *vakil al-raʿaya*, "people's representative" (the term for a traditional local ombudsman). He encouraged internal and foreign trade, granting the East India Company a base at Bushire, and rebuilt Shiraz (many of his fine buildings are still standing). A nominal Shiʿite, he practiced religious toleration, and did not actively seek the endorsement of the ulema. In 1776, after a year's siege, he captured the port of Basra in Ottoman Iraq, but his death in 1779 brought a withdrawal.

The Vakil, as he is affectionately known, has left a reputation as a strong but humane and unassuming ruler who restored a measure of peace and prosperity to Iran. His successors were by contrast cruel, rapacious, and unpopular, excepting the last, Lotf ʿAli Khan (1789–1794), and soon succumbed to the rising power of the Qajars.

BIBLIOGRAPHY

Perry, John R. "Justice for the Underprivileged: The Ombudsman Tradition of Iran." *Journal of Near Eastern Studies* 37 (1978): 203–215.

Perry, John R. *Karim Khan Zand: A History of Iran, 1747–1779.* Chicago: The University of Chicago Press, 1979.

John R. Perry

ZANZIBAR, SAʿIDI SULTANATE OF

The Omani dynasty of Zanzibar, under the able leadership of Sayyid Saʿid bin Sultan (1791–1856), inaugurated a new era in the commercial life of East Africa. Zanzibar had steadfastly remained loyal to Omani rule whether under the Yarubi dynasty, which had driven the Portuguese out of East Africa by the end of the seventeenth century, or under the Yarubi successors, the Busaʿidi dynasty, which came to power by the 1740s. Sayyid Saʿid was able to assert his sovereignty over much of the East African coastal strip but not over the Mazruʿi of Mombasa (his major competitor) who held out until 1837. He eventually moved his capital from Muscat to Zanzibar by the 1830s. The sultan was a master of intrigues and was able to deal with potential rivals such as Kimweri, the Kilindi ruler of Usambara, by disbursing gifts to Kimweri's officials, who were urged not to lose sight of the sultan's interests.

Major changes took place in East Africa after the arrival of Sayyid Saʿid. In fact, East Africa experienced what can be termed as a commercial revival, brought about by expansion in trading activities, new agricultural ventures (introduction of clove plantations), reforms in currency and customs administration, and encouragement of people with trading skills, such as Indians and Omani merchants, to settle in Zanzibar. The expansion in the coastal economy confirmed Zanzibar's privileged position as the hub of the international trade with its control of coastal ports through which products such as ivory and slaves filtered from the interior. The sultan's aggressive economic policies encouraged the trading

Sayyid Bargash Bin Saʿid, the Sultan of Zanzibar, circa 1880 with members of his court. The Zanzibar Sultanate fostered the growth of higher learning and of the intellectual community. HULTON ARCHIVE/GETTY IMAGES

caravans to venture into the interior of East Africa, and wherever the Arab and Swahili traders went Islam went with them. This is how Islam gained a foothold in the interior of East Africa along the trading routes as far as Buganda, where contact was made with the King of Buganda.

The nineteenth century also witnessed the growth of Islamic higher education in the whole coastal region. This growth was due primarily to the Omani presence and, in particular, the Zanzibar sultanate, which contributed to literacy and to the intellectual life of the community. Written texts became more readily available and this led to greater knowledge and adherence to the written orthodox tradition, which was stimulated by the Saʿidi sultanate. Religious scholars from Arabia—mainly from Hadramaut and Oman, the Comoros, and the Benadir coast—began to arrive in the coastal towns and especially in Zanzibar, which emerged as the leading center of Islamic learning in East Africa. Later some of the leading scholars in East Africa (such as Sayyid Smait and Abdalla Bakathir) traveled to the Middle East where they supplemented their education. Moreover, the Zanzibar sultans employed religious scholars, of both Shafiʿi and Ibadhi rites, as Muslim judges. Nevertheless, Omani Ibadhi influence was very superficial on the mainland. In fact, not only did the Ibadhis as a community lose Arabic as their first language (many had African mothers), but in addition

some of the leading Ibadhi families ended up following Shafiʿi rites.

See also **Africa, Islam in; Mazrui.**

BIBLIOGRAPHY

Farsy, Shaykh Abdalla Saleh al-. *The Shafi Ulama of East Africa, ca 1830–1970.* Edited by Randall Pouwels. Madison: University of Wisconsin, 1989.

Pouwels, Randall. *Horn and Crescent: Cultural Change and Traditional Islam on the East African Coast, 800–1900.* New York: Cambridge University Press, 1987.

Abdin Chande

ZAR

Zar refers to a type of spirits, the afflictions such spirits may cause, and the rituals aimed at preventing or curing these afflictions. It is one of the most widely distributed "cults of afflictions" in Africa and the Middle East. Its diffusion owes much to the slave trade and to the migration of people associated with the pilgrimage to Mecca. *Zar* spirits and *zar* practices are found throughout eastern North Africa and in areas of East Africa and the Middle East, including Tunisia, Algeria, Morocco, Sudan, Ethiopia, Egypt, Somalia, Arabia, Iran, and Israel. The *zar* cult has also influenced other possession practices in East and West Africa. Little is known of the cult's origins, but its presence has been documented in the Sudan since the mid-nineteenth century and in Ethiopia since at least the eighteenth century. Etymologically, most scholars consider the term *zar* to derive, not from Arabic, but from Persian or, more plausibly, from Amharic.

Popularly, however, the word is believed to originate from *zara*, "he visited," an Arabic word that was later corrupted. The geographic distribution of the word *zar* has led researchers to consider the many cults of spirit possession in northeast Africa as part of a single, historically connected phenomenon. While *zar* practices exhibit considerable variations from place to place, it is nonetheless possible to identify some shared characteristics of the spirit-host relation. Involvement with the *zar* generally follows a period of illness, during which all medical options have been exhausted. Eventually, the sufferer is diagnosed as being afflicted by a spirit. Treatment involves initiation into the *zar* cult during a propitiatory ceremony in which the initiate will ideally enter a trance, allowing the spirit to possess her or his body so as to affirm its identity and reveal its requirements. Once initiated, devotees must continuously negotiate the terms of their relationships with the possessing spirits. They express their commitment to intrusive *zar* by attending ceremonies, making offerings, and fulfilling ritual, moral, and social requirements. Getting well thus becomes a lifelong exercise, much of which is part of daily experience rather than being restricted to dramatic ritual.

In many areas, the *zar* cult has retained pre-Islamic or pre-Christian features. It has strongly been influenced by these two religions, and has influenced them, in turn. The complex and creative ways that *zar* has simultaneously competed with, adapted to, and borrowed from Islam or Christianity often means that spirit devotees see no incompatibility between their commitment to the *zar* and their identities as Christian or Muslims. To them, possession is part of a wider religious enterprise.

Not everyone agrees with this assessment, however. Some see *zar* as being antithetical to Islam or Christianity. Such divisions often follow gender lines. Thus, for northern Sudanese women, *zar* falls squarely within the purview of Islam, whereas their male counterparts find that relinquishing control of one's body to a possessing spirit is simply sinful and un-Islamic. Despite such condemnations, *zar* has continued to thrive in both rural and urban areas; in the latter it often provides supportive social networks for newcomers.

Men may criticize their wives' practices of assuaging the spirits, but they rarely interfere when their womenfolk stage a propitiatory ceremony. While they may want nothing to do with *zar*, men implicitly acknowledge the spirits' role in the preservation of fertility and prosperity. Though in some areas, men can become initiated, it is women whom *zar* most afflict, mainly with infertility. The preponderance of women has traditionally been explained as a strategy of redress for marginalized or powerless individuals in male-centered cultures. From this perspective, *zar* is nothing but a means to bring public attention to one's plight and achieve momentary power.

More recent interpretations have pointed to the multiple ways in which *zar* participants distill the lessons of history, reflect upon their subordinate status, and assess the relevance of cultural values by conjuring up images of amoral, foreign, and powerful spirits. Far from constituting a refuge from oppressive reality, *zar* is seen as a cultural resource that transcends the context of illness and is drawn upon by people to make sense of certain problems and experiences of everyday life.

See also **African Culture and Islam; Miracles.**

BIBLIOGRAPHY

Boddy, Janice. *Wombs and Alien Spirits: Women, Men, and the Zar Cult in Northern Sudan.* Madison: University of Wisconsin Press, 1989.

Lewis, Ioan M.; Al-Safi, Ahmed; and Hurreiz, Sayyid, eds. *Women's Medicine: The Zar-Bori Cult in Africa and Beyond.* Edinburgh: Edinburgh University Press, 1991.

Messing, Simon D. "Group Therapy and Social Status in the Zar Cult of Ethiopia." *American Anthropologist* 60, no. 6 (1958): 1120–1126.

Young, Allan. "Why Amhara Get Kureynya: Sickness and Possession in an Ethiopian Zar Cult." *American Ethnologist* 2, no. 3 (1975): 567–584.

Adeline Masquelier

ZAYTUNA

Zaytuna, an important mosque and cultural institution in the city of Tunis, was founded in 732 C.E. Zaytuna (in Arabic, "the Olive Tree") mosque became an organized Islamic university in the twelfth century and thereafter was considered one of the most important centers of Islamic scholarship and instruction in North Africa, together with Al-Azhar in Cairo and Al-Qarawiyyin in Fez. Qur'anic exegesis, Arabic grammar, and Islamic law (*shari'a*) were the main subjects offered at Zaytuna. Among the many historical figures who taught at Zaytuna were Muhammad Ibn 'Arafa, one of the greatest scholars of Islam's Maliki school, and the famous historian Ibn Khaldun.

Zaytuna suffered from the Spanish entry in Tunis in 1534, following which the mosque and library were pillaged. But under the Ottoman rule it recovered some of its prestige, and in 1842 its programs and teaching methods were institutionalized. After the establishment of the French Protectorate (1881), Zaytuna reformed its traditional programs to include a more modern and scientific system of instruction. In the beginning of the twentieth century it bred a generation of Islamic reformist thinkers and played an important role for Tunisian and Algerian nationalist movements.

After the independence of Tunisia (1956), Zaytuna became part of the state university and its library was integrated within the National Library of Tunis.

See also **Education; Law.**

BIBLIOGRAPHY

Abdel Moula, Mahmoud. *L'Université Zaytounienne et la société Tunisienne.* Tunis: Maison Tiers-Monde, 1984.

Claudia Gazzini

ZIYARA *See* **Pilgrimage: Ziyara**

Glossary

Pronunciation Key

	Symbol	Sound		Symbol	Sound
VOWELS	a	sat	CONSONANTS	dh	then
	a^h	father		h	horse
	au	mouse		kh	ch as in the German Dach
	ay	pay			or the Scottish Loch
	e	feet		sh	shake
	i	in		th	thin
	oo	boot		ʾ	glottal stop, the sound
	u	foot			in uh-oh (between the
					uh and the oh)
				ʿ	voiced pharyngeal fricative

*The syllable stress is indicated by italics. A doubled vowel such as in the word "ke-*taab*" indicates that the vowel should be said twice as long as a vowel in English.*

ʿAbd (Ar., a^hbd):
"Servant." Used with one of the names of God, such as ʿAbd Allah "Servant of God" or ʿAbd al-Rahim, "Servant of the Compassionate One" or ʿAbduh, "His servant." ʿAbd also means "slave," comparable to *ghulam* (Per.) or *mamluk* (Ar.)

Abu (Ar., a^h-boo):
"Father." Used in the construct "Abu + son's name," such as "Abu Husayn," to mean the father of Husayn. Often, it is the *kunya* or the name by which a person is known. Abu can also mean "the place of," such as Abu Dhabi (the place of the gazelle) or "the one that has." "Abu" can also be written as Aba or Abi, as in ʿAli b. Abi Talib.

Adhan (Ar., a-dhaan):
"Call to prayer." The early Muslim community in Medina is said to have debated how to summon their worshippers; Muhammad suggested the human voice. Thus, most mosques have their own *muezzin*, trained in the art of recitation, who calls worshippers to prayer five times a day.

Ahl al-kitab (Ar., ahl al-ke-taab):
"People of the Book." Mentioned in the Qurʾan, this phrase literally refers to religious communities who have a written scripture (the book), and specifically refers to Jews, Christians, and Sabians (Q. 5:72 "Those who believe [in the Qurʾan] those who follow the Jewish [Scriptures] and the Sabians and the Christians any who believe in Allah and the Last Day and work righteousness, on them shall be no fear nor shall they grieve.") Later Muslim rulers extended the interpretation of *ahl al-kitab* to include Zoroastrians, Hindus, Mandaeans, and Buddhists, among others. As such, *ahl al-kitab* have a specific protected status and freedom of religion within Muslim society, which the "pagan" Arabs did not enjoy.

Amir al-Muʾminin (Ar., a^h-meer al-muʾ-min-een):
"Commander of the Faithful." This title was adopted by ʿUmar ibn al-Khattab, the second leader of the Muslim community after the death of Muhammad, and was used by subsequent caliphs, heads of states, and sultans to signify their religiosity and religious authority.

Ansar (Ar., an-sa^hr):
"The helpers", a designation referring to the people of Medina who aided Muhammad following the *hijra* (emigration) from Mecca to Medina.

Aya (Ar., a^h-ya^h pl., Ayat a^h-yaat):
A verse in the Qur'an; a sign.

Ayatollah (a^h-ya^h-tul-la^h):
A Shi'ite theologian who has completed the following: 14 subjects of elementary study, independent study, and qualifications of a *mujtahid* (practitioner of independent legal reasoning) through oral examination. An ayatollah must also have attained a reputation amongst his peers, students and laity in knowledge and piety.

Baraka (Ar., ba^h-ra^h-ka^h):
Blessings of God.

Bid'a (Ar., bid-a^h):
"Innovation." A point of view or interpretation used in Islamic law or practice, but which is not present in the Sunna of the Prophet, and is therefore unacceptable to "traditionalists" who rely on the traditions (hadith) of Muhammad.

Bint (Ar., bint):
"Daughter." Used to designate the father-daughter relationship, such as Fatima bint Muhammad, and abbreviated in English as "bt."

Caliph:
"Successor." A title used by Muslim rulers to indicate their connection to Muhammad's leadership over the Muslim community. The title did not indicate, however, any sort of connection with the divine or spiritual supremacy.

Companions:
Most Sunni scholars believe that all those who converted to Islam during Muhammad's lifetime and who had contact with him are to be considered among his "Companions" with an ensuing righteous status. They are the primary transmitters of hadith, and it is to these people that the contemporary Salafiyya movements look for guidance. Because of the contentious relationships among some of this first generation of Muslims, Shi'a scholars are more selective in terms of who they consider a Companion.

Da'wa (Ar., da^hc-wa^h):
"Call." The missionary aspect of Islam in which Muslims encourage non-practicing Muslims to practice again (or practice according to a particular ideological view) and encourage non-Muslims to convert to Islam.

Dhikr (Ar., dhikr):
"Remembrance." An individual or collective ritual, usually involving chanting, where participants invoke the names and attributes of God. *Dhikr* is a central element in Sufi practice and spirituality.

Dhimmi (Ar., dhim-mee):
Protected groups of non-Muslims living under Muslim rule, primarily People of the Book (*ahl al-kitab*). *Dhimmi*s were required to pay a tax (*jiziya*) and were not allowed to serve in the army, although many rose to prominence as scholars, government advisors and officers, and physicians. Both *dhimmi* status and the *jiziya* tax do not exist in contemporary nation-states.

Dhu-l-Hijja (Ar., dhul-hij-ja^h):
The twelfth month of the Islamic calendar and the month in which the *hajj*, the pilgrimage to Mecca, takes place.

Emir/Amir (Ar., Per., a^h-meer):
A prince, ruler or commander, but early usage also included a military commander.

Faqih (Ar., fa-keeh):
A jurist, thus one who would be an expert in shari'a, especially *fiqh*.

Al-Fatiha (Ar., al-fa-tee-ha^h):
The opening chapter of the Qur'an, consisting of seven *ayat* (verses). This chapter is said in prayers as well as at significant times, such as marriage.

Fatwa (Ar., fat-wa^h):
"Legal opinion." Issued by a mufti or some other recognized and qualified scholar, a *fatwa* is a legal or advisory opinion in answer to a specific question or a broader issue facing the community.

Fiqh (Ar., fik):
"Jurisprudence." The science of studying the shari'a.

Fitna (Ar., fit-na^h):
First used to describe the violent factional dissension that took place in the early Islamic community, it denotes Muslims fighting Muslims, and as such signals the end of Muslim unity, and the domination of chaos and irreligiosity. *Fitna* is also used to describe temptations that test believers' religious commitments.

Futuhat (Ar., fu^h-tu^h-haat):
The conquest of territory by Muslim armies.

Hadith (Ar., ha-deeth, pl., ahadith a-ha-deeth):
The utterances, opinions, or rulings of the prophet Muhammad. According to the methods through which they have been collected and verified in the three centuries following his death, two elements are essential to a reliable hadith: a continuous, verifiable *isnad* (chain of transmitters), and a correspondence (or absence of contradiction to) the Qur'an. The Hadith, along with the Sunna and the Qur'an are the main sources for Islamic law. Sunnis and Shi'ites share many *ahadith*, but have different *isnad*s.

Hajj (Ar., haj):
The pilgrimage rite to Mecca, one of the essential requirement of being a Muslim. Muslims come from all over the world to participate once a year in the Hajj, commemorating Abraham's building of the Ka'ba and the difficult experiences of Hagar and Isma'il. The Hajj is required of Muslims once in their lifetime, but only if physically and financially able to do so—they cannot leave behind debts, and they must have paid the *zakat* on the resources they use to go on Hajj. After a person completes the pilgrimage, a man is called a Hajj or Hajji and a woman is called a Hajja.

Halal (Ar., ha^h-*laal*):
Permitted according to Islamic law. The use of the word also signifies a slaughtering technique that sanctifies meat for Muslims.

Hanafi (Ar., *ha*-na-fee):
One of the four Sunni schools of Islamic law, named after Abu Hanifa (699–767).

Hanbali (Ar., *han*-baal-ee):
One of the four Sunni schools of Islamic law, named after Ahmad ibn Hanbal (780–855)

Haram (Ar., ha^h-*raam*):
Forbidden in Islamic law, such as the consumption of pork and alcohol are haram.

Haram (*ha*^h-ram):
A holy place, a sanctuary. Mecca is referred to as Masjid al-Haram and the al-Haram al-Sharif in Jerusalem is the location of the Dome of the Rock and the Masjid al-Aqsa.

Hijra (Ar., *hij*-ra^h):
"Emigration." This term refers to the journey of Muhammad from Mecca to Medina in 622 c.e. and marks the beginning of the Muslim (lunar) calendar, known by the same name, abbreviated as A.H. (Arabic Hijra or Hegira)

Hizb (Ar., hizb):
A political party or movement, as in Hizb Allah (Party of God) in Lebanon.

'Ibadat (Ar., e-baa-*daat*):
Devotional acts of worship.

Ibadis (Ibadiyya) (Ar., e-ba^h-*de*-ya):
See Khawarij.

Ibn (Ar., *i*-bin):
"Son." Used in the construct of names to indicate the son-father relationship, thus Ibn Hasan is the "son of Hasan". Often it is the name by which people are known, their *kunya*, although it does not necessarily reflect their father's name, such as Ibn Sina or Ibn Rushd. In Arabic, when "ibn" occurs between names it is pronounced or written as "bin," as in 'Ali bin Abi Talib. "Ibn" is oftentimes abbreviated in English as "b." as in 'Ali b. Abi Talib.

'Id al-Adha (Ar., *eed*-ul-a^h*d*-ha^h):
"Feast of Sacrifice." This celebration marks the end of the hajj (pilgrimage) when pilgrims sacrifice an animal as part of their hajj ritual, and which Muslims also do all over the world (and donate a portion of it to the poor). It falls on the 10th of the month of Dhu-l-Hijja, and is also called al-'Id al-Kabir (the big Feast) or Bayram.

'Id al-Fitr (Ar., *eed*-ul-*fit*-r):
"Feast of Fast-breaking." This occasion marks the end of the month of Ramadan, the month of fasting. Special 'Id prayers are offered in the morning, and children and adults often get new clothes. Also called al-'Id al-Saghir (the smaller Feast).

Ijma' (Ar., ij-ma^h):
"Scholarly consensus," and one of the main methods for developing and interpreting Islamic law.

Ijtihad (Ar., ij-ti-haad):
"Independent legal judgement." The interpretation of law based on individual reasoning.

'Ilm (Ar., ilm, pl. 'Ulum, u-*luum*):
In religious terms, *'ilm* means knowledge and also gives us the word "ulema" (religious scholars) meaning those who are knowledgeable. In both the historical and contemporary Muslim world, *'ilm* also means "science."

'Ilm al-Rijal (Ar., ilm-ul-ri-*jaal*):
The study of the people who transmitted the hadith (sayings and practices of Muhammad) and who are mentioned in the *isnad*s (chains of transmission). Biographies of these early Muslims are the topic of many books and provides material for judging the soundness or believability of each hadith.

Imam (Ar., Per., ee-*maam*):
Among Sunnis, an imam is a legal scholar or the prayer leader in a mosque. Among Shi'ite communities, an imam is an infallible guide to the community, descended from the family of the Prophet. The Twelver Shi'ites believe that there were twelve imams, the last one of which went into occultation (hiding) and will return one day as the mahdi.

Imami (Ar., ee-*maam*-ee):
Twelver Shi'ites or Imamai Shi'ites. See Shi'ites.

Iman (Ar., ee-maan):
"Faith."

Islam (Ar., Is-*la*^hm):
The religion of Islam. Someone who follows Islam is a Muslim, which means that he or she believes that there is no god but God and that Muhammad is the Messenger of God. The word Islam, meaning "surrender" comes from the Arabic root (s-l-m) which denotes wholeness, peace, and safety, suggesting that these are the qualities one achieves through surrendering oneself to God.

Isma'ili (Ar., is-ma-ee-lee):
Shi'ites who disagreed with the main body of Shi'a over the identity of the seventh Imam. The Isma'ilis followed Ja'far al-Sadiq's eldest son Isma'il, while the majority (called the Imamis or Twelvers) followed his younger son Musa al-Kazim. Because of the split over the identity of the Seventh Imam, the Isma'ilis are also called Seveners, and the Agha Khan is the current head of the Nizari sect of the Isma'ilis.

Isra' (Ar., is-ra^h):
Muhammad's Night Journey (al-Isra' wal-Mi'raj); see *mi'raj*.

Jahiliyya (Ar., ja-hi-*lee*-ya^h):
"Time of Ignorance." The Arabic and Muslim way of referring to pre-Islamic history in the Arabian peninusula.

Jami' (Ar., *jaa*-mi):
A congregational mosque for Friday prayers, as opposed to a *masjid* or a *musalla*. Jami's are usually quite large in order to

hold the entire population who will pray and listen to the *khitab* or sermon of an *imam*.

Jihad (Ar., ji-*haad*):

"Struggle." Over time, the concept of a "jihad" has developed to include both the greater jihad, or the struggle by the individual to be a righteous Muslim, and the lesser jihad, or the struggle to fight oppression and defend the Muslim community. In the eighteenth and nineteenth centuries Asia and Africa witnessed reform movements that embarked on jihads to reform the Muslim communities and to fight colonial rule. More recently, certain groups have interpreted the concept of jihad to mean to fight non-Muslims.

Jinn (or Jinni) (Ar., jin):

Invisible, supernatural creatures, mentioned in the Qur'an, and who can be good or bad.

Jum'a (Ar., *joo*-ma^h):

"Friday." The word also is used to describe the Jum'a mosque of a particular city (see Jami') or *salat al-jum'a* (Friday prayers).

Ka'ba (Ar., *ka^h*-ba^h):

The name of the sacred, cube-shaped building located in the Haram in Mecca. The Black Stone is set in a silver frame in one of the lower corners and the whole building is covered by an embroidered cloth (*kiswa*). Muslims pray towards the Ka'ba and circumambulate it during *hajj*. Muslims believe that the Ka'ba was constructed by Abraham and Isma'il (see Q.2: 127–129).

Kalam (Ar., ka-*laam*):

"Theology."

Karbala (ka^hr-ba^h-*la*^h):

The burial site of Husayn bin 'Ali, the grandson of Muhammad, located in southern Iraq, south of Baghdad, and a popular place of pilgrimage for Shi'ites.

Khawarij (Kharajites) (Ar., kha-*waa*-rij):

An early sect of Islam that advocated a strict and puritanical interpretation of religious dogma. They believed that any Muslim was qualified to lead the community (in antithesis to Shi'a beliefs), but also held that mortal sins had the effect of making a Muslim into a non-believer and deserving of death. A group of Kharajites murdered 'Ali, thereby inadvertently facilitating the rise to power of the Umayyads, who suppressed them. Although largely wiped out, a major branch of the Kharajite movement, the Ibadiyya, continue to exist today in Oman and east Africa.

Al-Khulafa' al-Rashidun (The Rightly-guided Caliphs, Ar., al-khu-la-*fa*' ar-raa-shi-*doon*):

Sunni Muslims call the first four Caliphs who led the Muslim community the Rightly-guided Caliphs: Abu Bakr, 'Umar, 'Uthman, and 'Ali. After these men, who were selected by the community, rule was taken over by the Umayyad dynasty who assumed hereditary rule. Shi'a and Ibadis do not use the term "*al-khulafa' al-rashidun*."

Khutba (Ar., *khut*-ba^h):

The sermon during Friday prayers that is often delivered by an imam.

Kunya (*kun*-ya^h):

Another name by which a person is known, which is often the more commonly used and well-known than the person's given name. In many cases the *kunya* will be the "Father of," "Son of," "Mother of," or "Daughter of" construction. For example, the 11th century Persian scientist Abu 'Ali al-Husayn ibn 'Abdallah ibn Sina is referred to only as Ibn Sina and the ninth century writer Abu 'Uthman Amr b. Bahr al-Fuqaymi al-Basri is known as al-Jahiz (the bug-eyed).

Madhhab (Ar., *madh*-hab, pl., *madhahib*):

A school of thought in traditional Islamic scholarship, such as in law and theology. Among Sunni Muslims, four schools of law are recognized, named after the eminent scholars whose juridical works they were based on: Hanafi, Maliki, Hanbali, Shafi'i. The Shi'ites follow the Ja'fari school, named after the sixth Imam, Ja'far al-Sadiq, along with the *ijtihad* of living scholars of eminence.

Madrasa (Ar., *ma*-dra-sa):

"School." Historically a *madrasa* refers to a Sunni Muslim college where shari'a and other Islamic sciences were taught, while currently a *madrasa* refers to any school, religious or secular, private or public.

Maliki (Ar., *maa*-lik-ee):

One of the four Sunni schools of law, named after Malik Ibn Anas (715–795).

Masjid (Ar., *mas*-jid, pl., Masajid) :

Mosque.

Maulid (Mawlid) (Ar., *mau*-lid):

A yearly birthday celebration for the prophet Muhammad or a famous saint, common in Egypt and North Africa.

Mi'raj (Ar., mi-*ra^hj*):

Part of the *al-Isra' wal-Mi'raj*, Muhammad's night journey (Q. 17:1) that took him to the seven heavens.

Mihrab (Ar., mih-*ra^hb*):

The recessed arched niche in the mosque indicating direction of prayer towards Mecca. It is often highly decorated.

Minaret:

The tower or raised section of a mosque from where the muezzin gives the call to prayer. Historically, these towers have staircases inside so that the muezzin could climb the stairs and issue the call to prayer from a balcony. Today, most calls to prayer are broadcast from loudspeakers attached to the minaret.

Muezzin (Moo-*az*-zin, Ar., mu'*adh*-dhin):

The person who gives the call to prayer (*adhan*). Men or boys are chosen for this position for a variety of reasons, among them because of the quality of their voice; as an honor to that person for their service; or as a means of employment.

Mufti (Ar., *muf*-tee):

Chief Islamic jurist and a scholar who can issue *fatwa*s or legal opinions.

Muhajirun (Ar., mu-*haa*-ji-roon):
The Muslims who immigrated to Medina with Muhammad in 622 C.E., and who were helped by the Ansar, the Medinans who aided them and became part of the fledgling Muslim community.

Mujtahid (Ar., muj-*taa*-hid):
A religious scholar who practices independent legal judgement and reasoning (*ijtihad*) to form a legal opinion.

Muslim (Ar., *mus*-lim):
A follower of Islam.

Nabi (Ar., na-*bee*):
A prophet of God. In Islam, this includes the prophets from the Judeo-Christian tradition, such as Moses, Abraham, Jesus, among many others.

PBUH: See S.A.W.

Qadi (Ar., *ka*ʰ-dee):
A judge whose responsibilities are in the areas of religious law.

Qibla (Ar., *kib*-la):
The direction of prayer, i.e., the direction of Mecca. The direction is often marked in a mosque by a *mihrab*, which traditionally takes the shape of an arched niche in the *qibla* wall.

Qiyas (Ar., *kee*-yas):
Analogical reasoning used in Islamic law.

Qur'an (also written as Koran) (Ar., kuʰ-*ra*ʰn):
The Muslim Holy Book. Muslims consider the Qur'an to be the divine revelation of God to humankind and the basis for living a right and just life as a Muslim. As the word of God, it is untranslatable and is only the Qur'an in the language of revelation (Arabic). Muslims recite portions of the Qur'an in their prayers. The Qur'an consists of *sura*s (chapters) which are arranged by length; therefore, the Qur'an does not follow a narrative or chronological order.

Ramadan (Ar., ra*ʰ*-ma*ʰ*-*da*ʰn):
The lunar month in which Muslims fast from food, drink, smoking, sex, and gossip (among other things) from sunrise until sunset. It falls on the ninth month of the Muslim lunar calendar, and ends with the ʿId al-Fitr.

Rasul (Ar., ra*ʰ*-*su*ʰl):
A messenger of God.

S.A.W. (Sa*ʰ*l-*allah* ʿa*ʰ*-*lay*-he wa-*sal*-lam):
"Prayers and peace of God be upon him." Muslim invocation after writing or mentioning the name of Muhammad. Also rendered in English as PBUH (Peace be upon Him).

Sahaba (Ar., sa*ʰ*-*ha*ʰ-ba*ʰ*):
See Companions.

Salafi (Ar., *sa*-la-fee):
A term used by Muslims to denote a thinker or a movement who idealizes the time of the Prophet and thinks that contemporary Muslim societies must return to those standards and mores in order to achieve the best society. Originally coined by Muhammad ʿAbduh in the late 19th century, the term initially was meant as a reform movement to end corruption in society and to address the issues of the modern world. However, the term "Salafi" has come to have a much more extreme and coercive meaning, particularly as Wahhabi and other groups have forced their own definitions of Salafi ideals en masse on their populations (and others).

Salat (Ar., sa*ʰ*-*la*ʰt):
"Prayer." Prayer is one of the pillars of Muslim devotional life. Muslims pray five times a day, a practice which takes a few minutes and can be done in a mosque or any clean place. In order to pray, Muslims must be in a state of cleanliness, achieved by doing *wudu'* (ablutions).

Saum (Sawm) (Ar., saum, pl., *Siyam*):
"Fasting." For Muslims a fast from food and liquids takes place from sunrise to sunset, and occurs for a month during Ramadan as well as other special occasions and recommended times. See Ramadan.

Shafiʿi (Ar., *sha*-fi-ee):
One of the four schools of Sunni law, named after the Imam al-Shafiʿi (d. 820).

Shahada (Ar., sha-*haa*-da):
"Profession of faith." The *shahada* is the major pillar of Muslim doctrine and must be said with intention in order to become a Muslim: "There is no god but God and Muhammad is the messenger of God."

Shariʿa (Ar., sha-*ree*-a):
"Islamic law." The Qur'an, Hadith (sayings of the Prophet), and the Sunna (practices) are the basis for scholars and judges to determine shariʿa. With no central authority deciding legal issues, four schools (*madhhab*s) have emerged in Sunni law, although most scholars warn against blind adherence to a particular school (*taqlid*), and instead promote *ijtihad* (independent reasoning and legal judgement) as a means to best understand shariʿa at any particular time and situation. While Shiʿites follow their own Jaʿfari school, they do not follow a fixed canon of law because Shiʿite theologians continue to practice *ijtihad* to this day. Among the Shiʿa, there are a number of living scholars of eminence among whom the laity chose to follow in matters of shariʿa to find fresh answers to current problems.

Shaykh (Sheikh, Ar., shaykh):
Used as a title of respect, *shaykh* can refer to a religious scholar, the leader of a Sufi order, the head of a tribe or village, or an old man.

Shiʿite (she-ite):
Derived from their name, *shiʿt ʿAli*, or "the party of ʿAli", the Shiʿa are one of the major groups of Muslims; the other being Sunni. The Shiʿite believe that rule of the community (led by an Imam) should be through ʿAli and the descendants of the Prophet through his daughter Fatima who was married to ʿAli. They split into smaller divisions, over disagreements about the inheritance of the office of imam (see Ismaʿili). Today they make up about 15% of the Muslim population

and predominate or have significant minorities in Iran, Iraq, Lebanon, Yemen, and other Arabian Gulf states.

Sufism (Ar., *Tasawwuf*) :

An understanding of Islam that emphasizes mystical or spiritual practice. A Sufi is a practitioner of Sufism, and different groups or *tariqas* ("paths") have different relationships with orthodox practices, varying in time and place. Traditionally, Sufi orders have been run by a *shaykh* (Ar.) or a *pir* (Per.), whom students (*murids*) follow closely. Also associated historically with Sufism are *khanqas*, *zawiyas*, and *ribats*, residences and centers of spiritual practice.

Sunna (Ar., *sun*-na^h):

The practices, actions, and behavior of the prophet Muhammad. These are stories about him recorded by his companions and family in the same style as the hadith. The Sunna, along with the Hadith and Qur'an, comprise the main sources of Islamic law. "Sunna" is also a legal term used to describe a Muslim practice that is recommended (but not required), as in it is sunna to hold a celebratory feast (*walima*) for a wedding.

Sunni (Ar., *sun*-nee):

The largest group of Muslim adherents, the Sunni emphasize the Sunna (actions of Muhammad), the hadith (sayings of the Prophet) and the Qur'an. Through these sources they have developed four schools of law (*madhhabs*). They are the largest percentage of Muslims, making up approximately 85 percent of worshippers today.

Sura (Ar., *soo*-ra^h):

A chapter of the Qur'an. Each chapter is referred to by a number (114 total), and by a name, as in Surat al-Qamr (the Sura of the Moon) or Surat Maryam (the Sura of Mary), and contains any number of *ayat* (verses), ranging from 3 to 286.

Tafsir (Ar., taf-*seer*):

Interpretation of the Qur'an.

Tahara (Ar., ta^h-*ha*^h-ra^h):

"Purification," and can also refer to circumcision.

Tariqa (ta-*ree*-ka):

"Path or way." A term used in Sufi practices, to refer to a spiritual path or a specific discipline of Sufi thought following a particular master.

Ta'ziyeh (Per., ta-zee-*ya*^h) (Ar., ta'ziya):

Performances conducted among the Shi'ites commemorating the martyrdom of Husayn ibn 'Ali at Karbala.

Ulema (u^h-la^h-*ma*' Ar., sing. 'Alim, pl., 'Ulama'):

A scholar or learned person in the Islamic sciences, such as fiqh and shari'a.

Umma (Ar., *um*-ma^h):

The community of Muslim believers.

'Umra (Ar., *um*-ra)

A visit to Mecca outside of the *hajj* period, and thought of as a "lesser pilgrimage."

Wali (*waa*-lee):

"A friend of God." The term is used by Shi'ites to describe 'Ali. Sunnis also use the term when talking about Muslim holy men and women who they believe have intercessional powers with God, a popular practice and condemned by the orthodoxy.

Waqf (Ar., *wa*^hkf):

An endowment from which revenues from a particular property or business are allotted for a specific public service or building, often set up by an individual or his or her family. Many medieval mosques, *madrasas*, hospitals and other buildings had endowments associated with them that provided their running expenses, salaries, etc., and the practice continues to this day.

Wazir/Vizir/Vizier (Ar., wa^h-*zeer*, Per., va^h-*zeer*)

The advisor to a ruler, and usually a person with great power.

Wudu' (Ar., wu-*doo*'):

"Ablutions." Before prayer, Muslims must complete ablutions, cleaning their hands, feet, face, ears, mouth, and nose (in a prescribed process). Being in a state of *wudu'* can carry over from prayer to prayer if nothing takes place to break the state of cleanliness, such as going to the bathroom, passing gas, or sexual relations, among other things. Following sexual relations, menstruation, and childbirth, believers must perform *ghusul*, which requires the whole body to be cleaned.

Zakat (Ar., za-*kaat*):

"Tithe or alms." Another of the five pillars required of Muslims, *zakat* is a tithe that is to be paid each year by all Muslim adults in the amount of 2.5% of their income and wealth. Shi'ites also pay a *khums* or one-fifth on all excess wealth.

Ziyara (Ar., Per., zee-*ya*^h-ra^h):

Visits to a holy shrine, particular tombs of *wali*s and holy people.

Zuhd (Ar., zuhd):

Asceticism, a Sufi practice.

Appendix

Genealogies

Umayyad Caliphs

Tribe of Qaraysh (5th–8th centuries, C.E.)

Early Tariquas (Sufi brotherhoods) and their Founders

Isma'ili Imams

Shi'a Imams

Timelines

Islam in Central and East Asia 600–2003 C.E.

Islam in Europe and Africa 600–2003 C.E.

Islam in South and Southeast Asia 700–2003 C.E.

Islam in Southwest Asia 570–2003 C.E.

Life of Muhammad 570–632 C.E.

Appendix

Genealogies

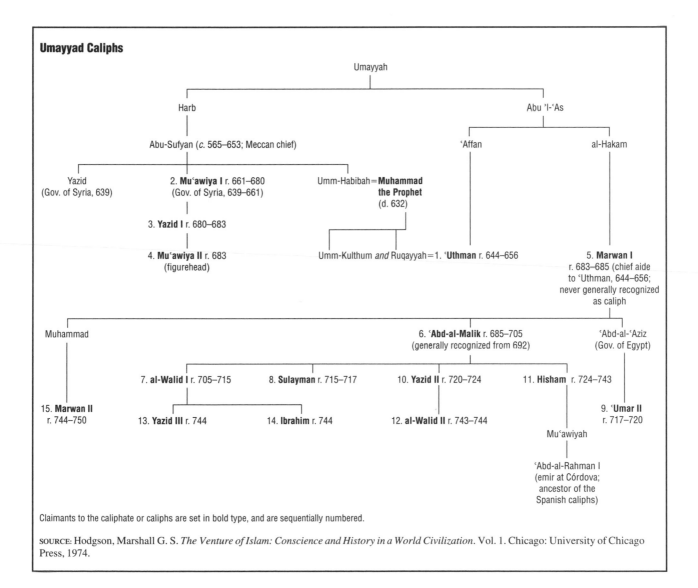

Umayyad Caliphs

Umayyah

Harb — Abu ʾl-ʿAs

Abu-Sufyan (c. 565–653; Meccan chief) — ʿAffan — al-Hakam

Yazid (Gov. of Syria, 639)

2. Muʿawiya I r. 661–680 (Gov. of Syria, 639–661)

Umm-Habibah = **Muhammad the Prophet** (d. 632)

3. Yazid I r. 680–683

4. Muʿawiya II r. 683 (figurehead)

Umm-Kulthum *and* Ruqayyah = 1. **ʿUthman** r. 644–656

5. Marwan I r. 683–685 (chief aide to ʿUthman, 644–656; never generally recognized as caliph)

Muhammad

6. ʿAbd-al-Malik r. 685–705 (generally recognized from 692)

ʿAbd-al-ʿAziz (Gov. of Egypt)

7. al-Walid I r. 705–715 **8. Sulayman** r. 715–717 **10. Yazid II** r. 720–724 **11. Hisham** r. 724–743

15. Marwan II r. 744–750

13. Yazid III r. 744 **14. Ibrahim** r. 744 **12. al-Walid II** r. 743–744

9. ʿUmar II r. 717–720

Muʿawiyah

ʿAbd-al-Rahman I (emir at Córdova; ancestor of the Spanish caliphs)

Claimants to the caliphate or caliphs are set in bold type, and are sequentially numbered.

SOURCE: Hodgson, Marshall G. S. *The Venture of Islam: Conscience and History in a World Civilization.* Vol. 1. Chicago: University of Chicago Press, 1974.

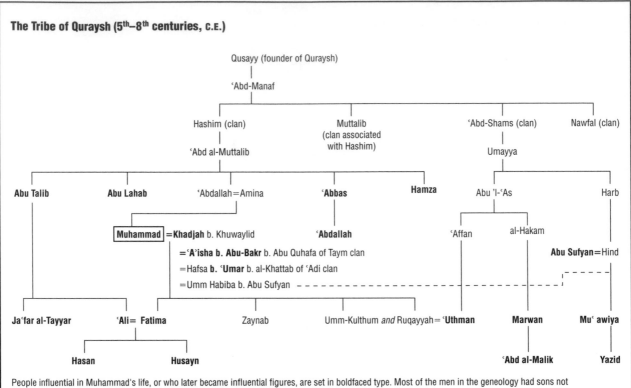

The Tribe of Quraysh (5th–8th centuries, C.E.)

People influential in Muhammad's life, or who later became influential figures, are set in boldfaced type. Most of the men in the geneology had sons not mentioned here due to space considerations.

SOURCE: Hodgson, Marshall G. S. *The Venture of Islam: Conscience and History in a World Civilization.* Vol. 1. Chicago: University of Chicago Press, 1974.

Early tariqas (Sufi brotherhoods) and their founders

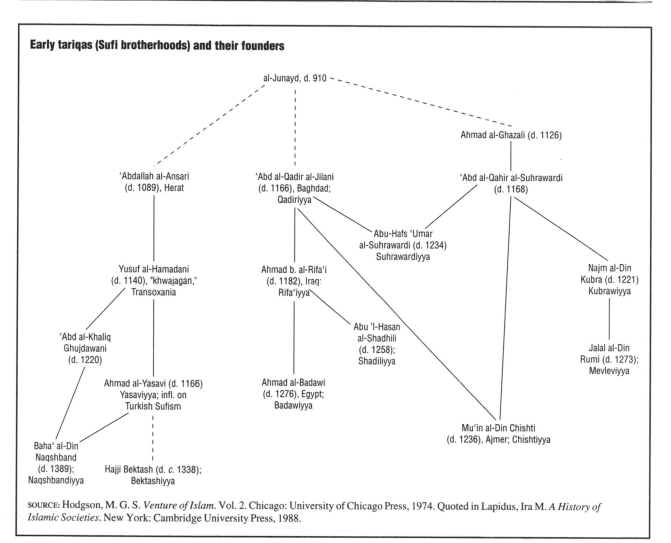

SOURCE: Hodgson, M. G. S. *Venture of Islam.* Vol. 2. Chicago: University of Chicago Press, 1974. Quoted in Lapidus, Ira M. *A History of Islamic Societies.* New York: Cambridge University Press, 1988.

Isma'ili Imams

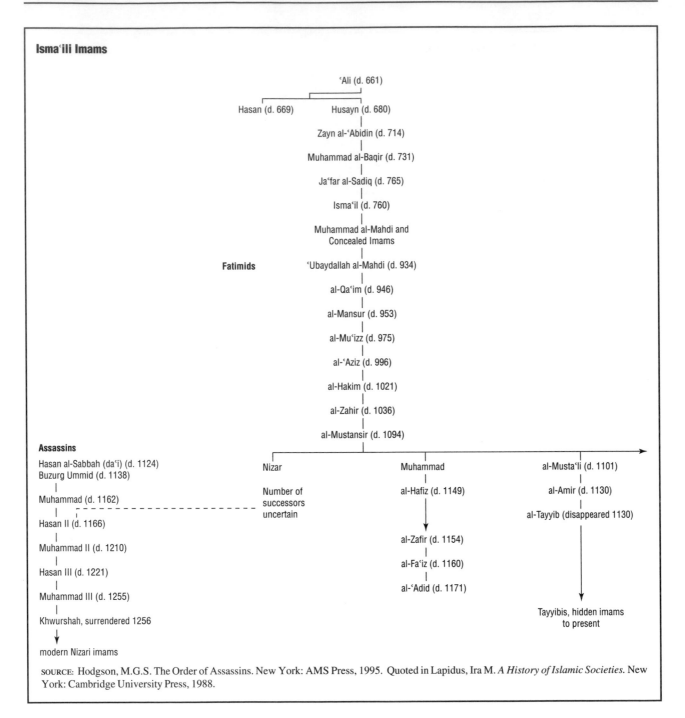

'Ali (d. 661)

Hasan (d. 669)   Husayn (d. 680)

Zayn al-'Abidin (d. 714)

Muhammad al-Baqir (d. 731)

Ja'far al-Sadiq (d. 765)

Isma'il (d. 760)

Muhammad al-Mahdi and
Concealed Imams

Fatimids   'Ubaydallah al-Mahdi (d. 934)

al-Qa'im (d. 946)

al-Mansur (d. 953)

al-Mu'izz (d. 975)

al-'Aziz (d. 996)

al-Hakim (d. 1021)

al-Zahir (d. 1036)

al-Mustansir (d. 1094)

Assassins

Hasan al-Sabbah (da'i) (d. 1124)   Nizar   Muhammad   al-Musta'li (d. 1101)
Buzurg Ummid (d. 1138)

Muhammad (d. 1162)   Number of   al-Hafiz (d. 1149)   al-Amir (d. 1130)
    successors
Hasan II (d. 1166)   uncertain   al-Tayyib (disappeared 1130)

Muhammad II (d. 1210)   al-Zafir (d. 1154)

Hasan III (d. 1221)   al-Fa'iz (d. 1160)

Muhammad III (d. 1255)   al-'Adid (d. 1171)

Khwurshah, surrendered 1256   Tayyibis, hidden imams
    to present

modern Nizari imams

SOURCE: Hodgson, M.G.S. *The Order of Assassins.* New York: AMS Press, 1995. Quoted in Lapidus, Ira M. *A History of Islamic Societies.* New York: Cambridge University Press, 1988.

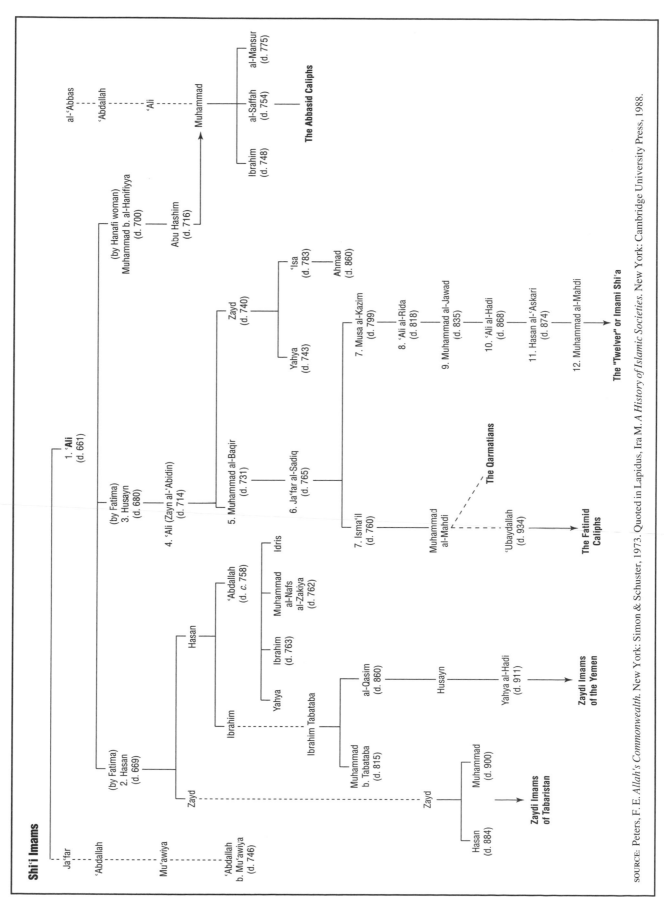

Shi'i Imams

Ja'far

'Abdallah

Mu'awiya - - - - - 'Abdallah - - - - -
b. Mu'awiya
(d. 746)

'Abdallah - - - - - al-'Abbas

'Ali - - - - - - 'Abdallah

Muhammad - - - - - 'Ali

1. 'Ali
(d. 661)

(by Fatima)
2. Hasan
(d. 669)

(by Fatima)
3. Husayn
(d. 680)

(by Hanafi woman)
Muhammad b. al-Hanifiyya
(d. 700)

Abu Hashim
(d. 716)

Ibrahim   al-Saffah   al-Mansur
(d. 748)   (d. 754)   (d. 775)

The Abbasid Caliphs

Zayd

Hasan

Ibrahim

Yahya

Ibrahim Tabataba

'Abdallah
(d. c. 758)

Muhammad
al-Nafs
al-Zakiya
(d. 762)

Ibrahim
(d. 763)

Idris

4. 'Ali (Zayn al-'Abidin)
(d. 714)

5. Muhammad al-Baqir
(d. 731)

6. Ja'far al-Sadiq
(d. 765)

Zayd
(d. 740)

Yahya
(d. 743)

'Isa
(d. 783)

Ahmad
(d. 860)

7. Musa al-Kazim
(d. 799)

8. 'Ali al-Rida
(d. 818)

9. Muhammad al-Jawad
(d. 835)

10. 'Ali al-Hadi
(d. 868)

11. Hasan al-'Askari
(d. 874)

12. Muhammad al-Mahdi

The "Twelver" or Imami Shi'a

7. Isma'il
(d. 760)

Muhammad
al-Mahdi

'Ubaydallah
(d. 934)

The Qarmatians

**The Fatimid
Caliphs**

Muhammad
b. Tabataba
(d. 815)

al-Qasim
(d. 860)

Husayn

Yahya al-Hadi
(d. 911)

**Zaydi Imams
of the Yemen**

Zayd - - - - - Zayd

Muhammad
(d. 900)

Hasan
(d. 884)

**Zaydi Imams
of Tabaristan**

SOURCE: Peters, F. E. *Allah's Commonwealth.* New York: Simon & Schuster, 1973. Quoted in Lapidus, Ira M. *A History of Islamic Societies.* New York: Cambridge University Press. 1988.

Shi'a imam lineage.

Timelines

ISLAM IN CENTRAL AND EAST ASIA 600–2003 C.E.

618
Tang begin to unite China.

664
Arab conquest of Kabul.

671
Arab armies cross Oxus (Amu Carya).

681
Arabs cross into Transoxania and spend winter.

683
Civil war in Khurasan.

689
Eastern Turks invade Transoxania.

691
Umayyad rule restored in Khurasan.

705
Qutayba ibn Muslim marches into Khurasan.

711
Eastern Turks conquer western Central Asia.

712
Arabs conquer Khwarizm; Eastern Turks take Samarkand.

713
Qutayba ibn Muslim reaches Ferghana; first mosque built in Bukhara.

725
Restoration of Balkh.

729
Muslim rule restored in Bukhara.

733
Famine in Khurasan.

737
Death of the Khan in Tukharistan.

739
Fall of the Western Turkish empire.

741
Sogdians restored to their native land.

742
Congregational mosque built in Balkh.

743
Partisans of 'Ali revolt in Khurasan.

745
Foundation of Uighur Empire in Central Asia (Chinese Turkestan, to 840).

747
Abu Muslim arrives in Khurasan.

748
Chinese destroy Suyab.

751
Defeat of Tang Chinese by Arab forces at battle of Talas River; end of Arab advances in Central Asia.

752
Prince of Ushrusana sends embassy to China.

753
Walls and defensive towers constructed at Samarkand.

763
Tang China is invaded by Tibetans.

766
Qarluqs occupy Suyab.

783
Defensive walls constructed near Bukhara.

792
Qarluqs expelled from Ferghana.

794

Subjugation of Ushrusana; new congregational mosque built in Bukhara.

806

Rafiʿ bin Layth revolts in Samarkand.

816

Famine in Khurasan.

819

Founding of Samanid dynasty in Khurasan and Transoxania (to 1005).

820

The Tughuzghuz take Ushrusana.

830

Tahirids proclaim independence at Khurasan.

867

Founding of Saffarid dynasty in east Persia (to 1495).

868

The Diamond Sutra, world's oldest surviving printed work.

907

End of the Tang dynasty in China, Arab disruption of trans-Asian trade.

916

Foundation of Khitan Empire.

947

Khitans invade northern China, establishing Lao dynasty at Beijing.

962

Foundation of Afghan Ghaznavid dynasty.

970

Paper money introduced in China.

979

Song dynasty unites China.

992

Establishment of Qarakhanid dynasty in Transoxania (to 1211).

1020

Firdowsi's *Shahnameh*—Book of Kings, Persia's national epic.

1038

Beginning of Seliuk dynasty, the first major Turkish Muslim empire (to 1194).

c. 1040

Seliuk Turks conquer Afghanistan and East Persia.

c. 1045

Movable type printing invented in China.

1077

Seljuk governors in Oxus region establish separate state of Khwarizm Shah (to 1231).

1090

Shiʿa Ismailis (of Alamut, Assassins) emerge as major force in North Persia (to 1256).

1123

Rubaiyat (quatrains) of Omar Khayyam; also his *Algebra*, for which he is more celebrated in his homeland, Persia.

1188

Nizami's *Layla and Majnun*, a Persian recasting of perennially popular pre-Islamic love story in verse.

1206

Mongols united by Temujin, proclaimed Genghis Khan; The Great Yasa, law code of the Mongols promulgated by Genghis Khan; Mongols begin conquest of Central Asia.

1211

Mongols begin conquest of northern (Jin) China.

1219

Mongol invasion of Khwarizm Empire.

1227

Death of Genghis Khan.

1229

Ogodai elected Great Khan.

1231

Mongols reconquer resurgent Empire of the Khwarizm Shah.

1233

Mongols take Jin capital, Kaifeng.

1235

Walled city built at Karakorum as fixed Mongol capital.

1237

Start of Mongol conquest of Russia.

1253–1255

William of Rubruck crosses Asia to Karakorum.

1256

Il-Khanate established in Persia, successor state to Mongols (to 1353); Hulegu crosses Oxus.

1258

Saʿdi's *Gulistan*, major popular classic of Persian literature.

1259

Great Khan Mongke dies.

1264

Kublai defeats rival for title of Great Khan, ending civil war.

1265

Death of Hulegu.

1271–1295

Marco Polo travels throughout Asia, returning by ship through Persian Gulf.

1274

First Mongol attempt to invade Japan defeated.

1275
Marco Polo reaches Kublai Khan's summer palace at Shangdu (Xanadu).

1279
Foundation of Yuan dynasty, Yuan take over Southern Song.

1281
Second failed Mongol invasion of Japan.

1292
Marco Polo given task of escorting Mongol princess to Hormuz.

1294
Death of Kublai Khan.

1295
Conversion of the Il-Khan Ghazan to Islam.

1320
Outbreak of plague in Yunnan province.

1320–1330
Mongol armies help spread plague throughout China.

1330
Plague reaches northeastern China.

1335
Rebellions against Mongol rule in China.

1335
Mongol wazir Ghiyath al-Din in Tabriz commissions an illustrated *Shahnameh*, a fine example of a Persian illuminated manuscript (called the Demotte Shahnameh).

1346
Plague reaches coast of Black Sea.

1368
Establishment of the Ming dynasty.

1379
Timur marches on Urgench.

1395
Sack of New Sarai, capital of Golden Horde.

1405
Beginning of Ming admiral Zheng He's seven voyages to Indian Ocean (to 1433).

1405
The Rigistan, Samarkand, built by Timur and one of the glories of his capital; End of Ming campaign against Mongols.

c. 1433
Construction of ocean-going junks banned by Ming.

1439
Poggio Bracciolini records Asian journeys of Niccolo Conti.

1449
Mongols defeat Chinese and capture the emperor.

1443
Great Library at Herat, Persia founded.

1499
Rise to power of Safavids in Persia.

1500
Shaybanid dynasty, of Mongol descent, assumes control of Transoxania (to 1598).

1501
Accession of Shah Isma'il I; beginning of Safavid dynasty in Persia (to 1732) .

1534–1535
Safavid war with Ottomans, who capture Tabriz and Baghdad.

1553–1555
Safavid war with Ottomans.

1557
Foundation of Portuguese colony at Macao.

1578–1590
Safavid war with Ottomans.

1581
Yermak begins Russian conquest of Siberia.

1598
Anthony and Robert Sherley travel to Persia, where they meet Shah 'Abbas.

1603
Foundation of Tokugawa Shogunate in Japan.

1627
Herbert's travels in Persia.

1636
Manchus establish Qing imperial rule at Mukden.

1644
Qing forces enter Beijing.

1689
Treaty of Nerchinsk agrees Russian and Chinese spheres of influence in East Asia.

1722–1736
Subjugation of Afghans by Persia.

1730–1734
Suppression of Khazaks by Russia.

1736
Nadir Shah becomes Shah of Persia.

1747
Foundation of Afghanistan by Ahmad Khan Abdali.

1751
Tibet, Dzungaria, Turkestan, and the Tarrm Basin overrun by Qing Chinese.

1758–1759
Qing campaigns against Kalmyks.

1786
Start of Qajar dynasty in Persia.

1839–1842
Afghans under Dost Muhammad defeat British in First Afghan War.

1840–1842
Opium War, British attacks force trading concessions from China.

1850s
Widespread Muslim rebellions against Qing rule in China.

1855–1873
Jihad of Yunnan Muslims, ends 1873.

1863–1873
Northwest uprising in Uighur domains of Qing empire, largest Muslim jihad in East Asia.

1864
Establishment of Russian control in Kalmykia (Semipalatinsk).

1868–1870
Suppression of Muslim states of Bukhara and Samarkand by Russia.

1878–1879
Second Afghan War, British attempt to invade Afghanistan, which is coming under Russian influence.

1909
Anglo-Persian Oil Company (later British Petroleum) founded in Iran.

1911
Qing dynasty overthrown by Sun Yat Sen's nationalists and Republic of China declared.

1925
Reza Shah deposes last Qajar shah and is proclaimed ruler of Iran. He introduces Western-style reforms.

1941
Abdication of Reza Shah, his son, Muhammad Reza Shah Pahlavi, succeeds him.

1945
Atomic bombs at Hiroshima and Nagasaki force Japanese surrender in World War II.

1945
(August) U.S.S.R. declares war on Japan.

1945
(August) Atom bomb dropped on Hiroshima.

1945
(September) Japanese surrender.

1945
Stalin begins transfer of ethnic-minority peoples to labor camps in Siberia.

1946–1949
Chinese Civil War between Nationalists and Communists.

1955
Afghan government supports movement for separation of Pakhtunistan from Pakistan.

1962
Land reform in Iran reduces power and influence of religious establishment.

1973
Rebellion in Afghanistan.

1979
Islamic revolution in Iran, deposition of shah, proclamation of Islamic republic.

1979
Deposition of monarchy in Afghanistan, Soviet invasion and civil war.

1989
Crushing of pro-democracy demonstrators in Beijing.

1989
Soviet troops withdraw from Afghanistan.

1990–1891
Collapse of U.S.S.R. creation of Central Asian republics; Islamic revival throughout region.

1995
Taliban militia reignites Afghan civil war.

1996
Taliban forces capture Kabul.

2001
Saudi millionaire Usama bin Ladin identified as mastermind behind al-Qa'ida attacks on New York and Washington on 11 September; U.S. demands his extradition from Afghanistan.

2001
U.S.-led coalition declares "war on terrorism," coalition forces attack and overthrow Taliban regime in Afghanistan in response to al-Qa'ida terrorist attacks.

2001
Reformist Iranian President Mohammad Khatami is relected with 77.4 percent of the votes, running on an Islamic democracy platform against hard-liners and conservative clerics.

2002
Chechen independence movement continues attacks on Russia; seizes theater with 700 hostages.

2002
Afghani *Loya Jerga*, or grand council, elects Hamid Karzai as interim head of state; he selects an administration to serve until 2004.

2003

Thousands fill the Iranian streets in wide scale anti-government protests of political and economic conditions.

Adapted from: Lunde, Paul. *Islam: Faith, Culture, History.* New York: DK Publishing, Inc., 2002.

ISLAM IN EUROPE AND AFRICA 600–2003 C.E.

624

Visigoths expel last Byzantine garrisons from southern Iberia.

626

Constantinople besieged by Sassanids, Avars, and Slavs.

635–642

Conquest of Egypt by Arabs.

642

Foundation of Fustat (Egypt) and Great Mosque by 'Amr ibn al-'As.

647

Arab invasion of Tripolitania.

663

Byzantine Emperor Constans II invades Italy and sacks Rome.

669

Arab conquest of North Africa extended beyond Tripoli to the West.

670

Annexation of Tunisia, founding of the city of Kayrawan.

680

Arab armies reach Atlantic at Morocco.

711

Invasion of Iberian Peninsula by Tariq, conquest of Visigothic kingdom (by 714).

712

Muslim capture of Toledo.

714

South and Central Spain effectively under Muslim control.

718

Christian victory at battle of Covadonga temporarily halts Muslim advance in Iberian Peninsula.

732

Arab armies halted at Poitiers, France.

755

Revived Umayyad dynasty established at Cordoba by 'Abd al-Rahman (to 1031).

785

Foundation of Great Mosque at Cordoba, extended in four phases (832–848, 929–961, 961–976, 987).

789

Idrisids establish power in Northwest Africa (Morocco, to 926).

790

Beginnings of Viking raids on western Europe.

800

Start of Aghlabid dynasty in Tunis.

c. 800

Emergence of trading towns such as Manda and Kilwa on East African coast.

800

Charlemagne crowned Holy Roman Emperor by Pope Leo III in Rome.

827

Crete and Sicily attacked by Aghlabids.

830

Foundation of Great Mosque at Kayrawan.

839

Swedes travel through Russia to Constantinople, opening of river trade from Baltic to Black Sea.

844

Vikings attack Seville.

847

Muslim raiders burn outskirts of Rome.

862

Novgorod founded by Rurik the Viking.

863

Saints Cyril and Methodius sent as Orthodox Christian missionaries to Moravia.

868

Ahmad Ibn Tulun founds the Tulunid dynasty in Egypt (to 905), control spreads to Syria.

876

Building of mosque of Ibn Tulun, Cairo, based on Great Mosque at Samarra.

884

Kiev becomes capital of new Russian state.

896

Magyars start to settle in Danube basin.

899–905

'Abbasid campaign against Egypt.

c. 900

Arab dhows (sailing ships) begin to ply the coastal routes of East Africa, as far south as Sofala.

c. 900

First sighting of Greenland by Viking seamen.

905
'Abbasids take over Egypt.

910
Shi'ite Fatimids expel Aghlabids from Tunis, extend power to Egypt and Syria and claim caliphate (to 1171).

928
Ruler of Cordoba, 'Abd al-Rahman III, takes title of caliph.

936
Cordoba palace complex of Madiniat al-Zahra begun.

969
Fatimids conquer Egypt, founded city of Cairo.

970
Al-Azhar University established in Cairo.

972
Zirid dynasty, of Berber origin, rule Tunisia and E Algeria, based at Kayrawan (to 1148).

976–1009
Decline of Arab power in Iberia.

992
Ghana captures Berber town of Awdaghost, gaining control of southern portion of trans- Saharan trade route.

c. 1000
Arab merchants begin to set up trading states in Ethiopian Highlands.

1015
Hammadids, offshoot of Zirids, rule East Algeria (to 1152).

1025
Death of great Byzantine emperor, Basil II (the Bulgar Slayer).

1031
Beginning of Christian reconquest (Reconquista) of Spain.

1041
Zirids of Ifriqiya gain independence.

1048
Fatimids lose control of Ifriqiya (Tunisia).

1050
King of Takrur converts to Islam.

1054
Final schism between Roman and Orthodox churches.

1066
Battle of Hastings, Norman conquest of England.

1071
Completion of St. Mark's basilica, focus of public religious life in Venice.

1076
Ghana falls to Almoravids.

1076
King of Ghana converts to Islam.

1085
Christian forces under Alfonso VI of Leon take Toledo.

1086
Almoravids enter Spain.

1091
Completion of Norman conquest of Sicily.

1094
Christian warlord El Cid takes Valencia.

1095
Byzantine empire appeals for aid to pope, who preaches in France to raise support.

c. 1110
Onset of serious desiccation of Sahel region.

1126
Birth of Muslim philosopher Averroes (Ibn Rushd) in Cordoba.

1128
Almohad religious revival order starts takeover of Almoravid dominions in North Africa and Iberia (1130–1269).

1132
Palatine Chapel at Palermo, unique blend of Romanesque, Byzantine, and Islamic architectural elements.

1136
Independence of Russian state of Novgorod.

1137
Union of Aragon and Catalonia.

1147
Almohads established in Morocco and southern Spain.

1147
Second Crusade; Lisbon taken from Moors; Holy Roman Emperor Conrad defeated by Turks at Dorylaeum.

1154
Building of Chartres Cathedral.

1169
Shi'ite Fatimid dynasty in Egypt suppressed by Saladin.

1171
Founding of Ayyubid sultanate in Egypt (to 1260).

1172
Great Mosque at Seville, intended to be the largest in the world, and the Giralda, a great square minaret.

1174
Saladin becomes Ayyubid sultan of Egypt and Syria (to 1193).

1184
Completion of citadel at Cairo.

1189
Start of Third Crusade.

1189
Succession of Richard I the Lionheart.

1194
Emperor Henry VI crowned King of Sicily.

1196
Marinids take control of Morocco (to 1485).

1200
Emergence of Hausa city-states, which come to dominate sub-Saharan trade.

1200
Rise of Mali in West Africa.

1204
Fourth Crusade never reaches Holy Land; Crusaders sack Constantinople; Venetian gains in Adriatic and Peloponnese.

1208
Crusade against Cathars, or Albigensians, in southern France.

1212
Battle of Las Navas de Tolosa, decisive defeat of Almohads by Christians in Iberia.

1226
Creation of the Golden Horde, Mongol state in south Russia (to 1502).

1228
Start of collapse of Almohad Empire in North Africa.

1228
Hafsid dynasty established at Tunis (to 1574).

1230
Establishment of Nasrid kingdom of Granada Muslim stronghold in southern Spain (to 1492).

1230
Establishment of the Mali Empire.

1236
Christian reconquest of Cordoba.

1241
Mongols invade Poland and Hungary.

1248
Christian reconquest of Seville.

1250–1254
First of Louis IX's crusades; Invasion of Egypt ends in defeat at Mansura; Louis captured and ransomed.

c.1250
Building of stone mosques in Swahili city-states.

1250
Mali Empire at its greatest extent.

1261
Michael Palaeologus recaptures Constantinople and restores Byzantine Empire.

1269
Marinids inflict final defeat on Almohads in Morocco.

1270
Death of Louis IX outside walls of Tunis.

1273
Foundation of Alhambra Palace at Granada.

1282
French driven from Sicily, which passes to Aragon.

1306–1310
Hospitallers conquer Rhodes, which becomes their base.

1312
Knights Templar Order accused of heresy and suppressed by Pope.

1324
Pilgrimage to Mecca by Mansa Musa of Mali.

1325
Ibn Battuta's first pilgrimage to Mecca.

1331
Ibn Battuta's voyage to the Swahili cities of East Africa.

1347
Marinids take Tunis.

1348–135
Black Death reaches Europe and North Africa.

1352
Ibn Battuta's travels to the Mali Empire.

1354
First Ottoman conquests in Southeast Europe at Gallipoli, Ottomans advance into Europe.

1366
Capture of Edirne (Adrianople) by Ottomans.

1378
Beginning of Great Schism in Catholic church (to 1417).

1381
Peasants' Revolt in England.

1389
Battle of Kosovo, Ottomans gain control of Balkans.

1393
Ottoman conquest of Bulgaria.

1396
Bayazid defeats crusader army at Nicopolis.

1415
Portuguese capture Ceuta in Morocco.

1430
Sultans of Kilwa begin grand building program.

1442
Al-Maqrizi writes detailed topographical survey of Egypt.

1453
Constantinople falls to Ottoman sultan Mehmed II.

1459
Annexation of Serbia by Ottomans.

1464
Beginning of Songay expansion under Sunni Ali.

1469
Marriage of Ferdinand of Aragon and Isabella of Castile, union of Castile and Aragon (1479).

1480
Muscovy throws off Mongol yoke.

1484
Ottoman Turks capture Akkerman at mouth of Dniester.

1492
Columbus, in search of Asia, reaches Caribbean.

1492
Muslim Granada falls to Spain.

1494
Treaty of Tordesillas divides western hemisphere between Spain and Portugal.

1502
First slaves taken to the New World.

1505
First Portuguese trading posts in East Africa.

1511
Sa'dian dynasty comes to power in Morocco (to 1659).

1517
Ottomans conquer Mamluks in Egypt.

1519
Charles V elected Holy Roman Emperor.

1519–1522
Magellan begins and del Cano completes first global circumnavigation.

1521
Sulayman takes Belgrade.

1521
Siege of Rhodes under Knights of St. John by Ottomans.

1526
Battle of Mohacs, Ottoman invasion of Hungary.

1529
Ahmad Gran leads jihad against Ethiopia.

1529
Unsuccessful Turkish siege of Vienna.

1538
Holy League against the Turks formed.

1540
Portuguese come to the aid of Ethiopia against Ahmad Gran.

1543
Death of Ahmad Gran, shot by a Portuguese musketeer.

1546
Songhay destroys Mali Empire.

1547
Negotiated peace acknowledges Ottoman control of most of Hungary.

1562
After inconclusive skirmishes, Ottomans gain Transylvania.

1565
Ottoman siege of Malta fails.

1571
Ottomans take Cyprus from Venetians, at battle of Lepanto Ottoman navy defeated by united Christian fleet off Greek coast.

1578
Moroccans crush invading Portuguese.

1580
Union of Spanish and Portuguese crowns.

1588
English defeat Spanish Armada.

1591
Moroccan invaders destroy Songhay Empire.

1618
Thirty Years War in Europe (to 1648).

c.1660
Collapse of Mali Empire.

1664
Turkish advance on Vienna turned back at battle of St. Gotthard.

1682
Peter the Great becomes czar of Russia.

1683
Siege of Vienna ends in Ottoman defeat.

1698
Arabs from Oman capture Mombasa.

1699
Peace of Karlowitz confirms Austrian conquests from Ottomans.

1701
Start of Asante's rise to prominence.

1705
Foundation of Husaynid dynasty in Tunis, which rules until 1957.

1716–1718
Further Austrian victories, including capture of Belgrade from Ottomans.

1729
Portuguese leave East Africa following attacks from Oman.

1730
Revival of Bomu Empire in central Africa.

c. 1730
Emergence of Fulbe confederation of Futa Jallon.

1757
Muhammad III becomes Sultan of Morocco.

1768
War between Russia and the Ottomans.

1776
Abd al-Qadir leads Muslims in jihad along the Senegal River.

1798
Occupation of Egypt by Napoleon Bonaparte, defeat of Egyptians at battle of the Pyramids Battle of the Nile, British fleet defeats French.

1804
Fulani leader, 'Uthman dan Fodio declares jihad and conquers Hausa city-states.

1804
Muhammad 'Ali becomes Viceroy of Egypt.

1804
Napoleon proclaimed Emperor of France.

1807
Hausa kings replaced by Fulani emirs.

1816
Inspired by 'Uthman dan Fodio, Amadu Lobbo launches jihad in Masina.

1820
Egyptians invade Sudan.

1820
'Uthman dan Fodio establishes Sokoto Fulani Kingdom.

1821–1833
Greek War of Independence from Ottomans.

1830
French invasion of Algeria, Algiers occupied.

1840
Ottoman Empire under threat from Egypt, saved by British and Austrian intervention.

1852
'Umar Tal conquers the Senegal valley.

1853
Russians defeat Turkish navy at Sinop.

1854–1856
Crimean War, French and British support Ottoman Turks against Russia.

1861
'Umar Tal's forces conquer Segu.

1861
Abolition of serfdom in Russia.

1863
Al-Hajj 'Umar Tal clashes with French in Senegal Valley and creates a Muslim empire, invades Timbuktu.

1864
'Umar Tal is killed attemping to suppress Fulani rebellion.

1869
Opening of Suez Canal.

1877–1878
Russia, Serbia, and Montenegro at war with Turkey.

1878
Treaty of San Stefano negotiated by Russia and Turkey.

1878
Berlin Congress independence of Serbia, Montenegro, and Romania from Ottomans.

1881
Tunisia occupied by French.

1882
Revolt in Egypt, occupation by British.

1882
Beginning of major Jewish emigration from Russian Empire.

1884
Berlin Conference on Africa; Samory Toure proclaims his Islamic theocracy in West Africa.

1885
Bulgaria granted Eastern Rumelia.

1887
Bulgaria independent of Ottoman empire.

1893
French conquer Dahomey.

1904
French create federation of French West Africa.

1908
Bulgaria declares full independence.

1908
Bosnia-Herzegovina annexed by Austro-Hungarian Empire.

1911
Libya occupied by Italy.

1912
Serbia, Bulgaria, Greece, and Montenegro form Balkan League, First Balkan War.

1912–1913
Balkan Wars. Ottomans lose most of their remaining European lands.

1914
Assassination of Archduke Franz Ferdinand in Sarajevo precipitates start of World War I (to 1918).

1914
(Oct) Turkey closes Dardanelles.

1915
Gallipoli landings Establishment of Salonican front.

1917
U.S. declares war on Central Powers, Bolshevik revolution in Russia.

1918
End of World War I.

1919
Treaty of Versailles creates a new European order.

1920
(Aug) Treaty of Sevres.

1920
Inauguration of League of Nations.

1922
U.S.S.R. (Union of Soviet Socialist Republics) is formed.

1929
Wall Street Crash.

1939
(September) Invasion of Poland by Germany and Soviet Union, outbreak of World War II.

1941
Germans and Italians advance into Egypt.

1942
British defeat Germans at El Alamein.

1942
Plans for Final Solution agreed at Wansee.

1945
(May) Germany surrenders.

1945
Yalta Conference, origins of Cold War.

1949
Formation of NATO.

1954
Algerian uprising against French rule.

1960
Fifteen African countries gain independence.

1963
Foundation of Organization of African Unity (OAU).

1974
Revised Yugoslav constitution grants Kosovo autonomy.

1981
President Sadat of Egypt assassinated by Islamic fundamentalists.

1983
Islamic law imposed in Sudan.

1986
U.S. bombs Libya in retaliation for terrorist attacks.

1987
Famine in Ethiopia.

1989
Fundamentalists seize power in Sudan.

1989–1990
Collapse of Communism in Europe.

1991
Islamic Salvation Front poised to win Algerian general election, army cancels second round of voting.

1991
Start of civil war in Yugoslavia.

1991
Unsuccessful coup attempt in U.S.S.R., disintegration of Soviet Union.

1991
Croatia, Slovenia, and Bosnia declare independence from Yugoslavia.

1992
Civil war in Georgia, Bosnia-Herzegovina.

1994
Russian troops invade Chechnya.

1995
Peace agreement (Dayton Accord) ends the Bosnian war, U.N. troops remain.

1998
U.S. bombs Sudan and Afghanistan in retaliation for al-Qa'ida bombing of U.S. institutions in Kenya and Tanzania.

1998
Slobodan Milosevic sends troops into areas controlled by Kosovo Liberation Army (KLA).

1999
Kosovo Peace talks collapse NATO begins bombing campaign.

2000
Milosevic forced to step down.

2001
Milosevic arrested to face charges of war crimes in Bosnia and Kosovo.

2003
European reluctance to support attack on Iraq; only Britain and Spain support the United States.

2003
Turkish parliament votes against the use of its soil for U.S. attacks on Iraq, despite the offer of $26 billion in aid and loan guarantees.

2003
(March 19) United States launches massive air attack on Iraq; U.S., British and Australian troops enter Iraq.

2003
Enormous anti-war protests rock Europe reaching as high as 750,000 in London.

2003
Liberian government and rebels sign a peace deal; outside forces enter the country to maintain stability and protect civilians.

Adapted from: Lunde, Paul. *Islam: Faith, Culture, History.* New York: DK Publishing, Inc., 2002.

ISLAM IN SOUTH & SOUTHEAST ASIA 700–2003 C.E.

711–712
Arab conquest of Sind introduces Islam to South Asia.

c. 750
Muslim merchants establish Islam in Kerala, southwest India.

c. 800
Arab ships sailing as far as China.

977
Founding of Ghaznavid dynasty in North India (to 1186).

997
Mahmud of Ghazni extends rule into northwest India.

c. 1025
Conquest of Punjab by Ghaznavids.

1030
Tower of Victory built by Mahmud of Ghazni, Muslim conqueror of North India.

1186
Raids by Muhammad al-Ghur herald decline of Ghaznavid dynasty, and of Buddhism, in North India.

1191–1193
Afghan Ghurids defeat Raiputs and seize Delhi and much of North India.

c. 1200
Muslim Sufi saint, Mu'in al-Din Chishti, founds first Sufi order in North Indian subcontinent.

1206
Breakaway Mamluk (Slave) dynasty, under Aibak, establishes Delhi Sultanate.

1258
First Mongol expedition to Annam.

c. 1280
Mongol invasions of Southeast Asia destroy Pagan and eclipse Dai Viet.

1283
Expeditions against Annam and Champa.

1287
Mongol expedition to Pagan.

1288
Kublai Khan abandons attempt to subdue Annam and Champa.

1293
Failed Mongol invasion of Java.

1295
Conversion of Sultan of Achin (Sumatra) to Islam, which spreads over much of the East Indies.

1320
Muhammad ibn Tughluq succeeds to Sultanate of Delhi.

1334–1341
Ibn Battuta serves as *qadi* (judge) in Delhi.

1336
Rebellion against Tughluqs marks beginning of Vijayanagara Empire.

1345–1346
Ibn Battuta visits Southeast Asia and China.

1345
Hasan Gangu, governor of Tughluq Deccani domains, revolts and founds Bahmani kingdom.

1398
Timur's invasion of India, sack of Delhi leads to fall of Tughluq dynasty.

1445
Conversion of Malacca (Malaya) to Islam.

c. 1450
Islam spreads over much of East Indies.

1487–1489
Portuguese Pero de Covilha sails through Red Sea to India.

1498

Vasco da Gama rounds Cape of Good Hope and reaches India.

1502

First published map to show correct general shape of India, by Alberto Cantino.

1507

Portuguese victory over Ottoman and Arab fleet at Diu.

1509–1516

Portuguese voyages to Moluccas, Malacca, and Macao.

1510

Portuguese conquest of Goa; Goa made capital of all Portuguese possessions in Asia.

1511–1512

Portuguese establish base in Malacca and reach Moluccas.

1517

First Portuguese trading mission to China.

1526

Babur conquers Delhi and founds Mogul Empire.

1538

Failure of Ottoman blockade of Portuguese at Diu.

1556

Akbar becomes Mogul emperor (to 1605); reign marked by territorial expansion and cordial Hindu-Muslim relations.

1600

Founding of British East India Company.

1627

Shah Jahan becomes Mogul emperor.

c. 1647

Completion of *Atlas of India* by Sadiq Isfahani.

1653

Completion of Taj Mahal for Shah Jahan's wife.

1658

Aurangzeb becomes Mogul emperor; empire reaches maximum extent during his reign (to 1701).

c 1660

Gujaratis make earliest known North Indian nautical charts.

c. 1700

Probable commencement of Mogul military mapping.

1707

Death of Aurangzeb heralds decline of Mogul power in North India.

c. 1720

Marathas start to expand over most of India.

1724

Independent rule over Deccan by Nizam of Hyderabad hastens disintegration of empire.

1728

Marathas defeat Nizam of Hyderabad and gain supremacy over Deccan with subsequent territorial expansion.

1739

Sack of Delhi by Persians and Afghans under Nadir Shah.

1744–1763

Anglo-French (Camatic) wars, eclipse of French power in South Asia.

1749

Mysore starts to become major power in southern North India.

1757

Expansion of Gurkha (Neiali) domains over much of Himalayas.

1757

Battle of Plassey, British victors, over combined French and Mogul force establishes British power in Bengal.

1761

Defeat by Afghans temporarily ends Maratha hegemony over northern North India.

1761

British destroy French power in North India following seizure of Pondicherry.

1767

Appointment of James Rennell as first Surveyor-General of Bengal, beginning of Survey of India.

1775

First Anglo-Maratha war (to 1782).

1782

Treaty ending first Anglo-Maratha war results in territorial losses for Marathas.

1788

Occupation of Delhi, Maratha territorial apogee, Mogul rulers become puppets of Marathas.

1799

Conquest of Mysore ends challenge to British power in southern North India.

1803

Second Anglo-Maratha war leads to British acquisition of Delhi.

1815

Victory in Anglo-Gurkha war extends British possessions into the Himalayas.

1818

Third Anglo-Maratha war ends in Maratha defeat.

1819

Stamford Raffles, of the British East India company, founds Singapore.

1849

British annex Punjab after two Sikh wars.

1857

Last Mogul emperor, the Maratha puppet Bahadur Shah II, dethroned and exiled by British.

1857–1859

Revolt (Mutiny) attempts to oust British from India May 30, 1857: Lucknow mutiny. June 27, 1857 massacre of British evacuees at Cawnpore.

1858

(March 22) British retake Lucknow after twenty-day siege.

1859

Timor divided between Netherlands and Portugal.

1873

Dutch attack on Achin sultanate in Sumatra.

1876

Queen Victoria declared Empress of India, and a viceroy appointed as her representative.

1885

Foundation of Indian National Congress.

1904

Partition of Bengal; nationalist agitation in North India.

1906

Foundation of All-India Muslim League.

1918

Indian contribution to World War I earns it membership in League of Nations.

1919

Amritsar massacre leads to surge in North Indian nationalism.

1920

Mahatma Gandhi gains control of Indian National Congress.

1920

Start of civil disobedience campaigns by Gandhi in support of independence struggle.

1926–1927

Rebellion against Dutch rule in Java and Sumatra.

1942

Indonesia, Indochina, Malaya, the Philippines, New Guinea, and Singapore seized by Japan.

1942

(February) Surrender of British forces to Japan in Singapore.

1942

(March) Dutch surrender East Indies to Japan.

1945

India becomes U.N. charter member.

1945

Sukarno and Ho Chi Minh declare independence for Indonesia and Vietnam respectively.

1947

India and Pakistan gain independence.

1947

New independent dominions of India (Hindu) and Pakistan (Muslim) are born.

1947

Start of Indo-Pakistani War fought over Jammu and Kashmir; U.N. ceasefire line agreed in 1949.

1949

Indonesia gains independence from the Dutch.

1952

First Indian general election won by Congress Party.

1954

Sukarno abrogates union with Dutch and declares unitary state of Indonesia.

1956

Pakistan constituted as Islamic Republic.

1957

Malaya granted independence from Britain, despite ongoing Communist insurrection.

1958

Abortive secessionist uprisings in Baluchistan, Pakistan.

1963

Federation of Malaysia incorporates Singapore, Sarawak, and Sabah, along with Malaya.

1965

Second inconclusive Indo-Pakistani war over Jammu and Kashmir.

1965

Failed Marxist coup and military countercoup in Indonesia ends Sukarno regime.

1971

Secession of East Pakistan leads to creation of Bangladesh; Third IndoPakistani war as India intervenes.

1975

Indonesia annexes East Timor.

1989–

Revival of violent insurrection against Indian rule in Jammu and Kashmir.

1998

Economic crisis in Indonesia leads to overthrow of government.

1999

Referendum in East Timor produces overwhelming vote for independence.

2001

Attack on North Indian parliament by Muslim terrorists leads to increased tensionbetween North India and Pakistan over Kashmir.

2002

East Timor officially declares independence from Indonesia.

2003

Indian and Pakistan resume diplomatic, trade, and transportation ties.

Adapted from: Lunde, Paul. *Islam: Faith, Culture, History.* New York: DK Publishing, Inc., 2002.

ISLAM IN SOUTHWEST ASIA 570–2003 C.E.

570

Birth of Muhammad in Mecca.

595

First marriage of Muhammad to Khadija, a merchant.

610

Muhammad receives first revelation.

611

Arabs invade Mesopotamia.

611–626

Sassanid armies capture Jerusalem and overrun Asia Minor.

622

Muhammad's emigration with followers to Yathrib (Medina), the Hijra, and the start of the Islamic calendar.

622

Qibla oriented toward Jerusalem.

624

Muhammad's rejection of links with Judaism.

629

Muhammad's pilgrimage to Mecca.

630

Orientation of *qibla* is altered toward Ka'ba in Mecca.

632

Death of Muhammad in Medina, sucession of Abu Bakr (to 634), beginning of Arab expansion in Arabian peninsula.

633–637

Muslims conquer Syria.

634

Caliphate of 'Umar (to 644), conquest of Palestine and Syria.

635

Arab armies cross Euphrates.

636

Byzantine army routed by Muslims on Yarmuk River.

637

Arab conquest of Mesopotamia.

637

Arabs capture Ctesiphon.

637

Arabs defeat Persians at al-Qadisiya; Jerusalem seized.

638

Foundation of first mosque in Kufa.

641

Arabs capture Nineveh and invade Armenia.

642

Muslims invade Persia, Sassanid Empire falls.

644

Death of ' Umar, 'Uthman appointed caliph.

656

Assassination of 'Uthman; 'Ali, son-in-law of Muhammad chosen as the fourth caliph but struggles for control of caliphate (to 661).

660

Mu'awiya proclaimed caliph in Damascus.

661

'Ali assassinated; beginning of Umayyad Caliphate (to 750).

670

Reconstruction of mosque in Kufa.

683

Anti-caliphate movement based in Mecca (to 693).

687

Building of Dome of the Rock in Jerusalem, completed 692.

693

Burning of the Ka'ba; anti-caliph executed.

707

Great Mosques of Damascus and Medina built, al-Aqsa Mosque in Jerusalem.

744

Abbasid Caliphate established in Baghdad.

750

Umayyad Caliphate is overthrown in Damascus, succeeded by the Abbasid Dynasty (to 1258).

754

Al-Mansur becomes caliph in Baghdad (to 775).

756

Under Abbasid Caliphate, new interest in seafaring, focused on Persian Gulf routes.

762

Abbasid capital moved to Mesopotamia; founding of Baghdad.

786

Harun al-Rashid becomes caliph; Baghdad becomes center of arts and learning.

809

Death of Harun al-Rashid, start of civil war between al-Amin and al-Ma'mun (ends 813).

813

Reign of al-Ma'mun, development of sciences and math in the Arab and Islamic world.

820

Death of al-Shafi.

836

Baghdad terrorized by Turkish slave troops. Abbasid Caliph al-Mu'tasim builds new capital at Samarra.

848

Foundation of Great Mosque at Samarra with monumental spiral minaret.

860

Zaidi Imams rise to power in Yemen; rule intermittently to 1281.

862

Qubba al-Sulaybiya mausoleum, Samarra; first monumental Islamic tomb.

863

Byzantines annihilate Arab forces to stem Muslim advance in Anatolia.

869

Revolt of black slaves in southern Iraq.

892

Capital of Abbasid Caliphate shifts back from Samarra to Baghdad.

894

Shi'ite Qarmatians establish power base in central Arabia.

932

Shi'ite Buwayhids (Buyids) establish power base in Persia, Iraq; rule in name of Abbasid Caliphate (to 1082).

935

Final text of Qur'an codified.

936

Turkic troops in pay of Buwayhids take effective control of Abbasid Caliphate.

945

Persian Buwayhids conquer Baghdad but allow caliph to reign as figurehead.

945

Hamdanids establish power base in Syria and Lebanon (to 1004).

950

Death of philosopher al-Farabi.

956

Al-Mas'udi's major historical/geographical work *The Meadows of Gold*.

970

Fatimids establish control of Damascus.

970

Seljuk Turks enter lands of caliphate.

976

Byzantine forces threaten to take Jerusalem.

1005

Al-Sufi's *Geography*, (now in St. Petersburg) probably oldest extant illustrated Arabic manuscript.

1009

Destruction of the Church of the Holy Sepulchre in Jerusalem.

1055

Seljuks capture Baghdad, ruling in the name of the Abbasid caliph.

1069

Seljuks take Konya (Iconium).

1071

Seljuks under Alp Arslan defeat Byzantines at Manzikert.

1077

Seljuk province established in Anatolia with capital first at Nicaea and then Konya, dynasty comes to be known as the Seljuks of Rum (to 1307).

1078

Seljuks take Damascus.

1079

Seljuks take Jerusalem.

1084

Fall of Antioch to Seljuks.

1092

Abbasid wazir Nizam al-Mulk murdered by Isma'ili assassin.

1094

Seljuk dynasty of Syria founded with capital at Aleppo.

1096

First Crusade.

1098

Crusaders take Antioch.

1099

Jerusalem captured by crusaders, Godfrey of Bouillon elected King of Jerusalem.

c. 1118

Crusading order of Knights Templar founded in Jerusalem.

1124
Crusaders capture Tyre.

1127
Zangid dynasty of Seljuk governors control Syria and Mesopotamia to 1222, initiate Muslim counteroffensive against crusaders.

c. 1130
Hospital of St John of Jerusalem (the Hospitallers) becomes military order.

1144
Edessa conquered by Zangi, governor of Mosul.

1145
The Friday Mosque at Isfahan.

1148
Crusaders abandon siege of Damascus.

1151
Last Christian stronghold in County of Edessa falls to Nur al-Din.

1163
Iplici Mosque at Konya, probably the first to have a campanile (tower) minaret.

1174
Saladin takes Damascus.

1183
Saladin takes Aleppo.

1187
Saladin defeats crusader armies at Hattin, takes Jerusalem and Acre.

1188
Saladin completes conquest of Latin kingdoms in Levant, Christians reduced to coastal enclaves.

1188
The Mosque at Rabat, like Seville, intended to be the largest in the world.

1190
Frederick I (Barbarossa) drowned in Anatolia on way to Holy Land.

1191–1192
Third Crusade, Richard I of England recovers some of territory taken by Saladin, including Jaffa and Acre, fails to take Jerusalem.

1192
Richard I of England makes treaty with Saladin.

1193
Death of Saladin.

1197
Order of Teutonic Knights established in the Holy Land.

1204
Maimonides' *The Guide to the Perplexed.*

1206
Citadel of Damascus completed.

1225
Holy Roman Emperor Frederick II inherits Kingdom of Jerusalem.

1229
Frederick negotiates agreement which wins back control over Jerusalem.

1229
Rasulids control Yemen (to 1454).

1237
Huand Khatun Mosque, mausoleum, madrasa, and baths at Kayser, central Turkey; major complex endowed by Seljuk noblewoman.

1250
Mamluks, military caste from Caucasus, take over Syria, Egypt, and Hejaz (to 1517).

1256–1257
Assassins' stronghold at Alamut falls to Hulegu.

1258
Sack of Baghdad and fall of Abbasid Caliphate, Hulegu founds Il-Khanate.

1260
Hulegu invades Syria; Mongols suffer first major defeat at 'Ayn Jalut.

1268
Mamluks capture Antioch from crusaders.

1281
Succession of Osman I, beginning of Ottoman dynasty (to 1924) and first phase of expansion.

c. 1302
Last Christian territory in Levant falls to Mamluks.

1314
Rashid al-Din's *Jami' al-tawarikh*, Persian history of Mongol conquest.

1326
Ottomans capture Byzantine city of Bursa and make it their capital.

1336
Birth of Timur.

1345
Ottomans annex Emirate of Karasi, empire reaches Dardanelles.

1347
Black Death reaches Baghdad and Constantinople.

1370

Beginning of Timur's conquests, Timurid successors rule his empire to 1506.

1372

Kitab hayyat al-hayyawan by al-Damiri, encyclopaedic collection of tales traditions and scientific observations concerning animals.

1378

Foundation of Ak Koyunlu, state based on Turkoman tribesmen in East Anatolia, Azerbaijan, Zagros mountains (to 1508).

c. 1380

Foundation of Janissary corps by Ottomans.

1380

Timur launches series of attacks on Persia.

1384

Herat rebels, Timur suppresses ruling dynasty.

1387

Isfahan rebels, in reprisal, Timur kills 70,000 people, building towers with their skulls.

1388–1391

Timur wages war against Mongol Khanate of the Golden Horde.

1389

Accession of Bayezid I.

1393

Sack of Baghdad by Timur.

1400

Sack of Aleppo and Damascus by Timur.

1401

Sack of Baghdad by Timur.

1402

Ottomans defeated by Timur at Ankara.

1405

Death of Timur.

1406

Ibn Khaldun's *Muqaddima*, the first attempt in any language to elucidate the laws governing the rise and fall of civilizations.

1461

Ottomans take Christian city of Trebizond.

1502

Italian Lodovico di Varthema visits Arabia disguised as an Arab.

1512

Accession of Ottoman ruler Selim I.

1514

Selim defeats Safavids at Caldiran.

1516–1517

Ottomans conquer Syria, Egypt, the Hijaz, and Yemen.

1517

Selim I orders construction of Ottoman fleet at Suez, Portuguese attack on Jedda repulsed.

1520

Sulayman the Magnificent becomes Ottoman sultan (to 1566).

1525

Ottomans defeat Portuguese fleet in Red Sea.

1528

Safavids take Baghdad from Kurdish usurper.

1534

Sulayman retakes Baghdad from Safavids.

1538

Ottomans subjugate Yemen and Aden and occupy port of Basra on Persian Gulf.

1546

Ottomans retake Basra after revolt.

1551–1552

Ottomans fail to oust Portuguese from Hormuz.

1566

Sulayman succeeded by Selim II.

1588

'Abbas I (the Great) becomes Safavid shah.

1592

Zaydi imans regain control of Yemen, and rule until 1962.

1598

Isfahan becomes imperial Safavid capital.

1603–1619

Safavid war with Ottomans, in first year 'Abbas recaptures Tabriz.

1604

'Abbas conquers Erivan, Shirvan, and Kars.

1672

Greatest extent of Ottoman Empire.

c. 1750

Emergence of Wahhabi reform movement in Arabia.

1774

Ottoman decline follows Treaty of Kucuk Kaynarca.

1806

Wahhabis take Mecca.

1812

Burckhardt first European to find Petra, ancient capital of Nabataea.

1812

Egyptian forces retake Mecca and Medina.

1814

Burckhardt visits Mecca.

1818

Sadleir is first European to make east-west crossing of Arabian peninsula.

1818

Wahhabi movement suppressed by Egyptian forces.

1839–1861

Sultan ʿAbd al-Majid I makes series of liberal Tanzimat decrees.

1843

Fortunes of Saʿud family restored by Faisal.

1853

Richard Burton visits Mecca and Medina in Arab disguise.

1876–1878

Doughty's Arabian journeys.

c. 1880

Birth of ʿAbd al-ʿAziz ibn Saʿud in Kuwait.

1887

Riyadh taken by Rashidis, who dominate Najd.

1888

Publication of Doughty's classic *Travels in Arabia Deserta*.

c. 1900

Baku oil fields in Azerbaijan producing half the world's oil.

1902

Ibn Saʿud reclaims his patrimony by capturing Riyadh.

1905

Jewish National Fund established to buy land in Palestine.

1908

Ottoman sultan deposed in Young Turk Revolution.

1914

Ottomans declare jihad, ally with Germany and Austria (Central Powers) against Allies.

1915

About one million Armenians massacred or deported by Turks.

1915

(February) First Turkish attempt to capture Suez.

1916

(February) Russians take Erzurum.

1916

(April) British surrender to Turks at Kut al-Amara in Mesopotamia.

1916–1918

Arab Revolt, Saudi tribes supported by British rise against Turks.

1917

Balfour Declaration declares British support for creation of Jewish state in Palestine; British take Baghdad; British take Jerusalem.

1918

Battle of Megiddo; Collapse of Ottoman Empire, Turkish surrender.

1919

Greek forces land at Smyrna; Kemal Pasha breaks away from authority of Istanbul government.

1920

Armenia cedes half its territory to Turkey.

1921

Turkish Nationalist government established in Ankara.

1922

Turks recapture Smyrna.

1923

Foundation of modern Turkey by Kemal Ataturk.

1923

(July) Treaty of Lausanne recognizes Turkish sovereignty over Smyrna and eastern Thrace.

1926

Ibn Saʿud crowns himself King of the Hejaz and Sultan of Najd.

1927

Oil discovered in Iraq.

1932

Kingdom of Saudi Arabia proclaimed.

1933

U.S. company, Standard Oil of California, granted concession in Saudi Arabia.

1936

Arab revolt in Palestine against British occupation and Jewish immigration.

1938

Commercial quantities of oil discovered in Saudi Arabia.

1944

Standard Oil reformed as ARAMCO (Arabian American Oil Company).

1945

Foundation of Arab League.

1947

U.N. partition of Palestine.

1948

Foundation of state of Israel leads to war, invading Arab armies repulsed in Israel; some 725,000 Palestinians made refugees.

1956

Suez crisis, Israel, France, and Britain invade Egypt; fail to block Egypt's nationalization of Suez Canal.

1958

Oil strikes in United Arab Emirates.

1961

Foundation of Organization of the Petroleum Exporting Countries (OPEC).

1967

Egypt closes Gulf of Aqaba to Israel; Israel defeats Egypt and other Arab nations in Six Day War; Israel occupies Sinai, Gaza, Golan Heights, and the West Bank including Jerusalem.

1973

Arab states fail to defeat Israel in Yom Kippur War.

1973

OPEC restricts flow of oil to world markets, raises price of crude oil by 200%, oil crisis causes inflation and economic slowdown.

1977

Start of Middle East peace process.

1978

Camp David summit between Egypt, Israel, and U.S.

1979

Egypt and Israel sign peace treaty based on Camp David accords.

1979

Islamic revolution in Iran, deposition of shah, proclamation of Islamic republic.

1980

Start of Iran-Iraq War.

1981

Fifty-two American embassy staff held hostage in Tehran since 1979 are freed.

1982

Israel invades Lebanon.

1988

End of Iran-Iraq War.

1990

(August 2) Iraq invades Kuwait, U.N. demands Iraq's immediate withdrawal.

1990

(August 7) U.S. troops sent to Gulf.

1990

(November 29) U.N. resolution authorizes members to use "all necessary means" against Iraq.

1991

(January) U.N. deadline for Iraqi withdrawal passes, Operation Desert Storm begins with bombing of Iraqi troops and installations.

1991

(February 24) Allied land offensive in Iraq.

1991

(February 28) Ceasefire in war in Iraq.

1993

Oslo Accords between Israel and PLO based on principle of "Land for Peace."

1993

Islamic countries issue Cairo Declaration to curb fundamentalism.

1995

Israeli-PLO agreement extends Palestinian self-rule within the West Bank.

2000

Ariel Sharon's visit to Dome of the Rock inflames Israeli-Palestinian violence.

2001

Sharon becomes Israeli premier, violence continues.

2002

(February 17) Saudi Crown Prince 'Abdallah proposes full Arab normalization with Israel in return for withdrawal to 1967 boundaries.

2002

Iraq allows unconditional return of U.N. weapons inspectors.

2002

Elections in Morocco, dominated by the Socialist Union of Popular Forces (USFP). The king appoints a non-party figure, former interior minister Driss Jettou, as Prime Minister.

2002

Parliamentary elections in Bahrain (the first in 30 years, and the first with female enfranchisement) are boycotted by the four main opposition parties, after amendment by Shaykh Hamad for an appointed second chamber. The turn-out is 53 percent with disproportionately low Shi'a representation.

2003

Turkish parliament fails to approve the use of its soil for U.S. attacks on Iraq, despite the offer of $26 billion in aid and loan guarantees.

2003

Yasser Arafat nominates Mahmud Abbas as Prime Minister in Palestine, who is approved by the Palestine Legislative Council.

2003

(March 19) U.S. and British invade Iraq and appoint an interim government.

2003

Bush administration announces the "Roadmap" for "a Permanent Two-State Solution" between the Israelis and the Palestinians.

Adapted from: Lunde, Paul. *Islam: Faith, Culture, History.* New York: DK Publishing, Inc., 2002.

LIFE OF MUHAMMAD 570–632 C.E.

570 C.E.

Abraha, the Christian king in South Arabia, leads an abortive attack on Mecca, "The Year of the Elephant." Death of 'Abdallah, the Prophet's father. Muhammad's birth (August 20).

570–575

Muhammad's nurture by Halima and residence at Banu Sa'd. Persian conquest of Yemen. Expulsion of the Christian Abyssinians.

575–

Persecution of Christians in Yemen by the Jewish King Dhu Nuwas.

575–597

Persian dominion in Yemen.

576

Death of Amina, the Prophet's mother.

578

Death of the Prophet's grandfather, 'Abd al-Muttalib. Guardianship of the Prophet passes to his uncle Abu Talib.

582

Muhammad's first journey to Syria. Meeting with Bahira, a Christian monk.

586

Muhammad's employment by Khadija.

595

Muhammad's second journey to Syria. Muhammad marries Khadija.

605

Muhammad helps rebuild the Ka'ba.

610

Beginning of the revelation of the Qur'an and the call to prophethood. Khadija, 'Ali, and Abu Bakr accept Islam in that order.

613

Muhammad begins publicly preaching Islam. Confrontation with the Meccans.

615

Hamza accepts Islam. First Muslim migration to Abyssinia. 'Umar becomes a Muslim.

616

General boycott of Banu Hashim. Return of the first emigrants.

617

Second migration of Muslims to Abyssinia.

619

Death of Abu Talib. Death of Khadija. Muhammad seeks tribal protection and preaches Islam in Ta'if.

620

Muhammad's engagement to 'A'isha bint Abu Bakr. First converts of Aws and Khazraj from Yathrib.

621

First meeting of al-'Aqaba. *Al-Isra'* and *al-Mi'raj* (night journey and ascent to heaven).

622

Second meeting of al-'Aqaba. Attempted assassination of the Prophet by the Meccans. July 16, the *Hijra*, the Prophet's migration to Yathrib, henceforth called Medina, from *madinat al-nabiyy* (the city of the Prophet).

622 C.E.

The Prophet builds a mosque and residence. Establishment of Islamic brotherhood as new social order. The Prophet founds the first Islamic state. The Covenant of Medina. Muhammad marries 'A'isha. The call to prayer (*adhan*) is instituted. 'Abdallah ibn Salam accepts Islam. The Jews attempt to split the Aws-Khazraj coalition.

623

Hamza's campaign against the Meccans near Yanbu'. Campaign of al-Kharrar.

623

Campaign against Waddan. The incident of Finhas. Campaign of Buwat. Campaign of al-'Ushayra.

624

Institution of Ka'ba in Mecca as *qiblah* (direction of prayer). Campaign of Badr (first Muslim victory). Campaign of Banu Qaynuqa'.

624

Campaign of Banu Sulaym. Campaign of Dhu Amarr. Campaign of al-Qarada.

625

Muhammad's marriage to Hafsa, widow, daughter of 'Umar.

625

Campaign of Hamra' al-Asad. Marriage of 'Ali to Fatima, the Prophet's daughter. Treachery against Islam at Bi'r Ma'una. Campaign of Banu al-Nadir.

626

Campaign of Uhud; martyrdom of Hamza.

626

First campaign of Dawmat al-Jandal.

627

Campaign of al Muraysi‘. *Hadith al-Ifk* (libel) against ‘A’isha. Campaign of al-Khandaq (The Ditch). Campaign of Banu Qurayda.

628

Second campaign of Dawmat al-Jandal. Campaign of Fadak. Campaign of Khaybar. Al-Hudaybiya Peace Treaty with Mecca. The Prophet sends delegates to present Islam to the neighboring monarchs.

629

First Muslim *hajj*. Khalid ibn al-Walid and ‘Amr ibn al-‘As become Muslims.

629

Killing of Muslim missionaries at Dhat al-Talh.

630

Campaign of Mecca. The Meccans accept Islam. Destruction of the idols and cleansing of the Ka‘ba. Conversion of the Arab tribes in the Hijaz. Campaign of Hawazin at Hunayn.

631

Second Muslim pilgrimage (led by Abu Bakr).

631

The Christian delegation of Najran (Yemen) visits Medina and is incorporated into the Islamic state as a constituent *umma* in that state. The Year of Deputations: the Arab tribes enter Islam and pledge their loyalty.

632

Death of Muhammad's son Ibrahim. Last pilgrimage of the Prophet. Completion of the revelation of the Qur’an.

632

Death of the Prophet. The campaign of Mu’ta.

Adapted from: al-Faruqi, Isma’il R., and Lamya’ al-Faruqi , Lois. *Cultural Atlas of Islam*. New York: Macmillan; London: Collier: 1986.

Index

Boldfaced *page numbers indicate main article on the subject.* Italicized *page numbers reference photos or illustrations.*

Fundamentalism, 147, 155, **261–263,** 536

    See also 'Abduh, Muhammad; Afghani, Jamal al-Din al-; Banna, Hasan al-; Ghazali, Muhammad al-; Ghazali, Zaynab al-; Ibn Taymiyya; Ikhwan al-Muslimin; Jama'at-e Islami; Khomeini, Ayatollah Ruhollah; Maududi, Abu l-A'la'; Political Islam; Qutb, Sayyid; Rida, Rashid; Salafiyya; Tablighi Jama'at; Velayat-e Faqih; Wahhabiyya

Fusha (al-'arabiyya, High Arabic), 60

Futuh al-Haramayn (The conquests of the holy sites), 129

Futuwwa, 120, **263–264,** 740

    See also Youth movements

G

Gabriel (Jibra'il, Jibril), 49, 170, 455

Gagnier, John, 516

Galawdewos, Ethiopian emperor, 29

Galen, 294, 446, 612

Gallus, Aelius, 52

Gandhi, Mohandas K. (Mahatma Gandhi), 39, *304,* 305, 391, 458, 640

Garad Abun, amir of Adal, 29

Gharbzadegi, 529

Gasprinskii (Gaspirali), Isma'il Bay (Bey), **265,** 469, 579, 609, 676

    See also Education; Feminism

Gazi Husrevbegova Mosque (Sarajevo), 103

GCC (Gulf Cooperation Council), 201, 519

Gehenna. See Jahannam

Gender, 22–23, 42–43, **265–272,** 710–711

    See also Divorce; Feminism; Ghazali, Zaynab al-; Marriage; Masculinities

Genealogy, **272–273**

    See also Biography and hagiography; Historical writing; Tariqa

Genghis (Chinggis) Khan, 112, 134, 211, 236

Genizot (religious treasuries), 53

Geography. See Cartography and geography

Geometric decorations, 79–80

Gerard of Lombardy, 296

Ghadiri of Medina, 320

Ghadir Khumm, 37, 621

Ghalib, 528, 689, 715

Ghaliyun, Burhan, 319

Ghana

    Islamic architecture of, 21

    Islam in, 18

Ghannoushi, Rashid al- (Ghannouchi, Rachid al-), **273,** 577, 616

    See also Political Islam

Ghassanids, 55

Ghayba(t), al- (the hiding), **273–274**

    See also Imamate; Shi'a: Imami (Twelver)

Ghazali, al- (Abu Hamid Muhammad bin Muhammad al-Ghazali), **274–275**

    accusations against ahl al-kitab by, 28

    biography of, 109

    on birth control, 229

    on conversion, 160

    criticism of Ibn Sina and al-Farabi by, 249, 274

    criticism of philosophy by, 248

    on disputation, 182

    ethical tradition of, 35, 226

    on hadith, 286

    on hell, 370, 502

    on knowledge, 397, 399–400

    on medicine, 296

    on political legitimacy, 122

    on renewal, 675

    respect for, 310

    on self, 250

    strict interpretation of shari'a by, 270

    on succession, 655

    on Sufism, 685–686

    on sunna, 667, 668

    as teacher, 83, 665

    on ulema, 704

    and Usuliyya, 717

    on welfare, 440

    See also Ash'arites, Ash'aira; Falsafa; Kalam; Law; Tasawwuf

Ghazali, Muhammad al-, **275–276,** 388, 523, 577

    See also Political Islam

Ghazali, Zaynab al- (Zaynab al-Ghazali al-Jabili), 110, 178, 271, **276,** 735

    See also Banna, Hasan al-; Ikhwan al-Muslimin; Political Islam

Ghazi, Ahmad b. Ibrahim al-. See Ahmad ibn Ibrahim al-Ghazi

Ghaznavid sultanate, 243, 528, 543, 635–636, **661–662**

    See also Persian language, literature, and poetry; Seljuk sultanate

Ghiyas al-Din Balban, 660

Ghulams (military slaves), 1, 218, 542, 661

Ghunaimi, Muhammad al-, 160

Ghurak, Sogdian king, 132

GIA (Groupe Islamique Armé), 366

Gibb, H. A. R., 696

Gibb, Hamilton, 515

Girls' Secrets, 459

Glassware, 77–78

Globalization, 147, 235, **276–279,** 615

    See also Internet; Networks, Muslim

Gnawa (spirit possession) cult, 19

Gnosticism, 397, 428, 620, 673

God-Worshiping Socialists, 619

Gokalp, Ziya, 505, 740

Gok Tepe, massacre at, 137

Golestan, 527–528

Gordianus III, Roman emperor, 55

Gordon, Gen. Charles, 422

Government, Islamic. See Hukuma al-Islamiyya, al- (Islamic government)

Grammar and lexicography, **279–281**

    See also Arabic language; Arabic literature; Qur'an

Granada (al-Andalus), 47, 236

Grand Mosque, floorplan of, *532*

Grand National Assembly, Turkey (Buyuk Millet Mejlisi), 425

Great Mosque (Jami' Masjid) of Delhi, 73, *439*

Great Mosque of Basra, 72

Great Mosque of Cordoba, 71

Great Mosque of Damascus, 70, 72, 79, 118, 376

    tomb of John the Baptist in, 144

Great Mosque of Djenné, 73

Great Mosque of Fatehpur Sikri, 73, 74, 213

Great Mosque of Isfahan, 73

Great Mosque of Kufa, 72

Great Mosque of Samarra, 72–73

Great National Assembly (Turkey), 89

Greece

    independence of, 102

    Muslim population of, 104

Greek civilization, **281–283,** 396, 427, 612, 695

    See also Africa, Islam in; Americas, Islam in the; Falsafa; Islam and other religions; South Asia, Islam in; Southeast Asia, Islam in

Green Book, 557

Gregorian calendar, 89

Groupe Islamique Armé (GIA), 366

Islamic Tendency Movement (harakat al-ittijah al-islami), 273

Islamic Union (Itihad-e Islami), 490

Islamic Union Party (Indonesia), 470

Islamic Unity Party of Afghanistan (Hizb-e Wahdat-e Islam-ye Afghanistan), 490

Islamic Work Party, 347

Islamization. *See* Islam: spread of

Islamization of Knowledge project, 147

Islam noir (black Islam), 18

Isma'il, son of Ja'far, 350

Isma'il I, Shah, 36, 99, 135, 217, **367,** 386, 626, 637, 704

    See also Safavid and Qajar Empires

Isma'il b. Mis'ada al-Isma'ili, 274

Isma'il II, Shah, 218

Isma'ili Shi'a. *See* Shi'a: Isma'ili

Isma'il Pasha, 116

Isma'il Samani, 133

Isma'il Shahid, Shah, 730

ISNA. *See* Islamic Society of North America

Israel

    creation of, 458

    defeat of Egypt by (1967), 4, 460, 521

    economy of, 199

    relations with Arab League, 69

Israfil, 49

Istiqlal (Independence) Party, 254

Ithna' 'Ashari, 393

Itihad-e Islami (Islamic Union), 490

Ittifak-i Muslumanlar (Union of muslims), 265

Ittisal (contact), 48

Iwan, 73

'Izra'il, 49

'Izz al-Din al-Qassam Briades, 291

J

Jabal 'Amil, 386

Jabbar, Kareem Abdul, 44

Jabbat al-Mithaq al-Islami (Islamic Charter Front), 347

Jabha al-Islamiyya li-l-inqadh, al-. *See* Islamic Salvation Front

Jabha-e Nijat-e Milli-ye Afghanistan (National Liberation Front of Afghanistan), 490

Jabir al-Hayyan, 369

Jabriyya, 631

Ja'da, 293

Ja'd b. Dirham, 427

Jadidism, 137, 579–580, 609

Ja'far, 678

Ja'far al-Khuldi, 632

Ja'far al-Sadiq, 121, 169, 170, **369–370,** 625, 628

    See also Imamate; Law; Succession

Ja'fari school, 369, 386, 625

Jahangir, Asma, 271

Jahangir, Hina Jilani, 271

Jahangir, Nur al-Din, 213, *302,* 637

Jahannam (hell), 175, **370,** 375, 501

    See also Calligraphy; Janna; Law; Muhammad; Qur'an; Tafsir

Jahiliyya (ignorance), **370–371,** 397, 444, 479, 538

    See also Arabia, pre-Islam; Modern thought; Political Islam; Qutb, Sayyid

Jahm b. Safwan, 427, 448

Jakhanke Muslims, 697–698

Jalal al-din al-Suyuti, 84, 107

Jama'a Islamiyya, 741

Jama'at-e Islami (JI, Islamic Community), 262, 304, **371–373,** *372,* 375, 444, 502, 641, 672, 676

    See also Maududi, Abu l-A'la'; Pakistan, Islamic Republic of

Jama'at izalat al-bid'a wa-iqamat as-sunna (Association for the removal of innovation and for the establishment of the sunna), 8

Jamalzadih, Mohammad-'Ali, 529

James, William, 250

Jami, 527

Jami' (to gather), 71, **373,** 437

    See also 'Ibadat; Masjid; Religious institutions

Jami'a Milli'a (Milliya) Islamiya, 39, 639

Jami'at al-Duwal al-'Arabiyya (League of Arab States), 68, 175

    See also Arab League

Jamil al-Amin, Imam (H. Rap Brown), 44, 45, **373–374**

    See also American culture and Islam; Americas, Islam in the; Nation of Islam

Jami' masjid (congregational mosque), 71, *439*

Jamishid b. 'Abdullah, 664

Jam'iyat al-Da'wah al-Islamiyya (Islamic Call Society), 173

Jami'yat al-Da'wah wal-Irshad, 172

Jam'iyat-e (Jam'iyat) Islami (Islamic Society), 238, 490

Jam'iyat-e (Jam'iyat) 'Ulama-e Hind (JUH), 177, 371, **374,** 375, 390, 443, 638

    See also Jam'iyat-e (Jam'iyat) 'Ulama-e Islam; South Asia, Islam in

Jam'iyat-e (Jam'iyat) 'Ulama-e Islam (JUI), 177, **374–375,** 676, 677

    See also Deoband; Jam'iyat-e (Jam'iyat) 'Ulama-e Hind; South Asia, Islam in; Taliban

Jam'iyat-e (Jam'iyat) 'Ulama-e Pakistan (JUP), **375,** 390

    See also Deoband; Jam'iyat-e (Jam'iyat) 'Ulama-e Hind; Jam'iyat-e 'Ulama-e Islam; South Asia, Islam in

Jam'iyyat al-ikhwan al-Muslimin (Society of the Muslim Brothers), 345

Jammu and Kashmir Liberation Front, 490

Janna (paradise), 175, **375–376,** 501

    See also Calligraphy; Jahannam; Law; Muhammad; Qur'an; Tafsir

Jannat 'Aden (Garden of Eden), 376

Jannat al Khuld (Garden of eternity), 376

Japan, Islam in, 189

Jariri school, 671

Javadi, Fattaneh Hajj Sayyed, 529

Jawhar al-Siqilli, Egyptian general, 92, 115

Jerusalem, 163, 164, 314–316, 332, 362

    See also Dome of the Rock; Holy cities

Jesus Christ, 28, 554, 615

Jevdet Pasha (Ahmet Jevdet Pasha; Cevdet Pasha, Ahmad), 270, **376–377**

    See also Modernization, political: Administrative, military, and judicial reform

Jihad

    as "cleansing of soul," 30, 158

    and martyrdom, 432

    meaning of, 158–160, **377–379,** *378*

    as obligation, 365

    and spread of Islam, 239, 590

    See also Conflict and violence; Terrorism

Jihad Organization (Tanzim al-Jihad), 365

JI (Jama'at-e Islami, Islamic Community), 262, 304, **371–373,** 375, 444, 502, 641, 672, 676

    See also Maududi, Abu l-A'la'; Pakistan, Islamic Republic of